THE EARLY WORKS OF ORESTES A. BROWNSON

VOLUME III: THE TRANSCENDENTALIST YEARS, 1836–38

Edited by

Patrick W. Carey

PRESS
2002

MARQUETTE STUDIES IN THEOLOGY NO. 29
Andrew Tallon, Series Editor

Library of Congress Cataloguing in Publication Data

Brownson, Orestes Augustus, 1803-1876.
[Selections. 2002]
The early works of Orestes A. Brownson: Volume III: The Transcendentalist Years, 1836-38 / edited by Patrick W. Carey.
p. cm. — (Marquette studies in theology ; no. 29)
Includes indexes.
ISBN 0-87462-678-1 (v. 3: pbk. : alk. paper)
1. Philosophy. 2. Theology. I. Carey, Patrick W., 1940- II. Title.
III. Marquette studies in theology ; #29.
B908 .B612 2000
191—dc21

99-050779

Member, THE ASSOCIATION OF AMERICAN UNIVERSITY PRESSES

MARQUETTE UNIVERSITY PRESS
MILWAUKEE

The Association of Jesuit University Presses

MARQUETTE UNIVERSITY PRESS
MILWAUKEE WISCONSIN USA
2002

TABLE OF CONTENTS

ACKNOWLEDGMENTS

I am especially grateful to Jeffrey Barbeau, a diligent and skilled graduate research assistant, who has been particularly helpful in preparing volume three for publication. From 1998 to 2000 he was responsible for formatting the text, locating biblical and philosophical citations, and assisting in the proofreading process. Another graduate research assistant, Constance Nielsen, provided careful proofreading of this volume. Karen Krueger, our good secretary in Marquette's Department of Theology, provided clean typed copies of original texts that were very difficult to decipher.

Over the years the Brownson project has been aided by the staffs of various archives and libraries, including those of the University of Notre Dame, where the Brownson papers are located, Harvard University, the American Antiquarian Society (Worcester, Mass.), Cornell University, and the Boston Public Library. I am especially obliged to the staffs of the Boston Public Library and the American Antiquarian Society for providing me with rare extant copies of the *Boston Reformer* and the *Boston Reformer and Anti-Monopolist*, both of which published a number of Brownson's essays that are included in or were used for the preparation of volume three. As ever, I am also indebted to Joan Sommers and the Reference and Interlibrary Loan staffs of Memorial Library at Marquette University. They have been assiduous beyond the call of duty in locating and obtaining for me numerous publications that contributed to the development of this volume. Father Thaddeus Burch, S.J., Dean of Marquette's Graduate School, has supplied me with a number of summer research grants to complete this project. Dr. Andrew Tallon, director of Marquette University Press, has provided encouragement and expert advice throughout the preparation of this and the previous volume. His associate Joan Skocir has also been of great service in providing technical assistance to me during the final stages of the publication of this volume.

INTRODUCTION

In May of 1836 Brownson moved his wife and four sons to Mt. Bellingham, Chelsea, a suburb of Boston, where he lived for the next twenty years. During the first two years of his work in Boston, the years covered in this volume, he became an articulate advocate in the Transcendentalist movement and one of the more outspoken clerical mouthpieces for the social as well as the spiritual regeneration of society. Although he abhorred partisan party affiliations, he did see himself as a member of the movement party in society, a proponent of the new, and a critic of the stationary party and the old school of philosophical empiricism, a philosophical system he interpreted to be as spiritually dead as the Lockean and Enlightenment-influenced Unitarian and traditional churches of Boston.

Brownson had been invited to Boston by George Ripley (1802-80), Ralph Waldo Emerson's cousin and a Unitarian minister at Purchase Street in Boston, and was apparently given some assurance of financial stability if he would come to preach to Boston's working class whom many Unitarians feared were either unbelievers or becoming such. Brownson came to Boston to fulfill these Unitarian expectations, but he also had a mission of his own in mind. Not only would he try to establish a religious society among the laboring class, he would set up a society that would transcend traditional religious boundaries, unite human beings with one another in their fundamental and natural religious affections, and upon the condition of this union work together to improve the economic, social, and cultural conditions of the poor and laboring classes. Young men dream dreams, and this was Brownson's.

In 1836, according to one contemporary Unitarian estimate, Boston had a population of about 78,000, and fifty Protestant and two Catholic churches. Only 29,000 to 30,000 (i.e., about 38% of the population) regularly attended Protestant public worship services, meaning that about 35,000 persons did not belong to or worship in Protestant churches (the report allowed for about 13,000 non-Protestants in Boston at the time). "This result," the report judged, "presents a serious view to the friends of virtue and social order." Five places of worship had recently been opened for the religious instruction of the poor of the city, but these, the report said, were not sufficient to meet the needs of the unchurched in Boston.[1] It was within the context of this

[1]"Places of Public Worship in Boston," *Christian Register* 15 (March 25, 1836): 49. The population estimate is verified by the Boston census of 1835. On this, see William H. Pease and Jane H. Pease, *The Web of Progress: Private Values and Public*

perception of religious life that Brownson came to Boston. His mission was to attract the unchurched poorer classes back to the church.

Even before he had moved his family to Chelsea, Brownson had appeared in Boston on a number of occasions to give lectures. In March of 1836, for example, while still living in Canton, Massachusetts, he gave a series of "Free Lectures on Christianity" in Boston's Swedenborgian Chapel, apparently to advertise his coming and to attract a congregation of followers. The lectures showcased his abilities and created an interest in his future ministry in Boston. The subject of these lectures, according to the *Boston Daily Advertiser*, was the "foundation of religion in the nature of man."[2] The essential character of religion, Brownson asserted in the terminology of the German theologian Friedrich Schleiermacher (1768-1834), was a "sense of the Infinite, the Invisible, the Perfect"; religion consisted in a "reverence of the Being, in whom these attributes are combined." Brownson had apparently been reading a manuscript translation of Schleiermacher's "Discourses on Religion, Addressed to the Educated Amongst Its Despisers"[3] in preparation for these lectures and for his first major book, *New Views of Christianity, Church, and Society* (1836). Brownson used this series of lectures to argue against those who claimed that religion was "merely a fiction of the imagination, the result of education, or the contrivance of statesmen and priests." According to the report in the *Daily Advertiser*, "It is rarely that the philosophy of religion is presented before a popular audience with more clearness of expression, strength of argument, or discrimination of thought, than were exhibited on this occasion."[4]

Styles in Boston and Charleston, 1828-1843 (New York: Oxford University Press,1985), 274 n. 32. Henry F. Brownson reported in his *Orestes A. Brownson's Early Life: From 1803 to 1844* [hereafter *Early Life*] (Detroit: H. F. Brownson, 1898), 138-39, that 20,000 to 30,000 members of the Boston community were unchurched or not regular church goers at the time. Church membership in Boston, as a census of 1845 indicated, differed from actual church attendance: 4,830 Congregationalists; 3,833 Baptists; 2,810 Unitarians; 2,331 Methodists; 1,631 Episcopalians; and 1,428 Universalists. The largest percentage of Boston's wealthy, however, were Unitarians. On this, see Pease and Pease, 301 n. 22.

[2]A Bostonian, "Mr. Editor," *Boston Daily Advertiser* (March 24, 1836): 2.

[3]Ripley had translated Schleiermacher's *Über die Religion. Reden an die Gebildeten unter iheren Verächtern*, 1799. Ripley apparently used the fourth edition (1831) for his translation, which he distributed to his friends in manuscript form. Ripley had also introduced "Schleiermacher as a Theologian" to Americans in *The Christian Examiner* 20 (March, 1836): 1-46. The English title for the translation of *Reden* comes from page 16 of Ripley's article.

[4]A Bostonian, "Mr. Editor," *Boston Daily Advertiser* (March 24, 1836): 2; see also "Mr. Brownson's Lectures," *Christian Register* 15 (April 2, 1836): 55.

These lectures were appealing because when he returned to Boston in May of 1836 he was able to attract a congregation to his Sunday sermons at the Lyceum Hall on Hanover Street. To support and to advertise his ministry in Boston, he published in the May issue of the *Christian Examiner* an article on the "Education of the People." There he presented his view that the Christian ministry should be the schoolmaster of the people, informing the people about the destiny of the human race and providing them with education, which is "the only efficient means of all social, as it is of all individual, progress."[5] Christian ministers must rise above mere "cure of souls" and concentrate instead upon the social welfare of human beings. Christianity was originally designed, he asserted, to aid the social as well as individual progress within a context of universal harmony and order. Concern for the social dimension of Christianity, Brownson averred, was the order of the day and was evident in the writings of the Saint-Simonians, the new French Catholics (e.g., Félicité Robert de Lamennais), Robert Owen, the French Revolution of 1830, and a host of other leading lights and movements of the age. Brownson's ministry in Boston would be, he implied, a participation in this new spiritual and social direction.

By the end of May he had named his congregation the "Society for the Promotion of Christian Union and Progress," a society he ministered to from 1836 to 1839.[6] The inaugural sermon for the last Sunday in May, entitled "The Wants of the Times," outlined the purposes of the society and was eventually published as a pamphlet. Harriet Martineau (1802-76)—a British political economist, journalist, and abolitionist who was a visitor to the United States between 1834 and 1836—apparently attended this inaugural lecture and later published parts of it in her *Society in America* (1837) when she returned to her native England.[7] Although Martineau was critical of American clergy, she called Brownson "a strong man, full of enlarged sympathies" and had nothing but high praise for Brownson's intellectual acumen and his new religious society in Boston.[8]

The Wants of the Times was Brownson's manifesto on the spiritual famine that existed in the country and especially among the working classes whose spiritual needs were not being met by the churches of

[5]20 (May, 1836): 155, 158.

[6]Brownson indicated that he preached from 1836 to 1839, then lived as a layman from 1839 to April of 1842 when he resumed his office as a preacher. On this, see "Introductory Address," *Boston Quarterly Review* 5 (July 1842): 366-71.

[7]2 vols. (London: Saunders and Otley, 1837), 2:402-15.

[8]Ibid., 2:358.

the day. Brownson tried to articulate, too, the grievances against the churches. The pew system, he argued, reflected the aristocracy of churches and created a painful distance between the rich and the poor; preachers were not addressing the real issues in society; free inquiry and social progress were not advocated in the churches but could be found in abundance in infidel associations that were springing up among the poor and the laboring classes. To his newly organized Society of Christian Union and Progress, Brownson promised, he would proclaim Jesus as the true liberator of the poor and the prophet of the masses. Unlike contemporary denominations, the new society would meet the wants of the times and clearly demonstrate that free inquiry and social progress were grounded in Christianity.[9]

By the first of July Brownson's new society had grown to such an extent[10] that he moved the Sunday services to the Masonic Temple in Boston. In July, moreover, he became the editor of the *Boston Reformer*[11]—a newspaper for the working class that focused on religion, morality, literature, and politics. Brownson edited it from July to October of 1836, and then again during the summer of 1837.[12] During his editorship many of the published articles fostered the principles of his Society and emphasized in particular the social dimensions of religion, presenting religion as indeed the principal "lever of reform." He also advocated the needs and rights of the laboring class, especially focusing upon their need of and right to an effective moral, cultural as well as occupational education that would elevate them and dignify the role of labor within the entire community. With this aim in mind he lobbied the state government, and

[9]*A Discourse on the Wants of the Times, Delivered in Lyceum Hall, Hanover Street, Boston, Sunday May 29, 1836* (Boston, 1836).

[10]At its peak the Society of Christian Union and Progress had a regular attendance of about 500 persons, but that attendance dwindled to about 300 persons by 1839.

[11]The *Boston Reformer*, a triweekly, existed under various titles since its first issue on November 3, 1834. It was edited by a former Universalist minister Theophilus Fisk prior to Brownson's editorship. Apparently it was still in existence in 1839, under the editorship of Arad H. Wood. On the history of the newspaper, see Arthur M. Schlesinger, Jr., *The Age of Jackson* (Boston: Little, Brown and Co., 1953), 170 n. 31. A few extant issues of the *Boston Reformer* are available from the Boston Public Library, the American Antiquarium Society in Worcester, Massachusetts, the New York Historical Society, the Library of Congress, and clippings of Brownson's *Reformer* essays are available on microfilm Roll # 4 of the Orestes Augustus Brownson Papers. See my *Orestes A. Brownson: A Bibliography, 1826-1876* (Milwaukee: Marquette University Press, 1997), 40-44, for a list of most of Brownson's extant *Reformer* articles.

[12]See Brownson's "To the Readers of the Reformer," *Boston Weekly Reformer* 4 (July 7, 1837): 1, for his account of his reasons for returning to the editorship.

especially the scholarly Massachusetts Governor Edward Everett (1794-1865, governor, 1835-39), for the establishment of manual labor schools. For Brownson, manual and mental labor were twin sources of or avenues to personal progress and cultivation. He also began to speak out against the moral evils of slavery and saw the cause of emancipation to be consistent with the cause of labor, even though he did not agree with the aggressive tactics of some in the Boston abolitionist party. By reviewing various literary publications (e.g., Emerson's *Nature*), moreover, he hoped to draw the laborers' attention to good literature and thereby provide for their cultural education and elevation. Although he claimed to support only the democratic principles of politics and no political party ("no party but mankind"), he clearly supported Democratic party politics and through George Bancroft (1800-91), historian and Democratic politician, Brownson became closely identified with the Democratic party.

It had been six years since Brownson had edited the *Genesee Republican and Herald of Reform*, also a working class paper. As in the past, so also in the present his articles and editorials received criticism from various sources. Some, the social elites, attacked the paper for its radicalism because it supported the demands of the working class for social equality and elevation, and especially for its advocacy of the ten hour working day. Such support was perceived as an extremist leveling of social ranks and could lead to nothing but class warfare or at least to unjustified expectations on the part of the "lower orders" of society. Although Brownson indeed supported some kind of social equity, a raising up of the working classes, as he called it, he opposed eccentric solutions like an "agrarianism" that championed an equal distribution of property and wealth. Nonetheless, there were those who charged that Brownson's advocacy of the working class was "agrarian." Others, apparently some of the working class themselves, opposed the direction of the paper because of its excessive preoccupation with religion and religious principles.[13] Opposition

[13]The proprietor of the *Reformer*, Arad H. Wood, fired Brownson as editor in October of 1836. While praising Brownson for his talents as a writer, theologian, and social critic, Wood indicated that his "habits of study, writing and association" made him "more valuable in many other departments of literature, than conducting a working man's paper." Brownson's "connection with a religious society, and the general character of his studies, disqualified him for the editorial charge of a paper that must of necessity partake very much of a practical, and miscellaneous character. This was obvious to all. The publisher therefore could lay hold of either horn of the dilemma, procure in part a new list of subscribers or dispense with his laborers. He chose the latter." See A. H. Wood, editorial and "History of the Reformer," 2 (October 21, 1836): 1, 2.

from both sides of Boston society, and the proprietor's dissatisfaction with Brownson's failure to give his undivided support to the Democratic party during the political campaigns of 1836, forced Brownson to give up his editorship; but in the summer of 1837 the proprietor convinced him to resume his position, which he did for a brief period before permanently resigning as editor in the fall of 1837.

In September of 1836, in the midst of his advocacy of the advancement of the working class, Brownson became one of the charter members of the so-called "Transcendentalist Club." "Transcendentalism" indicates a pivotal moment in American intellectual history, but it is a notoriously difficult term to define because it has been used to describe so many different philosophical and religious orientations. Although American Transcendentalism was indeed a philosophical and literary movement, it was primarily a spiritual crusade that had deep roots in Puritanism and Unitarianism. Transcendentalism, though, was distinct from both of those movements because of its new sensibility, which had been developing in the Western (mostly European) world of Romanticism and idealism since the late eighteenth and early nineteenth centuries, and in American Unitarian intellectual circles since the mid 1820s.

The term "Transcendentalism" itself, as Octavius B. Frothingham (1822-95), the first major historian of the American movement, acknowledged, comes from Immanuel Kant (1724-1804). It refers to those qualities of mind that lie outside of all "experience" and cannot be reached "either by observation or reflection, or explained as the consequence of any discoverable antecedents." For Kant there was something in the mind that was not first in the senses. Transcendental "designated fundamental conceptions, the universal and necessary judgments, which transcend the sphere of experience, and at the same time impose the conditions that make experience tributary to knowledge."[14] The transcendentals were those primitive or *a priori* elements of the mind that condition all knowledge. Kant used the term "Transcendental Philosophy" to describe his own project. In the post-Kantian world the term was used more broadly to describe those philosophies that focused on the primitive conditions or inspirations of thought and knowledge that were independent and indeed prior to all experience or empirical method.

Frederic Henry Hedge (1805-90), a Unitarian minister of Bangor, Maine, who had studied philosophy and theology in Germany, was perhaps the first American to use the term "Transcendentalism." In

[14] *Transcendentalism in New England: A History* (Boston: American Unitarian Association, 1903), 12-13.

an important article for the *Christian Examiner* in 1833, he defined the term in the way it would be used within the movement and in the way that Frothingham defined it later in his history. For Hedge the distinguishing element or fundamental presupposition of German transcendental philosophies, all having their origin in Kant, was their acknowledgment of an "active and not a passive" interior consciousness that conditioned all human knowledge. Such philosophies disclosed more effectively than Lockean sensualism the "spiritual in man."[15]

Although Brownson used the term "Transcendentalism" periodically before 1836, it was not until his review of Théodore Jouffroy's (1796-1842) works in May of 1837 that he gave any extensive treatment of the term. By that time "Transcendentalism" was used by its opponents to refer to "the ' fifth essence' of extravagance and absurdity."[16] Like Hedge and Frothingham, Brownson traced the term to Germany and particularly to Kant, but noted that it was a term "of uncertain import." In the United States, he asserted, Transcendentalism was used in a broad sense to include not just the Kantians and post-Kantian Germans, but also those who followed the French eclecticism of Victor Cousin (1792-1867) and Jouffroy. There were in his view very different kinds of American Transcendentalists: those who professed to be able to arrive at truth by logic, by mere reasoning without observation or scientific data; and those who reach the truth by observation and rely on the facts of consciousness as the only basis of all theory. By 1837, Brownson was participating in an American battle to define the term itself, and he made it clear that there were two American Transcendentalist schools of thought.

Historians have repeatedly used the term Transcendentalism to describe a cultural revolution in American life during the 1830s. For Perry Miller, Sydney E. Ahlstrom, Catherine Albanese and a number of other historians, American Transcendentalism was first of all a spiritual quest.[17] As a native spiritual movement—conditioned, of course, by British, French and German idealism and Transcendental-

[15]"Coleridge's Literary Character," *Christian Examiner* 14 (March, 1833): 108-29. See especially pp. 119-21 for Hedge's definition of "Transcendentalism."

[16]"Jouffroy's Contributions to Philosophy," *The Christian Examiner* 22 (May, 1837): 185.

[17]Perry Miller, ed., *The Transcendentalists: An Anthology* (Cambridge: Harvard University Press, 1959); Sydney E. Ahlstrom, *A Religious History of the American People* (New Haven: Yale University Press, 1972), 599; *The Spirituality of the American Transcendentalists: Selected Writings of Ralph Waldo Emerson, Amos Bronson Alcott, Theodore Parker, and Henry David Thoreau*, edited with introduction and notes, Catherine L. Albanese (Macon, Georgia: Mercer University Press, 1988); Lawrence Buell, *Literary Transcendentalism: Style and Vision in the American Renaissance* (Ithaca,

ism—it protested against materialism, sensualism, rationalism, exclusive empiricism, mechanism of society, and what Frothingham called a Protestant objection to literalism and formalism.[18] Perry Miller argued that American Transcendentalism was not so much a movement against the historical and philosophical corruptions of the eighteenth century, as were the transcendental movements in Germany, France, or England. American Transcendentalism had its own native source of discontent.[19] Transcendentalists were the first in American society, Miller claimed, to repudiate the American "business" civilization and the preoccupation with "making it" that deadened the soul. This native source of discontent made the American Transcendentalists receptive to the European post-Kantian philosophical world, and that world awakened what were already "latent propensities" in the souls of a few leading Unitarian thinkers.[20] The American movement was part of the Puritan and Unitarian preoccupation with finding a genuine spiritual life—one that transcended custom, tradition, and history. For Miller the American Transcendentalists discovered the authentic sources of the self in a "moral innocence which they identify with Nature, against the corruptions of civilization."[21]

Transcendentalism, however, was more than a protest or reform movement within American spiritual life. It was consistent, historians such as William Hutchison and others have argued, with the Unitarian preoccupation with uniting piety and reason[22] or, as David

New York: Cornell University Press, 1973), 4-5; as a form of "religious radicalism," see Paul F. Boller, Jr., *American Transcendentalism, 1830-1860: An Intellectual Inquiry* (New York: G. P. Putnam's Sons, 1974), 1-33; *Critical Essays on American Transcendentalism*, ed. Philip F. Gura and Joel Myerson (Boston: G. K. Hall & Co., 1982); William Hutchison, *The Transcendentalist Ministers: Church Reform in the New England Renaissance* (New Haven: Yale University Press, 1959); Clarence L. F. Gohdes, *The Periodicals of American Transcendentalism* (Durham: Duke University Press, 1931).

[18]Frothingham, 352.

[19]Perry Miller, "New England's Transcendentalism: Native or Imported?" in *Critical Essays*, 387-401.

[20]Ibid., 390, 393.

[21]Ibid., 399.

[22]William Hutchison, *The Transcendentalist Ministers*; Conrad Wright, *The Liberal Christians: Essays on American Unitarian History* (Boston: Beacon Press, 1970); Daniel Walker Howe, *The Unitarian Conscience: Harvard Moral Philosophy, 1805-1861* (Cambridge: Harvard University Press, 1970); Lawrence Buell, *Literary Transcendentalism: Style and Vision in the American Renaissance* (Ithaca: Cornell University Press, 1973); David Robinson "Unitarian Historiography and the American Renaissance," *Emerson Society Quarterly* 23 (2nd quarter, 1977): 130-37; and idem., *Apostle of Culture: Emerson as Preacher and Lecturer* (Philadelphia: University of Pennsylvania Press, 1982).

Robinson put it, "the complete merger of reason and experience in theology."[23] William Ellery Channing's (1780-1842) focus on the divinity within humanity as a means for individual self-culture and spiritual growth, moreover, was consistent with the later directions of Transcendentalism. Transcendentalism, thus, was a religious awakening within a Unitarian spiritual tradition that the Transcendentalists themselves, almost all of whom were Unitarians, sought to deepen, develop, and improve. For the Transcendentalists, though, unlike many of their fellow Unitarians, the religious life, though consistent with reason, was not an experience that was demonstrable by the use of reason. Religious life had its own powerful source of insight that transcended reason's meager capacity to understand.

Transcendentalism was also, as Frothingham and others have acknowledged, a philosophical movement. It was first of all a philosophical protest against the Lockean empiricism that had undergirded so much Unitarian life and thought. The Lockean system was thought to be materialist because it had relied so exclusively upon the senses and reflection as the source of all knowledge. Such a perspective made it impossible to justify knowledge of things spiritual because the senses were incapable of perceiving spiritual realities. Caleb Sprague Henry (1804-84), an American Episcopalian Transcendentalist philosopher, translated Victor Cousin's *Elements of Psychology* in 1834 because he believed that Cousin's work helped to establish the foundations for morality and religion against the "subversive principles of Locke and Paley."[24] Ripley, among others, agreed that the philosophy of Locke, pursued to its logical consequences, "undermines the foundation of religion."[25]

Philosophically Transcendentalism was not exclusively a protest movement; it offered an alternative view of human understanding that it considered more consistent with comprehending spiritual realities. Thus, they saw themselves as promoters and advocates of a more religious philosophy than Lockean sensualism and empiricism.

At the philosophical heart of the movement was a distinction between "reason" and "understanding," as Samuel Taylor Coleridge (1772-1834), the British Romantic poet and idealist philosopher, and many Americans following him, understood that distinction. That distinction, according to George Hochfield, became the "key

[23]Robinson, *Apostle of Culture*, 20.

[24](New York: Ivison and Phinney, 1856), xxiv.

[25]George Ripley, ed., *Specimens of Foreign Standard Literature*. Volume 2: *Philosophical Miscellanies from the French of Cousin, Jouffroy, and Benjamin Constant* (Boston: Hilliard, Gray, and Co., 1838), 270.

to nearly all Transcendentalist thinking."[26] "Reason" for most Transcendentalists meant intuition or immediate knowledge independent of the senses; it was an instantaneous grasp of the Infinite that arose out of the soul itself. It was the source of all spiritual knowledge, or the fundamental human capacity for spiritual revelations. "Understanding" was the mind's capacity to obtain knowledge by observation and reflection; such knowledge was dependent upon sense perception. Relying on sense and reflection, understanding could reach only the surface of things; it had no capacity, for example, to originate ideas of God, freedom or the immortality of the soul—spiritual realities that transcended sense or reflection. Not all Transcendentalists followed or accepted this precise definition of the distinction, as was clear in Brownson and some others who followed more closely the French Eclectic Cousin in distinguishing between spontaneous and reflective reason, a distinction that will become clear later in this introduction. For the present, though, it is enough to say that whether the Transcendentalists followed Coleridge or Cousin, they were definitely in the post-Kantian idealist world that opposed Lockean empirical approaches to knowledge and reality. The Lockean approach, they all agreed, provided insufficient or no intellectual grounds for spiritual experiences that transcended the senses or reflection.

As an historical movement, American Transcendentalism had its rise in the mid 1820s, progressed gradually during the early 1830s, became organized as a discussion group in 1836, reached its defining climax between the years 1836 and 1844 (i.e., when the *Dial* ceased publication), continued on as an organized movement until 1847 when Brook Farm ceased to exist as a community, and had a lingering influence upon American life and letters well into the late nineteenth century. From about 1829, the date of the publication of James Marsh's (1794-1842) edition of Coleridge's *Aids to Reflection*, until September of 1836, the date of the organization of the Transcendentalist Club, Transcendentalism was in a period of gestation. During that period, the Unitarian William Ellery Channing, Emerson's "bishop" of American Transcendentalism, had emphasized the divinity within humanity. Gradually other American Unitarians discovered not only the German Transcendentalists and Coleridge, but also the French Romantic and idealist tradition of Cousin, Benjamin Constant (1767-1830), and Jouffroy, European post-Kantian intel-

[26]"New England Transcendentalism," in *Critical Essays on American Transcendentalism*, 453-82, see especially, 458; on this issue, see also Buell, 5; Boller, 34-63; Arthur Versluis, *American Transcendentalism and Asian Religions* (New York: Oxford University Press, 1993), 12-13.

lectual traditions that corresponded with and provided a transcendental language and conceptual tools for the spiritual self-culture and perfectionism that characterized Channing's thought. In a sense, then, Emerson's often quoted characterization of Transcendentalism as a reaction to and rejection of the "corpse-cold Unitarianism of Brattle Street"[27] is a misleading description of the movement, emphasizing as it does the radical disjunction between Unitarianism and Transcendentalism. In fact, there is a great deal of historical and spiritual continuity between the two movements, especially in their preoccupation with cultivating the divinity within the individual soul and within society. The differences within Unitarianism, however, are clearly evident in the contrast between the Lockean and the emerging post-Kantian philosophical perspectives.

Those differences, which were quietly surfacing in the early 1830s, came fully to the fore in 1836, the *annus mirabilis* of the movement according to Ahlstrom,[28] in a number of publications that could be called manifestos of an emerging Transcendentalism. Emerson's *Nature*, Amos Bronson Alcott's (1799-1888) first volume of *Conversations with Children on the Gospels*, Ripley's review of James Martineau's *Rationale of Religious Inquiry* for the *Christian Examiner*[29] and his *Discourses on the Philosophy of Religion Addressed to Doubters Who Wish to Believe*, William H. Furness' (1802-96) *Remarks on the Four Gospels*, Convers Francis' (1795-1863) *Christianity as a Purely Internal Principle*, as well as Brownson's *New Views of Christianity, Society, and the Church*—all became declarations of liberation from old school Unitarianism and manifestations of the so-called movement party, the party of the future. The individual productions indicated a common distaste for the past and a yearning for a new and fresh liberation of the human spirit.

The organization of the Transcendentalist Club in 1836 was also an acknowledgment of the ideological differences that had been rising for some time within the Unitarian community. The Club gathered primarily progressive Unitarian ministers who desired to discuss the ideological movements of the day. Members of the Club were devoted to conversation and, as Lawrence Buell has pointed out, "much of its [Transcendentalism's] internal ferment and a good deal of its external impact" can be attributed to its reliance on the symposium as a forum for generating ideas for the pulpit, the lyceum, or

[27] *The Complete Works of Ralph Waldo Emerson*, ed. Edward Waldo Emerson, Centenary Ed. 12 vols. (Boston: Houghton Mifflin, 1903-04), 10:552.

[28] *A Religious History*, 600.

[29] 21 (November, 1836): 225-54.

the essay.[30] Initiated primarily by Hedge, the Club met about thirty times between September 8, 1836 and late September 1840.[31] At the first meeting between Hedge, Emerson, George Putnam, a Unitarian minister at Roxbury, and Ripley, the group decided to invite other like-minded thinkers to discuss and promote a more satisfactory philosophy and theology than the old sensuous one that had dominated American religious culture in the most recent decades. Brownson—together with Amos Bronson Alcott, an innovative lay educator, James Freeman Clarke (1810-88), a Unitarian minister in Cleveland, Ohio, and Convers Francis, a Unitarian minister in Watertown, Massachusetts—was invited to the second meeting on September 19 and participated in the next three meetings. The last meeting Brownson attended (on May 29, 1837) discussed the topic the "essence of religion."

Why Brownson never returned to the remaining meetings of the Club is not altogether clear from the available evidence. In his autobiography Brownson said nothing about the Transcendentalist Club or his participation in it, probably because by 1857 he had clearly separated himself ideologically, emotionally, and geographically from the American Transcendentalists. The whole episode of the Transcendentalist meetings is not even mentioned. Nonetheless, a few members of the Transcendentalist Club, as will be evident later in this introduction, have asserted that Brownson's own arrogance and philosophical fastidiousness made his separation from the group a desirable event. Brownson himself, moreover, felt alienated from the group's pantheism, which he thought tended toward infidelity.[32] His own writings during this period support the view that he had some sharp ideological disagreements with a few of the Transcendentalists. He criticized in particular Emerson and Alcott, both of whose emerging positions he considered logically pantheistic, even if they were not themselves pantheists. Although he separated himself from the Transcendentalist Club, Brownson continued to support the Transcendentalists' opposition to Lockean empiricism and materialism.

As the Transcendentalist movement was surfacing in the late 1820s and early 1830s, so also was the Unitarian opposition to the new Kantian, Coleridgean, and other post-Kantian philosophies. In 1829, for example, Alexander Hill Everett (1790-1847)—Boston intellectual, politician, and editor of the *North American Review* from 1830 to 1835—

[30]Buell, 77, and 77-101.

[31]On the history of these meetings, see Joel Myerson, "A History of the Transcendental Club," in *Critical Essays on American Transcendentalism*, ed. Philip F. Gura and Joel Myerson (Boston: G. K. Hall, 1982), 596-608.

[32]On this, see ibid., 598.

published a mild protest against Cousin's and Kant's idealism and reasserted the continuing value of Lockean empiricism.[33] For Everett the philosophies of Cousin and Kant were reactionary protests against the best of modern (i.e., Lockean) philosophy; those philosophies were trying to restore something like Descartes' innate ideas, a move that Locke had already demolished. The tone of Everett's article was one of confidence that the new reactionary philosophies represented no immediate threat to the supremacy of Locke in American intellectual life.

By 1836 the internal division within the Unitarian community was becoming much more public and the threat of the new philosophies was much more immediate than six years earlier. That year Andrews Norton (1786-1853), biblical scholar and professor at Harvard Divinity School, began what would be a four-year battle with Ripley on the nature and meaning of miracles, which Ripley considered unnecessary to confirm the truth of Jesus' teachings, and Norton considered the absolutely indispensable evidence of rational Christianity. For Ripley the "evidence of miracles depends on a previous belief in Christianity, rather than the evidence of Christianity on a previous belief in miracles." Norton attacked (without giving any particular arguments) Ripley's article as dangerous to religion because it tended "to destroy faith in the only evidence [miracles] on which the truth of Christianity *as a revelation* must ultimately rest."[34] This religious battle was primarily about the nature of religious knowledge—whether human beings had an intuitive insight into the spiritual or whether spiritual knowledge, like all other knowledge, came through the senses or through testimony (i.e., divine revelation authenticated by miracles).

In January of 1837, Francis Bowen (1811-90), a tutor at Harvard and one of the young conservative Unitarian critics of Transcendentalism, announced in a review of Emerson's *Nature* that "within a short period a new school of philosophy has appeared." For Emerson and the idealist school that he represented "matter is nothing, spirit is all." These Transcendentalists fly off into the realms of mysticism, where "pure intelligence usurps the place of humble research," obser-

[33]"A History of Intellectual Philosophy," *North American Review* 29 (July 1829): 67-123. Some authors (e.g., Cameron Thompson, in *Critical Essays on Transcendentalism*, 377) attribute this article, wrongly I believe, to Edward Everett. On this, see Perry Miller, ed., *The Transcendentalists*, 26-33.

[34]Norton reacted strongly in the *Boston Daily Advertiser* 42 (November 5, 1836) to Ripley's review of James Martineau's "Rationale of Religious Enquiry," *Christian Examiner* 21 (November, 1836): 225-54. Ripley's reply to Norton's attack is in the *Boston Daily Advertiser* (November 9, 1836). The controversy over the meaning of miracles would be waged again in 1839 and 1840.

vation, proofs, and arguments. They promoted their so-called new views, moreover, in a dogmatic, overbearing, and dictatorial manner.[35] Emerson and Brownson were clearly under attack in this review. The philosophical war was coming to a head.

By November of 1837, Bowen put the Unitarian reactions to *Nature* and the new philosophy into a much wider context in his "Locke and the Transcendentalists."[36] The article defended Locke and reflected Bowen's anxiety that the new philosophy was gaining a foothold among the Unitarians. Bowen listed a battery of charges against Transcendentalism that would become stock and trade for the opponents over the next few years. The Transcendentalists were mystical, unintelligible, elitist and sectarian. They separated speculation and practice, used obscure language and terminology, and were excessively subject to foreign (German, French, and British) intellectual influences that did not fit into the American intellectual tradition. They appealed, furthermore, to the passions and sentiments more than to understanding, focused more on persuasion than on conviction or argument, and, therefore, greatly depreciated reason. Their positions and their poetical and mystical (or mystifying) philosophy were radically opposed to the reasonable and practical Locke. Like other Lockean critics, Bowen believed that the Transcendentalist emphasis on intuition over reason would only lead to speculation without facts and eventually would end in atheism. By the end of 1837 the Unitarian opposition to Transcendentalism was mounting, and would become a notorious public spectacle after Emerson's "Divinity School Address" in 1838, but that part of the story must await the next volume. The present volume represents the first stages of Brownson's self-conscious development and defense of the new philosophical and religious perspective.

From the beginning of the Transcendentalist movement there were internal disagreements as well as some external opposition. The Transcendentalists, James Freeman Clarke quipped, were alike in this, that "no two of us thought alike."[37] They differed significantly over major religious and philosophical issues that apparently made little difference in the beginning of the movement as the participants were defining themselves *vis-á-vis* their external opposition. But, as the movement developed the internal ideological discord distanced some Transcendentalists from one another.

[35]"Transcendentalism," *The Christian Examiner* 21 (January, 1837): 371-85.

[36]*Christian Examiner* 23 (November, 1837): 170-94.

[37]Quoted in James Elliot Cabot, *A Memoir of Ralph Waldo Emerson*, 2 vols. (Boston: Houghton, Mifflin, 1887), 1:249.

The Transcendentalists differed among themselves in their understandings of religion, philosophy, and society. With respect to religion, first of all, there were those like Emerson who emphasized intuition and "reason" to such an extent that they saw no need of external revelation and historic Christianity; and those like Brownson who emphasized intuition and "Spontaneous Reason" as a primitive revelation or universal inspiration that provided the *a priori* condition for the reception of Christian revelation. Frothingham expressed the internal differences by calling the first group the "pure" and the second the "imperfect" Transcendentalists. The "pure" Transcendentalists were those who believed that human beings were already in possession of all supernatural truths. The "imperfects" were those who saw transcendental philosophy as a means for confirming their faith in supernatural realities; they held that human beings had only the capacity for receiving (not possessing) supernatural realities by means of a divine revelation.[38] Brownson would increasingly identify himself with the "imperfect" Christian Transcendentalists.

From the beginning of the movement, moreover, the Transcendentalists differed among themselves in understanding the all-sufficiency of nature. Even before joining the Transcendentalist Club, Brownson had clearly separated himself from the Emersonian segment of Transcendentalism. He hailed Emerson's *Nature* as a harbinger of a new kind of literature and praised Emerson as a good poet. *Nature*, however, was aesthetical rather than philosophical, and the less-than-adequate-philosophical elements in it reflected an extreme idealist orientation that Brownson thought led to pantheism.[39] Although he made little of the difference at the time, Brownson eventually saw Emerson's supposed pantheism as grounds for separating from him and others within the Transcendentalist group. By the time Brownson left the Transcendentalist Club in 1837, a number of other irreconcilable differences made conversation within the group uncomfortable, to say the least. Some Transcendentalists welcomed Brownson's separation from the Club because of his apparent arrogance in expressing his differences, a view shared by many subsequent historians. Intellectual arrogance may have contributed to the

[38]Frothingham, 198-99.

[39]"Nature," *Boston Reformer* 3 (September 6, 1836): 2. From the beginning of his association with the Transcendentalists, Brownson, like Andrews Norton and other Unitarian critics, charged Emerson with a tendency to pantheism—although for Brownson the charge was not a cause for separation from the overwhelming benefits of the new philosophy. Emerson's work needed correction, not destruction in Brownson's view.

alienation, but real ideological differences gradually divorced Brownson from the Emersonian branch of Transcendentalism, as will be evident in this volume and even more so in volumes four and five.

A second major difference within Transcendentalism was strictly philosophical. The Transcendentalists were all post-Kantian opponents of Lockean empiricism,[40] but they differed among themselves in the emphasis they placed on the role of understanding. One group, with Emerson at the head, followed Coleridge in their religious epistemology, emphasizing the distinction between reason and understanding; unlike Coleridge himself, Emerson and some of the other American followers of Coleridge placed little emphasis upon the role of understanding in matters of religious truth. A second group, with Brownson and Ripley at the head, followed Cousin in their religious epistemology, emphasizing indeed the role and priority of spontaneous reason, but asserting the need for understanding or, in Cousin's terminology, "reflective reason" to detect, explain and verify the ideas of consciousness that were supplied by an original inspiration or revelation. Ripley considered Coleridge an inspired poet and an "enthusiastic prophet of a spiritual philosophy," but he lacked the "philosophical clearness and precision" that were necessary for the practical building of the "temple of faith." Cousin, on the other hand, did all that Coleridge was able to do and "exhibits to the speculative inquirer, in the rigorous forms of science, the reality of our instinctive faith in God, in Virtue, in the Human Soul, in the Beauty of Holiness, and in the Immortality of Man."[41] For Brownson, too, human beings believe before they reflect, but in order to grow or progress as a human person human beings needed to reflect. Reflective reason enabled the human person to appropriate, appreciate and penetrate

[40]Brownson, following Cousin, repeatedly took issue with the Lockean philosophy, seeing it as a materialist philosophy that, despite its assertions to the contrary, logically led to atheism. In 1837 Brownson debated with the Boston atheist and Lockean Abner Kneeland, a former fellow Universalist whom Brownson once defended after he had been excommunicated from Universalism, arguing that all the phenomena of consciousness are not dependent upon the senses as Kneeland asserted. On the debate see, "A Discussion on the Question, Can All the Phenomena of Consciousness be Traced Back to Sensation?" *Boston Investigator* 7 (March 31, 1837): 2; (April 7, 14, 21, 28, 1837): 2; (May 5, 12, 19, 26): 2. The debate was also published in the *Boston Weekly Reformer* 4 (April 21, 1837; May 12, 1837), as these two extant copies indicate. Brownson's contribution to the debate is published in this volume.

[41]*Specimens of Foreign Standard Literature: Containing Philosophical Miscellanies, from the French of Cousin, Jouffroy, and Benjamin Constant*, ed. George Ripley, vol. 1 (Boston: Hilliard, Gray, and Company, 1838), 41-42.

gradually the mystery of the primitive data of consciousness. Reflective reason's role was not to prove or demonstrate, but to develop and help make manifest and intelligible what was primitive and unreflective in consciousness. Faith, or the primitive inspiration, in other words, demanded philosophy (or reflective reason) in order to make an individual mature.[42] Ripley and Brownson placed a great deal more emphasis, as Cousin did, upon understanding (reflective reason) than did the Coleridgeans. For Brownson human beings needed to give a rational account of their intuitions and inspirations because they were reflective creatures as well as inspired ones; and, the primitive revelations had a universal and necessary significance that demanded logical, consistent, and intelligible explanations.

Brownson saw himself as a member of the new school of thought in America even before the organization of the Transcendentalist Club, but he was much more influenced by the French eclecticism of Victor Cousin than he was by the British idealism of Samuel Taylor Coleridge. This would be a telling difference in the years to come as Brownson articulated his own views of how human beings come to a knowledge of God, nature, and humanity. Like others in the Transcendentalist Club he knew what he opposed in the old Lockean philosophical school. Like others, too, he was looking for a more spiritually satisfying philosophy, but still, unlike some Transcendentalists, he was searching for a philosophical tradition that could give a rational or philosophical account for the notions that were independent of the senses and prior to all forms of rational reflection.

In September of 1836 Brownson tried to define more systematically than he had ever done in the past his own philosophical and theological orientation. That month he sent his *New Views of Christianity, Society, and the Church* to press, and published in the *Christian Examiner* "Cousin's *Philosophy*." According to John McAleer, Brownson's *New Views* had more of an immediate impact on the Boston community than did Emerson's *Nature*.[43] When Ripley reviewed Brownson's corpus for the *Dial* in 1840 he noted that Brownson's *New Views*, although not widely read when first pub-

[42]For Brownson's distinction between spontaneous and reflective reason, see "Philosophy and Common Sense," *Boston Quarterly Review* 1 (January, 1838): 83-106.

[43]John McAleer, *Ralph Waldo Emerson: Days of Encounter* (Boston: Little, Brown and Co., 1984), 229. Frothingham, 122, claimed that only 500 copies of *Nature* were sold in twelve years. Ralph L. Rusk, *The Life of Ralph Waldo Emerson* (New York: Charles Scribner's Sons, 1949), 242, indicated that 500 copies were gone in the first month. Undoubtedly *Nature* had some immediate success in the Boston area, but it did not appear to have a widespread impact.

lished,[44] received considerable attention in subsequent years because of interests generated by Brownson's later writings. *New Views* was Brownson's response to the charges brought against Christianity by Henry Heine (1797-1856) and the Saint-Simonians who claimed that it was a "system of exclusive and extravagant spiritualism."[45] In Ripley's opinion, *New Views* "has already formed a conspicuous era in the mental history of more than one, who is seeking for the truth of things, in the midst of painted, conventional forms."[46]

Indebted to Schleiermacher, Constant, and Charles Follen (1796-1840),[47] *New Views* was Brownson's attempt to create an atonement between matter and spirit, calling for the Christianity of Christ to replace the Christianity of the historic church. But the book was also, as Brownson admits in his own 1842 review, an attempt to incorporate the truths and to "refute the errors" of the French Saint-Simonians and especially of Henry Heine's *De l' Allemagne*.[48] The Saint-Simonians and Heine had argued that Christianity had provided grounds for the social and religious development of the human race, but that it had had its day and must be replaced by a new religion or new philosophy. Brownson's book was written against this view of Christianity and to affirm the idea that Christianity was still a living religion and had the inherent power to raise up a new church of the future. *New Views* was Brownson's eclectic attempt to separate the truths from the errors of the historic church and the Saint-Simonians. The truths of both, he argued, were consistent with the teachings of Jesus.

To some extent, too, *New Views* was an apology or philosophy for his Society of Christian Union and Progress. The book called for a new church of the future, one that would reconcile the material and the spiritual orders of existence. Such a union would be a major

[44]In his "The Church of the Future," *Boston Quarterly Review* 5 (January, 1842): 1-2, and his autobiography (see *Works* 5:83) Brownson admitted the same.

[45]George Ripley, "Brownson's Writings," *The Dial* 1 (July, 1840): 25-30.

[46]Ibid., 30.

[47]See Brownson's *New Views of Christianity, Society, and the Church* (Boston: James Munroe and Co., 1836), viii, for his acknowledgment of his debt to Follen, Constant, and Schleiermacher. Brownson had read Follen's *Religion and the Church* (Boston: James Munroe, and Co., 1836), which is also republished in *The Works of Charles Follen, with a Memoir by His Wife*, 5 vols. (Boston, 1841-42), 5:254-313. According to Hutchison, 32, that small book was a "semi-transcendental work" that also drew heavily from Constant and Schleiermacher. It emphasized in particular that religious institutions must change as society itself advances and the religious sentiment itself seeks ever purer forms of expression.

[48]"The Church of the Future," *Boston Quarterly Review* 5 (January, 1839): 2.

new step toward human progress. The new church would be a grand synthesis of two extreme historical forms or rather "social systems" of Christianity: the excessive spiritualism of Catholicism and the equally excessive materialism of Protestantism. Originally Jesus had united spirit and matter in himself, reconciling the two social systems of the ancient world, the spiritualism of the Eastern world and the materialism of Greece and Rome. The true idea of the Christian Atonement was found in this original synthesis, but gradually in the course of Christian history the original synthesis came apart. The present task was to realize again that original reconciliation in order to overcome the rampant sectarian spirit that was abroad in the land. Brownson hoped that the new universal reconciliation would come out of the spiritual reforms currently taking place within Unitarianism. He interpreted Unitarianism as the historical culmination of the Protestant movement and therefore the final manifestation of materialism. If this reconciliation could take place within Unitarianism, a new church would be the result, a church that was neither Catholic nor Protestant, but transcending the weaknesses and errors of both social systems and incorporating the good and truth of each—a peculiarly eclectic idea. A new society would be formed by such a new church, and the age of the millennium would arrive. The whole world, every human being, was yearning for unity and progress, and the new church would be the agent of that universal aspiration. *New Views* contained a message of reform, but hidden in it were seeds of Brownson's subsequent criticisms of the exaggerated spiritualism of "pure" Transcendentalism.

In December of 1836 the *Boston Reformer*, under the editorship of Arad A. Wood, reviewed *New Views* and referred to Brownson's convictions as not only "new but important and entitled to careful consideration" because they were free from sectarianism.[49] Other reviewers were negative. An anonymous reviewer for the *Christian Examiner* predicted that it would not be widely circulated because of its utter "novelty." Brownson's peculiar use of such terms as spiritualism, materialism and atonement gave the book "a strange and foreign air."[50] The book mystified and confused many of those who read it because Brownson employed a social analysis of history that reflected more the contemporary French socialist intellectual tradition than it did the American Lockean tradition.

[49] *Boston Reformer* 3 (December 2, 1836): 1.
[50] *Christian Examiner* 23 (March, 1837): 128.

"Cousin's *Philosophy*" was a systematic presentation of and introduction to Victor Cousin's eclecticism.[51] Brownson saw in that philosophy a new and much needed defense for religion. He believed that religion had lost its hold upon the understanding and was left with little more than a primitive inspiration. The religious sentiment was indeed natural and universal, but contemporaries had not given an adequate philosophical explanation of it. Cousin's philosophy provided logically convincing arguments for the reality of this spiritual dimension. The existence of an inner spiritual light, which enlightened all human beings, was spontaneous and independent of the senses and the understanding, but it could be brought to conscious awareness by the power of reflective reason. Cousin's philosophy helped to provide the conceptual tools for such a task.

Brownson and Ripley were not the first Americans to call attention to or promote Cousin's idealist philosophy.[52] In 1829, Alexander Hill Everett was one of the first Americans to comment on Cousin's philosophy, criticizing its mystical and idealist tendencies in reaction to Locke.[53] In 1832, Henning Gotfried Linberg translated part of Cousin's *Introduction to the History of Philosophy* for an American audience.[54] That text was followed in 1834 by Caleb S. Henry's translation of Cousin's *Elements of Psychology: Included in A Critical Examination of Locke's Essay on the Human Understanding, and in Additional Pieces*.[55] Henry promoted Cousin's philosophy as a philosophical prolegomena for Christian revelation.[56] Cousin's philosophy was also reflected in the work of other Transcendentalists and in that of theologian Horace Bushnell (1802-76),[57] among others. By the mid 1830s Cousin's philosophy had been read by at least a small group of

[51] *Christian Examiner and Gospel Review* 21 (September, 1836): 33-64.

[52] On the influence of Cousin in the United States, see Walter L. Leighton, *French Philosophers and New-England Transcendentalism* (1908; New York: Greenwood Press, 1968); René Wellek, "The Minor Transcendentalists and German Philosophy," and Georges J. Joyaux, "Victor Cousin and American Transcendentalism," both in *American Transcendentalism: An Anthology of Criticism*, ed. Brian M. Barbour (Notre Dame: University of Notre Dame Press, 1973), 103-24, 125-38.

[53] "A History of Intellectual Philosophy," *North American Review* 29 (July 1829): 67-123.

[54] (Boston: Hilliard, Gray, Little, and Wilkins, 1832).

[55] (New York: Ivison and Phinney, 1834).

[56] On Henry, see Ronald Vale Wells, *Three Christian Transcendentalists: James Marsh, Caleb Sprague Henry, Frederic Henry Hedge* (New York: Columbia University Press, 1943), 49-95.

[57] For the influence of Cousin on Bushnell, see Irving H. Bartlett, "Bushnell, Cousin, and Comprehensive Christianity," *Journal of Religion* 37 (April 1957): 99-104.

Americans who had accepted his critique of Locke, his eclecticism, and his interpretation of the history of modern philosophy.

Cousin's philosophy was a synthesis of Thomas Reid's (1710-96) Scottish Common Sense Realism and German idealism, which he translated into French intellectual life during the first third of the nineteenth century. Cousin had at first been influenced by the Scottish tradition through his teacher Pierre Paul Royer-Collard (1763-1845) who had brought Reid's thought to Paris. Cousin and his American followers saw Reid's philosophy as a legitimate critique of the inherent materialistic and skeptical tendencies of Locke's philosophy, but as only a half-way measure to a full alternative philosophy, one that did emerge with Kant and the post-Kantian German idealism of Schelling, Fichte, and Georg Wilhelm Friedrich Hegel (1770-1831), all of whom Cousin knew and had studied with in Germany. From the Scots, Cousin retained what he called the psychological or empirical or Baconian or scientific method of observation. The Scots, though, had not applied that method as extensively as they could have. They did not, for example, apply it to the primitive facts of consciousness, facts which German idealism had done so much to reveal. The inductive method was for Cousin the starting point of all philosophy; it did not originate ideas, but it helped to discover and verify them by observation, analysis, and reflection. What Cousin called "reflective reason" (analogous to Coleridge's "understanding") enabled the human person to observe, analyze, and legitimate the primitive beliefs, which originated in what he designated "spontaneous" reason.

From the Germans, Cousin learned the absolute logical priority of spontaneous reason. The primitive facts of consciousness did not originate in the senses nor were they the result of the empirical method; they were, as the Germans insisted, *a priori* conditions of all knowledge. The Germans, however, had so emphasized the *a priori* method in philosophy that they had little or no room for the empirical method. On this score of method, Cousin separated himself from Kant and the German idealists, whose methods, he believed, led logically to subjectivism and to an extreme idealism. Cousin accepted a form of German idealism because he always emphasized the logical (though not chronological) priority of the primitive facts of consciousness, or, in other words, the logical priority of faith over science (meaning knowledge); but his idealism was modified by his stress upon the chronological priority of the Scottish empirical and Baconian method.

Although Cousin accepted the Germans' understanding of the *a priori* conditions of knowledge, he believed that Kant had identified the categories of knowledge with the human subject to such an extent that his system led logically to subjectivism. Kant could not account, therefore, for the world outside of the self. To avoid the problem of subjectivism, which ultimately led to a scepticism regarding the external world and the existence of God, Cousin developed his distinction between spontaneous and reflective reason. Spontaneous or impersonal reason was an activity or mode of reason that was disassociated from the will of the subject. Spontaneous reason was an original inspiration or revelation that enlightened all humans with the ideas of God, freedom, and the immortality of the soul—these ideas were primitive facts of consciousness, subject to observation and reflection, but not dependent upon or originating in the human will (and, therefore, such reason was impersonal as well as spontaneous). These truths of God, freedom, and immortality were subjective in the sense that they exist within human consciousness, but they were objective in that their origin was not dependent upon the subject's consciousness, but upon the activity of an impersonal reason that revealed them to consciousness.[58] In separating himself from Kant, and relying on the objective force of spontaneous reason Cousin had aligned himself more with the objective idealism of Schelling than with the subjective idealism of Fichte. This, too, would be Brownson's tendency in the post-Kantian world in which he operated and helps to explain his differences with the more subjective Emersonian Transcendentalism.

A third major difference among the Transcendentalists related to their divergent conceptions of society and social reform. Although a number of Transcendentalists opposed the Jacksonian Democrats who rejected corporate privilege and money power, most of them supported other social reform movements like women's rights, temperance, prison reform, abolitionism, children's aid, and educational reform, to name a few.[59] Most of the Transcendentalists, moreover, agreed, especially in the years prior to the economic crash of 1837, that all legitimate reform must begin with the reform of the individual through education and self-culture—the ingredients of social betterment. Despite their agreements on many social issues, there were, in John Farina's terminology,[60] at least two different theories of

[58]On this, see Cousin's *Introduction to the History of Philosophy*, Linberg's translation, 169-71.

[59]As a group the Transcendentalists "engaged wholeheartedly in the reforms of their day" according to Anne C. Rose, *Transcendentalism as a Social Movement, 1830-1850* (New Haven: Yale University Press, 1981), viii.

[60]I am relying on Farina's characterization in what follows. See *Isaac T. Hecker: The Diary*, ed. John Farina (New York: Paulist Press, 1988), 31-32.

social reform among the Transcendentalists. One group, the "solitary" Transcendentalists, with Emerson, Alcott, and Thoreau as representatives, so emphasized self-culture as the "necessary and sufficient" means to perfection that they denied the role of the church or any other institution in personal as well as social reforms. The "solitary" group emphasized the role of the individual to such an extent that it saw all society and social reform as a matter of coming to terms with the individual's inner consciousness as a means of reform. Progress belonged to the individual, not to society. Social progress did exist, but as a manifestation of the progress of individual self-culture. According to Catherine Albanese the Transcendentalists "tended to ignore collective and communal understandings to emphasize individual integrity and human freedom in the context of personal development."[61] All of the Transcendentalists, of course, did not, as she acknowledges, share this social vision.

The other group, the "communitarian" Transcendentalists, with Brownson, Ripley, and William Henry Channing as representatives, also emphasized self-culture but unlike Emerson, Thoreau, and Alcott they placed more stress on the social nature of all reality and upon the social conditions of and influences on all human life. This group, moreover, saw the importance of community, institutions, and other social systems in personal and individual salvation and reform. The community could and periodically was on the one hand a means and condition of reform, and on the other a source of social and individual sin. The second group focused upon the redemption of society as well as the individual. Brownson was particularly influenced in this direction by his association with the Workingmen's party in 1829 and 1830, by his reading of Constant, the Saint-Simonians and the French Democratic Christian socialism of Félicité Robert de Lamennais, and by his own social background, which made him personally sensitive to the oppression of the social and economic structures of society. Even in his *New Views* he had asserted that union or communion was itself the indispensable basis or condition of all human progress. For him self-culture, individual freedom, and progress all had their grounding in a new church of the future. He was, moreover, as Paul F. Boller had indicated, "the most socially active of all the Transcendentalists in the 1830's."[62] Only gradually, however, did he clearly separate himself from the Unitarian advocates of self-cul-

[61] *The Spirituality of the American Transcendentalists*, 10, see also p. 20.

[62] Boller, 29. See also Anne C. Rose, *Transcendentalism as a Social Movement, 1830-1850* (New Haven: Yale University Press, 1981).

ture as a means of social reform. The financial crisis of 1837 would have a transforming effect in this regard.

Although ideological and philosophical disagreements estranged Brownson from some of the other Transcendentalists, social background and personal attitudes also contributed much to Brownson's incompatibility with the inner circle of the Boston Transcendentalists. Brownson was a social outsider. Even before he came to Boston he was reminded by William Ellery Channing of his alien status. In 1834, Channing told Brownson in a generally friendly letter that "a stranger, like yourself, not brought up among us, and who has made important changes of religion, cannot be regarded immediately with the entire reliance which we place in a long known and tried friend."[63] Brownson would never gain that status of a "long known and tried friend" in Boston elite circles.

Although a Yankee, Brownson had not the refined manners, educational advantages, and economic status of the inner circle of Transcendentalists.[64] Unlike other Transcendentalists, he had been a Universalist and a religious skeptic for a brief period. He had lived in the wild and developing frontier country of western New York, had associated with radical socialists like Fanny Wright (1795-1852), supported the democratic leveling tendencies of the Workingmen's party, and had not the experience of living in the stable confines of Bostonian elite society. He, too, had habits of Vermont forthrightness, and even arrogance, in expressing his opinions—habits that irritated and alienated him from those who had lived in a polite society their entire lives.

Because of his social background and manners, a number of the Transcendentalists were uncomfortable with Brownson, to say the least, and some just did not trust him. Emerson, who had probably been stung more than once by Brownson's sharp tongue and forceful disagreements, thought him to be undisciplined emotionally and possessed of an "inordinate lack of intellectual restraint."[65] For Emerson "Brownson never will stop and listen, neither in conversation, but what is more, not in solitude."[66] Alcott, too, had a rather low opinion of Brownson. Although Alcott considered Brownson's *Quarterly* the best journal "on this side of the Atlantic," he thought it

[63]Channing to Brownson, January 11, 1834, in Brownson Papers, microfilm roll # 10. See also *Early Life*, 107.

[64]For a composite social profile of the Transcendentalists, a profile that does not fit for Brownson, see Buell, 7.

[65]The terminology here is not Emerson's but Gohdes', 43.

[66]An entry in Emerson's journal for October 26, 1842. See *Journals of Ralph Waldo Emerson, With Annotations*, ed. Edward Waldo Emerson and Waldo Emerson Forbes, 10 vols. (Boston: Houghton Mifflin, 1909-14), 6:297.

fell "far below the idea of the best minds among us."[67] The poet James Russell Lowell (1819-91) created an image of Brownson as an intellectual weathervane that influenced generations of historians who have emphasized Brownson's frequent, radical, and ultimately unstable ideological and religious changes. In *A Fable for Critics* (1847-48), Lowell noted Brownson's frequent changes of opinion and his demanding argumentative logic and irritating philosophical precision:

> The worst of it is, that his logic's so strong,
> That of two sides he commonly chooses the wrong;
> If there is only one, why he'll split them in two,
> And first pummel this half, then that, black and blue.[68]

Thomas Wentworth Higginson (1823-1911), one of Transcendentalism's most informed historians and an "apostle of Transcendental culture in Victorian guise,"[69] wrote in his biography of Margaret Fuller (1810-50), another member of the Transcendentalist Club, that Brownson was known for his "gladiatorial vigor."[70]

Whether accurate or exaggerations, these contemporary characterizations of Brownson demonstrate the distance—social, psychological, and personal, as well as ideological that separated the Boston Brahmins from the Vermont country boy. Even though Brownson remained a lifelong friend with Ripley, he did not fit socially in the polite intellectual society of Boston. But, that did not seem to bother the Vermont Yankee whose opinions he rarely kept to himself. He believed in the honest and candid expression of his views. And, he expected no less from others.

The Economic Panic of 1837

By the end of 1836 Brownson was clearly established in Boston. He had founded his Society of Christian Union and Progress, took over the editorship of the *Boston Reformer*, joined the Transcendentalist Club, and published his first major book. In the midst of this flurry of ministerial and intellectual activity and excitement were

[67]Thomas Wentworth Higginson, *Margaret Fuller Ossoli* (1884; Boston: Houghton, Mifflin and Co., 1899), 143, quoting Alcott's journal for 27 March 1836. Alcott also believed that Brownson's journal was too tied to Democratic party politics, see ibid., 147.

[68]*The Complete Poetical Works of James Russell Lowell. Cambridge Edition* (1848; Boston: Houghton Mifflin Co., 1911), 129.

[69]Kent P. Ljungquist's characterization, see *Biographical Dictionary of Transcendentalism*, ed. Wesley T. Mott (Westport, Conn.: Greenwood Press, 1996), 139.

[70]*Margaret Fuller Ossoli*, 144.

rumblings of economic disaster that would produce in 1837 an economic panic and crash that had a deep and long lasting influence on Brownson and particularly on the poor and laboring classes he served in Boston. The economic crash of 1837 brought forth from his pen a jeremiad, *Babylon is Falling*, on the American economic system, and his reflections on that system would continue to agitate his mind until they burst forth again during the elections of 1840 when he produced his classic diatribe on "The Laboring Classes."

During Andrew Jackson's Presidency (1829-1837) the Boston economy was relatively prosperous, but Jackson's war against the United States Bank, presided over by Nicholas Biddle, became a source of financial uneasiness in Boston and the nation.[71] On March 2, 1836, the federal government's charter of the United States Bank expired, and the Jacksonian administration did not renew it. That event, in the judgment of historian Reginald Charles McGrane, was the "first [step] in order of time as well as importance" in preparing the way for the financial panic of 1837.[72] The federal government removed its deposits from the United States Bank and put them in various state and local banks, who then proceeded to extend loans for various individual and local state projects. The excessively rapid expansion of the credit system, feeding and financing various get-rich-quick schemes as well as local governmental road and other infra-structural improvement plans, laid a foundation for economic calamity throughout 1836 and during the first months of 1837. On May 10, 1837, President Martin Van Buren (1782-1862), who had inherited the problems of the previous Democratic administration, closed the banks to stop the drain of funds and the imprudent extension of credit. The panic had set in and disaster struck as banks closed, credit was no longer easily available, state projects ceased to be funded, inflation increased, and unemployment consequently took a sharp rise.[73] Everyone was hit by the collapse, but the workers and working class were the ones most directly and immediately affected.

The Transcendentalists' protests against the business culture and the materialistic expectations and desires it created had no effect on the run-away economic pursuits of individuals and institutions eager for financial gain and material prosperity. Brownson, like other Transcendentalists of the day, was concerned with the damaging effects of

[71]On "Boston's Boom Years," see Pease and Pease, 23-39.

[72]*The Panic of 1837: Some Financial Problems of the Jacksonian Era* (Chicago: University of Chicago Press, 1924), 91.

[73]Pease and Pease, 204-06; see also Arthur M. Schlesinger. Jr., *The Age of Jackson*, 217-26.

such materialistic pursuits on the human soul, but in 1837 and increasingly thereafter he became preoccupied, unlike Emerson and a few other Transcendentalists, with the devastating effects of economic structures upon individuals and upon society as a whole. Individuals were caught in a web of economic forces that made them powerless to resist. Brownson tried to understand the economic system, but his immediate response to the economic crash was a bitter protest against the economy's unjust and debilitating power.

Eighteen days after the banks closed Brownson preached to his Society of Christian Union and Progress an apocalyptic sermon, *Babylon is Falling* (on Revelation 18:11: "And the merchants of the earth will weep and mourn over her [Babylon]; for no man buyeth their merchandize any more."),[74] that predicted the imminent collapse of an unjust economic system that had supported the "party of privilege" against the masses or producing classes of society. The current financial crash was only the beginning of the end of the sinful system. Babylon, that is, "the spirit of gain, the commercial spirit or system" was falling.

Brownson's sermon was his first major attempt to show how the universal human propensity for greed was more than simply an individual problem that might be resolved solely by personal reform or education. Greed, or the "spirit of gain" was actually incarnated in a social system that valued wealth and protected it by legislation. The real cause of the current financial ills was not the United States Bank or the deposit system, but an "unequal and therefore unjust legislation which fosters and sustains a privileged class."[75]

Within this economic context Brownson resumed his editorship of the *Boston Weekly Reformer* in the summer of 1837. He returned, he told his readers, because the nation was in the midst of a financial and commercial crisis that demanded that "right measures" be advocated and adopted to fix the situation or the country would experience ruin and calamity. In this predicament the mechanics, small farmers and workingmen needed a strong voice to articulate their concerns and their understanding of the new measures that were necessary to reform the corrupt American commercial system that had hitherto reigned. All measures that forget the workingmen's concerns "will be universally ruinous." Brownson asserted in this opening editorial that he identified himself with those who were termed Locofocos, represented the voiceless in American society, and opposed banks, the tariff, and indirect taxation. He stood in opposition

[74](Boston: I. R. Butts, 1837).
[75]Ibid., 19.

to slavery (and from the timidity that "shrinks from discussing it"), to mobs, and to the Lynch law. He was a friend to free discussion. He indicated his identification with the workingmen's issues, moreover, in a paragraph that summarized some long-standing issues:

> Universal education, manual labor schools, equalization of labor, shortening the hours of labor, elevation of the working class generally, the moral and religious improvement of the whole community, the production of perfect harmony between the American population and the American institutions—will of course be objects for which I shall contend, and contend earnestly.[76]

Brownson vowed to speak more forcefully than he had in the past—not because his views had changed, but because the times had changed.

The economic depression of 1837 forced Brownson to consider, for perhaps the first time, the devastating effects of economic, social and legislative systems upon individuals and society as a whole. Forces more powerful than individuals demanded a reconsideration of the contrary energies necessary to bring about true reform. Resorting to self-culture as a means of individual progress and societal reform would not be enough, Brownson began to realize during the collapse of the banks and the credit system. Although he continued to emphasize the role of self-culture as an indispensable means of reform, he began to see the ineffectiveness of that approach. One had to address the structures of society.

The experience of 1837 made him much more receptive and attentive to the social analyses he had been reading in Benjamin Constant and the Saint-Simonians for whom massive historical transformations were explained in terms of a clash of social systems or even of social classes. Constant, for example, described the progressive nature of history in terms of four great revolutions in the emancipation of the human spirit. Those historical revolutions were against the privileged orders of society bringing about in succession the destruction of theocracy, slavery, feudalism, and the nobility.[77] The Saint-Simonians wanted to extend the revolution into the nineteenth century by revolting against the rising privileged order of wealth in support of a new economic and social order that emphasized equality and equity in the economic distribution of the goods of the earth (while preserving the natural rights of private property). Brownson,

[76] "To the Readers of the Reformer," *Boston Weekly Reformer* 3 (July 7, 1837): 1.

[77] On this, see Constant's "On the Perfectibility of the Human Race," in *Mélanges de Littérature et de Politique*, in George Ripley, ed., *Specimens of Foreign Standard Literature*, 2:259-60.

too, would see the present struggle of the working class as part of the progressive historical emancipation of the human race.

Babylon is Falling was a first step in this kind of social and economic class analysis that Brownson developed in subsequent years. The real battle in society, the one underlying the present economic crisis, Brownson asserted, was between "a decided and steady tendency of the masses towards equality in political, social and property relations," and the "collecting and concentrating of forces in defense of old privileges, old abuses, and the hitherto universally prevalent inequality."[78] The war between the masses of productive workers and the privileged was a battle against the artificial distinctions and factitious influences of the privileged classes and for a restoration of "virtue, truth, justice, in their rightful dominion as sovereigns of the world."[79] This was a social analysis that perceived the current problems in terms of a clash of classes in society—part of an ongoing historic battle against the privileged, or, what is the same thing, private law made "expressly to favor an individual." Even science and technology have come to the aid of the commercial and manufacturing classes, increasing their wealth and reducing the need for the working class by their labor-saving machinery.[80]

Babylon is Falling was a protest against economic and social inequalities, against privilege, and against the structures that upheld them. Brownson offered no practical solution to the problems in society, but called upon his listeners to choose sides in the historic battle that was in its initial stages and whose ultimate destiny was victory for the advocates of equality. The published sermon was a message of hope in a time of economic despair. In apocalyptic fashion it predicted the fall of the forces of artificial favor that ultimately opposed the divine design in nature and history.

Those with agrarian tendencies reviewed the sermon favorably, commending Brownson for tracing the causes of the current economic crises to the forces of greed and not to the United States Bank, the deposit system, Jackson, or Biddle. Agrarians, too, agreed with Brownson's declaration that the war against inequality had commenced.[81] Others in the community were afraid that Brownson's depiction of an apocalyptic battle between the privileged and the masses would stir up the lower classes and lead to class warfare.

[78]*Babylon is Falling,* 5-6.

[79]Ibid., 9.

[80]Ibid., 15-16.

[81]See J. M., "Rev. O. A. Brownson's Discourse Respecting the Fall of Babylon," *Boston Investigator* 7, no. 331 (July 28, 1837): 1.

Brownson did not back down from the criticisms his *Babylon* sermon evoked. The current and future economic war, he wrote in the summer of 1837, was and would be between capitalists and workers, a view he would articulate increasingly between 1837 and 1840. "The contest," he proclaimed in the *Boston Reformer*, "is now between Capital or Money and Labor." The moneyed interests in society have had their chance to run the government, but they have botched it: "They may disguise the matter as they will, the laboring class comes up and demands its turn in the government of the world and its turn it will have."[82]

Brownson continued to assess the economic situation in the United States throughout 1837 and 1838, focusing in particular on the Sub-Treasury Bill in Congress. The Van Buren administration had suggested and promoted the creation of an independent federal treasury (i.e., the Sub-Treasury Bill) that would divorce the state from the banks and establish a system of two or three federal depositories in the states under the charge of federal commissioners. Eventually the Democrats and John C. Calhoun (1782-1850), United States Senator of South Carolina, favored the proposal while the Whigs—under the leadership of Henry Clay (1777-1852), Senator of Kentucky, and Daniel Webster (1782-1852), Senator of Massachusetts—opposed it. In July of 1838, Brownson reviewed the Congressional arguments for and against the Bill, siding with Calhoun and the Democrats. Brownson believed at the time that dispensing with the state banks, which had held federal deposits after the cessation of the United States Bank, would free the government and Congress to manage its own fiscal concerns with independence from the control and influence of the banks. The Bill, moreover, would help to prevent one portion of the community—the banks, merchants and manufacturers—from taking excessive advantage of taxes collected for the common good. In a conclusion to his article on the Bill, Brownson argued that it would promote a real social as well as a political democracy. "The moneyed interests will be prevented from converting our government from a democracy into a timocracy, and the people, the whole people, will be in fact, not in name only, the state, under justice, the real sovereign."[83]

[82]Quotation from the *Boston Reformer* (August 4, 1837), in Arthur M. Schlesinger, Jr., *The Age of Jackson* (Boston: Little, Brown and Co., 1953), 255. I have not been able to locate extant copies of this essay. See, however, "Rich and Poor," *Boston Weekly Reformer* 3 (July 21, 1837), available from the New York Historical Society, and quoted in "Conversation with a Radical," *Boston Quarterly Review* 4 (April 1841): 145-51 (see also EW, 6, Chapter 1), where Brownson also fulminates against those who support the privileged order in the American economic system.

[83]"Sub-Treasury Bill," *Boston Quarterly Review* 1 (July, 1838): 333-60, quote on 359.

The proposed Sub-Treasury Bill, however, became a very unpopular measure because it provided (at least according to Webster's argument) financial relief for the government but none for the people. The proposal to divorce the bank and the state, which Brownson and other hard-money Democrats had supported, according to Arthur M. Schlesinger, Jr., found "its only backing among intellectuals and radicals."[84] Brownson's position was a minority one. The Whig argument apparently had some popular appeal because in 1837 and 1838 Whig political candidates gained significant victories at the polls. In Massachusetts, for example, an overwhelming majority of 59,595 voted for the Whigs, while the Democrats gained only 32,987 votes. The people sided with the deposit bank party against the Van Buren Administration.[85] Brownson's position, which he thought supported the people because it tended to keep taxes low, was rejected by the voters. What was happening at the polls in 1837 and 1838 forecast the doom of the Van Buren administration, an event that did not take place until the elections of 1840. The whole episode with the Sub-Treasury Bill demonstrated that Brownson's economic views in 1837 were unpopular long before the 1840 election and his "Laboring Classes" bombshell that fell upon the politicians' playground.

During 1837 and 1838 Brownson became involved in the abolition movement as never before. In the past he had written a paragraph here and there against slavery and in his *New Views* he presented the abolition movement, though not its tactics, as part of the progressive emancipation of humankind.[86] Brownson stood behind the work of emancipation and periodically came to the support of various causes of liberation, though he was never very precise about what form of emancipation he favored in his early years. On 4 August 1836, for example, Brownson criticized a "mob" of Southern pro-slavery advocates who had disrupted and protested against a Boston Anti-Slavery Society anniversary celebration of the emancipation of slaves in the British West Indies. Brownson led the Anti-Slavery Society in a prayer after the protests and then members retired to their homes. Brownson's account of the affair criticized the financial interests in the North that sympathized with the slaveholders, but his strongest attack was directed at the lawless mobocracy. The abo-

[84]*Age of Jackson*, 227, see also 227-41.

[85]McGrane, 160-67.

[86]Brownson first presented this view in "An Essay on the Progress of Truth," *Gospel Advocate and Impartial Investigator* 6 (March 15, 1828): 90; see EW, 1:75 n. See also *New Views*, 99; "Influence of Slavery on Labor," *Boston Reformer* 3 (July 26, 1836): 1-2; "The Slave Cause," *Boston Reformer* 3 (August 4, 1836): 2.

litionists' liberating cause, he asserted, must now be the cause of "every freeman, every patriot, every philanthropist and every Christian."[87]

The Boston abolitionist movement and William Lloyd Garrison (1805-79) in particular had come under repeated verbal assault in the early and mid 1830s. Brownson periodically gave the movement moral support. In July of 1837, for example, five Boston Congregationalist ministers published "An Appeal of Clerical Abolitionists on Anti-Slavery Measures," which criticized the Massachusetts Anti-Slavery Society (MAS) for supporting Garrison's newspaper, *The Liberator*, and censured Garrison and his paper for its "abuse" of ministers who did not follow Garrison's radical party line of immediate emancipation of the slaves. In the midst of this heavy clerical attack, on 27 September 1837, Brownson backed Garrison and spoke out against the annexation of Texas at a MAS meeting in Worcester, Massachusetts.[88] Brownson considered his Worcester talk an implied criticism of Garrison's clerical opponents as well as his own clerical encouragement for Garrison.[89]

On 8 December 1837, Brownson again joined the Massachusetts anti-slavery cause. On that day William Ellery Channing had convoked an anti-slavery meeting to memorialize Elijah Lovejoy, a Presbyterian minister and anti-slavery editor in Alton, Illinois, who had been killed by an angry mob in November of 1837. Brownson was one of the anti-slavery protesters invited to speak before the five thousand people who jammed Faneuil Hall for the occasion.[90] He called Lovejoy a martyr to free speech and liberty.[91] Brownson had frequently championed the cause of free inquiry and free speech and some mistook his advocacy of such procedural issues as support for the abolitionist principles of immediate emancipation, which was certainly not the case as some abolitionists were soon to learn.

Although Brownson had supported the emancipation of slaves, he had never formally joined the abolitionist movement. Like many other clerics in the Boston community he did not believe immediate emancipation was best for the slaves or the country, and he said so in an article for his *Boston Quarterly Review*. Garrison was outraged by

[87]"Slavery—Mobs, &c," *Boston Reformer* 3 (August 4, 1836): 1.

[88]On the MAS September meeting and Brownson's participation in it, see *The Liberator* 7 (October 6, 1837): 163. See also "Remarks of Dea[con] John Gulliver," *The Liberator* 7 (October 20, 1837): 170-71.

[89]For Brownson's interpretation of this speech, see "Letter to William Lloyd Garrison," *The Liberator* 8 (May 11, 1838): 73.

[90]On the protest meeting in Faneuil Hall, see Henry Mayer, *All on Fire: William Lloyd Garrison and the Abolition of Slavery* (New York: St. Martin's Press, 1998), 238.

[91]"Rev. Mr. Brownson's Speech," *The Liberator* 8 (January 5, 1838): 1-2.

the article and verbally assaulted Brownson as he had previously condemned other clergy who did not agree with his immediatism. Brownson found the attack particularly ungenerous since he had previously come to Garrison's aid at the Worcester meeting.[92] Like a number of others in Boston, Brownson was marked by Garrison's sharp pen and he never forgot it. For the remainder of his life he opposed the abolitionist movement because of its radical immediatism, its one-idea reformerism, and its lack of concern for constitutional order in society.

At the beginning of 1837, in the midst of the economic depression, George Bancroft, the historian and newly appointed Collector of the Port of Boston, chose Brownson to be the Steward of the Marine Hospital of Chelsea, a position that carried with it a salary of fifteen hundred dollars a year, a substantial sum that freed Brownson from financial worries during the depression. He also received a house on the Hospital grounds as part of his compensation for superintending the operations of the Hospital. The post was part of the political patronage system. Brownson and Bancroft had become close friends since July of 1836 when Brownson had given Bancroft a very favorable review of his Fourth of July address. The two were ardent Democrats and Brownson's nomination was the fruit of his friendship with Bancroft and his support of the Democratic party. He held the position until the presidential election of the Whig William Henry Harrison in 1841, when new appointments were made by the new administration. Brownson's stewardship—which entailed little more than visits of inspection, superintendence, making reports, and ordering supplies[93]—allowed Brownson to continue his ministerial work and his writing, and, he was assured by Bancroft, his political independence from the party in power. Brownson's new financial stabil-

[92]For the article see "Slavery—Abolitionism," *Boston Quarterly Review* 1 (April, 1838): 238-60 (see also Chapter 18 in this volume). For Garrison's response, see William Lloyd Garrison, "Extraordinary Somerset," *The Liberator* 8 (April 13, 1838): 59, and "Boston Quarterly Review," *The Liberator* 8 (April 27, 1838): 2. For Brownson's counter, see "Letter to William Lloyd Garrison," *The Liberator* 8 (May 11, 1838): 73. This "Letter" was originally published in the *Boston Reformer and Anti-Monopolist* 16 (April 20, 1838): 1-2. For further defense of his own antislavery position, see "To the Editor of the Liberator," *Boston Reformer and Anti-Monopolist* 19 (May 11, 1838): 2—a manuscript of this letter was later republished in *The American Catholic Historical Researches* 11 (April, 1894): 50-52, with no indication of where the original was published. "To the Editor" was Brownson's response to an attack upon his character by an anonymous correspondent, Elia. See "A Crooked Course No Deviation from a Straight Line," *The Liberator* 8 (May 4, 1838): 71.

[93]*Early Life*, 211.

ity also allowed him to consider a fresh adventure, namely the establishment of a journal of opinion, which he began to organize during the closing months of 1837.

Brownson had for some time conceived of the idea of starting a journal that would be devoted to extensive examinations of religion, philosophy, politics, and general literature. The idea had been germinating perhaps since his days in the Transcendentalist Club where the idea had first been raised. A more immediate motivation, however, came from Francis Bowen's attack on Emerson's *Nature* in the January 1837 issue of the *Christian Examiner.* That attack demonstrated that that journal would no longer be sympathetic to the Transcendentalist leanings and Brownson, along with other Transcendentalists, saw the necessity of establishing an organ for the dissemination of the new school philosophy. Whatever Brownson's motives may have been, there is no doubt that he had clearly planned the entire first issue of the *Boston Quarterly Review* during the last two months of 1837 and had it ready for publication in January of 1838.

In November of 1837 Brownson wrote to Bancroft to tell him, among other things, about the new publication that he had been preparing since he left the *Boston Reformer.* "My design in publishing it," he told Bancroft "is by means of a higher philosophy of man than Reid's or Locke's to christianize democracy and *democratize* the church."[94] The production of the journal was motivated primarily, as Ripley pointed out, by "the inward promptings of the author's own soul."[95]

Brownson intended his new journal to be the mouthpiece of the Transcendentalist or the "movement party" within Unitarianism. To accomplish this he invited a number of the new lights to write for the journal and published articles from George Bancroft, Ripley, Amos Bronson Alcott, Sarah Margaret Fuller (1810-50), Anne Charlotte Lynch (Botta) (1815-91), Sarah H. Whitman (1803-78), R. A. Tyler, Elizabeth Peabody (1804-94), B. H. Brewster, Henry S. Patterson, Alexander Hill Everett (1790-1847), Theodore Parker (1810-60), Albert Brisbane (1809-90), and John F. Tuckerman (1815-55). Emerson, who was also invited to participate, declined to do so on the grounds that he was over committed already in 1837.[96] Theodore Parker noted in his copy of the first volume of the journal (1838) that John Sullivan Dwight (1813-93), William Henry Channing (1810-84), Samuel D. Robbins (1812-84), Bancroft, and Parker him-

[94]Brownson to Bancroft, November 10, 1837, in microfilm # 9 of the Brownson Papers.

[95]"Brownson's Writings," 30-31.

[96]*Early Life*, 214, 215, 220, 227, 230, 231, 233, and 237.

self had written articles for that volume.[97] Although a number of writers contributed to the first volume and a few wrote for subsequent volumes, it appears that Brownson himself wrote most of the articles throughout the five years of its existence.

In his "Introductory Remarks" for the first issue, Brownson outlined the journal's aims. It was an organ, he insisted, of no religious sect, school of thought, or political party; but, he admitted, it would be an advocate for "the great movement party of mankind" that had its origins in Jesus and was gathering momentum day by day. He would support that great movement party "whether it be effecting a reform in the church, giving us a purer and more rational theology; in philosophy seeking something profounder and more inspiring than the heartless sensualism of the last century; or whether in society demanding the elevation of labor with the loco-foco, or the freedom of the slave with the abolitionist, I own I sympathize, and thank God that I am able to sympathize."[98] He wanted the journal to excite and stir up thought, and intended his own articles to be provocative, inviting criticisms that would help clarify thought for the new society that he felt was dawning.

The journal had something of a national reputation during its five years of existence and at its peak it had over 1000 subscribers.[99] It had a much wider subscription list, for example, than did the semi-official organ of the "pure" Transcendentalists, the *Dial* (1840-44), which never had more than 300 subscribers throughout its existence. The *Quarterly* took a leading role in advocating the new philosophy and particularly in spreading a knowledge of French idealism and eclecticism, and the more radical French socialist tradition of the Saint-Simonians, the later Félicité de Lamennais, and Pierre Leroux. In the judgment of Clarence L. F. Gohdes, the authority on Transcendentalist journals, the *Quarterly* was "the most philosophical of all the periodicals connected with the [Transcendentalist] movement."[100]

From the beginning of the *Quarterly* Brownson wanted to make it clear that, even though he considered himself a member of the movement party, he was not a "Transcendentalist," at least not in the sense that that term was being understood by many opponents of the new philosophy—that is, as a term of derision, meaning those who advocated a mindless mysticism, obscurantism, metaphysical non-

[97]On authorship of unsigned articles in the *Boston Quarterly Review*, see Gohdes, 47-50.

[98]*Boston Quarterly Review* 1 (January, 1838): 6.

[99]Charles Carroll Hollis, "The Literary Criticism of Orestes Brownson," Ph.D. dissertation, University of Michigan, 1954, 35.

[100]Gohdes, 80.

sense, or groundless German idealism. In fact, Brownson, like Emerson and a few others, periodically wrote about Transcendentalism, according to Arthur Versluis, "as if they were separated from it." For those who were called Transcendentalists, this was a kind of conventional "rhetorical trick" that helped them distinguish their own views from the interpretations put upon them by their opponents.[101] Brownson employed this tactic for quite another reason. He wanted to promote French eclecticism as the philosophy of the day, and, like Cousin himself, Brownson tried to show how the "psychological method" employed by the French eclectics clearly separated them from the transcendental starting point of the German and Coleridgean schools of the new philosophy.

In one of the first articles for the *Quarterly*, "Philosophy and Common Sense," Brownson, taking issue with the young Francis Bowen's attack on Transcendentalism, asserted that he knew of no one who followed the Transcendental philosophy.[102] Brownson argued that the "genius of our country is for Eclecticism." Eclecticism was particularly appropriate for a democratic country like the United States because it acknowledged, through its emphasis on spontaneous reason or inspiration, that all human beings have common sense, that is, a common cognitive faculty and common or universal beliefs. Thus, eclecticism could put trust in the masses because, unlike the Lockeans who saw in the mind of the masses only a *tabula rasa*, it acknowledged their dignity and their instinctive beliefs. Philosophy, or reflective reason, did not instruct the masses on the universally valid beliefs of common sense; philosophy's role was to accept, explain, and legitimate those instinctive beliefs of humankind. The eclectic philosophy, therefore, was "in perfect harmony" with common sense and the American democratic tradition.

The first issue of the *Quarterly*, moreover, began a series of articles that defined Christianity as an historical force in the shaping of religion, culture, politics and economics. Christianity, in other words, had a social bearing, social implications, and an inherent force that could change the course of history and contemporary society. In "Christ Before Abraham" Brownson defined Christianity, much as Coleridge had done before him,[103] as a life, not a system of doctrines,

[101]Versluis, 12.

[102]*Boston Quarterly* Review 1 (January, 1838): 83-106. Brownson refers here to Bowen's "Locke and the Transcendentalists," *Christian Examiner* 23 (November, 1837): 170-94.

[103]In *Aids to Reflection*, vol. 9 of *The Collected Works of Samuel Taylor Coleridge. Aids to Reflection*, ed. John Beer (Princeton, N.J.: Princeton University Press, 1993),

or morals, or theologies. The life that Jesus and his apostles led was one of "pure disinterested love." That power of a life of love, furthermore, did not originate with Jesus; it existed before Abraham, and, therefore, Christianity was not original with Jesus but preceded him. Christianity was the idea and ideal of love that transcended historical forms even while it was incarnate in those forms.[104] This idealistic view of Christianity, which put the Christianity of Christ against the Christianity of the church, was a recurring theme in his previous thought but it was becoming much clearer in these early articles in the *Quarterly*.

What was original in Jesus and the Christian movement was, Brownson argued, his character, not his nature, not any new doctrine, not because the Christ (i.e., disinterested love) was in him, and not because he died a martyr. What was original in Jesus was that "the Christ attained to universality, and that his love was no longer the love of family . . . but a love of Humanity; it was no longer mere piety, . . . it was Philosophy."[105] Christianity, in Brownson's opinion, added philanthropy to Judaism. Love of humanity was the heart of the matter. In fact, love was the mediator between God and man; it was the universal atoner or reconciler. The force of this love was evident in the "history of the progress of philanthropy for the last two thousand years."[106] In this respect, Brownson continued to argue in the first issue, the newly organized Boston Association of the Friends of the Rights of Man, a workingmen's society, was consciously or unconsciously carrying on the inherent mission of Christianity in the present.[107] He warned his readers that a battle would rise up between the capitalist, the power of privilege, and the laboring classes unless the great doctrine of the universal brotherhood of humanity were incarnated in contemporary social structures.

Brownson also used the *Quarterly* to call for reforms in church, state, society, and politics. These institutions had to make visible and actual the primitive revelation of the life of love and universal brotherhood. Brownson sided with the various movements for reform, but he had an aversion to what he called the "one-idea reformers" or the "ultraist," that is, those reformers like the abolitionists who fixated

202, Coleridge argued: "Christianity is not a Theory, or a Speculation; but a *Life*. Not a *Philosophy* of Life, but a Life and a living Process."

[104]"Christ Before Abraham," *Boston Quarterly Review* 1 (January, 1838): 12-13, 15, 16, 17.

[105]"The Character of Jesus and the Christian Movement," *Boston Quarterly Review* 1 (April, 1838): 133.

[106]Ibid., 149.

[107]"Tendency of Modern Civilization," *Boston Quarterly Review* 1 (April, 1838): 206.

upon one issue and did not clearly see the fundamental principles that should guide the reformation of society and individuals. Individuals in contemporary society were left with no peace because they were bombarded on every side with reforms for one thing or another.[108] "Ultraism," whether religious or secular, was a characteristic of American society that he criticized throughout his life.

Brownson also abhorred political party politics, as was said earlier. In fact, he was removed from the editorship of the *Boston Reformer* in 1836 because he did not support the Democratic party with the kind of vigor the proprietors deemed necessary. Nonetheless he was involved in politics and was particularly interested in articulating a philosophy of the American political system. Democracy was an abiding interest for him and in the first issue of his paper he outlined his own philosophy of democracy. He despised the equation of democracy with the idea of the sovereignty of the people. For him, sovereignty ultimately belonged to justice, not to the people—this was not a new philosophy that developed only after the election of 1840, as some historians have contended.[109] In his idealist understanding of democracy, "Justice is the political phasis of God, it is identical with God."[110] For him, therefore, the power of the people and the sovereignty of the state were limited by justice "or, what is the same thing, the inalienable Rights of Man."[111] Periodically Brownson, like Lamennais, identified democracy with the spirit of Christianity, seeing in democracy the political manifestation of the Christian spirit of freedom and equality. What had been successful in American life was the emergence of political liberty; what remained to be unfolded was social equality. His struggles in the Workingmen's Association and his work for his own religious society supported a social democracy in the United States.

Religion, and Christianity in particular, according to Brownson, had an influence upon politics, but not the kind of influence some in American society were promoting. The United States was not, as some claimed, a Christian Commonwealth. Brownson had in the past repeatedly opposed that assertion; in 1838 he again rejected it and

[108]"Ultraism," *Boston Quarterly Review* 1 (July, 1838): 377-84.

[109]Schlesinger, *The Age of Jackson*, 401-02, 405-06, 495, and a number of historians after him have asserted that after the election of 1840 Brownson gradually rejected popular or egalitarian democracy and moved more closely to authoritarianism, finally ending up in Catholicism. Brownson, however, even in the early 1830s, did not include popular sovereignty as an essential characteristic of democracy.

[110]"Democracy," *Boston Quarterly Review* 1 (January, 1838): 54.

[111]Ibid., 59.

argued that the Christian idea of freedom and equality was the constitutive idea of the nation. That idea was located in the primitive consciousness of all humans; it was unfolded historically through human effort. Christians, and particularly Christian ministers, should be involved in the historical process of implementing these ideals in society.[112] For Brownson, democracy was a grand principle of freedom and equality; he could not sympathize with those who feared that it meant a leveling of all social and individual distinctions and gifts. Democracy meant, though, that all should work for equal opportunity and that those in positions of political responsibility ought to "level upwards" those who were disadvantaged in the community.[113] He tried to assuage the fears of those in the community who thought that democracy, and Brownson's advocacy of it, was a revolutionary attempt to bring down those in power and position in the community. He repeatedly asserted that he wanted to raise up the lowly, not bring down the mighty. But his disclaimers were ineffective even with his Transcendentalist cohorts, many of whom thought he was an uncouth Democrat and believed his journal was the organ of the Democratic party.[114] Even Ripley, Brownson's closest friend among the Transcendentalists, had only recently converted to Democracy, Brownson told Bancroft in 1837.[115]

Brownson launched the first three issues of his journal in 1838 and defined his view of the Christian basis of democracy as well as the democratic dimensions of Christianity and the church. Religion and the primitive revelation inherent in human consciousness, *á la* Cousin, he argued throughout the first issues, needed to be brought to a progressive realization by reflection and human effort. Even though Brownson had an idealist conception of Christianity, he still emphasized the role of human reflection and effort in making the spirit of Christianity actual in time and space. By the end of the year some Transcendentalists were put on the defensive by the mounting public attacks upon Emerson's "Divinity School Address." Brownson joined the defense, but he also saw the radicalism of Emerson's address as it related to the historic role of Christianity. Emerson's idealism was much more subjective than Brownson's and that difference would surface over the next few years. Volume four tells that story.

[112]"Religion and Politics," *Boston Quarterly Review* 1 (July, 1838): 310-33.

[113]"The *American Democrat*," *Boston Quarterly Review* 1 (July, 1838): 360-77.

[114]Gohdes, 64.

[115]Brownson to Bancroft, November 10, 1837, in microfilm # 9 of the Brownson Papers.

The editorial principles and procedures followed in this volume are the same as those in volume one of *The Early Works of Orestes A. Brownson*,[116] which is referred to in the footnotes in this and subsequent volumes as EW.

[116] *The Universalist Years, 1826-29* (Milwaukee, Wis.: Marquette University Press, 2000), 30-34.

WORKS

1.

EDUCATION OF THE PEOPLE[1]

Christian Examiner and General Review
20 (May, 1836): 153-69

M. Matter brings to the question of the reciprocal influence of manners and laws, proposed by the French Academy, an acute mind, a philosophical spirit, and extensive erudition. He succeeds in disengaging and bringing forth to the light truths of the greatest importance to the statesman and the philanthropist. The work before us is only a *résumé* of a larger one not yet completed. It is divided into four parts. The first part is taken up with general remarks on the question to be discussed, and on the sense in which the terms *manners* and *laws* are used by the author. The second part treats of the influence of manners upon laws; the third of the influence of laws on manners; and the fourth contains views and observations on the means offered by the reciprocal influence of manners and laws for the social melioration of nations.

The general facts, which, according to M. Matter, should serve as the basis of every political measure and every species of legislation having for their object the glory and prosperity of nations, are these.

1. The influence of manners, tastes, habits, customs, morals, on laws, and of laws on manners, is not always equally strong. It depends on circumstances, is variously modified, but it is always profound. Manners inspire laws, laws modify manners. Generally one is the copy, the expression, of the other. Sometimes, however, they are not in harmony. When they are not, the social state is deranged, is in peril. But when the tendency of either is generous, moral, popular, and when the authority that directs them is the same, the danger of the conflict is not great. In opposite cases there is only disorder and revolt, or corruption and decline, in empires.

2. Manners exercise a stronger action than laws. They are anterior, they belong more intimately to man, are, so to speak, the man, the nations themselves. Laws come later than manners. They must

[1][Ed. Review of Jacques Matter's (1791-1864) *De l' influence des moeurs sur les lois, et de l' influence des lois sur les moeurs* (Paris: Firmin Didot Frèrer, 1832).]

necessarily resemble them, support themselves on them, and borrow from them their power. They have a strong and permanent authority only as they are recommended by established habits, dictated by general opinion, and sanctioned by the public adhesion. In this happy condition, laws give to manners the most august sanction, protect them, honor them, and assure them a salutary ascendancy in all classes of society.

3. Manners without laws lose their purity, fail in force and influence. Laws without manners are null. "In vain," says Socrates, "are the walls of the Portico covered with laws. It is not by decrees, but by principles of justice deeply imprinted in the hearts of its citizens, that a state is well governed."[2]

4. In the progress of the moral and legal civilization of nations, sometimes the laws, sometimes the manners are found in advance. Here it is the development of manners, there it is the development of legislation, that precedes. But whichever may precede, one always gains by what the other gains. The progress of law always leads to a progress of morality or of the individual, and a legislation having at all times in view the moral interests of humanity, so far from being a chimera, is the only legislation deserving the name. Every other is insufficient, defective, pitiable.

5. Manners have a greater importance than laws for the prosperity of empires. Where they are very bad, good laws are impossible. Without good manners the best laws have but a feeble influence, and are often inoperative or mischievous. Without good manners or without good laws there is no life for nations, and the corruption of both is the most active cause of their ruin.

According to M. Matter, to labor "to establish, preserve, and perfect the public morality is the most sacred duty of government." It should attach itself to the dominant sentiment, idea, tendency of a people, and direct all its laws to this end. This is the first means offered by the reciprocal influence of laws and manners for the social melioration of nations. The second means to be adopted to obtain the same end, is the moral and political education of the people, and the third, the education of the young. The first means will never be successfully applied without the other two. Education then, both of the people and of children, is in reality the only efficient means of all social, as it is of all individual, progress.

But there may be a question as to the schoolmaster. Who shall determine and impart the education? The king of Prussia has de-

[2][Ed. Unable to identify quotation.]

cided in favor of government.[3] He has made himself the schoolmaster of his people, and is taking good care to educate them to be faithful to an authority which does not tolerate one particle of political liberty. In his hands, education, instead of being a means of social progress, becomes a means of preventing it. Despotism was never so politic before. It is turning the weapons of reformers against themselves. In the hands of the Catholic Church, education would be made to uphold the popedom and prevent the increase of religious light and liberty. In the hands of our own government, it would be turned to the especial benefit of the opinions or interests of the party in power for the time being. For ourselves we have no great faith in the fitness of any government, nor of any constituted body, civil, political, or religious, to be charged with the education of the people or of children. All constituted bodies have, or are prone to imagine that they have, peculiar rights and interests, and these peculiar rights and interests will almost invariably preside over the education they command or tolerate.

But waiving this, no government, no government on earth, is qualified to determine the education to be given the people. The wisdom of government can never rise above the average of the wisdom of the individuals who compose it. Allow that these individuals, which is far from being the fact in any country, are the wisest and best men of the nation, and it by no means follows that they are qualified to decide, authoritatively, what ideas, what sentiments are proper for the people, or what instruction should be given to children. There are few who would not call in question their infallibility, and the expediency of giving up their own understandings to theirs. No education can be complete, can be what it ought to be, that does not instruct both people and children in reference to the end for which man was made, and fit them to attain it. The destination of man and of society, and the means of marching steadily and straight forward towards it, are the subject matter of all useful education; and surely it is no want of charity to say, that governments are in respect to these, at least, but very little in advance of the people. They need education themselves as well as the people; and they must in fact receive theirs from the people, for the people always exercise a stronger action on government, than government does on them. Government then, cannot be the schoolmaster for the people, nor for chil-

[3][Ed. Reference is to Frederick William III (1770-1840), King of Prussia from 1797, who after 1807 accepted some reforms in his government, but he had a constant fear of "Jacobin" reformers and sought to reinforce royal prerogatives.]

dren. It may, as it is in duty bound, make all the provision for the education of both that it can, but it must not attempt to decide what the education shall be.

But it is necessary that both people and children be rightly educated. The education of the people is even more important than that of children; for it is their education which decides the character and measures of government, and determines the education of the young. The importance of educating the young, the rising generation, is, in this country at least, widely and deeply felt. We allow, we contend, that all children should be well educated, and we have done and are doing much that they may be. But our own education, so far as relates to ideas, sentiments, to that which constitutes the soul of our education, will be the measure of that we give to our children. Allow that we of the present, acting generation have incorrect notions on the destiny of man and of society, that we do not rightly perceive and fully comprehend the true end which man in his individual and social acts should always keep in view, and it would evidently follow that we are not qualified to instruct dogmatically those who are to take our places. The education we give to our children must be incomplete, erroneous, if not mischievous. Not a little of the education received by a large portion of the children of our country is perhaps only better than none. We need but look into a multitude of tracts and Sabbath-school books, which are constantly issuing from the orthodox presses of the country, to be convinced of this fact. Those tracts and books educate to a certain extent our children; but they educate them not for their true destiny, not for the future, but for the past. Now, there is no remedy for this, but in the education of the grown-up generation, but in having the people possess right ideas on the destination of man and of society, in having them clearly perceive and fully comprehend, so far as it is given to finite beings, what man and society may be, and what they ought to be.

We would not have it understood by these remarks that we wish to relax exertions for the education of children. We believe with the Spartan lawgiver, that "the principal part of legislation is the right education of youth,"[4] and with a wiser than he, "Train up a child in the way he should go, and when he is old he will not depart from it"

[4][Ed. Reference is to Lycurgus (flourished in seventh-century B.C.) to whom the foundations of many ancient Spartan institutions are ascribed. Brownson may have derived the quote from an edition of Plutarch's *Life of Lycurgus*. On this, see, for example, *Plutarch: The Lives of the Noble Grecians and Romans*, trans. John Dryden; revised Arthur Hugh Clough (New York: The Modern Library, 1932), 58-59.]

[Prov. 22:6]. But this we contend is impossible, unless the people themselves know the way in which he should go. It is vain to ascribe this knowledge to any great extent to the people of any country. Enlightened as we think ourselves in this country, we do not fully possess it. Our notions on what education should be are vague and contradictory. If our own government were qualified to determine for us, its determinations would have no weight. Some want their children educated to be Calvinists, some to be Catholics, some to be Episcopalians, some to be Methodists, some to be Universalists, some to be Unitarians, and some to be believers in no religion. In this case the most government can do is, so far as its own schools are concerned, to disregard the wants of all parties, and prohibit all sectarian and, as things are, virtually all religious instruction; which is, in fact, prohibiting instruction in what it most concerns us to know.

This evil is a great one. It is beginning to be widely and deeply felt. But there is no remedy but in the education of the people. The education of children has long held a prominent place, but the education of the people has not till lately received much direct attention. Neglected it has not been, but it has not been provided for and pursued systematically, designedly. It has seldom been presented as a distinct topic of consideration, and as an indispensable prerequisite to the right education of children. But we think it highly important that it should be. Let the people be educated, that is, let them have just ideas on whatever can affect man as a moral, religious, or social being, and they would soon devise and carry into effect the proper education for children. Ideas are not powerless. They may operate silently, slowly, but in the end they prove themselves omnipotent. They pass from mind to mind, from heart to heart, and generate a moral force, that breaks out eventually with irresistible energy and changes the whole face of society. Just ideas are what is needed. The most important service which man can render his fellow beings is to diffuse just ideas on the destiny of man and society. To do this is to educate the people; and when the people are truly educated, enlightened, a sound and vigorous national and individual morality will not be slow to follow.

But the question now recurs, who are to be the educators of the people? Not governments, we have decided, because they need to be educated themselves. We want the influence of a body of men from which both governments and people shall receive their character. Where is this body to be found? We answer, unhesitatingly, it ought to be found in the Christian ministry. The Christian clergy are designed to be the chief educators of the people. They act directly on the ideas of the people. They are concerned with every sphere of man's duty, with that which relates to his neighbor and society, as well as with that which relates to himself and to his God. They are the schoolmasters for adults, "public teachers of piety, religion, and morality," as they are denominated in our "Bill of Rights,"[5] and it is their mission to give lessons on whatever affects man as an individual or a social being, for time or for eternity.

In pronouncing the Christian clergy the educators of the people, we would not be understood as claiming for them the right to teach dogmatically. The question of the destiny of man and of society is not yet settled, and, till it be, instruction should be as little dogmatic as possible. The clergy, no more than governments, are infallible. There are few of them who do not need instruction themselves. They must inquire rather than dogmatize. They must educate by arousing and directing the attention of the people, by revealing to their minds their unexerted powers, and pointing them to the means of individual and social progress not yet adopted. They must study to set the people to work in the right direction, and educate them by inducing them to educate themselves. They are to act on free minds, and that not to control them, but to quicken and strengthen them. They must convince, not dictate; persuade, not compel.

But we may be told that the clergy are doing all this now. Not all of it. They seem to us to restrict themselves to one part, an important part, we admit, of their mission. They seem to consider that the individual element is the only element of religion, and that that element is mainly important simply as it relates to another world. They confine their mission too exclusively to what is technically called the "cure of souls," and seem to think that they should depart from their duty, if they should labor for the social well-being of man in his present mode of existence. They interpret in a wrong sense the words of Jesus, "My kingdom is not of this world" [John 18:36], so as to make them mean, not that the moral kingdom of Jesus was to be based on principles wholly different from those on which were based the moral and political kingdom of his epoch, but that he really intended to establish no kingdom except for the world after death.

[5][Ed. Brownson attributes this provision to the "Bill of Rights," but it actually is from the third article of the "Northwest Ordinance of 1787" (July 13): "Religion, morality, and knowledge being necessary to good government and the happiness of mankind, schools and the means of education shall forever be encouraged." On this, see Clarence Edwin Carter, ed., *The Territorial Papers of the United States*, 26 vols. (Washington, D. C.: U. S. Government Printing Office, 1934-62), 2:47.]

This world, society and all its direct interests, they seem to imagine to belong of right to some other class of instructors. The consequence is that they give no direct instructions on the destination of society, do little to awaken a zeal and quicken exertions for social progress. They aim indeed to perfect the individual but not society. In this they overlook the social, if we may so speak, the material elements of religion.

Now we affirm that Christianity was designed to aid social as well as individual progress; and if so, the clergy have no more right to overlook the social element than they have to overlook the individual element. Undoubtedly the first concern of Christianity is to perfect the individual, to fit him for that glorious social state into which the good will enter after death; but it contemplates also the fitting of him for a more perfect social state here. The angels sang "*On earth*, peace and good will toward men," as well as "Glory to God in the highest" [Luke 2:14]. It was on earth that Jesus proposed to establish a kingdom of righteousness and peace, as well as in the world after death. And, indeed, so far as he gave us any instruction on the subject, he taught us that the surest pledge of a heaven hereafter is the creation of one here. In perfecting the individual, reference then may be had to his earthly mode of being. That mode of being comes within the precincts of the clerical mission. If it does, we know not why the clergy have not a right to touch upon society, point out social abuses, what society is, what it may be, what it ought to be, what are the means of its progress, what man has a right to demand of it, and what it in return has a right to exact of him.

Allow, however, that the perfection of the individual is the sole object of Christianity, this subject can never, to any considerable extent, be obtained without the perfection of society. Man has his social side, social faculties, duties, rights, and interests. Leave out these and his character will want symmetry, fail in completeness. Perfect every individual, and undoubtedly you would perfect society; but it is necessary that the perfection of both be carried along together. Out of society, in a cave or cloister, a part of man's nature must remain undeveloped, or be developed but to wither and die. Man can live and grow only in society. His growth effects a growth of society, and that growth of society reacts upon him and effects a new growth. But, in some states of society, there must be a social growth before there can be, in relation to a part of the community, an individual growth. Many individuals may occupy a position in the social state that precludes the possibility of the growth of any part, except the animal part, of their nature. These individuals never compose the whole of any community, but their number may be great. Of themselves they cannot rise. The man within them cannot germinate and spring up and expand into beauty or ripen into moral worth, unless watered and cherished by those who occupy a more favorable position. Society bears them down, tramples them in the dust; and may not the clergy urge their claims, and urge them even in loud and earnest tones? May they not point to the imperfections of that social state, where multitudes of human beings, endowed with a noble nature, are by the action of causes which exceed their energy or power to control, doomed to live and die mere animals. And in pointing out these imperfections may they not direct attention to the discovery and application of a remedy? If they may not, how can they labor successfully for the perfection of all the individuals composing a community?

But it may be objected to this, that it would carry the clergy from the *actual* to the *possible*, from what is to what ought to be. We hope it would. The church from its beginning has been strangely inconsistent. In relation to the individual it has always been going from the actual to the possible, from what is to what should be. It never tells the sinner his actual condition must be preserved, that he must indulge in no visionary schemes of improvement, that innovations are dangerous, and that it is safest not to depart from the old landmarks. But it always attempts to make him discontented, and feel that his condition is most miserable. And it presents him, too, visions of a better state, and urges him by motives attractive as heaven, and terrible as hell, to gain it. In relation to society all this has changed. Here the actual is approved and departure from it condemned. "Undoubtedly, indirectly, by softening the manners, exalting the sentiments, decrying or abolishing many barbarous practices, the church has powerfully contributed to the improvement of man's social condition."[6] But directly it has done nothing. It has done worse than nothing. It has generally given its aid to despotism, lent its spiritual aegis to shelter the civil tyrant in his war against the progress of society. Why this difference? In the most favored parts of the world society is imperfect, and its imperfections must in the eyes of a just God excuse many of the imperfections of individuals: why not then labor to perfect it? What, indeed, is the great mission of life, but to

[6][Ed. Brownson's footnote refers to "the influence of the church" in François Pierre Guillaume Guizot's (1787-1874) *Histoire générale de la civilization en Europe, depuis la chute de l'Empire romain jusqu' a la révolution française* (Paris: Pichon et Didier, 1828), Leçon vi.]

go from the imperfect to the perfect? And can it be less Christian to go from the imperfect to the perfect in relation to society, than it is in relation to the individual?

It may be alleged that, should the clergy bring out the social element and labor for the perfection of society, they would soon lose themselves in a land of shadows, and merely amuse the people with dreams. Be it so then. Even dreams are sometimes from God. Those visions of something better than what is, which are for ever coming to the minds and the hearts of the gifted and the good, are our pledges of higher destiny. They familiarize us with loftier excellence, enchant us with a beauty superior to that of earth, and quicken within us the power to do and to endure everything to realize them. They may never be realized. It may be best that they should not. But the soul's struggles to realize them always make us stronger and better. We envy no one who has them not. No one ever attained to eminence who did not see mountains rising far above the highest he could reach. There flit before the "mind's eye" of the greatest masters in painting and sculpture, forms of beauty which infinitely surpass their skill to transfer to the canvass or the marble. The immortal sons of song have visions of intellectual greatness and moral worth, of which even their happiest numbers can give us but a faint conception. Yet it is to their daily and nightly communing with these beings of the ideal, to their continual efforts to seize and embody them, that they are indebted for the excellence they attain. It is, in fact, to the soul's power to go off from the actual to the possible, to conceive something greater and better than what is, that we are indebted for all our improvements. The soul goes before the body. It seizes upon heaven while its clog of clay drags upon the earth. It is well that it is so. It is the condition of all progress. Let the soul then be ever breaking away from the present, seeking a serener heaven, a warmer sun, and greener fields in the future; it is but its effort to return to God, of whom it carries with it, wherever it goes, an inward sentiment and an undying love.

Of course we would not lose sight of the practicable. But where does the practicable end? Till the limits of thought be discovered, and the depths of love be sounded, no one can tell. Man has within him powers which have slept from creation; and who is prepared to say what he may not achieve, when they shall be once awakened and put forth in all their energy? Certainly we would not lose ourselves in the ideal, nor indeed do we think there is much danger of doing it in this materializing age. There may be epochs when men are too much engaged in building castles in the air, and in peopling them with the creatures of their own imagination. But ours is not one. We are too much engrossed with the outward, the tangible, the material, to be in much danger of losing ourselves in the ideal. We say, then, let the clergy bring out the social element of Christianity, and direct their attention, and that of their congregations, to the work of perfecting society. Let them take generous views of what society ought to be, and of what it may be. And if they turn out to be dreamers, let them not lose their self-respect. We would rather dream with Plato, than reason with Hobbes and Machiavelli.

We trust we shall not be misinterpreted. We are not urging governments to attempt to realize the crude projects of mere day-dreamers. We are among those who are willing that government should move "slowly and surely," never departing from a settled line of policy without urgent and satisfactory reasons. We are not now speaking of the duty of governments, but of the clergy as educators of the people. In the education they give, we would have the clergy connect the present with the future. We would have them educate the people with special reference to progress both in the individual and in society. We would have them preach the progress of humanity and of society, progress in the spiritual and in the material order, turn all minds and hearts towards it, convince them of its practicability, and kindle a deep and becoming enthusiasm to effect it.

If, however, we may be our own interpreters, we would not have progress preached to the detriment of order. We yield to none in our love of order. Order is heaven's law. But order, except in a very incomplete sense, is nowhere as yet attained. Disorder now reigns in the individual and in the social state; and this is the reason why we desire progress, which, if it be progress and not retrogression, is only a continued approach to order, a continued effort of man and society to place themselves in harmony with the universal order which is God.[7] Nor would we have progress so preached as to arouse angry feelings. We want no indignation, no condemnation. Jesus Christ came not to condemn the world, but to save it. The *Christian* ministry can follow no example but his. It will indulge no bad feelings itself, and it will avoid as much as possible the arousing of any in others. Love is the dominant principle of all good education, whether for old or young; and love is the lever with which the clergy must raise man and society to their destiny.

[7]See "Mélanges Philosophiques, par Théodore Jouffroy." Paris: 1833. Article, "Du Bien et du Mal."

In contending that the clergy should labor more directly for the melioration of society than they have hitherto done, we by no means forget the excuse, if not the justification, of their past conduct. It is easy to perceive the reason why this world has entered so little into their instructions. Christianity was like "leaven" deposited in the mighty mass of religious notions generated by the Grecian and Oriental worlds. For a time it must be concealed, and seem lost; and it was only after ages of silent and secret working, that it could succeed in leavening the "whole lump." Those religious notions, which Greece and the East had given the world, must therefore for a long time be predominant; and the history of the church proves that they did reign for a long time, and that some of them have been very powerful down to our own times. The Grecian world was indeed human, material, social. But its religion was from the East, from Egypt and India, and there all is mysticism. Not all, perhaps, but mysticism predominates there, gives its character and direction to men's thoughts, feelings, and pursuits. From them mysticism passed into the church, sometimes reigned, or nearly reigned in it, and at all times tinged its doctrines and exerted an influence over its practice.

Now what is the view which mysticism gives us of this life, of this world? In the eyes of the mystics, this world is not worth a thought or a wish. The earth is a "wretched land," unable to "yield us any supply." Sublunary bliss is impossible. Man sees around him only the spectacle of sin and misery. His life is a continual warfare. He obtains not a morsel of bread, not a covering for his body, without a war with matter. Nothing is obtained without an effort, and all effort must end in fatigue, and generally in disappointment. Man's condition here is that of punishment. Everything is opposed to his well-being. The body with its wants, society with its importunities, its petty ambitions, its vain pursuits, its friendships, its sorrows, its temptations, its vices and crimes, are forever interposing between the soul and its good, rending it away from God, and compelling it to sigh and seek in vain for repose.

With this view of man's earthly mode of being, how could the thought of laboring for it find admittance? Life was death, and society the grave. We were not placed in this world to live, but to endure. It is not our home. We are strangers and sojourners here. We are pilgrims, seeking a city whose maker is God, as though God were not the maker of this as well as of all other worlds. Here all is toil and fatigue; and what would we have religion to be but a star of hope to guide us over "life's tremulous, ocean," to the haven of everlasting rest, to our eternal home, where all our toils will be over, where there will be no more fatigue, where the soul may repose forever beneath the sunlight of the Lord? What is life, what is the world, that they should detain us here? Scorn them, deny them, think only of heaven, only of gaining a blissful "mansion in the skies."[8]

This view of life, of this world, of the true object of pursuit, though it has never completely triumphed in the church, has always made the grand staple of its sermons, exhortations, prayers, and hymns. With this view, it would hardly seem a duty for the clergy to labor for the melioration of society. And this view is not without some show of truth. It is true that we can in this world obtain only a part of the good promised us by our nature, and it is true that we gain nothing without effort, and that all effort is followed by fatigue. All this is true. But, if we cannot obtain all the good our nature promises, we may obtain a part of it; if we cannot achieve our destiny here, we may commence it and march towards our end.[9] If we can obtain nothing without effort, it is in effort that we grow, in effort that the soul is developed and becomes strong and healthy. Repose after toil is sweet, but endless repose were endless death. Give to the soul perfect rest, and you annihilate it. Action is its life. And for action this world is fitted. It has its pains and its pleasures, its joys and its sorrows, its hopes and its fears, its struggles and its rests, its alternations of light and darkness, everything needed to touch the soul on every side, to quicken and exert all its faculties. It is then rather a state of trial than of endurance, of discipline, and not of punishment. It need not be condemned. It is useful to the soul. It is God's world, and to slight it were to fail in reverence to God.

The New Testament also in some places seems to favor this view of the mystics. But it is only in appearance. It condemns worldly-mindedness, but worldly-mindedness can hardly be confounded with the philanthropic desire to make the world the abode of peace and love. It forbids us to expect happiness from the world, but not to hope and labor for it in the world; it assures us the earth cannot yield us a supply, but not that no supply can be obtained while we are on the earth. It requires us to mortify the body; yet it does not mean that the body has not its place, its rights, and its uses,

[8][Ed. "Mansion in the skies" comes from Isaac Watts (1674-1748) "Hymns and Spiritual Songs," Book 2, Hymn 65, Line 2. See Selma L. Bishop's *Isaac Watts Hymns and Spiritual Songs 1707-1748: A Study in Early Eighteenth Century Language Changes* (London: Faith Press, 1962), 229.]

[9]We refer our readers for a fuller development of the views offered in this and the two preceding paragraphs, to Professor Jouffroy's "Cours [for 1833 and 1834,] de Droit Naturel. Cinquième Lecon. Système Mystique."

but that we should not be governed by its propensities, that we should yield ourselves servants only to our higher, our spiritual nature. It teaches us that our main effort should be to gain heaven, but heaven may be here, in a degree, as well as hereafter; that our only good is in God, but God is on this side [of] the grave as well as on the other. He is in every good man's heart. He is found only in being good and in doing good. We may be good in this world and for this world, and do good for this world, without in the least unfitting ourselves for another. Man has a destiny on earth in time as well as in eternity, and the path that leads to his destiny here is the true road to that hereafter, for both are but one and the same destiny. If he has a destiny here, he has duties here, and if duties here, the world is not beneath his notice.

While, however, the notion prevailed that this world is but a place of punishment, while it was considered an enemy, life a wearisome load, and heaven after death the only thing worth laboring for, the clergy could not preach and act much otherwise than they did. There was then no place for the social element. If they had brought it out, it would have been unheeded. The state of society itself, during the centuries which immediately succeeded the introduction of Christianity, was such as must almost inevitably turn men's minds in the direction of mysticism. Everything was unsettled. There was nowhere any security. All was fleeting. The earth seemed abandoned by its Maker to the merciless hordes of barbarians that overrun it. There was no faith in it, no heart to labor for its improvement, and no cause to wonder at the thousands of monks and anchorites who filled the deserts and monasteries.

But this state of things is now changed and the clergy must change with it, or lose their influence, and be themselves numbered with the things that were. The clergy, no more than governments, can have any authority without attaching themselves to the dominant sentiment or idea of the people. The secret of their influence is in their being the best representatives, impersonations, of the sentiments of their age and country, or of those on whom they are to act. The dominant spirit of their epoch is their *point d' appui*, which must cover and support all their operations. The history of the clergy since the Reformation, affords lamentable proof of the truth of this assertion. Before the Reformation, the church was hardly called to preach social progress. The spiritual order then was everything, the material order nothing, except as it served the church. Man was something, but society was not. Individual progress might then be preached, but not social progress. The time had not yet come. The Reformation changed the face of things. It was in many respects the installation of society. It brought up the state, and prepared the way for the social element to become operative. This was a new state of things. The clergy should have accepted and conformed to it. As men, some of them did; but, as clergymen, the greater part rejected it and continued to pray, sing, and preach, in the spirit of the church before the change had been effected.

And what has been the consequence? Its consequences have been, in the first place, to lessen the influence of the clergy, till in those countries in which social progress has been the greatest, it is now almost too trivial to be named; and, in the next place, to throw the direction of the social progress into the hands of those whose enmity the church had aroused, and whose minds were embittered against religion itself from its supposed hostility to social reform. It is therefore, that infidelity is so prominent a feature in modern civilization. The social element, being refused by the clergy, was taken up by unbelievers; and, in proportion as the social element gained upon the individual element, unbelievers gained upon the clergy. And their gain has been great. In literature, perhaps we do not hazard too much in saying the infidel sentiment reigns. Scarcely a writer who takes a wide and deep hold upon the public mind, but seems to owe his success to his sympathy with doctrines generally disavowed by the clergy. Religion and society are at war. To a great extent the clergy adhere to the progress of humanity alone, while the opponents of the clergy are clamorous for the progress of society. Exceptions we know there are, but we are speaking merely of dominant tendencies; and what we say of these was, perhaps, much truer at the close of the last century than now. Since then the influence of ministers of religion may have been on the increase. But their increased influence must be traced to the fact, that since then they have labored much more for society than they ever did before.

We say to the *fact*, and we say it designedly, for we do not perceive that there has been any material change of theory. The principle contended for is the same as it was. Social melioration, except in a theological sense, as it is to be effected by proselytizing and converting, does not seem to be yet allowed by the clergy generally to be a Christian object, any more than it was before the Reformation. The energy, which would have been directed to the improvement of society properly so called, has been beguiled into an apparently social channel, but it will soon discover that it is not yet in the right channel, and then, if the clergy do not accept it, they are prostrate. The real dominant sentiment of our epoch is that of social progress.

It is in vain to war against it. The clergy, during their centuries of labor for individual progress, have prepared the way for it. It has come. It will have its day. It will reign till the progress of society equals that which has been made by individuals. It should be accepted. To accept this is what we are urging upon the clergy. We believe it their duty to accept it, and we are confident that to accept it is the only means they have left to recover their influence and save the world from infidelity.

We say the dominant sentiment of our epoch is that of social progress. We think we cannot be mistaken in this. If the development and growth of the social element be not the dominant sentiment of the age, we would ask, what mean these demands for social reform which come to our ears on every breeze, from every land? What mean these movements among the people, these combinations of even workingmen to meliorate society? What mean these shakings of thrones, these fears, which penetrate the hearts of kings, fill courts with consternation, and make those who live by existing abuses turn pale? There is no mistaking the spirit of the times. We see it everywhere, we see it in new sects, in the abortive attempts of the Saint-Simonians, in the new French Catholic Church, insignificant as it may be. We saw it in the deep sensation produced by the whimsical Owen, when he first announced his new social system;[10] we felt it in the thrill which ran through our hearts, and heard it in the loud burst of sympathy which broke from the whole civilized world, at the news of the French Revolution of July, 1830.[11] We see it in the influence of such writers as Jeremy Bentham, Byron, and Bulwer.[12] We see it, and not the least plainly, in the humble but powerful min-

[10][Ed. By 1836 the Saint-Simonian movement to produce a new Christianity had failed to develop much of a following in France. The "new French Catholic Church" was clearly a reference to Félicité Robert de Lamennais (1782-1854) and his movement to align Christianity and modern democracy. Brownson was familiar with Lamennais' *Paroles d' un croyant* (1834) that, among other things, presented a picture of an ideal community in which production and consumption were harmoniously balanced. On Robert Owen, see the introduction to EW, 1.]

[11][Ed. The bloodless revolution of July 1830 made Louis Philippe of Orléans the "Citizen King" of France (1830-48).]

[12][Ed. Jeremy Bentham (1748-1832), British philosopher and legal theorist, stimulated the rise of utilitarianism in England and tried to put legal and social criticism on a scientific basis. George Gordon Byron (1788-1824) was an English Romantic poet and satirist. Edward George Earle Bulwer-Lytton (1803-73) was a British novelist, politician, poet, and critic. Bulwer was a prolific and popular novelist, some of whose many works Brownson periodically reviewed in his journals.]

istry to the poor in *this* city as well as in some others.[13] All these and a thousand other circumstances we could mention, had we room, are proofs to us that men's minds and hearts are busy with the social state, and that the real sentiment of our epoch is the sentiment of social progress. To this sentiment the clergy must attach themselves. The time for star-gazing has gone by. They must look on the earth and exert themselves to make it the abode of peace and love. This is the only way in which they can recover a permanent influence and be widely and lastingly useful. They neglected to accept the social element when they might have done it to better advantage. That element is now mainly in the hands of laymen and to a great extent in the hands of men who either disavow or do not love religion. In their hands it is abused, it takes a tinge of infidelity, receives a character and a direction foreign to its nature. The clergy should now be instant to redeem their past neglect, to recover and accept the rejected element, to cultivate it and give it a religious direction. By so doing they will recover their influence, so far as they ought to recover it, and be again in men's minds and hearts, with power to lead them up to God.

But, in contending that the clergy should take up the social element, we would by no means have them neglect the individual element of religion. Both are elements of Christianity, and both are responded to in the deep sympathies of human nature. They should be united, carried along together, as mutual friends constantly assisting each other. We believe in no social progress that is not demanded and sustained by individual progress. But the latter cannot reach perfection without the cooperation of the former. Therefore we advocate the progress both of humanity and of society. Nor would we have a heaven after death neglected. That is our everlasting home; it is only then that we shall be able to finish our destiny; and, in thinking more of that portion of our destiny which may be accomplished here, we would by no means think less of that which will always remain to be accomplished hereafter.

[13][Ed. Reference is to a Unitarian-led effort, which had its origins in the 1820s, to meet the religious needs of the working class in Boston. The effort was pioneered by the Unitarian minister Joseph Tuckerman (1786-1840). On Tuckerman, see Daniel T. McColgan, *Joseph Tuckerman: Pioneer in American Social Work* (Washington, D.C.: The Catholic University of America Press, 1940). Brownson was himself involved in this Unitarian work in his ministry to the Society for the Promotion of Christian Union and Progress.]

2.

A DISCOURSE ON THE WANTS OF THE TIMES[1]

The Apostle Paul remarks in one of his letters, that he became all things to all men, that he might gain some [1 Cor. 9:22]. From this, it has been inferred, that he varied his opinions, and shaped his doctrines to suit the views of those he chanced to address. But he probably meant to assert nothing more than that he adapted himself to all capacities, and to the peculiar wants of those to whom he preached.

[1][Ed. Delivered in Lyceum Hall, Hanover Street, Boston; Sunday, May 29, 1836. (Boston: James Munroe and Company, 1836). The following was prefaced to the Discourse:

"The Discourse, the substance of which, by request, I hereby offer to the public, was a hasty, extemporaneous performance, given to the congregation which for a few Sabbaths has assembled at Lyceum Hall, without the remotest idea to publication. In preparing it for the press, I have felt it my duty, to reproduce it with as much fidelity as possible. This must be my apology for suffering a Discourse to be printed, so imperfect in its form and dress as I know this to be.

The subject matter of this Discourse, however, has long occupied my thoughts, and I may say, I have here given some of the results to which I have arrived only after years of close application, varied experience, and intense thought. I ask, therefore, for my statement, that respect, that attention, which every man has a right to claim, when he speaks on that which has been his favorite topic of study, and to the investigation of which he has given his best moral and intellectual energies.

I speak without reserve of the object I am anxious to accomplish, because it is not *my* object. I stand in awe before it, and ask "who is sufficient for it?" That I wish to effect some changes in the mode of dispensing Christian truth, that I do contemplate great moral and social alterations, meliorations, I would say, as the effect of new views of Christianity clearly exhibited and fearlessly defended, I have no disposition to deny. Neither the state of morality, nor of society, comes up to my ideal of the perfect, nor of the possible. Christ, as the manifestation of God, does not seem to me as yet to be formed, to any great extent, in either the individual or the social heart; but I would have him, and I believe he may and will be incarnated in the heart of every man, and in the universal heart of humanity.

With regard to the charge of radicalism, which some have thrown out against myself and my friends, I have only to remark that the same word by contending parties is often, perhaps generally, taken in different senses; and that as I and my friends understand the word radical, we have no objection to be called radicals; but as the term is generally understood by the community, it cannot be justly applied to us. We are not destructionists. We do not touch the rights of property, and

I allude to this remark of Paul, for the purpose of obtaining a principle which ought to preside over all instruction, and which is applicable to all times and places. This principle is that we should always consult the wants of our age, and especially of the community to which we address ourselves. What is very proper to preach at one time, in one country, to one description of persons, may be very improper at another. Instruction must change with the changes of time and the progress of events, or it will fail to reach the mind or influence the heart.

The age, and especially the country, in which we live, are peculiar. They, therefore, require a peculiar kind of instruction, and, I may say, a peculiar mode of dispensing Christian truth. They are unlike any which have preceded us. They are new, and consequently demand what I have called a new Dispensation of Christianity, a dispensation in perfect harmony with the new order of things which has sprung into existence. Yet of this fact we seem not to have been generally aware. The character of our religious institutions, the style of our preaching, the means we rely upon, for the production of the Christian virtues, are such as were adopted in a distant age, and fitted to wants which no longer exist, or which exist only in a greatly modified shape.

It is to this fact that I attribute that *other* fact of which I have heretofore spoken, that our churches are far from being filled, and that a large and an increasing portion of our community take very little interest in religious institutions, and manifest a most perfect indifference to religious instruction. These persons do not stay away from our churches because they have no wish to be religious, no desire to meet and commune in the solemn temple with their fellow men, and with the great and good Spirit which reigns everywhere around and within them. It is not because they do not value this communion, that they do not come into our churches, but because they do not find it in our churches. They cannot find, under the costume of our institutions, and our instructions, the Father-God, to love and adore, with whom to hold sweet and invigorating communings; they are unable to find that sympathy of man with man, which they crave—to obtain that response to the warm affec-

would not, except to render them more secure. We are, indeed, levelers, but *we would level upward, not downward.* We see no one too high, too great, too learned, too refined, or too good, and the extent of our radicalism is to bring up the low, and place every man, if possible, in such a position, that he can fulfil the great end of his being."]

tions of the heart, which would make them love to assemble together and bow together before one common altar.

We may complain of people as much as we please for not attending public worship, for not laboring to sustain religious institutions, but they will not do it to any great extent unless their wants are met. They will not attend church, listen to preaching, unless they are interested, unless they are *fed*. If they do not find themselves fed in our churches, they will not attend them. When, therefore, we see large and increasing portions of a community staying away from church, showing themselves indifferent to everything bearing the name of religion, we may be assured that there is some defect in the form with which religion is clothed, or in the methods by which it is dispensed; and since this is obviously the fact with our country at the present moment, we may be assured that there are in our community religious wants which no denomination among us fully meets. The people are not really fed; their spiritual wants are unsupplied, and they are spiritually starving.

I am for myself at no loss to account for this fact, to perceive in what this defect consists. I see much in our places of worship which is offensive to a large portion of the community. One pew is marked worth five hundred dollars, another at half that sum, another at a fourth, and another a *free* seat. Everybody is struggling for the highest priced pews, or counting them the most honorable seats, and nobody will sit in one of the free seats, unless he be willing to write himself down a *pauper*. The painful distance between the rich and the poor, the cause of so many heart-burnings out of the temple, is thus preserved within it, where all should meet as equals before our common Father. It is unpleasant to see these distinctions in the house of God, and where they are not abolished, none but those who are able to occupy the high seats will be willing to appear. I wish they were abolished, so that there might be one spot on earth, where we might forget the factitious distinctions of an artificial society, and appear, as we are, children of the same Father, brothers and sisters of the same family.[2]

[2][Ed. Pew rents created an appalling distinction in many of the American religious congregations. The new Irish Catholic bishop of Charleston, South Carolina, John England, found the system a violation of Christian equality and community when he first came to the United States in 1820. He tried to abolish it, but without much success. On England's views, see my *An Immigrant Bishop: John England's Adaptation of Irish Catholicism to American Republicanism* (Yonkers, New York: United States Catholic Historical Society, 1982), 100-01.]

There are many who would attend some of our churches if they could afford it. They are too spirited to sit in the *pauper's* seat, and they are not able to own a pew, nor to rent one, much less to pay the tax levied upon it in addition. This fact keeps away large numbers, who, though they may not be rich, yet have souls worth as much in the sight of God, as those of their more favored fellow beings; and it keeps them away when there are seats enough unoccupied. There is room enough in the churches in this city for nearly all the people who can conveniently at one time attend them; but that room is too expensive to be obtained. Pews are held as freehold estates; men call them their religious *homes*, and seem to be more anxious that their privacy should not be disturbed, or their cushions soiled, than they are, that the temple of God should be filled with worshipers. Let this evil be remedied, the aristocracy of our churches abolished, or let us cease to blame people for not filling them.

But were this difficulty obviated, were seats easily obtained by all, and so obtained as to imply on the part of no one an assumption of superiority, or a confession of inferiority, the preaching which is most common is far from being satisfactory, and the wants of the times would by no means be met. I say the preaching which is most common is far from being satisfactory; but not because it is not true. I accuse no preacher of not preaching the truth. The truth is, I believe, preached in all churches, of all denominations, to a certain extent at least; but not the right kind of truth, or not truth under the aspects demanded by the wants of the age, and country. All truth is valuable, but all truths are not equally valuable; and all aspects of the same truths are not at all times, in all places, equally attractive. The fault I find with preaching in general is, that it is not on the right kind of topics to interest the masses in this age and country. The topics usually discussed may once have been of the highest importance; they may now be very interesting to the scholar, or to the student in his closet, or with his fellow students; but they are, to a great extent, matters of perfect indifference to the many. The many care nothing about the meaning of a Greek particle, or the settling of a various reading; nothing about the meaning of dogmas long since deprived of life, about the manners and customs of a people of whom they may have heard, but in whose destiny they feel no peculiar interest; they are not fed by descriptions of a Jewish marriage feast, a reiteration of Jewish threatenings, nor with beautiful essays, and rounded periods on some petty duty, or some insignificant point in theology. They want strong language, stirring discourses on great principles, which go deep into the universal mind, and strike a chord which vibrates through the universal heart. They want to be directed to the deep things of God and humanity, and enlightened and warmed on matters with which they every day come in contact, and which will be to them matters of kindling thought and strong feeling through eternity.

That our religious institutions, or our modes of dispensing Christian truth, are not in harmony with the wants of the times, is evinced by the increase of infidelity and the success infidels have in their exertions to collect societies and organize opposition to Christianity. There is sustained in this city a society of infidels, free inquirers, I believe they call themselves. Why has this society been collected? Not, I will venture to say, because their leader is an infidel.[3] People do not go to hear him because he advocates atheistical or pantheistical doctrines; not because he denies Christianity, rejects the Bible, and indulges in various witticisms at the expense of members of the clerical profession; but because he opposes the aristocracy of our churches, and vindicates the rights of the mind. He succeeds, not because he is an infidel, but because he has hitherto shown himself a democrat.

Men are never infidels for the sake of infidelity. Infidelity, I use not the term reproachfully, has no charms of its own. There is no charm in looking around on our fellow men as mere plants that spring up in the morning, wither and die ere it is night. It is not pleasant to look up into the heavens, brilliant with their sapphire gems, and see no spirit shining there—over the rich and flowering earth, and see no spirit blooming there—abroad upon a world of mute, dead matter, and feel ourselves—alone. It is not pleasant to look upon the heavens as dispeopled of the Gods, and the earth of men, to feel ourselves in the center of a universal blank, with no soul to love, no spirit with which to commune. I know well what is that sense of loneliness which comes over the unbeliever, the desolateness of soul under which he is oppressed, but I will not attempt to describe it.

I say, then, it is not infidelity, that gives the leader of the infidel party success. It is his defense of free inquiry and of democracy. In vindicating his own right to disbelieve Christianity, he has vindicated the rights of the mind, proved that all have a right to inquire fully into all subjects, and to abide by the honest convictions of their own understandings. In doing this he has met the wants of a large

[3][Ed. The reference here is to Abner Kneeland (1774-1844), a former Universalist minister like Brownson, who abandoned his earlier Christian tradition, became a free enquirer and severe critic of Christianity, and edited the *Boston Investigator* as an organ for the Boston "infidels." On Kneeland, see introduction to EW, 1: 18, 27.]

portion of the community, and met them as no church has ever yet been able to meet them. I say not that he himself is a free inquirer, but he proclaims free inquiry as one of the rights of man; and in doing this, he has proclaimed what thousands feel, though they may not generally dare own it. The want to inquire, to ascertain what is truth, what and wherefore we believe, is becoming more and more urgent; we may disown, unchurch, anathematize it, but suppress it we cannot. It is too late to stay the progress of free inquiry. The dams and dykes we construct to keep back its swelling tide are but mere resting places, from which it may break forth in renovated power, and with redoubled fury. It is sweeping on, and, I say, let it sweep on, let it sweep on; the truth has nothing to fear.

Next to the want to inquire, to philosophize, the age is distinguished by its tendency to democracy, and its craving for social reform. Be pleased or displeased as we may, the age is unquestionably tending to democracy; the democratic spirit is triumphing. The millions awake. The masses appear, and every day is more and more disclosed

> "The might that slumbers in a peasant's arm."[4]

The voice of the awakened millions rising into new and undreamed of importance, crying out for popular institutions, comes to us on every breeze, and mingles in every sound. All over the Christian world a contest is going on, not as in former times between monarchs and nobles, but between the people and their masters, between the many and the few, the privileged and the unprivileged, and victory, though here and there seeming at first view doubtful, everywhere inclines in the party of the many. Old distinctions are losing their value; titles are becoming less and less able to confer dignity; simple tastes, simple habits, simple manners are becoming fashionable; the simple dignity of man is more and more coveted and with the discerning it has already become far more honorable to call one simply a MAN than a gentleman.

Now it is to this democratic spirit that the leader of the infidel party appeals, and in which he finds a powerful element of his success. Correspondents of his paper attempt even to identify atheism and democracy.[5] I myself once firmly believed that there could be no social progress, that man could not rise to his true dignity, without the destruction of religion; I really believed that religious institu-

[4][Ed. Unable to identify quotation.]

[5][Ed. Brownson again refers to Abner Kneeland.]

tions, tastes, and beliefs were the greatest, almost the sole, barrier to human improvement; and what I once honestly believed, is now as honestly believed by thousands who would identify the progress of humanity with the progress of infidelity.

It is, I own, a new state of things for infidelity to profess to be a democrat. Hobbes, one of the fathers, if not the father, of modern infidelity, had no sympathy with the masses; Hume and Gibbon dreamed of very little social progress, and manifested no desire to elevate the low, and loosen the chains of the bound. Before Thomas Paine, no infidel writer in our language, to my knowledge, was a democrat, or thought of giving infidelity a democratic tendency. Since his times, the infidel has been fond of calling himself a democrat, and he has pretty generally claimed to be the friend of the masses and the advocate of progress. He now labors to prove the church aristocratic, to prove that it has no regard for the melioration of man's earthly mode of being. Unhappily in proportion as he succeeds, the church furnishes him with new instruments of success. In proportion as he seems to identify his infidelity and the democratic spirit, the church disowns that spirit, and declares it wholly opposed to the faith. When, some years since, the thought passed through my head, that there were things in society which needed mending, and I dreamed of being a social reformer, I found my bitterest opponents, clergyman as I was, among the clergy, and those who were most zealous for the faith. That I erred in the inference I drew from this fact, as unbelievers now err in theirs, I am willing to own; but the fact itself *has* the appearance of proving that religion and religion's advocates are unfriendly to social progress.

These are the principal reasons why infidelity succeeds. Its advocates meet two great wants, that of free inquiry, and that of social progress, two wants which are at the present time, and in this country, quite urgent, and meet them better than they are met by any of our churches. We need not, then, ascribe their success to any peculiar depravity of the heart, nor to any peculiar obtuseness of the understanding. They are right in their vindication of the rights of the mind and in advocating social progress. They are wrong only in supposing that free inquiry and the progress of society are elements of infidelity, when they are only, in fact, its accidents. They constitute, in reality two important elements of religion; as such I own them, accept them, and assure the religious everywhere that they too must accept them, or see religion for a time wholly obscured, and infidelity triumphant.

Infidels are wrong in pretending that infidelity can effect the progress of mankind. Infidelity has no element of progress. The purest morality it enjoins is selfishness. It does not pretend to offer man any higher motives of action than that of self-interest. But self-interest can make no man a reformer. No great reforms are ever effected without sacrifice. In laboring for the benefit of others, we are often obliged to forget ourselves, to expose ourselves, without fear and without regret, to the loss of property, ease, reputation, and sometimes of life itself. He who consults only his own interest will never consent to be so exposed. Or admitting that we could convince men, that to labor for a universal regeneration of mankind is for the greatest ultimate good of each one, the experience of every day proves that no one will do it, when a small, immediate good intervenes which it is necessary to abandon. A small, immediate, present good always outbalances the vastly greater, but distant good. The only principle of reform on which we can rely is love. We must love the human race in order to be able to devote ourselves to their greatest good, to be able to do and to dare everything for their progress. But we cannot love what does not appear to us *loveable*. We cannot love mankind unless we see something in them which is worthy to be loved. But infidelity strips man of every quality which we can love. In the view of the infidel, man is nothing more than an animal, born to propagate his species and die. It is religion that discloses man's true dignity, reveals the soul, unveils the immortality within us, and presents in every man the incarnate God, before whom he may stand in awe, whom he may love and adore. Infidelity cannot, then, effect what its friends assert that it can. It cannot make us love mankind, and not being able to make us love them, it is not able to make us labor for their melioration.

But I say this without meaning to reproach infidels. I do and must condemn infidelity; but I have taught myself to recognize in the infidel a man, an equal, a brother, one for whom Jesus died, and for whom I, too, if need were, should be willing to die. I have no right to reproach the infidel, no right to censure him for his speculative opinions. If those opinions are wrong, as I most assuredly believe they are, it is my duty to count them his misfortune, not his crime, and to do all in my power to aid him to correct them. We wrong our brother, when we refuse him the same tolerance for his opinions which we would have him extend to ours. We wrong Christianity, whenever we censure, ridicule, or treat with the least possible disrespect any man for his honest opinions, be they what they may. We have often done violence to the gospel in our treatment of those who have, in our opinion, misinterpreted or disowned it. We have not always treated their opinions, as we ask them to treat ours. We have not always been scrupulous to yield to others the rights we claim for ourselves. We have been unjust, and our injustice has brought, as it always must, reproach upon the opinions we avow and the cause we profess. There was, there is, no need of being unjust nor uncharitable to unbelievers. We believe we have the truth. Let us not so wrong the truth we advocate as to fear it can suffer by any encounter with falsehood. Let us adopt one rule for judging all men, infidels and all, not that of their speculative opinions, but their real moral characters.

I prefer to meet the infidel on his own ground; I freely accept whatever I find him advocating which I believe true, and just as freely oppose whatever he supports which I believe to be false and mischievous. I think him right in his vindication of free inquiry and social progress. I accept them both, not as elements of infidelity, but as elements of Christianity. Should it now be asked, as it has been, what I mean by the new dispensation of Christianity, the new form of religion, of which I have often spoken in this place and elsewhere, I answer, I mean religious institutions, and modes of dispensing religious truth and influences, which recognize the rights of the mind, and propose social progress as one of the great ends to be obtained. In that New Church of which I have sometimes dreamed, and I hope more than dreamed, I would have the unlimited freedom of the mind unequivocally acknowledged. No interdict should be placed upon thought. To reason should be a Christian, not an infidel, act. Every man should be encouraged to inquire, and to inquire not a little merely, within certain prescribed limits; but freely, fearlessly, fully, to scan heaven, air, ocean, earth, and to master God, nature, and humanity, if he can. He who inquires for truth honestly, faithfully, perseveringly, to the utmost extent of his power, does all that can be asked of him; he does God's will, and should be allowed to abide by his own conclusions, without fear of reproach from God or man.

In asserting this I am but recalling the community to Christianity. Jesus reproved the Jews for not of themselves judging what is right, thus plainly recognizing in them, and if in them in us, both the right and the power to judge for themselves. "If I do not the works of my Father," says Jesus, "believe me not" [John 10:37]; obviously implying both man's right and ability to determine what are, and what are not, "works of the Father," that is, in other words, what is or what is not truth. An Apostle commands us to "stand fast in the liberty wherewith Christ has made us free" [Gal. 5:1], "to prove all things," and to "hold fast that which is good" [1 Thess. 5:21]. In fact the very spirit of the gospel is that of freedom, it is called a "law of liberty" [James 1:25, 2:12] and its great end is to free the soul from all restraint but that of its obligation to do right. They wrong it who would restrain thought, and hand-cuff inquiry; they doubt or deny its truth and power who fear to expose it to the severest scrutiny, the most searching investigation; and, were I in an accusing mood, I would bring the charge of infidelity against every one who will not or dare not inquire, who will not or dare not encourage inquiry in others.

I have said that social progress must enter into the church I would have established as one of the ends to be gained. Social progress holds a great place in the sentiments of this age. Infidels seize upon it, find in it one of the most powerful elements of their success. I too would seize upon it, give it a religious direction, and find in it an element of the triumph of Christianity. I have a right to it. As a Christian I am bound to rescue social progress, or, if you please, the democratic spirit, from the possession of the infidel. He has no right to it. He has usurped it through the negligence of the church. It is a Christian spirit. Jesus was the man, the teacher of the masses. They were fishermen, deemed the lowest of his countrymen, who were his Apostles; they were the "common people" who heard him gladly; they were the Pharisee and Sadducee, the chief priest and scribe, the rich and the distinguished, in one word the aristocracy of that age who conspired against him and caused him to be crucified between two thieves. He himself professed to be anointed of God *because* he was anointed to preach the gospel to the poor, to proclaim liberty to them that are bound, and to let the captive go free [Luke 4:18]. To John he expressly assigns the kindling fact, that the poor had the gospel preached unto them, as the most striking proof of his claims to the Messiahship [Luke 7:22-23].

And what was this gospel which was preached to the poor? Was it a gospel suited to the views of the autocrat of the Russias, such as despots ever love? Did it command the poor in the name of God to submit to an order of things of which they are the victims, to be contented to pine in neglect and die of wretchedness? No, no. Jesus preached no such tyrant-pleasing, and tyrant-sustaining gospel. The gospel which he preached was the gospel of human brotherhood. He preached the gospel, the holy Evangel, good news to the poor, when he proclaimed them members of the common family of man, when he taught that we are all brethren, having one and the same Father in heaven; he preached the gospel to the poor, when he declared to the boastingly religious of his age that even publicans and harlots would go into the kingdom of heaven sooner than they; when he declared that the poor widow, who out of her necessities cast her two mites in the treasury of the Lord, cast in more than all the rich; and whoever preaches the universal fraternity of the human race preaches the gospel to the poor, though he speak only to the rich.

There is power in this great doctrine of the universal brotherhood of mankind. It gives the reformer a mighty advantage. It enables him to speak words of an import, and in a tone, which may almost wake the dead. Hold thy hand, oppressor, it permits him to say, thou wrongest a brother. Withhold thy scorn, thou bitter satirist of the human race, thou vilifiest thy brother. In passing by that child in the street yesterday, and leaving it to grow up in ignorance and vice, notwithstanding God had given thee wealth to train it to knowledge and virtue, thou didst neglect thy brother's child. Oh, did we but feel this truth, that we are all brothers and sisters, children of the same parent, we should feel that every wrong done to a human being was violence done to our own flesh.

I say again that Jesus was emphatically the teacher of the masses, the prophet of the workingmen if you will, of all those who "labor and are heavy laden" [Matt. 11:28]. Were I to repeat his words in this city or elsewhere, with the intimation that I believed they meant something, were I to say, as he said, "It is easier for a camel to go through the eye of a needle, than for a rich man to enter the kingdom of heaven" [Matt. 19:24, Mark. 10:25, Luke 18:25], and to say it in a tone that indicated I believed he attached any meaning to what he said, you would call me a "radical," an "agrarian," a "trades unionist," a "leveler," a "disorganizer," or some other name equally barbarous and horrific. It were more than a man's reputation for sanity, or respectability as *a Christian*, is worth, to be as bold even in these days in defense of the "common people" as Jesus was.

I say still again, that Jesus was emphatically the teacher of the masses, the prophet of the people. Not that he addressed himself to any one description of persons to the exclusion of another, not that he sought to benefit one portion of the human race at another's expense, for if any one thing more than another distinguished him, it was, that he rose above all the factitious distinctions of society, and spoke to universal man, to the universal mind, and to the universal heart. I call him the prophet of the people, because he recognized the rights of humanity brought out, and suffered and died to establish principles, which, in their legitimate effect, cannot fail to bring up the low and bowed down, and give to the many, who, in all ages, and in all countries have been the tools of the few, their due rank and social importance. His spirit, in its political aspect, is what I have called the democratic spirit; in the most general aspect, it is the spirit of progress in the individual, and in the race towards perfection, towards union with God. It is that spirit which for eighteen hundred years has been to work in society, like the leaven hidden in three measures of meal, before which slavery, in nearly all Christendom, has disappeared, which has destroyed the warrior aristocracy, nearly subdued the aristocracy of birth, which is now struggling with the aristocracy of wealth, and which promises, ere long, to bring up and establish the true aristocracy, the aristocracy of merit.

If it be now asked, as it has been asked, to what denomination I belong, I reply, that I belong to that denomination, whose starting point is free inquiry, which acknowledges in good faith, and without any mental reservation, the rights of the mind, and which proposes the melioration of man's earthly mode of being, as one of the great ends of its labors. I know not that such a denomination exists. I know, in fact, of no denomination, which, *as a denomination*, fully meets the wants of the times. Yet let me not be misinterpreted. I am not here to accuse, or to make war upon, any existing denomination. I contend with no church. I have no controversy with my Calvinistic brother, none with my Arminian, Unitarian, or Trinitarian brother. Every church has its idea, its truth, and more truth, much more, I believe, than any one church will admit of in those from which it differs. For myself, I delight to find truth in all churches, and I own it wherever I find it; but still I must say, I find no church which owns, as its central truth, the great central truth of Christianity, a truth which may now be brought out of the darkness in which it has remained, and which it is now more than ever necessary to reinstate in its rights.

Let me say, then, that though I am here for an object, which is not, to my knowledge, the special object of any existing church, I am not here to make war upon any church, nor to injure any one in the least possible degree. I would that they all had as much fellowship for one another, as I have for them all! I interfere with none of them. I am here for a special object, but one so high, one so broad, they may all cooperate in gaining it. My creed is a simple one. Its first article is, free, unlimited inquiry, perfect liberty to enjoy and express one's own honest convictions, and perfect respect for the free and honest inquirer, whatever be the results to which he arrives. The second article is social progress. I would have it a special object of the society I would collect, to labor to perfect all social institutions, and raise every man to a social position, which will give him free scope for the full and harmonious development of all his faculties. I say, *perfect*, not destroy, all social institutions. I do not feel that God has given me a work of destruction. I would improve, preserve, whatever is good, and remedy whatever is defective and thus reconcile the CONSERVATOR and the RADICAL. My third article is, that man should labor for his soul in preference to his body. Man has a soul; he is not mere body. He has more than animal wants. He has a soul, which is in relation with the absolute and the Infinite; a soul which is for ever rushing off into the unknown, and rising through a universe of darkness up to the "first Good and the first Fair." This soul is immortal. To perfect it is our highest aim. I would encourage inquiry; I would perfect society, not as ultimate ends, but as means to the growth and maturity of man's higher nature—his soul.

These are my views, and views which, I believe, meet the wants of the times. They make war upon no sect of Christians. They are adopted in the spirit of love to humanity, and they can be acted upon only in the spirit of peace. They threaten no hostility, except to sin; with that, indeed, they call us to war. We must fight against all unrighteousness, against spiritual wickedness in high places, and in low places; but the weapons of our warfare are not carnal, but spiritual. We must go forth to the battle in faith and love, go forth to vindicate the rights of the mind, to perfect society, to make it the abode of all the virtues, and all the graces, to clothe man in his native dignity, and enable him to look forth in the image of his Maker upon a world of beauty.

This is my object. I am not here to preach to workingmen, nor to those who are not workingmen, in the interests of aristocracy, nor of democracy. I am here for humanity; to plead for universal man, to unfurl the banner of the cross on a new and more commanding position, and call the human race around it. I am here to speak to all who feel themselves human beings, to all whose hearts swell at the name of man, to all who long to lessen the sum of human misery, and increase that of human happiness, to all who have any perception of the beautiful and the good, and a craving for the infinite, the eternal, and indestructible, on whom to repose the wearied soul and find rest—to all such is my appeal, to them I commit the object I have stated, and before which I stand in awe, and entreat them by all that is good in their natures, holy in religion, or desirable in the joy of a regenerated world, to unite and march to its acquisition, prepared to dare with the hero, to suffer with the saint, or to die with the martyr.

3.

SOCIETY FOR CHRISTIAN UNION AND PROGRESS

Boston Reformer 3 (June 30, 1836)

This is the name of a new society which has just been organized in this city under the preaching of the present editor of this paper. It has thus far held its meetings in Lyceum Hall, Hanover Street; but will hereafter meet for religious worship in the Masonic Temple.[1] As this society is something new, it may not be improper for us to say a few words of its object.

Let it be understood, then, that its first object is to present a broad ground of union for all the various divisions and subdivisions of the Christian church. This it supposes may be done by seizing upon what is now held in common by all sects. Though all sects differ one from another, and have their peculiar ideas, yet there is a broad ground of Christian truth common to them all. This is a high table land, elevated far above all their differences, and which overlooks them all. On this high table land, it is proposed to erect a Christian Temple, within whose spacious courts may meet all, of all sects, names, and creeds, in peace and love, and depositing at its entrance all their badges of distinction, prostrate themselves with one heart before the one altar of a Universal Father.

This object may seem to some unattainable; but we have faith in it. We think the time to make the effort for it has come. And we think moreover this city is the place to make the experiment. In no other city in the Union can be found all the necessary elements of success. But all these elements are here. Here are intelligence, philosophy, benevolence, liberality, a love for moral and religious investigation. Religious differences count for less here than elsewhere; and since from this city went forth the voice which called into existence our Republic and gave it freedom, from the same place must in the order of things go forth the voice which shall from its scattered elements call together the new Christian church, and secure it true

[1][Ed. In July of 1836 he preached his sermon on the "Wants of the Times," which was the inaugural sermon at Masonic Temple where the new society would meet regularly until 1839.]

Christian liberty. The voice in fact has been sounding out from here for more than twenty years, and the preparatory work is done, and the foundation for the new Temple is laid, or rather, the true foundation which was laid by Jesus and the Apostles, and which had long been buried in the earth is rediscovered, the builders may come forth with joy to their work, and continue it until the capstone is brought forth amid the shouts of "grace, grace unto it."

Another object of the society is to encourage progress, moral and religious, individual and social progress. Its views on social progress, its connection with Christianity, the designs of Jesus in relation to society are so well set forth in the following communication from a highly esteemed friend, addressed to the former editor of the *Reformer*,[2] that we insert it instead of any remarks of our own.[3] We only remark that the Social Reform Society, to which he alludes, strictly speaking, has never had any existence. The name was assumed, in giving the earlier notices of our meetings, but was soon dropped as being expressive of only one part of our object. The Society is composed principally of intelligent mechanics, and has thus far succeeded beyond our expectations.

(July 7, 1836)

Another reason assigned in our discourse before this society on Sunday last,[4] why so large a portion of the community, is becoming indifferent to religious institutions, was the fact that the church in other countries, has been pretty uniformly leagued with the despot and identified with abuses in the state. Before the Reformation the church controlled the state; but after the Reformation, the state obtained the control of the church. The first effect of the Reformation which rent one half of Europe from the Catholic Church, was to raise up the state and to enlarge the powers and prerogatives of the monarch, and the first instance of absolute monarchy in Europe, after the decline of the Roman Empire, is subsequent to the Reformation. The Reformation by weakening the church strengthened the monarchy, and enabled the state to make the church its servant.

This new state of things could not fail to array those who desired a reform in the state against the church. Obedient to its masters the

[2][Ed. The former editor was Theophilus Fisk (1801-67), a former Universalist minister who, like Brownson, became a strong Democratic advocate of the laboring classes. On Fisk, see Arthur M. Schlesinger, Jr., *The Age of Jackson* (1945; Boston: Little, Brown and Co., 1953), passim.]

[3][Ed. On the communication, see "For the Reformer," *Boston Reformer* 3 (June 30, 1836).]

[4][Ed. Reference is to the previous essay on the "Society for Christian Union and Progress," *Boston Reformer* 3 (June 30, 1836).]

church arrayed itself against the reformer. The church was founded on absolutism; and, though the Protestant churches, under one aspect, in their character of Protestants, recognized the rights of the mind, they have always retained as churches the same principle; the church, whether Catholic or Protestant, therefore of its own accord could not but oppose the progress of society. Hence the friends of social progress, identifying the church with hostility to liberty, deemed it necessary to destroy it.

This was in some degree necessary in France, perhaps, it is in some degree necessary in England, but it is not necessary here. The church here is not unfriendly to social progress; but a tradition of what was true, and an echo of what is still true in many parts of the world, influence many individuals, who take not much note of time and place, and cause them to manifest the same sort of hostility to religion as it exists here, which might be commendable as it exists elsewhere. Be this as it may, the social reformers of the last century deemed it necessary to destroy the church, and that to be reformers they must be infidels, and those who echo their philosophy and arguments deem the same necessary now and here. And this keeps aloof from religious institutions a larger portion of the community.

There is in this a great error. Though the infidel may be a strenuous advocate of social progress, and may do something for it, it is not by virtue of his infidelity. Infidelity can do nothing for social progress. It shows nothing in man worth laboring for. What is the use of laboring for man, who, if infidelity be true, is but an animal, born to propagate his species and die, nothing more than the dew-drop on the flower, to sparkle for a moment, but which the morning sun soon evaporates! Infidelity is powerless, and those who deem it an element of reform will find it impotent — worse, an insurmountable obstacle.

(July 8, 1836)

This society met on last Sunday at the masonic Temple. In our capacity as minister to this society, we attempted to give some idea of its objects and principles. We began by stating the causes which had led to its organization. These were the fact that it was sometime since published that in this city there were between twenty and thirty thousand people not regular attendants upon any religious meeting, and the fact which no one can fail to observe, that there is in our whole country a growing indifference to religious institutions.[5]

[5][Ed. The sentence is obscure, but accurately recorded. The report referred to is probably "Places of Public Worship in Boston," *Christian Register* 15 (March 25, 1836): 49. On religious participation in public worship, see the Introduction to this volume.]

The statement with regard to the numbers in this city who attend no religious meeting, was believed to be exaggerated, but we all know that there is among us as well as elsewhere vast numbers who neither attend religious meetings or value religious institutions. The reasons why it is so are to be sought in the new modes of thought and feeling which have become predominant, and in the history of the church. These reasons we shall take an early opportunity to disclose and lay before our readers.

The first form which Christianity assumed, that is, the first external institution in which men embodied what they comprehended of it, was *Catholicism*. Catholicism was based on absolutism. It allowed no liberty to thought, admitted no right in the mind to inquire why it should believe what it was commanded to believe. It was commanded, and that was enough, all it had a right to know. Absolutism, or despotism in the church led to despotism in the state. In the church and state absolutism, authority, was the only principle recognized. But as men advanced they must feel that they had rights. This manifested itself first in the effort to assign a reason for believing what the church commanded. But as the church would not allow this, those who could not believe without a reason revolted against the church and finally effected in the early part of the 16th century what is known as the Reformation.

The Reformation was at bottom a revolution in behalf of the rights of the mind. But none of the Protestant churches have fully understood this and have attempted rather to parcel out Catholicism, the popedom, than to destroy it. No church fully recognizes the rights of the mind, consequently as under Catholicism Christianity and absolutism were identified, so in a vast majority of cases they are still identified under Protestantism. This is one reason why so many now reject the church. They do not believe that they can be Christians and at the same time free inquirers, and as they are conscious of their right and their duty to be free inquirers, they will not join any existing church.

4.

MR. HALLET'S [*sic*] ORATION[1]

Boston Reformer 3 (August 9, 1836): 1

This Oration is just what we should expect from Mr. Hallet, spirited and able, but destitute of sound, statesmanlike views. It is the production of a political partizan, not of a political philosopher. It is loud for democracy but *the* democracy for which it is loud, might better be called demagogy.

We do not like his definition of democracy. He understands by the term the sovereignty of the people, and their fitness to rule; both of which we deny. Sovereignty, in its true sense, is no attribute of the people, neither of the many, nor of the few. Sovereignty resides only in the right, and God is its only impersonation. And as for the fitness of the people to govern, nothing is further from the truth. How many individuals can be found in our whole country, who know anything about the objects of government, the bearing and effects of this or that law? Nothing is more nonsensical than to pretend that the people are fit to govern.[2]

But in saying this, we do not contend that a few raised to independence of the people should govern. The aristocracy are even less qualified than the people to govern. They always have governed and so long as in power, they always will govern, the many for the interests of the few. We have no faith in the Democratic, nor in the Old Federal doctrines. We believe in the government neither of the many nor of the few.

Democracy in our definition of it, means fitting the people to dispense with government; that is, writing just laws, on the hearts of the people, instead of on parchment. And the true democratic faith is the belief that this can be done, and the real democratic party is the one that labors to do it.

[1][Ed. Brownson's article against Hallett's Oration at Palmer Hampden Co.; July 4, 1836. Brownson has incorrectly spelled Benjamin Franklin Hallett's (1797-1862) name. The oration is Hallett's *An Oration delivered July 4th 1836, at Palmer, in Hampden County, Massachusetts, by the request of a committee of Democratic citizens of sixteen towns . . . in the eighth congressional district* (Boston: Printed by Beals & Greene, 1836).]

[2][Ed. It has frequently been said that Brownson's views of democracy changed radically after the election of 1840 when he lost complete confidence in the voice of the people. This is not the case as the skeptical comments here on popular sovereignty indicate.]

5.

NATURE[1]

Boston Reformer 3 (September 10, 1836)

This is a singular book. It is the creation of a mind that lives and moves in the beautiful, and has the power of assimilating to itself whatever it sees, hears or touches. We cannot analyze it; whoever would form an idea of it must read it.

We welcome it however as an index to the spirit which is silently at work among us, as a proof that mind is about to receive a new and a more glorious manifestation; that higher problems and holier speculations than those which have hitherto engrossed us, are to engage our attention; and that the inquiries, what is perfect in art, and what is true in philosophy, are to surpass in interest those which concern the best place to locate a city, construct a railroad, or become suddenly rich. We prophesy that it is the forerunner of a new class of books, the harbinger of a new literature as much superior to whatever has been, as our political institutions are superior to those of the old world.

This book is aesthetical rather than philosophical. It inquires what is the beautiful rather than what is the true. Yet it touches some of the gravest problems in metaphysical science, and may perhaps be called philosophy in its poetical aspect. It uniformly subordinates nature to spirit, the understanding to the reason, and mere hand-actions to ideas, and believes that ideas are one day to disenthrall the world from the dominion of semi-shadows, and make it the abode of peace and love, a meet temple in which to enshrine the spirit of universal and everlasting beauty.

The author is a genuine lover of nature, and in a few instances he carries his regard for woods and fields so far as to be in danger of forgetting his socialities, and that all nature combined is infinitely inferior to the mind that contemplates it, and invests it with all its charms. And what seems singular to us is, that with all this love for nature, with this passion for solitary woods and varied landscapes, he

[1][Ed. Review of Ralph Waldo Emerson's *Nature* (Boston: J. Munroe & Co., 1836).]

seems seriously to doubt the existence of the external world except as an picture which God stamps on the mind. He all but worships what his senses seem to present him, and yet is not certain that all that which his senses place out of him, is not after all the mere subjective laws of his own being, existing only to the eye, not of a necessary, but of an irresistible faith.

Some great minds have, we know, had this doubt. This was the case with the acute and amiable Bishop Berkeley, the audacious Fichte and several others we could mention[2]. Taking their standpoint in the creative power of the human soul, and observing the landscape to change in its coloring as the hues of their own souls change, they have thought the landscape was nothing but themselves projected, and made an object of contemplation. The notion is easily accounted for, but we confess that we should think so acute a philosopher as our author would easily discover its fallacy.

The reason is undoubtedly our only light, our only criterion of certainty; but we think the reason vouches for the truth of the senses as decidedly and as immediately as it does for its own conceptions. He who denies the testimony of his senses seems to us to have no ground for believing the apperceptions of consciousness; and to deny those is to set oneself afloat upon the ocean of universal scepticism. The whole difficulty seems to us to be in not duly understanding the report of the senses. The senses are the windows of the soul through which it looks out upon a world existing as really and as substantially as itself; but what the external world is, or what it is the senses report it to be, we do not at first understand. The result of all culture, we think will not be as our author thinks, to lead to Idealism, but to make us understand what it is we say, when we say, there is an external world.

The author calls the external world phenomenal, that is, an appearance; but he needs not to be told that the appearance as really exists, though it exists as an appearance, as that which appears, as the Absolute. Man is phenomenal in the same sense as is the universe, but man exists. The author calls him "the apparition of God." The apparition exists as certainly as God exists, though it exists as an apparition, not as absolute being. God is absolute being. Whatever is

[2][Ed. George Berkeley (1685-1753) was an Irish philosopher and bishop in the Anglican Church of Ireland whose metaphysical idealism was intended to be a safeguard against skepticism. Johann Gottlieb Fichte (1762-1814) was a German philosopher whose subjective or transcendental idealism was intended to reinforce human freedom.]

absolute is God; but God is not the universe, God is not man; man and the universe exist as manifestations of God. His existence is absolute, theirs is relative, but real.

But we are plunging too deeply into metaphysics for our readers and perhaps for ourselves. In conclusion, we are happy to say that however the author may deviate from what we call sound philosophy, on his road, he always comes to the truth at last. In this little book he has done an important service to his fellow men. He has clothed nature with a poetic garb, and interpenetrated her with the living spirit of beauty and goodness, showed us how we ought to look upon the world round and about us, set us an example of a calm, morally independent, and devout spirit discoursing on the highest and holiest topics which can occupy the human soul, and produced a book which must ever be admired as a perfect specimen of art. We thank him for what he has done and commend his book — his poem we might say — to every lover of the true, the beautiful and the good.

6.

COUSIN'S *PHILOSOPHY*[1]

Christian Examiner and Gospel Review 21
(September, 1836): 33-64

Whoever would see the American people as remarkable for their philosophy as they are for their industry, enterprise, and political freedom, must be gratified that these works have already attracted considerable attention among us, and are beginning to exert no little influence on our philosophical speculations. It is a proof that our philosophical speculations are taking a wholesome direction, and especially that the great problems of mental and moral science are assuming in our eyes a new importance, and calling to their solution a greater and an increasing amount of mind. We are, in fact, turning our attention to matters of deeper interest than those which relate merely to the physical well-being of humanity. We are beginning to perceive that Providence, in the peculiar circumstances in which it has placed us, in the free institutions it has given us, has made it our duty to bring out the ideal man, and to prove, by a practical demonstration, what the human race may be, when and where it has free scope for the full and harmonious development of all its faculties. In proportion as we perceive and comprehend this duty, we cannot fail to inquire for a sound philosophy, one which will enumerate and characterize all the faculties of the human soul, and determine the proper order and most efficient means of their development.

These works will, we think, afford us important aid in rescuing the church, and religious matters in general, from their present lamentable condition. Religion subsists among us, and always will, for it has its seat in the human heart; but to a great extent it has lost its hold upon the understanding. Men are no longer satisfied with the arguments by which it has heretofore been defended; the old forms,

[1][Ed. Review of Victor Cousin's *Introduction to the History of Philosophy*, Trans. H. G. Linberg (Boston: Hilliard, Gray, Little, and Wilkins, 1832); *Elements of Psychology, included in a critical Examination of Locke's Essay on the Human Understanding*, Trans., Intro., Notes, and Additions by Caleb Sprague Henry (1840-84) (Hartford, Conn.: Cooke and Co., 1834); *Fragmens philosophiques*, 2d edition (Paris: Ladrango, 1833).]

in which it has been clothed, fail to meet the new wants which time and events have developed, and there is everywhere, in a greater or less degree, a tendency to doubt, unbelief, indifference, infidelity. We have outgrown tradition, and authority no longer seems to us a valid argument. We demand conviction. We do not, as in the Middle Ages, go to religion to prove our philosophy, but to our philosophy to prove our religion. This may or may not be an evil, but it is unavoidable. We must accept and conform to it. Henceforth religion must, if sustained at all, except as a vague, intangible sentiment, be sustained by philosophy. To doubt this, is to prove ourselves ignorant of the age in which we live.

But the philosophy, which has hitherto prevailed, and whose results now control our reasonings, cannot sustain religion. Everybody knows that our religion and our philosophy are at war. We are religious only at the expense of our logic. This accounts for the fact that on the one hand we disclaim logic, unchurch philosophy, and pronounce it a dangerous thing to reason; while, on the other, we reject religion, declaim against the clergy and represent it exceedingly foolish to believe. This opposition cannot be concealed. It is found not only in the same community, but to a great extent in the same individual. The result cannot be doubtful. Philosophy will gain the victory. The friends of religion may seek to prevent it, labor to divert men's minds from inquiry by engaging them in vast associations for practical benevolence, or to frighten them from philosophizing by powerful appeals to hopes and fears; but the desire to philosophize, to account to ourselves for what we believe cannot be suppressed. Instead, then, of quarreling with this state of things, instead of denouncing the religious as do professed free inquirers, or the philosophizers, as is the case with too many of the friends of religion, we should reexamine our philosophy, and inquire if there be not a philosophy true to human nature, and able to explain and verify, instead of destroying, the religious belief of mankind? We evidently need such a philosophy; such a philosophy we believe there is, and we know of no works so well fitted to assist us in finding it, as those of M. Cousin.

We welcome the appearance of M. Cousin's works also as indications, perhaps we should say, results, of a revolution which, within a few years, has been effected in French philosophy. As Americans, we cannot be indifferent to France. She is associated with what is most soul-stirring in our national history, and with much that is most hallowed in our memories. She has exerted by her opinions, her literature, and especially by her philosophy, and must long continue to exert, a great influence on our destiny. Aside, then, from the general concern which we take in what affects our race for good or for evil, and the deep sympathy we feel with man wherever and whatever we find him, we cannot but take a very great interest in everything which relates to France; and we consider it of vast importance to ourselves, the future welfare of our own country, that she has renounced that chilling materialism, which was preached with such fervent and fanatical zeal by her philosophers of the last century.

What has been known, and what is now considered by many, in an especial sense, as French philosophy, is sensualism, so called from its professing to trace back all the facts of consciousness to sensation. France was ready for this philosophy when Voltaire[2] introduced it to her acquaintance, from England, where he had borrowed it from Locke and his disciples. Condillac[3] simplified it, gave it systematic unity, constructed its logic, and fitted it for empire, which it obtained and held for nearly a century, without contradiction and without example in the whole history of philosophy. It penetrated everywhere, into the court and saloons,[4] into literature, the sacred desk, and, as the most decisive proof of its popularity, even into all the branches of instruction.[5] The Revolution in 1789 came to swallow it up for a time, as it did everything else but unchained passion, exalted enthusiasm, and terrible energy in action; but, as soon as the storm abated and there was a momentary calm, under the Directory, it reappeared and resumed its dominion. No one thought of questioning its legitimacy. That brilliant *coterie* who philosophized with so much eclat at the close of the last century and during the first days of the present, among whom were Cabanis, Destutt de Tracy, Volney,

[2][Ed. Voltaire is a pseudonym of François-Marie Arouet (1694-1778), a French deist author.]

[3][Ed. Étienne Bonnot de Condillac (1714-80), French empiricist, was considered the great analytical mind of his generation. For Brownson as well as Cousin his sensualism (all knowledge depends on the senses) represented the logical extension and reduction of British or Lockean empiricism.]

[4][Ed. Brownson has "saloons" in the original. He consistently uses the British "saloons" for "salons."]

[5]See Damiron's *Essai sur l'Histoire de la Philosophie en France du XIXe Siècle*, in 2 vols., 8vo. A work we can recommend without reserve, to all who would become acquainted with French philosophy during the present century. We think we have seen a third edition of it. Ours is the second: Paris, 1828.

Degerando, and Laromiguière,[6] however they might differ among themselves on some minor point, all received sensualism, systematized and perfected by Condillac, as the last word of philosophy. In their opinion, so far as its essential principles are concerned, Condillac had finished philosophy, and left nothing for future workmen but to illustrate and adorn it. Even down to the last moments of the Empire, sensualism was philosophy *par excellence*, and scarcely a scientific voice above a whisper was heard against it.

But its reign is now ended, and its glory departed. The works before us, together with their popularity in France, and that of their author, are sufficient proof of it. Providence, doubtless, assigned it an important mission; but that mission ended with the destruction of the old Catholic Church and the feudal monarchy, and, though it continued to reign some time after, it was as a tradition rather than as a living system. It indeed maintained nearly the same extent of territory, exhibited the usual emblems, and preserved the customary forms of authority; but its internal power was much weakened and its vital energy nearly exhausted. Napoleon disliked it, not because it was sensualism but because its most zealous adherents were the friends of liberty, and the firm but orderly opponents of the despotism he established, and the weight of his displeasure, together with the fact that he exerted the whole energy of his government to make soldiers instead of philosophers, could not fail to hasten its downfall. Some of its friends, especially Laromiguière, in order to improve it and facilitate its defense, departed from some of its essential principles, and aided in destroying, while intending to preserve it. Several individuals, without having any clear perceptions of a different system, opposed it by their strong instinctive tendency to spiritualism. Among those were Bernardin de Saint-Pierre, Chateaubriand, and Madame

[6][Ed. Georges Cabanis (1757-1808) was a French ideologue and physician whose *Rapports du physique et du moral* contributed to the rise of empirical anthropology. Antoine Destutt de Tracy (1754-1836) was a French philosophical ideologue who identified thought and feeling. Constantin-François Volney (1757-1820) was also a child of the French Enlightenment whose *Les Ruines* on the fall of empires and whose love of progress Brownson had studied as a young man. Joseph-Marie Degérando (1772-1842) was a French ideologue who wrote, among other things, on the nature of human knowledge. Pierre Laromiguière (1756-1837) was a French philosopher who taught at a number of institutions in France before ending his career at the Sorbonne where he became one of Victor Cousin's influential teachers. He was a close student of Condillac, but departed from his teachings, among other things, in emphasizing that the mind was not totally passive. His *Leçons de philosophie*, a popular philosophical text, went through six editions between 1815 and 1844.]

de Staël,[7] who by their love and praise of nature, their sense of the beautiful, their enthusiasm, their appeals to the heart, the moral and religious sentiments and regrets which they awakened, prepared the way for a sounder philosophy, one loftier in its conceptions and truer to human nature. In 1811, M. Royer-Collard,[8] a disciple of the Scotch school, was raised to the chair of philosophy, from which, up to 1814, he attacked sensualism without scruple and without mercy. It was not able to survive his blows. Dr. Broussais, in 1828, published a work on *Irritation et Folie*, in its defense;[9] but he did little more than show himself *irritated* at the general disrespect with which it was treated, and the extreme *folly* of undertaking to restore it to power. In 1815, M. Victor Cousin, whose attention had been drawn to philosophy by the instruction of M. Laromiguière, and who had been taught to analyze the will by M. de Biran,[10] and converted by M. Royer-Collard from sensualism, was made professor of philosophy in the Normal School and the Faculty of Literature. Young, ardent, penetrating, and eloquent, he soon produced a powerful movement, completed the revolution commenced by M. Royer-Collard, and prepared for France a new philosophical future. If he have not, as some may believe, given to France the philosophy which must reign during that future, he has at least given the method for its creation, and rendered the return to sensualism impossible.

[7][Ed. Jacques-Henri Bernardin de Saint-Pierre (1737-1814) was a French philosophical writer whose works (e.g. *Paul et Virginie*) reveal a philosophy of nature that swings back and forth between the Enlightenment and the Romantic world views. François René Chateaubriand (1768-1848), a Romantic author whose *Le Génie du christianisme* (1802) was widely read as an apology for Christianity against the critiques of the Enlightenment rationalists. Germaine Necker, Madame de Staël-Holstein (1766-1817) , author of *De l'Allemagne* (1808-10), was at the center of the French Romantic movement's reaction to the preceding age.]

[8][Ed. Pierre Paul Royer-Collard (1763-1845) was foremost in establishing the Scottish Common Sense Tradition in Paris. His spiritual philosophy, moving away from the reigning sensualism of Condillac, had a great influence on his most famous student, Victor Cousin.]

[9][Ed. François Broussais (1772-1838) was a French physician who believed that diet and bleeding were the exclusive remedies for all illnesses. He also asserted in *Traité de l'irritation et de la folie* a similar solution to cure psychological maladies.]

[10][Ed. Marie François Pierre Gontier de Brian (1766-1824) was one of the early nineteenth century French philosophers who separated himself from the reigning sensualism of Condillac by affirming the fundamental unity of conscience, emphasizing in particular the role of the human will in self-consciousness. His philosophy gradually moved toward a kind of mystical spiritualism.]

M. Cousin calls the system of philosophy which he and his friends profess and advocate, ECLECTICISM; because it recognizes the leading principles of all the great schools into which the philosophical world has been divided, and attempts to mold them into one grand whole, which shall include them all, and yet be itself unlike any of them. It went into power with the King of the Barricades,[11] and will undoubtedly preside over the new system of schools and instruction which the government is preparing for France. We already see it in the most popular French journals, and in many of the most fashionable literary productions; and we can hardly persuade ourselves but that (in these and other ways) its influence on the destinies of France is at present, and must be for the future, very great. But without going into any speculations on the influence and prospects of this philosophy, we proceed to give our readers as clear and as satisfactory a statement of what it is, as we can within the limits to which we are necessarily restricted. In doing this we shall draw liberally from the Preface to the second edition of the *Philosophical Fragments*, the third work on our list, in which the author has given us a summary of his system, together with answers to some objections which are raised against it, and some account of its formation and growth in his own mind. We shall arrange what we have to offer under the heads of, 1. Method; 2. Application of Method to Psychology; 3. Passage from Psychology to Ontology; 4. Passage from God to Nature, and 5. General Views on the History of Philosophy.

I. The adoption of a method decides the destinies of a philosophy; for any given system of philosophy is only the development and application of a given method. The method of all sound philosophy is that of observation and induction. Our first step is to study human nature, by observation to ascertain what is in the consciousness; our next and last step is to draw from observation by induction, by reasoning, all the consequences contained in the facts it has collected. Philosophy is the science of facts, and also the science of reasoning. It begins with observation, but it ends only with the limits of the reason itself. It observes and it reasons. In physical science we begin with observation of facts, but we do not end with it; we rise from observation, by reasoning, to general laws and to the system of the world. We should pursue the same method in mental and moral sci-

[11][Ed. The reference is probably to the July 1830 revolt of the French middle classes against King Charles X. The insurrection occurred in opposition to Charles X's reactions and restrictive government measures. Street barricades and fighting cleared Paris of royal troops.]

ence. If we receive as true whatever legitimately follows from the facts of the external world, which we have observed, we should do the same with whatever legitimately follows from the facts of the internal world, which we have scrupulously observed and profoundly analyzed.

In philosophizing, we must guard against rushing too precipitately, from hasty and incomplete observation, to hazardous inductions; and also against confining ourselves, in spite of all the craving of our nature, to mere observation, against never venturing upon an induction, a synthesis of the facts observed. To neglect observation is to fall into hypothesis; to restrict ourselves to mere observation is, whether we know it or not, to place philosophy on the road to scepticism. Scepticism and hypothesis are the two rocks, which philosophy must study to avoid. True method avoids them both. It does not end at the beginning; it does not begin at the end. It acknowledges no limits to induction but those of the reason itself, but it supports induction on a sufficient observation. Reserving to itself the right to the ulterior employment of the faculties of the understanding, philosophy cannot observe too scrupulously. It can no more than physical science, proclaim too loudly, insist too earnestly, that observation is its necessary point of departure. There is, in fact, no difference between philosophy and physical science, except in the nature of the phenomena to be observed. The proper phenomena of physical science are those of external nature, of that vast world of which man makes so small a part; the proper phenomena of philosophy are those of internal nature, of that world which each man carries within himself, and which is observed by that inward light called consciousness, in like manner as the other is observed by the senses.

Philosophy begins by observing the phenomena of the world within us. A mere glimpse of those phenomena is not observation. They are as truly open to our inspection as those of the world without us; but they appear and disappear so rapidly, that the consciousness perceives and loses sight of them almost at the same instant. To merely glance at them as they are passing over the varying theater of consciousness, is not enough; we must retain them as long a time as possible, recall them from the darkness into which they vanish, demand them anew of the memory, reproduce them, that we may examine them at our leisure, vary the lights in which we observe them, survey each one under all its aspects, that we may embrace each one in its entireness. We must reflect; not only listen to nature, but question her; not only observe, but make experiments. Whatever be the objects to which it is applied, experience has the same conditions and rules; and it is only by following them, in the science of man as in that of nature, that we can arrive at exact classifications.

These classifications, when their subject is human nature, the human soul, are called psychology. Psychology, an exact classification of the mental phenomena, is the first part, the foundation, but not the whole of philosophy. This is a point of great importance. The principal peculiarity of M. Cousin's system results from the fact, that he makes psychology the foundation, but not the superstructure, the beginning, but not the end of philosophy. By making psychology the basis of philosophy, he connects his philosophical enterprise with modern philosophy itself, which from Descartes, Bacon, and Locke,[12] tolerates only the experimental method. In this he does not dissent from the philosophy which reigned in France during the last century. That philosophy was indeed sensualism, but it was also experimental; as experimental M. Cousin accepts, and though he modifies, continues it. This deserves the especial notice of those, who have supposed that he rejects experience and ought to be confounded with the hypothesis-constructing Germans. In method, he is as free from hypothesis as he is from scepticism. By beginning with psychology, making it the only door of entrance into the temple of philosophy, he not only connects himself with the old French, but separates himself from the new German school. The new German school, represented by Schelling and Hegel,[13] begins where he ends, and ends where he begins. It begins by an hypothesis, rises at once without means, or by means of which it takes no account, to the Absolute, to the Being of beings, and attempts to reach nature and humanity through ontology. When we have once placed ourselves in ontology, in absolute being, the passage to the phenomenal, to nature and humanity, is without difficulty; psychology may most assuredly be found in ontology; but how can we attain to ontology? How shall we place ourselves in the Absolute as our point of observation? We must attain the summit by a slow and toilsome ascent from the valley, where is our starting-point, not by dropping from the heavens. Our only true method is to begin by ascertaining what is; from what is, the

[12][Ed. René Descartes (1596-1650), Francis Bacon (1561-1626), and John Locke (1632-1704) emphasized method and became, in Cousin's and Brownson's perspectives, the fathers of modern philosophy.]

[13][Ed. Friedrich Wilhelm Joseph Schelling (1775-1854), German idealist philosopher, modified Fichte's absolute idealism by his philosophy of nature which emphasized the role of the object in the identity between the objective and the subjective. Georg Wilhelm Friedrich Hegel (1770-1831), German idealist philosopher, was well know for his philosophy of history and religion.]

actual, we may pass to its origin, from that to its legitimacy, and thus attain the Absolute. Should we adopt the method of the new German school, and by some lucky divination obtain the truth, which M. Cousin considers to be the case with the school in question, the truth thus obtained, not having been scientifically obtained, would be without any scientific validity.

II. But if M. Cousin separates himself, so far as it concerns method, from the new German school and approaches the old French school, he separates also from this last, as soon as he proceeds to the application of his method to psychology. Their method is the same, but the French school is not true to it. It applies it with the prejudices of a system. It observes, but it observes only what suits its convenience. It mutilates the consciousness, and observes only the facts of the sensibility. Its analysis is, therefore, necessarily too narrow for its generalizations.

There is, undoubtedly, a class or order of phenomena in the consciousness, which may be traced back to sensation. That this class exists, and is of large extent, is incontestable. The manner in which the phenomena it includes, are generated, although somewhat complicated, is easily comprehended; and they have the advantage of reposing on a primitive fact, which, by connecting them with the physical sciences, seems to vouch for their reality. This fact is, that of the impression produced on the organs of sensation and reproduced by the brain in the consciousness. The illusion of believing that this order includes all the phenomena of which we can be conscious, was therefore very natural. If there be only a single order of phenomena in the consciousness, there can be only a single faculty to which we can refer those phenomena, and which in its transformations must produce all the others. This faculty is that of sensation, or, if we may adopt the etymological instead of the common meaning of the word, the sensibility; but if sensibility be the root of all our intellectual faculties, it must be the root of all our moral faculties. This reduces man to a mere creature of sensation. He can then know nothing which is not cognizable by some one or all of his five senses. Our senses can take cognizance of only material objects; if other objects exist we cannot know them; they are for us as though they were not. When we recognize only material existences, thought itself becomes materialized; painting, sculpture, poetry, all the fine arts, take a tinge of materiality, cease to reveal the infinite, and merely represent some small portions of the finite. All our notions of God, of the soul, of the beautiful, the right, inasmuch as they are not copies of outward material objects, which are observed alike by the senses, are illusions, mere fantasies, no more to be trusted than the dreams which disturb our nightly slumbers; religion withers into a mere form, hardens into a petrifaction, or entirely disappears; or, at least, can be retained only as an inconsequence or as an instrument; morality freezes into selfishness; pleasure and pain become the synonyms of right and wrong; and that alone which gives pleasure, not to the soul but to the senses, can be dignified with the name of *good*; the soul, having no longer any employment, takes its departure, and the man sinks in the animal, recognizing and laboring only for animal wants. This is the unavoidable result of recognizing in the consciousness the phenomena of the sensibility alone, and of reducing the whole nature of man to the faculty of receiving a sensation. The history of France in the last century proves this. She began with Condillac, who reduced the soul to sensation, and ended with Helvétius, who reduced morality to the simple maxim, "Seek pleasure, fly pain," with D'Holbach, who raved for materialism and atheism as a fanatic, and Lamettrie, who discoursed eloquently of the Man-Machine and the Man-Plant.[14] But is this a true account of man? Who does not find in himself the ideas of the just and the unjust, the beautiful and its opposite, the holy and the unholy, the true, the true in itself? An impartial observation refutes both the principle and the system which is deduced from it, by making it appear that there are in the consciousness phenomena which no effort can legitimately trace back to sensation, numerous ideas, ideas which are perfectly real, both in human life and in language, which sensation cannot explain. After having been struck with the relations of the human faculties, we are struck also with their differences, and a rigorous method enlarges the field of psychology.

M. Cousin recognizes in the consciousness three classes of phenomena, which result from the great elementary faculties which comprehend and explain all the rest. These faculties are Sensibility, Activity, and Reason. They are never found isolated one from another. Yet they are essentially distinct, and a scrupulous analysis distinguishes them in the complex phenomena of intellectual life without dividing

[14][Ed. Claude Adrien Helvétius (1715-71) articulated his maxim in *De l'esprit* (1758). See *De l'esprit; or Essays on the Mind and Its Several Faculties* (Poultry: Albion Press, 1810), 251 for the maxim. *De l'esprit* caused quite a sensation for its sensualist notions and rejection of religious ethical foundations. Paul Heinrich Dietrich Holbach (1723-89) was a French encyclopedist who produced a number of volumes dedicated to the destruction of religion. Julien Offray de La Mettrie (1709-51), French physician and materialist philosopher, proposed in *L'Homme machine* (1748) and other works that humans are but superior animals subject to the laws of self-organizing nature.]

them. To sensibility belong all the internal phenomena, which are derived from sensation, through our senses, from the external world; to the activity belong those, which we are conscious that we ourselves produce; and under the head of reason must be arranged all our ideas of the Absolute, the Supersensible, and all the internal facts which are purely intellectual, which we know we do not produce, and which cannot be derived through sensation from external nature. The activity is developed only by sensation. Activity and sensibility can generate no idea without the reason; and without sensibility and activity the reason would have no office. This psychology destroys sensualism and leads to a philosophy of a totally different character. The philosophy to which it leads has already made some progress. It is represented on the theater of the nineteenth century by the Scotch school, but more especially by the Kantian school, which, professing the same method as the Scotch, applies it with a very different rigor and extent. This school has enriched psychology by so many ingenious and profound observations, and is above all so distinguished by the beauty and grandeur of its morality, that it must always be held in deserved honor.

The sensualist school admits and studies with great success the facts of the sensibility; but overlooking those of the activity and the reason, or not making a sufficient account of them, it mutilates the soul, and becomes false in its inductions. The Scotch school avoids this error; it distinguishes between the reason and sensibility, but without much scientific precision. The Kantian school has done it with more care and accuracy; it has also described with great clearness and precision the laws of the reason, but it has not discerned with sufficient exactness the distinction between the reason and the activity. This deficiency has ruined the school. The activity is personal. *We* are in the activity; that alone is our *self.* To confound the reason with the activity, as Kant[15] and his followers do, is to make the reason personal, and to deprive it of all but a subjective authority; that is, to make it of no authority except in relation to the individual in whom it is developed. To deprive the reason of all but a subjective authority, to allow it no validity out of the sphere of our own personality, is to deprive it of all legitimate authority, and to place philosophy on the route to a new and original scepticism. If the reason have

[15][Ed. Immanuel Kant (1724-1804) was a German philosopher whose critical philosophy had a major impact on all subsequent modern philosophy. His *Der Kritik der reinen Vernunft* (1781, 1787) underlined the synthetic and conditional nature of all human knowledge. Brownson's knowledge of Kant was derivative, coming primarily from Cousin. He did not read Kant's *Kritik* until 1838.]

no authority out of the sphere of the personality, out of the individual consciousness in which its phenomena appear, it can reveal to us no existences which lie beyond ourselves. Such may be the laws of our nature, that we cannot help believing that we are, that there is an external world, and God; but our belief can repose on no scientific basis. There is nothing to assure us, that it is not a mere illusion; nothing can demonstrate to us, that anything really exists to respond to it. All certainty resolves itself into a mere personal affection. To this conclusion all are driven who assert the subjectivity of the reason. This may be seen by going from Kant, the circumspect master, to Fichte, the audacious disciple, who shrinks from no logical results, and even ventures to represent the external world, and God himself, as productions of that mysterious something we mean, when we say, *I, Me*!

To avoid this extravagance, we must distinguish between the reason and the activity, and show that, though intimately connected, they are nevertheless fundamentally distinct. The reason, though appearing in us, is not our *self*. It is independent of us, and in no sense subject to our personality. If it depended on our personality, or if it constituted our personality, we could control its conceptions, prescribe its laws, and compel it to speak according to our pleasure. Its conceptions would be ours, as much and in the same sense, as our intentions; its revelations would be our revelations, that is, revelations of ourselves, and its truths would be our truths. Who is prepared to admit such a conclusion? We may say, "my actions, my crimes, my virtues," for we consider ourselves very justly as their cause; we may even say, "my error," for our errors are in some degree attributable to ourselves; but who dare say "*my* truth"? Who does not feel, who does not know, that the truth is not his, is nobody's, but independent of everybody? If, then, we are conscious that the conceptions of the reason are not ours, that the truths it reveals are not our truths, are not truths which are in any sense dependent on us, we must admit that the reason is independent of us, and, though appearing in us, is not our *self*.

Nobody doubts the independence of the reason in the consciousness itself. Who doubts the reality of the mental phenomena of which we are directly conscious, who doubts the apperceptions of consciousness, apperceptions on which is founded the knowledge of our own existence? No skeptic doubts these, for no skeptic doubts that he doubts. But not to doubt that we doubt, is to know that we doubt, is to know something, is, in fine, *to know*. Now, what is it that *knows*? What is that inward light we call consciousness, which has these apperceptions in which we confide, which knows in any degree, which knows at all? Is it not the reason? If the reason may be trusted in one case, why not in another? If the knowledge, which the reason gives us of what is passing within us, be undeniable, why shall not all other knowledge, which the same reason gives, be considered equally certain? The reason is the same in all its degrees, and we have no right arbitrarily to restrict or extend its limits.

III. The reason, once established in its true nature and independence, becomes a legitimate authority for whatever it reveals. A true analysis of it shows, that, instead of being imprisoned in the consciousness and compelled to turn forever within the sphere of the subjective, it extends far beyond, and attains to beings as well as to phenomena. It reveals to us God and the world on precisely the same authority as our own existence, or the slightest modification of it. Ontology thus becomes as legitimate as psychology; since it is psychology, which, by disclosing to us the true nature of the reason, conducts of itself to ontology.

We suppose that few, comparatively speaking, feel much interest in, or have any very clear conceptions of the precise problems, which it is the object of the higher metaphysics to solve. There are but few who wish to pass from the subjective to the objective, from psychology to ontology. Once convinced that man is determined by a law of his nature to believe in an external world and in God, most men are satisfied without seeking anything farther. But there are those who would have the legitimacy, as well as the existence, of that law established. This was the case with Hume.[16] He saw very clearly that man was determined by his nature to believe in an external world and in God; but, as this determination was no result of experience, he counted it of no scientific value, and asserted that the existence neither of the world nor of God, could be proved, and, though every man in his senses must believe in the existence of both, that philosophy must forever remain in relation to them a skeptic. The Scotch school, honorable for its good intentions, undertook to refute him; but, incapable of comprehending him, it alleged against him the very fact which he admitted, and which he acknowledged that no man in his senses could deny. It alleged as a proof of God and the external world, that we were compelled to believe in them by a law, a first, a constituent principle of our nature. So said Hume. But what is the authority of that principle? What is its legitimacy? What vouches for its veracity? The Scotch school answered only by a paralogism. The Kantian school advances not a step beyond Hume. It describes the conditions on which the belief is formed; but it denies that we can know the

[16] [Ed. See Chapter 7, n. 16.]

Absolute, that we can, in relation to God and the world, have anything more than an irresistible belief, founded on the subjective laws of our own nature. Schelling and his school assume, by a bold hypothesis, the Absolute, the objective, and give us a magnificent poem, which we believe to be mainly true, but which is nevertheless no philosophy, and can in no degree solve the difficulty stated by Hume. The psychological truth of God and the world, we think, has been demonstrated over and over again, in a manner that must be satisfactory to the most skeptical, who are not ignorant of the demonstrations which have been given; but no philosopher, with whom we are acquainted, unless it be M. Cousin, has demonstrated their ontological truth. M. Cousin professes to have demonstrated, that we not only have the belief, and cannot help having it, but that it is well founded, that there is something out of us to respond to it. This he supposes he has done by establishing the independence of the reason; by proving that the reason is objective in relation to our personality, he thinks he has obtained a legitimate witness of the objective; and since this witness unquestionably deposes to the existence of God and of the world, he thinks he has proved their validity.

He asserts that the reason—the only faculty in us which knows, the only principle of all certainty, the only rule of the true and the false, of the right and the wrong, which alone perceives its own aberrations, disabuses itself when deceived, recovers its path when led astray, accuses, acquits, or condemns itself—the reason gives us ontology, the science of being, the knowledge of our own personal existence, and of the existence of external nature and of God, by precisely the same title as the least knowledge which we possess, and gives it too without waiting for any long developments, immediately, wholly and in each of its parts, in every fact of consciousness, in the first as well as in the last. It is on psychology that he supports himself in this assertion, but on a psychology to which only a profound reflection can attain.

Can there be any fact of consciousness without some attention? Our thoughts, if we do not attend to them, become confused, fall into indistinct reveries, very soon vanish away, and become for us as though they were not. Even the perceptions of our senses, without attention, degenerate into mere organic impressions. An organ is struck, and even with force, but the mind, if engaged elsewhere, does not perceive it; there is then no sensation, and, if no sensation, of course no consciousness. In every fact of the consciousness, therefore, the attention does and must intervene.

Now is not every act of the attention more or less voluntary? Is not every voluntary act marked with this character, that we consider ourselves its cause? And is it not this cause, whose effects may vary while it remains itself unvaried, this power, which its acts alone reveal to us, and which its acts do not exhaust, is it not this cause, power, force, that we call *I*, *me*, our individuality, our personality, that personality of which we never doubt, which we never confound with any other, because we never refer to any other the voluntary acts which give us an intimate sentiment and an unalterable conviction of it? The *I*, the personality, is then given us in every fact of consciousness. There can be no fact of consciousness without a conception of our own existence.

We find *ourselves* then, in the fact of consciousness, and we find ourselves a cause, a creative force. This is the radical idea which we have of ourselves. We know ourselves under no other character than that of a cause, and we exist for ourselves no farther than we are a cause. The bounds of our causality are the bounds of our existence. Can this cause, which we are, do whatever it will? Meets it no resistance, no obstacles? It does, at every step, and of every kind. To the sentiment of our strength is ever added that of our weakness. Thousands of impressions from without continually assail us. If we do not attend to them, they come not to the consciousness; but, as soon as we attend to them, sensation begins. Now, here is the intervention of a new element. We refer to ourselves the act of attending to the impressions made upon our organs of sense, but we do not, and we cannot, refer to ourselves, as their cause, the impressions to which we attend. We receive sensations, we do not cause them. But, if we cannot refer them to ourselves as their cause, we cannot help referring them to some cause, and necessarily to a cause which is out of us, exterior. The existence of this exterior cause is as certain to us as our own existence; for the phenomenon—sensation—which suggests it, is as certain to us, as the phenomenon, act of attention, which suggests to us our existence. Both too, are given together, in the same phenomenon. There is then, in every fact of consciousness, not only a conception of our own existence, of our personality, but also a conception of something which is not ourselves, something independent of our personality and exterior to it, external nature.

If anyone should doubt this, he is required to conceive of himself without also conceiving of that which is not himself, or of that which is not himself without conceiving of himself. I cannot have a clear conception of myself without distinguishing myself from all other existences. To assert that I exist, is to assert that I am, and that I am myself and not another. In the complex phenomena of consciousness, we have seen there necessarily intervene activity and sensibility. There are the impressions from a cause which we are not, and attention, which is our act, applied to those impressions, giving us a consciousness of them. These two causes, one of which we are, the other of which we are not, external nature, are then unquestionable in every fact of consciousness and both equally certain. But with what characters do we find these two causes? Certainly they appear as relative, imperfect, bounded, finite. The cause, which we are, meets resistance, obstacles, bounds, in that variety of causes to which we refer the phenomena of which we are conscious, which we do not produce and which are purely affective and involuntary; and these causes themselves are limited and bounded by that voluntary cause which we are. We resist them as they resist us, and, to a certain extent, limit their action as they limit ours. It is only in the meeting, the clashing of the two causes, it is only in their conflict, that either is revealed to us. There is no question that we always conceive of them, and cannot help conceiving of them, as relative and as finite causes. Now, what is it to conceive of these two causes as relative and finite? It is to distinguish them in our minds as such; it is to assert that they are not absolute, infinite causes, but relative and finite causes. If, then, whenever these two causes are in the consciousness, they are there as relative, as finite, they must be there as contrasted with the infinite, the absolute. But they cannot be contrasted with, or distinguished from, the infinite and the absolute, without a conception of the infinite and the absolute; and, without being so contrasted or distinguished, they cannot be conceived as relative and finite. In every fact of consciousness, then, there is a conception of ourselves, or of personality, and of something which is not ourselves, external nature, both as relative, finite causes; and of the infinite, the absolute, to which they are by the reason necessarily referred, and with which they must be contrasted in order to be conceived.

The reason, which is developed in the consciousness, and which perceives there at the same time attention and sensation, as soon as it has the apperception of them, makes us conceive immediately of the two sorts of distinct, but correlative and reciprocally finite causes to which they are referred. But the reason does not stop here. The notion of finite and limited causes once given, we cannot help conceiving of a superior, absolute, and infinite cause, which is itself the first and last cause of all causes. The internal and personal cause which we are, and the exterior causes which we call nature, are undeniably causes in relation to their own effects; but the same reason which gives them as causes, giving them as relative and limited causes, prevents us from stopping with them as causes which are sufficient for themselves, and forces us to refer them to a supreme Cause, which produces and sustains them, which is relatively to them what they are relatively to their own phenomena, and which, being the Cause of all cause, and Being of all being, is sufficient for itself, and for the reason which seeks nothing and finds nothing beyond.

If this analysis of a fact of consciousness be accurate, we are authorized to say that no fact of consciousness is possible without the conception of our own existence, the existence of the world, and that of God. The ideas, of ourselves as a free personality, of nature, and of God as the substance, the cause, of both us and nature, constitute a single fact of the consciousness, are its inseparable elements, and without them consciousness is impossible. Ourselves, nature, and God are, then, necessarily asserted in every word, in every affirmation, in every thought. The skeptic who professes to doubt their existence, in that he can assert that he doubts, asserts that they exist. Atheism is, then, impossible; some men may want the term, the word, but all men believe in God.

The world and ourselves are found in the fact of consciousness as causes, and God is also found in the same fact, as a cause, the infinite, the absolute cause, which is the cause and substance of the relative and finite causes which we and nature are. God, then, exists to us under the character of a cause. A little reflection soon discovers the identity of cause and substance. We call ourselves and the world substances for the simple reason that they are causes, and in our conception the limits of their causality are the limits of their substantiality. God, being absolute cause, is absolute substance. If absolute, he must be one, for two absolutes are an absurdity. The relative, free, intentional causality, personality, which we are, implies absolute intentional causality, absolute personality; and, as the absolute can be found only in the absolute, it follows that God is not a blind, fatal causality, but a free, intentional cause, that is, a person. Descending again into the reason, we find there the absolute principles of the just and the beautiful. These principles, being absolute, belong to the absolute. Hence, from the absolute principles of causality, substance, unity, intentionality, the just, and the beautiful, we obtain the absolute God, Cause of causes, Being of beings, substance of substances, unity of unities, intentionality of intentionalities, morally just, beautiful, righteous—our Father.

It should be remarked, that we do not *infer* the Absolute from the relative, the Infinite from the finite, God from nature and humanity. The Absolute is no logical creation, no production of reasoning. It could not be deduced from the relative. No dialectic skill has ever yet been able to draw the infinite from the finite, the unconditioned from the conditioned. Both terms are given together, both are primitive *data*, without which no reasoning could possibly take place. Remove from man the idea of the infinite, or of the finite, and he would be incapable of a single intellectual act. A man, to reason, must assert something, and must assert that something to be either infinite or finite. But no man can say that a thing is finite without having at the same time the conception of the infinite; or that a thing is infinite without at the same time conceiving the finite. Neither, then, can be deduced from the other; both coexist in the intelligence as its fundamental elements, and not only coexist, but coexist as cause and effect. Hence the ideas of the infinite, the finite and their relation, not of mere coexistence but as cause and effect, are inseparable and essential elements of all intellection. This being true, all three, embracing all existence, ourselves, God, and the world, must have existed in the understanding, before ever an intelligent act was possible. They are, then, so far from being inferred, some from the others, that all then must exist before an inference is possible. They are the primitive *data* of the intellect, the starting-points of all reasoning. That is, when they are considered in relation to their logical origin, though in point of fact they are not developed in the understanding, till the understanding begins to act. All three, however, are developed simultaneously in the first fact of the intellectual life.

But if the absolute logically precedes the relative, and if the conceptions of the infinite, the finite, and their relation be indispensable conditions of all reasoning, it follows of course that our belief in God, in nature, in our own existence, is the result of no reasoning. When we first turned our minds inward in the act of reflection, we found that belief. We had it, and every man has it, from the first dawn of the intellect. It does not proceed then from reflection; and, as reflection is the only intellectual act in which we have any agency, it follows that it does not exist in consequence of anything we have willed or done. It is prior to *our* action, and independent of it. Whence then its origin? It must be a primitive, spontaneous belief, the result of the spontaneity of the reason. The reason sees by its own light, is itself active; and, being in relation with the objective and the absolute, it can and does of itself reveal to the consciousness God and the world, giving by its own vigor the belief in question. The reason, being in its nature independent, and in its spontaneity acting independently of us, and though developing itself in us, is a good and legitimate witness for what lies beyond us, and exists independent of us.

Is this a legitimate passage from the subjective to the objective, from psychology to ontology, from the phenomenon to being, from the relative to the absolute, from the conditioned to the unconditioned? Is there here a verification of that law of our nature, which determines us to believe in God and an external world? Is there here a proof, that our belief in the existence of the world and of God has any objective reality to respond to it? The reason is independent, it is objective; therefore, it is a legitimate authority for the objective. The reason is objective, it is absolute, and therefore a sufficient witness for the absolute. The reason reveals the absolute, therefore the absolute exists. This conclusion, which we believe to be correct, rests upon an assumption of the credibility of the reason. The reason may declare itself to be independent, absolute, but how can we prove that it is not a law of thought, a mere mode of intellectual activity? It is true we may so define personality, as to make the reason objective in relation to what we are pleased to term *ourself*, but a definition is not a demonstration. We have only the reason with which to prove the reason's independence; consequently, we have only its own word that it is not subjective. We attain the objective on the faith of the reason, but we have no voucher for that faith.

We dissent from M. Cousin with no little distrust of ourselves; but we confess that we are unable to conceive the possibility of absolutely demonstrating, logically proving, the objective, till we can obtain an independent witness to vouch for the independence and veracity of the reason. This witness we have not, and cannot have. If such a witness could be supposed, he could give his testimony to us only through the reason, and we should still have only the reason's authority for it. We must take the reason's word that the reason has correctly reported what the witness has testified. But at the same time that we deny the possibility of demonstrating the objectivity of the reason in relation to *man*, though we may do it in relation to the *will*, we contend that there is no need of doing it. The reason sees, and knows, and truly reveals the absolute, the infinite, the unconditioned, the spiritual world, God. It sees and reveals the spiritual world, the world of reality, by its own light and energy; and this is the highest degree of certainty we ever have, the highest we ever ask, for none of us have ever asked that the reason be proved reasonable. M. Cousin, we think, has demonstrated all that he was required to demonstrate. He has shown beyond a question that the reason, which is our only light, gives us the Absolute, God, and external nature, as positively and on the same authority as our own existence or the apperceptions of consciousness. We have no authority for either but the reason, and that is given as decidedly for one as the other. We may be as certain, then, that there is a God as that we exist. But we cannot prove it. We cannot prove that we exist, because, in every attempt to prove our existence, we are obliged to assume it, and because we have nothing more evident than our existence with which to prove it. But are we less certain that we exist on this account? That which we best know is least susceptible of being proved. The proof must be more certain than that which is to be proved. When, therefore, the proposition in question is one of those which have the highest degree of certainty, it of course cannot be proved. But it is certain without being proved. The Deity knows all things; but could he, if he would, prove to himself this fact? With what should he prove it? What is more evident to him than the fact that he knows all things? We are now engaged in writing, we know what we are doing, but we should be at a loss to prove to ourselves that we are writing. But, to our very great relief, we discover no necessity of having it proved. So, in relation to ontology, we know it, but cannot prove it. With what shall we prove it? The reason is the only eye with which we see it, and we have no witness but the reason to bring to prove that the reason's eye really sees it. But as the deposition of the reason is always all the proof we ask, we need no other witness.

The whole matter, then, turns on the credit due the reason. Grant reason tells the truth, we know the Absolute, the Unconditioned, God. Deny the reason, or declare the reason unworthy to be believed, and we neither know God, the world, ourselves, nor anything else. We are reduced to a worse strait than to "doubt that doubt itself be doubting,"[17] a strait in which we cannot possibly remain even in thought so long as it takes to name it. Thus much, we think, M. Cousin has done, and, we believe, it is all that he considers himself as having done, though he calls it a demonstration, which we contend it is not. The demonstration would require him to prove the credibility of the reason, a thing which he cannot do, because he has only the reason with which to establish the truth of the reason. But this is no cause of regret. We want no higher authority than the reason. The reason in all its essential elements is in every man. It is the light, "the true light that lighteneth every man that cometh into the world" [John 1:9]. As it reveals spontaneously, in every man's consciousness, the vast world of reality, the absolute God, the cause and substance

[17][Ed. Quotation is from George Gordon Byron's (1788-1824) *Don Juan* (1823), Canto ix, Stanza 17, Line 136, in *Lord Byron: The Complete Poetical Works*, ed. Jerome J. McGann, vol. 5 (Oxford: Clarendon, 1986).]

of all that APPEARS, it follows that every man has the witness of the spiritual world, of the Absolute, the Infinite, God, in himself.

IV. The reason can reveal nothing which it has not in itself. If it reveal the absolute, it must itself be absolute. If absolute, it must be the Being of beings, God himself. The elements of the reason are then the elements of God. An analysis of the reason gives, as its elements, the ideas of the infinite, the finite, and their relation as cause and effect. Then these ideas are the elements of all thought, of thought in itself, of God. God then, is thought, reason, intelligence in itself. An intelligence which does not manifest itself, is a dead intelligence, a dead thought; but a dead thought, a dead intelligence, is inconceivable. To live, to exist, intelligence must manifest itself. God, being thought, intelligence in itself, must necessarily manifest himself. To manifest himself is to create, and his manifestation is creation.

In going from humanity and nature to God, we found him a cause. If he be a cause, he must create, that is, cause something. A cause which does not create is no cause at all. Creation then is necessary. God ceases to exist to us in exact proportion as he ceases to be a creator. But out of what can God create? Not out of nothing as is easily shown. The hypothesis of the independent existence of matter is also inadmissible. If matter can exist independent of God, then it is sufficient for itself; if sufficient for itself, it is almighty, absolute. There would then be two absolutes. Two independent existences, matter on the one side, and God on the other, would be a gross absurdity. God, then, can create only out of himself; that is, by developing, manifesting, himself.

But God can manifest only what is in himself. He is thought, intelligence itself. Consequently there is in creation nothing but thought, intelligence. In nature, as in humanity, the supreme Reason is manifested, and there, where we had fancied all was dead and without thought, we are now enabled to see all living and essentially intellectual. There is no dead matter, there are no fatal causes; nature is thought, and God is its personality. This enables us to see God in nature, in a new and striking sense, and gives a sublime meaning to the words of Paul: "The invisible things of him from the creation of the world, even his eternal power and Godhead, are clearly seen, being understood by the things which are made" [Rom. 1:20]. Well may we study nature, for, as a whole and in the minutest of its parts, it is a manifestation of the Infinite, the Absolute, the Everlasting, the Perfect, the universal Reason—God. It should be loved, should be reverenced, not merely as a piece of mechanism, but as a glorious shining out of the Infinite and the Perfect. How much more, however, should we study, love, reverence and stand in awe of humanity, the still brighter manifestation, more perfect type, image of the supreme Intelligence, the true God—our Father!

This idea of creation is suggested and explained by what is continually passing in ourselves. We will to raise an arm. It may be paralytic, and consequently does not move. Nevertheless we have created something, we have created an intention. Here is the type of creation. God wills; the universe is; he speaks, and it stands fast. It is but God's volition, his intention. This gives us an affecting view of our dependence on God. We are his volition, as dependent on him as our volitions are dependent on us. We will to raise our arm, the volition to raise it exists; we cease to will, and our volition is gone, is—nothing. God wills, we are, ceases to will, and we are not. How truly was it said, "In him we live, and move, and have our being" [Acts 17:28]!

If this view of creation be admissible, that notion which presents the Deity waking from the sleep of an eternity, putting forth for a moment his omnipotent energy, creating, arranging, and adorning the world, assigning it certain laws by which to govern itself, setting its machinery in motion, and then returning to his sleep, or departing to form new world-machines, world-automata, or seating himself on a solitary throne far back from and above his creation, and contemplating his works in eternal silence—this notion of God, we say, must be forever abandoned. "God is at once true and real, substance and cause, always substance, always cause, being substance in that he is a cause, one and many, eternity and time, space and number, essence and life, individuality and totality, beginning, middle, and end, alike infinite and finite at the summit and at the lowest round of existence."[18] God is above, over and in all, cause and substance, life and reality of all.

This is not Pantheism. Pantheism considers the universe as a God; but this presents God as the cause, and the universe as the effect. God is as inseparable from the universe as the cause is inseparable from the effect; but no one who can discern any distinction between an appearance and that which appears, between the phenomenon and being, the manifestation and that which is manifested, can ever confound him with the universe. The cause is always in the effect. I am in my intention, but I am not my intention. All there is in the intention is of me, but it does not exhaust me. I create an intention, and I remain with all my creative energy. So of God. The universe is his intention. It is what he wills, and he is in it, the sub-

[18][Ed. The substance of the quotation reflects Victor Cousin's position, but I could not identify the source.]

stance of his volition; it is what he speaks, and he is in it, as a man is in his words; but he is distinct from it, by all the distinction there is between the energy that wills, and that which is willed, between him who speaks, and the words he utters.

The reason, taken absolutely, we have said is identical with God. The consequences of this are numerous and grand. The reason is God; it appears in us, therefore God appears in us. The light of reason, the light by which we see and know all that we do see and know, is truly the light of God. The voice of the spontaneous reason is the voice of God; those who speak by its authority, speak by the authority of God, and what they utter is a real revelation. This explains inspiration, accounts for the origin of prophecies, pontificates, and religious rites, and justifies the human race for having believed that some men had been the confidants and interpreters of God. He in whom the spontaneous reason was more active than in his fellow beings, had a closer communion with God, could better interpret him than they, and was rightly termed the inspired, for he was inspired; not indeed in a sense different from the rest of mankind, but in a different, a special, degree.

This idea that God really appears in us, that it is by his light that we see, though it may be an approach to the "vision in God" of Malebranche,[19] is one that we value for its religious as well as its philosophical bearing. It has some affinity with Fichte's doctrine of a twofold personality, one phenomenal, individual, the other absolute, real. We are, as individuals, only APPEARANCES. Our real being is in God. Back of us and through us, there is always shining out something which is not phenomenal, relative, but absolute, substantial, which may be called person in itself. Person in itself is God. God then, is our higher, our absolute personality. This explains the mystery of the incarnation, of the two natures in Jesus, and shows how Jesus was, and how we may be, one with the Father. Jesus was one with the Father—"God manifest in the flesh," if one chooses—because his phenomenal personality was absorbed in the absolute, his individual will was lost in the Divine, the absolute will. The Divine, the God in man, was conspicuous in Jesus above the human. In proportion as our will, our lower, phenomenal personality, becomes lost

[19][Ed. Nicholas Malebranche (1638-1715), French Catholic priest of the Oratory and unorthodox proponent of Cartesian philosophy whose *The Search After Truth* (1674) presented his most characteristic contributions to philosophy: the vision in God and occasionalism. According to the ontologist Malebranche the innate ideas in the human mind are in God, and as such they are eternal and independent of finite minds.]

in our higher, our absolute personality, we approach God, become one with him, pass from the phenomenal to real being, from death to life, from the mortal to the immortal, from the corruptible to the incorruptible—from earth to Heaven. We cannot proceed; but, if we do not deceive ourselves, we have indicated here a train of thought which may lead to grand results, and throw a new, a clear, and a strong light on some of the darkest passages in our religion.

V. Man's intellectual life begins with the spontaneous reason. We believe, we confide before we reflect. In the infancy of the individual and of the race, God himself, as a tender father, is the guide and teacher. The child a little advanced, wishes to go alone, to be guided by his own light, to follow his own will, and rely on his own strength. A dangerous wish! but one which must be gratified if the child is ever to become a man. After a while man finds he has believed, and he desires to know why he has believed, to account to himself for the phenomena he discovers. There is now a new element developed within him, the reflective reason; and henceforth, instead of confiding, he must reflect, and instead of faith he must have philosophy. No more repose, no more careless glee of the child; active life begins: its cares, its burdens, its duties must be met and borne and performed. The father gives the child his blessing, his counsel, and sends him, at his request, forth into the world to seek his fortune as best he may.

Philosophy begins the day that man begins to reflect; it is the creation of reflection, and, since reflection is our act, it is our creation. It is to humanity, what nature and humanity are to God. As there can be nothing in nature and humanity which is not in God, so there can be nothing in philosophy which is not in humanity. He who comprehends humanity, comprehends not only true philosophy, but all systems of philosophy which have heretofore obtained, or which can obtain hereafter. He who comprehends all the systems of philosophy which have been, comprehends humanity as far as it is now developed. The study of human nature then, throws light on the history of philosophy, and the study of the history of philosophy in return, throws light on human nature. Since all the systems of philosophy which have been, embrace the entire development of humanity in the past, it follows that he who should comprehend those systems, would comprehend thus far the whole history of our race. History in general, as throwing light on humanity, the history of philosophy in particular, as enlightening all other branches of history, and as the practical, the experimental test of a philosophy, should be ranked among the very highest objects of human study.

There can be nothing in philosophy which is not in humanity. There is nothing in humanity but intelligence. Philosophy then is a development of intelligence. But it is a development only of the human intelligence, which is itself only a fragment of the absolute intelligence. It cannot, therefore, embrace intelligence in itself. The human intelligence being itself defective, incomplete, the most perfect development of it, can be only an imperfect development of truth. To be incomplete, imperfect, consequently more or less erroneous in its creations, is the inevitable lot of humanity. No system of philosophy, then, can be obtained, however clear and far-reaching its vision, that will take in the whole horizon of truth. The most perfect system attainable must always be incomplete, leaving out vast, undefined regions of the true. But as all philosophy is a development, more or less complete, of intelligence; and, as intelligence in all its degrees is true, an absolutely false philosophy is impossible.

Although there can be nothing in philosophy which is not in humanity, there may be much in humanity which is not in philosophy. A philosophy which does not embrace the whole of human nature is false, not only in relation to the Absolute, but in relation to man, and false because it is defective, and in its defectiveness. All that is in our past history is but a development of human nature, and, in that it is a development of human nature, it is true. All systems, all creeds, all events, in that they have been, are true, true as far as they go, though by no means the whole truth. It is necessary then to accept all. Now, if our philosophy exclude any portion of them, if it cannot find in each an element of truth, if it do not explain them all, and find itself in all, it is itself defective, and in that it is defective, false. In this way history becomes a test of a philosophy. A philosophy which accepts the entirc history of humanity, and which finds in itself precisely the same number of elements as in that history, excluding nothing, owning and enlightening all, may be pronounced the true philosophy, that which exactly represents the development of humanity. No philosophy does this, except that which finds in each system, creed, event, an element of the true, which it extracts and brings together into one vast, harmonious whole. This philosophy is ECLECTICISM. Every sound philosopher, then, must be an Eclectic.

Three ideas constitute the human as the Divine intelligence; the idea of the infinite, the idea of the finite, and the idea of their relation. These three ideas must be found in every philosophy, but they may be found in different degrees of development; sometimes one and sometimes another may be predominant. The predominance of one or another makes the different epochs of humanity, and of philosophy. The number of these ideas determine the number of philosophical systems which are possible. These ideas are represented in the consciousness by three great faculties, the reason, activity, sensibility. The reason represents the infinite, the sensibility the finite, the activity the relation of the two. Attention, reflection, may be directed exclusively to the facts of the sensibility; it will then overlook, or see but in the background, the facts of the reason and the activity, and refer all the mental phenomena to sensation. Hence SENSUALISM, which is true in relation to the facts of the sensibility, the only ones it analyzes; but it is not true of a larger number which are as really in the consciousness as those derived from sensation.

We may direct our attention exclusively to reflection, the reflective reason, which represents the activity in the world of philosophy, and which is purely personal. Plunged into ourselves, we there overlook the facts of the spontaneous reason and of the sensibility, and refer to ourselves, to the energy of our own thoughts, all the phenomena which we observe. Hence IDEALISM, which, being unable to come out of the consciousness, denies an external world, in like manner as sensualism denies the existence of whatever is not observable by the senses.

A sober-minded man may be disgusted by the contentions of these two schools, and led to question, not only the truth of both, but the truth of the reason itself; that is, the possibility of knowing at all. Hence SCEPTICISM, which is sometimes needed to check the rage of dogmatism, to bring back system-makers to common sense, and to compel them to examine anew their means of construction, their premises, and the logic by which they have attained their conclusions.

In fine, disgusted with the perpetual wranglings of sensualism and idealism, wearied with the endless doubt and perplexity of scepticism, unable to resist the cravings of the soul to believe, we take refuge in a primitive fact, hitherto overlooked, and, rejecting reflection, repose on the spontaneous reason. Hence MYSTICISM, a philosophy which is founded on a real element of our nature, and consequently true, but, taken exclusively, like all the others becomes the occasion of more or less error.

Each of these schools has a truth, and embraces and explains a certain number of the phenomena of our nature; but neither embraces and explains them all. Transport now either of these schools into history, and it will do what it does in psychology; it will mutilate history, as it has mutilated consciousness. It will either give no account of the facts which do not suit its purpose, or it will pervert them, give a false account of them. It will at once declare war against three fourths of history. Now in this fact, each proves itself inadequate to the explanation of the history of philosophy. Each then, is false as a whole, though it may be true as a part. These four schools embrace all the phenomena of consciousness, the whole of humanity; consequently embrace the whole history of humanity. A philosophy then, which embraces and explains the principles of these four schools is proved by history to be the true philosophy. Thus history and psychology reciprocally prove each other. By psychology we determine the number of elements which there can be in history, and by history the number there can be in psychology. When the number is the same in both cases, we may be sure that we are right. Erudition and criticism on the one hand, and profound psychological analysis on the other, are the instruments of a sound philosophy.

The four schools designated are found in all the philosophical epochs of the human race. They have all appeared on the stage of modern philosophy; each has played its part, accomplished its mission, and exhausted itself. Neither school has any longer anything to do. All it can do as an exclusive school has been done, and is now known. What then remains for philosophy? Either to take shelter under the aegis of authority, cease to be, or become an eclectic. The first is impossible. With Descartes it broke away from the ecclesiastical authority which ruled in the Middle Ages, declared itself independent, and its subjection is henceforth impossible. To say that it will cease to be, that the human race will no longer seek to render an account to itself of what it is, believes, and does, is to declare one's self ignorant of the wants of the human soul, that intelligence will cease to develop itself, that thought is dead, the human race extinct. Nothing, then, but the last remains as possible. Eclecticism is then the philosophy of our age.

We must be eclectics, excluding no element of humanity, but accepting and melting all into one vast system, which will be a true representative of humanity so far as it as yet developed. We must take broad and liberal views, expect truth and find it in all schools, in all creeds, in all ages, and in all countries. The great mission of our age is to unite the infinite and the finite. Union, harmony, whence proceed peace and love, are the points to be aimed at. We of the nineteenth century appear in the world as mediators. In philosophy, theology, government, art, industry, we are to conciliate hostile feelings, and harmonize conflicting principles and interests. We must bind together the past and the future, reconcile progress and immobility, by preserving what is good and studying to advance, that is, by meliorating instead of destroying; enable philosophy and theology to walk together in peace and love, by yielding to theology the authority of the spontaneous reason, inspiration, and vindicating for philosophy the absolute freedom of reflection.

Such is a very imperfect outline of M. Cousin's philosophy. As he has nowhere, to our knowledge, published a systematic development of his entire system, it is very possible that we have not correctly seized it in all its parts, and consequently may have in some instances misconceived it in relation to the points on which we have touched. We can only say, that our respect for M. Cousin himself, and our general approbation of his philosophy, if not our love of truth, must have preserved us from all voluntary misconceptions. It was our intention to notice some objections to his system; but we have exceeded all reasonable limits already, and must therefore refer the reader to the *Preface* to the second edition of the *Fragmens Philosophiques*; and we must refer him also to the same source, together with Mr. Henry's introduction to his translation of the "Criticism on Locke," for some personal details which we intended to offer, and which will be found sufficiently interesting.

M. Cousin has been charged with a want of originality. It were, perhaps, presumptuous for us to attempt to discuss a charge of this nature. He himself replies to it in some degree in the Preface referred to. He acknowledges that he has had masters, and hopes that he shall have many more. He avows himself indebted to Laromiguière, De Biran, Royer-Collard, Kant, Schelling, and Hegel. He says he has borrowed much from Schelling and Hegel, which he thinks it need not demand much humility on his part to acknowledge. He does not claim originality. He has, he informs us, always sought, and he still seeks truth, first to nourish and penetrate himself, and afterwards to communicate to his fellow-beings. The several parts of his system, it is very possible, may be found elsewhere; but we confess we know not where else to find it as a whole. We should claim for him originality in his reduction of the elements of the reason to the ideas of the infinite, the finite, and their relation, in his development of the distinction between the spontaneous and reflective reason, and, consequently, in the manner in which he reaches the objective and the Absolute; though we must confess we can find elsewhere some things from which we can, now that we know his views on these points, derive something like them, although it may be very doubtful whether we could have done it without the aid he has furnished us. Once in the Absolute, he does not differ essentially from the new German school. He follows Schelling and Hegel very nearly, in going from God to nature and humanity, and in his march through history. But his method, as has already been observed, is wholly different from theirs. He begins with the study of human nature; they, with a flight more admirable for its loftiness than its science, soar at once to the Absolute. But after all, the great question, and the only one which it becomes us to ask is, not, is this philosophy original? but, is it true?

We have no room to discuss this question. Our opinion may have been already gathered. We approve his method; it is the only true method. It is simply, what is in the consciousness? How did it come there? What is its legitimacy? In psychology, he applies his method with singular sagacity and success. He describes the actual consciousness with great acuteness and precision, and treats the primitive, the origin of our ideas, in a manner to merit our confidence; as is evinced by his "Criticism on Locke," translated by Mr. Henry, the production of a consummate metaphysician, and beyond question, one of the finest pieces of philosophical criticism in the world. That he has really thrown a bridge over the gulf which separates ontology from psychology, we have above disputed; but, after what he has shown us on the nature and development of the reason, we believe we can leap it, and consequently dispense with the bridge. In erudition, in eloquence, as a writer and a lecturer, his merit cannot be easily exaggerated. His publications make an epoch in philosophical literature. The French language in his hands, poor and deficient as Englishmen suppose it, becomes equal to the profoundest thought, the warmest emotion, and the nicest metaphysical distinctions. We wish someone would appear to do a similar service to our own language, which, though possessed of ample resources, is now, in consequence of the loose manner in which it is used, and the repugnance to abstraction which characterizes those who use it, so vague, so equivocal in its philosophical department, that the metaphysician is sure to be baffled even in his most strenuous efforts to make himself intelligible, or at least to express himself without ambiguity. Mr. Linberg and Mr. Henry have had to contend with this difficulty in translating M. Cousin; but their success has been such as to do them great credit.

In the application of his system to war and European politics, perhaps it is no want of charity to M. Cousin, to believe that the Frenchman got the better of the philosopher. However that may be, though we are decidedly opposed to war, we believe what some call his defense of it, and for which they condemn him, is substantially correct; and, till men become wise enough and good enough to tolerate individual and national differences of opinion, the shock of ideas will issue in bloodshed. But, should it be found that in the application of his system he is not always correct, it would not lessen him in our opinion. We want no man to apply his system for us. Let him give us his method and his premises; we will do the rest for ourselves. We wish there were less judging a man by the applications which he makes of his system himself, and more attention directed to its principles.

We cannot conclude without thanking M. Cousin for the sympathy he uniformly expresses with humanity. He does not tell the truth with a sneer like Gibbon, with a cold regard to obtaining mere power over man with Machiavelli, nor with a malignant scowl at man's weakness with Hobbes. He feels himself a man, is penetrated with what the French happily call the sentiment of humanity. He contemplates the progress of the race with delight, and stands in awe before the dignity of human nature, which unveils itself before the light of his philosophy. So long have we been accustomed to see man's weaknesses paraded with a sort of savage exultation, to have our hopes damped, our noblest energies repressed, by eternal declamations against human depravity, that we hold him our personal friend and benefactor for having vindicated humanity, and showed that he feels it no disgrace to be a MAN.

In conclusion we would commend the study of his works to everyone who would know himself; and especially to every young man whose soul burns to take an active part in the scenes around him, and to leave his trace on the age in which he lives. He who would hereafter become a great and good man, must be a great philosopher. We know there are those, who will contradict this assertion; we know there are those, who think very meanly of philosophy, and continually exclaim, "Give us practical men, not theorizers; actions, not systems"; but, without meaning to be discourteous, we bid all such persons go and study history. The mere actor passes off, is forgotten, and there remains no trace of his actions; but the philosopher, the mere theorizer, as he is contemptuously called, by the force of a few ideas which he throws out into the mass of thought, putteth down or setteth up kings, and prepares a new future for the human race. He who best comprehends and best develops ideas, is earth's mightiest sovereign. A Sesostris, a Cyrus, an Alexander, may be gathered to their fathers, and their empires be forgotten;[20] a Moses, a Socrates, a Plato, live and reign forever.

[20]Ed. Sesostris III, king of Egypt (c. 1836-18, B.C.), reshaped Egypt's government and became in the course of time the patron deity of Egyptian Nubia. Cyrus II (c. 590-529, B.C.), Persian conqueror, who is famous in the Bible for freeing Jewish captives in Babylonia and allowing them to return to their homeland. Alexander III, the Great, (c. 356-323, B.C.), king of Macedonia, was a great general and conqueror who laid the foundations for the Hellenistic empire.]

7.

NEW VIEWS OF CHRISTIANITY, SOCIETY, AND THE CHURCH[1]

PREFACE

It must not be inferred from my calling this little work New Views that I profess to bring forward a new religion, or to have discovered a new Christianity. The religion of the Bible I believe to be given by the inspiration of God, and the Christianity of Christ satisfies my understanding and my heart. However widely I may dissent from the Christianity of the church, with that of Christ I am content to stand or fall, and I ask no higher glory than to live and die in it and for it.

I believe my views are somewhat original, but I am far from considering them the only or even the most important views which may be taken of the subjects on which I treat. Those subjects have a variety of aspects, and all their aspects are true and valuable. He who presents any one of them does a service to humanity; and he who presents one of them has no occasion to fall out with him who presents another, nor to claim superiority over him.

Although I consider the views contained in the following pages original, I believe the conclusions, to which I come at last, will be found very much in accordance with those generally adopted by the denomination of Christians, with whom it has been for some years my happiness to be associated. That denomination, however, must not be held responsible for any of the opinions I have advanced. I am not the organ of a sect. I do not speak by authority, nor under tutelage. I speak for myself and from my own convictions. And in this way, better than I could in any other, do I prove my sympathy with the body of which I am a member, and establish my right to be called a Unitarian.

In what I have written here as well as in all I have written elsewhere and on other occasions, I have aimed to set an example of free thought and free speech. I ask no thanks for this, for it was my duty and I dared not do otherwise. Besides, theology can never rise to the

[1][Boston: James Munroe & Company, 1836. Ed. The book was dedicated to the members and friends of the Society for Christian Unity and Progress.]

rank and certainty of a science till it be submitted to the free and independent action of the human mind.

It will at once be seen that I have given only a few rough sketches of the subjects I have introduced. Many statements appear without the qualifications with which they exist in my own mind, many parts are doubtless obscure for the want of fuller developments, and the whole probably needs to be historically verified. But I have done all I could without making a larger book, and a larger book I could hope that nobody would buy or read. I may hereafter fill up my sketches and complete my pictures; but it would have been useless in the present state of the public mind to attempt more than I have done.

For my literary sins I have a right to some indulgence. My early life was spent in far other pursuits than those of literature. I make no pretensions to scholarship. For all my other sins—except those of omission, for which I have given a valid excuse—I ask no indulgence. I hope I shall be rigidly criticized. He who helps me correct my errors is my friend.

Those who feel any interest in "The Society for Christian Union and Progress," a society collected during the past summer, and of which I am the minister, may find in this volume the principles on which that society is founded, and the objects it contemplates. To the members of that society and to those who have listened to my preaching these views will not be new.

If any of my readers wish to pursue the subject touched upon in my Introduction, I would refer them to Benjamin Constant's great work *De la Religion considérée dans sa Source, ses Formes et ses Développements*; to *Religion and the Church*, a book by Dr. Follen, which he is now publishing in a series of numbers; and especially to Schleiermacher's work *Ueber die Religion: Reden an die Gebildeten unter ihren Verächtern* or, *Discourses on Religion, Addressed to the Cultivated among its Despisers*, a work which produced a powerful sensation in Germany when it first appeared, and one which cannot fail to exert a salutary influence on religious inquiry among ourselves.[2] A friend, to whom I am proud to acknowledge myself under many obligations, has translated this work in the course of his own private studies and I cannot but hope that he may be induced ere long to publish it.[3]

[2] [Ed. On Constant, Follen, and Schleiermacher, see the introduction to this volume.]

[3] [Ed. The friend was George Ripley.]

With these remarks I commit my little work to its fate. It contains results to which I have come only by years of painful experience; but I dismiss it from my mind with the full conviction, that He, who has watched over my life and preserved me amidst scenes through which I hope I may not be called to pass again, will take care that if what it contains be false it shall do no harm, and if it be true that it shall not die. Boston, Nov. 8, 1836.

INTRODUCTION

Religion is natural to man and he ceases to be man the moment he ceases to be religious.

This position is sustained by what we are conscious of in ourselves and by the universal history of mankind.

Man has a capacity for religion, faculties which are useless without it, and wants which God alone can satisfy. Accordingly wherever he is, in whatever age or country, he has—with a few individual exceptions easily accounted for—some sort of religious notions and some form of religious worship.

But it is only religion, as distinguished from religious institutions, that is natural to man. The religious sentiment is universal, permanent, and indestructible; religious institutions depend on transient causes, and vary in different countries and epochs.

As distinguished from religious institutions, religion is the conception, or sentiment, of the Holy, that which makes us think of something as reverend, and prompts us to revere it. It is that indefinable something within us which gives a meaning to the words venerable and awful, which makes us linger around the sacred and the time-hallowed, the graves of heroes or of nations, which leads us to launch away upon the boundless expanse, or plunge into the mysterious depths of being, and which, from the very ground of our nature, like the Seraphim of the prophet, is forever crying out, "Holy, holy, holy, is the Lord of hosts; the whole earth is full of his glory" [Isa. 6:3].

Religious institutions are the forms with which man clothes his religious sentiment, the answer he gives to the question, What is the holy? Were he a stationary being, or could he take in the whole of truth at a single glance, the answer once given would be always satisfactory, the institution once adopted would be universal, unchangeable, and eternal. But neither is the fact. Man's starting-point is the low valley, but he is continually, with slow and toilsome effort it may be, ascending the sides of the mountain to more favorable positions, from which his eye may sweep a broader horizon of truth. He begins in ignorance, but he is ever growing in knowledge.

In our ignorance, when we have seen but little of truth, and seen that little but dimly, we identify the Holy with the merely terrible, the powerful, the inscrutable, the useful, or the beautiful; and we adopt as its symbols, the thunder and lightning, winds and rain, ocean and storm, majestic river or placid lake, shady grove or winding brook, the animal, the bow or spear by means of which we are fed, clothed, and protected; but as experience rolls back the darkness, which made all around us appear huge and spectral, purges and extends our vision, these become inadequate representatives of our religious ideas; they fail to shadow forth the holy to our understandings; and we leave them and rise to that which appears to be free from their limited and evanescent nature, to that which is unlimited, all-sufficient, and unfailing.

We are creatures of growth; it is, therefore, impossible that all our institutions should not be mutable and transitory. We are forever discovering new fields of truth, and every new discovery requires a new institution, or the modification of an old one. We might as well demand that the sciences of physiology, chemistry, and astronomy should wear eternally the same form, as that religious institutions should be unchangeable, and that those which satisfied our fathers should always satisfy us.

All things change their forms. Literature, art, science, governments change under the very eye of the spectator. Religious institutions are subject to the same universal law. Like the individuals of our race, they pass away and leave us to deck their tombs, or in our despair, to exclaim that we will lie down in the grave with them. But as the race itself does not die, as new generations crowd upon the departing to supply their places, so does the reproductive energy of religion survive all mutations of forms, and so do new institutions arise to gladden us with their youth and freshness, to carry us further onward in our progress, and upward nearer to that which "is the same yesterday, to-day, and forever" [Heb. 13:8].

CHAPTER I. CHRISTIANITY

About two thousand years ago, mankind, having exhausted all their old religious institutions, received from their heavenly Father through the ministry of Jesus of Nazareth a new institution which was equal to their advanced position, and capable of aiding and directing their future progress.

But this institution must be spoken of as one which was, not as one which is. Notwithstanding the vast territories it acquired, the mighty influence it once exerted over the destinies of humanity, and its promises of immortality, it is now but the mere shadow of a sovereign, and its empire is falling in ruins. What remains of it is only the body after the spirit has left it. It is no longer animated by a living soul. The sentiment of the holy has deserted it, and it is a by-word and a mockery.

Either then Jesus did not embrace in his mind the whole of truth, or else the church has at best only partially realized his conception.

No institution, so long as it is in harmony with the progress of the understanding, can fail to command obedience or kindle enthusiasm. The church now does neither. There is a wide disparity between it and the present state of intellectual development. We have discovered truths which it cannot claim as its own; we are conscious of instincts which it disavows, and which we cannot, or will not, suppress. Whose is the fault? Is it the fault of humanity, of Jesus, or of the church?

Humanity cannot be blamed, for humanity's law is to grow; it has an inherent right to seek for truth, and it is under no obligation to shut its eyes to the facts which unfold themselves to its observation. It is not the fault of Jesus, unless it can be proved that all he contemplated has been realized, that mankind have risen to as pure, and as happy a state as he proposed; have indeed fully comprehended him, taken in his entire thought, and reduced it to practice. Nobody will pretend this. The fault then must be borne by the church.

The church even in its best days was far below the conception of Jesus. It never comprehended him, and was always a very inadequate symbol of the holy as he understood it.

Christianity, as it existed in the mind of Jesus, was the type of the most perfect religious institution to which the human race will, probably, ever attain. It was the point where the sentiment and the institution, the idea and the symbol, the conception and its realization appear to meet and become one. But the contemporaries of Jesus were not equal to this profound thought. They could not comprehend the God-Man, the deep meaning of his assertion, "I and my Father are one" [John 10:30]. He spake as never man spake, uttered truths for all nations and for all times; but what he uttered was necessarily measured by the capacity of those who heard him, not by his own. The less never comprehends the greater. Their minds must have been equal to his in order to have been able to take in the full import of his words. They might, as they did, apprehend a great and glorious meaning in what he said; they might kindle at the truths he revealed to their understandings, and even glory in dying at the stake to defend them; but they would invariably and inevitably narrow them down to their own inferior intellects, and interpret them by their own previous modes of thinking and believing.

The disciples themselves, the familiar friends, the chosen apostles of Jesus, notwithstanding all the advantages of personal intercourse and personal explanations never fully apprehended him. They mistook him for the Jewish Messiah, and even after his resurrection and ascension, they supposed it to have been his mission to "restore the kingdom to Israel" [Acts 1:6]. Though commanded to preach the gospel to "every creature," they never once imagined that they were to preach it to any people but the Jewish, till the circumstances, which preceded and followed Peter's visit to Cornelius the Roman centurion, took place to correct their error, it was not till then that any one of them could say, "Of a truth, I perceive that God is no respecter of persons; but in every nation he that feareth him and worketh righteousness is accepted with him" [Acts 10:34-35]. If this was true of the disciples, how much more true must it have been of those who received the words of Jesus at second or third hand, and without any of the personal explanations or commentaries necessary to unfold their meaning?

Could the age in which Jesus appeared have comprehended him it would have been superior to him, and consequently have had no need of him. We do not seek an instructor for our children in one who is not able to teach them. Moreover, if that age could have even rightly *apprehended* Jesus, we should be obliged to say his mission was intended to be confined to that age, or else to admit that the human race was never to go beyond the point then attained. Either Jesus did not regard the future of humanity, or he designed to interrupt its progress, and strike it with the curse of immobility; or else he was above his age and of course not to be understood by it. The world has not stood still since his coming; the church has always considered his kingdom as one of which there is to be no end; and we know that he was not comprehended, and that even we, with the advantage of nearly two thousand years of mental and moral progress, are far, very far, below him.

If the age in which Jesus appeared could not comprehend him, it is obvious that it could not fully embody him in its institutions. It could embody no more of him than it could receive, and as it could receive only a part of him, we must admit that the church has never been more than partially Christian. Never has it been the real body of Christ. Never has it reflected the God-Man perfectly. Never has it been a true mirror of the holy. Always has the holy in the sense of the church been a very inferior thing to what it was in the mind and heart and life of Jesus.

But we must use measured terms in our condemnation of the church. We must not ask the man in the child. The church did what it could. It did its best to "form Christ" [Gal. 4:19] within itself, "the hope of glory" [Col. 1:27] and was up to the period of its downfall as truly Christian, as the progress made by the human race admitted. It aided the growth of the human mind; enabled us to take in more truth than it had itself received; furnished us the light by which we discovered its defects; and by no means should its memory be cursed. Nobly and perseveringly did it discharge its duty; useful was it in its day and generation; and now that it has given up the ghost, we should pay it the rites of honorable burial, plant flowers over its resting place, and sometimes repair thither to bedew them with our tears.

To comprehend Jesus, to seize the holy as it was in him, and consequently the true idea of Christianity, we must, from the heights to which we have risen by aid of the church, look back and down upon the age in which he came, ascertain what was the work which there was for him to perform, and from that obtain a key to what he proposed to accomplish.

Two systems then disputed the empire of the world; spiritualism[4] represented by the eastern world, the old world of Asia, and materialism represented by Greece and Rome. Spiritualism regards purity or holiness as predicable of Spirit alone, and matter as essentially impure, possessing and capable of receiving nothing of the holy, the prison house of the soul, its only hindrance to a union with God, or absorption into his essence, the cause of all uncleanness, sin, and evil, consequently to be condemned, degraded, and as far as possible annihilated. Materialism takes the other extreme, does not recognize the claims of Spirit, disregards the soul, counts the body everything, earth all, heaven nothing, and condenses itself into the advice, "Eat and drink; for tomorrow we die" [1 Cor. 15:32].

This opposition between spiritualism and materialism presupposes a necessary and original antithesis between spirit and matter. When spirit and matter are given as antagonist principles, we are obliged to admit antagonism between all the terms into which they

[4]I use these terms, spiritualism and materialism, to designate two social, rather than two philosophical systems. They designate two orders, which, from time out of mind, have been called *spiritual* and *temporal* or carnal, *holy* and *profane*, *heavenly* and *worldly*, etc.

are respectively convertible. From spirit is deduced by natural generation, God, the priesthood, faith, heaven, eternity; from matter, man, the state, reason, the earth, and time; consequently, to place spirit and matter in opposition, is to make an antithesis between God and man, the priesthood and the state, faith and reason, heaven and earth, and time and eternity.

This antithesis generates perpetual and universal war. It is necessary then to remove it and harmonize, or unite the two terms. Now, if we conceive Jesus as standing between spirit and matter, the representative of both, God-Man, the point where both meet and lose their antithesis, laying a hand on each and saying, "Be one, as I and my Father are one" [John 17:11], thus sanctifying both and marrying them in a mystic and holy union, we shall have his secret thought and the true idea of Christianity.

The Scriptures uniformly present Jesus to us as a mediator, the middle term between two extremes, and they call his work a mediation, a reconciliation, an atonement. The church has ever considered Jesus as making an atonement. It has held on to the term at all times as with the grasp of death. The first charge it has labored to fix upon heretics has been that of rejecting the atonement, and the one all dissenters from the predominant doctrines of the day have been most solicitous to repel is that of "denying the Lord who bought us" [2 Pet. 2:1]. The whole Christian world, from the days of the apostles up to the moment in which I write, have identified Christianity with the atonement, and felt that in admitting the atonement they admitted Christ, and that in denying it they were rejecting him.

Jesus himself always spoke of his doctrine, the grand idea which lay at the bottom of all his teaching, under the term "Love." "A new commandment give I unto you, that ye love one another" [John 13:34]. "By this shall all men know that ye are my disciples, if ye have love one to another" [John 13:35]. John, who seems to have caught more of the peculiar spirit of Jesus than any of the disciples, sees nothing but love in the gospel. Love penetrated his soul; it runs through all his writings, and tradition relates that it at length so completely absorbed him that all he could say in his public addresses was, "Little children, [...] love one another" [John 13:33-34]. He uniformly dwells with unutterable delight on the love which the Father has for us and that which we may have for him, the intimate union of man with God, expressed by the strong language of dwelling in God and God dwelling in us. In his view there is no antagonism. All antithesis is destroyed. Love sheds its hallowed and hallowing light over both God and man, over spirit and matter, binding all beings and all being in one strict and everlasting union.

The nature of love is to destroy all antagonism. It brings together; it begetteth union and from union cometh peace. And what word so accurately expresses to the consciousness of Christendom, the intended result of the mission of Jesus, as that word peace? Every man who has read the New Testament feels that it was peace that Jesus came to effect, peace after which the soul has so often sighed and yearned in vain, and a peace not merely between two or three individuals for a day, but a universal and eternal peace between all conflicting elements, between God and man, between the soul and body, between this world and another, between the duties of time and the duties of eternity. How clearly is this expressed in that sublime chorus of the angels, sung over the manger-cradle, "Glory to God in the highest, on earth peace and good-will to men" [Luke 2:14]!

Where there is but one term there is no union. There is no harmony with but one note. It is mockery to talk to us of peace where one of the two belligerent parties is annihilated. That were the peace of the grave. Jesus must then save both parties. The church has, therefore, with a truth it has never comprehended, called him God-Man. But if the two terms and their products be originally and essentially antagonist; if there be between them an innate hostility, their union, their reconciliation cannot be effected. Therefore in proposing the union, in attempting the atonement, Christianity declares as its great doctrine that there is no essential, no original antithesis between God and man; that neither spirit nor matter is unholy in its nature; that all things, spirit, matter, God, man, soul, body, heaven, earth, time, eternity, with all their duties and interests, are in themselves holy. All things proceed from the same holy Fountain, and no fountain sendeth forth both sweet waters and bitter. It therefore writes "HOLINESS TO THE LORD" [Exod. 28:36] upon everything, and sums up its sublime teaching in that grand synthesis, "Thou shalt love the Lord thy God with all thy heart and mind and soul and strength, and thy neighbor as thyself" [Luke 10:27].

CHAPTER II. THE CHURCH

The aim of the church was to embody the holy as it existed in the mind of Jesus, and had it succeeded, it would have realized the atonement; that is, the reconciliation of spirit and matter and all their products.

But the time was not yet. The Paraclete was in expectation. The church could only give currency to the fact that it was the mission of Jesus to make an atonement. It from the first misapprehended the conditions on which it was to be effected. Instead of understanding Jesus to assert the holiness of both spirit and matter, it understood him to admit that matter was rightfully cursed, and to predicate holiness of spirit alone. In the sense of the church then he did not come to atone spirit and matter, but to redeem spirit from the consequences of its connection with matter. His name therefore was not the Atoner, the Reconciler, but the Redeemer, and his work not properly an atonement, but a redemption. This was the original sin of the church.

By this misapprehension the church rejected the mediator. The Christ ceases to be the middle term uniting spirit and matter, the *hilasterion*, the mercy-seat,[5] or point where God and man meet and lose their antithesis, the Advocate with the Father for humanity, and becomes the avenger of spirit, the manifestation of God's righteous indignation against man. He dies to save mankind, it is true, but he dies to pay a penalty. God demands man's everlasting destruction; Jesus admits that God's demand is just, and dies to discharge it. Hence the symbol of the cross, signifying to the church an original and necessary antithesis between God and man which can be removed only by the sacrifice of justice to mercy. In this the church took its stand with spiritualism, and from a mediator became a partisan.

By taking its stand with spiritualism the church condemned itself to all the evils of being exclusive. It obliged itself to reject an important element of truth, and it became subject to all the miseries and vexations of being intolerant. It became responsible for all the consequences which necessarily result from spiritualism. The first of these consequences was the denial that Jesus came in the flesh. If matter be essentially unholy, then Jesus, if he had a material body, must have been unholy; if unholy, sinful. Hence all the difficulties of the Gnostics[6]—difficulties hardly adjusted by means of a Virgin

[5][Ed. The "mercy seat" was a rectangular slab of refined gold that covered the Ark of the Covenant (see Exod. 25:17; 37:6). It was important in the Bible as the place of the revelation of God's word to Moses (Exod. 25:22; Num. 7:89) and as the place where blood was sprinkled on the Day of Atonement (Lev. 16). The term is used in the New Testament, as in much of the Old, to denote the expiation of sins.]

[6][Ed. There were various forms of Christian Gnosticism. Although very difficult to define, the Christian gnostics had their origin in pagan religious circles but flourished in the second century of the Christian era. Most believed, though, that Jesus merely appeared to be human or that his humanity was merely a mask for his divinity. This was at least Brownson's understanding of the Christian sect. Since the discovery of the Coptic Nag Hammadi texts in Upper Egypt in 1945 and

Mother and the Immaculate Conception; for this mode of accommodation really denied the God-Man, the symbol of the great truth the church was to embody. It left the God indeed, but it destroyed the man, inasmuch as it separated the humanity of Jesus by its very origin from common humanity.

Man's inherent depravity, his corruption by nature followed as a matter of course. Man by his very nature partakes of matter, is material, then unholy, then sinful, corrupt, depraved. He is originally material, therefore originally a sinner. Hence original sin. Sometimes original sin is indeed traced to a primitive disobedience, to the Fall; but then the doctrine of the Fall itself is only one of the innumerable forms which is assumed by the doctrine of the essential impurity of matter.[7]

From this original, inherent depravity of human nature necessarily results that antithesis between God and man which renders their union impossible and which imperiously demands the sacrifice of one or the other. "Die he or justice must."[8] Man is sacrificed on the cross in the person of Jesus. Hence the vicarious atonement, the conversion of the atonement into an expiation. But, if man was sacrificed, if he died as he deserved in Jesus, his death was eternal. Symbolically then he cannot rise. The body of Jesus after his resurrection is not material in the opinion of the church. He does not rise God-Man, but God. Hence the absolute Deity of Christ, which under various disguises has always been the sense of the church.

From man's original and inherent depravity it results that he has no power to work out his own salvation. Hence the doctrine of human inability. By nature man is enslaved to matter; he is born in sin and shapen in iniquity. He is sold to sin, to the world, to the devil. He must be ransomed. Matter cannot ransom him; then spirit must, and "God the mighty Maker" dies to redeem his creature, to deliver the soul from the influence of matter.

But this can be only partially effected in this world. As long as we live, we must drag about with us this clog of earth, matter, and not till after death, when our vile bodies shall be changed into the likeness of Christ's glorious body, shall we be really saved. We are not then saved here; we only hope to be saved hereafter. Hence the doc-

1946, there has been a great deal of scholarly attention to the various gnostic systems. For a good introduction, see Robert M. Grant, *Gnosticism: An Anthology* (London: Collins, 1961).]

[7][Ed. Brownson's interpretation of the doctrine of original sin, of course, is Manichean, not Christian.]

[8][Ed. John Milton, *Paradise Lost*, Book 3, line 210.]

trine which denies holiness to man in this world, which places the kingdom of God exclusively in the world to come, and which establishes a real antithesis between heaven and earth, and the means necessary to secure present well-being and those necessary to secure future blessedness.

God has indeed died to ransom sinners from the grave of the body, to redeem them from the flesh, to break the chains of the bound and to set the captive free; but the effects of the ransom must be secured; agents must be appointed to proclaim the glad tidings of salvation, to bid the prisoner hope, and the captive rejoice that the hour of release will come. Hence the church. Hence too the authority of the church to preach salvation to save sinners. And the church is composed of all who have this authority and of none others, therefore the dogma, "Out of the church there is no salvation."[9]

The church is commissioned; it is God's agent in saving sinners. It is then his representative. If the representative of God, then of spirit. In its representative character, that is, as a church, it is then spiritual, and if spiritual, holy; and if holy, infallible. Hence the infallibility of the church.

The holy should undoubtedly govern the unholy; Spirit then should govern matter. Spirit then is supreme; and the church as the representative of spirit must also be supreme. Hence the supremacy of the church.

The church is a vast body composed of many members. It needs a head. It should also be modeled after the church above. The church above has a supreme head, Jesus Christ; the church below should then have a head, who may be its center, its unity, the personification of its wisdom and its authority. Hence the pope, the supreme head of the church, vicar of Jesus, and representative of God.

The church is a spiritual body. Its supremacy then is a spiritual supremacy. A spiritual supremacy extends to thought and conscience. Hence on the one hand the confessional designed to solve cases of conscience, and on the other creeds, expurgatory indexes, inquisitions, pains and penalties against heretics.

The spiritual order in heaven is absolute; the church then as the representative of that order must also be absolute. As a representative

[9][Ed. The quotation is attributed to Bishop Cyprian of Carthage (d. 258), who, in letter # 4, asserted that "there can be no salvation for anyone except in the church." On this, see *Saint Cyprian Letters (1-81)*, trans. Rose Bernard Donna, vol. 51 of *The Fathers of the Church* (Washington, D.C.: Catholic University of America Press, 1964), 13. Bishop Augustine of Hippo (354-430) cited Cyprian as the source of the phrase in *On Baptism, Against the Donatists*, 4:24.]

it speaks not in its own name, but in the name of the power it represents. Since that power may command, the church may command; and as it may command in the name of an absolute sovereign, its commands must be implicitly obeyed. An absolute sovereign may command to any extent he pleases—what shall be believed as well as what shall be done. Hence implicit faith, the authority which the church has alleged for the basis of belief. Hence too prohibitions against reason and reasoning which have marked the church under all its forms, in all its phases and divisions and subdivisions.

Reason too is human; then it is material; to set it up against faith were to set up the material against the spiritual; the human against the divine; man against God: for the church being God by proxy, by representation, it has of course the right to consider whatever is set up against the faith it enjoins as set up against God.

The civil order, if it be anything more than a function of the church, belongs to the category of matter. It is then inferior to the church. It is then bound to obey the church. Hence the claims of the church over civil institutions, its right to bestow the crowns of kings, to place kingdoms under ban, to absolve subjects from their allegiance, and all the wars and antagonism between church and state.

The spiritual order alone is holy. Its interests are then the only interests it is not sinful to labor to promote. In laboring to promote them, the church was under the necessity of laboring for itself. Hence its justification to itself of its selfishness, its rapacity, its untiring efforts to aggrandize itself at the expense of individuals and of states.

As the interests of the church alone were holy, it was of course sinful to be devoted to any others. All the interests of the material order, that is, all temporal interests, were sinful, and the church never ceased to call them so. Hence its perpetual denunciation of wealth, place and renown, and the obstacles it always placed in the way of all direct efforts for the promotion of well-being on earth. This is the reason why it has discouraged, indeed unchurched, anathematized, all efforts to gain civil and political liberty, and always regarded with an evil eye all industry not directly or indirectly in its own interests.

This same exclusive spiritualism borrowed from Asia, striking matter with the curse of being unclean in its nature, was the reason for enjoining celibacy upon the clergy. An idea of sanctity was attached to the ministerial office, which it was supposed any contact with the flesh would sully. It also led devotees, those who desired to lead lives strictly holy, to renounce the flesh, as well as the world and the devil, to take vows of perpetual celibacy and to shut themselves up in monasteries and nunneries. It is the origin of all those self-inflicted tortures, mortifications of the body, penances, fastings, and that neglect of this world for another, which fill so large a space in the history of the church during what are commonly called the "Dark Ages." The church in its theory looked always with horror upon all sensual indulgences. Marriage was sinful, till purified by holy church. The song and the dance, innocent amusements, and wholesome recreations, though sometimes conceded to the incessant importunities of matter, were of the devil. Even the gay dress and blithesome song of nature were offensive. A dark, silent, friar's frock was the only befitting garb for nature or for man. The *beau ideal* of a good Christian was one who renounced all his connections with the world, became deaf to the voice of kindred and of friends, insensible to the sweetest and holiest emotions of humanity, immured himself in a cave or cell, and did nothing the live-long day but count his beads and kiss the crucifix.

Exceptions there were; but this was the idea, the dominant tendency of the church. Thanks, however, to the stubbornness of matter, and to the superintending care of Providence, its dominant tendency always found powerful resistance, and its idea was never able fully to realize itself.

CHAPTER III. PROTESTANTISM

Everything must have its time. The church abused, degraded, vilified matter, but could not annihilate it. It existed in spite of the church. It increased in power, and at length rose against spiritualism and demanded the restoration of its rights. This rebellion of materialism, of the material order against the spiritual, is Protestantism.

Matter always exerted a great influence over the practice of the church. In the first three centuries it was very powerful. It condemned the Gnostics and Manicheans as heretics, and was on the point of rising to empire under the form of Arianism.[10] But the oriental influence predominated, and the Arians became acknowledged heretics.

After the defeat of Arianism, that noble protest in its day of rationalism against mysticism, of matter against spirit, of European against Asiatic ideas, the church departed more and more from the atonement, and became more and more arrogant, arbitrary, spiritual-

[10][Ed. The Manicheans, or followers of a certain Mani (c. 216-76) from the Persian empire, had a basically dualistic philosophy that, among other things, held matter to be the source of evil. The Arians, followers of the Alexandrian priest Arius (c. 250-c. 336), denied the full divinity of Jesus Christ. They were condemned as heretics at the Council of Nicea (325).]

istic, papistical. Still matter occasionally made itself heard. It could not prevent the celibacy of the clergy, but it did maintain the unity of the race and prevented the reestablishment of a sacerdotal caste, claiming by birth a superior sanctity. It broke out too in the form of Pelagianism,[11] that doctrine which denies that man is clean gone in iniquity, and which makes the material order count for something. Pelagius was the able defender of humanity when it seemed to be deserted by all its friends, and his efforts were by no means unavailing.

Matter asserted its rights and avenged itself in a less unexceptionable form in the convents, the monasteries and nunneries, among the clergy of all ranks, in that gross licentiousness which led to the reformation attempted by Hildebrand;[12] and finally it ascended—not avowedly, but in reality—the papal throne, in the person of Leo X.[13]

The accession of Leo X to the papal throne is a remarkable event in the history of the church. It marks the predominance of material interests in the very bosom of the church itself. It is a proof that whatever might be the theory of the church, however different it claimed to be from all other powers, it was at this epoch in practice the same as the kingdoms of men. Poverty ceased in its eyes to be a virtue. The poor mendicant, the bare-footed friar, could no longer hope to become one day the spiritual head of Christendom. Spiritual gifts and graces were not now enough. High birth and royal pretensions were required; and it was not as a priest, but as a member of the princely house of Medici that Leo became pope.

The object of the church had changed. It had ceased to regard the spiritual wants and welfare of mankind. It had become wealthy. It had acquired vast portions of this world's goods, and its great care was to preserve them. Its interests had become temporal interests, and therefore it needed, not a spiritual father, but a temporal prince. It is as a prince that Leo conducts himself. His legates to the imperial, English and French courts, entered into negotiations altogether as ambassadors of a temporal prince, not as the simple representatives of the church.

Leo himself is a sensualist, sunk in his sensual pleasures, and perhaps a great sufferer in consequence of his excesses. It is said he

[11][Ed. Pelagianism was a Christian heresy that held that human beings, through the exercise of their free will apart from divine grace, could obtain salvation. The heresy took its name from Pelagius, a British monk who taught in Rome during the end of the fourth and beginning of the fifth centuries.]

[12][Ed. Hildebrand was Pope Gregory VII from 1073 to 1085.]

[13][Ed. Leo X was pope from 1513 to 1521.]

was an atheist, a thing more than probable. All his tastes were worldly. Instead of the sacred books of the church, the pious legends of saints and martyrs, he amused himself with the elegant but *profane* literature of Greece and Rome. His principal secretaries were not holy monks but eminent classical scholars. He revived and enlarged the university at Rome, encouraged human learning and the arts of civilization, completed St. Peter's, and his reign was graced by Michael Angelo and Raphael.[14] He engaged in wars and diplomacy and in them both had respect only to the goods of the church, or to the interests of himself and family as temporal princes.

Now all this was in direct opposition to the theory of the church. Materialism was in the papal chair, but it was there as a usurper, as an illegitimate. It reigned in fact, but not in right. The church was divided against itself. In theory it was spiritualist, but in practice it was materialist. It could not long survive this inconsistency, and it needed not the attacks of Luther to hasten the day of its complete destruction.

But materialism must have become quite powerful to have been able to usurp the papal throne itself. It was indeed too powerful to bear patiently the name of usurper; at least to be contented to reign only indirectly. It would be acknowledged as sovereign, and proclaimed legitimate. This the church could not do. The church could do nothing but cling to its old pretensions. To expel materialism and return to Hildebrand was out of the question. To give up its claims, and own itself materialist, would have been to abandon all title to even its material possessions, since it was by virtue of its spiritual character that it held them. Materialism, as it could reign in the church only as it were by stealth, resolved to leave the church and to reign in spite of it, against it, and even on its ruins. It protested, since it had all the power, against being called hard names, and armed itself in the person of Luther to vindicate its rights and to make its claims acknowledged.

The dominant character of Protestantism is then the insurrection of materialism, and what we call the reformation is really a revolution in favor of the material order. Spiritualism had exhausted its energies; it had done all it could for humanity; the time had come for the material element of our nature, which spiritualism had neglected and grossly abused, to rise from its depressed condition and contrib-

[14][Ed. Michelangelo di Lodovico Buonarroti Simoni (1475-1564) was an Italian Renaissance sculptor, painter, poet, and architect who was the chief designer of St. Peter's Basilica in Rome. Raffaello Zanzio (1483-1520) was another master painter and architect of the Italian Renaissance. Many of his major works, too, are displayed in the Vatican in Rome.]

ute its share to the general progress of mankind. It rose, and in rising it brought up the whole series of terms the church had disregarded. It brought up the state, civil liberty, human reason, philosophy, industry, all temporal interests.

In Protestantism, Greece and Rome revived and again carried their victorious arms into the East. The reformation connects us with classical antiquity, with the beautiful and graceful forms of Grecian art and literature, and with Roman eloquence and jurisprudence, as the church had connected us with Judea, Egypt and India.

CHAPTER IV. PROTESTANTISM

That Protestantism is the insurrection of matter against spirit, of the material against the spiritual order, is susceptible of very satisfactory historical verification.

One of the most immediate and efficient causes of Protestantism was the revival of Greek and Roman literature. Constantinople was taken by the Turks, and its scholars and the remains of classical learning which it had preserved were dispersed over western Europe. The classics took possession of the universities and the learned, were studied, commented on, appealed to as an authority paramount to that of the church and Protestantism was born.

By means of the classics, the scholars of the fifteenth century were introduced to a world altogether unlike and much superior to that in which they lived—to an order of ideas wholly diverse from those avowed or tolerated by the church. They were enchanted. They had found the ideal of their dreams. They became disgusted with the present; they repelled the civilization effected by the church, looked with contempt on its fathers, saints, martyrs, schoolmen, troubadours, knights and minstrels, and sighed and yearned and labored to reproduce Athens or Rome.

And what was that Athens and that Rome which seemed to them to realize the very ideal of the perfect? We know very well today what they were. They were material; through the whole period of their historical existence, it is well known that the material or temporal order predominated over the spiritual. They are not that old spiritual world of the East which reigned in the church. In that old world—in India for instance—where spiritualism has its throne, man sinks before God, matter fades away before the presence of spirit, and time is swallowed up in eternity. Industry is in its incipient stages, and the state scarcely appears. There is no history, no chronology. All is dateless and unregistered. An inflexible and changeless tyranny weighs down the human race and paralyzes its energies. Ages on ages roll away and bring no melioration. Everything remains as it was, monotonous and immovable as the spirit it contemplates and adores.

In Athens and Rome all this is reversed. Human interests, the interests of mankind in time and space, predominate. Man is the most conspicuous figure in the group. He is everywhere, and his imprint is upon everything. Industry flourishes; commerce is encouraged; the state is constituted, and tends to democracy; citizens assemble to discuss their common interests; the orator harangues them; the aspirant courts them; the warrior and the statesman render them an account of their doings and await their award. The people, not the gods, will, decree, make, unmake, or modify the laws. Divinity does not become incarnate as in the Asiatic world, but men are deified. History is not theogony, but a record of human events and transactions. Poetry sings heroes, the great and renowned of earth, or chants at the festal board and the couch of voluptuousness. Art models its creations after human forms, for human pleasure or human convenience. They are human faces we see; human voices we hear; human dwellings in which we lodge and dream of human growth and human melioration.

There are gods and temples, and priests and oracles, and augurs and auguries, it is true; but they are not like those we meet where spiritualism reigns. The gods are all anthromorphous. Their forms are the perfection of the human. The allegorical beasts, the strange beasts, compounded of parts of many known and unknown beasts which meet us in Indian, Egyptian, and Persian mythology, as symbols of the gods are extinct. Priests are not a caste, as they are under spiritualism, springing from the head of Brahma and claiming superior sanctity and power as their birthright, but simple police officers. Religion is merely a function of the state. Socrates dies because he breaks the laws of Athens—not, as Jesus did—for blaspheming the gods. Numa[15] introduces or organizes polytheism at Rome for the purpose of governing people by means of appeals to their sentiment of the holy; and the Roman Pontifex Maximus was never anything more than a master of police.

This in its generality is equally a description of Protestantism, as might indeed have been asserted beforehand. The epoch of the re-

[15][Ed. Numa Pompilius (flourished c. 700 B.C.) was, according to Roman tradition, the second of seven kings who ruled Rome before the founding of the Republic (c. 509 B.C.). He is suppose to have formulated the religious calendar and established other early religious institutions in Rome.]

vival of classical literature must have been predisposed to materialism or else it could not have been pleased with the classics, and the influence of the classics must have been to increase that predisposition, and as Protestantism was a result of both, it could be nothing but materialism.

In classical antiquity religion is a function of the state. It is the same under Protestantism. Henry VIII of England declares himself supreme head of the church, not by virtue of his spiritual character, but by virtue of his character as a temporal prince. The Protestant princes of Germany are protectors of the church; and all over Europe, there is an implied contract between the state and the ecclesiastical authorities. The state pledges itself to support the church on condition that the church support the state. Ask the kings, nobility, or even church dignitaries, why they support religion, and they will answer with one voice, "Because the people cannot be preserved in order, cannot be made to submit to their rulers, and because civil society cannot exist without it." The same or a similar answer will be returned by almost every political man in this country; and truly may it be said that religion is valued by the Protestant world as a subsidiary to the state, as a mere matter of police.

Under the reign of spiritualism all questions are decided by authority. The church prohibited reasoning. It commanded, and men were to obey or be counted rebels against God. Materialism, by raising up man and the state, makes the reason of man, or the reason of the state, paramount to the commands of the church. Under Protestantism, the state in most cases, the individual reason in a few, imposes the creed upon the church. The king and Parliament in England determine the faith which the clergy must profess and maintain; the Protestant princes in Germany have the supreme control of the symbols of the church, the right to enact what creed they please.

Indeed the authority of the church in matters of belief was regarded by the reformers as one of the greatest evils, against which they had to contend. It was particularly against this authority that Luther protested. What he and his coadjutors demanded was the right to read and interpret the Bible for themselves. This was the right they wrested from the church. To have been consequent they should have retained it in their hands as individuals; it would then have been the right of private judgment and, if it meant anything, the right of reason to sit in judgment on all propositions to be believed. To this extent, however, they were not prepared to go. Between the absolute authority of the church, and the absolute authority of the individual reason, intervened the authority of the state.

But as the state was material, the substitution of its authority for the authority of the church was still to substitute the material for the spiritual.

But the tendency, however arrested by the state, has been steadily toward the most unlimited freedom of thought and conscience. Our fathers rebelled against the authority of the state in religious matters as well as against the authority of the pope. In political and industrial speculations, the English and Americans give the fullest freedom to the individual reason; Germany has done it to the greatest extent in historical, literary and philosophical, and to a very great extent, in theological matters, and France does it in everything. All modern philosophy is built on the absolute freedom and independence of the individual reason; that is, the reason of humanity, in opposition to the reason of the church or the state. Descartes refused to believe in his own existence but upon the authority of his reason; Bacon allows no authority but observation and induction; Berkeley finds no ground for admitting an external world, and therefore denies it; and Hume finding no certain evidence of anything outward or inward, doubted, philosophically, of all things.[16]

Philosophy is a human creation; it is the product of man, as the universe is of God. Under spiritualism, then, which, in theory, demolishes man, there can be no philosophy; yet as man, though denied, exists, there is a philosophical tendency. But this philosophical tendency is always either to scepticism, mysticism, or idealism.[17] Scepticism, that philosophy which denies all certainty, made its first appearance in modern times in the church. The church declared reason unworthy of confidence, and in doing that gave birth to the whole skeptical philosophy. When the authority of the church was questioned and she was compelled to defend it, she did it on the ground that reason could not be trusted as a criterion of truth, and that there could be no certainty for man, if he did not admit an authority independent of his reason, not perceiving that if reason were struck with impotence there would be no means of substantiating the legitimacy of the authority.

[16][Ed. David Hume (1711-76), Scottish philosopher and historian, was thought to be a skeptic by many in the early nineteenth century. He insisted that philosophy could not go beyond experience.]

[17][Ed. Victor Cousin's interpretation of the various philosophical tendencies that are inherent in human nature, and manifested in history, shows through in this passage. Only empiricism is left out of this catalogue of the four basic philosophical tendencies of human nature.]

On the other hand, the church having its point of view in spirit, consulted the soul before the body, became introspective, fixed on the inward to the exclusion of the outward. It overlooked the outward; and when that is overlooked it is hardly possible that it should not be denied. Hence idealism or mysticism.

Under the reign of materialism all this is changed. There is full confidence in the reason. The method of philosophizing is the experimental. But as the point of view is the outward—matter-spirit is overlooked; matter alone admitted. Hence philosophical materialism. And philosophical materialism, in germ or developed, has been commensurate with Protestantism. When the mind becomes fixed on the external world, inasmuch as we become acquainted with that world only by means of our senses, we naturally conclude that our senses are our only source of knowledge. Hence sensualism, the philosophy supported by Locke, Condillac, and even by Bacon, so far as it concerns his own application of his method. And from the hypothesis that our senses are our only inlets of knowledge, we are compelled to admit that nothing can be known which is not cognizable by some one or all of them. Our senses take cognizance only of matter; then we can know nothing but matter. We can know nothing of the spirit or soul. The body is all that we know of man. That dies and there ends man, at least all we know of him. Hence no immortality, no future state. If nothing can be known but by means of our senses, God, then, inasmuch as we do not see him, hear him, taste him, smell him, touch him, cannot be known; then he does not exist for us. Hence atheism. Hence modern infidelity, in all its forms, so prevalent in the last century, and so far from being extinct even in this.

The same tendency to exalt the terms depressed by the church is to be observed in the religious aspect of Protestantism. Properly speaking, Protestantism has no religious character. As Protestants, people are not religious, but co-existing with their Protestantism, they may indeed retain something of religion. Men often act from mixed motives. They bear in their bosoms sometimes two antagonist principles, now obeying the one, and now the other, without being aware that both are not one and the same principle. With Protestants, religion has existed; but as a reminiscence, a tradition. Sometimes, indeed, the remembrance has been very lively, and seemed very much like reality. The old soldier warms up with the recollections of his early feats, and lives over his life as he relates its events to his grandchild,

"Shoulders his crutch and shows how fields are won."[18]

If the religion of the Protestant world be a reminiscence, it must be the religion of the church. It is, in fact, only Catholicism continued. The same principle lies at the bottom of all Protestant churches, in so far as they are churches, which was at the bottom of the church of the Middle Ages. But materialism modifies their rites and dogmas. In the practice of all, there is an effort to make them appear reasonable. Hence commentaries, expositions, and defenses without number. Even where the authority of reason is denied, there is an instinctive sense of its authority and a desire to enlist it. In mere forms, pomp and splendor have gradually disappeared, and dry utility and even baldness have been consulted. In doctrines, those which exalt man and give him some share in the work of salvation have gained in credit and influence. Pelagianism, under some thin disguises or undisguised, has become almost universal. The doctrine of man's inherent total depravity, in the few cases in which it is asserted, is asserted more as a matter of duty than of conviction. Nobody, who can help it, preaches the old-fashioned doctrine of God's sovereignty, expressed in the dogma of unconditional election and reprobation. The vicarious Atonement has hardly a friend left. The Deity of Jesus is questioned, his simple humanity is asserted and is gaining credence. Orthodox is a term which implies as much reproach as commendation; people are beginning to laugh at the claims of councils and synods, and to be quite merry at the idea of excommunication.

In literature and art there is the same tendency. Poetry in the last century hardly existed, and was, so far as it did exist, mainly ethical or descriptive. It had no revelations of the Infinite. Prose writers under Protestantism have been historians, critics, essayists, or controversialists; they have aimed almost exclusively at the elevation or adornment of the material order, and in scarcely an instance has a widely popular writer exalted God at the expense of man, the church at the expense of the state, faith at the expense of reason, or eternity at the expense of time. Art is finite, and gives us busts and portraits, or copies of Greek and Roman models. The physical sciences take precedence of the metaphysical, and faith in railroads and steamboats is much stronger than in ideas.

In governments the tendency is the same. Nothing is more characteristic of Protestantism than its influence in promoting civil and

[18][Ed. See Oliver Goldsmith (1728-74), "The Deserted Village," line 158, in *Collected Works of Oliver Goldsmith*, ed. Arthur Friedman (Oxford: Clarendon, 1966), 4:293.]

political liberty. Under its reign all forms of governments verge towards the democratic. "The king and the church" are exchanged for the "constitution and the people." Liberty, not order, is the word that wakes the dead, and electrifies the masses. A social science is created, and the physical well-being of the humblest laborer is cared for, and made a subject of deliberation in the councils of nations.

Industry has received in Protestant countries its grandest developments. Since the time of Luther, it has been performing one continued series of miracles. Every corner of the globe is explored; the most distant and perilous seas are navigated; the most miserly soil is laid under contribution; manufactures, villages and cities spring up and increase as by enchantment; canals and railroads are crossing the country in every direction; the means of production, the comforts, conveniences and luxuries of life are multiplied to an extent hardly safe to relate.

Such, in its most general aspect, in its dominant tendency, is Protestantism. It is a new and much improved edition of the classics. Its civilization belongs to the same order as that of Greece and Rome. It is in advance, greatly in advance, of Greece and Rome, but it is the same in its groundwork. The material predominates over the spiritual. Men labor six days for this world and at most but one for the world to come. The great strife is for temporal goods, fame or pleasure. God, the soul, heaven and eternity are thrown into the background, and almost entirely disappear in the distance. Right yields to expediency, and duty is measured by utility. The real character of Protestantism, the result to which it must come, wherever it can have its full development, may be best seen in France, at the close of the last century. The church was converted into the pantheon, and made a resting place for the bodies of the great and renowned of earth; God was converted into a symbol of the human reason, and man into the man-machine; spiritualism fell, and the revolution marked the complete triumph of materialism.

CHAPTER V. REACTION OF SPIRITUALISM

What I have said of the Protestant world cannot be applied to the present century without some important qualifications. Properly speaking, Protestantism finished its work and expired in the French revolution at the close of the last century. Since then there has been a reaction in favor of spiritualism.

Men incline to exclusive spiritualism in proportion to their want of faith in the practicability of improving their earthly condition.

This accounts for the predominance of spiritualism in the church. The church grew up and constituted itself amidst the crash of a falling world, when all it knew or could conceive of material well-being was crumbling in ruins around it. Greece and Rome were the prey of merciless barbarians. Society was apparently annihilated. Order there was none. Security for person, property, or life, seemed almost the extravagant vagary of some mad enthusiast. Lawless violence, brutal passion, besotting ignorance, tyrants and their victims, were the only spectacles presented to win men's regard for the earth, or to inspire them with faith and hope to labor for its improvement. To the generation of that day, when the North disgorged itself upon the South, the earth must have appeared forsaken by its Maker, and abandoned to the devil and his ministers. It was a wretched land; it could yield no supply; and the only solace for the soul was to turn away from it to another and better world, to the world of spirit; to that world where tyrants do not enter, where wrongs and oppression, sufferings and grief, find no admission; where mutations and insecurity are unknown, and where the poor earth-wanderer, the time-worn pilgrim, may at length find that repose, that fullness of joy which he craved, which he sought but found not below. This view was natural, it was inevitable; and it could lead only to exclusive spiritualism–mysticism.

But when the external world has been somewhat meliorated, and men find that they have some security for their persons and property, that they may count with some degree of certainty on tomorrow, faith in the material order is produced and confirmed. One improvement prepares another. Success inspires confidence in future efforts. And this was the case at the epoch of the reformation. Men had already made great progress in the material order, in their temporal weal. Their faith in it kept pace with their progress, or more properly, outran it. It continued to extend till it became almost entire and universal. The eighteenth century will be marked in the annals of the world for its strong faith in the material order. Meliorations on the broadest scale were contemplated and viewed as already realized. Our republic sprang into being, and the world leaped with joy that "a man child was born." Social progress and the perfection of governments became the religious creed of the day; the weal of man on earth, the spring and aim of all hopes and labors. A new paradise was imaged forth for man, inaccessible to the serpent, more delightful than that which Adam lost, and more attractive than that which the pious Christian hopes to gain. We of this generation can form only a faint conception of the strong faith our fathers had in the progress of society, the high hopes of human improvement they indulged, and the joy too big for utterance, with which they heard France in loud and kindling tones proclaim LIBERTY and EQUALITY. France for a moment became the center of the world. All eyes were fixed on her movements. The pulse stood still when she and her enemies met, and loud cheers burst from the universal heart of humanity when her tricolored flag was seen to wave in triumph over the battlefield. There was then no stray thought for God and eternity. Man and the world filled the soul. They were too big for it. But while the voice of hope was yet ringing, and *Te Deum*[19] shaking the arches of the old cathedrals, the convention, the Reign of Terror, the exile of patriots, the massacre of the gifted, the beautiful, and the good, Napoleon and the military despotism came, and humanity uttered a piercing shriek, and fell prostrate on the grave of her hopes!

The reaction produced by the catastrophe of this memorable drama was tremendous. There are still lingering among us those who have not forgotten the recoil they experienced when they saw the republic swallowed up, or preparing to be swallowed up, in the empire. Men never feel what they felt but once. The pang which darts through their souls changes them into stone. From that moment enthusiasm died, hope in social melioration ceased to be indulged, and those who had been the most sanguine in anticipations, hung down their heads and said nothing; the warmest friends of humanity apologized for their dreams of liberty and equality; democracy became an accusation, and faith in the perfectibility of mankind a proof of disordered intellect.

In consequence of this reaction, men again despaired of the earth; and when they despair of the earth, they always take refuge in heaven; when man fails them, they always fly to God. They had trusted materialism too far; they would now not trust it at all. They had hoped too much; they would now hope nothing. The future, which had been to them so bright and promising, was now overspread with black clouds; the ocean on which they were anxious to embark was lashed into rage by the storm, and presented only images of dismasted or sinking ships and drowning crews. They turned back and sighed for the serene past, the quiet and order of old times, for the mystic land of India, where the soul may dissolve in ecstasy and dream of no change.

[19][Ed. *Te Deum* is a famous early Christian Latin hymn to God the Father and the Son. The origins of the hymn are obscure, but its use was already prescribed in the Rule of St. Benedict in the early sixth century.]

At the very moment when the sigh had just escaped, that mystic land reappeared. The English, through the East India Company, had brought to light its old literature and philosophy, so diverse from the literature and philosophy of modern Europe or of classical antiquity, and men were captivated by their novelty and bewildered by their strangeness. Sir William Jones gave currency to them by poetical paraphrases and imitations; and the Asiatic Society by its researches placed them within reach of the learned of Europe.[20] The church rejoiced for it was like bringing back her long lost mother whose features she had remembered and was able at once to recognize. Germany, England, and even France became Oriental. Cicero, and Horace, and Virgil, Aeschylus, Euripides, and even Homer, with Jupiter, Apollo, and Minerva were forced to bow before Hindoo bards and gods of uncouth forms and unutterable names.

The influence of the old Braminical or spiritual world, thus dug up from the grave of centuries, may be traced in all our philosophy, art and literature. It is remarkable in our poets. It molds the form in Byron, penetrates to the ground in Wordsworth, and entirely predominates in the Schlegels.[21] It causes us to feel a new interest in those writers and those epochs which partake the most of spiritualism. Those old English writers who were somewhat inclined to mysticism are revived; Plato, who traveled in the East and brought back its lore which he modified by western genius and molded into Grecian forms, is re-edited, commented on, translated, and raised to the highest rank among philosophers.[22] The Middle Ages are re-examined and found to contain a treasure of romance, acuteness, depth, and wisdom, and are deemed by some to be "Dark Ages" only because we have not light enough to read them.

[20][Ed. Sir William Jones (1746-94) was a British Orientalist and jurist who did much to encourage interest and study of Oriental sources in the West. In 1784 he founded the Asiatic Society of Bengal to encourage Oriental studies. On Jones, see Garland Cannon and Kevin R. Brine, eds., *Objects of Enquiry: The Life, Contributions, and Influences of Sir William Jones, 1746-1794* (New York: New York University Press, 1995).]

[21][Ed. William Wordsworth (1770-1850) was a major English Romantic poet and co-author of *Lyrical Ballads* (1798), among other works. Friedrich von Schlegel (1772-1829) was a German Romantic literary critic and philosopher who converted to Catholicism in 1808. Together with his equally Romantic brother August Wilhelm (1767-1845), he edited the *Athenaeum* (1798-1800), the primary theoretical organ of German Romanticism.]

[22][Ed. Both Cousin and Schleiermacher translated Plato for the French and the Germans.]

Materialism in philosophy is extinct in Germany. It is only a reminiscence in France, and it produces no remarkable work in England or America. Phrenology, which some deem materialism, has itself struck materialism with death in Gall's work,[23] by showing that we are conscious of phenomena within us which no metaphysical alchemy can transmute into sensations.

Protestantism, since the commencement of the present century, in what it has peculiar to itself, has ceased to gain ground. Rationalism in Germany retreats before the Evangelical party; the Genevan Church makes few proselytes; English and American Unitarianism, on the plan of Priestley and Belsham,[24] avowedly material, and being, as it were, the jumping-off place from the church to absolute infidelity, is evidently on the decline. There is probably not a man in this country, however much and justly he may esteem Priestley and Belsham, as bold and untiring advocates of reason and of humanity, who would be willing to assume the defense of all their opinions. On the other hand Catholicism has revived, offered some able apologies for itself, made some eminent proselytes, and alarmed many Protestants, even among ourselves.

Indeed everywhere is seen a decided tendency to spiritualism. The age has become weary of uncertainty. It sighs for repose. Controversy is nearly ended and a sentiment is extensively prevailing that it is a matter of very little consequence what a man believes, or what formulas of worship he adopts, if he only have a right spirit. Men, who a few years ago were staunch rationalists, now talk of spiritual communion; and many, who could with difficulty be made to admit the inspiration of the Bible, are now ready to admit the inspiration of the sacred books of all nations; and instead of stumbling at the idea of God's speaking to a few individuals, they see no reason why he should not speak to everybody. Some are becoming so spiritual that they see no necessity of matter; others so refine matter that it can

[23][Ed. Franz-Joseph Gall (1758-1828), a Viennese doctor, promoted phrenology, that is, a study of the conformation of the skull as indicative of mental faculties and traits of character. Gall's method was purely empirical. Brownson's attempt to defend it from the charge of materialism is a stretch, to say the least. George Combe (1788-1858), a Scottish education reformer and moral philosopher, made phrenology a semi-popular movement in antebellum America, presenting phrenology as a system of moral improvement and educational reform.]

[24][Ed. Joseph Priestley (1733-1804), scientist and theologian, was a founder of the Unitarian movement in England and had an influence on its development in the United States. Thomas Belsham (1750-1829) accepted Priestley's Unitarian pulpit at Hackney, England when Priestley moved to the United States. He wrote frequently in defense of Unitarianism.]

offer no resistance to the will, making it indeed move as the spirit listeth; others still believe that all wisdom was in the keeping of the priests of ancient India, Egypt, and Persia, and fancy the world has been deteriorating for four thousand years, instead of advancing. Men go out from our midst to Europe, and come back half Catholics, sighing to introduce the architecture, the superstition, the rites, and the sacred symbols of the Middle Ages.

A universal cry is raised against the frigid utilitarianism of the last century. Money-getting, desire for worldly wealth and renown, are spoken of with contempt, and men are evidently leaving the outward for the inward, and craving something more fervent, living, and soul-kindling. All this proves that we have changed from what we were; that, though materialism yet predominates and appears to have lost none of its influence, it is becoming a tradition; and that there is a new force collecting to expel it. Protestantism passes into the condition of a reminiscence. Protestant America cannot be aroused against the Catholics. A mob may burn a convent from momentary excitement, but the most Protestant of the Protestants among us will petition the legislature to indemnify the owners.[25] Indeed, Protestantism died in the French revolution, and we are beginning to become disgusted with its dead body. The East has reappeared, and spiritualism revives; will it again become supreme? Impossible.

CHAPTER VI. MISSION OF THE PRESENT

We of the present century must either dispense with all religious instructions, reproduce spiritualism or materialism, or we must build a new church, organize a new institution free from the imperfections of those which have been.

The first is out of the question. Men cannot live in a perpetual anarchy. They must and will embody their ideas of the true, the beautiful, and the good, the holy, in some institution. They must answer in some way the questions, What is the holy? What is the true destination of man?

To reproduce spiritualism or materialism, were an anomaly in the development of humanity. Humanity does not traverse an eter-

[25][Ed. Reference here is to a mob's burning of the Catholic Ursuline convent in Charlestown, Massachusetts on 11 August 1834. Many Unitarians, the "most Protestant of the Protestants" did indeed protest the mob's action and petitioned the legislature for indemnification, but the petition was voted down. On the event itself and the reactions, see Jeanne Hamilton, "The Nunnery as Menace: The Burning of the Charlestown Convent, 1834," *U. S. Catholic Historian* 14 (Winter 1996): 35-65.]

nal circle; it advances; it does not come round to its starting point, but goes onward in one endless career of progress towards the Infinite, the Perfect.

Besides, it is impossible. Were it desirable, neither spiritualism nor materialism can to any considerable extent, or for any great length of time, become predominant. We cannot bring about that state of society which is the indispensable condition of the exclusive dominion of either.

Spiritualism just now revives; its friends may anticipate a victory; but they will be disappointed. Spiritualism, as an exclusive system, reigns only when men have no faith in material interests; and in order to have no faith in material interests, we must virtually destroy them; we must have absolute despotism, a sacerdotal caste, or we must have another decline and fall like that of the Roman empire, and a new irruption like that of the Goths, Vandals and Huns.

None of these things are possible. There are no more Goths, Vandals or Huns. The north of Europe is civilized. Northern and central Asia is in the process of civilization through the influence of Russia; England is mingling the arts and sciences of the West with the spiritualism of India; France and the colony of Liberia secure Africa; the Aborigines of this continent will in a few years have vanished before the continued advance of the European races; merchants and missionaries will do the rest. No external forces can then ever be collected to destroy civilization and compel the human race to commence its work anew.

Internally, modern civilization has nothing to fear. It contains no seeds of destruction. A real advance has been made. A vast fund of experience has been accumulated and is deposited in so many different languages, that we can hardly conceive it possible that it should be wholly lost or greatly diminished. The art of printing, unknown to Greek and Roman civilization, multiplies books to such an extent, that it is perfectly idle to dream of any catastrophe, unless it be the destruction of the world itself, which will reduce them to a few precious fragments like those left us of classical antiquity.

There is, too, a remarkable difference in the diffusion of knowledge. In the best days of classical antiquity, the number of the enlightened was but small. The masses were enveloped in thick darkness. Now the masses have been to school, and are going to school. The millions, who then were in darkness, now behold light springing up. The loss of one individual, however prominent he may be, is not felt. Another is immediately found to fill his place.

Liberty exists also to a much greater extent. The rights of man are better comprehended and secured. The individual man is a greater being than he was in Greece or Rome. He has a higher consciousness of his worth, and he is more respected, and his interests are felt to be more sacred.

Labor has become more honorable. In Greece and Rome labor was menial; it was performed by slaves, at least by the ignorant and brutish. Slavery is disappearing. It has only a small corner of the civilized world left to it. As slavery disappears, as labor comes to be performed by freemen, it will rise to the rank of a liberal profession, and men of character and influence will be laborers.

The improvements in the arts of production have become so extensive, and the means of creating and accumulating wealth are so distributed, and the amount of wealth has already become so great and is shared by so many, that it is impossible that there should ever come again a scene of general poverty and wretchedness to make men despair of the earth, and abandon themselves wholly to the dreams of a spirit-land. There must always remain something to hope from the material order, and consequently, whatever may be the influence of a sudden panic, or a momentary affright, always a check to the absolute dominion of spiritualism.

Nor can materialism become sovereign again. It contains the elements of its own defeat. The very discipline, which materialism demands to support itself, in the end neutralizes its dominion. As soon as men find themselves well off in a worldly point of view, they discover that they have wants which the world does not and cannot satisfy. The training demanded to ensure success in commerce, industrial enterprises, or politics, strengthens faculties which crave something superior to commerce, to mere industry, or to politics. The merchant would not be always estimating the hazards of speculation; he dreams of his retirement from business, his splendid mansion, his refined hospitality, a library, and studious ease; the mechanic looks forward to a time when he shall have leisure to care for something besides merely animal wants; and the politician to his release from the cares and perplexities of a public life, to a quiet retreat, to a dignified old age, spent in plans of benevolence, in aiding the cause of education, religion, or philosophy. This low business world, upon which the moralist and the divine look down with so much sorrow, is not quite so low after all, as they think it. It is doing a vast deal to develop the intellect. It is full of high and expanded brows.

It is true that money getting, mere physical utility has at this moment a wide influence, and may absorb the mind and heart quite too much. Still the evil is not unmixed. That man who tortures his brain, spends his days and nights to accumulate a fortune, is much superior to him who is content to rot in poverty, who has no courage, no energy to attempt to improve his condition. He is a better member of society, is worth more to humanity. It is a great day, even for spiritualism, when all the people of a country are carried away in an industrial direction. Speculation may be rife, frauds may be common; many may become rich by means they care not to make known; many may become discontented; there may be much striving this way and that, much effort to get up, keep up, to pull or to push down; but the many will sharpen their faculties, and gain the leisure and the means and the disposition to attend to the spiritual part of their being. It does my heart good to witness the industrial activity of my countrymen. I see very clearly the evils which attend it; but I also see every year the general level rising, and the moral and intellectual power increasing. So is it too with our political struggles. They quicken thought, give the people the use of language, a consciousness of their power, especially of the power of mind, and upon the whole they do much to elevate the general character. Those quiet times we look back upon and regret, either were not as quiet as we think them, or they were quiet because they had not enough of thought to move them. They were, as still, but too often as putrid, as the stagnant pool.

The science which is now introduced into commerce, into the mechanic arts and agricultural pursuits, and which is everyday receiving a greater extension and new applications, while it preserves the material order, also keeps alive the spiritual, and gives us a check against the absolute ascendancy of materialism.

We cannot then go back either to exclusive spiritualism, or to exclusive materialism. Both these systems have received so full a development, have acquired so much strength, that neither can be subdued. Both have their foundation in our nature, and both will exist and exert their influence. Shall they exist as antagonist principles? Shall the spirit forever lust against the flesh, and the flesh against the spirit? Is the bosom of humanity to be eternally torn by these two contending factions? No. It cannot be. The war must end. Peace must be made.

This discloses our mission. We are to reconcile spirit and matter; that is, we must realize the atonement. Nothing else remains for us to do. Stand still we cannot. To go back is equally impossible. We must go forward, but we can take not a step forward, but on the condition of uniting these two hitherto hostile principles. PROGRESS is our law and our first step is UNION.

The union of spirit and matter was the result contemplated by the mission of Jesus. The church attempted it, but only partially succeeded, and has therefore died. The time had not come for the complete union. Jesus saw this. He knew that the age in which he lived would not be able to realize his conception. He therefore spoke of his "Second Coming." The church has always had a vague presentiment of its own death, and the birth of a new era when Christ should really reign on earth. For a long time the hierophants have fixed upon ours as the epoch of the commencement of the new order of things. Some have gone even so far as to name this very year, 1836, as the beginning of what they call the millennium.[26]

The particular shape which has been assigned to this new order, this "latter day glory," the name by which it has been designated, amounts to nothing. That some have anticipated a personal appearance of Jesus, and a resurrection of the saints, should not induce us to treat with disrespect the almost unanimous belief of Christendom in a fuller manifestation of Christian truth, and in a more special reign of Christ in a future epoch of the world. All the presentiments of humanity are to be respected. Humanity has a prophetic power. "Coming events cast their shadows before."[27]

The "Second Coming" of Christ will be when the idea which he represents, that is, the idea of atonement, shall be fully realized. That idea will be realized by a combination, a union, of the two terms which have received thus far from the church only a separate development. This union the church has always had a presentiment of; it has looked forward to it, prayed for it; and we are still praying for it, for we still say, "Let thy kingdom come." Nobody believes that the gospel has completed its work. The church universal and eternal is not yet erected. The cornerstone is laid; the materials are prepared. Let then the workmen come forth with joy, and bid the temple rise. Let them embody the true idea of the God-Man, and Christ will then have come a second time; he will have come in power and great glory, and he will reign, and the whole earth will be glad.

[26][Ed. Brownson himself certainly saw 1836 as a crucial year in ushering in a new order of the ages, as his writings for this year reveal, particularly his *New Views*.]

[27][Ed. See Thomas Campbell (1777-1844), "Lochiel's Warning," line 56, in *The Complete Poetical Works of Thomas Campbell*, ed. J. Logie Robertson (New York: Haskell House, 1968), 159.]

CHAPTER VII. CHRISTIAN SECTS

This age must realize the atonement, the union of spirit and matter, the destruction of all antagonism and the production of universal peace.

God has appointed us to build the new church, the one which shall bring the whole family of man within its sacred enclosure, which shall be able to abide the ravages of time, and against which "the gates of hell shall not prevail" [Matt. 16:18].

But we can do this only by a general doctrine which enables us to recognize and accept all the elements of humanity. If we leave out any one element of our nature, we shall have antagonism. Our system will be incomplete and the element excluded will be forever rising up in rebellion against it and collecting forces to destroy its authority.

All sects overlook this important truth. None of them seem to imagine that human nature has or should have any hand in the construction of their theories. Instead of studying human nature, ascertaining its elements and it wants, and seeking to conform to them, every sect labors to conform human nature to its own creed. No one dreams of molding its dogmas to human nature, but everyone would mold human nature to its dogmas. Everyone is a bed of Procrustes.[28] What is too short must be stretched, what is too long must be docked. No sect ever looks to human nature as the measure of truth; but all look to what they are pleased to call the truth, as the measure of human nature.

This were well enough if human nature had only been made of wax, or some other ductile material. But unfortunately it is very stubborn. It will not bend. It will not be mutilated. Its laws are permanent and universal; each one of them is eternal and indestructible. They war in vain who war against them. Be they good or be they bad, we must accept them, we must submit to them and do the best we can with them.

But human nature is well made, its laws are just and holy, its elements are true and divine. And this is the hidden sense of that symbol of the God-Man. That symbol teaches all who comprehend

[28][Ed. According to Greek legend Procrustes was a robber dwelling somewhere in Attica. He had an iron bed upon which he compelled his victims to lie. If a victim was shorter than the bed, Procrustes stretched him by hammering or racking the body to fit, and if shorter he cut off his legs. A "Procrustean bed" has become proverbial for arbitrarily or ruthlessly forcing someone or something to fit into an unnatural scheme or pattern.]

it, to find divinity in humanity, and humanity in divinity. By presenting us God and man united in one person, it shows us that both are holy. The Father and Son are one. Therefore we are commanded to honor the Son as we honor the Father, humanity as divinity, man as well as God. But the church has never understood this. No sect now understands it. Hence the contempt with which all sects treat human nature, and their entire want of confidence in it as a criterion of truth. They must correct themselves. "The Word was made flesh and dwelt among us" [John 1:14].

To reject human nature and declare it unworthy of confidence as the church did, and as all sects now do, is, whether we know it or not, to reject all grounds of certainty, and to declare that we have no means of distinguishing truth from falsehood. Truth itself is nothing else to us than that which our nature by some one or all of its faculties compels us to believe. The fact that God has made us a revelation does not in the least impair this assertion. God has revealed to us truths which we could not of ourselves have discovered. But how do we know this? What is it but the human mind that can determine whether God has or has not spoken to us? What but the human mind can ascertain and fix the meaning of what he may have communicated? If we may not trust the human mind, human nature, how can we ever be sure that a revelation has been made? Or how distinguish a real revelation from a pretended one? By miracles? But how determine that what are alleged to be miracles, really are miracles? Or the more difficult question still, that the miracles, admitting them to be genuine, do necessarily involve the truth of the doctrines they are wrought to prove? Shall we be told that we must believe the revelation is a true one, because made by an authorized teacher? Where is the warrant of his authority? What shall assure us that the warrant is not a forgery? Have we anything but our own nature with which to answer these and a hundred more questions like them and equally important?

If human nature has the ability and the right to answer these questions, where are the limits of its ability and its right? If we trust it when it assures us God has spoken to us, and when it interprets what he has spoken, where shall we not trust it? If it be no criterion of truth, why do we trust it here? And if it be, why do we disclaim it elsewhere? Why declare it worthy of confidence in one case and not in another? It is the same in all cases, in all its degrees; and whether it testifies to that which is little, or to that which is great, it is the same, and its testimony is of precisely the same validity.

If we admit that human nature is the measure of truth—of truth for us, human beings—then we admit that it is the criterion by which all sects must be tested. It is then the touchstone of truth. Every sect must be approved or condemned according to its decision. No sect must blame humanity for not believing its doctrines. If after they have been fairly presented and fully comprehended they are rejected, they are proved to be false, or at least to be only partially true. It is no recommendation to advocate doctrines repugnant to human nature; nor is it any reproach to defend those which are pleasing to the natural heart. Humanity loves the truth and can be satisfied with nothing else. The sect, then, which ceases to make converts should abandon or enlarge its creed.

Sects in general are and will be slow to learn this truth. Each sect, because it has all the truth to be seen from its standpoint, takes it for granted that it has the whole truth. It does not even dream that there may be other standpoints, from which other truths may be seen, or the same truths under other aspects; and therefore it concludes when its doctrines are rejected, that they are rejected because human nature is perverse or impotent, because men cannot or will not see the truth, or because they naturally hate it. Let it change its position and it will soon learn that the horizon, which it took to be the boundary of truth, was in fact only the boundary of its own vision.

All sects, however, have their truth and are serviceable to humanity. Each one has a special doctrine which gives prominence to some one element of our nature, and is therefore satisfactory to all in whom that element predominates. But as that element, however important a one it may be, is not the whole of human nature, and as it can hardly be predominant alike in all men, no sect can satisfy entire humanity. Each sect does something to develop and satisfy the separate elements of humanity, but no one can develop and satisfy all the elements of humanity and satisfy them as a whole.

Spiritualism and materialism are the two most comprehensive sectarian doctrines which have ever been proclaimed. But neither of these is comprehensive enough. Either may satisfy a large class of wants, but each must leave a class equally as large unsatisfied. One has always been opposed by the other, and mutual opposition has finally destroyed them both. Humanity is still sighing for what it has not. It is seeking rest but finds none. And rest it will not find, till its untiring friends gain a standpoint, from which, as with one grand panoramic view, they may take in all elements in their relative proportions, and exact distances, in their diversity and in their unity, till they have gone up and down the earth and collected and brought together its disjointed members, which contending sects have torn asunder, and molded them into one complete and lovely form of truth and holiness.

Where is the Christian sect that is engaged in this work? Where is the one that deems it desirable or possible? All the sects of Christendom, so far as it concerns their dominant tendency, fall into the category of spiritualism, or into that of materialism. Catholicism is virtually the church of the Middle Ages. It is but a reminiscence. It has no life, at least no healthy existence. It belongs to spiritualism. Calvinism, bating some few modifications produced by Protestant influence, is only a continuation of Catholicism. It is decidedly spiritualistic. Its prayers, its hymns and homilies are deeply imprinted with spiritualism. It repels the material order, and exhorts us to crucify the flesh, to disregard the world and to think only of God, the soul and eternity.

In the opinion of the Calvinist, the world lies under the curse of the Almighty. It is a wretched land, a vale of tears, of disease and death. There is no happiness below. It is vain, almost impious, to wish it till death comes to release us from the infirmities of the flesh. As long as we live we sin; we must carry about a weary load, an overwhelming burthen, a body of death. Man is a poor, depraved creature. He is smitten with a curse, and the curse spreads over his whole nature. There is nothing good within him. Of himself he can obtain, he can do nothing good. He is unclean in the sight of God. His sacrifices are an abomination, and his holiest prayers are sinful. His will is perverted; his affections are all on the side of evil; his reason is deprived of its light, it is blind and impotent, and will lead those who trust to its guidance down to hell.

By its doctrine of "foreordination," Calvinism annihilates man. It allows him no independent causality. It permits him to move only as a preordaining and irresistible will moves him. It makes him a thing, not a person, with properties but without faculties or rights. Whatever his destiny, however cruel, he has no right to complain. Spirit is absolute and has the right to receive him into blessedness or send him away into everlasting punishment, without any regard to his own wishes, merit or demerit. Hence Calvinists always give supremacy to the spiritual order. They fled from England to this then wilderness world, because they would not conform to a church established by the state; and when here they constituted the church superior to the state. In theory the Pilgrims made the state a mere function of the church. In order to be a citizen it was necessary that one should first be a church member. And for the last twenty years the great body of Calvinists throughout our whole country have been exerting all their skill and influence to raise the church to that eminence from which it may overlook the state, control its deliberations and decide its measures.

His doctrine of "hereditary total depravity" has always compelled the Calvinist to reject reason and to rely on authority—to seek faith, not conviction. Protestant influences prevent him in these days from submitting to an infallible pope, but he indemnifies himself by infallible creeds, councils, synods and assemblies. Or if these fail him, he can ascribe infallibility to the "written Word." Always does he prohibit himself the free exercise of his own understanding, and prescribe bounds beyond which reason and reasoning must not venture.

By the dogma of Christ's vicarious death, he takes his stand decidedly with spiritualism, denies the atonement, loses sight of the mediator, and rejects the God-Man. He cannot then build the new church, the church truly universal and eternal. It is in vain that we ask him to destroy all antagonism. He does not even wish to do it; before the foundations of the world, its origin and eternity were decreed. God and the devil, the saint and the sinner, in his estimation, are alike immortal.

Universalism would seem to a superficial observer to be what we need. Its friends call it the doctrine of universal reconciliation, and they group around the love of God that which constitutes the real harmony and unity of creation. But Universalists do not understand themselves. They have a vague sense of the truth, but not a clear perception of it. As soon as they begin to explain themselves, they file off either to the ranks of spiritualism, or of materialism.

The larger number of Universalists, among whom is, or was, the chief of the sect, contend that all sin originates in the flesh and must end with it.[29] The flesh ends at death, when it is deposited in the tomb; therefore, "he that is dead is freed from sin" [Rom. 6:7]. Sin is the cause of all suffering; when sin ends, suffering ends. Sin ends at death, and therefore after death no suffering, but universal happiness.

This doctrine is as decidedly spiritualism as oriental spiritualism itself. If the body be the cause of all sin, it certainly deserves no respect. It is a vile thing, and should be despised, mortified, punished, annihilated. Universalists do not draw this inference, but they avoid it only by really denying that there is any sin, or at least by considering the consequences of sin of too little importance to be dreaded.

[29][Ed. By the "chief of the sect" Brownson probably means Hosea Ballou (1771-1852). On Ballou, see introduction to EW, 1:5, 24.]

The body, however, according to this doctrine is a curse. Man would be better off without it than he is with it. It deserves nothing on its own account. Wherefore then shall I labor to make it comfortable? I shall be released from it tomorrow, and enter into a world of unutterable joy. Let my lodging tonight be on the bare ground, in the open air, destitute of a few conveniences, what imports it? Can I not afford to forego a pleasant lodging for one night, since I am ever after to be filled and overflowing with blessedness? Universalism, then, according to this exposition of it must inevitably lead to neglect of the material order. Its legitimate result would be, not licentiousness, but a dreaming contemplative life, wasting itself away in idleness, watching the motion of the sun, and wishing it to move faster, so that we may be the sooner translated from this miserable world, where nothing is worth laboring for, to our Father's kingdom where is music and dancing, songs and feasting forever and ever.

Universalists have, however, existing side by side with this exclusive spiritualism, some strong tendencies to materialism. Spiritualism and materialism are nearly balanced in their minds, and constitute, not a union of spirit and matter, but a parallelism which has no tendency to union. But when the true doctrine of the atonement is proclaimed, Universalists will be among the first believers. None will rejoice more than they, to see the new church rise from the ruins of the old, and none will attend more readily or with more zeal at its consecration.

Unitarianism belongs to the material order. It is the last word of Protestantism, before Protestantism breaks entirely with the past. It is the point towards which all Protestant sects converge in proportion as they gain upon their reminiscences. Every consistent Protestant Christian must be a Unitarian. Unitarianism elevates man; it preaches morality; it vindicates the rights of the mind, accepts and uses the reason, contends for civil freedom, and is social, charitable and humane. It saves the Son of man, but sometimes loses the Son of God.

But it is from the Unitarians that must come out the doctrine of universal reconciliation; for they are the only denomination in Christendom that labors to rest religious faith on rational conviction; that seeks to substitute reason for authority, to harmonize religion and science, or that has the requisite union of piety and mental freedom, to elaborate the doctrine which is to realize the atonement. The orthodox, as they are called, are disturbed by their memory. Their faces are on the back side of their heads. They have zeal, energy, perseverance, but their ideas belong to the past. The Universalists can do nothing till someone arises to give them a philosophy. They must comprehend their instincts, before they can give to their doctrine of reconciliation that character which will adapt it to the wants of entire humanity.

But Unitarians are every day breaking away more and more from tradition, and every day making new progress in the creation of a philosophy which explains humanity, determines its wants and the means of supplying them. Mind at this moment is extremely active among them, and as it can act freely it will most certainly elaborate the great doctrine required. They began in rationalism. Their earlier doctrines were dry and cold. And this was necessary. They were called at first to a work of destruction. They were under the necessity of clearing away the rubbish of the old church, before they could obtain a site whereon to erect the new one. The Unitarian preacher was under the necessity of raising a stern and commanding voice in the wilderness, "Prepare ye the way of the Lord, make his paths straight" [Isa. 40:3; Matt. 3:3; Mark 1:3; Luke 3:4]. He raised that voice, and the chief priest and Pharisees in modern Judea heard and trembled and some have gone forth to be baptized. The Unitarian has baptized them with water unto repentance, but he has born witness that a mightier than he shall come after him, who shall baptize them with the Holy Ghost and with fire.

When the Unitarian appeared, there was on this whole earth no spot for the temple of the living God, the temple of reason, love and peace. For such a spot he contended. He has obtained it. He has began the temple; its foundations already appear, and although the workmen must yet work with their arms in one hand, he will see it completed, consecrated, and filled with the glory of the Lord.

CHAPTER VIII. INDICATIONS OF THE ATONEMENT

The church was the result of three causes, the Asiatic conquests of the Romans, the Alexandrian school of philosophy, and the Christian movement of the people.

By the Asiatic conquests of the Romans, spiritualism and materialism were brought together upon the same theater and placed in the condition necessary to their union. Eastern and western ideas were mingled in strange confusion throughout the whole of the Roman empire during the first three centuries of our era, and the attempt to unite them, to combine them into a regular and harmonious system, could hardly fail to be made.

This attempt was made by the Alexandrian philosophers.[30] These philosophers called themselves eclectics. Their avowed object was to unite the East and the West, European and Asiatic ideas, to reduce to a regular system the ideas of all the various schools of philosophy. They did it as perfectly as they could with the lights they had and the experiments they had made.

The Christian movement of the people was apparently very unlike that of the Alexandrian. The early Christians were the farthest in the world from being philosophers. They were inspired. They were moved by an impulse of which they asked, and could have given no account. God moved in them, and spoke through them; gave them lofty enthusiasm, a resistless energy of character, and prepared them to do, to dare, and to suffer anything and everything. At his command they went forth to conquer the world, and they did conquer it; not, as it has been well remarked, by killing, but by dying.

We understand today what it was that moved the early Christians. What was inspiration in them is philosophy in us. They had an instinctive sense of the synthesis of spirit and matter. Yet they thought nothing of spirit and matter. They disturbed themselves not in the least with spiritualism and materialism, with the East and the West, with Europe and Asia. They saw mankind sunk in sin and misery, weary and heavy laden, and they went forth strong in the Lord to raise them to virtue, to convert them to Christ and to give them rest. They did not speculate, they did not reason, they saw and felt and acted.

These and the Alexandrians met, and the church was the result. The share of the Alexandrians in the construction of the church has always been acknowledged to be very great. Perhaps it was greater than any have suspected. Certain it is that they furnished the Fathers their philosophy, and they may be pronounced without much hesitation, the real elaborators—not of Christianity, but—of the dogmas of the church.

All men feel more or less the desire to account to themselves for what they are. For a time they may be carried away by a force not

[30][Ed. By the Alexandrian philosophers, Brownson, following Cousin, meant Ammonius Saccas, Plotinus, Proclus, Porphyry, Jamblichus, Eunapius, Julian (the Emperor)—that is, all those from the so-called school of Alexandria who were eclectic in their desire to unite the Greeks and the Orientals, the Greek philosophy with the Oriental religion. The culmination of this movement was a scientific mysticism. Throughout his life Brownson would give pride of place to this Alexandrian effort. To some extent he tried to carry out this project in his own spiritual philosophy.]

their own, and they may be so engrossed with varied and exciting action and events, that they have no time to think; but at the first moments of calmness and self-consciousness they will ask what has moved them, what was the power which carried them away and whither have they been borne. This was the case with the early Christians. The first excitement over, and the visits of inspiration having become less frequent, they desired to explain themselves to themselves, to give a name to the instincts they had obeyed, to the Divinity which had moved them, and to the destiny they had been fulfilling. The Alexandrians answered all their questions. They explained the Christians to themselves, and henceforth their explanations were counted Christianity.

These three causes of the old church, or analogous ones, reappear today for the first time since that epoch; and is not their reappearance an indication that a new church is about to be built?

The East and the West are again on the same theater. The British by means of the East India Company have reconquered the father-land of spiritualism, and brought up from the graves of ages its old literature and philosophy, and mingled them with those of the West, the father-land of materialism.[31] The church itself has introduced not a little spiritualism into Christian civilization, while Protestantism by encouraging the study of the classics has reproduced Greece and Rome. The two worlds, the two civilizations, the two systems to be atoned or united are now in very nearly the same relative condition as they were at the birth of the church. They are thrown together into the crucible.

Alexandria, too, is reproduced with the modifications and improvements which two thousand years could not fail to effect. Eclecticism is declared to be the philosophy of the nineteenth century. Not one of the exclusive systems, which obtained during the last century, has now any life. Materialism is a tradition even in France; idealism has exhausted itself in Germany, and England has no philosophy.

Schelling had at least a presentiment of eclecticism in his doctrine of identity; Hegel has greatly abridged the labors of its friends; Fries and his disciples observe its method, and Jacobi virtually em-

[31][Ed. On American Transcendentalism and Asian religions, see Arthur Christy, *The Orient in American Transcendentalism: A Study of Emerson, Thoreau, and Alcott* (New York: Octagon, 1972) and Arthur Versluis, *American Transcendentalism and Asian Religions.*]

braced it.[32] In our own country it has produced no great work, and perhaps will not; but it is avowed by many of the best minds among us, and is the only philosophy we have, that has not ceased to make proselytes.

In France, however, eclecticism has received its fullest developments. M. Cousin has all but perfected it. He has presented us the last results of the philosophical labors of his predecessors and contemporaries, and furnished us with a method by which we may construct a philosophy which may truly be called the science of the absolute, a philosophy which need not fear the mutations of time and space, and may be sure that its sovereignty will be complete and undisputed as fast and as far as it comes to be understood.

M. Cousin has not only given, us, as it were, a geometrical demonstration of the existence of nature and of God, but he has also demonstrated that humanity, nature and God have precisely the same laws, that what we find in nature and humanity we may also find in God, and that when we have once risen to God we may come back and find again in nature and humanity all that we had found in him. This at once destroys all antithesis between spirit and matter, between God and man, gives man a kindred nature with God, makes him an image or manifestation of God, and paves the way for universal reconciliation and peace.[33] If God be holy, man, inasmuch as he has the very elements of the divinity is also holy. God and man may then unite in an everlasting and holy union, justice and mercy kiss each other, and all antagonism is destroyed.

The third cause, the inspiration of the people, is no less remarkable now than it was in the first centuries of our era. When God would produce a great result, one which requires the cooperation of vast multitudes, he does not merely inspire one man; he does not speak plainly in distinct propositions to a few, and leave them to

[32][Ed. Jacob Friedrich Fries (1773-1843) was a German post-Kantian philosopher who opposed the speculative idealism of Fichte, Schelling, and Hegel. He accepted the Kantian *a priori*, but claimed that it was knowable through the observation of our faculties, a position that is sometimes categorized as psychologism. In general he took Kantianism in a moralistic and empiricist, rather than a speculative idealist, direction. Friedrich Heinrich Jacobi (1743-1819) subjected Kant's remarks on "things-in-themselves" to a devastating critique, criticized the limits of reason and science, and espoused a fideistic approach that in effect grounded human knowledge in faith.]

[33]See my article on Cousin's Philosophy in the *Christian Examiner*, for September, 1836. Also, Cousin's Philosophical Works everywhere, especially the V. and VI. Lectures of his "Cours," in 1828, and the Preface to the 2d Edition of his *Fragmens philosophiques*.

speak to the many; but he gives an impulse to the masses, and carries away all the world in the direction of the object to be gained. People seem to themselves to be acting from their own impulses, and to be obeying their own convictions; but they are borne along by an invisible and resistless power towards an end of which they have a vague presentiment, but no distinct vision.

This is the case now. The time has come for a new church, for a new synthesis of the elements of the life of humanity. The end to be attained is union. How would an inspiration designed to give the energy, the power to attain this end be most likely to manifest itself; in what way could it manifest itself but by giving the people an irresistible longing for union, and a tendency to unite, to associate on all occasions and for all purposes not inconsistent with union itself? And what is the most striking characteristic of this age? Is it not the tendency to association, a tendency so strong that it appears to the cool spectator like a monomania?

This tendency shows itself everywhere. All over Christendom, men seem mad for associations. They associate for almost everything, to promote science, literature, art and industry, to circulate the Bible, to distribute religious tracts, to diffuse useful knowledge, to improve and extend education, to meliorate governments and laws, to soften the rigors of the prison house, to aid the sick, to relieve the poor, to prevent pauperism, to free the slave, to send out missionaries, and to evangelize the world. And, what deserves to be remarked, all these associations, various as they are, really propose in every instance a great and glorious end. They all are formed for useful, moral, religious, philosophical, philanthropical or humane purposes. They may be badly managed, they may fail in accomplishing what they propose, but that which they propose deserves to be accomplished. Sectarians may control them; but in all cases their ends are broader than any sect, than all sects, and they alike commend themselves to the consciences and the prayers of mankind. In some of these associations, sects long and widely separated come together, and find to their mutual satisfaction that they have a common ground, and a ground which each one instinctively admits to be higher and holier than any merely sectarian ground.

This tendency too is triumphing over all obstacles. Sects, which opposed this or that association because principally under the control of this or that sect, have slowly and reluctantly ceased their opposition, and have finally acquiesced. Individuals, who for a time resorted to ridicule and abuse to check associations, are now silent and they stand amazed as did those who listened to the Apostles on the day of Pentecost.[34] Those who apprehended great evils from them now seek to withstand them only by counter associations. To resist them is in fact out of the question. One might as well resist the whirlwind. There is a more than human power at the bottom of them. They come from God, from a divine inspiration given to the people to build the new church and realize the atonement, a universal and everlasting association.

This tendency or inspiration will, in a few days, meet the eclectic movement, if it have not already met it; and what shall prevent a result similar to that which followed the meeting of the early Christian inspiration and the Alexandrian eclecticism? This inspiration is, indeed, at this moment, apparently blind, but it and modern philosophy tend to the same end. They have then the same truth at bottom. They must then have a natural affinity with one another. They will then come together. The philosophy will explain and enlighten the inspiration. They who are now mad for associations will comprehend the power which has moved them, they will see the end towards which they have been tending without their knowing it, and they will give to the philosopher in return zeal, energy, enthusiasm, and there will then be both the light and the force needed to construct the new church.

And I think I see some indications that this meeting of inspiration and philosophy is already taking place. Something like it has occurred in Germany, in that movement commenced by Herder,[35] but best represented by Schleiermacher, a man remarkable for warmth of feeling, and coolness of thought, a preacher and a philosopher, a theologian and a man of science, a student and a man of business. It was attempted in France, where it gave birth to "Nouveau Christianisme,"[36] but without much success, because it is not a new Christianity but a new church that is required.

But the plainest indications of it are at home. In this country more than in any other is the man of thought united in the same person with the man of action. The people here have a strong ten-

[34][Ed. Brownson is apparently one of those who had been recently converted to those benevolent societies he once so severely criticized during his Universalist years, 1826-1829.]

[35][Ed. Johann Gottfried von Herder (1744-1803), German philosopher and literary figure, was primarily interested in the interrelations of language, culture, and history, rejecting in the process supernatural or providential explanations and interpretations. James Marsh's translation of Herder's *The Spirit of Hebrew Poetry* (1833) became very popular among American Transcendentalists.]

[36][Ed. On the Saint-Simonian attempts to create a new Christianity, see the introduction to this volume.]

dency to profound and philosophic thought, as well as to skillful, energetic and persevering action. The time is not far distant when our whole population will be philosophers, and all our philosophers will be practical men. This is written on almost every man's brow in characters so plain that he who runs may read. This characteristic of our population fits us above all other nations to bring out and realize great and important ideas. Here too is the freedom which other nations want, and the faith in ideas which can be found nowhere else. Philosophers in other countries may think and construct important theories, but they can realize them only to a very limited extent. But here every idea may be at once put to a practical test, and if true it will be realized. We have the field, the liberty, the disposition, and the faith to work with ideas. It is here, then, that must first be brought out and realized the true idea of the atonement. We already seem to have a consciousness of this, and it is therefore that we are not and cannot be surprised to find the union of popular inspiration with profound philosophical thought manifesting itself more clearly here than anywhere else.

The representative of this union here is a body of individuals rather than a single individual. The many with us are everything, the individual almost nothing. One man, however, stands out from this body, a more perfect type of the synthesis of eclecticism and inspiration than anyone else. I need not name him.[37] Philosophers consult him and the people hear his voice and follow him. His connection with a particular denomination may have exposed him to some unfriendly criticism, but he is in truth one of the most popular men of the age. His voice finds a response in the mind and in the heart of humanity.

His active career commenced with the new century, in that place where it should, and in the only place where it could, in the place where a republic had been born and liberty had received her grandest developments and her surest safeguards. There he has continued, and there he has been foremost in laying the foundation of that new church which will soon rise to greet the morning ray, and in which a glad voice will chant the hymn of peace to the evening sun. Few men are so remarkable for their union of deep religious feeling with sound reflection, of sobriety with popular enthusiasm. He reveres God and he reverences man. When he speaks he convinces and kindles.

When rationalism was attacked he appeared in its defense and proclaimed, in a language which still rings in our ears, the impre-

[37] [Ed. William Ellery Channing.]

scriptible rights of the mind. After the first shock of the war upon rationalism had been met, and a momentary truce tacitly declared, he brought out in an ordination sermon the great truth which destroys all antagonism and realizes the atonement. In that sermon, the most remarkable since the Sermon on the Mount, he distinctly recognizes and triumphantly vindicates the God-Man. "In ourselves are the elements of the Divinity. God, then, does not sustain a figurative resemblance to man. It is the resemblance of a parent to a child, THE LIKENESS OF A KINDRED NATURE."[38] In this sublime declaration, the Son of God is owned. Humanity, after so many years of vain search for a Father, finds itself here openly proclaimed the true child of God.

This declaration gives us the hidden sense of the symbol of the God-Man. By asserting the divinity of humanity, it teaches us that we should not view that symbol as the symbol of two natures in one person, but of kindred natures in two persons. The God-Man indicates not the antithesis of God and man; nor does it stand for a being alone of its kind; but it indicates the homogeneousness of the human and divine natures, and shows that they can dwell together in love and peace. The Son of Man and the Son of God are not two persons but one, a mystery which becomes clear the very moment that the human nature is discovered to have a sameness with the divine.

CHAPTER IX. THE ATONEMENT

The great doctrine, which is to realize the atonement and which the symbol of the God-Man now teaches us, is that all things are essentially holy, that everything is cleansed, and that we must call nothing common or unclean.

"And God saw everything that he had made, and behold it was very good" [Gen. 1:31]. And what else could it have been? God is wise, powerful and good; and how can a wise, powerful and good being create evil? God is the great fountain from which flows everything that is; how then can there be anything but good in existence?

Neither spiritualism nor materialism was aware of this truth. Spiritualism saw good only in pure spirit. God was pure spirit and therefore good; but all which could be distinguished from him was evil, and only evil, and that continually. Our good consisted in resemblance to God, that is, in being as like pure spirit as possible. Our duty was to get rid of matter. All the interests of the material order

[38][Ed. The reference here is to "Likeness to God." See *William Ellery Channing Selected Writings*, Ed. David Robinson (New York: Paulist, 1985), 150.]

were sinful. St. Augustine declared the flesh, that is the body, to be sin;[39] perfection then could be obtained only by neglecting, and as far as possible annihilating it. Materialism, on the other hand, had no recognition of spirit. It considered all time and thought and labor bestowed on that which transcends this world as worse than thrown away. It had no conception of inward communion with God. It counted fears of punishment or hopes of reward in a world to come mere idle fancies, fit only to amuse or control the vulgar. It laughed at spiritual joys and griefs, and treated as serious affairs only the pleasures and pains of sense.

But the new doctrine of the atonement reconciles these two warring systems. This doctrine teaches us that spirit is real and holy, that matter is real and holy, that God is holy and that man is holy, that spiritual joys and griefs, and the pleasures and pains of sense, are alike real joys and griefs, real pleasures and pains, and in their places are alike sacred. Spirit and matter, then, are saved. One is not required to be sacrificed to the other; both may and should coexist as separate elements of the same grand and harmonious whole.

The influence of this doctrine cannot fail to be very great. It will correct our estimate of man, of the world, of religion and of God, and remodel all our institutions. It must in fact create a new civilization as much in advance of ours as ours is in advance of that which obtained in the Roman Empire in the time of Jesus.

Hitherto we have considered man as the antithesis of all good. We have loaded him with reproachful epithets and made it a sin in him even to be born. We have uniformly deemed it necessary to degrade him in order to exalt his Creator. But this will end. The slave will become a son. Man is hereafter to stand erect before God as a child before its father. Human nature, at which we have pointed our wit and vented our spleen, will be clothed with a high and commanding worth. It will be seen to be a lofty and deathless nature. It will be felt to be divine, and infinite will be found traced in living characters on all its faculties.

We shall not treat one another then as we do now. Man will be sacred in the eyes of man. To wrong him will be more than crime, it will be sin. To labor to degrade him will seem like laboring to degrade the Divinity. Man will reverence man.

Slavery will cease. Man will shudder at the bare idea of enslaving so noble a being as man. It will seem to him hardly less daring than

[39][Ed. Brownson is here articulating a Manichean, not an Augustinian, view of the body and flesh.]

to presume to task the motions of the Deity and to compel him to come and go at our bidding. When man learns the true value of man, the chains of the captive must be unloosed and the fetters of the slave fall off.

Wars will fail. The sword will be beaten into the ploughshare and the spear into the pruning hook. Man will not dare to mar and mangle the shrine of the Divinity. The God looking out from human eyes will disarm the soldier and make him kneel to him he had risen up to slay. The warhorse will cease to bathe his fetlocks in human gore. He will snuff the breeze in the wild freedom of his native plains, or quietly submit to be harnessed to the plough. The hero's occupation will be gone, and heroism will be found only in saving and blessing human life.

Education will destroy the empire of ignorance. The human mind, allied as it is to the divine, is too valuable to lie waste or to be left to breed only briars and thorns. Those children, ragged and incrusted with filth, which throng our streets, and for whom we must one day build prisons, forge bolts and bars, or erect gibbets, are not only our children, our brother's children, but they are children of God, they have in themselves the elements of the Divinity and powers which when put forth will raise them above what the tallest archangel now is. And when this is seen and felt, will those children be left to fester in ignorance or to grow up in vice and crime? The whole energy of man's being cries out against such folly, such gross injustice.

Civil freedom will become universal. It will be everywhere felt that one man has no right over another which that other has not over him. All will be seen to be brothers and equals in the sight of their common Father. All will love one another too much to desire to play the tyrant. Human nature will be reverenced too much not to be allowed to have free scope for the full and harmonious development of all its faculties. Governments will become sacred; and while on the one hand they are respected and obeyed, on the other it will be felt to be a religious right and a religious duty to labor to make them as perfect as they can be.

Religion will not stop with the command to obey the laws, but it will bid us make just laws, such laws as befit a being divinely endowed like man. The church will be on the side of progress, and spiritualism and materialism will combine to make man's earthly condition as near like the lost Eden of the eastern poets, as is compatible with the growth and perfection of his nature.

Industry will be holy. The cultivation of the earth will be the worship of God. Workingmen will be priests, and as priests they will be reverenced, and as priests they will reverence themselves and feel that they must maintain themselves undefiled. He that ministers at the altar must be pure, will be said of the mechanic, the agriculturist, the common laborer, as well as of him who is technically called a priest.

The earth itself and the animals which inhabit it will be counted sacred. We shall study in them the manifestation of God's goodness, wisdom, and power, and be careful that we make of them none but a holy use.

Man's body will be deemed holy. It will be called the temple of the living God. As a temple it must not be desecrated. Men will beware of defiling it by sin, by any excessive or improper indulgence, as they would of defiling the temple or the altar consecrated to the service of God. Man will reverence himself too much, he will see too much of the holy in his nature ever to pervert it from the right line of truth and duty.

"In that day shall there be on the bells of the horses, HOLINESS UNTO THE LORD; and the pots in the Lord's house shall be as the bowls before the altar. Yea, every pot in Jerusalem and in Judah shall be Holiness unto the Lord of hosts" [Zech. 14:20-21]. The words of the prophet will be fulfilled. All things proceed from God and are therefore holy. Every duty, every act necessary to be done, every implement of industry, or thing contributing to human use or convenience, will be treated as holy. We shall recall even the reverence of the Indian for his bow and arrow, and by enlightening it with a divine philosophy preserve it.

"Pure religion, and undefiled before God and the Father is this, to visit the fatherless and the widows in their affliction, and to keep one's self unspotted from the world" [James 1:27]. Religious worship will not be the mere service of the sanctuary. The universe will be God's temple, and its service will be the doing of good to mankind, relieving suffering and promoting joy, virtue and well-being. By this, religion and morality will be united, and the service of God and the service of man become the same. Our faith in God will show itself by our good works to man. Our love to the Father, whom we have not seen, will be evinced by our love for our brother whom we have seen.

Church and state will become one. The state will be holy, and the church will be holy. Both will aim at the same thing, and the existence of one as separate from the other will not be needed. The church will not be then an outward visible power, coexisting with the state, sometimes controlling it and at other times controlled by it; but it will be within, a true spiritual—not spiritualistic—church, regulating the heart, conscience and the life.

And when this all takes place the glory of the Lord will be manifested unto the ends of the earth, and all flesh will see it and rejoice together. The time is yet distant before this will be fully realized. We are now realizing it in our theory. We assert the holiness of all things. This assertion becomes an idea, and ideas, if they are true, are omnipotent. As soon as humanity fully possesses this idea, it will lose no time in reducing it to practice. Men will conform their practice to it. They will become personally holy. Holiness will be written on all their thoughts, emotions and actions, on their whole lives. And then will Christ really be formed within, the hope of glory. He will be truly incarnated in universal humanity, and God and man will be one.

CHAPTER X. PROGRESS

The actual existence of evil, the effects of which are everywhere so visible, and apparently so deplorable, may seem to be a serious objection to the great doctrine of the atonement, that all things are essentially good and holy; but it will present little difficulty, if we consider that God designed us to be progressive beings, and that we can be progressive beings only on the condition that we be made less perfect than we may become, that we have our point of departure at a distance from our point of destination. We must begin in weakness and ignorance; and if we begin in weakness and ignorance we cannot fail to miss our way, or frequently to want strength to pursue it. To err in judgment or to come short in action will be our unavoidable lot, until we are instructed by experience and strengthened by exertion.

But this is no ground of complaint. We gain more than we lose by it. Had we without any agency of our own been made all that by a proper cultivation of our faculties we may become, we should have been much inferior to what we now are. We could have had no want, no desire, no good to seek, no end to gain, no destiny to achieve, no employment, and no motive to action. Our existence would have been aimless, silent and unvaried, given apparently for no purpose but to be dreamed away in an eternal and unbroken repose. Who could desire such an existence? Who would prefer it to the existence we now have, liable to error, sin and misery as it may be?

Constituted as we are, the way is more than the end, the acquisition more than the possession; but had we been made at once all that is promised us by our nature, these would have been nothing; we should indeed have had the end, the possession, but that would have been all. We should have been men without having first been children. Our earlier life, its trials and temptations, its failures and its successes, would never have existed. Would we willingly forego that earlier life? Dear to all men is the memory of childhood and youth; dear too is the recollection of their difficulties and dangers, their struggles with the world or with their own passions. We may regret, do regret, suffer remorse, that we did not put ourselves forth with more energy, that the enemy with which we had to contend was not more manfully met; but who of us is the craven to wish those difficulties and dangers had been less, or that the enemy's forces had been fewer and weaker?

God gave his richest gift when he gave the capacity for progress. This capacity is the chief glory of our nature, the brightest signature of its divine origin and the pledge of its immortality. The being which can make no farther progress, which has finished its work, achieved its destiny, attained its end, must die. Why should it live? How could it live? What would be its life? But man never attains his end; he never achieves his destiny; he never finishes his work; he has always something to do, some new acquisition to make, some new height of excellence to ascend, and therefore is he immortal. He cannot die, for his hour never comes. He is never ready. Who would then be deprived of his capacity for progress?

This capacity, though it be the occasion of error and sin, is that which makes us moral beings. Without it we could not be virtuous. A being that does not make himself, his own character, but is made, and made all he is or can be, has no free will, no liberty. He is a thing, not a person, and as incapable of merit or demerit as the sun or moon, earthquakes or volcanoes. As much superior as is a moral to a fatal action, a perfection wrought out in and by one's self to a perfection merely received, as much superior as is a person to a thing, albeit a glorious thing, so much do we gain by being made for progress, by having a capacity for virtue, notwithstanding it be also a capacity for sin, so much superior are we to what we should have been had we been created full grown men, with all our faculties perfected.

But moral evil, by the superintending care of Providence and the free will of man, is often if not always a means of aiding progress itself. The sinner is not so far from God as the merely innocent. He who has failed is farther onward than he who has not been tried. The consequences of error open our eyes to the truth; the consequences of transgression make us regret our departure from duty and try to return; the effort to return gives us the power to return. Thus does moral evil ever work its own destruction. Rightly viewed, it were seen to be no entity, no positive existence, but merely the absence of good, the void around and within us, and which by the enlargement of our being, we are continually filling up. It is not then a person, a thing, a being, and consequently can make nothing against the doctrine, which asserts the essential holiness of all things.

But men formerly supposed evil to be a substantial existence, as much of an entity as goodness. But then came the difficulty, whence could evil originate? It could not come from a good source, for good will not and cannot produce evil. But evil exists. Then all things do not come from the same source. One good and holy God has not made whatever is. There must be more gods than one. There must be an evil god to create evil, as well as a good God to create good. Hence the notion of two gods, or two classes of gods, one good and the other bad, which runs through all antiquity, and under the terms God and the devil, is reproduced even in the Christian church.

But this notion is easily shown to be unfounded. If one of the two gods depend on the other, then the other must be its cause, its creator. In this case, nothing would be gained. How could a good God create a bad one, or a bad god create a good one? If one does not depend on the other, then both are independent, each is sufficient for itself. A being that is sufficient for itself, that has the grounds of its existence within itself, must be absolute, almighty. There are then two absolutes, two almighties; but this is an absurdity, a contradiction in terms. This notion then must be abandoned. It was abandoned, and the evil was transferred to matter. But matter is either created or it is not. If it be created, then it is dependent, and that on which it is dependent is answerable for its properties. How could a good God have given it evil properties? If it be not created, then it is sufficient for itself; it has the grounds of its own existence within itself; it is then absolute, almighty, and the absurdity of two absolutes, of two almighties, is reproduced.

Still we need not wonder that men, who saw good and evil thickly strewn together up and down the earth, the tares everywhere choking the wheat, should have inferred the existence of two opposite and antagonist principles, as the cause of what they saw. Nor is it at all strange that men, who felt themselves restrained, hemmed in, by the material world, who carried about with them a material body forever importuning them with its wants and subjecting them to a thousand ills, should have looked upon matter as the cause of all the evil they saw, felt and endured. As things presented themselves to their observation they judged rightly. We may, by the aid of a revelation, which shines further into the darkness and spreads a clearer light around us and over the universe than any they had received, be able to correct their errors, and to perceive that the antagonism, in which they believed, has no existence in the world of reality; but we must beware how we censure them for the views they took. They saw what they could see with their light and from their position, and we can do no more. Future generations will have more favorable positions and a stronger and clearer light than we have, and they will be to us what we are to the generations which went before us. As we would escape the condemnation of our children, so should we refrain from condemning our fathers. They did their duty, let us do ours, serve our own generation without defaming that to which we owe our existence and all that we are. All things are holy, and all doctrines are sacred. All the productions of the ever-teeming brain of man, however fantastic or unsubstantial their forms, are but so many manifestations of humanity, and humanity is a manifestation of the Divinity. The Son of Man is the incarnate God. He who blasphemes the spirit with which he works and fulfils his mission in the flesh, blasphemes the Holy Ghost. Silent then be the tongue that would lisp, palsied the hand that would write the smallest censure upon humanity for any of the opinions it has expressed, however defective, however far from embracing the whole truth, future or more favored inquirers may find them. Humanity is holy, let the proudest kneel in reverence.

This doctrine of progress, not only accounts for the origin of evil and explains its difficulties, but it points out to us our duty. The duty of every being is to follow its destiny, to seek its end. Man's destiny is illimitable progress; his end is everlasting growth, enlargement of his being. Progress is the end for which he was made.[40] To this end, then, it is his duty to direct all his inquiries, all his systems of religion and philosophy, all his institutions of politics and society, all the productions of genius and taste, in one word all the modes of his activity.

This is his duty. Hitherto he has performed it, but blindly, without knowing and without admitting it. Humanity has but today, as it were, risen to self-consciousness, to a perception of its own capacity, to a glimpse of its inconceivably grand and holy destiny. Heretofore it has failed to recognize clearly its duty. It has advanced, but not designedly, not with foresight; it has done it instinctively, by the aid of the invisible but safe-guiding hand of its Father. Without knowing what it did, it has condemned progress, while it was progressing.

[40][Ed. By 1843, particularly in his articles on the "Mission of Jesus" in the *Christian World*, Brownson would begin to ask: what is the end of progress itself? Union with God would be his answer, but at this point in his life, as during his Universalist period, he was preoccupied with the idea of progress itself.]

It has stoned the prophets and reformers, even while it was itself reforming and uttering glorious prophecies of its future condition. But the time has now come for humanity to understand itself, to accept the law imposed upon it for its own good, to foresee its end and march with intention steadily towards it. Its future religion is the religion of progress. The true priests are those who can quicken in mankind a desire for progress, and urge them forward in the direction of the true, the good, the perfect.

CONCLUSION

Here I must close. I have uttered the words UNION and PROGRESS as the authentic creed of the new church, as designating the whole duty of man. Would they had been spoken in a clearer, a louder and a sweeter voice, that a response might be heard from the universal heart of humanity. But I have spoken as I could, and from a motive which I shall not blush to own either to myself or to him to whom all must render an account of all their thoughts, words, and deeds. I once had no faith in him, and I was to myself "a child without a sire."[41] I was alone in the world, my heart found no companionship, and my affections withered and died. But I have found him, and he is my father, and mankind are my brothers, and I can love and reverence.

Mankind are my brothers, they are brothers to one another. I would see them no longer mutually estranged. I labor to bring them together, and to make them feel and own that they are all made of one blood. Let them feel and own this, and they will love one another; they will be kindly affectioned one to another, and "the groans of this nether world will cease";[42] the spectacle of wrongs and outrages oppress our sight no more; tears be wiped from all eyes, and humanity pass from death to life, to life immortal, to the life of God, for God is love.

And this result, for which the wise and the good everywhere yearn and labor, will be obtained. I do not misread the age. I have not looked upon the world only out from the window of my closet; I have mingled in its busy scenes; I have rejoiced and wept with it; I have hoped and feared, and believed and doubted with it, and I am

[41][Ed. Brownson overstates the case here of his infidelity, as he did in his autobiography. In 1830, indeed, he did experience a period of skepticism and doubt, but existing evidence does not indicate that he ever lost faith in God. I am unable to identify the quotation, one which Brownson frequently used.]

[42][Ed. Unable to identify quotation.]

but what it has made me. I cannot misread it. It craves union. The heart of man is crying out for the heart of man. One and the same spirit is abroad, uttering the same voice in all languages. From all parts of the world voice answers to voice, and man responds to man. There is a universal language already in use. Men are beginning to understand one another, and their mutual understanding will beget mutual sympathy, and mutual sympathy will bind them together and to God.

And for progress too the whole world is struggling. Old institutions are examined, old opinions criticized, even the old church is laid bare to its very foundations, and its holy vestments and sacred symbols are exposed to the gaze of the multitude; new systems are proclaimed, new institutions elaborated, new ideas are sent abroad, new experiments are made, and the whole world seems intent on the means by which it may accomplish its destiny. The individual is struggling to become a greater and a better being. Everywhere there are men laboring to perfect governments and laws. The poor man is admitted to be human, and millions of voices are demanding that he be treated as a brother. All eyes and hearts are turned to education. The cultivation of the child's moral and spiritual nature becomes the worship of God. The priest rises to the educator, and the schoolroom is the temple in which he is to minister. There is progress; there will be progress. Humanity must go forward. Encouraging is the future. He, who takes his position on the "high table land" of humanity, and beholds with a prophet's gaze his brothers, so long separated, coming together, and arm in arm marching onward and upward towards the perfect, towards God, may hear celestial voices chanting a sweeter strain than that which announced to Judea's shepherds the birth of the Redeemer, and his heart full and overflowing, he may exclaim with old Simeon, "Lord, now lettest thou thy servant depart in peace, for mine eyes have seen thy salvation" [Luke 2:29-30].

8.

JOUFFROY'S CONTRIBUTIONS TO PHILOSOPHY[1]

Christian Examiner and Gospel Review 22
(May, 1837): 181-217

Before proceeding to a special examination of these very interesting and valuable volumes on the ground of moral obligation, we propose to offer a few remarks on philosophy in general, and on French Eclecticism in particular. We do this because both, in our estimation, are somewhat misapprehended, and, as a consequence of being misapprehended, they receive far too little or else a wrong kind of consideration.

We almost every day meet people by no means deficient in good sense and general information, who entertain strong prejudices against philosophy, and manifest no slight contempt for all philosophical pursuits. These people, in general, profess a great attachment to common sense, and count it a great piece of folly to look for anything superior to that. In their estimation, philosophy is mere speculation, and to philosophize is merely to construct, out of the phantasies of one's own brain, a various and ever-varying hypothesis on God, the human soul, and human duty and destiny; hypotheses which disdain the aid of fact and experience, and which, however pleasing they may be to the professed metaphysician, can answer no good purpose in practical life, and must ever vanish away before the first breath of common sense. They therefore regard philosophy as a vain pretense, as a worthless pursuit, and not only as worthless but mischievous, inasmuch as it consumes that time and thought which we need for other purposes. If they be right, we are most certainly wrong in filling up any portion of our pages with notices of philosophical works; and did we believe them right, we should by no means take the trouble to review philosophical works, or even to read them.

But, with all becoming modesty be it said, we do not believe that they are right. The conclusions appear to us to be drawn from false

[1][Ed. Review of *Cours de Droit Naturel*, by Theodore Simon Jouffroy. Premiere partie, Prolégomènes àu Droit Naturel, 2 vols. (Paris: 1834, 1835).]

premises. Their objections to philosophy are founded on mistaken views of what philosophy really is, of what is its legitimate province, and of what, in point of fact, it professes to be able to accomplish. Unless we have ourselves greatly misapprehended it, philosophy is something widely different from mere speculation. The true philosopher eschews all hypotheses as scrupulously as the good man eschews evil. He is far from doing business on credit, from speculating on merely fictitious capital; he must have facts, good substantial facts; and when his stock of facts is exhausted and he feels unable to increase it, he retires from business, and counts his work achieved. He does not undertake to manufacture the truth, nor does he profess to have any means of discovering it, which are not equally within the reach of every one who will but use the faculties which God has given him. Philosophy originates and can originate none of our ideas. It works and must work with materials which have been furnished without its aid, and which are furnished to the simplest ploughboy in equal quantity and variety as to the profoundest philosopher. The difference between the philosopher and the mere common sense man does not consist in the fact that the one has any means of knowing or any ideas which the other has not, but in the fact that the one does and the other does not know, does not comprehend what he knows. The common sense man knows as much of the nature of things, of God, the soul, man and man's destinies as the philosopher; but his knowledge is vague, obscure, confused, and independent of his control; whereas the philosopher's knowledge is clear, definite, precise, and entirely subject to his will.

This distinction is intelligible, and in our estimation very important. Men who find, when they want them, all the great truths needed for the chief practical purposes of life, and who, nevertheless, are not conscious of having ever philosophized at all, are not a little puzzled to discover the very great worth which the philosopher ascribes to his favorite pursuit; but we think their difficulties would be in a great measure removed, if they would observe the distinction we have here indicated, distinguish between knowing and comprehending, and learn that the province of philosophy is not to know, but to comprehend; not to give us knowledge, but to enable us to comprehend what we already know; to explain and verify what we have already received as true on the faith of common sense. We all believe that we exist. For this belief we are not indebted to philosophy. Philosophy can neither give it nor take it away. What then is the use of philosophy, in relation to this particular belief? Simply to enable us to comprehend what we do when we believe that we exist; what is involved in the fact that we believe in our existence. All the world, or nearly all the world, believe in God, in Immortality, and Duty, and believe too without the aid of philosophy. The first man who philosophized found the world believing in these, and these were the facts on which he first philosophized. What then in relation to these is the value of philosophy? Not to give us the idea of God, the idea of Immorality, and that of Duty, but to explain these ideas to the understanding, and to determine their worth. Common sense, if that be the term preferred, gives these ideas, places them in the consciousness; philosophy detects, explains, and verifies them.

To detect, explain, and verify our ideas, is no mean service. Under common sense we believe, and believe the truth; but we believe blindly, without knowing why or wherefore; without being able to justify our belief to ourselves. We take everything on trust. But as soon as our intellect is awakened, and we begin to think with some degree of earnestness, we can no longer be satisfied with taking things on trust; we can no longer repose in blind belief; a new want, an imperious want is developed within us, and we ask ourselves, why we have believed? Wherefore we have trusted? And what authority we have for believing what we find we have believed? All men may not, we admit, ask themselves these questions, for there are not a few who die children, though they die in old age; but many more ask them than we commonly imagine. There are thousands who pass along apparently unthinking, with unperturbed looks and careless speech, in whom these questions lie fermenting, or who call upon all nature, upon the seen and the unseen, upon the living and the dead, to answer them. There is more passing beneath those leathern bosoms which men seem to wear, in those secret chambers of thought into which no stranger enters, than we can easily divine. All who attain to self-consciousness ask themselves these questions; and when these questions have once been asked, when they have once been raised, they "will not down at the bidding."[2] Pleasure may distract, business may divert, authority may frighten us awhile from their consideration; but at the first moment of release, at the first moment of calmness and self-collectedness they return with all their primitive force and importune us for an answer. Is it a mean service to answer them? Worthless are his labors who helps us to silence their importunate clamor and to restore peace to the soul? Let him who has been tormented by this everlasting Why, and this ever-recurring Wherefore, which one of the most urgent wants of our nature never ceases, from

[2][Ed. Unable to identify quote.]

the first awakening of reason, to ask—let him answer. But to ask why? Wherefore? And to seek for an answer, is to philosophize. Philosophy is nothing more nor less than the answer which we obtain by reflection, to the Why and the Wherefore. Why then speak slightingly of it? Why condemn the philosopher? Wherefore attempt to dissuade from philosophizing? Would we doom our race to perpetual infancy, and forbid the sleep of the cradle ever to be broken? Would we place an interdict upon reflection, and oblige men forever to forego conviction, to know without comprehending, to believe without knowing why or wherefore? If not, we must have and cannot but have philosophy.

To answer the questions of the Why? And the Wherefore? Philosophers in their infancy framed hypotheses; and, ignorant as yet of the legitimate province of philosophy, and of the true method of philosophizing, they answered merely by guesses. They were unwilling to wait, to inquire. Their wants were too troublesome; their need of dogmatizing was too urgent to allow them to seek an answer by slow and scrupulous analysis. They wanted the patience to untie the knot, to unravel the mysteries of our being; and hence the failures of philosophy, and the reproaches with which she has been visited. But her real friends have profited by experience. They have grown wiser, and prefer research to dogma. They are willing to wait. They have learned that it is in vain to give hypothetical answers; in vain to create answers; and that their only proper method of proceeding is to seek by patient and accurate observation of the facts of consciousness, the answer which God himself has written with his own finger on the tablets of our being. They now know that their business is not to construct, but to reflect; and so long as they pursue the path of reflection, we are unable to perceive why the gravest common sense man should wish to impede their march. They do but bear the torch of reflection over the dark field of consciousness, and labor to enable us to see and comprehend the mysteries of our spiritual nature. They do only that which every one does to a greater or less extent who turns his mind in upon itself, communes with his own heart, and seeks to solve the problem of his being and destiny. Who is there that is willing to admit that he never does this, or at least that he never attempts to do this? No one, we will take it upon us to answer; that is, no one who has ever become conscious that he is an intellectual being. Let philosophy and philosophers then be acquitted; let philosophy no longer be confounded with mere speculation; and, above all, let the philosopher no longer be counted the synonym of the mere builder of castles in the air.

Similar objections to some of those we have been considering, we have occasionally heard alleged against French Eclecticism. We do not take notice of this fact because we would give in our adherence to that philosophy. To us all truth is sacred and desirable, and we are ready to own and obey it, let it come from what quarter and under what name it may; but we choose to see it for ourselves, and to accept and obey it because we ourselves are convinced by our own examination that it is the truth, not because it is the dogma, or the theory of a school. We do not hold ourselves responsible for the doctrines of the French Eclectics, nor do we propose them for the adoption of our countrymen. But we do place a high value on the labors of the French Eclectics, and we believe an acquaintance with their philosophical researches a very important acquisition in the work of elaborating a better philosophy than any which has hitherto obtained among us. We would, therefore, see their works studied, and studied without prejudice, for what they are, and not for what they are not. And this is our apology, if an apology be needed, for taxing the time and attention of our readers with some remarks designed to place French Eclecticism in its true light.

Many among us confound French Eclecticism with German Transcendentalism; and German Transcendentalism they suppose to be the very "fifth essence" of extravagance and absurdity.[3] They who thus confound the two philosophies seem to take it for granted that German Transcendentalism names a particular school, designates a special metaphysical doctrine. But this is a mistake. German Transcendentalism is a phrase of uncertain import. It may include systems which have hardly anything in common. As used by the Germans themselves it is nearly synonymous with the term metaphysics, and metaphysics, among the Germans, vary with almost every individual devoted to their pursuit. German philosophy has, in point of fact, no unity which authorizes us to predicate anything of it as a whole, unless it be its freedom and independence, and the fact that the reason, instead of the sensibility, is in all cases its point of departure. It is not just to condemn the whole because a part may be unsound; one man's views, because another's, which are different, are judged to be erroneous. For their freedom, for their bold and uniform assertion and maintenance of the independence of the reason,

[3][Ed. The "fifth essence" or quintessence means the most subtle extract of a body that can be procured. The ancient Greeks thought that there were four elements (water, earth, fire, and air) in which matter can exist. The Pythagoreans added a fifth that they called ether, which was more subtle and purer than the others.]

we respect the whole body of German metaphysicians, whatever the systems they may have severally arrived at, or supported; in this particular they cannot be praised too warmly; but we are not aware that any of them, nor that all of them, have as yet given us a true philosophy of man. They have contributed valuable materials for the construction of that philosophy; but that philosophy, or what we deem such, we have not found in any of their systems which have fallen under our notice. Kant, the ablest and soberest of them all, has unquestionably done much. He has explored the human understanding, and determined the conditions of all experience, or what must be the nature of the understanding to render experience possible. In doing this, he has created a new era in the history of metaphysical science; but he has not given us a philosophy; he has merely fixed the starting point, and opened the route for future philosophers. Fichte was a bold speculator, an ardent friend of freedom and humanity. For this last we honor him, and cherish his memory; but we have yet to learn the important service he has rendered to philosophy. Had he lived, he might have done something worth remembering, as he had before his death hit upon the path, which, if followed, conducts to true philosophy; but cut off as he was in the prime of his life, philosophy has gained little by his talents, genius, and labors. Jacobi had some dim visions, some vague presentiments of a superior philosophy, but he wanted the intellectual vigor to obtain results truly scientific. He did something, however, to open the way for Fries, from whom philosophy is receiving valuable contributions. Fries adopts the true psychological method of philosophizing and upholds the experimental against the hypothetical or constructive philosophy. Schelling, whose reputation as a philosopher will diminish with time, attempted a philosophy of man, and of nature; but both he and Hegel, who in respect to method agrees with him, have vitiated their labors by adopting the hypothetical or constructive instead of the psychological or experimental method of philosophizing; and notwithstanding they have, as we believe, divined the truth to a great extent, [and] in consequence of the original sin of their method, they have been unable to give it any scientific value. It is their vicious method which constitutes the real objection which may be urged against those German metaphysicians, who are, we suppose, generally understood by the Transcendentalists, and it is the only objection which we deem it necessary to bring against them. They build on hypothesis and construct a theory with which to explain facts, instead of observing facts as the only basis of all just theory. A theory, which is anything else than the true statement of what there is of the general in facts, as distinguished from the particular, has no value in our eyes. The facts should elicit the theory, and not the theory the facts. Some of the Germans reverse this maxim, and if they who do it are the ones, as we presume they are, intended by the Transcendentalists, we most certainly have no disposition to appear in their defense. But these are not the only ones who bear the name of Transcendentalist, for the term, instead of being restricted to these, is used in a much broader sense, so as to include those who adopt the psychological as well as those who adopt the hypothetical or constructive method, the philosophizers as well as the systematizers. Whenever, then, we speak of German Transcendentalists, we should be careful to discriminate, and let it be known of whom we intend to speak; and whenever we judge it to be our duty to condemn Transcendentalism, we should state distinctly whether we mean to condemn metaphysics in general, or only some special system of metaphysics; and, if this last be the case, as is most likely, what special system we mean.

It is desirable also, that this same discrimination should be made, when speaking of Transcendentalism as it is beginning to be manifested among ourselves, and some injustice has already been done in consequence of neglecting it. Men are classed together under the general term, Transcendentalist, who have scarcely anything in common but their fondness for philosophical pursuits. There are men among us who have a most hearty dislike for observation, who disregard experience, ask no aid of facts, and who deem themselves competent to construct a true philosophy of man and the universe by means of speculation alone. If they who condemn the Transcendentalists mean these; they are bound to say so; for there are others among us also called Transcendentalists, who adopt the psychological method, and pursue it with the most rigid fidelity, who will attach no scientific value to any metaphysical system, whatever its pretensions, which is not a legitimate induction from facts patiently collected, scrupulously analyzed, and accurately classed. These last are no more to be confounded with the first, than a modern chemist is to be confounded with an old alchymist, or a Bacon with a Paracelsus.[4]

[4][Ed. Paracelus is the pseudonym of Theophrastus Bombastus von Hohenheim (1493-1541), a Swiss chemist, physician, and natural philosopher. He insisted upon observation and experiment in medical practice, and drew on a combination of biblical sources, German mysticism, alchemy, and Neo-platonic magic to present a unified view of the universe and humankind. His views were an advance over the classical medical inheritance of Claudius Galen (c.130-200), the Greek physician and writer on medicine.]

If it be meant that the French Eclectics are Transcendentalists in the sense these last are, we have no objection to offer. But this is not the case. They, who call them Transcendentalist with the feeling that Transcendentalism is an accusation, mean to identify them with the other class, with the speculators, the systematizers, with those who profess to be able to arrive at truth by logic, by mere reasoning without observation or scientific data to reason from. But in this sense the Eclectics are not Transcendentalists. M. Cousin, their acknowledged chief, so far as they acknowledge any chief, bases his whole system, as we have shown when reviewing his philosophy,[5] on psychology. He does not, like Schelling and Hegel, commence by a construction. He tolerates no hypothesis, no divination, no guessing at truth, but iterates and reiterates that the only legitimate starting-point for the philosopher is the observation of facts. According to him, there is and there can be no sound philosophy which does not begin with the observation or analysis of the facts of consciousness. He does not begin by inquiring what ought to be in the consciousness, how what may be supposed to be in the consciousness entered there, but simply what is there, what are we conscious of in ourselves. The first question with him is always, What is? If from the question of what is, if from the observation of facts he passes to the induction of principles, of laws, it is because observation itself forces induction upon us, and we cannot avoid it, even if we would. We cannot remain in the observation of facts. We do never content ourselves with saying two and two, two and two, but always find ourselves obliged to say two and two are four. Facts taken singly never satisfy us; we are always compelled to add them together and find their sum total. Our right to do this may be questioned; it may be said that we have no authority for passing from the observation of facts to the induction of principles, of laws; but he who should say so would in the very act of saying so do that which he says we have no right to do. His assertion would be an induction, not a fact. One may have observed the extravagances and absurdities into which men have fallen in their inductions, and therefore *infer* that we ought never to attempt an induction; another may, from what he has observed of the power of the reason to rectify its own mistakes, to recover itself from its own aberrations, and of the miracles wrought by induction in the physical sciences, infer directly the opposite, and assert the legitimacy of induction; another still may assert that we are too ignorant to assert

[5][Ed. See "Cousin's *Philosophy*," *Christian Examiner and Gospel Review* 21 (September, 1836): 33-64.]

anything about the matter; but all alike make an induction, and the last not less than the other two, his induction being that we are too ignorant to know whether we have or have not the right to make an induction. Whoever will regard the facts of his own consciousness cannot fail to discover that, whether induction be or be not a legitimate exercise of the reason, be or be not warranted, we do always make an induction, and we cannot help doing it. It is a necessary mode of the activity of the reason, and altogether independent of our control. It is forced upon us by a power which we are not. We can make no assertion, whether of affirmation or denial, without making an induction. This necessity, under which we labor in regard to induction, is sufficient to justify induction in the minds of all who comprehend anything of the matter, and exonerates us from all blame in not struggling in vain to resist it. If this be admitted, as nobody questions the legitimacy of observation, we may assert that both observation and induction are legitimate. These two modes of activity of the reason, observation and induction, constitute M. Cousin's method. His method, then, is legitimate, and if legitimate, if faithfully followed, it must conduct to scientific results.

The method of philosophizing, which we adopt, is that which determines the character and value of the system of philosophy to which we arrive. All philosophers and all systems of philosophy are to be classed, in the first instance, according to their method. If their method be scientific, they cannot be without value; if their method be vicious, no matter how much talent and genius they display, they are worth nothing for science. It is their vicious or unscientific method, which prevents us from attaching any importance to the systems of philosophy of many who are called Transcendentalists both at home and abroad, notwithstanding they embosom no small share of truth. The truth they have has not been obtained on scientific principles. They have obtained it by a sort of divination or guess, as when a schoolboy we sometimes from sheer indolence used to guess out the answers to the questions given us in arithmetic. Our old schoolmaster always sent us back to first principles, and made us solve the problems scientifically, even when we had chanced to guess aright. But with the French Eclectics there is none of this guessing at truth. Their method of solving all philosophical problems is, as we have seen, strictly scientific. It is the experimental method, that of observation and induction. This method, though virtually the method of Descartes, is called the Baconian method. Bacon introduced it into modern philosophy, at least defended it, and applied it to the physical sciences. Locke applied it to the study of the Human Understanding, and applied it too with greater fidelity than any of his predecessors, and herein lies his merit as a philosopher. But his fidelity was not strict enough; almost at the first step he departed from his method, and hence the defects of his system as a system of philosophy. He was too eager to construct a system, and rushed into dogmatism before he had completed his observation, or psychological analysis. He did not remain long enough in the sphere of consciousness to become thoroughly acquainted with its phenomena. He spent too little time in ascertaining and describing the facts of consciousness as they actually appear in the consciousness, and passed too soon to the question of the origin of our knowledge, of our ideas. This was his fatal error, the rock on which he stranded. What reasonable hope could he have of giving a correct account of the origin of our ideas before he had determined what ideas we have? By going to the question of the origin of our ideas before he had settled the question of the number and character of our ideas, he departed from the path of science and fell into that of hypothesis, and dogmatized instead of philosophizing. This has destroyed the scientific value of his *Essay on Human Understanding* but it has not destroyed his merits as a man. Great as were his metaphysical errors, he deserves, and had they been ten times as great as they were, he would still have deserved the gratitude of posterity for his ardent love of humanity, his labors in the cause of civil liberty and Christian charity, and the much he has unquestionably done to simplify metaphysical science, and to abridge the labor of comprehending ourselves.

The French School of the last century adopted the same method, and was really, though but partially, experimental. So far forth as it was experimental, it was powerful, and deserves our respect. But it fell into the same fundamental error, which we have pointed out in its master, Locke. We say its master, Locke, for we suppose everybody, who knows anything about the matter, knows that the French philosophy, as expounded by Condillac and his disciples, was borrowed from Locke, and introduced into France by Voltaire. Condillac and his disciples drew conclusions from Locke's philosophy, which Locke himself did not draw, and which he would very likely have rejected; but they were all warranted by his premises, were but the legitimate consequences of the principles he laid down. Like him, the French School, instead of studying the facts of consciousness, and ascertaining what we know, ran against the question of how we know; and deciding after his example, *a priori*, that we know only by means of our five senses, it overlooked or denied in its subsequent psychological analysis all the facts of consciousness which it could not succeed in transforming into sensations. We say not this in a spirit of hostility to that school, nor out of any want of respect for its English master. It was a great school, it did some service to humanity; more, perhaps, than many, who depart less from it than we do, are willing to admit; but its early departure from the strictly psychological method proved its ruin, compelled it to be exclusive, and it has died as must die all exclusive systems, whether in philosophy or in theology.

Now nobody, we presume, ever dreams of calling this school or its founders, Locke and Condillac, Transcendental in the odious sense in which some are pleased to use that term; but why not? Why not call the old French School, Locke and Condillac, Transcendental, as well as M. Cousin? He bears a much closer affinity to them in a scientific relationship, than he does to those commonly understood by the Transcendentalists. His method is the same as theirs; and if he obtains different results it is because he applies it differently, because, as he would say, he follows it with more fidelity and severity, because he is more strictly experimental, a more rigid psychologist. They, by ascribing the origin of all our ideas to sensation, and allowing the understanding on materials on which to work but such as could come through the senses, necessarily condemned themselves to a mutilated psychology. They were restricted in their analysis to the facts of the sensibility; but M. Cousin, postponing the question of the origin of our ideas till he has ascertained what are our ideas, analyzes the whole consciousness, whether its elements be the sensibility, the activity, or the reason, and is thus enabled to form a psychology as broad as the human soul itself. This is what he professes to have done. Whether he has or has not done it, makes no part of our present inquiry. We do not undertake the defense of the results he professes to have obtained. We are concerned now only with his method, and that method we do contend is scientific, the only method which can lead to scientific results. Locke and the French School adopted it, but they applied it with systematic views, with the design to maintain a system previously adopted; he applies it without any reference to a system, before he forms his theory, and, therefore, is able to apply it without prejudice. This is his method, this is his profession. He indeed may not be true to his method, he may not practice what he professes, but that is a question which every one may and can decide for himself. By giving us his method he has enabled us to correct him where he errs, and to verify him where he is right. All we have to offer on this point is, that not every one who speculates a little on metaphysical subjects should feel himself qualified to sit in judgment on M. Cousin.

Whoever would do him justice should take up his method and bring to its test all the results he professes to have obtained. They who will do this will, we do not say, adopt all those results, but at least acquit him of being a bold theorizer, a fanciful constructer of hypotheses, a Transcendentalist in the sense in which they use the term who deem Transcendentalism an accusation. They will find him an eloquent, an enthusiastic preacher of philosophy, but at the same time a sober psychologist, a clear and able experimental philosopher. He has not, we own, this reputation among some of our friends; but we are at no loss to discover the reason why he has not. The eloquence and poetry of his style mislead many, who have imbibed the notion that whatever is warm and glowing, whatever is pleasing and inspiring, must be wanting in soberness and depth. His merits are also estimated among us principally by his Introduction to the History of Philosophy, and of that work not by its general spirit and method, but by some few of its generalizations or inductions, as the one on war for instance.[6] The method by which those generalizations or inductions are obtained, and by which their legitimacy may be determined, is, it is true, in the same volume; but to master that method and its application, and to bring the generalizations to its decision, requires some trouble, some hard thinking, some introspection, all of which are things an author must be very much out of his wits to ask of readers in this age of superficial writing and light reading.

It should also be borne in mind that French Eclecticism is not, as they who declaim against Transcendentalism would seem to infer, of German origin. Germany has indeed made many important contributions to it, but the movement of which it is a result was produced by the introduction and study in France of the works of Dr. Richard

[6][Ed. See the introduction to this volume for an analysis of Cousin's influence in the United States. In his *Introduction to the History of Philosophy* (Linberg's translation, 1832), 272-91, Cousin asserted the philosophical inevitability, necessity, utility, and historical importance of war as a means of reconciling conflicting ideas that had become incarnated in different peoples. For Brownson's opposition to this perspective, see "Wars must Cease—Cousin's Argument for Wars," *Boston Quarterly Review* 1 (April, 1838): 152-61.]

Price, and of the Scotch philosophers, Dr. Reid and Dugald Stewart.[7] French Eclecticism received its impulse, its method, and its direction from M. Royer Collard, who was, as everybody knows, a disciple of Dr. Reid, the founder of the Scotch School. M. Cousin was made professor of philosophy through the influence of M. Royer Collard, and his first year's instruction in the Normal School was confined to the defense and development of the Scotch philosophy. Up to this day he has continued in the path marked out by the Scotch School. He is the continuator of Dugald Stewart. He has gone beyond Stewart, but it has been in the same direction. It is true he has followed in that direction with a freer and a bolder step than comports with Scotch timidity and caution; but he has followed with a step as firm and secure as Dugald Stewart himself. This fact is often overlooked. We have not infrequently been amused to hear M. Cousin condemned by the very eulogists of Reid and Stewart, when he is, in point of fact, only their complement, and can claim to have done little else than to complete what they commenced, and to have furnished the means of verifying what they took for granted.[8] It is worthwhile also to notice

[7][Ed. Richard Price (1723-91) was a Welch dissenting minister and moral philosopher whose *A Review of the Principal Question in Morals* (1758) was particularly influential upon William Ellery Channing and Ralph Waldo Emerson, among other Unitarians. Price argued that an intuitive knowledge of moral truths is accompanied by feelings of approval and disapproval that are responsible for moral motivation. Thomas Reid (1710-96), philosopher at Aberdeen and then Glasgow, was the founder of the Scottish Common Sense tradition in philosophy. Reid asserted that human beings have common sense convictions that are accounted for by the power of innate faculties which have first principles that can be trusted. Dugald Stewart (1753-1828), a disciple of Reid and the Common Sense school, was a systematic philosopher at Edinburgh whose published works were used in American colleges after 1820 to replace Locke's *Essay on Human Understanding*, which had been used throughout much of the eighteenth and early nineteenth centuries. Both Reid and Stewart modified pure empiricism by their emphasis upon the intuitive powers of intelligence. Cousin and Brownson believed they were on the right philosophical path, but did not go far enough in the direction of Immanuel Kant in recognizing the *a priori* conditions of all knowledge.]

[8]Dugald Stewart, in the Preface to his "Philosophy of the Active and Moral Powers of Man," and in the very last paragraphs, we believe, which he wrote for publication, speaks as follows of the French philosophers mentioned above. "I cannot conclude this Preface without expressing the satisfaction I have felt in observing, among the more liberal writers in France, a reviving taste for the Philosophy of the Human Mind. To this no one has contributed more than M. Victor Cousin, so well known and so honorably distinguished, as the object of Jesuitical persecution; a persecution which appears to have followed him beyond the limits of his own country. To him the learned world is indebted, not only for his own very valuable writings, but for a French translation, accompanied with notes, of the whole works

that those old English writers, whom it is just now the fashion to praise, and we believe in some instances to read, had some anticipations of what the Eclectics have done, and relied for the worth of their conclusions on the very philosophy, more or less clearly seen by them, which we now call French Eclecticism.

We have spoken of M. Cousin; we have done this, because he is at the head of French Eclecticism, and because his method is that of all his disciples. We have spoken too of the Eclectics as a School; but in this we are not sure that we have done them justice. They seem to us to have too little of the spirit of system to be able to form a school. They are not exclusive enough for that. They cast free and impartial looks over all systems and schools, and expect and seem to themselves to find truth in them all, and truth they are ready and willing to receive, let it come whence it may, and whatever be the name or character it may bear; and this not because it makes for their theory, but because it is the truth. They are very indifferent as to theory, and their indifference in this respect, their subordination of theory to truth, to facts, or rather their habit of deducing their theory from

of Plato; for an edition of the works of Proclus, the Platonic philosopher, from a manuscript in the Royal Library of Paris, and, last of all, for a complete edition of the works of Descartes, a most important publication in the present state of science in France. M. Royer Collard, whose great talents have long been zealously devoted to the same pursuits, has, if I am not misinformed, already made considerable progress in a translation of Dr. Reid's *Essays on the Intellectual Powers of Man*, a report to which I give the more credit, from the account of his previous studies given by a most respectable writer, M. Jouffroy, in a work which appeared at Paris in 1826. And here I may be pardoned for gratifying a personal feeling, by mentioning the pleasure which I have lately received from a perusal of the very elegant translation, by M. Jouffroy, of my *Outlines of Moral Philosophy*, preceded by a long introduction, full of original and important matter. This publication, together with the space occupied in the *Fragmens Philosophiques* of M. Cousin, by large extracts from the same work, comprising nearly the whole of its contents, encourage me in the hope, that the volumes I now publish, which may be considered as a comment on the ethical part of my outlines, may perhaps, find a few who will not only read, but study them with attention, (for a cursory perusal is altogether useless) in some other countries as well as my own. *Kinneil House, April 16, 1828*." [Ed. References in the above texts are to the Scottish Common Sense philosopher Dugald Stewart's (1753-1828) *The Philosophy of the Active and Moral Powers of Man* (Edinburgh: Printed for Adam Black, 1828) and his *Outlines of Moral Philosophy; for the Use of Students in the University of Edinburgh* (Edinburgh: W. Creech, 1793). Thomas Reid's (1710-96) *Essays on the Intellectual Powers of Man* (Edinburgh: J. Bell, 1785) was translated in *Oeuvres complètes de Thomas Reid, chef de l'école écossaise, publiées par M. Th. Jouffroy, avec des fragments de M. Royer-Collard et une introduction de l'éditeur*, 6 vols. (Paris: V. Masson, 1828-36). Victor Cousin's *Fragmens philosophiques* (Paris: A. Sautelet and Company, 1826).]

facts, instead of constructing a theory with which to explain facts, has exposed them to a charge the very opposite of the one we have been considering. They are accused of having no theory, no system, no systematic unity; of jumbling together all systems and theories, according to their own caprice, without rule or measure. We have neither the time nor the room to answer this objection. All we can say is that though we have studied French Eclecticism with some attention, we have never felt it, and cannot conceive how any fair-minded man could have ever entertained it. In our judgment, French Eclecticism is not, as some allege, mere syncretism, but genuine Eclecticism. It recognizes a truth in all systems, and it selects from all, but not by caprice or at hazard. It has certain principles, according to which it does it. It is true, its friends do not seek for a systematic, a theoretic unity in philosophy, which is not to be found in human nature itself. They recognize more than one element in human nature, and they look for as many elements in philosophy as they find in human nature. Their method of proceeding is, in the first place, to form their psychology, that is, by observation and induction in the bosom of consciousness itself, to ascertain the number and character of the elements of human nature; these elements being ascertained, their second step is to bring to their test all the systems or schools furnished by the history of philosophy. Their psychology becomes, therefore, their measure of the true and the false in the systems and schools which they examine. Nobody can object to this method of proceeding. Philosophy, we all know, is a human creation, a manifestation of the human reason. It can then contain nothing which is not in the human consciousness. All systems and schools, then, must contain one element or more of the human consciousness. A study of systems of philosophy, a knowledge of their real elements becomes, therefore, a means of determining the elements of the human consciousness, and of course of verifying our psychology. This last method, the historical method, is also pursued by the Eclectics, and it is a scientific method; but the other, or the psychological method, holds the highest rank, and is always to precede the historical.

We trust we need make no apology for having detained our readers so long from the main object of this article. The work we have introduced to their notice is a philosophical work, and the production of one of the most distinguished of the French Eclectics, and we could not in good conscience have proceeded to review it, without having first said something to vindicate the general subject with which it is connected, and the particular philosophy to which it belongs.

We have also wished to throw out a few hints, which might be of some service to those young men among us, who are beginning to have a taste for philosophizing. The number of these young men is already far from being small, and it is every day increasing. It is of the very highest importance, that they at first adopt a truly scientific method. Method is to the philosopher what Demosthenes[9] declared action to be to the orator. Before one enters upon the broad field of speculation, he should have some tolerable notions of what it is, of its outlines, and some clear and definite directions as to the route he ought to pursue. Thousands have entered it, and thousands have been lost in it and thousands too of the very elect of mankind, because they fell at first into a wrong path, into one which compelled them to traverse it in perpetual circles, without ever being able to make the least advance. After having gone round and round a few times, their heads have grown dizzy, and they have found themselves unable to see anything distinctly, or any longer to recognize their point of departure. We have wished to do something to save others from their fate. If our remarks contribute anything to this end, they will not have been made in vain. With the educated among us blind belief is passing away, and it is even so with the uneducated, and everywhere is the young heart tormented with the questions of the Why, and the Wherefore. The young mind craves no longer authority, but conviction, and around, with eager eyes and anxious thoughts, does it look to find it. To the young man craving conviction we say, obtain a truly scientific method; understand that the field of its application is your own consciousness; the facts to be known and classed are the facts which every man carries about in himself, and if you have but a mind of tolerable sobriety and patience, and some little logical sequence of thought, you shall not fail to arrive at results consoling and nourishing to yourself and beneficial to humanity.

The work before us, as we have said, is the production of one of the most distinguished of the French Eclectics; and, we may add, of one of the ablest men of the age. Its author, M. Jouffroy, was first a pupil, then an assistant of M. Cousin in the Normal School, and is

[9][Ed. Demosthenes (384-322 B.C.), Athenian statesman and orator. It appears from this assertion and from other evidence throughout his writings that Brownson may have gained his knowledge of Demosthenes and other Greek classical authors from one of the many English translations of Plutarch's *Lives*, which were available to him in any number of editions from the 1820s and 1830s. On Demosthenes' view of action, see *Plutarch: The Lives of the Noble Grecians and Romans*, trans. John Dryden; revised Arthur Hugh Clough (New York: The Modern Library, 1932), 1028.]

now his successor in the chair of modern philosophy at the *Facultié des Lettres of Paris*. He is about forty years of age, and has already attained to a high reputation, both as a lecturer and as a philosophical writer. In 1826, he gave the French public a translation of Dugald Stewart's *Outlines of Moral Philosophy*, preceded by a very interesting and valuable Preface, in which he demonstrates the possibility of psychology, or of a science of the facts of consciousness, and makes an unanswerable plea for the moral sciences.[10] He collected and published in 1833 his *Melanges Philosophiques*,[11] an octavo volume of philosophical miscellanies, for the most part consisting of articles previously inserted in the *Globe* and other French periodicals, but of very great value to the student of philosophy and even to the general reader. He is remarkable for his soberness and little anxiety as to the systematic results to which he may be conducted. His object seems everywhere to be simply the interpretation of human nature. He seeks to analyze the facts of consciousness, not to obtain a system, but to obtain the truth. His style is not so animated, nor so poetical as that of M. Cousin, but it is strong, elevated, transparent, and is in fact one of the best specimens of style for philosophical disquisition with which it has been our lot to be acquainted. While reading him, he strikes us as less peculiarly French than most French writers with whom we meet; and the cast of his mind, and his combinations of thought, seem to us to have something of the Scotch character (though without anything of the Scotch timidity and shallowness), a fact, if it be one, which may, perhaps, be attributed to his long and profound study of the Scotch philosophy.

The two volumes before us comprise the first part of his course of lectures on natural right, which he commenced in 1833, and which is not yet completed. The whole course is to be divided into *five* parts, the second of which, under the title of *Morale Personelle*, is to include the system of duties which man owes to himself; the third part, under the title of *Droit Réel*, is to expose the principles of the conduct which man should observe towards things, or towards irrational creation; the fourth part, or *Morale Sociale*, will embrace the science of the rights and duties which result from men's relations to one another; and as these relations are various, it will be subdivided into several distinct parts; the fifth and last part, or *Religion Naturelle*,

[10][Ed. See Dugald Stewart's *Esquisses de philosophie morale*, trans. Théodore Jouffroy (Paris: A Johannean, 1826; 2nd ed., 1833).

[11][Ed. Théodore Simon Jouffroy (1796-1842), *Mélanges philosophiques* (Paris: Paulin, 1833).]

is to have for its object man's relations to his God, and the duties which spring from those relations. From this statement, it will at once be seen that M. Jouffroy takes the term natural right in its broadest acceptation, so as to include the whole range of man's duties; whether they be duties to himself, to things, to his like, or to God; and it will also be seen that his plan is so comprehensive, that it must take several years to complete his course. When his course is completed, his plan filled up, judging from the specimen before us, we think we hazard nothing in saying it will be one of the most valuable contributions ever made to moral science, to the philosophy of natural right.

But before proceeding to discuss our rights and duties, to ascertain the special enactments of natural legislation, there is a preliminary question of some importance to be disposed of; a question of no less magnitude than that of determining whether there be a natural right, any natural legislation at all. The idea of law, of rule, of duty, of right, implies that of obligation. To seek the laws, the rules of human conduct, man's rights and duties, is to seek what man ought and what he ought not to do; what it is his duty to do and to respect, and what he has the right to cause to be respected and done. But if there be for him nothing obligatory, if he be bound to nothing, and if others are bound to nothing in regard to him, then there are no rights and duties, no laws, no rules of human conduct to seek, no science of natural rights and duties to construct; the object of the science, the science itself escapes, disappears. Several philosophical systems, not without reputation in the world, have denied that there is anything binding upon man, that he is placed by nature under obligation to pursue one course of conduct rather than another. If these systems be correct, then it is perfectly idle to talk of natural right, of moral science, for morality must dwindle down to a few counsels or considerations of prudence. It is evident, therefore, that the first step for the moral philosopher is to determine whether there be anything obligatory upon man, anything he is naturally bound to do or not to do, the right to do or cause to be done. To this question the volumes before us are devoted, and they contain the solution which M. Jouffroy himself gives to it, and a critical review of the principal solutions which it has received from others.

Since we know the school to which M. Jouffroy belongs, since we know the method of that school, we know the method he will take to solve this momentous question. He will not begin by assuming that there is or that there is not something obligatory for man, and then seek for proofs of the position assumed; he will neither praise nor declaim against those who deny moral obligation; he will waste no time in appealing to our prejudices, in depicting the consequences which must inevitably follow from the position that man is not a moral being, and in deploring the wretched condition to which society would be sunk without morality; he will do nothing of all this; he will mingle with the question no considerations of what is desirable or undesirable, of what is useful or what is harmful; but proceeding on the conviction that truth is to be sought for its own sake, that it is alike truth, whether it meet men's wishes or cross them, and without offering any reasons why we should or why we should not believe there is something obligatory, he will enter into the consciousness, ascertain the moral facts of our nature, and thus determine whether moral obligation be or be not one of those facts. This is his method. He does not speculate, he does not reason; he inquires, he observes. He answers the question, not by balancing opposite arguments, and determining which are the weightiest, but by ascertaining what is the psychological fact. If moral obligation be a psychological fact, a fact of human nature, that is enough. Then there is moral obligation for man, there is a law which man is bound to obey, and the only question is, what is that law, and what are its enactments? In accordance with this method, he begins by giving us a brief statement of what he calls the *Moral Facts of Human Nature*. In making this statement of the moral facts, he gives us a summary of what may be considered his system on the point in question. To do him full justice with those of our readers who are unacquainted with the volumes under review, we ought to give this statement without any abbreviation; for as he himself has given it, it is as condensed as it well can be. But we are obliged, out of regard to the patience of our readers, to condense it still more; and if, in doing this, we render his system somewhat obscure, the obscurity must be charged to our account, and not to his; to the necessity we are under of giving indications of what his system is, rather than a development of it, and not to the system itself, which is perfectly intelligible to every man who can look steadily at the moral phenomena of his own nature. With these remarks we proceed to lay his system before our readers, with as much distinctness and detail as the space which remains to us will admit.

The idea of law implies that of duty; the idea of duty implies that of obligation; several systems of philosophy have said there is no obligation, and several other systems, though they have admitted moral obligation, have given such an account of it as greatly to impair its force. Before we can proceed to determine what is enjoined by natural law, or natural right, what is our duty, and what is the value of these philosophical systems, we must ascertain whether moral obligation be a fact of our nature, and if it be, what it is. Both questions, it must be obvious, are matters of fact and not of speculation, and are to be answered by simply observing or ascertaining what are the moral facts of human nature. We must, then, sit down and patiently examine these facts.

In his account of these facts, M. Jouffroy distinguishes the end for which man is made, the instinctive tendencies by which he aspires to that end, the faculties given him with which to attain it, the liberty or voluntary power by which he may govern his faculties, and the reason which furnishes him the motives of his conduct. He also distinguishes three different moral states in the development of human life, characterized by three different modes of determination. In the first, or primitive state, our actions are determined by our instinctive tendencies, passion; in the second, by regard to our own personal good, selfishness; in the third, by respect to the universal, absolute good, the good in itself.

The end of a being is determined by its nature. Every being has a nature peculiar to itself, and consequently a special end, to which its nature predetermines it. Did we know thoroughly the nature of a being we could deduce from it the destination or end of that being. The end of a being is what is meant by its good. The good of a being is to fulfil its destiny, to go to the end for which it has been organized. As each being has a special nature, and by virtue of that a special end, so has each one necessarily the faculties required for accomplishing it. It would be a contradiction to condemn a being by its very constitution to a certain end, and not to give it the faculties which are indispensable in attaining it; and an examination of the end imposed, and the faculties provided, will show that this is never the case. In being predetermined by its constitution to make honey, the bee has the instruments with which to make it.

It follows from these principles, that man, having a special nature, has a special end, the accomplishment of which is his good, and that being organized, fitted expressly for this end, he necessarily has the faculties which are requisite for accomplishing it.

As soon as man exists, and it is the same with all organized beings, and even with unorganized beings, though this is less apparent, as soon as man exists there take place within him certain movements, which, without any reflection or calculation on his part, bear him towards a certain number of particular ends, which, taken together, make up his total end. These instinctive movements, which occur in him as soon as he comes into the world, and which grow in intensity with his growth, M. Jouffroy calls the *primitive and instinctive Tendencies of Human Nature.* It is these tendencies, what they have in common in all men and particular in each individual, that Gall and the Phrenologists have sought to determine and to enumerate in an exact manner, by showing what variations they undergo in different individuals and in the same individual, and of which, we venture to say, they have given a tolerable account, though they have, improperly enough, called them faculties, and made them the sole determining mode of our actions through life. These tendencies have attracted the attention of a small number of philosophers, and although they have had some influence on their systems, they have not yet received the distinct consideration they deserve.

Simultaneously with the development of the instinctive tendencies which impel man to his end, his good, the faculties, which God has given him so that he may attain it, are also set in motion under the influence of these tendencies and seek to seize the objects towards which they bear him. As soon, then, as man exists, there are awakened within him on one part the tendencies which are the expression of his nature, and on the other, the faculties which have been given him in order that these tendencies may obtain satisfaction. This is not merely the beginning of human life, it is its very ground, and on this ground, which never changes, must be traced all the phenomena humanity presents.

M. Jouffroy believes that he has demonstrated in a previous course, that when these faculties are first developed it is in an indeterminate manner, and without any precise direction. What gives them a determinate and precise direction, is the fact, that they everywhere find obstacles, meet resistance in the pursuit of their objects, which compels them to concentrate their forces upon one point. Whenever they meet resistance, they bring together spontaneously all the forces which had before radiated in all directions, and make an effort to overcome it. If this world were the harmony of the forces of all the beings which compose it, and were the forces of all these beings, instead of contradicting, opposing one another, developed as harmonious and parallel forces, this would never occur. But the world is a vast assemblage of contradictions, where all destinations and the forces of all the beings of which it is composed are placed in opposition. Our faculties, therefore, cannot seize at once upon their objects. Their spontaneous, instinctive development does not suffice to obtain satisfaction for the tendencies of our nature. Man attains not his end without an effort, a conflict with hostile and opposing forces.

And even with it, with all the concentration of his forces and his mightiest effort, he never more than partially realizes it in this life. He never fulfils on earth the destiny appointed him by his nature, his organization. Hence the idea and the promise of another life, a life beyond this life.

When our faculties, by concentration, by an effort, succeed in obtaining satisfaction for our tendencies, in conquering for us a portion of the good to which our nature aspires, there is produced in us a phenomenon called *pleasure*, and when they fail, there is produced another phenomenon called *pain*. We must not confound these with good and evil. Good and evil are success or failure in the pursuit of the ends to which we are determined by the constitution of our being. Conceive man as having been made capable of acting, but not of feeling; he would, nevertheless, have had an end to accomplish, the accomplishment of which would be his good, and the non-accomplishment of which would be his evil; he would have tendencies aspiring to his end, faculties with which to obtain it, but he would feel no pleasure when he succeeded, no pain when he failed. We enjoy when we obtain satisfaction for our tendencies, and suffer when we fail, because we are not merely active beings, but also sensitive beings. Pleasure is a consequence, a sign of the realization of some portion of our good; pain the consequence, the sign of the privation of good; but pleasure is not the good, nor is pain the evil.

Inasmuch as we aspire to our good, enjoy when we obtain it, suffer when deprived of it, we love and seek all that which, though it be not itself our good, can aid us in procuring it, and dislike, entertain an aversion for whatever interposes an obstacle to its acquisition. When, therefore, our faculties, on being developed, meet objects which second or oppose their efforts, we experience for the first, sentiments of affection and love, and aversion and hatred for the other. This makes the tendencies, that is, the great, the real passions of our nature, to branch out and subdivide themselves, in going to the accomplishment of their end, into a multitude of particular tendencies, which may also be called passions, but only in a secondary sense. We must be careful to distinguish them from the others, the primitive passions, which are developed spontaneously, independently of all external objects, and which aspire to their end, even before reason has disclosed it. These secondary passions are produced only on the occasion of some external object, which aids or opposes the development of our primitive passions. Those objects, which second our primitive tendencies or passions, we qualify as *useful*; those which oppose them we qualify as *harmful.* Hence the origin of the secondary passions, and the ideas of useful and harmful.

Some of our primitive tendencies, as sympathy, are benevolent for others; some of them are not, as curiosity, or the desire to know, ambition, or the love of power. Consequently, even in childhood, while as yet all our tendencies are developed without any conscious reference to our own interest, there are some of our tendencies which have no other result than our own personal good. This, however, is not the case with sympathy; for that has for its result both our own good and that of others. It is always by our tendencies, never by virtue of reason—by sympathy, which, independently of all idea of duty, of all the calculations of interest, impels us to seek the good of others as its proper and ultimate end—that we are benevolent. The principle is personal, but the object to which it aspires is out of ourselves, the good of others. Man is, therefore, benevolent for others, even when he is governed solely by his instinctive movements.

The facts we have indicated constitute the primitive state of man, childhood, the period which elapses before the appearance of the reason. The reason, when it appears, effects two important changes in this state, from which result two other states, distinct from it and from each other. The characteristic of this primitive state, that which distinguishes it from every other, is the domination of passion. There is, undoubtedly, in the fact of the concentration of our faculties, induced by the resistance they find, the beginning of self-government, and of the direction of his faculties by the personal power or the will of the man himself; but this power, the will, is as yet blind, and wholly subject to the passions, which determine necessarily both the action and the direction of our faculties. It remains in this condition till reason appears. It is the reason alone that withdraws the will from the exclusive dominion of the passions. Till it appears, then, the present passion, and among present passions the strongest, bears away the will in its own direction, because the will can as yet have no foresight of evil. Hence the law of human determination, in this state, is the triumph of the present passion over the future passion, and among the present passions the triumph of the strongest passion. We pass now to examine the changes the presence of the reason produces in this state, which, be it remembered, is the state of childhood.

The reason, in its most simple definition, is the faculty of comprehending. We must distinguish this faculty from that of knowing. Animals know, but they do not appear to comprehend, and it is this which distinguishes them from man. If they could comprehend they would be like us, and instead of remaining all their life as they do in the state we have just described, they would rise successively, like man, to the two other states which the intervention of reason produces in us.

The reason, when first awakened in man, finds human nature in full development, all the tendencies in full play, and all the faculties in action. By virtue of its own nature, its power of comprehending it very soon penetrates the meaning of the spectacle it beholds. In the first place, it comprehends that all these tendencies, that all these faculties, aspire and go to one and the same end. This end is the satisfaction of human nature. The satisfaction of human nature is the sum, and, as it were, the resultant of all its tendencies. It is, then, its true end, its real good. It is this good to which it aspires by all its tendencies, and which it strives to gain by all the faculties it exerts. From this, the reason forms the general idea of *good*, and, though it be as yet only the idea of our individual good, it nevertheless marks no slight advance from that primitive state in which it did not and could not exist.

Observation and experience of what is perpetually passing within us show the reason that the complete satisfaction of human nature is impossible, that it is vain to pretend to anything more than a partial good, and, therefore, that we should aim only at the realization of our greatest possible good. By this the reason rises from the idea of our good to that of our greatest possible good, the greatest possible satisfaction of our nature. It very soon conceives that whatever contributes to this satisfaction is good on that account alone, and that whatever hinders it is evil. But it never confounds this double property, which it finds in objects with good and evil themselves; that is to say, with the satisfaction or non-satisfaction of human nature. It makes a fundamental distinction between good in itself, and the things proper to produce it, and generalizing the common property of things to produce good, it rises to the idea of *utility*. It distinguishes also this satisfaction or this non-satisfaction of human nature from the agreeable or disagreeable sensations which accompany it. Pleasure is never in its eyes the same thing as good or utility, nor is pain the same thing as evil, or as that which is harmful. As it had created the general idea of good and that of utility, it sums up whatever is common to all agreeable sensations, and creates the general idea of *happiness*. These three ideas, *good*, *utility*, *happiness*, the reason very soon deduces from the spectacle of human nature, and they are distinct in all languages, for all languages have been made by common sense, the most faithful expositor of the reason. As soon as the reason has conceived these ideas, man has the secret of what is passing within him. Before, he had it not. He had lived without comprehending it; now he understands it. These passions, he sees whence they come and whither they would go; these faculties, he knows how they are determined, and what purpose they serve; what he loves, what he hates, he knows why he loves, why he hates it; what of pleasure and pain he experiences, he knows wherefore he experiences it. All this is now clear to his understanding, and it is the reason that has made it so.

But the reason does not stop here. It comprehends also, that in the actual condition in which man is placed, dominion over oneself, the government of his faculties, or forces, by the man himself is the only means by which he can obtain the greatest possible satisfaction of his nature. So long as our faculties are under the dominion of the passions, they always obey the one, which, for the time being, is the dominant one. This has a double inconvenience. Nothing is more variable than passion. The domination of one passion is rapidly displaced by that of another, and one passion may reign this moment, another passion the next. Under the dominion of the passions, then, our faculties can have no sequence in their action, and must, therefore, be hindered from producing anything of value. The good, too, which results from the satisfaction of an actually dominant passion, may be the cause of a great evil, and the evil which would result from its non-satisfaction the principle of a great good. Consequently, nothing is less adapted to the production of our greatest possible good, than the subjection of our faculties to the passions. The reason is not slow in discovering this, and it concludes from it, that in order to obtain our greatest possible good, it would be better that the human force, the will, should not remain a prey to the mechanical impulse of the passions, that instead of being driven by that impulse to satisfy, at each instant, the actually dominant passion, it would be better to rescue it from that impulse, and direct it to the realization of a calculated interest, the interest of all our passions: that is, the greatest good of human nature. The reason, in conceiving this as something better, conceives it also as possible. It depends on us to calculate our interest. To do it, we have only to employ our reason. It depends on us also to gain possession of our faculties, and to employ them in the service of the idea which the reason has conceived. We have the power to do it. This has been revealed to us—at least, we have had a presentiment of it—in the spontaneous effort by which we concentrated all our forces upon a single point, in order to satisfy the demand of passion. What we have done heretofore spontaneously, we have only to do voluntarily now, and the power, the will, is created. This important revolution is no sooner conceived, than it is accomplished. A new principle of action springs up within us, interest well understood, a principle which is not a passion, but an idea, which does not proceed blind and instinctive from the tendencies of our nature, but descends clear and intelligent from the reflections of our reason—a principle, which is not a moving force *(mobile)* but a *motive*. The natural power, which we have of controlling our faculties, finding in this motive a point of support, becomes developed and strengthened. The will escapes from the inconsequent, variable, and stormy reign of the passions, and submits only to a law of the reason, which calculates the greatest possible satisfaction of our nature, our greatest good. Interest well understood, instead of those partial ends towards which our passions impelled us, is now the end to be sought; self-control is the means. The immediate dominion of the passions over our faculties, the characteristic of the primitive state, is broken. Between the power of the passions, and that of the faculties, now intervenes a third power, that of the reason and the will, the reason holding out an object to our conduct, and the will directing the faculties to its acquisition.

But we must not suppose that the will henceforth finds no support in the passions. Our nature, as we have seen, sends out its secondary passions for whatever seems capable of affording it satisfaction. It is *passionate* for utility. It believes this system of conduct, which the reason presents it under the character of interest well understood, is a useful system; it, therefore, approves it, loves it, and deviates from it only with regret. Through interest well understood passion is, therefore, led to support the will. Consequently, in this second state, there is a harmony between the instinctive and rational elements of human nature. But this harmony is far from being perfect. The idea of our greatest good, conceived by the reason, does by no means suppress our instinctive tendencies. They subsist, for they are imperishable. They develop themselves, they act, demand immediate satisfaction, the same as they did before the idea was conceived. They continue to strive, as in the primitive state, to carry away the faculties in pursuit of their immediate satisfaction, and they not infrequently succeed. If interest well understood finds sympathy in passion, it finds in it also a multitude of obstacles to be overcome. In this second state, then, the will is far from being wholly withdrawn from the immediate dominion of the passions. They are very often able, especially in weak minds, to disturb not a little the calculations of interest. In short, when the reason has appeared, when it has risen to the idea of interest rightly interpreted, a new moral state, a new mode of determination, is created; but it does not destroy the primitive mode, nor so completely supplant it that a return to it becomes impossible. Man floats between the two states, now going to the one and now to the other, now resisting the impulses of the passions and conforming himself to the counsels of interest, and now succumbing to those impulses, and leaving them to bear him whither they will; nevertheless, a new mode of determination is created within us and introduced into human life.

This new mode is the selfish mode. Selfishness consists in our knowingly and intentionally acting with sole reference to our own personal good. Our own good is the end we have distinctly in view, and we regard it as our ultimate end. Selfishness cannot occur in the primitive state. The child, in the beginning, is not selfish. In him the instinctive tendencies reign without a rival. These tendencies aspire, each to its end, as to its ultimate end. The child sees these ends, loves them, strives to attain them, but sees nothing beyond them. At bottom it is the satisfaction of his nature to which all his passions aspire, but he is not their accomplice. He is not therefore selfish, in the true acceptation of the word. He is as innocent as Psyche,[12] who loves without knowing love. Reason is in man the torch of Psyche. That alone reveals to him the ultimate end of his passions, and by revealing it substitutes a rational motive to his conduct for the varying impulses of passion, which he had previously obeyed. Reason is then the sole creator of selfishness.

But we have not yet reached the state which properly deserves to be called moral. We have proceeded as far as the selfish moralities ever proceed, but we have not proceeded far enough. We have not yet found an obligatory law, without which, as we have seen, there can be no morality. We have risen to the idea of good, but we are immeasurably below that of duty, of right, of obligation. The idea of good obtained is only that of our own personal good. With this the reason is not satisfied. The selfish mode of determination conceals a vicious circle. Selfishness calls the satisfaction of the tendencies of our nature good; but when asked why this is good, it gravely replies that it is good because it is the satisfaction of the tendencies of our nature. In vain is it that in order to come out of this vicious circle, it seeks, in the pleasure which follows the satisfaction of the tendencies of our nature, the proofs of the equation it attempts to establish be-

[12][Ed. In Greek and Roman mythology, Psyche is a maiden beloved by Cupid (Eros). After many tribulations caused by jealousy, because of her beauty, Psyche is united with her lover and is accorded a place among the gods as a personification of the soul. The tale of Cupid and Psyche is known only from *The Golden Ass* of Lucius Apuleius.]

tween this satisfaction and our good; the reason finds no more evidence in the equation of pleasure and good, than in the equation of the satisfaction of our nature and good, and the wherefore of this last equation is always a mystery to it. If we ask the selfish philosophers, why we are bound to perform a given action, they answer, because it will contribute to the satisfying of our nature; if we ask them why we are bound to contribute to the satisfying of our nature, they may answer, because that will yield us happiness; but if we proceed to ask, why are we bound to seek our own happiness, they have nothing to answer. We all feel that we are bound to consult the good, to obey the right; but how can we prove that the satisfaction of our nature is really a good, that to consult our own good is right? This is the problem which tortures the reason, and which it solves by revealing to us an absolute good, and our good as an element of it.

Escaping from the exclusive consideration of individual phenomena, the reason conceives that what passes in us, passes also in all possible creatures; that all, having their special nature by virtue of that, aspire to a special end, which is also their good; and that each one of these different ends is an element of a total ultimate end, which embraces them all. This end is that of creation itself, an end which is identical with universal order. The realization of this end, of universal order alone, in the eyes of reason, merits the title of good, alone answers to its idea of good, and alone forms with that idea a self-evident equation, which we have no need to prove. When the reason has risen to this conception, then, but only then, we have the idea of good. We had it not before. We had, by a confused sentiment, applied the term good to the satisfaction of our nature; but we were unable to give any account of that application, or to justify it. By the light of this discovery, that application becomes clear and legitimate. We perceive good, veritable good, good in itself, absolute good, to be the realization of the absolute end of creation; that is, universal order. The end of each element of creation, that is, the end of each being, is an element of this absolute end. Each being then aspires to this absolute end in aspiring to its individual end, and this universal aspiration is the universal life of creation. The good of each being is then a fragment of the absolute good, and it is by virtue of this fact that it is a good. It is from this source alone that it can derive this character. If the absolute good be honorable and sacred for the reason, the good of each being, the realization of the end of each being, the fulfilment of the destiny of each being, the development of the nature of each being, the satisfying of the tendencies of each being, all meaning one and the same thing, must also be sacred and venerable for the reason.

Now no sooner does the reason conceive this idea of order, of the ultimate end of creation itself, than there is between it and this idea a sympathy so profound, so true, so immediate, that it prostrates itself before it, acknowledges it sacred and obligatory, reverences it as its legitimate sovereign, honors and submits to it as to its natural and eternal law. To violate order is ever an indignity in the eyes of reason; to realize order, as far as it is given to our weakness, this is good, this is beautiful. A new motive of acting has now appeared, a new rule really a rule, a new law truly a law, a motive, rule, law, which bears in itself the warrant of its legitimacy, which obliges immediately, and which has no need of calling in anything foreign, anterior, or superior to itself to make itself reverenced and acknowledged.

To deny there is for us, beings endowed with reason, something holy, sacred, obligatory, is to deny either that the reason rises to the idea of the good in itself, the absolute good, universal order; or that, after having conceived this idea we do not bow down before it, and feel immediately and intimately that we have encountered our true law, a law which we had not encountered before, two things which it is impossible to mistake or to call in question.

This idea, this law, is luminous and fruitful. By showing us the end of each creature as an element of universal order, it clothes the end of each being, and the instinctive tendencies by which each being aspires to its end, with the same sacred and venerable character with which order itself is clothed. Before we had discovered this law we were determined to satisfy the tendencies of our nature by the very impulse of those tendencies themselves, or by the attraction of the pleasure which followed their satisfaction. The reason might judge that satisfaction convenient, useful, or agreeable, it might calculate the best means of obtaining it; but it could not decide that it was legitimate, an intrinsic good, whether it was or was not our duty to pursue it, our right to obtain it. Our right and duty to seek our own good begin only when our end is presented to us as an element of the absolute end of creation, our good as a fragment of the absolute good. That moment our good is clothed with legitimacy and absolute goodness. But not ours only. The good of each creature is at the same time and by the same title clothed with the same characters as our own. Before we had conceived that other creatures had tendencies to satisfy, that there was a good for them as well as for us, we might indeed, impelled by sympathy, instinctively desire their good, find pleasure in promoting it, and consequently make its production enter into the calculations of interest; but that it was legitimate in itself, that it should be sought for anything but for our own sake, that it ought to be as sacred and honorable in our eyes as our own, this our reason could neither discover nor even conceive. But the idea of the absolute good once conceived, what was not visible becomes apparent; the good of others being then shown to be an element of the absolute good, is shown to be a good by the same title as our own. To deny henceforth that we are bound to consult it, will be the same as to deny that we have any right to pursue ours. All difference between our right to pursue our own good and our duty to respect and contribute to the good of others loses itself, and is confounded in the bosom of the absolute good, which, being legitimate by itself, necessarily imparts legitimacy to all its elements.

All duty, all right, all morality flows from one and the same source, the idea of good in itself, the idea of universal order. Suppress this idea and there is nothing sacred for the reason, nothing obligatory, no moral difference in the ends to be pursued, in the actions to be performed, creation is unintelligible, and all notion of destiny an enigma. Reestablish this idea, and all in the universe and in man becomes transparent; there is an end for all and for each; there is a sacred order, which every being gifted with reason is bound to respect and labor to accomplish, both in himself and out of himself; there are duties and rights, there is a morality, consequently a natural legislation for human conduct.

The conception of the idea of order, of absolute good, of obligation as we have described it, introduces us into the third state, to a mode of determination altogether different from the two previous ones. The mode of determination in this state is not the impulse of passion, as in the primitive state, nor reference to our own personal welfare, as in the selfish state, but reference to order, to the intrinsically good. It is fundamentally distinct from the instinctive and selfish modes. It agrees with the selfish mode in this, that it is possible only in a being endowed with reason; but the lines by which it is separated from that mode are so broad and so characteristic, that they can hardly escape the observation of any one. As passion and selfishness may urge the performance of the same action, so indeed selfishness and the moral motive may prescribe in a multitude of cases the same conduct; but it is precisely in this coincidence that is most clearly seen the difference which distinguishes them. The selfish motive counsels, the moral motive obliges. The first sees only the greatest possible satisfaction of our nature, and is selfish even when it counsels the good of others; the second considers only what is intrinsically good, and remains disinterested even in prescribing our own good. In yielding to the counsels of selfishness, it is ourselves that we obey; in yielding to the moral motive, we submit to something which is not ourselves, and we submit to it simply because in our own eyes it is good. In this last case there is a devotedness to something besides ourselves; in the first there is not and cannot be. Now for a being to be devoted to that which he is not, and which he believes to be good, is precisely what is meant by virtue, by moral goodness. Virtue, moral goodness, can appear in us only in the third state, and is a phenomenon peculiar to the third mode of determination. We have moral goodness whenever we knowingly and with intention obey the law which is the rule of our conduct; moral evil whenever we knowingly and with design disobey it. This is the true definition of moral good and evil. But moral good and evil are wholly distinct from absolute good and evil themselves. Absolute good and evil are order and disorder. They are distinct too from that portion of absolute good and evil which we call the good and evil of man, and which consist in the satisfaction and non-satisfaction of the tendencies of his nature.

The difference between the moral mode of determination and the two other modes may be seen also in the phenomena which result from it. Among these phenomena there is one which is peculiar to the moral law. When we have voluntarily fulfilled the moral law, independently of the special pleasure received by our sensibility, we judge ourselves worthy of esteem and recompense; and in the opposite case we consider ourselves deserving blame and chastisement. This is what is called the pleasure of well-doing, and the pain or remorse of evil-doing. This judgment of merit or of demerit is necessarily a consequence of every moral action, and it can be a consequence of no other. When we have acted contrary to our interest, we may be out of humor with ourselves, may accuse our weakness or want of address; in the contrary case, we may laud our prudence, our wisdom, or our ability; but these phenomena are altogether distinct from moral approbation and disapprobation. We do not feel remorse for failing to be true to our interest; the most we feel is regret. Imprudence never excites our remorse, unless our interest has been identified with the absolute good, and then only when we believe that in neglecting our interest we have compromised the good. In this case it is the last consideration, not the first, that produces our remorse. It may be seen from this that M. Jouffroy does not condemn enlightened self-interest, but on the contrary that he legitimates it, and makes a duty of it. But it is not as our interest that he makes a duty of it, but simply as an element of universal order, as a fragment of the absolute good.

To complete the picture of the moral facts of human hature, so far as we can complete it in the space to which we are limited, two observations are wanting, which we proceed to adduce, and which we pray our readers, in justice to M. Jouffroy, not to overlook.

To what do the primitive tendencies of our nature aspire? The true end, the real good of our nature. To what tends our conduct, when directed by enlightened self-interest? The highest realization possible of our tendencies, the fullest possible accomplishment of our destiny, our end, our good. And what, when it makes its appearance, does the moral law prescribe? Respect for and the greatest possible realization of absolute good, or of order. But our good is an element of absolute good, of absolute order; the law of order then legitimates and imperatively prescribes the accomplishment of the very good, to which we are impelled by our nature and counseled by selfishness. It is true that it prescribes it without any reference to us, with a view to order, to the good in itself; it is true that it prescribes not our good only, but also that of all other beings; but our nature on the one side instinctively aspires to the good of others, and on the other side selfishness shows us that the pleasures which flow from beauty and benevolence are two of the greatest elements of our happiness, and that order in our conduct and respect for the rights and well-being of others are among the very best calculations of interest. There is then no contradiction, but a harmony between the primitive tendencies of our nature, interest properly understood and the moral law. They all point in the same direction, to the same end. The moral motive does not then come for the purpose of destroying the other two, but to explain and control them. Indeed, how could man conduct himself aright, if he were condemned to those absolute struggles imagined by philosophers, if it were necessary in the name of the obligatory principle conceived by our reason to sacrifice continually in order to be virtuous both the impulses of instinct, by which our nature is driven, and the counsels of prudence, by which it is engaged, to pursue its good? Nobody would be virtuous if virtue were possible only on such conditions. Certainly the ends of passion and selfishness differ from that of virtue; but so far from being contradictory or opposed to it, they coincide with it; and hence is it that there is not a virtue which does not find an auxiliary in passion and in interest properly understood. Hence is it also that in a great variety of cases we conduct ourselves by instinct, or by selfishness, precisely as we should were we to obey the moral law. Thus does the child, thus do the greater part of mankind, and it is by virtue of this agreement that society subsists. If all acts which are not done in view of duty were on that account alone contrary to the moral law and hostile to order, society could not merely not subsist, but it could not even be formed. It is necessary then to renounce these false notions, and see things as they are. Struggles we undoubtedly have and must have. Passion will sometimes oppose prudence, and prudence will sometimes counsel disobedience to right; but it will only be because passion is blind, and prudence not clear-sighted. For at the bottom of things it is ordinarily the greatest interest of passion to be sacrificed to prudence, and the greatest interest of prudence to be sacrificed to order.

We have spoken thus far of the three states which we have distinguished in man, as though they appertained to three wholly distinct epochs in human life. This is not exactly true. Neither of the three modes of determination we have pointed out in making its appearance abolishes the one which preceded it; it merely adds to it; so that when once produced the three modes henceforth coexist in human life. As to the order of their appearance, it is certain that the instinctive mode chronologically precedes the two others; but it would be difficult to affirm a similar succession from the selfish to the moral state. Although the reason appears very early, nobody will maintain that it rises at once to the sublime conception of order which is the moral law. Moreover, and everybody knows it, in a large portion of mankind the sublime conception of the moral law never receives a precise formula. Is it necessary to conclude from this that there is no morality till a certain age, and that there is never any in the majority of men? Not at all. We must distinguish two things, the confused view and the clear view of the moral law. A confused view of the moral law is contemporaneous with the first appearance of the reason; it is one of the reason's first conceptions; and with the majority of men this obscure conception remains through life, and is never transformed into a clear idea. What is called conscience is nothing else than this confused or obscure idea of order, and hence it is that its effects resemble less those of a conception of the reason than those of an *instinct* or a *sense*. Its judgments do not seem to be derived from general principles, which it applies to particular cases; they seem rather to result from a sort of tact, which in each particular case enables it to feel what is good and what is evil. But the obligatory character of good and evil is not affected by this dimness of perception. However confusedly conscience may perceive it, it always presents the good as that which we ought to do, and the evil as that which we ought to avoid; and we feel for obeying or disobeying it as lively approbation or remorse, as we should had we obeyed or disobeyed a more elevated and clear conception of the moral law. Thus conscience, or this confused view of order, is sufficient to make men virtuous and vicious, criminals and heroes. And still he who conceives clearly this moral law, and the sacred obligation it imposes, is much more culpable for violating it, than he who has only a confused conception of it, for he violates it with a clearer understanding of what he does, he sins against greater light. It is not without reason then that human laws make distinctions among the guilty, and mete out severer or less severe punishments, according as they judge their understandings to have been more or less developed, and consequently as they are supposed to have a more or less clear knowledge of good and evil.

These details show us that as soon as the reason appears it introduces at once the moral motive and the selfish motive, and that therefore these two modes of determination, which have been separated in the description, are very nearly, if not quite contemporaneous. The development of the reason does not abolish the instinctive mode which reigns exclusively in childhood; thus after its development man's life is a perpetual alternation between the three states, a perpetual passage from one to the other, as passion, interest, or the moral law by turns controls the will and presides over its determinations. No life is exempt from this alternation. What distinguishes men is the nature of the motive which most frequently triumphs. Some habitually obey passion, they are *passionate* men; others interest, they are selfish men; others in fine the moral motive, they are virtuous. As one or the other of these modes of determinations predominate, such or such is the character of the man. No one obeys exclusively and constantly either of the three; however powerful and habitual the predominance of the one, the other two always preside over some of our determinations. Moreover in the majority of cases the three, by virtue of the harmony which at bottom unites them, concur and act together, and probably there are few human actions which can be referred exclusively to either alone. Thus man is never wholly virtuous, wholly selfish, or wholly a creature of passion. With that one of these moving forces, which seems to determine him, there is always mingled more or less of the secret impulse of the two others.

Such is the picture of the moral facts of human nature according to M. Jouffroy, as faithfully as we have been able in the space allotted us to present it. We may not have seized his exact meaning in all cases, and in some cases where we have ourselves seized it, we may have failed to impart it to our readers. Discussions of this nature are always attended with difficulty. Not that the moral facts of our nature cannot be seized as well as any other, are not, if we may so speak, as tangible as those of physiology; but they are less studied, and the faculties requisite for observing them are less exercised than those requisite for observing the facts of the body. Our psychological language too is vague, and not yet settled. We are obliged to use popular terms; but in using them we give them a definite and precise sense which they have not in popular usage, and which to the general reader will often seem unwarranted. But enough of this. We have no wish to exalt our merit by magnifying the difficulty of our task. Everybody, who has attempted to discourse metaphysics to those who are not somewhat acquainted with metaphysical thought, will censure us but lightly, even if we seem to many of our readers dark and unintelligible.

We might offer very easily some reflections on the system of morality of which we have here given the outlines, and reflections which might not be without interest to our readers, but we have trespassed too long already upon their patience. They will find, if we mistake not, though in some instances he may appear to be open to criticism, that M. Jouffroy throws a clear and cheering light on many dark passages of moral philosophy, and enables us to settle to our satisfaction several important questions, on which philosophers have long disputed, and divided and subdivided into schools and sections of schools, much to the grief of the friends of philosophic truth, and to the amusement of the eulogizers of common sense.

We hope in a future number to be able to recur to these volumes, and give our readers some account of the criticisms on different ethical doctrines which they furnish us, and which, if not of the highest value, are at least intensely interesting to the moral philosopher.

9.

PHENOMENA OF CONSCIOUSNESS

A Discussion on the Question, *Can all the Phenomena of Consciousness be traced back to Sensation?*[1]

Boston Investigator 7 (April 7, 1837): 2

Mr. Kneeland[2] must permit me to thank him for his liberality in allowing me to enter his columns to controvert what he considers the truth. Such liberality is as honorable as it is rare. Were it more common, controversy would lose much of its acerbity, and the progress of truth be accelerated.

The question to be discussed is one of grave import. It is, in point of fact, the question on which now turns the whole controversy between the advocates of religion and their opponents. If the answer Mr. Kneeland gives it, be the true one, it is perfectly idle to talk of religion, of God, duty or immortality. Whatever transcends the reach of the senses is and forever must be to us as though it were not. Christendom must essentially modify its creed; thought and exertion must seek out new channels, and receive new ends and aims. The question, then, is surely worth examining. It is not a matter of idle curiosity to enquire whether Mr. Kneeland's answer be or be not the true one.

But we must answer this question without any reference to the consequences which may result from the answer adopted. Truth is truth whatever may be its consequences; and we gain nothing by denying or refusing to see it. This, too, is a philosophical question, and as such, it is not to be solved by appeals to fear or hope, by declamation, by tradition, by the authority of names, by personal reproach or commendation, nor even by personal allusion. The combatants themselves must stand aside, and let reason gain the victory.

[1][Ed. This essay was not listed in my *Orestes A. Brownson: A Bibliography, 1826-1876* (Milwaukee: Marquette University Press, 1997).]

[2][Ed. Abner Kneeland (1774-1844) was at the time of this debate the editor of the *Boston Investigator*. Brownson had known of Kneeland since 1829 when Kneeland was excommunicated from the Universalist Church, an excommunication that Brownson considered unjustified. On this, see the introduction to EW, 1:18, 27.]

Passion must be calm, and prejudice must hold her voice. Witticism, logical or rhetorical artifice, evasion, equivocation, subterfuge—none of these things can be of any avail. The question needs to be met fairly and honestly, with an eye single to the discovery of the truth; with the docility of the child, but with the reasoning strength of the man.

The question relates to the origin of our ideas; and the discussion which is to ensue, is designed to determine whether we have or have not any other source of ideas than that of sensation or sensibility. Mr. Kneeland affirms that we can know only by means of our senses, and that there are no phenomena in the consciousness which are not the products of sensation. He admits, if I have rightly learned his views, a sort of sixth sense or faculty, by means of which we take cognizance of our internal phenomena; but he contends that this faculty or sense is a result of the combined action of the five senses, or at least is in some way or other a creation of the five senses, so that in the last analysis we know only by means of sensation. I believe I state his views correctly, when I say he affirms that there can be nothing in the consciousness which has not been previously in the senses, and which has not entered the consciousness through the gate of sensation. Is he right? Is it true that there are no phenomena of consciousness which are not the products of sensation?

Before answering this question, we must ascertain what are the phenomena of consciousness. We must determine what is really in the consciousness before we can determine the means by which it found its way there. We cannot undertake to decide on the origin of our ideas, before we know what are our ideas, without danger of falling into grievous mistakes. We may assert that sensation is our only source of ideas, and then deny that we have this or that idea, because it could not have been furnished by the senses; but this will avail nothing, if upon examination it be ascertained that we really have this or that idea which it is said we cannot have. Hypothesis cannot withstand facts. The only true method of philosophizing is to eschew all hypotheses on the origin of our ideas and enquire simply what are our ideas.

But let this matter be fairly understood. We have not finished our work when we have proved that this or that is a fact or phenomenon of consciousness. It is still necessary to determine its value. The simple fact that an idea is in the consciousness is not a proof that it has anything in the world of reality to respond to it. The question concerning the ground of human knowledge, subdivides itself into three other questions: 1. What are the facts or phenomena of consciousness? 2. What is their origin? 3. What is their value? We have not verified what we call our knowledge until we have answered all three of these questions. But the first question must take precedence in our enquiry. It must be answered before the other two can be. I therefore begin with the question, What are the phenomena of consciousness?

I do not propose to give an exact enumeration of the phenomena of consciousness. To do that I should need more time and space than I have at my command; besides, it is not necessary to the design of this discussion. It is enough for my present purpose to adduce a single phenomenon of consciousness which must have its origin in something else than sensation. A phenomenon of this description I proceed to adduce. From several equally as good which I might adduce, I select the notion, idea or conception, which all men have, and which is expressed by the word *cause*. This idea, conception or notion, is unquestionably a phenomenon of consciousness. What is its precise character? I will try to describe it, not indeed as it exists in the world of reality, but as it really exists in the world within us.

I am now writing. I see my pen move. I am convinced that I move it. I believe I am the *cause* of the motion of my pen. When for a long time I have seen two events occurring in the relation of invariable antecedent and consequent, I call the first the *cause* of the second. But what is meant[3] by this word *cause*? What is the fact of consciousness which it names? Certainly I mean, and everybody means, by the word cause, a productive force, a power which produces something. Everybody means by cause something more than mere antecedence. When I believe my will is the cause of the motion of my pen, I certainly believe that my will does more than simply precede that motion. I believe it produces that motion. When one thing is said to be the cause of another, something more is most certainly meant than that one thing merely precedes another in the order of time. We always believe the cause is that which really produces what we term its effect. This is the notion of cause as it exists in the consciousness. Now, do or can our senses give us this notion of cause? Mr. Kneeland will bear in mind that I do not now enquire the value of this notion, that I do not say that there is out of the consciousness any causality to answer to this notion, and to justify it.

[3][Ed. Kneeland, the editor, changed Brownson's original "meant" to "meaned," and Brownson protested the change in *Boston Investigator* 7 (April 14, 1837): 2. "P S.—In my former communication I observe the past tense of the verb to *mean* is printed in all cases where it occurs, mean*ed*. This is not as I wrote it, and is contrary to good usage. I pray the Editor not to force me to make all irregular verbs regular."]

That is a question which will come up in its place. I now merely state the fact as it exists in the consciousness and ask if the senses could have placed it in the consciousness.

It is admitted or contended, I believe, by all philosophers, that our sense cannot give us a notion of cause in the sense in which I have defined it. The senses can give us no other notion of cause than that of antecedence. You tell me the appearance of the sun is the cause of light; but all I know by my senses is that the appearance of the sun is followed by light. I put my hand in the fire; it is burned, and I feel the smart. These three phenomena are all that my senses give me. They can disclose to me not secret power in the fire which *causes* the burning and the smarting I feel. They merely show the putting of the hand into the fire as the antecedent of the burning, and the burning as the antecedent of the smarting. A musket ball is discharged; a man falls dead. I hear the report, I see where the ball has passed through the heart of the man who has fallen. Can my senses give me any assurance of any other connection between the discharge of the musket ball and the man's death than that of simple antecedence and consequence? Can they assure me that the passage of the ball through the man's heart has caused his death? I think they cannot. The senses can give us only what they can themselves discover. They can furnish us with ideas only of that of which they can take cognizance. The secret connection supposed they do not see. Moreover, they can present us no fact from which we can *infer* it. Because such and such phenomena have followed such and such other phenomena, I demand what right have I to infer that the last have produced the first, and that there is such a connection between them that when I see the first I have a right to infer that the last have been, or that when I see the last I have a right to infer that the first will be?

I repeat it, then, that our senses do not give us the notion of the cause in question. They can only show us certain things, events, or phenomena, in certain relations in time and space. The occult power by which one thing produces another, if any such power there be, wholly transcends their reach. If we have no other source of ideas than our senses, we must deny all causality, or at least say with Brown, that we have no conception of any causality but that of invariable antecedence.[4] I need not dwell upon this point. Miss Frances Wright,

[4][Ed. Thomas Brown (1778-1820) was a Scottish Common Sense philosopher who followed Thomas Reid's emphasis upon intuitive truths, but was critical of Reid's lack of philosophical analysis. Brown was widely read in the United States, especially his *A Treatise on the Philosophy of the Human Mind, being Lectures of the Late Thomas Brown,* abridged by Levi Hedge (Cambridge: Hilliard and Brown,

in one of the chapters of her Few Days in Athens, has shown, beyond the possibility of cavil, that our senses can give us no other idea of cause and effect than that of invariable antecedence and consequence.[5]

But this notion of causality, as furnished by the senses, is very different from that which we find by observation in the consciousness. When it is said that priestcraft and superstition have been the causes of incalculable mischief to mankind, most assuredly something more is meant than that priestcraft and superstition merely *preceded* those mischiefs. When we say a severe contusion on one's head has been caused by a blow from an angry fellow, we mean more than that the blow was the simple antecedent of the contusion. When the philanthropic reformer demands the promulgation of truth as the means of regenerating mankind, he certainly believes that truth is to be something more than the forerunner of that regeneration. But the notion of this *something* more, which is unquestionably a fact of consciousness, cannot be given by the senses, for they cannot observe it. Then the senses are not the sole origin of the facts of consciousness. There is at least one fact or phenomenon of consciousness which is not and cannot be a product of sensation. Mr. Kneeland will probably either admit that I am right, or show wherein I am wrong.[6]

NO. 2. 7 (April 14, 1837): 2

Mr. Kneeland says that "the word cause no more expresses a conscious idea, or a phenomenon of consciousness, when applied to inanimate things, or when applied to other animals except ourselves, than any other word which might be named."[7] That is, if I rightly apprehend him, causes, so far as the external world is concerned are

1827) and his *Inquiry into the Relation of Cause and Effect*, third edition, (Edinburgh: A Constable, 1818). On his influence in the United States, see Terence Martin, *The Instructed Vision* (Bloomington, Ind.: Indiana University Press, 1961).]

[5][Ed. Frances Wright's [D'Arusmont] (1795-1852) *A Few Days in Athens* (London: Longman, Hurit, Rees, Orme, and Brown, 1822) was a fictitious account of the discovery of a long lost letter that was a defense of Epicureanism. In the fictitious piece Wright outlines her view that knowledge of cause and effect was not available through the senses.]

[6]P. S. Mr. Kneeland will please pardon the length of this communication, which some necessary preliminary remarks have swelled beyond the limits I had prescribed myself. I have studied to be brief as I could without leaving my argument unintelligible. Trust me, that I will do my best to avoid all undue prolixity. [Ed. Kneeland responded to each one of Brownson's essays. Those responses were printed immediately after Brownson's articles.]

[7][Ed. This was part of Kneeland's first response to Brownson's first article in *Boston Investigator* 7 (April 7, 1837): 2.]

not in us but in the external world itself. In this he is undoubtedly correct.

The causes which are at work in the world round and about me are not phenomena of my consciousness. They are facts existing beyond or out of the sphere of consciousness. It was not the *causes* themselves, as Mr. Kneeland supposes, that I alleged to be facts or phenomena of consciousness; but the *notion*, idea or conception of cause or causality. At least, such was my intention. All notions, ideas or conceptions are phenomena of consciousness. If, then, we have in our mind [a] notion, idea or conception of cause or causality, it—the notion, idea or conception—is a phenomenon of consciousness.

Have we a notion, idea or conception of causality? What is the notion we really have? What is its origin?

1. That we have a notion of causality, few I presume will deny. We all think and speak of causes, causality and causation. What we think and say may be very foolish, or very false, but we think and say something. No man can look into himself and not detect the notion in question. Individual causes may be various; but every man conceives more or less clearly of something which must be common to all causes, so far forth as they are causes, and without which they would not be causes. This *something* we call causality. The conception of this is what I mean by the idea, or notion of cause or causality. And it is this conception—not that of which it is a conception—that I alleged to be a phenomenon of consciousness. Mr. Kneeland, in his reply, says nothing against this allegation; whether because he agrees with me in this respect, or whether because he supposed I was speaking of *causes* themselves, and not of the *notion* of causality, I shall not attempt to decide.

2. But what is this notion, idea or conception? I do not ask what is a cause, what it is to be a cause, what causality is in itself? But what is the notion, idea or conception which we have of causality? What do we conceive to be the common property of all causes, that without which they would not and could not be causes? This question evidently relates—not to causes as they may exist in the world of reality, but simply to the notion of causality as it—the notion—exists in the consciousness. Every man believes—rightly or not is not now the question—that the common property of all causes, that without which they would not and could not be causes, is the power of causing, creating or producing effects. This is the notion of causality which we have. It is very different from the notion of simple antecedence with which it is sometimes confounded. To avoid all occasion of being misunderstood, I repeat it, the notion of causality,

as it—the notion—exists in the human consciousness, is *the notion of a creative or productive power or force*. To prove that this notion is entertained, that it is a phenomenon of consciousness, and to illustrate its character, reference was made in my former communication to the motion of my pen in writing. That reference was not made, as Mr. Kneeland in his reply seems to have supposed, for the purpose of indicating the *origin* of our notion of causality, but to establish the fact that the notion of causality is a phenomenon of consciousness, and that we do always conceive a cause to be a creative or productive force or power, and not a mere antecedent. These two facts, or alleged facts, which it was the main purpose of my communication to set forth, seem not to have arrested Mr. Kneeland's attention. He does not take the slightest notice of them; not, however, I am sure, because he deems them unworthy of notice, but probably because I failed to set them forth in the clear and prominent light which was requisite.

That the notion of causality is a phenomenon of consciousness, Mr. Kneeland does not deny; and that we always conceive a cause to be a creative, a productive force, I think the facts I adduced sufficiently prove. Mr. Kneeland does not pretend that they are insufficient. He does not deny that we conceive of a cause under the character I stated, but in point of fact he even assumes that we do. It is true, he denies that my *will* is the cause of the motion of my pen in writing, as I asserted; but he does not deny the causative force for which I contended. All he does is merely to transfer it from my will to my fingers. He takes the notion of causality, for which I contend, for granted, when he says, "the will is an effect which sensation creates or produces." Mr. Kneeland is too good a master of language, and too accurate in his selection of words, to say, sensation *creates* or *produces* the will, when he means only that sensation *precedes* the will. I shall then assume it as admitted by Mr. Kneeland, that the notion of causality is a phenomenon of consciousness, and that the notion of causality is the notion of an agency, power, or force, causing, creating, or producing effects. May I take this much to be settled?

3. What is the origin of this notion? I do not mean by this question what has merely preceded it in the order of time, but what has produced it, placed it in the consciousness? I have contended that it could not be sensation. The senses can give us no notion of anything of which they can take no cognizance. They do not and cannot take cognizance of causes. In no case whatever do the senses take cognizance of the power or force which causes, creates or produces. They give us the phenomena which fall under their observa-

tion, but nothing more. They merely present us the phenomena of the external world in certain relations in time and space. I see a rifle pointed towards a man, I hear a report, see the man fall, and observe where the ball passed through his heart. This is all my senses give me. "All I see," says Mr. Kneeland, "are precedents and consequents." He is right. The senses, and of course sensation, can go no further. But my mind goes further. I conceive of *something more* than "precedents and consequents." I believe, and so does Mr. Kneeland, that the rifle ball did more than *precede* the man's death, that it actually caused his death, as much as my "fingers" cause the motion of my pen in writing.

Now, I ask the origin of this notion of *something more* than "precedents and consequents?" According to Mr. Kneeland himself, sensation stops with simple "precedents and consequents"; how, then, can sensation give us a conception of something which transcends simple "precedents and consequents?" Of this something they must give a conception, or they do not give the notion in question.

Mr. Kneeland says that he *infers* the causative force from the facts and circumstances presented by his senses; but how can he infer that of which he has and can have no conception? He contends that he can have no notion of anything which has not its prototype in the world which falls under the observation of the senses, what is not recognizable by some one or all of his senses is absolutely inconceivable. Now causes, we have already determined, do not fall under the observation of the senses, are not recognizable by any nor by all of the senses. They are then absolutely inconceivable. How then are they to be inferred?

I can very easily infer a particular cause in a particular case, because I have already the general notion of causality in my mind. So may Mr. Kneeland, for he has also the general notion of causality. But suppose him destitute of this idea, I ask how could he infer the presence of a causative force from the simple phenomena of "precedents and consequents?" Previously unfurnished with the notion of cause, I ask how could the sensible phenomena suggest the presence of a cause? From the SEEN are we able to infer the UNSEEN, and that too, when we have and can have no conception of the UNSEEN?

I have thus far alleged that the notion of causality is a phenomenon of consciousness; that this notion is the notion of a creative or productive force; and that this notion cannot be given by the senses. It now remains for Mr. Kneeland to show that the notion in question is not a phenomenon of consciousness, or that it is not what I have alleged it to be, or that by the senses we can obtain notions or ideas of that which is not recognizable by the senses, or else to admit that there is at least one phenomenon of consciousness which cannot be traced back to sensation.

NO. 3. 7 (April 21, 1837): 2

Mr. Kneeland admits that the notion of causality is a phenomenon of consciousness and that it is what I alleged it to be. These two points, then, are disposed of. We have the notion of causality, and it is the idea or conception of a productive power or force.

Mr. Kneeland also admits that the senses do not detect this power or force in the external world. Causes in that world are not objects of sense. The senses perceive there only certain phenomena in certain relations in time and space. The notion of causality comes from within ourselves. It is suggested, or obtained, by detecting ourselves in the act of causing or producing some effect. In this I entirely agree with Mr. Kneeland.

But, though he admits that our senses discover nothing in the external world to answer to our notion of causality, and that the notion comes from within and not from without, Mr. Kneeland still contends that it is a product of sensation.

Sensation is an effect of an impression made on the organs or an organ of sense. It cannot be produced without an organ and some object capable of affecting that organ. That, too, which is incapable of making an impression upon an organ of sense, is incapable of producing a sensation. Consequently, no notions can be transmitted by sensation to the consciousness of that which cannot make an impression upon an organ of sense, or which is the same thing, of that which is not an object of sense, which is not recognizable by some one or more of the senses.

Mr. Kneeland will now permit me to ask him if he knows of anything not belonging to the external world, capable of making an impression upon an organ of sense? According to him, and he is right, in order to produce a sensation, the nerves of sensation must be affected. Is there anything, not belonging to the external world, capable of affecting the nerves of sensation? If so, what is it? And to what world does it belong?

If the notion of causality be transmitted to the consciousness by sensation, then causality itself must be an object of sense, something which one or more of our senses can recognize. Of which of our senses is causality, that is, the causative power or force of which we conceive, of which of the senses is it an object? Can we see it? touch it? hear it? smell it? taste it? Is it visible, tangible, audible, odorous, or savory? Not at all. Then it is no object of sense. Then it is not recognizable by the senses. Then no notion of it can be transmitted by sensation to the consciousness. But a notion of it is there.

Mr. Kneeland removes, to his apprehension, all the difficulty which may be supposed to be lodged here, by making use of the word *feeling*. We may not see, touch, hear, smell or taste causes, but we may *feel* them. Be it so. But in what sense does he use the word *feeling*? Does he mean by it an external sense? If so, does he mean what is usually termed the sense of touch, or something else? In what does he distinguish it from the sense of touch? Does he mean by it an internal sense? If so, I demand its organ and the objects capable of affecting that organ. Or am I to understand him as asserting that we are furnished with a sense that needs no organ, and consequently no organic impressions in order to perform its functions? Mr. Kneeland says that all the mental phenomena may be included under the general term *feeling*. When he so includes them, in what sense does he use the term *feeling*? Is it not as designating an effect produced by an impression upon the organs or an organ of sense? If so, he uses it as the synonym of *sensation*. His assertion, then, that all the mental phenomena may be embraced under the general term feeling, is nothing but asserting in other words, that all the phenomena of consciousness may be traced back to sensation. If this is not what he means by the assertion, will he tell me what he does mean?

Mr. Kneeland also asserts, that the senses, be they five, six or more, may all be reduced to *feeling*. In what sense is the word feeling used here? Is it not as naming our capacity to receive sensations, that is, what we commonly call the sensibility? If not, I ask what else he would designate by the word in this case? If he does use it in this sense, his assertion is merely that all our senses have the common property of *sensing* or receiving sensations; and when he asserts that we know only what we feel, he merely assumes the point in debate, to wit, all the phenomena of consciousness can be traced back to sensation. I presume Mr. Kneeland did not intend to beg the question. The very point in dispute between us is whether *feeling* be our only means of *knowing*.

As this word *feeling* is so important a word to Mr. K., I am anxious to have the meaning of it determined. Mr. K. will pardon me, then, for requesting him to tell me distinctly, whether he means by the word *feeling* that one of our external senses usually denominated the sense of touch, simply sensation, or merely our capacity for receiving sensation? Does he mean by it one of these? Then which one? Does he mean all of them? Something diverse from then all? If this last, what is that something diverse? Or does he wish me to understand him to assert that the external sense of feeling, that is, the touch, the effect of an organic impression, that is, a sensation, our capacity to receive sensations, that is, the sensibility are one and the same thing? I am willing Mr. Kneeland should use such words as he pleases, and how he pleases; all I ask is, that he attach to them a definite meaning, and inform me precisely what that meaning is.

Mr. K. is anxious to have me recur to the motion of my pen in writing. All in due time. I have no wish to go over the ground in debate more than once. I wish to finish my work as far as I go. Some progress we have made. We have ascertained one phenomenon of consciousness, agreed what it is, and that it cannot be transmitted to the consciousness by sensation from the external world. By this our question is much simplified. We have nothing now to do but to determine whether the cause which we are, or the causative force we are conscious of exerting, be or be not an object of sense.

Mr. K. and I both agree that the notion of causality originates within ourselves and not in what we perceive by our senses in external nature. We have the notion of causality, and it is suggested by the fact that we are conscious of causing, or producing. Now the question is, is that *We* who causes, or is conscious of being a cause, or of causing, an object of sense, recognizable by any of the senses? If it be an object of sense, of which of the senses is it an object? Of the sense of feeling? If Mr. K. gives this answer, he shall have his reply when he has answered the questions I have proposed in relation to feeling.

NO. 4. 7 (April 28, 1837): 2

1.[8] Mr. Kneeland defines the word feeling to mean, "all that is or can be *felt*, more or less."[9] That is, he means by feeling all that is feeling. This, to my understanding, is a definition that needs defining.

2. Mr. Kneeland appears to have been misled and seduced by this word feeling into much unsound reasoning. This has been because the word has several meanings, and he has not, in all cases, guarded against confounding one meaning with another. The word feeling, so far as we have anything to do with it in this discussion, may be used to designate *four* phenomena of human nature: 1st, one of the five senses—the sense of touch; 2d, the effect of an organic impression—sensation; 3d, the capacity of perceiving by the senses—sensibility; and 4th, apperception of our internal phenomena—con-

[8][Ed. From this issue onward Kneeland numbered each paragraph so that he could respond to them one at a time.]

[9][Ed. See *Boston Investigator* 7 (April 21, 1837): 2.]

sciousness. In philosophical matters, the term feeling is usually restricted to the first named phenomenon. But these four phenomena, however designated, are really distinct phenomena in human nature.

3. Mr. Kneeland, so far as I can judge from his replies to me, is in the habit of calling these four phenomena by the general name of feeling; and being accustomed to call them by the same name, he has naturally been led to regard them much more attentively in their sameness than in their difference. He has a laudable aversion to "hair-splitting," but he does not seem to be aware that if he would succeed in philosophical matters, he must deem no shade of difference between any of the phenomena of human nature, too slight to be observed.

4. Had Mr. Kneeland kept these four phenomena as distinct in his argument as they are in nature, he would never have fallen into the following sophism:

> Sensation is feeling;
> Consciousness is feeling;
> Therefore, consciousness is sensation.

Nor into this:

> All that can be called by the same name is identical.
> Sense, sensation, sensibility, consciousness, may all be called by the name feeling.
> Therefore, sense, sensation, sensibility, consciousness, are identical one and the same thing.

5. The fact that all these phenomena are sometimes called by the same name is no proof that they are one and the same phenomenon. Because one of our senses is called feeling, and because sensations are sometimes called feelings, we are not to infer that there is no difference between a sense and a sensation. Because sensations are said to be *felt*, and because the phenomena of consciousness are also said to be *felt*, we are not to infer that the phenomena of consciousness are sensations.

6. Mr. Kneeland's argument in defense of the position he has assumed, appears, however, to be based on a practical forgetfulness of this fact.

7. His argument, so far as I have been able to collect it, is, when simply stated,

> Sensations are said to be *felt*;
> The phenomena of consciousness may also be said to be *felt*;
> Therefore, the phenomena of consciousness are sensations;

We know only what we feel, or, what is the same thing, by feeling;
To know by feeling is to know by sensation;
Therefore, all our knowledge comes by sensation.

Is this a fair statement of Mr. Kneeland's argument? According to the best of my judgment it is; but if it be not, he will please to set me right.

8. The soundness of this argument depends on the hypothesis that *to feel* a phenomenon of consciousness is the same thing as *to feel* an organic impression, or a sensation. I *feel* (the phraseology is constructed according to Mr. Kneeland's use of language, not mine), I *feel* the notion of causality; I feel a blow upon my head. Is the *feeling* the same in both cases? Mr. Kneeland asks, "Is it not equally *feeling*?" Yes, if he choose to say so; but not equally *sensation*. If he mean by *feeling*, sensation, then I deny that we feel a notion. If he says we do, then he must prove it. The fact that he *calls* it *feeling*, I hardly need say, is no proof that it is a *sensation*.

9. When Mr. Kneeland says, that the phenomena of consciousness are *felt*, he merely begs the question; or else, he uses *to feel* as the synonym of *to be conscious*. This is what he has done in his last reply. Suppose we take this reading. Consciousness is then a feeling; sensation, too, is a feeling. We must, therefore, correct our question accordingly: "Can all the phenomena of consciousness be traced back to sensation?" The words *consciousness* and *sensation* must be substituted by the word *feeling*; our question will then be, "Can all the phenomena of feeling be traced back to feeling?" or, more simply, but with the same import, "Can all the phenomena of feeling be *felt*?" A grave question, surely, and grave men are we to engage in its discussion!

10. All this comes of Mr. Kneeland's aversion to splitting hairs, or to noting minor shades of difference; but we must see and admit things as they are, not as it would suit our convenience to have them, if we would avoid confusion and falsehood in our reasoning. It costs one some mental labor, some hard thinking, to analyze and accurately classify all the phenomena of human nature; but it becomes no Free Enquirer to shrink from this labor, or to shun this hard thinking. A man may, in the opinion of some, be made a saint in the "twinkling of an eye" [1 Cor. 15:52], but he can become a philosopher only by long years of patient and unremitting mental labor. He must think, observe, reason, reflect.

11. Mr. Kneeland must allow me to say that sensation and consciousness, being distinct in nature, two fundamentally distinct phe-

nomena, he cannot, whatever he may think, express the same thing by the word *feeling*, when he applies it to the one, that he does when he applies it to the other. If he contend that they are not two phenomena, but one and the same phenomenon, he must prove it, and by something else than the fact that he chooses to call them both by the name of feeling. Words are not things, nor can they annihilate the natural difference of things? [*sic*]

12. Mr. Kneeland must bear in mind that in his use of the word, I do not admit that all feelings are sensations. Sensation is "the perception of external objects by means of the senses"; or, as I have heretofore defined it, the effect of an impression made by some object on the organs or an organ of sense. It is, briefly, an effect of an organic impression. If Mr. Kneeland, then, choose to call the phenomena of consciousness feelings, I shall not object; but he must prove that they are perceptions of external objects by means of the senses, or the effects of an organic impression, before I shall admit that they are *sensations*, and before he will have done what he is required to do by the terms of the question in debate.

13. I call phenomenon of consciousness every notion, idea or conception, we are conscious of entertaining. When the notion in question is a notion of something which is perceptible or recognizable by the senses, I call the notion a product of sensation. When *that of which it is a notion* is not perceptible or recognizable by one or more of the senses, I say it is not a product of sensation. There is no question whether the notion be or be not a feeling, be or be not *felt*; but a simple question whether that of which it is a notion, be or be not perceptible or recognizable by some one or more of the senses.

14. The notion of causality I have adduced as one phenomenon of consciousness which is not a product of sensation. My reason for this assertion is the fact that that of which it is a notion, to wit, causality itself, is never an object of sense, is not perceptible or recognizable by any one of the senses. Now, this is a very simple matter. It requires no disputation for it is a simple question of fact. If causes themselves be in any case recognizable or perceptible by the senses, I am wrong so far as concerns the notion of causality; if they be not, Mr. Kneeland must abandon his position, which he may do, for aught that yet appears, without changing his belief in relation to religious matters.

15. Now has Mr. Kneeland been able to adduce the cause—that is, the causative, productive force—which is perceptible or recognizable by the senses? Not in the external world, he admits. There nothing is seen but "precedents and consequents." Well, in ourselves,

then? I admit, I contend, that I am a cause, and it is the fact that I cause or produce effects that suggests to me the general notion of causality. But how know I that I am a cause? By my senses? I deny it, and I defy Mr. Kneeland to prove by aid of the senses that either he or I is a cause.

16. I recur now to the motion of my pen in writing. Mr. Kneeland denies that my will is the cause of the motion of my pen in writing, for although I might will to write the same after as before, yet I could not write if my arm were paralyzed. Admit it. Surely I am not conscious that my will moves my pen. What does move it then? My fingers. How know I that? All that my senses show me is my pen and fingers in certain relations, and the motion of my pen following the motion of my fingers. Nothing but the phenomena in this case are perceptible by the senses; the *power* which moves the fingers and the pen escapes them.

17. I am unable to prove by my senses that I am a cause, or that I cause anything. I will to walk; my feet move. What connection do my senses discover between my feet and my will? I will to move my hand; my hand moves. Can my senses tell me anything more than this? I sling a stone, that is, I will to sling a stone; a stone is slung, a bird is killed. I defy Mr. Kneeland to connect, by and of his senses, these three phenomena in the relation of cause and effect. I make an internal effort, a certain muscular contraction succeeds, a sensation passes, if you please, into the consciousness; what more? Where is the proof that the effort was the *cause* of the muscular contraction, and that the muscular contraction was the *cause* of the sensation? Nothing is perceptible to the senses, even to Mr. Kneeland's sense of feeling, but certain phenomena succeeding one another in a certain order.

18. These remarks will show Mr. Kneeland that we no more take cognizance of causes themselves by our senses, in ourselves, than we do in the external world. My senses can never assure me that I am a cause. In ourselves as out of ourselves, the senses are limited in their action to phenomena; they attain not to causes. "I sling a stone," says Mr. Kneeland. How does he know that *he* slings it? All he knows by his senses, even according to his own understanding of the word sense, is, 1st, that he wills to sling a stone; 2d, a certain muscular contraction succeeds the act of willing; and 3d, that a motion of the stone succeeds the muscular contraction, or, if he prefer, muscular effort. This is all. The relation of cause and effect is not perceptible by sense. Nothing is perceptible by the senses, but certain phenomena, but "precedents and consequents." Yet we have a notion of something

which is not "precedents and consequents"; we have a notion of causality. Mr. Kneeland believes there is between his willing, or the effort he is conscious of putting forth, and the slung stone, the relation of cause and effect, and yet that relation is recognizable by none of his senses. This is so plain a case I presume he will not pretend to deny it; and as he has admitted the notion in question, probably nothing more will need be said on my part to settle the matter in dispute; and this is my apology for the undue length to which this communication has extended.

NO. 5. 7 (May 5, 1837): 2

1. Thus far Mr. Kneeland has replied to me by mere double and twisted mystification. Does he ask me to define what I mean by double and twisted mystification? I shall not attempt to answer him in words, for words are very feeble signs of ideas, and are liable to be misapprehended. I refer him, therefore, to the *thing* itself, to his replies.

2. Mr. Kneeland thinks his definition of feeling does not need defining. Here is his definition: I mean by feeling all that is or can be *felt*, more or less. All that is felt, then, is feeling. I feel my pen; my pen, then, is *felt*, consequently my pen is a feeling. We know, according to Mr. Kneeland, only what we feel. All that we feel is feeling. Feelings are in us, not out of us, consequently we know only what is in us. Is it said that we know crow-bars, sledges, horses, ships, trees, an external world? Mr. Kneeland answers, we know only what we feel; all that we feel is feeling; all the external world then, so far as known, is feeling; and as feeling is within us and not without us, the external world, so called, is neither more nor less than a collection of feelings existing within us, in man. Does Mr. Kneeland mean this? I presume not; but his words imply this. What does he mean, then? I know not, but I presume he means that feeling is feeling. If so, if he say merely that feeling is feeling, does he give a definition that defines anything?

3. Mr. Kneeland wishes me to prove that the causality of which there has been a question, is not an object of sense. It will be time enough to do that when he shall have offered a shadow of an argument to prove that it is. If Mr. Kneeland chooses to say black is white, he must prove his assertion. It were unreasonable in the extreme to ask me to prove that black is not white.

4. Mr. Kneeland appears to ask, though not in so many words, "if the notion of causality be not a product of sensation, of what is it a product?" I will answer him when he shall inform me that the evidence on his part to prove that it is a product of sensation is closed.

I have no wish merely to *deny*; I have evidence enough against his position, which I shall adduce as soon as I can find a place for it. As he affirms, I choose he should give in his affirmative evidence. He need not be afraid. I have no disposition to shrink from any part of the work which properly devolves on me. All I want is to proceed methodically, and not confound my opponent by double and twisted mystifications.

5. It must be obvious to our readers that Mr. Kneeland and I do not discuss the same question. He is discussing one question, and I am discussing another. I understand very well the question which he is grappling with, and I would meet him on that question; but as it is not, in my opinion, the question under debate, I cannot consistently do it. I have some doubts about his understanding the question I am discussing; for if he does, he must be merely throwing dust in the eyes of his readers. I read over my statement of the question to a boy nine years old. I found he could understand it, and he laughed at Mr. Kneeland's reply, for its inappropriateness to his understanding of the question; I can hardly believe, therefore, that I am misunderstood. Perhaps a little double and twisted mystification was nearer at command than a refutation of my arguments. If so, I do not complain.

6. It is sheer folly to proceed as we are proceeding. I, therefore, close this communication with a few direct questions, designed to produce a mutual understanding and agreement as to the point to be discussed.

1. Can all the phenomena of consciousness be traced back to sensation? This is our question in the very terms in which we adopted it. We adopted it, too, without any intimation on either side of any peculiar significance to be given to any of the terms in which the question was expressed. Now I ask Mr. Kneeland if he and I are not under these circumstances bound to use these terms in their ordinary philosophical acceptation? If not, will he tell me why he thinks we are not? And also, whether he supposes he has any more right to use these terms to signify what they do not signify in their ordinary philosophical sense than I have? And if we may both use the words in any sense we please, and insist that whatever alteration we make in the use of the words, we make none in the purport of the question as expressed in them, how he expects either of us can be proved in the right or in the wrong?

2. Does Mr. Kneeland mean by sensation the perception of external objects by means of the senses? If not, will he tell me what he does mean by sensation?

3. Does Mr. Kneeland recognize any distinction between consciousness and a *phenomenon* of consciousness?

4. Does Mr. Kneeland recognize any distinction between the subjective and objective, that is, between a notion and that of which it is a notion? For instance, does he consider causality itself and the notion of causality to be one and the same thing?

5. Does Mr. Kneeland mean to assert that *causality* is recognized by the sense of feeling or that merely the *notion* of causality is felt?

6. Does Mr. Kneeland mean by his internal sense of feeling, a sense proper, as much so as the sight, the hearing, and the touch?

7. Does Mr. Kneeland consider that we *receive* or that we *produce* a sensation? In the matter of sensation, are we active or are we passive? If active, will he be good enough to tell me what he means by action in a philosophic sense?

These questions, I think, will pave the way for Mr. Kneeland and I to come together. I pray him to answer them, to answer one way or other as he pleases, but to answer them, and as definitely as he can.

NO. 6. 7 (May 12, 1837): 2

1. As my candor and politeness are not the question in debate, Mr. Kneeland, I hope, will forgive me for declining to take a special notice of his allusion to them.

2. My logic will bear the test. If we can know only what can be felt, and if all that is or can be felt, be feeling, then all that is known is feeling. Do we know the external world? Then it is feeling. Feelings are within us; consequently what we call the external world, if known, is nothing but feeling existing, or occurring, in us, in man. This conclusion is inevitable. Mr. Kneeland must admit it or abandon his premises.

3. If I "presumed" in my last that this conclusion was not intended, it was because I thought Mr. Kneeland more likely to use words without a strict regard to their import, than to contradict, knowingly, what I had taken to be, his philosophy. I hope there was nothing uncharitable in this.

4. Upon a review of the matter, I am not certain but I *presumed* too much. The conclusion which I presumed he would disavow, I find warranted, not merely by an unlucky sentence, of which I should scorn to take advantage, but by the general tenor of his reasoning throughout this discussion. He does not appear to recognize any distinction between *knowledge* and the *objects* of knowledge, between *notions* which are phenomena of consciousness, and the *objects* of

which they are notions. For him the notion and object are identical; causality, and the notion of causality, are one and the same thing, and both are feeling. If this be so, he cannot believe in any objective reality. All is subjective, mere modifications[10] of the one who feels. This has the air of being Mr. Kneeland's doctrine. If it be, he admits and intends the construction I put upon his language. But enough of this. If I am wrong in this respect, he can say so.

5. I am glad that Mr. Kneeland does not hold me bound to prove negatives for negatives are sometimes very hard things to prove.

6. Mr. Kneeland informs me that he has closed the evidence on his part. To what, in *his estimation*, does that evidence amount? Does he deem it sufficient to prove the affirmative? Far from it; so far from it, that he admits the question cannot be answered in the affirmative. He says, after giving me two other alternatives, that it "*will answer his purpose equally as well*," if I will admit, in relation to the disputed point, that "we cannot tell, and that the question cannot be answered either in the affirmative or the negative."[11] It is fair to presume that nothing but truth can answer Mr. Kneeland's purpose. Consequently, no admission of mine, not in accordance with what he believes the truth, can answer his purpose. To say, then, that it would answer his purpose, if I would admit the question cannot be answered either in the affirmative or the negative, is only saying, in other words, that he really believes it cannot be.

If this be Mr. Kneeland's meaning, he has conceded the question. If all the phenomena of consciousness *can* be traced back to sensation, the question *can* be answered in the affirmative. To say the question *cannot* be answered in the affirmative is precisely the same thing as to say that all the phenomena of consciousness *cannot* be traced back to sensation. Mr. Kneeland has, therefore, very honorably yielded the question. It was what might have been expected from his candor and love of truth.

7. To my mind, Mr. Kneeland has also admitted the point in dispute by assenting to my definition of sensation: "Sensation is the perception of external objects by means of the senses." We may distinguish, then, in the matter of sensation, 1st, the subject, the *He* who perceives and is the recipient of the sensation; 2d, the sense or senses by means of which he perceives; and 3d, the object perceived. This object must be external. That is, the object perceived is exterior to

[10][Ed. Originally "mystifications." Brownson made the correction to "modifications" in *Boston Investigator* 7 (May 19, 1837): 2.]

[11][Ed. See *Boston Investigator* 7 (May 5, 1837): 2.]

the subject that perceives; for sensation is the perception of *external* objects, not of *internal* objects.

This premised, I ask if causality, of which we have the notion, be an *external* object perceptible by the senses? No. Mr. Kneeland admits that we do not and cannot perceive causes by our senses in the world out of ourselves. We may *infer* a cause out of us, but we *perceive* it only *within* ourselves. This, then, is conclusive. The perception of causality is not, then, a sensation. The notion of it, then, cannot be traced back to sensation. The question, then, cannot be answered in the affirmative. The position assumed by Mr. Kneeland is, then, conceded.

This ought to have been done before. The moment Mr. Kneeland admitted that causality is not an *external* object perceptible by the senses, he in reality gave up the question; and ever since that I have been doing my best to make him perceive it. I must own that I have been surprised that he did not perceive it sooner and have been much puzzled to find him arguing on even after he was, to my comprehension, logically vanquished.

8. If I have made no account of the extract Mr. Kneeland furnishes from Darwin,[12] it is because Darwin's design in that passage is not so much to define sensation as to tell how it is produced, and because I perceive nothing in his definition to conflict with the one I have adopted. I hope Mr. Kneeland has never considered me quite so foolish as to contend that joy and grief, pain and pleasure, indeed all our sentiments, are not facts of the sensibility. He may call them feelings, sensations. I certainly do not object. They are so called in popular language, and I have never complained of him for calling them so. In our account of these, I presume Mr. Kneeland and I do not essentially differ.

9. There is a point, and to me the vital point, in the question before us, to which, so far as I can discover, Mr. Kneeland has not sufficiently attended. He has had, hitherto, to contend with very ignorant opponents, who would bring against his philosophic views

[12][Ed. Reference here is probably to Erasmus Darwin (1731-1802), the grandfather of Charles Darwin and a scientist (botanist) and philosopher, whom Abner Kneeland had quoted on the definition of "sensation," a definition Kneeland found in "Webster's quarto Dictionary": "*Sensation* is an exertion or change of the central parts of the sensorium, or of the whole of it, beginning at some of those extreme parts of it which reside in the muscles or organs of sense. The secretion of tears in grief is caused by the *sensation* of pain. Efforts of the will are frequently accompanied by painful or pleasurable *sensations*. *Darwin*." See Kneeland's remarks in the *Boston Investigator* 3 (May 5, 1837), 2.]

very unphilosophical objections. Now, he seems to me to have taken it for granted, that my objections were of precisely the same kind as those he has so often and so successfully brushed away. He has, therefore, interpreted me by others, and dealt out his arguments against others, and not against me. This is the way in which I account for his misapprehension of my meaning. I must, therefore, ask leave to call his attention to the precise point, on which, to my understanding, the whole matter turns. I will do it as simply and as clearly as I can.

10. Mr. Kneeland, I presume, may have been asked, for instance, how he knows that he loves? Does he see love, hear it, taste it, smell it, touch it? To which he may have answered, "I *feel* it," and this is answer enough. It is the true answer, and the only answer to be given, for love is a sentiment. Again, he may have been asked how he knows that he thinks, has a thought? With which of his senses does he take cognizance of the fact that he thinks? To this he may have answered, "I feel that I think." This is proper enough. Suppose, now, the following questions and answers between him and me on causality:

B.—Have you a notion of causality?

K.—Yes.

B.—How know you that you have the notion of causality? You, I believe, contend that we can know only what can be recognized by the senses. Can you see, hear, touch, taste or smell a notion?

K.—No. But I feel the notion—that is, I am conscious of having it.

Now to these answers I have by no means objected, for I have not asked the questions here supposed. I have not asked how do we know that we have the notion of causality? Nor anything like it. I have not asked, in a single instance, *the origin of consciousness*? How we are conscious? By what means we take cognizance of the facts of consciousness? Yet, Mr. Kneeland appears to me to have replied to such questions, and to such questions alone. I have asked one question, and he has answered another.

But what *is* the question? *How do we take cognizance of causality? By what means do we conceive the existence of causality?* Causality, I conceive to be something which exists out of the sphere of consciousness—that is, exterior to the percipient subject. It is an object of thought. We conceive of it, talk of it, and have such strong faith in regard to it, that we may say, "similar causes produce similar effects"; and when we see certain effects, we say at once, certain other events have been, or will be. There is here, 1st, the subject, myself, who has the conception, who is conscious; 2^{d}, the conception, the phenomenon of consciousness; and 3^{d}, the object, causality, of which I conceive. Now my question is not, how I learn that I do conceive of causality? How I learn that I have the conception of causality? But how do I conceive of causality? How do I learn that there is causality at all? Mr. Kneeland answers, "by sensation." To this I object that sensation is the perception of *external* objects by means of the senses; and causality, by Mr. Kneeland's own admission, is not an *external* object, perceptible by the senses—consequently, the conception of it is not capable of being traced back to sensation.

11. I hope this explanation will be found to be intelligible. If so, Mr. Kneeland will see clearly that all I have said has been pertinent to the question, and that I have done all that the terms of the question and the nature of the case demanded of me. He will see, too, why I have complained of his want of fairness. But as he admits that he has nothing more to offer, and that what he has offered leaves the matter, to say the least, doubtful, I will proceed, in my next, to offer my negative proofs.

NO. 7. 7 (May 19, 1837): 2

1. Can all the phenomena of consciousness be traced back to sensation?

2. This question asks not the origin of consciousness, but of the phenomena of consciousness.

3. Phenomena of consciousness are the notions, ideas or conceptions, of whatever name, nature or value, we are conscious of entertaining.

4. Sensation is the perception of external objects by means of the senses. That is, external to sense or senses by which they are perceived.

5. When the notion, idea or conception, is a notion, idea or conception of an object which is perceptible by the senses, it is a product of sensation. All such phenomena may be traced back to sensation. I have the notion of a pen, a stone, a house, a ship. This notion may be traced to sensation, because a pen, a stone, a house, a ship, are objects perceptible by the senses. The same may be said of the notion we have of light, heat, pleasure, pain, joy, grief, love and hatred, and the like. They may all be traced back to sensation, because the objects of which they are notions are perceptible by the senses or by sensibility.

6. When the notion, idea or conception, which we are conscious of entertaining, is not a notion of an object perceptible by the senses, it is not a product of sensation.

7. Now if *all* the notions which can be detected in the consciousness can be shown to be notions of objects perceptible by the senses,

the question in debate must be answered in the affirmative; if *one* notion can be detected which cannot be shown to be a notion of an object perceptible by the senses, it must be answered in the negative.

8. Mr. Kneeland says that all the notions which can be found in the consciousness are notions of objects perceptible by the senses. This is the point for him to prove. I assert that there are phenomena of consciousness which are not of this description, notions which have no sensible objects or prototypes. This is the point for me to prove.

9. My only possible way of proving my position is to take some one phenomenon of consciousness and show that it could not have had a sensible origin. This I have aimed to do.

10. The phenomenon I have selected is the notion of causality. Now if Mr. Kneeland, on his part, can show that this notion can be traced back to sensation, he by no means proves his position, for there may be other notions which I may adduce. If I fail in proving that the notion of causality is what I have alleged it to be, it by no means follows that I must abandon the negative of the question. It merely follows that I have not been fortunate in the selection of my example. But if I prove that this notion could not have come from sensation, then Mr. Kneeland is completely refuted.

11. I have adduced the notion of causality as an instance of a phenomenon of consciousness which cannot be traced back to sensation. Can it be? This is the question.

12. That *a* notion which some pretend is the notion of causality can be traced back to sensation, I admit. Hume, Brown, Frances Wright, Robert Dale Owen, all philosophers, except Mr. Kneeland, who derive all our knowledge from sensation, call the idea of invariable antecedence, or the constant relation of antecedence and consequence between phenomena, the idea of causality. This, they say, is our only idea of causality, and they say we can have no other because the senses can give us no other. That this idea *can be* traced to the senses, I admit. But I deny that it is *the* idea of causality which all men have. I say the idea of causality is the idea of a productive power or force. And so say Mr. Kneeland. The question now is, do or can the senses give us this idea of cause, the idea of cause as a productive power or force?

13. It is something new to me to be told that the senses can give us this idea of cause. I never heard the thing pretended by any body but Mr. Kneeland, and I never even once dreamed that he would pretend it, till he astonished me by the assertion. It is admitted by all philosophers of all schools, that our senses never attain to anything

but phenomena. The senses cannot take cognizance of the Invisible. They may observe the phenomena of gravitation, but they do not and cannot observe the cause, the power or force—if such power or force there be—which produces them. They can assure us an apple falls, but they can tell us nothing more. They present us the phenomena of magnetism, but they cannot show us the power that causes the needle to vibrate to the pole. A thousand instances may be adduced to show that the senses perceive only phenomena. If any one doubts on this point, I would recommend him to read Hume's famous Essay on Power, Brown on Cause and Effect, and especially Frances Wright's Lectures on Knowledge.[13] I refer not to these writers as authority; I merely refer to them for a fuller discussion of the subject than I have the time or the space to go into.

14. Indeed Mr. Kneeland himself admits that the senses perceive nothing but phenomena in the external world. Consequently, then, we must either say that the senses do not give the idea of cause, or deny that we have it. But Mr. K. owns that we have it.

15. Mr. K. dissents from this conclusion on two grounds: 1st. It is true, he says, that the senses do not take cognizance of causes in the external world, but they do take cognizance of them in ourselves. 2d. The causality which we believe to exist out of us is *inferred* from the causality we are conscious of in ourselves. We feel ourselves sling a stone, for instance; and in doing this we get an idea of cause, from which we *infer* the action of causes in the world round and about us. Is he right? This is the question now.

16. I contend he is not. My reasons are at hand: 1st. Mr. Kneeland proceeds on the ground that we are a cause and that our senses advertise us of this fact. I deny this, because a thing to be perceived by the senses must be *exterior* to the sense by which it is perceived. I do not mean to say that it must be exterior to the body, but exterior to that

[13][Ed. Reference to the Scottish philosopher and historian David Hume's (1711-76) "Essay on Power" is probably an allusion to Hume's *An Enquiry Concerning Human Understanding* (1748, 1758), "Of the Idea of Necessary Connection," sections 48 to 61, and/or to his *A Treatise on Human Nature* (1740), Part 3, "Of Knowledge and Probability," section 14, "Of the Idea of Necessary Connection." In both places Hume argues that we cannot observe the so-called concealed "powers" in causes and that we simply infer their existence from the conjunction we observe between causes and their effects. Other references are to Thomas Brown's *Inquiry into the Relation of Cause and Effect* (1818), which combined an empiricist analysis and the principle of intuitive belief to defend Hume's account of causal relations; and Frances Wright's *Course of Popular Lectures* (New York: Free Enquirer, 1829) whose first three public lectures on the nature of knowledge Wright gave in New York, Philadelphia, Boston, and various other cities in the United States.]

which perceives. But Mr. K.'s argument requires it to be interior. I object to his statement because we do not perceive by our senses what it alleges to be perceived by them. Eliminate everything but sensation, reduce me to my senses alone, and I cannot obtain the idea that I am a cause. I sling a stone. Analyze this assertion, ascertain precisely what it is the senses give. I am conscious of an internal effort. Be it so. This is not a fact of the sensibility. This, therefore, must be eliminated. I feel a muscular contraction or effort; this is the first fact which sensibility perceives. To the muscular contraction or effort succeeds the motion of the sling and stone. This is all my senses give me. Now, I believe that I sling the stone. This belief supposes that the I—that which constitutes myself—causes the muscular contraction or effort, which in its turn causes the motion of the sling and stone. The senses give two phenomena which succeed one another, but the proposition requires them to be connected as cause and effect, and connected as effects to an invisible cause which I call *me* or myself. Now I do not question the truth of the proposition. A man must be out of his wits indeed, to doubt that he slings the stone. What I do allege, and what I think I have shown, is that the belief involves the conception of something which has not and cannot have a sensible origin.

2^d. I object to Mr. Kneeland's account of the matter, that, even admitting the senses to take cognizance of the cause within ourselves, that the cause which I am conscious of being does not warrant the inference to the causes which I believe to exist in the world around me. Mr. Kneeland says that the senses give us the conception of ourselves as a cause, and having thus obtained the conception of causality, we *infer* its existence whenever we see occasion for it. For instance, because I am conscious of being the cause which slings a stone, I infer that the rifle shot causes the man's death. Is this inference legitimate? Because I am the cause that slings the stone, have I a right to say the rifle ball kills the man?

I have always been taught that a conclusion not contained in the premises, is unwarranted. To infer from a thing is merely to deduce one thing from another; and I confess I am unable to conceive how that can be inferred or deduced from another which that other does not contain. The inference from my causality to that of the rifle ball can be legitimate only on the ground that the causality of the rifle ball is involved or contained in my causality. But this will not be pretended. The inference, then, is not warranted. If the causality which I recognize in the case of the rifle ball be not my causality, it cannot be inferred from mine. Because John slings a stone, it hardly follows that Peter is a good swimmer, or that James catches fish.

Again: If the causality which is believed to exist out of us, be inferred from our causality, then it must be merely our own causality projected. This was what Fichte, the prince of German Idealists, asserted.[14] He believed that the causality which we are, is the only causality which we can know. Consequently, that all the causality we can conceive of as existing out of us, must be our own causality projected. Hence, he taught that the *We*, the personality, the cause which we are, makes the external world, God and all things we think we see, or believe to exist. Mr. Kneeland's doctrine, if pursued by a logical mind to its last results, must end in the same system of Idealism. That Mr. Kneeland is aware of this, I do not pretend; that he would reject this result with something like horror I have no doubt; but it is not every maker of a system that is able to foresee all its consequences, or that has the courage to own all its results.

The idea of causality obtained by the act of slinging a stone, is not the idea of causality in general, but the idea of a specific cause. But the notion we have of causality differs essentially from this. The idea as it exists in the consciousness is universal and necessary, not particular and contingent. Everybody believes, not merely that he slings a stone, in case he slings one, but that *no event* can take place, or begin to be, without a cause, a power or force which causes it to be. Now I ask how from the fact that I am a specific cause, that I sling a stone for instance, I obtain the universal and necessary idea that no event can take place, that nothing can begin to be, without a cause? Now, it is not enough to say that the universal and necessary, the abstract, can be inferred from the specific, the particular and contingent, the concrete. I require the process of reasoning by which it can be done. Assertion is not argument, and will not pass for argument.

The cause which slings the stone, in the case I sling the stone, is not only particular and contingent, but it is personal and voluntary. I am that cause. I refer the slinging of the stone to myself, and I can refer it to no one else. Now the cause which kills the man, on the supposition that the rifle ball kills him, is not believed to be personal or voluntary, nor is it referred to myself. I am not that causality. It is wholly distinct from me. I have not the slightest connection with it.

[14][Ed. Brownson, following Cousin, always considered Fichte an absolute subjective idealist who took Kant's philosophy to its logical subjectivist consequence. For Fichte, according to Brownson, the ego was the only verifiable cause, and therefore he could not legitimately and logically conclude to a cause outside of the self.]

Now will any one be good enough to show me how this totally distinct causality can be inferred from mine? By what process of reasoning, I repeat it, do I prove the fact that I sling a stone come to the conclusion that a rifle ball kills a man?

17. This article is too long, but I could not well make it shorter. The discussion will terminate the sooner for it. If I be fairly answered, I shall probably write one or two more; but I pledge myself not to exceed in any case two communications more; and unless something unlooked for occurs, I shall close all I have to say in my next. If my arguments be passed over as they have been heretofore, self-respect will prohibit me from writing even one communication more.[15]

A NOTE

7 (May 26, 1837): 2

Mr. Kneeland having expressed his regret in his last that my articles occupy his columns to the exclusion of what he calls valuable matter, I must be stupid indeed not to perceive that he desires our discussion to be discontinued. I, therefore, so far as depends on me, discontinue it.

I have said enough to convince all who are capable of philosophic thought, that I am right; I might talk or write till doomsday, without convincing any others. If any one doubts this conclusion, give me a champion of the philosophy which Mr. K. avows, capable of feeling the force of an argument, and I hold myself pledged to demonstrate it.

As it concerns the victory to which Mr. Kneeland has more than once alluded, I have nothing to say. Mr. Kneeland has continued to talk to the end; he has the last word, and *therefore* he will doubtless claim the victory. Be it so. Let him claim it, and wear its laurels.

[15]P. S.—If F. W. D. wishes to take the place of Mr. Kneeland, and he is willing, I have no objection to discussing the question with her, only I do not much like to dispute with women. Or if she will define her terms, I will answer the question she puts to me.

I thank "A Man of the People" for the information that "Republicans have but *five senses.*"—This, however, is not new to me. I have never believed in more than five senses, and if Mr. Man-of-the-People would contrive to convince Mr. Kneeland that man has only five senses, I should be very much obliged to him. If he would persuade Mr. Kneeland to read Frances Wright's *Lectures on Knowledge*, I think he would also do something to give a profitable termination to this debate. I should not then have to use all my powers to make him admit his own philosophy.[Ed. F. W. D. and A Man of the People were two correspondents to the *Boston Investigator* who commented on the exchange between Brownson and Kneeland. On this, see *Boston Investigator* 7 (May 12, 1837).]

Many such victories as the present has he won; many more such may he win. Let his friends decree him an ovation; for they may be assured that,

> In arguing, too, the parson owned his skill,
> For e'en though vanquished; he can argue still.[16]

My thanks to Mr. Kneeland for the use of his columns, and my congratulations that he is in no danger of being one of those who have need to use the old Scotch prayer, "O Laird! give us a good conceit o'oursel's."[17]

[16][Ed. Oliver Goldsmith, "The Deserted Village," lines 211-12, in *Collected Works*, 4:295.]

[17][Ed. Unable to identify quotation.]

10.

BABYLON IS FALLING[1]

"And the merchants of the earth shall weep and mourn over her; for no man buyeth their merchandise anymore." Revelations 18:11.

This was said in reference to the fall of Babylon. Its force can be appreciated only by settling in our minds what the writer of this book, called Revelation, intended to shadow forth by the city of Babylon. On this point doctors disagree. Some suppose that he intended pagan Rome, others Catholic Rome, and others still suppose that he designed to indicate in this way some great and widely influential heresy or false doctrine. Without attempting to reconcile conflicting opinions, or calling in question the justness of any of the interpretations which have been offered, I am, for my part, inclined to understand by the city of Babylon the SPIRIT OF GAIN, the commercial spirit, or system, which has in these last centuries spread over the world, corrupted and intoxicated all people.

I do not propose this interpretation as being certainly the true one; I will not say positively that this is what the Revelator meant; but I think it answers better to his symbolical language than any other interpretation thereof which has been offered. The spirit of gain, viewed simply in connection with the commercial system it has created, the direction it has given to men's minds and hearts, the evil propensities it has fostered, the wicked passions it has strengthened, and the worldliness and sensuality in which it has buried kings, governments and people, may well be called, it seems to me, "the mother of harlots and abominations of the earth" [Rev. 17:5]. All nations have been maddened, "intoxicated with the wine of the wrath of her fornication, and the kings of the earth have committed fornication with her, and the merchants of the earth are waxed rich through the abundance of her, delicacies" [Rev. 18:3].

In saying that the spirit of gain, the commercial spirit, or system, is shadowed forth under the type of the city of Babylon, I do not mean to express any opinion hostile to commerce, when commerce

[1][Ed. *A Discourse Preached in the Masonic Temple, to the Society for Christian Union and Progress; Sunday, May 28, 1837* (Boston: I. R. Butts, 1837).]

is confined within its legitimate province, when made, as it should be, the simple carrier of the productions of agriculture and manufactures from one place or from one country to another; nor do I mean to say aught against merchants, or to intimate that the men engaged in commerce are not as good, as virtuous as the rest of the community. I speak not against men, but against a prevailing spirit which all men partake more or less of—against a system which spreads its meshes over the whole community and for which the whole community, not any one division of it, is accountable. The spirit against which I speak in strong terms of reprobation extends beyond what is technically called commerce, prevails elsewhere than in cities, and works its iniquities by others than merchants.

Understanding then by the city of Babylon of the Apocalypse, the spirit of gain, the commercial spirit, or if you choose, the modern commercial system, a system of universal fraud and injustice, a system which lays the whole earth under contribution to make "princes merchants and merchants princes,"[2] the chapter from which my text is taken may be considered a prediction of its downfall. God has for the encouragement and consolation of the saints, foretold that the system must end, that they who have lived on the toil, and sweat, and groans, and often the blood of their brethren, are to stand one day afar off weeping and wailing over the ruin of her by whom they were made rich. And unless I greatly deceive myself, there are at this moment some not to be mistaken signs that this prediction is about to be fulfilled. The system of fraud, deception and injustice, which men's greediness for wealth, for this world's goods, has built up, if I am not grossly in error, stands tottering, ready at every moment to fall with a crash that shall make the world tremble.

The embarrassment in the commercial world, of which we hear and feel so much, is no temporary embarrassment produced by local and temporary causes. It proceeds from causes which lie deep, which go to the very heart of every community. It is one of the indications of a contest which is commenced between two forces into which the whole human race is now divided, of the shock occasioned by the meeting of the two causes which have drawn mankind out into two opposing and hostile camps. It is not the United States Bank, it is not the deposit system; it is not a mere question of government, or finance, which divides the human family today. Governments and

[2][Ed. The quotation appears to be a paraphrase of Isa. 23:8: "who hath taken this counsel against Tyre, the crowning city, whose merchants are princes, whose traffickers are the honorable of the earth?"]

banks, finance regulations, and treasury circulars are but the instruments or the effects of the contest now raging, the means made use of by one party or the other to gain some advantage or to ward off some attack. He who would comprehend the real cause of the present financial convulsion must look far beyond such things as these.

Whoever has paid much attention to the movements which have occurred in our own times, the controversies which have been stirred up, the measures proposed, adopted or rejected by governments and rulers, and the divisions which are everywhere taking place, cannot have failed to perceive that there is on the one hand a strong, decided and steady tendency of the masses towards equality in political, social and property relations, and that on the other hand there is a collecting and concentrating of forces in defense of old privileges, old abuses, and the hitherto universally prevalent inequality. No one who has eyes, it seems to me, can fail to see that the human race is drawn out and arrayed under separate banners on which are inscribed words of far different import. On the banner which I see floating over one of the camps, I read the to me, I will confess it, inspiring words, LIBERTY, EQUALITY, PEACE; and on that which waves over the other I read PRIVILEGE, INEQUALITY, WAR. These two banners wave in view of each other; these two armies are waiting but the signal to rush to the terrible encounter, if indeed the battle have not already begun.

I ask your attention, my friends, for a few moments, to the consideration of the two causes espoused by these two hostile divisions of our brethren. Stand aloof as we will, we shall be drawn into the combat, and be compelled to give or receive our share of the blows, which must pass and repass. Well then doth it behoove us to make ourselves acquainted with the question at issue, the cause espoused by either party, that we may choose our side understandingly, and enlist under the banner of truth and justice, not under that of falsehood and iniquity. Let us then, in our minds, place ourselves upon an eminence which overlooks the two camps, and inquire what mean these words inscribed upon their respective banners.

What mean these words, liberty, equality, peace? Or, to simplify the inquiry, and to give something like unity to my remarks, What means this word equality? What do they mean by it who have inscribed it on their banners? Do they mean that all men are equally wise, equally good, entitled to equal shares of the products of art and industry? Not at all. Do they mean that all men are born with equal capacities, able to reach the same intellectual heights, and that they deserve equal consideration and influence? Not at all.

No man with his eyes open can adopt the doctrine that all men are born with equal capacities. All are born with the same nature, with the elements of the same virtue and intelligence, the same moral and religious greatness, but they are born with varying capacities. Their abilities differ. One man is weak and timid, another is strong and brave; one is low in his aims, feeble in his resolves, and narrow in his views, another has lofty purposes, invincible resolutions, far-reaching thought and creative genius; one perceives only a few objects just around him, and is utterly incapable of putting three ideas together, another opens up to himself new worlds upon worlds, forms plans for national and individual melioration and progress at once minute, complex, bold, comprehensive and practical. The soldiers in the camp of equality are by no means prepared to war for the principle that all men are born with equal powers of mind, though they may contend, and perhaps justly, that God has made less difference between man and man than is commonly believed.

There are differences in men's capacities which it is impossible wholly to obliterate. Education may modify, lessen or exaggerate them, but it never has been able, and I do not believe that it ever will be able, to destroy them. No education can make every man a Homer, a Milton, a Locke, a Washington, a Franklin. Perhaps it is well that there are differences. If all men had minds of precisely the same compass, precisely the same thoughts, and hearts of precisely the same feelings and aspirations, this would be a dull and monotonous world. There would be little room for enterprise, few inducements to exertion, small ambition to excel, and nothing to urge men onward and upward in the glorious career of perfectibility.

Nor do the soldiers of equality contend that all men should have equal influence, equal power over political and social matters. They do not, as some suppose, war against aristocracy, when by aristocracy is understood, as should be, the government of the wisest and best. The wisest and best, wisdom and virtue, have a legitimate right to rule in church, society and state. No friend to equality objects to this. No man, no full grown man, desires the rule, or rather misrule, of ignorance and vice. Every wise and good man is an aristocrat, and no one, however staunch a democrat he may be, contends for a government in which ignorance, in which the base and corrupt bear sway.

The controversy which has raged on this point, arises from the adoption of a false standard of worth, in consequence of which they who are not have often been called the wisest and best. The test of wisdom and virtue usually adopted is a false test. Men are placed in the ranks of the aristocracy who have no business there, and invested with authority, when they have nothing to support their right to it but a worldly success, obtained by craft, adroitness and inhumanity. It is against these that they war, who are supposed to war against aristocracy. Not against wisdom and virtue do they gird on their armor and bend the bow, but against their counterfeits; not against the legitimate sovereign do they rush to the battle, but against the usurper, who by craft and cunning, by his baseness and iniquity, or by the carelessness, corruption, or too great confidence of the people, has placed himself in the throne to which he has no right.

That young soldier of equality, whose step is so proud and whose eye flashes such deep indignation, wars not against the legitimate influence of mental and moral superiority. He complains not that others have stronger minds, sounder judgments, warmer hearts, a more passionate love of the true and beautiful, and a more commanding influence than he. He is not disturbed that the republic has greater, wiser, better men than he. They wrong him who accuse him of envy, and allege that he enlists on the side of equality because he cannot bear to see any one above him. It is not so. Err he may, but he is not without a soul, without a heart. His bosom burns, it may be, with as generous a love of virtue, his heart swells with as noble and as disinterested sentiments, and he moves by as pure and as lofty motives as any of them who war against him. Say not that he is envious, that he seeks only to bring down to his own level, the wisdom and virtue he is conscious he cannot equal. It is not so. He stands in religious awe of the God-created, the God-patented nobility of our race, and prostrates himself before the truly great man as the outspeaking symbol of the Divinity.

I repeat it, he wars not against aristocracy as such, in itself, but against the false and unjust standard of greatness which now obtains—against clothing directly or indirectly with power over their brethren, men whose influence proceeds from no real merit, who have neither wisdom or virtue to sustain them, and who are at the topmost round of the social ladder only by virtue of their success in deceiving their fellow beings, or in availing themselves of the talents and industry of others. He wars against that social system in which they who best understand the art of buying and selling human beings, or working them as men work their oxen and horses, are accounted the wisest and best, and do really control all the affairs of the nation, devise all financial schemes, governmental and educational measures, and have in their own hands the molding of individual character and the forming of the public conscience. He and his comrades band together to dethrone the misbegotten power of wealth, of fraud and injustice, to destroy artificial distinctions and factitious influences, and to restore, reinaugurate virtue, truth, justice in their rightful dominion as sovereigns of the world. He is indignant at hearing men lauded to the heavens, whose ends are selfish, whose thoughts are low, whose aspirations are downwards, and who are strangers to whatever ennobles man, or dignifies human nature. He is ready to own that he is unworthy to unloose even the latchet of the shoes of him whom God sends to baptize the people with the Holy Ghost and with fire, but he has sworn in the very depths of his being that he will not fall down at the sound of sackbut, psaltery and harp, before the golden image set up for him to worship. Rather than do that, he will brave the fiery furnace, though heated seven times hotter than it is wont to be heated.

Nor do the advocates of equality contend for equal wealth. They do not ask that all shall share equally the gains of industry. But they do believe that God has given the earth to the children of men and they demand that it be left open to all. They contend that the few have no right to spread their broad hands over the whole surface of the globe, so that the many shall not find whereon to set their feet, so that the poor man shall find no obscure corner on which he may erect an humble cabin, in which his children may behold the light,[3] or his bones at last be laid to be absorbed into their mother's bosom. The whole soil of the globe is monopolized. The few hold it for themselves, and their children, and their children's children. And therefore must the children of the poor be born naked and destitute indeed, be naked, destitute, wretched, so long as God lets them live, unless by ingenuity, by fraud, by some means or other they can contrive to dispossess the children of the few of some portions of that which was left them by their fathers. Hence the war which men have been carrying on. Society for long ages has been in perpetual strife. They who have a portion of this world's goods have been struggling

[3]Vide Paroles d' un Croyant. Par M. de La Mennais.[Ed. Brownson cites in a footnote Félicité Robert de Lamennais' *Paroles d'un croyant* (Paris: E. Renduel, 1834). English translations were also available to him. See *Words of a Believer* (London: B. D. Cousins, 1834; New York: DeBehr, 1834). Brownson's reference to *Paroles* was one of the first signs that Brownson had been reading Lamennais whom he considered the leader of the new French Catholic movement. Earlier, in 1836, he translated part of an essay on absolutism and liberty that had been attached to the seventh edition of *Paroles.* On this, see "Absolutism and Liberty," *Boston Reformer* 3 (September 13, 1836): 2. It is not clear how much he knew about Lamennais at this time, but it is clear that Lamennais' position resonated with his own views of the relationship between Christianity and democracy.]

to keep what they have and to get more, and they who have not, have been struggling to dispossess them who have. This struggle passes in the business world by the respectable name of competition, but, be its name what it may, that of saint or sinner, it is an ungodly struggle, and the ill effects of it are now becoming apparent to every man, woman and child throughout Christendom.

The soldiers of equality have taken up arms to put an end to this struggle, and that is what they mean by that word PEACE you see inscribed on their banner. This struggle can be ended only by giving to all, not equal wealth, but equal chances to wealth. They do not fight for equal property, but for equal chances, that all may have equal chances to wealth opened to them. Now the chances are unequal. Some are born with the right to live in ease and luxury, to every advantage which wealth can purchase, while others are born only with the right to work or starve. There is nothing equal in this. One is set forward, to say the least, two-thirds of the distance, and the other must run three times as far in the same time, in order to reach the goal at the same instant. And what is, perhaps, more aggravating than all, he who has three times the distance of the other to run, is set down as a poor runner if he do not come out ahead.

To have equal chances all must have the same starting-point, and this is all that the advocates of equality demand in relation to wealth. They say, "The prize to the swiftest runner," but at the same time, "Let all start together." They say it is wrong to give one an advantage by setting him forward or by compelling his competitor to carry weight. Their principle is, "Equal chances to all, and to each one according to his ability." But this cannot be realized until we revise our notions in some respects concerning what ought to be, or ought not to be, accounted property, and the tenure by which property can be legitimately held. It is generally contended, that property is a creature of legislation, and that man has, and can have, no right to property but that which the law gives him. But this I deny. Man has a natural right to property and the law can give him no valid right to call that his property which is not so by a natural right. Law never does, and never can, create right. Right is prior to law, superior to law, and is the only thing which can give to the legislative enactment the character of law. So long as the legislative enactment remains, especially in a free government like ours, whatever its character, it should be respected and obeyed; but if it be not founded in justice, it may and should be altered, amended, annulled, or superseded. That only, in truth and justice, is a man's property, which he himself creates or produces by his own industry, or, which is the same thing, that which he obtains in equitable exchange for his own productions. If I call anything my property which I have not produced, or obtained in exchange for what I have produced, I call something my property which is the production of another, or I contend that my claims to the gifts of God are paramount to those of my equals. All men have an equal right to the gifts of God. God is a common father, he showers his blessings upon all, but upon no one in particular. I have, then, no right to monopolize them. If I call that my property which another has created or produced, I strike at the foundation of all property, and do violence to the only principle by which I can legitimate my right to my own productions.

In saying that the earth should be open to all her children, and that all should have equal chances, I say nothing in favor of an equal division, nor in favor of any division of property. Nothing seems to me more unjust than what is commonly understood by an equal division of property. Every man with the least possible claims to correct moral feelings must at once revolt at the bare thought of giving one man's property, or any portion of the gains of his industry, to another. Every man has a sacred and divine right to the proceeds of his own industry, and if one produces more than another, he should have more. This is just and whatever is just is equal. Enable all to start fairly, with no other disadvantages than nature herself imposes, secure to every man the gains of his own industry, and you have established all the equality as to property relations which can be demanded, and all the inequality of which anyone ever dreams of complaining, will be removed, or at least will very soon wear itself out.

When this shall be done, men will be so nearly equal in their property that the equality most desired will be easily secured. Equality in property is not, or should not, be desired as an end, but as a means; and is desirable no farther than it tends to secure equality as it concerns mental, moral and religious progress. The means for this progress are now very unequally and artificially distributed. Millions of children are now so born that they must live and die, and leave no trace, but the corruption they breed, of their having been. Nineteen twentieths of the human race, taking the world over, are doomed by the very condition in which they are born to mere brutishness. Forever must they grope in darkness. No star glimmers through the gloom of their eternal night, presaging a day-dawn and the uprising of a sun of science to shed on them his beams of life and glory. How many of them are born, too, with the germs of a godlike virtue, born with all the intrinsic power to be the prophets of humanity! How many of them, but for the cold and friendless hand which smooths their infant pillow, or rocks their cradle, might outdo and outshine the mightiest and most world-renowned of those whose names have now a magic spell to kindle the youthful spirit and urge it on to deeds of true glory! Say not that God has made them inferior to their more favored brethren; say not that God blasts them in the bud and dooms them to eternal barrenness; say not that God creates such richly endowed beings as is the most miserably furnished human soul, but to live and die and be no more as the beasts of the field or the reptiles of the dust. It is not so. While one portion are favored with libraries, instructors, with all that wealth, art, science and genius can do to develop their minds, and make them grow up men, others are pent up in workshops, stifled in factories, or compelled to work beyond their strength to support an impoverished, a wretched, an idle, drunken, improvident or avaricious father.

If the advocates of equality contend for equal chances to wealth, it is not because they crave wealth for its own sake; it is not because they are supreme lovers of wealth; but it is because they would command the means of training up all the children of the community to be really men and women; because they would obtain an "open field and fair play," a theater on which man may enact all his greatness, develop all his faculties harmoniously in all their beauty and majesty; because they would place all the riches of intellect, taste, refinement, virtue, rational religion within the reach of every human being; and could they but do this they would care little who should have mere physical wealth. If men would not monopolize the lights of science, and the pleasures of refined culture, they might be welcome to God's physical gifts. Poverty we can bear; we care not that our hands are hard, that our faces are sun-burnt, and our bodies bent with toil; we care not that our coats are threadbare and patched and that our food is scanty and coarse, if we be not debarred from access to the pleasures of intellect and taste, if we but have free scope for the full and just development of our nobler and diviner nature. Let science open to us his treasures, and art lavish upon us her beauties, and take, if ye will, partisans of privilege, take if ye will the mere pelf. Ye can at best enjoy it but for a day before ye will deposit it at the mouth of the tomb to be as poor and destitute as the poorest.

Such is the cause espoused by the camp, over which floats in the breeze, the banner on which are inscribed, liberty, equality, peace. The division of mankind arranged under this banner demands equal rights, equal chances, equal chances to wealth, knowledge, virtue, freedom; equal opportunities to develop and exert all the faculties of human nature in the service of truth and justice; and it promises as the result, love, union, peace. If it triumph it assures us that men will feel and live as brothers, and that the songs of brotherly love shall rise on the air, and swell the sublime chorus of heaven itself.

Let us now turn to the other camp. We need not gaze long to perceive what it is and to learn the cause it espouses. The words inscribed on its banner, *privilege*, *inequality*, *war*, are intelligible enough, and we have the experience of a thousand ages to explain them. Privilege, what means this word privilege? In its literal import it means a private law, a law made expressly to favor an individual. It is distinguished from the municipal law in that the municipal law is general, and is intended to effect all the members of the city alike, while the privilege or private law is special, and intended to confer an exclusive benefit or advantage upon some one or more individuals. It is at once the offspring and the parent of injustice. By giving to one member of the city or of the community an advantage over another, it creates an artificial inequality between the one favored, and the rest of the community, which cannot fail on one side to provoke a strife for like or greater special favors, and on the other to excite envy and hostility towards the specially favored, and the result can be nothing but *war*.

I regret that I have neither the time nor the room to sketch to you the history of the party of privilege. I assure you it would be interesting and instructive, and someday I may attempt it. The principle of this party is to reap without sowing and to enjoy without producing. It would be wrong to say that its members are not working men. They work and I am inclined to believe that they work harder than the workingmen, properly so called; but they work not to produce, but to make what others produce pass into their own possession. The people, in their estimation, were created for them to ride, or to appropriate to their pleasure or profit.

Formerly the main business of this party was war and plunder, latterly it has become commerce and manufacture. To a great extent it has now laid aside the sword and taken up the pen; and instead of military tactics, it now studies arithmetic and leaving off killing it takes to what properly deserves to be called swindling. That many of this party are ignorant of the real tendency of their practices is most cheerfully conceded. Very few of them comprehend the system they adopt. They do not perceive that though it may be sport to them, it is death to others. They have always heard it dignified with the titles of honorable and respectable; they know the advantages they derive from pursuing it, and there is no dearth of priests to tell them that the sufferings they can but see around them is not occasioned by their injustice, but is a mere godsend, sent by the Deity for some inscrutable, but to himself, no doubt, satisfactory reason. Did they know what they are doing, did they comprehend that they can be what they are only at the expense of millions of victims, it is no stretch of charity to believe that they would desist, yield up their privileges, and consent to take their chance with the rest. God, let us hope, will forgive them, and let us too, their victims, forgive them, for they know not what they do.

In former times this party was less numerous than at present. The result of the progress of civilization thus far has not been to elevate in any conceivable degree the producing classes, as such, but merely to increase the number of those the producing classes must feed. The progress of science, the various improvements and new inventions in the arts of production and for abridging labor, and of which we hear such loud boasts, have not as yet, so far as I can see, in the least lightened the burdens of working men and working women, properly so called; they have merely facilitated the means by which a poor man, a producer, may pass to the class of the non-producers, from one of the ridden to be one of the riders. This may indeed be thought a benefit in his particular case, but no man can fail to perceive that it adds to the number of those the producers must feed, while it diminishes the number who are to feed them. It increases the weight while it decreases the strength which is to sustain it. This increase of the burden on the one hand and decrease of strength on the other would have made the burden long since intolerable, it is true, had it not been for science and the introduction of labor-saving machinery. By means of this machinery the producing classes have been able to sustain a weight which they otherwise could not have sustained. But with this machinery, as a class, they have had their burdens not in the least diminished. The working men, fewer in proportion indeed than they were, work as hard as ever, and in point of fact, much harder than formerly.

But the fact I have mentioned the increase of the riders and the diminution of the ridden has not been without immense results. In those old times which some regret, and which, had the present no future, I too should regret, when the number of riders was pretty well fixed, and the people knew the weight they must carry, [and] were withal accustomed to their burdens and acquainted with the road they must travel, when it never chanced, or rarely chanced, that a footman became a rider, or that a rider was unhorsed and degraded to the rank of a footman, things moved along somewhat quietly, and, to say the least, in tolerable order. So long as riders were deemed such by virtue of their birth, or by the grace of God, the footmen-born, or the God-neglected, never dreamed of becoming riders. They considered themselves, if they considered at all, born to be ridden, at least to go on foot, and they studied to be contented with their lot. They supposed themselves in their true position and they dared aspire to no other. But these multiplied facilities for passing from a footman to a rider, from one who feeds others to one whom others feed, from one who works for others to one for whom others work, have unsettled everything. When one man by his native energy, by the force of his own talents, leaped the chasm which separated the plebeian from the patrician, when one of the lowest footmen was seen to make himself a graceful, renowned and lordly rider, bearing away the prize even from the native-born cavalier, a strange, an unwonted, an unaccountable feeling seized the whole class of footmen, a new and daring ambition took possession of their souls. As one after another was seen to pass from their ranks to the ranks above them, another after another, another and another wished to do it. The whole class soon became dissatisfied with their condition. Everyone felt himself in a false position, became weary and disgusted with his lot, and desirous of following the example of those who had exchanged it for a more favored one. Each one said to himself, "Why may I not reap without sowing, and enjoy without producing, as well as others?"

It is in this dissatisfaction with their lot, occasioned by the example of so many of their number passing into the ranks of the privileged, that we must look for that universal strife we everywhere witness among the workingmen to become members of the more favored classes. It is hardly possible to conceive of the eagerness with which they have pressed forward after privileges, to become members of the privileged classes. In former times this eagerness would have been repressed by the sword or gunpowder; but in these days the sword and gunpowder are going out of fashion; besides, it is found that they are dangerous tools to handle, and may sometimes be employed with advantage against those who first resort to their use. The only method of repression which has been left is, for the privileged to be less exclusive, and to share their privileges with the most forward and importunate of the clamorers. The footmen have always rallied round certain men, whom they look upon as their friends, whom the riders call the ringleaders of the mob. When the mob has become too strong or too impetuous, the privileged have found that the best way to disperse them, is to buy up their leaders, to receive them into their own ranks and make them gentlemen. By this means they deprive the people of their leaders, satisfy the people for a time with the belief that their demands are granted because their leaders are received into favor, or throw them into confusion and compel them to disperse and desist from their purpose till they can find new leaders. This process has been going on ever since the old fashioned military nobility formed an alliance with the commercial nobility.

As the door into the upper classes was found to be opened to some of the working men or producers, from the fact, that hundreds were seen to enter, and afterwards beheld on the balconies hand and glove with the privileged, so all the producers pressed forward to enter. But as wealth was the only passport, the only certain right to entrance, hence the universal passion for wealth which disgraces humanity, the perfect madness of the people everywhere to become suddenly rich; hence the increased activity given to the productive arts, the enterprise and the numerous schemes for becoming quickly rich, and hence too banks and banking, stocks, fancy stocks, stock-jobbing, speculation, overtrading, and whatever else may have tended to produce the present widespread and ruinous commercial embarrassment.

Whatever we may think of the times in which we are struggling to live, of the commotions we see everywhere around us, however we may blame government and its recent measures, the United States Bank, the deposit banks, all other banks and their friends or opponents, we must look for the real cause of what we see and deplore in that one word, privilege; in the unequal and therefore unjust legislation which fosters and sustains a privileged class, which obtains its wealth and consideration by transferring the earnings of others to its own pocket, and to the fact, strange as it may seem, that people almost everywhere would rather ride than be ridden.

The camp we are now considering is filled with the privileged and their retainers, with those who have hitherto arranged all things in state, society, and church, to their own liking, for their own private advantage. Their right to continue to be the privileged and to arrange all things for their own private advantage is called in question, is denied, is opposed, and it is in defense of this pretended right that they have taken up arms. They are, you see, about to fight for privilege, for a system of legislation and a social order of which the best fruits are inequality and universal war. Not willingly will they give up their advantages. Their power has been somewhat weakened but they are yet strong, and they will make a desperate defense.

The immediate cause of hostilities is the fact that the privileged have become alarmed and find it necessary to close their doors to the admission of new members. If all men should become sharers in their privileges, their privileges would cease to be privileges. If all should become riders, it would be precisely the same thing as to have no riders at all. When there are none to be ridden, there are none that can ride, and if all rise to the class of riders, there will be none to constitute the class of the ridden. This the unprivileged classes have themselves at length become able to comprehend. They have heretofore thought nothing of elevating their class, but have struggled with all their might to become as individuals members of the privileged classes, but they now perceive that though some of their number have passed and many now may pass from among them and swell the number of those they must support, all cannot, nor even the majority, and they have therefore wisely concluded to dispense with privilege altogether. Against privilege then, in defense of equal rights, equal chances then, these have armed themselves, and taken the field.

Such are the camps before us, such are the two parties into which mankind are now divided, and such is the contest which now rages. Peace between these two parties is henceforth out of the question. There may be a truce, a cessation of hostilities from time to time, but no solid enduring peace. Do what we will, say what we may, ever will hostilities break out afresh, and ever too with increased rancor and fierceness. The two causes are hostile in their very nature, and can never co-exist but in a state of war. One party or the other must be exterminated before the war will end.

It has been said that we are in the midst of a revolution. They who said so perhaps were not aware of the truth they uttered. We are in the midst of a revolution, a bloodless one I hope, but a revolution to which all those which have been will be counted mere child's play. Calm as society may seem to a superficial spectator, I assure you it is moved to its very foundations and is in universal agitation. The question which is now debated and to which entire humanity listens is one which reaches infinitely further than the most celebrated of the questions heretofore debated. The question today is not between one reigning family and another, between one people and another, between one form of government and another, but a question between privilege and equal rights, between law sanctioned, law fenced in privilege, age-consecrated privilege, and a hitherto unheard of power, a new power just started from the darkness in which it has slumbered since creation day, the *power of honest industry*. The strange name borne by this new-born power, may deceive some as to its strength and merits, but though they may deem it an infant, they may be assured they will find it an Herculean one. The contest is now between the privileged and the unprivileged and a terrible one it is. The slave snaps his fetters, the peasant feels an unwonted strength nerve his arm, the *people* rise in stern and awful majesty, and demand in strange tones their ever despised and hitherto denied rights. They rise and swear in a deep and startling oath that *justice shall reign*. Let those who feed on the labors of others hear, and know, that not with a look or a word will they frighten or charm them down.

Not to this country alone, nor chiefly, is this revolution confined. It reaches the old world. The millions down-trodden for ages by kings, hierarchies, and nobilities, awake. Kings put their hands to their heads to feel if their crowns be there; hierarchies lash themselves and cry mightily unto Baal; nobilities tremble for their privileges; time-cemented and moss covered state fabrics reel and totter; all who live on abuses seem to themselves to see the hand-writing on the walls of their palaces and to feel everything giving way beneath them.

How this contest will end God alone knows. The period in which we live is indeed an eventful one. Events are hourly occurring of the most grave significance, and where all will end I hardly dare conjecture. There are moments when I despair, when the future is overspread with thick clouds, and no light reaches my eye, except now and then a lightning flash, which merely makes the darkness more awful. I look on with fear and trembling. It is a time for men to hold their breath in expectation. Still the prevailing state of my mind inclines to a favorable termination of this fearful war. As a lingering lightning flash throws back the darkness, I seem to catch a glimpse of the Son of Man seated in the clouds of heaven, surrounded by the ministers of his justice, and the agents of his power; and there comes to my ear, as the voice of many waters, "The doom of Babylon is sealed," I seem to see the storm commissioned, to hear the rushing of the mighty wind that is to sink her ships in the ocean, and to prostrate herself with a thunder crash that shakes the world. This may be all a mere vision. But I must believe that the great day of reckoning has come, that the saints are to be avenged, and justice and truth henceforth to govern the world. God grant that I be not deceived.

11.

AN ADDRESS ON POPULAR EDUCATION[1]

My friends, I take the liberty of calling your attention to the subject of education. This is a subject on which everybody speaks, on which many write, but which is yet far from being exhausted. Much yet remains to be said, and done too, in reference to education, before we can have anything like the education befitting a free people or demanded for the development and perpetuity of our free institutions.

Education is something more than is commonly understood by the term. Education is something more than the ability to read and write and cipher, with a smattering of grammar, geography and history into the bargain. Education is the formation of character. It is not acquired in schools only, in the few months or the few years our children are in the school-room. It begins with the first impression made on the senses of the infant, and ends only with the last made on those of the man before he sinks into the grave; and it embraces the results of all the circumstances and influences which have, or which have had, the least possible bearing in making up or determining the individual character. Its process is ever going on. The conversation, habits and conduct of parents; the spirit, manners and morals of brothers and sisters, of playmates, companions, associates and of the whole society, all contribute to it and aid in determining its character. These influences make up the real education received. Our schools do and can do but little. Even their good influences may be more than overbalanced by the evil influences at home, in the streets, or in society at large.

Education will go on; there is no earthly power that can stop it. Our children will be educated in spite of all our efforts. But shall they be educated for good or for evil? This is a question for the community to determine. They are educated for good only when they are educated for their destiny; trained up, fitted to discharge the mission which God Almighty has given to each one. No education is

[1][Ed. Delivered in Winnisimmet Village, on Sunday evening, July 23, 1837 (Boston: J. Putnam, 1837).]

a good one which does not take the child from its mother's arms, and train it up to be a Man, with a lofty soul, with generous sympathies, high aims, conscious of his destiny, and prepared to leave his trace on his age and country for good. God has given to each human being born into the world a high and important mission, a solemn and responsible charge; and that only is a good education which recognizes that mission, charge, and creates the power, and forms the character to fulfill it. This is the education we want.

This is the education we want; and the education we must have too, or vain are all our boasts of freedom and fallacious will prove all our hopes of preserving our free institutions. Freedom is not a thing to be written on paper, engrossed on parchments, or preserved in the archives of state; it must be written in the heart; it must be a well of living waters, springing up in the soul, and diffusing its fertilizing streams over the whole man and the whole life. Liberty comes not from without; it is not a child of decrees, of conventions and legislative enactments; it comes, if it come at all, from within, from the very ground of the moral and intellectual man. It is only a free people that can make a free government; and it is only the freedom of the individual soul that can create and preserve freedom in the state.

We have instituted a free government; we have adopted the principle of universal suffrage; we have made, in some sort, every man in the country a legislator, given him a direct legal voice in all the affairs of the state and nation. This we have done. Some, indeed, may regret it, may blame the policy which has done it; but done it is, and it is in vain to attempt to undo it. We cannot go back to a property qualification in electors even if we would. We might as well attempt to go back to the old feudal system, and revive the old seignors and their vassals, lords and lords paramount. The whole tendency of modern civilization is against such a retrograde movement. He who would do it, must war not only against the whole spirit of modern civilization, but against the design of Christianity, against the whole force of humanity, and even against the omnipotence of humanity's Maker, God himself. Power has passed out of the hands of the few; it has passed down into the hands of the many, of the millions, and there it is, there it will be; there, too, thank God, it ought to be, and was intended by the Creator to be.

But this fact imposes upon every friend of law and order, upon every friend of the human race, and lover of individual or social progress, a solemn and imperious duty. Power, in the hands of an ignorant and vicious populace, is a dangerous thing. With the power should go the virtue and intelligence needed to wield it with safety and with beneficial results to humanity. This virtue and this intelligence do not yet exist in any community on earth. They do not exist with us. We are yet far, very far, from the virtue which wills nought but the public good, and the intelligence which clearly perceives what that good is and seizes at once the proper means for securing it. Few, very few, of our whole community, not one in a hundred, understand the principles of legislation or can comprehend the full bearings of a single important law or influential public measure. In this case, what safeguard have we for liberty? What certainty of just legislation and wholesome public measures? How can men vote understandingly when they comprehend not the course that they whom they vote for should pursue? The history of our past legislation, and the present condition of the country, may read us a useful lesson on this subject if we are not among those who are incapable of being taught, even by experience.

No man can have observed the events, which have of late transpired in our country, without grief and alarm. The frequent occurrence of mobs, and lynching, shows us plainly that a lawless spirit is abroad, and a spirit not the less alarming because not in all cases confined to the lower classes.[2] Let this spirit prevail and where are we? And how will you check it? By riot laws? By preaching? By moral or patriotic lectures? No. You may read riot laws "till your throats are sore," preach till you are exhausted, give moral and patriotic discourses from sunrise till sundown, and from sundown to sunrise, and mobs will occur; Judge Lynch[3] will occupy the bench, and Justice will desert her throne, and Liberty cover herself with sackcloth and ashes. Nor will the military save you: insubordination will enter its ranks and the soldier called out to defend may be the first to trample on law and order. You have no security, no arm of defense, so long as there are among you the materials out of which mobs are

[2][Ed. Some mob activity had already occurred in Charlestown, Massachusetts, in the burning of the Ursuline Convent in August of 1834, in Boston when Southern sympathizers had mobbed a peaceful anti-slavery anniversary celebration in 1836, and in various other places across the country where lawless mobs and secret lynchings had taken place. On the rise of violence and mob activity in the United States, especially between 1833 and 1838 when ninety-six incidents were reported, see Leonard L. Richards, *Gentlemen of Property and Standing: Anti-Abolition Mobs in Jacksonian America* (New York: Oxford University Press, 1970), 7-19, especially 14 for statistics. See also James Elbert Cutler, *Lynch-Law: An Investigation into the History of Lynching in the United States* (New York, 1905), chap. 4.]

[3][Ed. The reference here is to Charles Lynch (1736-96), a Virginia planter and justice of the peace whose name has been associated with executing criminals or those suspected of criminal activities without due process of law.]

made, or tools for the lawless or the ill-disposed to use. Your only safety is in education, in an education which trains up the whole people to love law and order, which trains them up to love virtue and freedom, and which fits them to maintain freedom in the state by first maintaining it in themselves.

And the *whole* people: the education, even the right education, of a few, will not suffice. Athens had her learned, her educated few; she has left us models in the arts, given us poets and orators, we yet emulate in vain, and philosophers, whose depths we are not yet able to fathom: but Athens has fallen, and for long ages sighed under the whip of the despot. Rome, too, once the haughty mistress of the world, boasted of her freedom; but she has fallen, and solitude reigns on the Seven Hills of her power. Wherefore? Not for the want of an educated few, not for the want of poets, orators, statesmen, jurists, philosophers; but for the want of an educated, an enlightened people. The feeble lights gleaming out from the windows of a few solitary students were lost in the thick darkness which brooded over the many. And so will it ever be. We must have an *educated people*; the many must go to school, and stay there too, till they are formed into freemen, into men in whose souls liberty lives, and in whose minds are the ideas that will ensure her universal empire and immortal life.

The *whole* people must be educated; not one half only; not man only, but woman as well as man. In forming the character and determining the fate of a people, woman's is the more important, the more influential sex. She nurses us in our infancy, she plays with us in childhood, she is our companion in the vigor of manhood, she soothes us in the gloom of old age, bends over our dying bed, and drops her tear into our graves. Her rank determines the rank of the race. Ask nothing great of that nation where woman is man's slave or the mere plaything of his pastime, the mere appanage of his pleasures. Man is often selfish and easily discouraged; he wavers before a difficult undertaking, and shrinks from even the righteous cause when it demands of its adherents the sacrifice of ease, reputation, rank or wealth. He needs a voice that shall bid him be firm, be true to the righteous cause, in evil as well as in good report, true to duty though he stand alone—though he be obliged to beg—though he die. It is woman alone from the fullness of her inspiration and the disinterestedness of her sympathies that can give utterance to that voice. Let her then be educated—be educated to be the mother and the companion of Men—of such men, too, as a free government demands, as this country demands to fulfill its destiny, to perfect its mission. All the children of the land must be educated, both male and female; and educated thoroughly, morally, intellectually, physically, religiously. Nothing else can save us. Liberty is a mere dream when not coupled with universal education.

These, after all, are but common-place remarks. Everybody among us who pretends to have any thoughts at all admits all I have thus far said. It comes to us in Fourth of July orations; it comes to us from the pulpit, in public addresses, in Lyceum lectures, in legislative reports; but, as yet, we have done little more than to admit its necessity, and to spend our energy in talking on and about it. Education, in the broad sense in which I have defined it, nowhere exists among us, and nowhere is there provision made, or begun to be made, that it may exist among us. While we are talking about the importance of education, the lawless spirit is passing over the land, and our children are growing up to be leaders of mobs, the mere tools of demagogues, or, what is worse, to be demagogues themselves. It is time that something be done, and be done quickly, and be done effectually.

But what can be done? The citizens of one town alone cannot do all that ought to be done. The citizens of this town have it not in their power to do all that is required to train up all the children of the town even to be what they should be. But we can do something; and we may do much to improve our public schools, our district schools. This system of schools, which is the boast of New-England, may require in time, to be re-cast, and after a somewhat different model. It perhaps will not be found equal to the increasing educational wants of the people. It may hereafter be ascertained and believed that colleges, universities for the few, and district schools for the many is not the most republican usage possible; but the system is worth something—it has its merits and is susceptible of new developments, and may be made to yield richer and far more precious fruits than it ever yet has yielded. At present, the first duty of the friends of education is to carry these district schools to the highest degree of perfection of which they are capable.

This may be done by the parents and guardians in each school district taking a deeper and more personal interest in whatever relates to the school. They must not absent themselves from the meetings of the district, and leave its affairs to be managed merely by three or four. Everyone should show that he feels a personal interest in the affairs of the district, that he is willing to do his share of the labor and to take his share of the responsibility. This will keep the school up as a topic of thought and conversation, and by being made a constant topic of thought and conversation, it will stand a chance of receiving more than one valuable improvement.

Parents and guardians ought to interest themselves more in the school. They should all of them know precisely how the school is conducted, how it is managed in all respects, what progress children are making in their studies, what good influences they are under, or what bad influences obtain in school, or out of school on the playground. Many men can trace more of the evil which has appeared in them, in after life, to the evil influences at work out of the school, in the play-hours, on the playground, than to any other source whatever. A careful inspection of district schools throughout the country would, perhaps, show us that many of them are as much nurseries of vice as of virtue. It is sometimes a trying thing for the parent to send his little son to a district school. However tenderly he may have watched over him, whatever good precepts he may have instilled into him, or whatever virtuous instincts he may have awakened, a few months at the district school is often enough to send him home with a large stock of bad habits, of impudence, profanity, and disobedience. I know not how this can be wholly prevented; but much may be done to lessen the evil, if parents and guardians will but do their duty, in keeping a personal eye on the school and its pastimes.

In order to improve our district schools, we must pay more attention to the construction of schoolhouses. Hitherto, schoolhouses seem to have been constructed on the principle of occupying as little room and of being as inconvenient as possible. A small box, some eighteen feet by twenty, placed at the corners of the streets or crotch in the roads, with some four or five small windows, and furnished with a few hard benches without stay or support for the backs of the little occupants, has been deemed ample accommodation for thirty, forty, fifty or a hundred scholars, ranging from four to eighteen years of age. Into this narrow space they are crowded, compelled to breathe a confined and unwholesome air, to sit, with but a few minutes recess, to sit still too, for three long hours, poring over a dull and unintelligible lesson, and we wonder our children are not more healthy and more fond of the school and of study! It is impossible that our children should love study, that they should study with advantage or preserve their health, in such confined rooms and in such an impure and unwholesome atmosphere. Who of us could, or would, submit to what we, in this respect, exact of our children? We can remedy the evil only by enlarging our schoolhouses, making them spacious, light and airy; in which there shall be room for the lungs and the mind to expand—for the young thoughts to grow. We should furnish, on the score of schoolhouses, every possible accommodation. The schoolroom should be as richly and tastefully fitted up as the drawing room.

The next and last thing, I shall mention for the improvement of our district schools, is more care in the selection of teachers. They who teach our schools have heretofore, in innumerable instances, been persons fit for almost anything else rather than for that of teaching the young idea how to shoot; at least, how to shoot as it should. Of this, we are becoming pretty generally sensible. There is at present no small complaint made about the incompetency of teachers. But, in point of fact, good teachers, first rate teachers, have not generally been in any very great request, nor has anything like an adequate provision been made for securing their services. There has always been too low an estimate formed of what constitutes a good teacher. In some places, the good teacher is one who will teach for low wages; in others, he is the good teacher who pays great attention to some one branch, reading, or arithmetic, or penmanship, for instance, or who is a good disciplinarian; but in very few places, indeed, is there anything like an adequate conception formed of what it is to be a good teacher, a first rate educator.

The business of education is first in time, and in a free country first in importance. Legislations and administrations sink into insignificance before education. The legislator, the minister of state, the lawyer, the divine are quite subordinate personages compared with the schoolmaster. The schoolmaster, if he be the schoolmaster, makes and executes our laws, pleads our cases, writes our sermons; for he forms the mind from which these emanate. It is plain then to every man's common sense that the educator should be no common man—that his should be no ordinary mind. He should be a man of the first order of talent, of an enlarged and comprehensive intellect, of a warm heart and generous sympathies. He should be a man of thought, of a wide field of observation, of profound reflection, of pure moral feelings, and a correct moral and religious deportment. He should be well versed in the philosophy of mind, thoroughly acquainted with the laws of its development, with the laws by which it grows and may be perfected; he should know men and things, the philosophy of history and of society; he should fully comprehend man's destiny in this world, and the means by which it is to be achieved. This is something of what an educator should be, and if we cannot always obtain men who possess it all, we must aim at procuring those who possess the most of it. We must come up to the standard which I have erected, as nearly as possible. We must not take up with anything and everything calling itself a schoolmaster. A little "school-master larnin'" must not be accounted sufficient. We must seek out and employ and sustain the best and greatest men among us, the greatest and best we can find, and count no expense too great that secures their services.

Still, there is a great deficiency of good schoolmasters. There is not, in the country, the requisite number of good, of real educators for our children. One great cause of this deficiency is the little demand there has been for real educators; and another, perhaps, is in the fact that the people themselves need educating more than they have been before they will recognize or sustain the real educator, the one who will educate their children as they ought to be educated. Moreover, school teaching, in this money-making and money-loving country, has not been sufficiently lucrative to command the requisite talents and acquisitions. It has usually been a temporary and a precarious business; very few engage in it with the determination to make it a profession for life. It is in most cases an occasional pursuit, adopted as a stepping-stone to something else. This needs to be corrected; but it can be corrected only by making the business of teaching a high and honorable profession, a profession offering sufficient inducements to our young men to engage in it as their business for life. They will then qualify themselves for it, and will pursue it for itself, not merely as a means of helping them to something they account more honorable, and which society permits to be more profitable.

But were this done, there would be still a serious difficulty. We have no schools in which young men can qualify themselves to be teachers. This is a grand defect. There ought to be in every state and in every county, normal schools, schools for preparing educators for their profession. We have schools for lawyers, for physicians, for clergymen; but none for the educator. We are not willing to rely on chance for a supply of lawyers, physicians and clergymen, but apparently willing to rely on nothing else for a supply of educators, more vitally essential to the life and health and virtue of the people than they all. I trust this will not be so much longer. I hope the legislature, ere long, will take this matter up, and authorize the people in the several counties of the Commonwealth to establish the requisite number of normal schools, to make adequate provision for the supply of the demand for educators of children and youth. But till this be done, resort must be had to our higher schools, to our academies and higher seminaries.

In this point of view, the Winnisimmet Academy is deserving of your attention and patronage. This institution, which our Legislature has incorporated and which I hope will before long go into operation, may be an able auxiliary in furnishing a supply of good teachers for our common schools. It may be made, and I believe, to some extent, is intended to be made, a school in which young men, and young women too, may fit themselves for the profession of teaching, from which they may go out able and accomplished teachers.

Now that I have referred to this Academy, which is proposed to be established in our beautiful and healthy village, you must allow me to enlarge a little on its claims to your support. Do the best we can with our common schools and we shall find them inadequate to the educational wants of the community. Very few of us will or can be satisfied with giving our children no better, more thorough education, than can be given them in the common schools. I would not speak disrespectfully of common schools; they do something to supply the want of a good education, but they do not, and cannot do all. The very wealthy can, indeed, send their children to distant schools, or employ private tutors; but the great mass of our citizens cannot do this; it must transcend their means. But with an academy of a high order at their own doors, as it were, the great mass of our citizens can find, can command the means of giving their children a good academical education. By this means, the sons and daughters of our poorer citizens would be so educated as to compete successfully with those of the more wealthy, and thus a practical equality would be maintained, republican habits would be strengthened, and additional security be given to our free institutions.

Academies are valuable institutions to the poor and to the middle classes. The rich, as I have intimated, can do without them. To them it is, comparatively, of little importance whether there be an academy in each town or not. But the case is very different with the majority of the people, especially with those in moderate or indigent circumstances. The poor boy cannot go off fifty or a hundred miles to attend an academy—he has not the means; but he can avail himself of nearly all the advantages of academic instruction, if the academy be within reach of his own home. I am fond of taking this view of academies; and I believe it is the true view, though many have looked upon them as aristocratic institutions, designed chiefly to benefit the children of the rich; but if they are of any more benefit to one section of the community than to another, it is to the poorer.

And this view of them should commend them to the love and support of the wealthy; certainly should not alienate from them those who have a superabundance of this world's goods. There is always, or there always should be, a high satisfaction in aiding those who need aid, in contributing to the well-being of those who, in a worldly point of view, are less favored than ourselves. No wealthy man ever had cause to repent his contributions to the educational wants of the community. No man ever yet really applauded himself but for the good he had been instrumental in doing. Man applauds himself only when he is conscious of being of some service to his race. This is as it should be. Man was made to be the friend, the helper, the brother of man; and it is only in befriending, helping, manifesting a brotherly love for man, that he tastes the sweets of existence and learns how blessed it is to live.

But if selfish considerations, considerations for which I have no great respect, and to which I seldom appeal—if selfish considerations must have a place, they are not wanting. Duty and interest are seldom, if we view the matter rightly, disconnected. The establishment of an academy in our village, especially on the pleasant spot selected for it—a fine airy location, commanding one of the most beautiful prospects in the world, and the grand amphitheater in which have taken place some of the most important and soul-kindling events in the world's history, will by no means diminish the value of property, or render ours a less delightful place of residence. It will bring to us an additional number of the best inhabitants of our neighboring city, who are anxious to escape the confinement, dust, noise and impure atmosphere of a city, for the green fields, pure air, freshness and tranquillity of the country; and who are deterred now from coming only for fear that they shall lose some educational advantages they now enjoy. Our vicinity to the city, making it perfectly convenient to reside here and do business there, together with the healthiness and beauty of the place, must always make it a desirable place of residence. Let our schools be equal to the first and best of those of the city, and everyone who has a lot to sell shall find a purchase, and every vacant lot shall have erected on it a dwelling, and every dwelling shall be filled with a happy, virtuous and intelligent family.

12.

INTRODUCTORY REMARKS

Boston Quarterly Review 1 (January, 1838): 1-8

In adding another to the numerous periodicals of our country, I have not much to say by way of introduction and nothing by way of apology. I undertake the present publication, with a deep feeling of responsibleness and with the hope of contributing something to the moral pleasure and social progress of my countrymen.

Had I consulted my ability to conduct a periodical as I would see one conducted, or had I listened to the counsels of some of my warmest and most judicious friends, I had not engaged in my present undertaking. But I seem to myself to be called to it by a voice I dare not and even cannot disobey if I would. Whether this voice, which I have long heard urging me to the work, be merely an illusion of my own fancy, the promptings of my own vanity and self-esteem, or whether it be an indication of duty from a higher source, time and the result must determine. It speaks to me with Divine authority, and I must obey.

No man is able to estimate properly the value of his own individual experience. All are prone to exaggerate more or less, the importance of what has happened to themselves. This it is altogether likely is the case with me. Yet in my own eyes my experience possesses some value. My life has been one of vicissitude and trial. My mind has passed through more than one scene of doubt and perplexity. I have asked in the breaking up, as it were, of my whole moral and intellectual being, What is the destiny of man and of society? Much of my life has been spent—wasted perhaps—in efforts to decipher the answer to this question. In common with others, I have tried my hand at the riddle of the Sphinx; and in common with others too, I have, it may be, faith in my own explanation. In seeking to solve the problem which has pressed heavily on my heart, as well as on my mind, I have been forced to appeal from tradition and authority to the universal reason, a ray of which shines into the heart of every man that cometh into the world; and this, which has been forced upon me, I would force upon others. The answer, which I have obtained and which has restored peace and serenity to my own soul, I would urge others to seek, and aid them to find. For this purpose I undertake this Review.

I have not sought to solve the problem of the destiny of man and of society, without thinking for myself. By thinking for myself, I have found myself a solitary being, in a great measure shut out from communion with my race. Whoever thinks for himself will find himself thinking differently from the majority around him, and by this fact he will be alone in their midst. He will find few who can sympathize with his soul, recognize his voice, or comprehend his language. However his heart may yearn towards his brethren and however affectionately he would fold them in his bosom, he must submit to be regarded as a stranger, as an alien. He cannot speak to them and make them acquainted with what is concealed within him, through popular organs, or the established channels of communication. Those channels, though readily opened to others, are closed to him. They, who have it in their power to open them to whom they will, and shut them to whom they will, are afraid of him; they are ignorant of the value of what he would utter, and they see no mark by which they can even guess what it will pass for in the market. His thoughts have not been through the mint of public opinion, and therefore must be debarred from general circulation. In this case he must have his own medium of communication, organs of his own through which he can speak, or else he must remain silent. Perhaps the world would lose nothing were he to remain silent; but silence, when one's thoughts are pressing hard for utterance, when they are even rending one's bosom, and resolving they will out and to the world, is a thing not entirely at one's command. There are times when I experience something like this, and when, do what I will, hold my peace I cannot. I must and will speak. What I say may be worth something, or it may be worth nothing, yet say it I will. But in order to be able to do this, I must have an organ of utterance at my own command, through which I may speak when and what I please. Hence, the *Boston Review*.

I ought in justice to the periodical press of the country to say that it has always been at my service as far as I have sought to use it. With one or two insignificant exceptions, I have never asked the privilege of inserting an article, which has not been granted. The *Christian Examiner*, a periodical for freedom and freshness unsurpassed in the world, has always been open to me; and, for aught I have reason to think, still would be; but that removes not the difficulty. There is a possibility of refusal. The editor's imprimatur must be obtained. The censorship may be indulgent, liberal, obliging yet it is censorship, and that is enough. The oracle within will not utter his responses when it depends on the good will of another whether they shall to the public ear or not. The evil of the thing does not consist in the refusal to publish what is written, but in hindering one from writing what he otherwise might. This is after all a small affair, but who is there that is not disturbed by small affairs more than by great?

I undertake this Review, then, for myself; not because I am certain that the public wants it, but because I want it. I want it for a medium through which I may say to those who may choose to listen to my voice, just what I wish to say, and through which I may say it in my own way and time. This is the specific object for which I undertake it. I cannot say whether what I shall utter will be for the public good or not. What is for the public good ? Who knows? I do not. This or that may seem to me today for the public good, and tomorrow's eve proves me mistaken; and yet how know I that? That which I shall tomorrow's eve account a public evil, may turn out to have been a public blessing. Man seeth not the end and knoweth not the termination of events. He cannot say which is the blessing or which is the curse. All that is for him is what his hand findeth to do, to do it, and the word which is pressing for utterance, to utter it, and leave results to God, to whom alone they belong. I am not wise enough to say dogmatically what is or what is not for the public good; but I know what I think, what comes to me as truth; and as a watchman I would tell what I see, or seem to see, and let them of the city treat it as they will. Man is a seer and it is each man's duty to declare simply what he sees, without attempting to fix its precise value, and without allowing himself to be disturbed because others may not rate its value precisely as he does.

I would not, however, leave it to be inferred from this, that I am indifferent to the welfare of my fellowmen. Perhaps their interest is dear to me; and it may be that I would do them good; but I dare not say that this or that is for their good, and that they must do as I bid them. Once in my life I set up to be a reformer, a bold innovator, but not now. I would aid a reform, it is true, but I dare not say, that what I may propose, or what seems to me as desirable, ought to be adopted, and must be adopted, in order to obtain that greater good, after which humanity yearns and struggles. All I can do, all I have a right to do, is to throw my opinion into the common mass of opinion, and let it go for what it is worth. It may be worth something, as is every man's independent opinion, but it cannot be worth much. No man's opinion is worth much, except to himself. Men themselves, in the great movements of humanity, count for less than they imagine. There is a power above man, call it fate, necessity, or God, that carries all things along as they should and must go, without any deference to individuals, and without any aid from human volitions. What a man wills, says, and does, is of grave import, as concerns himself, his own moral character, his acquittal or condemnation before the august tribunal of conscience; but it alters not the fate of nations, and neither hastens nor retards the progress of humanity. The Power above achieves his own work with or without human cooperation in his own way and time, and in my humble belief, makes all things at last turn out for the best. With this belief my mind rests easy as to the final result. With this belief I come forward merely to play my part, utter my word, do my duty, and then pass off, satisfied if I have executed my mission, whatever it may be, to the acceptance of my Master, I would say, my Father, that I need not be at all uneasy about the consequences.

It may easily be inferred from what I have said, that I have no very definite objects to accomplish. I establish no journal to carry this or that proposed measure, to give currency to this or that doctrine, to support this or that party, this or that class. I belong to no party under heaven, to no sect on earth, and swear allegiance to no creed, to no dogma. I have no wish to build up one party or to pull down another, to aid one sect or to depress another, or to recommend this school in preference to that. I would discourse freely on what seem to me to be great topics, and state clearly and forcibly what I deem important truths; push inquiry into all subjects of general interest, awaken a love of investigation, and create a habit of looking into even the most delicate and exciting matters, without passion and without fear. This is all.

I own, however, that I am desirous of contributing something to the power of the great movement party of mankind, or rather of showing that I have the will, if not the ability, to aid onward the great movement commenced by Jesus of Nazareth, and which acquires velocity and momentum in proportion as it passes through successive centuries, and which is manifesting itself now in a manner that makes the timid quake and the brave leap for joy. With this movement, whether it be effecting a reform in the church, giving us a purer and more rational theology; in philosophy seeking something profounder and more inspiriting than the heartless sensualism of the last century; or whether in society demanding the elevation of labor with the Loco foco,[1] or the freedom of the slave with the abolitionist, I own I sympathize, and I thank God that I am able to sympathize. I sympathize with the progress of humanity wherever I see it; and it is my life and my delight to contemplate and try to aid it.

But I am growing too egotistical; what I have said will disclose the character of this Review as far as it needs to be disclosed in an introduction. I will only add that it will probably be very heretical, and show a fellow feeling for heretics of every name and nature. All, who are afraid of heresy, who want the nerve to look even the most arch-heresy in the face, had better not patronize it, nor even undertake to read it. It is not designed for them and will by no means do them any good. It is addressed only to those who love truth and are willing to follow wherever her light may lead, to those only who are willing to "prove all things" and have the desire to "hold fast that which is good" [1 Thess. 5:21]. How many such there be I know not; perhaps I shall not find out; but I venture to say that they are three times more numerous than most people think and their number is every day increasing.

One word as to the name I have selected. I call it a Review because that term is indefinite and allows me to discourse on anything I please. Moreover it has nothing in it offensive like the name "New Views," which I was sometime ago so foolish, not to say presumptuous, as to give to a little work I thought worth the publishing, though hardly anybody seems to have thought it worth the reading.

I add the epithet Boston, both to designate the place whence it is published, and to pay a sort of compliment to this goodly city. Boston is, of all the cities in the Union, the one in which thought is freest and boldest, and in which progress finds its warmest and most enlightened friends. I may say this for I am not a Bostonian. I know Boston is called an aristocratic city and I know also that democracy is a word for which it has no slight aversion; but in point of fact, it has less aristocracy than any other of our cities and is more truly democratic in its practice. One may indeed see now and then the representative of a by-gone generation, walking the streets with an antique air and dress, but he is, after all, one who makes us doubt whether we

[1][Ed. Locofoco refers to a radical wing of the Democratic party in the mid 1830s. Locofocos were those who opposed the so-called "bank Democrats" and supported the old Workingmen's party. Locofocos took their name from the trade name of a friction match used to light the candles at one of the early party meetings. On the Locofocos, see Arthur M. Schlesinger, Jr., *The Age of Jackson* (1945; Boston: Little, Brown and Co., 1953), 190-209.]

have advanced much on our fathers. True, there is here and there a purse-proud *parvenu*, and a poor worshiper of fashion, but even these it has been conjectured, and not without reason, have souls, and even hearts[2] which may with proper applications be made to beat with something like sympathy with humanity, and admiration of a generous sentiment or a heroic deed. Boston is, say what you will of it, the city of "notions," and of new notions too; and in the progress of liberal ideas in this country, it ever has and ever will take the lead. Elsewhere there may be more bustle, more pretense, more profession of liberty, of reform, of progress, of democracy; but when it comes to the reality, Boston need not blush in the presence of any of her sisters. This being the case, it is proper that I should call my Review the *Boston* Review, intimating thereby that it contains in some sort *Boston* notions; and sure am I that in Boston shall I find for it the most sympathy and its best friends.

In conclusion, I merely add that, as this Review is the organ of no party, nobody but its editor, and those of his friends who may contribute to its pages, must be at all implicated in its sins and heresies. It is a free journal. It will be open to the discussion of all subjects of general and permanent interest, by any one who is able to express his thoughts—providing he has any—with spirit, in good temper, and in good taste.

[2]Sartor Resartus. [Ed. Thomas Carlyle (1799-1881), *Sartor Resartus. In Three Books* . . . (1831; Boston: J. Munroe, 1836).]

13.

CHRIST BEFORE ABRAHAM[1]

Boston Quarterly Review 1 (January, 1838): 8-21

Christianity is generally, at least extensively, taken to be an original revelation, a set of moral and religious doctrines communicated to mankind for the first time by Jesus of Nazareth. Two controversies have thence arisen, which have not been without their effect on the faith and prosperity of the church. The first has been among professed Christians themselves, and has had for its object to ascertain and settle the precise doctrines Jesus revealed. The other has sprung up in modern times between professed Christians and unbelievers.

Unbelievers, raking together a modicum of erudition, have attempted, by an appeal to the records of antiquity, to show that all the doctrines and precepts contained in the New Testament were known in the world long before the time of Jesus. Some of the defenders of the faith have denied this, and set themselves at work to find out the doctrine or the precept which was peculiar to Jesus, and of which there is no historical trace anterior to the Christian era. But in this, so far as I am informed, they have not succeeded. At one time they have claimed one doctrine, at other times another; now this moral precept and now that. Some have insisted upon it that the command to forgive or to love one's enemies is the original and peculiar revelation; others have claimed the doctrine of the resurrection or the immortality of the soul; and others, that of a future retribution; and others still, the doctrine of the ultimate holiness and happiness of all mankind. But none of these are peculiar to the gospel. Plato, as well as Jesus, teaches the forgiveness of enemies; and all antiquity believed in a future life; and all the views which now obtain in regard to that life were prevalent long before Jesus lay in his manger-cradle. Indeed, if the truth of Christianity depended on the fact that it was an original revelation with Jesus, we should be obliged to give it up. Nothing

[1][Ed. The title of this article is "Christianity not an Original Revelation with Jesus, nor a System of Theological Doctrines, Properly so Called." The running title is "Christ Before Abraham." On the peculiarity and originality of Jesus, a companion article to "Christ Before Abraham," see "The Character of Jesus and the Christian Movement," *Boston Quarterly Review* 1 (April, 1838): 129-52.]

is more evident to them who have investigated the subject, than that all the doctrines and precepts of the New Testament were known in the world at least many hundred years before the time of Jesus; and they who contend to the contrary do great disservice to the Christian cause, besides exposing themselves to a certain and even shameful defeat.

On the other hand, the controversy among professed Christians themselves, as to the precise doctrines Jesus taught, is very far from being ended, and does not seem likely to be brought very soon if ever to a satisfactory termination. Each party appeals to the Bible; but, little is done save to pit text against text and commentary against commentary. Each, according to its own reading, finds the Bible expressly in its own favor, and pointedly against its opponent; and each may fight on and fight on with no danger of exhausting its ammunition. For nearly two thousand years the wordy war has been waged, and for aught we can see it may be waged for two thousand years to come, without any prospect of peace or even of a temporary cessation of hostilities. The truth is—and we may as well own it as not—that it is very nearly if not quite impossible to settle definitely, to the satisfaction of all concerned, what are the precise doctrines taught or implied in the New Testament. The book itself is none of the clearest, and its language, on most occasions, is far from being definite. And then it was written long ago, amidst peculiar circumstances, by peculiar men, and in an idiom altogether different in its genius and complexion from ours. Its exact meaning, it appears to me, must forever remain a matter of doubt and dispute to the ablest philologists and the most experienced critics. Each interpreter, notwithstanding his most strenuous efforts to the contrary, will interpret it according to the peculiar cast and biases of his own mind; and as these vary in each interpreter, each must necessarily interpret it differently from the other.

Now it strikes me that both of these controversies are needless and uncalled for. Christianity, according to its usual interpretation, that is, as a particular set of moral and theological doctrines, is not an original revelation with Jesus, and when interpreted as it should be, it is not the revelation of any specific doctrines or dogmas at all.

All truth is immutable and eternal. There is no new truth; there is no old truth. Relatively to us, truth may indeed be new or old, but not in itself. It is from everlasting to everlasting, the same yesterday, today, and forever.[2] It is not made, not created, but is, ever was, and ever will be. We may be ignorant of it; that is, it may be unrevealed to us; but it exists not the less, is the same, just as much the truth before

[2][Ed. Brownson refers here to Heb. 13:8.]

as after we become acquainted with it. The time when, or the individual by whom it is made known do not affect it. The age in which it is first revealed can add nothing to its truthfulness, and the individual who first declares it can add nothing to its legitimate authority. The truth of Christianity can, then, in no way, be made to depend on the time when or the individual by whom it was first taught. Say it was taught thousands of years before Jesus, by nobody knows whom. What then? If true, it is not the less true on that account. If it be not true, the fact, that it was taught about eighteen hundred years ago by Jesus of Nazareth, cannot make it true. In order to determine whether it be true or not, it is needless to inquire when or by whom it was first taught. The teacher does not make the truth; he but teaches that which is as true without him as with him. Grant then to the unbeliever that all the doctrines of the New Testament were known to the world long before the age of Jesus, you grant him nothing to the detriment of Christianity.

But in point of fact, the New Testament writers and even the early fathers do not profess to regard Christianity as an original revelation with Jesus. Several of the early fathers stated expressly in their apologies for Christianity that it was no new religion; that they did not consider themselves as teaching any new faith or philosophy, but merely that which had been embraced by the sages, patriarchs, and philosophers of old. Paul, in his Epistle to the Galatians, assures us that he was teaching no new religion; "for the scriptures, foreseeing that God would justify the heathen through faith, preached before the gospel unto Abraham" [Gal. 3:8]. And he contends earnestly that they who believe are justified with "faithful Abraham" [Gal. 3:9]; that is, as I interpret it, on the same ground, by the same faith or religion as that on or by which Abraham was justified. Jesus himself says to the Jews, "Abraham rejoiced to see my day; and he saw it and was glad" [John 8:56]. The Jews say unto him, "Thou art not yet fifty years old; and hast thou seen Abraham?" "Before Abraham was, I am" [John 8:58], was his reply. The New Testament writers all teach us, so far as they teach us anything on this point, that the "Lamb of God which taketh away sin" [John 1:29], was "the Lamb slain from the foundations of the world" [Rev. 13:8]. Indeed, had they not regarded the doctrines they were teaching as having been previously taught, how could they, with the least show of propriety, have made the use they did of previous writings? Whenever they preach or address themselves to the Jews, they appeal to Jewish writings, and undertake to prove from them that what they were preaching was not only in harmony with, but actually contained in "the law and the prophets." Paul, when he preaches to the gentiles, quotes or refers to gentile writings, apparently for the purpose of proving to them that he was but teaching what had already been taught by their own poets, wise men, and philosophers. Whence the propriety of this, if they were the teachers of a new, original, and peculiar revelation?

Now these considerations satisfy me that neither Jesus nor his apostles ever pretended to teach a new religion, that they did not regard themselves as setting forth doctrines essentially different from those which had long been entertained, and perhaps widely diffused. They laid no claims to originality. They appeared to themselves to be but reviving the faith which had been from the beginning. They were reformers, but not innovators. And this has in reality been the uniform belief of the great majority of the Christian world. In ascertaining the doctrines of the gospel, until quite lately, at least, the Christian world has considered the Old Testament of equal authority with the New.

But in the next place, I contend that Christianity, understanding it as Jesus and his apostles seem to have understood it, is not a system of moral and religious doctrines. It was not the doctrines Jesus and the apostles preached, as we usually understand the word doctrines, that produced the Christian movement, the Christian revolution; but the life they lived, the spirit and disposition they displayed. The doctrines they preached had been preached before, and by others, but without the effect Jesus and his apostles produced. The simple preaching of those doctrines never could have revolutionized the world. The new power they seemed to acquire was the power of a new life. Not they, but the new life arrested men's attention, moved men's hearts, changed their dispositions, commanded their assent, and made them new creatures. The power of Jesus to live and die for man as man, of the apostles to endure hardships, and perils, and death, in the cause of humanity, was the moving power, the creator of that mighty change in the face of the moral world effected by preaching the gospel.

This is the view which all the New Testament writers seem to me to take of Christianity. They never, if I rightly recollect, represent the gospel as a proposition for the intellect to grapple with. They always propound it to the heart; never, I believe, to the understanding. It is the faith indeed, but the faith of the heart, not of the head. It is a life. It is spirit and an influence. Contrasted with Judaism, which the New Testament writers frequently designate as the flesh and as the world, it is spirit, the power of God, and the kingdom or reign of God. It is the spirit of power, of love, and a sound mind; God dwelling in the soul, presiding over the inner man, and guarding all the issues of life. It is the word of God, but not a mere doctrinal proposition which God reveals, for it is "quick and powerful, sharper than any two-edged sword, piercing even to the dividing asunder of soul and spirit, and of the joints and marrow, and is a discerner of the thoughts and intents of the heart" [Heb. 4:12]. The same view is taken by Paul, when he says to the Corinthians, "We preach Christ crucified, unto the Jews a stumbling-block and unto the Greeks foolishness. But unto them who are called, Christ the power of God and the wisdom of God" [1 Cor. 1:23-24].

Jesus speaks of himself as a way, and as the life. "I am the way and the truth—the resurrection and the life" [John 14:6]. "He that believeth on me shall never die" [John 11:26] and "the dead, who hear my voice, shall live."[3] "That," says John, "which was from the beginning, which we have heard, which we have seen with our eyes and looked upon, which our hands have handled of the word of life, that declare we unto you; for the life was manifested, and we have seen it, and do bear witness, and show unto you that eternal life, which was with the Father and which was manifested unto us" [1 John 1:1-2]. Now it is evident from the whole tenor of this first epistle of John, that this "word of life," this "life," this "eternal life, which was with the Father," is not an intellectual but a spiritual life. John did not call Christianity a life because by believing it one would be entitled to life and immortality in the world to come, but because it was life in itself, an endless life, the only life acceptable and well pleasing to God the Father.

We are exhorted to come to Jesus. "Come unto me," says Jesus, "all ye who are weary and heavy laden, and I will give you rest" [Matt. 11:28]. "Ye will not come to me that ye may have life" [John 5:40]. In order to be what God requires us to be, we must "receive the Son," — "believe on the Son" [John 9:35]—"eat his flesh and drink his blood" [John 6:53]; and we are assured that if we do not, we have "no life in us,"—"have not eternal life,"—"are dead,"—"condemned,"—with the "wrath of God abiding on us" [John 3:36]. Paul teaches us the same thing by the phrases, being in Christ, and Christ in us, which he so frequently uses. "There is therefore now no condemnation to them who are in Christ Jesus" [Rom 8:1]. "If any man be in Christ Jesus he is a new creature" [2 Cor. 5:17]. "If a man have not the spirit of Christ he is none of his" [Rom. 8:9]. "If Christ be in you the body is dead" [Rom. 8:10]. "Christ liveth in me" [Gal. 2:20].

[3]The King James Version [Jn. 5:25] reads: "the dead shall hear the voice of the Son of God: and they that hear shall live."

"Of whom I travail in birth again until Christ be formed in you" [Gal. 4:19]. "That Christ may dwell in your hearts" [Eph. 3:17]. "Christ who is our life" [Col. 3:4]. Now all this, and much more like it, is explained to my understanding by the exhortation, "Let this mind be in you which was also in Christ Jesus" [Phil. 2:5]. We are taught by it, that in order to be a Christian; to have true, spiritual, eternal life; to be a saint; to be saved; accepted with God; one must have that mind in him, which was in Jesus, be filled with the spirit with which he was filled; in a word, be what he was, a son of God, as he was a son of God, a joint-heir with him of the kingdom of heaven. That, by virtue of which one becomes a true Christian, must of course be Christianity; and nothing is more certain than that one becomes a true Christian according to the New Testament by living and only by living the life which Jesus lived—not by believing what he may have taught, but by being what he was, righteous as he was righteous.

Now nothing is more evident than that the life which Jesus lived was the life of pure, disinterested love, manifesting itself, on the one hand, in warm and unaffected piety towards God, and, on the other hand, in an abiding and all-enduring friendship for man—a friendship which led him to taste death on the cross for the human race. All his divine worth and exalted virtues are integrated in pure, disinterested love. He therefore is able to sum up all his commands in that simple declaration, "Thou shalt love the Lord thy God with all thy heart, and with all thy soul, and with all thy strength, and with all thy mind; and thy neighbor as thyself" [Luke 10:27]. Or more simply still in that new commandment he gave to his disciples, that "they should love one another as he had loved them" [John 13:34; 15:12]. They who observed this commandment were his disciples, and by observing it they were to be known as such. The simple fact, of loving one another as Jesus loved them, was to be a proof unto all men of their discipleship. "By this shall all men know that ye are my disciples, if ye have love one towards another" [John 13:35].

If this be accepted, and I see not how it can be avoided, it is certain that Christianity is not a system of theological doctrines, a set of propositions propounded to the understanding, but a life, the life of pure, disinterested love.[4] This conclusion to which I have arrived,

[4][Ed. Brownson's view of Christianity is similar to Samuel Taylor Coleridge's. On this, see Coleridge's *Aids to Reflection*, ed. John Beer, in vol. 9 of *The Collected Works of Samuel Taylor Coleridge*, 27 vols. (Princeton, N.J.: Princeton University Press, 1969), 9: 202. "Christianity is not a Theory, or a Speculation; but a *Life*. Not a *Philosophy* of Life, but a Life and a living Process."]

if duly considered, will carry us much further, and perhaps help us to solve several important and oftentimes troublesome problems.

The possession of the love which Jesus manifested proves one to be a true disciple. A true disciple is unquestionably a true Christian, one who has true, spiritual, eternal life, and is a subject of the kingdom of God. By possessing this love, then, one becomes precisely what he would be, by coming to Christ, receiving the Son, possessing the Son, by being in Christ, or by having Christ in him. The Christ, the Son, and love, then, are identical. The Christ which sanctifies, the Son which gives life, and the love which proves discipleship are, then, one and the same thing; and the three terms are only so many different terms for expressing the same spirit, power, influence, state, or disposition of the inner or spiritual man.

Now this fact implies a distinction which is sometimes overlooked, a distinction between Jesus and the Christ. Jesus, it is true, is called Christ, the Christ, but I apprehend only by that figure of speech by which the attribute is put for the subject, the character, office, or endowment for the individual. The term Christ was applied to Jesus because it was supposed that he answered to the Jewish prophecies of a Messiah. But the Jewish Messiah, in strictness, was not a person, but an impersonation of an idea, principle, or power. This I think will readily appear to all who will study the Jewish prophets carefully and without prejudice.

The Jewish prophets were dissatisfied with the state in which they found their nation and the world. In their view, the earth was abandoned to tyranny and oppression, to ignorance and gross idolatry. Darkness covered the land and gross darkness the people.[5] The nations sat in the region and shadow of death. Justice and judgment were not executed; truth and holiness had no dominion, and peace no dwelling-place. Men knew not God and loved not one another. But this could not last forever. By the Holy Spirit with which they were inspired, they foresaw that the period must come round when this state of things would cease to exist. They saw in that distant future into which God gave them to look, and from which they derived wherewithal to cheer their drooping spirits, that there was an unattained good in reserve for poor, suffering, struggling, downtrodden humanity; that the night would run out, a glorious morning dawn, a new sun arise with healing in his beams, to dispel the darkness and dry up pollution; that the sword and spear would be broken, the tyrant overthrown, the captive set free, wrongs and oppres-

[5][Ed. A reference here to Isa. 60:2.]

sions ended, the true God universally known and worshiped, and the whole earth filled with love and peace.

But how is this God-sent vision to be realized? The movement towards its realization, whether it be of the Jewish or gentile world, will need a leader, someone who may guide it to the end desired. Hence the conception of the Messiah, of a personage one day to appear, God-anointed, consecrated, commissioned to achieve the universal palingenesia of man and society.[6] The Messiah of the prophets was a deliverer, a renovator, the father of the age, the new order of things, which they foresaw, would in its appointed time be introduced. At one time they regard him as a prince of the line of David, far surpassing his renowned ancestor, a wise and judicious king reigning in righteousness, the father of his people, caring for the poor and needy; at another time, as a conquering hero, taking vengeance on the enemies of the Jewish nation, breaking the rod of the oppressor, and subjecting the heathen by his might in battle to the Jewish dominion; then again, as a priest, a prophet, an inspired teacher of truth and righteousness, converting the world by moral and spiritual means to the worship of the true God. But these are only the different forms which their fancy, their wants, or prejudices, as individuals or as Jews, necessarily led them to give, if I may be allowed the expression, to the Messianic idea. Divested of these forms, which are accidental and not necessary to the idea, the real Messiah of the prophets was the spirit, power, or agency by which the new order of things, in which they believed, was to be introduced and established.

Now if we can determine what is the spirit, power, or agency, which really introduces and establishes this new order of things, we can at once determine who or what is the real Christ. Whatever may have been the opinions of the Jewish prophets, the expectations of the Jewish people, or early notions of the disciples themselves, we know well today what it is. It is love, pure, disinterested love of God and humanity. Nothing but love is able to achieve a work so vast and

[6][Ed. Palingenesia refers to the new birth, or regeneration, from an older and lower state of existence to a higher and better life. This idea of regeneration was at the heart of Brownson's idea of progress in the 1830s, but Brownson's understanding of the term palingenesia, which he used repeatedly throughout his life, would change significantly as his theology moved from an inherent naturalism in the 1830s to various forms of supernaturalism in the early 1840s and thereafter. Brownson, like some in the French social tradition, emphasized the social as much as the individual dimension of palengenesia. Such a view would be at the heart of his own developing philosophy and theology of history. On the use of palingenesia in French social tradition, see Arthur McCalla, *A Romantic Historiosophy: The Philosophy of History of Pierre-Simon Ballanche* (Leiden: Brill, 1998), 135-72.]

so glorious. Nothing but love can make the wolf and the lamb lie down together, dethrone the tyrant, break the chains of the captive, unbar the prison door, beat the sword into the ploughshare and the spear into the pruning-hook, wipe the tears from off all faces, and fill the earth with gladness and peace. Love, then, is the true Messiah, the real Christ. And this is what I have before proved.

But Jesus is not love. He was an individual and is no more to be called love, or the Christ, than Socrates is to be called philosophy, Demosthenes eloquence, or Washington patriotism. The term Christ applies to him merely as the term eloquent to the great orator, or as we call the man, most eminent for oratory, the orator. Jesus in strictness was not the Messiah, the Christ; but he possessed the Christ; he was the individual who possessed, and in the most, eminent degree of any of the sons of men, that which brings in the new age, and effects the regeneration which the prophets foresaw and foretold. This is why he is called the Christ. The Christ was in him and without measure. This distinction between the individual Jesus and the Christ explains, if I mistake not, the mystery of the two natures which have been attributed to Jesus. The Scriptures plainly teach us that Jesus was a man, but they also seem to teach that he was more than man, that he was divine, if not God. Understand all that is said of Jesus Christ as a man, as applying to the individual Jesus, and what is said of him which seems to imply that he was more than man, as applying to the Christ that was in him, and you will have no difficulty.

By means of this distinction, we can easily dispose of the difficulty concerning the alleged preexistence and Deity of Jesus. Jesus was a man, and no more existed before he was born than other men. In a certain sense, preexistence may be affirmed of all men. In this sense, it may be affirmed of Jesus, but in no other. But the Christ preexisted and was divine. The Christ, I have proved, is love; but love existed long before Jesus was born. The Christ existing in Jesus was love incarnated, or made flesh, or manifested by one in the flesh. But God is love. The Christ being love, then, must be one with God. The Christ being, as I have shown, identical with the Son, it follows also that the Son is one with the Father, with this difference merely, that the Son is love incarnate, and the Father is love universal, constituting the ground and being of all that is. Christ, the Son, is then literally and truly God, only God under accident, God revealing himself in and through humanity. The Christ was in Jesus. Jesus loved; therefore God was in him. He dwelt in love; therefore he dwelt in God and God in him; as John says, "He that dwelleth in love dwelleth in God, and God in him" [1 John 4:16].

This distinction enables us to understand what Jesus meant when he said, "Before Abraham was, I am" [John 8:58]. He did not mean that he, the literal man, the man after the flesh, was before Abraham, for that was not true; but that the Christ, the Divine Love, which was in him, and in whose name he spoke, whose words he was uttering, and for which he was suffering reproach, was that by virtue of which Abraham had been raised to the dignity of being called the friend of God; that in which Abraham rejoiced, which he saw, though it may be but through a glass darkly, and in which he was glad. This Christ was before Abraham; it was eternal; it was in the beginning with God, and was God. And Jesus, by the passage referred to, would also teach the Jews that what he was urging upon them, the love he was urging them to possess and show forth, had been before Abraham, even from the beginning, the only savior of men, the only way of life, the only sacrifice, all-sufficient sacrifice, for sin, and the only means of justification and acceptance with God. The way of salvation is the same in all ages of the world. It is now what it ever was and ever will be. No man is accepted with God, till he is reconciled to him, at one with him; and what, but the possession of love, can reconcile or make us at one with a God who is love? Love only can make at one with love.

It is easy to see now why Jesus and his apostles gave the world no new religion. There had been good men before Jesus. But goodness, or that by virtue of which one is good, is the same in all ages and in all countries of the world and in all individuals too. They, who had been good before Jesus, had been good in the same sense, though it may be not in the same degree in which he was good. There is none good, absolutely considered, but one, and that is God. Men at best are only relatively good, and good only as they approach or partake of God. God is love; consequently men become good in proportion and only in proportion as they love or are filled with love.

Of the millions who had lived before Jesus, had none ever loved? Shall we say none of them had ever known anything of that love which was manifest in Jesus? If we may not say so, then Christianity was no new religion. It revealed no new truth; for every man, who had loved, had experienced and known its truth. To that truth Jesus may have given a fuller meaning; he may have developed and quickened the life of love, as it never had been before; but the truth he taught had always been in the world, and borne witness to by every man, in whose heart love had found a resting-place.

If I am right, I gain this important conclusion; to wit, a man's creed does not constitute his Christianity. He who fears God and works righteousness, that is, loves, is accepted with him, whatever be his creed, sect, nation, or mode of worship. The man who loves the Divinity with all his heart and soul, and his neighbor as himself, be he Jew or Moslem, be he Pagan or a professed Christian, is a Christian in the highest and only worthy sense of the term. He is a member of the true Christ's Church, and is one in the unity of his love with the good of all ages and nations, one with Jesus, and one with God. Thank God, there is and there never was but one church, and all who love are its members, and are brethren of the same religion, and will one day come together, however they may be separated now.

14.

DEMOCRACY[1]

Boston Quarterly Review 1 (January, 1838): 33-74

We have introduced this Address, because it gives us an opportunity for expressing ourselves on the vexed and sometimes vexatious question of democracy. In common with the great body of our countrymen, we are sturdy democrats; and, do what we can to prevent it, democracy will more or less tincture all that we write. But in order to avoid all just occasion of offence to those—if such there be—in whose minds the word *Democrat* calls up unpleasant associations, and to save ourselves from being misapprehended or misinterpreted, we design, in this article, to give as clear and as satisfactory an exposition, as we can, of what we understand by democracy, and of the sense in which we consider ourselves and wish others to consider us democrats.

1. We may understand by democracy a form of government under which the people, either as a body or by their representatives, make and administer their own laws. This is the original and etymological sense of the word; and in this sense, a democrat is one who believes in, or contends for a popular form of government. All, or nearly all Americans are democrats in this sense of the word. We have established a democratic government, both for the confederacy and for the several states; and there are few among us, if any, who would exchange it for another. Some may have less faith than others in the utility or permanence of this form of government; here and there one, perhaps, may be found with an individual preference for a limited monarchy; but virtually the whole people are seriously and honestly bent on preserving the institutions the wisdom of our fathers adopted. There may be those who question the propriety of this or that public measure, who object to this or that law, but none who object very strenuously to the form of the government itself. The American people are not revolutionists. They are conservatives, and to be a conservative in this country, is to be a democrat.

[1][Ed. Brownson's comments on "Address of the Democratic State Convention of Massachusetts," holden at Worcester, September 20, 1837.]

2. By the word *Democracy* we may designate the great body of the people, the unprivileged many, in opposition to the privileged few. In this sense of the word, a democrat is one who sympathizes with the masses, and who contends that all political and governmental action should have for its end and aim the protection of the rights and the promotion of the interests of the poorest and most numerous class. The whole, or nearly the whole American people are democrats also in this sense of the term. There may be differences of opinion, as to the means of promoting the good of the many, as to what constitutes their good, and as to the amount of good God has made them capable of receiving, obtaining, or enjoying, but none as to the principle that the government is bound to seek "the greatest good of the greatest number."

3. The term *Democracy* may also be applied, as it is applied in this country, to a certain political party. There is a political party in this country called the Democratic party. It sprang up on the adoption of the Federal Constitution, to which it was opposed, and which it refused to accept without some important amendments. It came into power with Mr. Jefferson, in 1801, and has had at least the nominal control of the general government ever since, though it has seldom had a majority in all the states. Its first party appellation was that of Anti-Federalist; in 1798 it was called the Republican party; since 1812, especially since 1825, it has assumed the name of the Democratic Republican or Democratic party. When we use the word *democracy* to designate this party, we call an adherent of this party a democrat. A democrat in this sense, however, does not imply so much the one who believes in the general doctrines of the Democratic party, and who countenances its principal measures, as the one who enters its ranks, puts on its livery, submits to its rules and usages, and feels himself bound by his duty to his party to vote for its candidates and to support its policy, whether he like them or not. He must be a good man and true, one on whom the party can count, and who will not disturb it by any obstinate adherence to the convictions of his own understanding, or the dictates of his own conscience. In the sense of a member of this party, a considerable number of the American people are not democrats. Some are not democrats because they disapprove the doctrines and measures of the Democratic party; others, because they have a very great aversion to being swallowed up in a multitude that goes hither and thither, just as some irresponsible will directs.

We are of the latter class. We do not call ourselves democrats in a party sense, because we have a great dislike to party tyranny, and because, wherever we are, we must speak according to our own convictions, and act as seemeth to us good, without asking the leave of a party. In a party sense, we are nothing. There is no party that can count on our fidelity. In politics, as in morals, theology, and philosophy, we are eclectics, and hold ourselves free to seek, accept, and support truth and justice wherever we can find them. No party is always wrong; no one is always right. We agree with all parties where they agree with us; but where they do not agree with us, we cannot and will not surrender our own convictions for the sake of agreeing with them or with any one of them.

4. The word *Democracy,* in the last place, may be taken as the name of a great social and political doctrine, which is now gaining much in popularity, and of a powerful movement of the masses towards a better social condition than has heretofore existed. In this sense the word is used in England and on the continent of Europe, though not often in this country. A democrat, in this sense of the word, is rather a philosophical, than a party democrat. He takes the word, not in a party and historical sense, but in a broad, philosophical sense. He distinguishes between party democracy as it exists in this country, and philosophical democracy, or democracy as it should be. With the first we do not concern ourselves. In the second, we take a deep interest, both as a man and as a citizen; and this Review will ever be found its fearless and untiring advocate.

But, what is philosophical democracy? Or the social and political doctrine, which may be called, not in an historical and party sense, but in a philosophical sense, the democratic doctrine? This is not a question without significance. It is a question it behooves every American citizen to ask, and, as far as he can, to answer. It needs a deliberate answer, such an answer as it has never yet, to our knowledge, received. Not a few of those who call themselves democrats are entirely ignorant of what democracy is, and wholly unable to legitimate the doctrines or the measures they support. Notwithstanding the much that has been said and written about democracy, it is yet more of an instinct, an impulse, a sentiment, than an idea. The masses feel its power and yield to its direction, but they see not whither they are going, and they comprehend not wherefore they ought to suffer themselves to be borne along on its current. They go, perhaps, where they ought to go, but they go blindly, without legitimating or being able to legitimate their course. It will not be useless then to attempt to seize this vague sentiment, this democratic instinct, and to do something to present it in a form that shall enable men to perceive what it is, and what are the grounds on which it may be legitimated.

Democracy, in the sense we are now considering it, is sometimes asserted to be the sovereignty of the people. If this be a true account of it, it is indefensible. The sovereignty of the people is not a truth. Sovereignty is that which is highest, ultimate; which has not only the physical force to make itself obeyed, but the moral right to command whatever it pleases. The right to command involves the corresponding duty of obedience. What the sovereign may command, it is the duty of the subject to obey.

Are the people the highest? Are they ultimate? And are we bound in conscience to obey whatever it may be their good pleasure to ordain? If so, where is individual liberty? If so, the people, taken collectively, are the absolute master of every man taken individually. Every man, as a man, then, is an absolute slave. Whatever the people, in their collective capacity, may demand of him, he must feel himself bound in conscience to give. No matter how intolerable the burdens imposed, painful and needless the sacrifices required, he cannot refuse obedience without incurring the guilt of disloyalty; and he must submit in quiet, in silence, without even the moral right to feel that he is wronged.

Now this, in theory at least, is absolutism. Whether it be a democracy, or any other form of government, if it be absolute, there is and there can be no individual liberty. Under a monarchy, the monarch is the state. "*L'Etat, c'est Moi,*"[2] said Louis the Fourteenth, and he expressed the whole monarchical theory. The state being absolute, and the monarch being the state, the monarch has the right to command what he will, and exact obedience in the name of duty, loyalty. Hence absolutism, despotism. Under an aristocracy, the nobility are the state, and consequently, as the state is absolute, the nobility are also absolute. Whatever they command is binding. If they require the many to be "hewers of wood and drawers of water" [Josh. 9:21] to them, then "hewers of wood and drawers of water" to them the many must feel it their duty to be. Here, for the many, is absolutism as much as under a monarchy. Everybody sees this.

Well, is it less so under a democracy, where the people, in their associated capacity, are held to be absolute? The people are the state, and the state is absolute; the people may therefore do whatever they please. Is not this freedom? Yes; for the state; but what is it for the individual? There are no kings, no nobilities, it is true; but the people may exercise all the power over the individual that kings or nobilities may; and consequently every man, taken singly, is, under a democ-

[2][Ed. French for "I am the State."]

racy, if the state be absolute, as much the slave of the state as under the most absolute monarchy or aristocracy.

But this is not the end of the chapter. Under a democratic form of government, all questions, which come up for the decision of authority, must be decided by a majority of voices. The sovereignty, which is asserted for the people, must, then, be transferred to the ruling majority. If the people are sovereign, then the majority are sovereign; and if sovereign, the majority have, as Miss Martineau[3] lays it down, the absolute right to govern. If the majority have the absolute right to govern, it is the absolute duty of the minority to obey. We who chance to be in the minority are then completely disfranchised. We are wholly at the mercy of the majority. We hold our property, our wives and children, and our lives even, at its sovereign will and pleasure. It may do by us and ours as it pleases. If it take it into its head to make a new and arbitrary division of property, however unjust it may seem, we shall not only be impotent to resist, but we shall not even have the right of the wretched to complain. Conscience will be no shield. The authority of the absolute sovereign extends to spiritual matters as well as to temporal. The creed the majority is pleased to impose, the minority must in all meekness and submission receive; and the form of religious worship the majority is good enough to prescribe, the minority must make it a matter of conscience to observe. Whatever has been done under the most absolute monarchy or the most lawless aristocracy may be reenacted under a pure democracy, and what is worse, legitimately too, if it be once laid down in principle that the majority has the absolute right to govern.

The majority will always have the physical power to coerce the minority into submission; but this is a matter of no moment in comparison with the doctrine which gives them the right to do it. We have very little fear of the physical force of numbers, when we can oppose to it the moral force of right. The doctrine in question deprives us of this moral force. By giving absolute sovereignty to the majority, it declares whatever the majority does is right, that the majority can do no wrong. It legitimates every possible act, for which the sanction of a majority of voices can be obtained. Whatever the majority may exact, it is just to give. Truth, justice, wisdom, virtue can erect no barriers to stay its progress; for these are the creations of

[3][Ed. Harriet Martineau (1802-76), British Unitarian author, published a widely read account of her travels to the United States. Her *Society in America* (3 vols., 1837) gave a favorable review of Brownson's work among the working class. On her, see *American National Biography* (1999), 14: 613-15.]

its will, and may be made or unmade by its breath. Justice is obedience to its decrees, and injustice is resistance to its commands. Resistance is not crime before the civil tribunal only, but also *in foro conscientiae.* Now this is what we protest against. It is not the physical force of the majority that we dread, but the doctrine that legitimates each and every act the majority may choose to perform; and therefore teaches it to look for no standard of right and wrong beyond its own will.

We do not believe majorities are exceedingly prone to encroach on the rights of minorities; but we would always erect a bulwark of justice around those rights and always have a moral power which we may oppose to every possible encroachment. The majority, we believe, always leave the minority in possession of the greater part of their rights, not however as rights, but as favors. It is to this we object. We cannot, and will not, consent to receive as a boon, what we may demand as a right. Our liberties belong to us as men; and we would always feel that we hold them as our personal property, of which he who despoils us is a thief and a robber.

The effects of this doctrine, so far as believed and acted on, cannot be too earnestly deprecated. It creates a multitude of demagogues, pretending a world of love for the *dear* people, lauding the people's virtues, magnifying their sovereignty, and with mock humility professing their readiness ever to bow to the will of the majority. It tends to make public men lax in their morals, hypocritical in their conduct; and it paves the way for gross bribery and corruption. It generates a habit of appealing, on nearly all occasions, from truth and justice, wisdom and virtue, to the force of numbers, and virtually sinks the man in the brute. It destroys manliness of character, independence of thought and action, and makes one weak, vacillating— a time-server and a coward. It perverts inquiry from its legitimate objects, and asks, when it concerns a candidate for office, not, who is the most honest, the most capable? But, who will command the most votes? And, when it concerns a measure of policy, not, what is just? What is for the public good? But, what can the majority be induced to support?

Now as men, as friends to good morals, we cannot assent to a doctrine which not only has this tendency, but which declares this tendency legitimate. That it does have this tendency needs not to be proved. Everybody knows it and not a few lament it. Not long since it was gravely argued by a leading politician, in a Fourth of July Oration, that Massachusetts ought to give Mr. Van Buren her votes for the presidency, because, if she did not, she would array herself against her sister states, and be compelled to stand alone, as the orator said with a sneer, "in solitary grandeur." In the access of his party fever, it did not occur to him that Massachusetts was in duty bound, whether her sister states were with her or against her, to oppose Mr. Van Buren, if she disliked him as a man, or distrusted his principles as a politician or a statesman. Many good reasons, doubtless, might have been alleged why Massachusetts ought to have voted for Mr. Van Buren, but the orator would have been puzzled to select one less conclusive, or more directly in the face and eyes of all sound morals, than the one he adduced. The man who deserves to be called a statesman never appeals to low or demoralizing motives, and he scorns to carry even a good measure by unworthy means. There is within every man, who can lay any claim to correct moral feeling, that which looks with contempt on the puny creature who makes the opinions of the majority his rule of action. He who wants the moral courage to stand up "in solitary grandeur," like Socrates in face of the Thirty Tyrants,[4] and demand that right be respected, that justice be done, is unfit to be called a statesman, or even a man. A man has no business with what the majority think, will, say, do, or will approve; if he will be a man, and maintain the rights and dignity of manhood, his sole business is to inquire what truth and justice, wisdom and virtue demand at his hands, and to do it, whether the world be with him or against him, to do it, whether he stand alone "in solitary grandeur," or be huzzaed by the crowd, loaded with honors, held up as one whom the young must aspire to imitate, or be sneered at as singular, branded as a "seditious fellow," or crucified, as was Jesus, between two thieves. Away then with your demoralizing and debasing notion of appealing to a majority of voices! Dare be a man, dare be yourself, to speak and act according to your own solemn convictions, and in obedience to the voice of God calling out to you from the depths of your own being. Professions of freedom, of love of liberty, of devotion to her cause, are mere wind when there wants the power to live, and to die, in defence of what one's own heart tells him is just and true. A free government is a mockery, a solemn farce, where every man feels himself bound to consult and to conform to the opinions and will of an irresponsible majority. Free minds, free hearts, free souls are the materials, and the only materials, out of which free governments are constructed. And is he free in mind, heart, soul, body, or limb, he

[4][Ed. Socrates was tried on charges of refusing to recognize the gods of the city and of corrupting the youth of the city. The charges came before a large jury and if thirty of the jurors had voted differently he would have been acquitted.]

who feels himself bound to the triumphal car of the majority, to be dragged whither its drivers please? Is he the man to speak out the lessons of truth and wisdom when most they are needed, to stand by the right when all are gone out of the way, to plead for the wronged and down-trodden when all are dumb, he who owns the absolute right of the majority to govern?

Sovereignty is not in the will of the people, nor in the will of the majority. Every man feels that the people are not ultimate, are not the highest, that they do not make the right or the wrong, and that the people as a state, as well as the people as individuals, are under law, accountable to a higher authority than theirs. What is this higher than the people? The king? Not he whom men dignify with the royal title. Every man, by the fact that he is a man, is an accountable being. Every man feels that he owes allegiance to some authority above him. The man whom men call a king, is a man, and inasmuch as he is a man, he must be an accountable being, must himself be under law, and, therefore, cannot be the highest, the ultimate, and of course not the true sovereign. His will is not in itself law. Then he is not in himself a sovereign. Whatever authority he may possess is derived, and that from which he derives his authority, and not he, in the last analysis, is the true sovereign. If he derive it from the people, then the people, not he, is the sovereign; if from God, then God, not he, is the sovereign. Are the aristocracy the sovereign ? If so, annihilate the aristocracy, and men will be loosed from all restraint, released from all obligation, and there will be for them neither right nor wrong. Nobody can admit that right and wrong owe their existence to the aristocracy. Moreover, the aristocracy are men, and as men, they are in the same predicament with all other men. They are themselves under law, accountable, and therefore not sovereign in their own right. If we say they are above the people, they are placed there by some power which is also above them, and that, not they, is the sovereign.

But if neither people nor kings nor aristocracy are sovereign, who or what is? What is the answer which every man, when he reflects as a moralist, gives to the question, Why ought I to do this or that particular thing? Does he say because the king commands it? The aristocracy enjoin it? The people ordain it? The majority wills it? No. He says, if he be true to his higher convictions, because it is right, because it is just. Every man feels that he has a right to do whatever is just and that it is his duty to do it. Whatever he feels to be just, he feels to be legitimate, to be law, to be morally obligatory. Whatever is unjust, he feels to be illegitimate, to be without obligation, and to be that which it is not disloyalty to resist. The absolutist, he who contends for unqualified submission on the part of the people to the monarch, thunders, therefore, in the ears of the absolute monarch himself, that he is bound to be just; and the aristocrat assures his order that its highest nobility is derived from its obedience to justice; and does not the democrat, too, even while he proclaims the sovereignty of the people, tell this same sovereign people to be just? In all this, witness is borne to an authority above the individual, above kings, nobilities, and people, and to the fact, too, that the absolute sovereign is justice. Justice is then the sovereign, the sovereign of sovereigns, the king of kings, lord of lords, the supreme law of the people, and of the individual.

This doctrine teaches that the people, as a state, are as much bound to be just, as is the individual. By bounding the state by justice, we declare it limited; we deny its absolute sovereignty; and, therefore, save the individual from absolute slavery. The individual may on this ground arrest the action of the state, by alleging that it is proceeding unjustly; and the minority has a moral force with which to oppose the physical force of the majority. By this there is laid in the state the foundation of liberty; liberty is acknowledged as a right, whether it be possessed as a fact or not.

A more formal refutation of the sovereignty of the people or vindication of the sovereignty of justice is not needed. In point of fact, there are none who mean to set up the sovereignty of the people above the sovereignty of justice. All, we believe, when the question is presented, as we have presented it, will and do admit that justice is supreme, though very few seem to have been aware of the consequences which result from such an admission. The sovereignty of justice, in all cases whatsoever, is what we understand by the doctrine of democracy. True democracy is not merely the denial of the absolute sovereignty of the king, and that of the nobility, and the assertion of that of the people; but it is properly the denial of the absolute sovereignty of the state, whatever the form of government adopted as the agent of the state, and the assertion of the absolute sovereignty of justice. Still, we are not insensible to the fact, that the doctrine of the sovereignty of the people marks an immense progress in political science, and in the sense in which they, who assert it, mean to assert it, it is no doubt true.

Sovereignty may be taken either absolutely or relatively. When taken absolutely, as we have thus far taken it, and as it ought always to be taken, especially in a free government, it means, as we have defined it, the highest, that which is ultimate, which has the right to command what it will, and which to resist is crime. Thus defined it is certain that neither people, nor kings, nor aristocracies are sovereign for they are all under law and accountable to an authority which is not theirs, but which is above them, and independent on them.

When taken relatively, as it usually is by writers on government, it means the state, or the highest civil or political power of the state. The state, we have seen, is not absolute. It is not an independent sovereign. It is not, then, in strictness, a sovereign at all. Its enactments are not in and of themselves laws, and cannot be laws, unless they receive the signature of absolute justice. If that signature be withheld they are null and void from the beginning. Nevertheless social order, which is the indispensable condition of the very existence of the community, demands the creation of a government, and that the government should be clothed with the authority necessary for the maintenance of order. That portion of sovereignty necessary for this end, and, if you please, for the promotion of the common weal, justice delegates to the state. This portion of delegated sovereignty is what is commonly meant by sovereignty. This sovereignty is necessarily limited to certain specific objects, and can be no greater than is needed for those objects. If the state stretch its authority beyond those objects, it becomes a usurper, and the individual is not bound to obey, but may lawfully resist it, as he may lawfully resist any species of injustice—taking care, however, that the manner of his resistance be neither unjust in itself, nor inconsistent with social order. For instance, the state assumes the authority to allow a man to be seized and held as property; the man may undoubtedly assert his liberty, his rights as a man, and endeavor to regain them; but he may not, in doing this, deny or infringe any of the just rights of him who may have deemed himself his master or owner. The Israelites had a right to free themselves from their bondage to the Egyptians, but they had not the right to rob the Egyptians of their jewelry.

Now this qualified, limited sovereignty, which in the last analysis, as we have said, is no sovereignty at all, is the sovereignty which has been asserted for the people, and to this sovereignty they are undoubtedly entitled. This sovereignty, which is the sovereignty of the state, may be vested in one man, and then the government is a monarchy; it may be vested in a few, and then the government is an aristocracy, or an oligarchy; it may be vested in the priesthood, and then the government is a hierarchy, or a theocracy, as it is more frequently called, because the priesthood never claim the sovereignty in their own name, but in the name of God, the priestly name for justice, the absolute sovereign; or, in fine, it may be vested in the people, and then it is a democracy, and a democracy, although the exercise of authority be in fact assigned to one man or to a few nobles, if the one man or the few nobles are held to derive their authority to govern from the people. France, in theory, was a democracy under Napoleon, although the exercise of authority was delegated to one man, and made hereditary in his family.

If the question come up, which of these various forms of government is the best, we answer unhesitatingly, that which vests sovereignty in the people. One thing may be affirmed of all forms of government. Wherever the supreme power of the state is lodged, they who are its depositaries always seek to wield it to their own exclusive benefit. Government is, whatever its form, invariably administered for the good of the governors. Theorists, indeed, tell us that government is instituted for the good of the governed; but that they are wrong is proved by the experience of six thousand years. Some have thought that governments were made for the good of the people; they who think the people were made for the good of governments, think more conformably to fact. They who have the power invariably seek to derive the greatest profit possible from it for themselves. Thus, in a monarchy, all things must be held subordinate and subservient to the interests and glory of the monarch; in a theocracy, all succumbs to the priesthood; in an aristocracy, the few must ride, though the many trudge on foot; in a democracy, the many are cared for, though the few be neglected. Without claiming any peculiar merit for the governing class in a democracy, we say, therefore, that a democracy is the best form of government for humanity—as much better as it is that the many shall be well off, though the few suffer, than it is that the few should be clothed in purple and fine linen, and fare sumptuously every day, while the many lie at their gates, covered over with the rags and bruises of poverty and abuse, begging to be fed with the few crumbs which may chance to fall from their tables. So far, then, as sovereignty is to be affirmed of the state, we say let it be affirmed of the people. If we be told that the people are incapable of using it to their own good, we say, let them use it to their own hurt then. They will have a hard time of it, even with a good share of infernal aid to boot, to govern themselves worse than kings, nobilities, and hierarchies have hitherto governed them.

We suppose all that any body really means by the sovereignty of the people is that the highest civil or political power in the state is the people; and that all officers of the government, whether bearing royal, patrician, or plebeian titles, are to be regarded, not as the governors or rulers of the people, but as the simple agents of the people, to whom they are directly accountable for their official conduct. This we hold to be a truth; and the fault we find with them who assert the sovereignty of the people is not with the doctrine they seem to themselves to be setting forth, but with their neglect of the obvious limitations of that sovereignty. The advocates of popular sovereignty have taken good care to limit the authority, to circumscribe and define the powers of the government, so as to keep it in due subordination to the people, from whom it derives its existence; but they have not taken as good care to guard the people, as individuals, against the people, as a body politic. They have limited the government, which is a creature of the body politic, but they have left the body politic itself in possession of unlimited sovereignty. In denying the sovereignty of the people, we mean to deny to the body politic unlimited authority, or the right to act at all, in any way, or by any agents whatever, on any except certain specific objects, indispensable to the maintenance of social order, and, if the phrase will be taken strictly, the common weal.

But the doctrine of the popular sovereignty, whatever its unsoundness or dangerous tendency, when asserted without any qualifications, has had an important mission to execute, and it has done no mean service to humanity. From the moment it was first asserted up to the present, it has been the rallying point of the friends of freedom and progress; and, as things have heretofore been, neither freedom nor progress were possible to be attained without it. It is not for nothing, then, that the friends of freedom and progress, in this and other countries, cling to the sovereignty of the people; and we are not to be astonished, if they now and then stretch it somewhat beyond its legitimate bounds, and continue to defend it, even after its mission is perfected. We do not willingly let go a doctrine which has stood us in good stead in our days of darkness and trial; nor is it an easy matter for us to determine with precision the exact amount of good it has done, or may yet do us. Moreover, we are slow to learn that in contending for the same form of words, we are not always contending for the same doctrine, and that in giving up an old form of words, we do not necessarily give up the old truth we had loved. Words ever change their import as change the circumstances amid which they are uttered. The form of words, which yesterday captained the doctrine of progress, today contains a doctrine which would carry us backward. The watchword of liberty under one set of circumstances becomes under another set of circumstances the watchword of tyranny. It is the part of the wise man to note these changes, and to seek out new watchwords as often as the old ones lose their primitive meaning.

So long as the sovereignty of the people was the denial of the sovereignty of kings, hierarchies, and nobilities, it was true, and was the doctrine of progress. The assertion of the sovereignty of the people was necessary to legitimate popular liberty. In every human heart, there is a more or less lively sense of legitimacy. Men revolt from one authority, not because it oppresses them, or restrains them in the free use of their persons or property, but because they regard it as illegitimate, as a usurper; they submit to another authority and uphold it, although it impose severe burdens, take the fruits of their labors to squander on its pleasures, their daughters for its debaucheries, and their sons for its battles, because they hold it to be legitimate, the rightful sovereign, which they are bound in conscience to obey. To uphold the first, or to resist the last, would in their estimation be alike disloyal. This sense of legitimacy meets us every where throughout the whole of modern history. It has made the people sustain a corrupt and demoralizing hierarchy, cling to old forms of government, and fight for old abuses, long after the reformer has appeared to demand meliorations from which they could not fail to profit. It is so deeply rooted in modern civilization—indeed, in human nature itself—that to eradicate it is impossible. In point of fact, we ought not to eradicate it even if we could, for at bottom, it is one of the noblest attributes, we may say the distinguishing attribute, of man himself, that, without which man would cease to be man. It is, in the last analysis, identical with the sense of right, the correlative of the sense of duty. Take it away and right and wrong would be empty names, man could acknowledge no sovereign, feel no obligation, and never be made to comprehend the fact that he has rights. The principle in itself is good and must be retained if man is to be preserved. But it depends almost entirely on circumstances, whether the sense of legitimacy shall be combined with a truth, or with a falsehood. If the individual be enlightened so as to discern the true sovereign, then this sense of legitimacy makes him invincible in the support or defense of the right, of freedom, of progress; but if he be darkened by ignorance or warped by prejudice, so as to mistake the true sovereign for the one who is no sovereign, then does it make him equally invincible in the support and defense of the wrong, the bitter and untiring foe of freedom and progress.

Now at that period of modern history when the popular movement began to manifest itself, legitimacy was almost exclusively attached to the hereditary monarch, and passive obedience was the order of the day. Opposition to the monarch was revolting to the general sense of right; and yet, the cause of the people could not advance without opposing him, and in some instances not without dethroning and even decapitating him. The monarch was held to be sacred and inviolable; but so long as he was so held, the cause of the people must sleep. The people must desist from their efforts to meliorate their condition, unless they could discover some means by which opposition to the hereditary monarch should become sacred and venerable in the eyes of conscience. To act against their sense of right, is what the people never do. A mob may be excited; and, in the intoxication of the moment, it may trample on justice and humanity; but the people are always serious, conscientious in what they do. Long ages will they endure the most grievous wrongs and the most grinding oppression; but to relieve themselves at the expense of what they conceive to be justice—that will they do never. Knowingly, intentionally, they never do wrong. When they have laid it down or found it laid down in their conscience that the hereditary monarch is the legitimate sovereign, they gather round each, the smallest even of his prerogatives, and defend it at the sacrifice of their lives.

Here, we perceive, was a serious difficulty to be removed. The physical power was on the side of the people; but physical power is as chaff before the wind whenever it has to encounter spiritual might. The people had numbers and the physical strength to gain their freedom but they dared not. Conscience disarmed them. They felt that they were bound to obey the monarch and they had no courage to resist him. The stoutest and bravest are children and cowards in a war against conscience. What could be done? How could opposition to the monarch be made to appear justifiable to those who had been taught and long accustomed to hold him sacred and inviolable? Assuredly, by denying his absolute sovereignty, that is, his legitimacy. But this alone was not enough. Sovereignty must be somewhere. There must be a sovereign; we feel that there is somewhere an authority we are bound to obey. Where is it? If the monarch be not sovereign, who or what is? Had this question been asked at Runnymede,[5] it might have been answered that the nobles were sovereigns; but Louis XI in France and the Tudors in England had rendered such an answer invalid.[6] The old feudal chiefs had succumbed to the lord paramount and ceased to be regarded as legitimate sovereigns by the

[5][Ed. Runnymede was a borough and district in the northwestern part of the county of Surrey, England. It was made famous as the place where on June 15, 1215 King John (1167-1216) granted the Magna Carta, the charter of English liberties.]

[6][Ed. Louis XI (1423-83), king of France (1461-83), repeatedly warred against provincial nobles. The Tudor kings and queens of England (Henry VII, Henry VIII, Edward VI, Mary I, Elizabeth I) also asserted their own authority over nobles as well as people.]

people. If the question had been asked of Hildebrand,[7] he might have said, that God is the legitimate sovereign; but this, at the time of which we speak, would only have been reasserting the supremacy of the church, which Protestantism had denied. The philosopher might have answered it, as we have answered it today, in favor of justice; but the people were not philosophers then, and to have told them to submit to justice would only have been to tell them to obey the laws, which again would only have been telling them to obey the monarch from whom the laws emanated.

Under these circumstances it is evident, that the legitimacy of the monarch could be denied only in favor of the people. The people was the only competitor of the king for the throne that it was possible to set up. The people, not the king, is the legitimate sovereign, was the only answer the question admitted. All government is for the good of the people and every government, which fails to effect the good of the people, is by that fact rendered illegitimate and may be lawfully opposed. Kings are crowned to protect the rights and promote the interests of the people, and are, therefore, answerable to the people for the use they make of the power given them. The people, in fine, are superior to kings and may judge them. The people then are the sovereign authority. "The people are sovereign"; what words, when first they were uttered! The moment they were uttered, the people sprang into being and were a power—a power clothed with legitimacy and capable of imparting sanctity and inviolability to its adherents. The people could now legitimate their opposition to the hereditary monarch. In opposing him, they were but calling its servant to an account of his stewardship. They were not contending against just authority, for license, for disorder, but for order, for liberty, for the legitimate sovereign against the usurper. They were able, therefore, to shelter the reformer, and to save him from those compunctions of conscience with which, otherwise, he would have been visited for opposing an authority he had been taught to reverence and long accustomed to obey. The doctrine of the sovereignty of the people made their cause a legitimate, a holy cause, and gave men the right and made it their duty to assert and maintain it.

In this way, the doctrine of the popular sovereignty has wrought out deliverance for the people. It has made the people kings and

[7][Ed. The monk Hildebrand (1020-85) became Gregory VII (1073-85), a reforming pope of the Middle Ages who sought to free the church from a subordination to the state and to political and lay powers. He emphasized the superiority of the spiritual over the temporal.]

priests and declared it sacrilege to touch the least of their prerogatives. This is its victory for humanity. In the old world, where the masses are trodden down by the privileged orders, it may still have a mission. There it may not have ceased to be the doctrine of progress and may yet need its soldiers, battles, and martyrs. But here its mission is ended and its work done. Here it is the doctrine of yesterday and not of tomorrow. To assert it, is not to deny the sovereignty of kings, hierarchies, and nobilities; for kings, hierarchies, and nobilities, thank God! are not at home on American soil; and, if by some mischance they should be transplanted hither, they would not thrive, they would soon droop, die, and be consumed in the fires of freedom, everywhere burning. The assertion of the sovereignty of the people with us, can be only the assertion of the right of the majority to tyrannize at will over the minority, or the assertion that the people taken individually, are the absolute slaves of the people, taken as a whole. No; the sovereignty of the people, has achieved its work with us, and the friends of freedom and progress must anoint a new king. Democracy today changes its word and bids its sentinels require of those who would enter its camp, not "The sovereignty of the people," but "The sovereignty of justice."

Democracy, as we understand it, we have said, is, on the one hand, the denial of absolute sovereignty to the state, whatever the form of government adopted, and on the other hand, the assertion of the absolute sovereignty of justice. It therefore commands both the people and the individual to be just. It subjects both to one and the same law; and, while it commands the citizen to obey and serve the state with all fidelity, so long as it keeps within its legitimate province, it takes care not to forget to remind the state that it must leave the citizen, as a man, free to do or to enjoy whatever justice permits, commands, or does not forbid.

According to our definition of it, democracy reconciles conflicting theories and paves the way for the universal association of the human race. By enthroning justice it accepts and explains the leading ideas of theories apparently the most contradictory. Every theory, which obtains or ever has obtained currency, embraces some essential element of truth. He, who has yet to learn that the human mind never does, never can believe unmixed falsehood, has no reason to boast of his progress in philosophy. The monarchist has a truth. His truth is that sovereignty is necessarily absolute, one and indivisible. This truth the democrat accepts. In declaring justice the sovereign, he declares the sovereign to be absolute, one and indivisible. The authority of justice is unbounded, and there are not two or more justices, but one justice—one God. The error of the monarchist is in confounding the absolute sovereign, in practice at least, with the man whom men call a king. This error the democrat escapes.

The theocrat has a truth, a great truth. His truth is that the highest and best,—God, is the sovereign. The democrat asserts the same thing. Justice is the political phasis of God, it is identical with God, and in asserting its sovereignty, the democrat asserts precisely the same sovereignty as does the theocrat. The error of the theocrat is in making the priesthood the symbol of this sovereignty and the authoritative expounders of its decrees. This error the democrat escapes by adopting no symbol of sovereignty, but the universal reason which is ever shining in the human soul, and in making the people in a few instances, and the individual in all the rest, the only authoritative expounders of its decrees.

The truth of the aristocrat is that some men are greater and better than others, and that the greatest and best should govern; that is, that wisdom and virtue, not vice and folly should rule. This truth the democrat by no means rejects. He believes as strongly as any aristocrat that there are diversities and even inequalities of gifts, that in all communities there are a few men, God-patented nobles, who stand out from the rest, the prophets of what all are one day to be; and he contends that these are the natural chiefs of the people, and that they ought to govern. In asserting that justice is sovereign, he necessarily asserts that they in whom justice is most manifest, in whom God dwells in the greatest perfection, should have the most influence, the most power; but at the same time, he asserts as a necessary consequence of this, that their power should be moral, spiritual, not physical. The error of the aristocrat is in looking for these God-patented noblemen in a particular class, in an hereditary order, or in a special corporation; and in seeking to give them in addition to the superior power with which they are naturally endowed, the physical power of the state and the factitious authority of an established regime. This error the democrat avoids. He proclaims equal chances to equal merit, and leaves every man free to find the place and to wield the authority for which nature, God, has fitted him.

The old-fashioned democrat's truth is that there shall be no political authority in the state which does not emanate from the people, and which is not accountable to the people; that where there must be state action, it shall be the action of the whole people, not of one man, or of a few men, who may have an interest directly hostile to the interests of the great body of the people. His error is in the fact that he does not take sufficient care to mark the bounds of the people's authority and to preserve to the citizen his rights as a man. The democrat, in our sense of the word, accepts the truth, and avoids the error.

It may be seen from these few examples that democracy accepts and explains all. It is not monarchy, it is not aristocracy, it is not theocracy, in the sense in which the word has been appropriated, nor is it democracy as some would teach us to understand it, but it is a sort of chemical compound of them all. It is a higher and a broader truth than is contained in any one of these systems, one which comprehends and finally absorbs them all.

Democracy is the doctrine of true liberty. The highest conception of liberty is that which leaves every man free to do whatever it is just to do, and not free to do only what it is unjust to do. Freedom to do that which is unjust according to the laws of God or, which is the same thing, the law of nature, is license, not liberty, and is as much opposed to liberty as lust is to love. "A free government," say the Old English lawyers, "is a government of laws," and they say right, if law be taken absolutely and not merely as the enactment of the human legislature. Where there is an arbitrary will above the law, be it the will of the one, the few, or the many, there is, in theory at least, absolutism, and the room for pure despotism. A free government must be a government, not of the will of one man, nor of the will of any body of men, but a government of law; not of a law which a human authority may make or unmake, but of that which is law in the very nature, constitution, and being of this system of things to which we belong. Under a government of law in this sense, where authority may never do, command, or permit, only what the immutable law of justice ordains, men are free; they live under the "perfect law of liberty" [James 1:25], and may attain to the full and harmonious development of all their faculties.

Governments have not yet been brought under this law. Hitherto, they have all been more or less arbitrary, and have sought to make the law, rather than to discover and publish it. They have, therefore, often declared that to be law which is not law, imposed burdens on the individual, for which nature, God, never designed him, and attempted to do what they have no capacity to do, what ought not to be done at all, or if done, to be done by the individual. Forgetful of their legitimate province, transcending the bounds which nature had marked out for them, they have created an artificial state of society, disturbed the natural relations between man and man, invaded the individual's rights in all directions, and cursed the human race with the unutterable woes of tyranny and oppression. The democrat enlightened by the study of past ages, and still more by the study of human nature as it unrolls itself to the observer, in the consciousness of the individual, comes forward today, and summoning all governments, whatever their forms, to the bar, tells them in the name of God and humanity, that they have no law-making power, that they must limit their legislative functions to the discovery and promulgation of the law, that they must lay aside the robe and diadem, the scepter and the sword, and sit down at the feet of nature as simple disciples; that they must study to conform their enactments to the enactments of God, which are written in God's book, the universe, and especially in the universe in man; and that they must deem it their duty and their glory, to leave man and society free to achieve the destiny to which God hath appointed them. It will be long before this lesson will be heard or regarded. The mania for governing has become too universal to be speedily cured. But we need not despair. The world rolls on and becomes wiser with each revolution. Governments are meliorating themselves. The doctor of medicine begins to admit that, notwithstanding the efficacy of his drugs, nature is the best physician; and the time may not be so far distant as our fears would indicate, when the doctor of laws shall own that nature is the best and only lawgiver. That time must come. The human and divine laws must become identical, the Son must be one with the Father, and the God-Man be realized.

Democracy takes care not to lose the man in the citizen. In the free states or rather free cities of antiquity, there were rights of the citizen, but no rights of man. As a citizen, the individual might use his personal influence and exertions in making up the decision of the city; but when the decision was once made up, he was bound in conscience, as well as compelled by physical force, to yield it, whatever it might be, the most unqualified submission. He had no rights sacred and inviolable beyond the legitimate authority of the city. In a question between the city and himself, he could demand nothing as his right. The city was in no way responsible to him; but he owed it everything he had, even to his life. Athens condemns Socrates to death, and sends him to prison to await his execution. His friends provide the means, and urge him to escape. No; Socrates is a conscientious man. He knows his duty. Athens has condemned him to die, and he is bound, as a good citizen, to submit to her sentence. He drinks, therefore, the hemlock at the appointed time, of his own accord, and dies in discharge of his duty to the laws of the city of which he acknowledged himself a citizen. As a citizen of Athens, Socrates knew he could not save his life without incurring the guilt of disloyalty. He had no rights as a man that he might plead. He felt himself as much the slave of Athens as the Persian was of the "Great King."[8] His rights as a man were sunk in those of the citizen and those of the citizen were sunk in those of the city.

Here was the great defect of ancient democracy. In Athens, in any of the ancient republics, there was no personal liberty. One individual might indeed call in the city to maintain his rights, in a dispute with another individual; but beyond this, he had no rights. There was municipal liberty, but no individual liberty. The city could bind or loose the individual at its will, declare him a citizen, or degrade him to a slave, just as she deemed it most expedient. The city differed in no respect from an absolute monarchy, save in the fact, that the absolute sovereignty, in the case of the city, was supposed to be vested in the majority of the citizens, instead of being vested in one man, as in the monarchy. But she was as absolute, and in case she could get a majority of voices, she might go as far and play the tyrant to as great an extent, as the king of Persia himself. Her democracy was then by no means liberty. It was liberty, if you will, for the city, but none for the individual man. The individual man was not recognized as an integer; he was, at best, only a fraction of the body politic. He was, in truth, merely a cipher; without inherent value, augmenting the value of the city, indeed, if placed at her right hand, but counting for nothing if placed at her left hand. But, thanks to the feudal system, and still more to Christianity, an element is introduced into the modern city, which was unknown in the ancient, the element of individuality, by virtue of which the individual man possesses an intrinsic value which he retains in all positions, and instead of a fraction, becomes a whole.

Modern democracy, therefore, goes beyond the ancient. Ancient democracy merely declared the people the state; the modern declares, in addition, that every man, by virtue of the fact that he is a man, is an equal member of the state—universal suffrage and eligibility, two things the ancients never dreamed of— and that the state is limited by justice, or, what is the same thing, the inalienable rights of man. These inalienable rights of man are something more than the rights of citizenship, or certain private rights, the rights of one man in relation to another, which the state is bound to protect; they stretch over nearly the whole domain of human activity, and are, in the strictest sense of the word, rights of the individual in relation to the state, rights of which the state may not, under any presence whatever, de-

[8][Ed. Reference probably is to Alexander the Great (356-323 B. C.) who conquered Persia after 327 B.C.]

prive him, and to whose free-exercise it may, in no case whatever, interpose any obstruction. In the ancient democracies the individual, if a member of the ruling race, was a citizen with duties; in the modern, he adds, in theory, to the citizen with duties, the man with rights. Democracy, as we understand it, does not give all the rights to the state, and impose all the duties on the individual. It places the state under obligation to the citizen, in the same manner, and to the same extent, that it places the individual under obligation to the state.

This, if we mistake not, is a novelty. The old doctrine, and the one yet prevalent, recognizes in the state nothing but rights and in the individual nothing but duties. We bear not a little of the responsibility of citizens to the state. Patriotism, although not recognized in the Christian code, is made one of the cardinal virtues. Men must love their country, support its government, give it their time, their talents, their property, and, if need be, their lives. But what may they claim in return; that is, demand as their right? The privilege of paying taxes and—a grave. The responsibility of society to the individual sounds as a strange doctrine in our ears. Few admit it and fewer still comprehend it. The state, we deny not, owns that it is bound to act the part of judge, between man and man, and to vindicate him whose rights a brother invades; but it owns no obligation, in a question between itself and the individual man. It may take all he hath, and give him nothing in return, unless it please. If he trespass on its rights, it may send him to the tread-mill, the galleys, the dungeon, the scaffold, or the gibbet; but he has no right to do aught in his own defense against its invasions. He has no rights which he may hold up, and in the name of God and of humanity, command it to respect. However rudely authority may treat him, grossly invade what in truth are his rights, however insupportable the burdens it may lay on his shoulders, he must not even protest. It can do no wrong. But happily this old doctrine is giving way. Governments are beginning to comprehend that they are not created merely for the purpose of laying and collecting taxes, that they are servants, or rather agents, and not masters, and that it is their mission merely to see that what eternal justice ordains, be respected and obeyed alike by themselves and the individual.

Democracy declares that the state as well as the individual has rights and duties. Where the rights and duties of the individual begin, there end those of the state; where those of the state begin, there end those of the individual. Where is this point? This is the great political problem of our epoch. The conciliation of individual with social and of social with individual rights, and the subordination of all social and individual action to the laws of justice, the law of nature, or the law of God, is the mission of the moralist and politician throughout humanity's whole future.

Something in reference to the first of these problems has been attempted in all countries, which have adopted constitutional governments. In this work, England claims precedence of all other nations. She has been the first, we believe, to establish a constitutional government. She has done more than any other nation for the extension of the practice of individual liberty, though, it must be admitted, she has done less than some others to enable the world to legitimate that liberty as a right. Her citizens have a large share of practical freedom; but, in theory, they hold it not as a right, but as a grant. And they defend it not by an appeal to the rights of man, but by an appeal to certain parchment rolls, carefully preserved in the archives of state. Magna Carta[9] is not an enumeration of natural rights, but a grant—a forced grant, if you will—of certain specified privileges. Her bill of rights,[10] drawn up in 1688, is the same. Her Parliament assembles by virtue of a writ from the king, not by virtue of the right of the people of England to be represented. Her liberty, in a word, is an admirable thing as a fact, but totally indefensible on the only ground on which liberty is defensible at all, that of natural right. Of this the Englishman has an instinctive sense at least, for he never calls his liberty by the broad name of the natural liberty of man, but *English* liberty; and the English nation, while it has everywhere contended for liberty as a grant, has spared neither money nor blood to suppress it, wherever it has been asserted as a right. English liberty rests solely on compact and is defended solely by an appeal to charters and precedents. Hence, the contempt with which all English statesmen speak of "abstract right," and their uniform practice of legitimating their measures, not by justice but by precedent. The minister of state entrenches himself behind a wall of precedents; the member of parliament asks for precedents; the lawyer alleges precedents in favor of his client; the judge decides according to the precedents; and no one thinks of inquiring what is right, but what are the precedents? This is all in perfect keeping. An Englishman has no business to inquire for justice; for his liberty is a precedent and not a

[9][Ed. On June 15, 1215 King John (1167-1216) granted the Magna Carta, the charter of English liberties. These liberties were perceived as grants of government, not natural rights.]

[10][Ed. England's "Bill of Rights" as well as a toleration act actually passed Parliament in 1689.]

right, founded on precedent not on justice; though it must be said in his favor that his precedents are often coincident with justice.

France, if we mistake not, has taken a step beyond England. We do not mean to say that France has more liberty than England, as a fact, but she has more as a right. The king has ceased to *octroyer* the charter; he accepts it, and in theory, it emanates from the people. The French people are therefore the sovereign of the king. This is much; it is at least the entering wedge to freedom. The old monarchy of Louis XIV is abolished, the old feudal nobility is extinct, and the *Bourgeoisie,* or middle class, is now on the throne. This class is the one in every community the most praised; and it is always accounted the most virtuous. Perhaps it is so. It certainly has some very respectable virtues. It is composed of merchants, bankers, manufacturers, lawyers, large farmers, in a word of the stirring, business part of the community. It has no affection for hereditary nobility and none for the doctrine of equality. It has no objection to leveling down to itself those who are above it, but it has an invincible aversion to leveling up to itself those who are below it. It demands a laboring class to be *exploited,* but it loves order, peace, and quiet. These, however, it knows are incompatible with the existence in the community of an ignorant, vicious, and starving populace; it, therefore, will attend to the wants of the lower classes up to a certain point. It will build them, if need be, churches, and establish ministries for the especial purpose of teaching them to be quiet; it will furnish them with the rudiments of education, see that they are fed, clothed, maintained in a good working condition, and supplied with work. All this it will do for those below itself; and this, though not enough, is more than a little; and when this is done more will be undertaken. This is the first step; and when the first step is taken, the rest of the way is not difficult. The *prolétaires* soon disappear, and the *canaille* become men and citizens. We are, therefore, far from deprecating, with some of our friends, the "monarchy of the middle classes." We believe its reign in a certain stage of social progress, not only inevitable, but desirable. We believe no worse calamity could at this moment befall France, than the overthrow of the present dynasty of the *Bourgeoisie.* Its reign will and must be salutary, however far short it may come of satisfying the wishes, or the views of the ardent friends of liberty. It has a mission to execute and when it shall have executed its mission it will then give way to the monarchy, not of a class, not of an order, but of humanity, of justice. France appears to us to be on the route to freedom. May she obtain it! With her fine social qualities, and after all her toils, and struggles, and sacrifices, she deserves it.

But it is to our own country that we must look for constitutional government in the worthiest sense of the word. In the bills of rights which precede several of our constitutions, we have attempted to draw up an inventory of the natural rights of man, rights, which authority must ever hold sacred and which the people, in their associate capacity, can neither give nor take away, in no shape or manner, alter or abridge. In the Constitution of the United States, and in those of the several states, we have attempted to define the natural boundaries of the state, to fix its authority, and to determine the modes of its action. These constitutions and these bills of rights may be very imperfect; they may not enumerate all the rights of the individual, and they may not accurately define the powers of the people in their capacity as a state; but if so we may perfect them at our leisure. They recognize the great principle for which we contend, that the people are not absolute, that the individual has rights they cannot alter or abridge, and which it is the duty and the glory of authority to preserve untouched, and which it may neither invade nor suffer to be invaded. They teach us that if society has powers the individual must obey, the individual has rights society must respect; that if the people as a body politic may do some things, there are some things they may not do; and that if majorities may go to a certain length, there is a line they may not pass. They teach us then what we have denominated the great democratic doctrine and they prove that doctrine to be the doctrine of the American people, however far short they may fall of its perfect realization.

There may, indeed, be some among us, who, affected by their reminiscences of English Whiggism, regard our constitutions and bills of rights, not as attempts to enumerate the natural rights of man, and to define the natural powers of government, but as compacts between the people as individuals, and the people as a state, or, more properly, as declarations of what the people in convention assembled have willed to be the rights of individuals, and have ordained to be the powers of government. According to these persons, our liberties are not, in the strict sense of the word, rights, but grants. They are not grants from what is technically called the government, but from the people in convention assembled. They are not limitations of the supreme authority of the state, but favors which that authority is pleased to confer on its subjects. The people in convention assembled might have willed, had they chosen so to do, that the powers of government should be more or less than they now are, or that our rights should be different from what they are now declared to be. They were competent to draw the boundary line between the authority of the state and the rights of the individual where they pleased. By meeting again in convention, they may unmake all our present rights, and make such new ones as seems to them good.

But this view of our bills of rights and constitutions we are not prepared to admit. It implies the absolute sovereignty of the people, a doctrine we have denied and refuted. The people, neither in convention nor out of it, can make or unmake rights. If they can, if they may bind or unbind as they please, then are we, as we have already shown, absolute slaves as individuals to the will of the majority. If we allow that the people make the rights of the individual, we deny the validity of his rights, and deprive him of everything to oppose to the tyranny of the many. Bills of rights and constitutions can avail him nothing when it is a question, not between him and the ministers of state, but between him and the state itself. They limit the action of his majesty's ministers, but not of his majesty himself. But this is not the fact. If these bills of rights and constitutions enumerate on the one hand all our natural rights, and recognize nothing to be a right which is not a right by decree of justice; and if they on the other hand accurately define the powers of government, they are unalterable, and are as much binding on the people in convention, as they are on the people's ministers of state, or on the individual. In denying sovereignty to the people, we deny that the people can make or unmake rights, bind or unbind; we limit their functions to the discovery and promulgation of the law, as it is in justice, which is anterior and superior to all conventions. Consequently our rights, in truth, are the same before as after the sitting of the convention. If we had no rights before, we have none now.

It is true that, in the form of our bills of rights and constitutions, there are some things which would seem to authorize this English interpretation of them; and no doubt many statesmen and most lawyers, have so interpreted them, and done it very honestly too; but in reality our institutions are fundamentally distinct from the English, based on an entirely different idea; and instead of interpreting our bills of rights as grants, we ought to interpret them as an attempted inventory, more or less exact, of the natural rights of man; and our constitutions, instead of compacts, should be regarded as attempts to determine and fix the legitimate powers of government. They are shields interposed between the minority and the majority, between the individual and the people. The people say to the individual and the majority say to the minority, by these instruments, not merely that they *will* exercise their authority according to the rules herein specified, but that, errors excepted, they have no *right* to exercise it according to any other rules. Constitutions are not needed by majorities; they are needed merely as a moral force by the minority, who want the physical force to protect themselves against the aggressions of the majority. They are not needed, as some suppose, to constitute the people a body politic. The people are as much a body politic, before assembling in convention and adopting a constitution as afterwards. Bodies politic, rights of societies or of individuals, are not things to be created by a few arbitrary slopes, curves, and angles on parchment. Right and wrong, for governments, individuals, and societies, for cities and citizens, are eternal and immutable.

For ourselves, we have no patience with the notion that we hold our liberties as grants. We do not like to be sent to rummage in the dark and dusty cabinets of old state papers, and to decipher old worm-eaten parchments, in order to find out what our liberties are, and what is the authority by which we may legitimate them. The charter, by virtue of which we legitimate our rights, is no charter engrossed on parchment, but one which God Almighty has engrossed on the human heart. The Magna Carta, to which we appeal, is no grant forced from King John, King Edward, King Harry, King William,[11] nor any other king, from no hierarchy, no aristocracy, from no democracy or conventions of the people, but that which God gave us, when he made us men, and by virtue of which we are men. We consult no constitution to learn what our rights and duties are, but the constitution of human nature itself. And all constitutions which do aught but faithfully transcribe that, we declare null and void from the beginning. We are free, not because the king wills, not because it is the good pleasure of the nobility, not because the priesthood grants permission, not because the people in convention ordain, but because we are men. It is not a privilege of American citizenship, but a right of universal humanity.

By assuming this position, democracy gains a vantage ground for humanity. If we hold our rights not by virtue of compacts, grants, or decrees of conventions, then we hold them by virtue of our human nature. Our rights and duties belong to us as men, as human beings. Then all who are men, human beings, have the same rights and duties. If all have the same rights and duties, then, in matter of right and duty, all men are equal. Hence, the grand, the thrilling, tyrant-killing doctrine of EQUALITY—THE DOCTRINE THAT MAN MEASURES MAN THE WORLD OVER. Men may be di-

[11][Ed. Brownson is clearly referring to the Magna Carta of King John of England (1167-1216), but it is unclear what other English kings he has in mind.]

verse in their tastes, dispositions, capacities, and acquirements; but so long as they all have the same rights and the same duties, so long it may be affirmed of them with truth that they are equal one to another, in all respects in which equality does not tend to lose itself in identity. This doctrine will not remain unfruitful.

If all men have equal rights and duties as individuals, then is society bound to treat them as equals. If she exalt one or depress another, confer a favor on this one and not on that, place one in a more favorable position for the enjoyment of his rights or the performance of his duties than another, then is she partial, and therefore unjust, therefore illegitimate; then does she disturb the original equality, which God established between man and man, and therefore does she become an usurper, to be driven back to her legitimate province. This rule is broad; it reaches far, but society will one day observe it.

No government or society has ever yet respected this equality. In the Grecian and Roman city, the individual, as we have seen, counted for nothing. There were municipal rights but no rights of man. The city might do what it pleased. The same remark may be made of all aristocratic and monarchical governments. All, like the English parliament, have called themselves omnipotent, have usurped all the rights of man, and claimed them, as their own property. Claiming, as their own property, all possible rights susceptible of being exercised by individuals, they have claimed, as a natural consequence of this, the right to parcel out the exercise of these rights to individuals or to corporations, as they pleased. Hence PRIVILEGE, a private law, by which authority confers a special favor, or grants to an individual or a corporation, the right to do what he or it had not the right to do before, or exempts him or it from a duty, which was previously obligatory. Authority, under the character of a privilege, confers on this man the exclusive right of baking all the bread for a given number of people, upon that one the right to distill corn into whiskey, upon this company the exclusive right to buy and sell slaves, and upon that one the right to traffic at a certain place in certain kinds of foreign productions, upon this one the right to wear a certain ribbon or garter, and of receiving the income of certain lands or offices. We need not be particular on this head. Society is and ever has been filled, and covered over, with privileges of every name and nature.

Our first emotion on contemplating this immense system of privilege, which has grown up through successive ages, is that of indignation. We go even so far as to rail at the privileged, and to charge the whole to their selfishness and rapacity. But after a while, after having penetrated more deeply into the matter, we calm ourselves, and suppress our wrath and indignation. The evil lies not at the door of the privileged alone. Few, at least not many, of the unprivileged would have refused to accept these privileges, had they been offered them. Of those who declaim against privilege now, not the smallest half do it somewhat on the principle that the fox declaimed against the grapes. The error is not in the privileged, the evil is not in the fact that one set of men rather than another enjoy the privileges; but in the fact that authority ever presumed to have any privileges to grant, any favors to confer. The evil lies not in the fact that privileges have been conferred, but in the fact that governments have been allowed to usurp, and hold as its own, all the rights of the people as individuals. Having usurped these rights, having robbed them from individuals, governments could, perhaps, do no better than to parcel them out under the name of privilege. It was only under this name, only by favor, that individuals could get back some portion of that of which authority had robbed them. Unequal as this must necessarily be in its bearing on the whole mass of individuals, it was nevertheless better to get back something in this way than to be left entirely destitute. He, who has been robbed of his all by the highwayman, can sometimes do no better than to accept back part of the contents of his purse as a present.

It is true that what was granted as a favor should, if granted at all, have been granted as a right; but every favor granted weakened, in the end, the government which granted it, and did something towards raising it up a successful rival. Every individual who became one of the privileged, became one who would not easily be reduced to slavery again. When the crisis came between him and authority he would claim his privilege as his right and defend it with his life. Paradoxical as it may seem, modern liberty is the natural, if not the legitimate, child of privilege. These special grants and monopolies, which are so abhorrent to democracy, have been the means, or one of the means, by which the mighty Demos[12] has broken himself loose from the grasp of the monarch, and become strong enough and wise enough to demand, as his right, what he had formerly been proud and most thankful to receive as a boon. These special grants and monopolies have, in reality, been victories gained by the people over their masters, so many provinces wrested from the dominion of the usurper. The system of privilege, therefore, though founded on usurpation, and unjust and unequal in its bearing, has been the means or one of the means, under God, of carrying onward the progress of

[12][Ed. Demos was an ancient Greek country district or village. It also referred to the common people in Greek. Brownson seems to be personifying the term here to refer to the people.]

society and of restoring to individuals, in some measure, the exercise of rights of which authority had violently dispossessed them.

But while we admit all this, while we admit and even contend, that during the past under the circumstances which existed, privilege was one of the means by which individual freedom was to be obtained, we contend that democracy is right, today, and in this country, in asserting herself, as she does in the Address before us, as "equality against privilege." For a time privilege was to be resorted to, as we sometimes resort to one evil to cure another; but it needs no argument to prove that that time has gone by and that the doctrine of privilege has ceased to be the doctrine of progress. Humanity demands today her rights; she has ceased to solicit favors. She makes no war upon the privileged few; for, aside from their character as the privileged, they are her children and equally as dear to her heart as any of the other members of her vast family; but she proclaims in a voice which all must hear and shall respect, that all which anyone may, in obedience to justice, enjoy, he may demand as a right, and that he needs no patent from human authority to empower him to do whatever is right in the sight of God, and that all the patents in the world cannot make it just for him to do what in the sight of God it is wrong for him to do.

Democracy, we repeat it, does not declaim against men for having accepted privileges when it was admitted that governments had them to bestow; but it tells governments, and the people in this country, as the only government we acknowledge, that they have no privileges to grant, no favors to confer. They have nothing to deal out to individuals. If they have favors to bestow, will they be good enough to tell us where they got them. Did they take them from individuals? Then have they no right to them. What belongs to the individual can never become the rightful property of the government. If it was ever the property of individuals, it is now, and individuals may possess it without asking permission of the government. If the powers in question be not individual rights, the property of individuals, then has government no right to confer them and the individual no right to receive them. Governments can confer on individuals no powers which God has not given them; and, if individuals claim, by authority, that which is not theirs by Divine right, or do, under cover of man-made law, what is not authorized by God's law, they are guilty, and must be condemned, if not in the civil court, at least in the court of conscience. Governments have, therefore, no privileges to confer, and individuals have no right to ask or to receive them. The government can confer on one individual only what it has robbed from him or from another. Has it a right to rob one individual for the sake of enriching another? Or is it desirable that it should first rob a man of his rights, and then give them back to him in the form of a present or a privilege? Whenever governments forbid this man to do what he has a natural right to do, or authorize that man to do what he has not a natural right to do, it assumes the power to readjust the regulations of Infinite Wisdom, and to recast the handy work of God. We know of no governments that have the right to assume so much. We have a profound respect for the wisdom and governmental skill, manifested by those who are charged with the management of our state and national governments; but we very much distrust their capacity to enter the courts of heaven as cabinet ministers to the All-Wise. It is enough for even our enlightened governments, in this most enlightened country, to sit down at the feet of Great Nature, as humble disciples, content to learn and obey what God ordains.

The great error of government, in all ages of the world, has been that of counting itself the real owner and sovereign disposer of the individual—that of disfranchising all individuals and then pretending to redistribute individual rights according to its own caprice, interests, or necessities. To put an end to this system of privilege is now the great aim of democracy. Its object is to restrict governments, whether royal, aristocratical, or popular, to their legitimate province, and individuals to their natural rights and to teach both to perform those duties and those duties only, which everlasting and immutable justice imposes. To this it steadily makes its way; for this it struggles; and this it will ultimately achieve.

The reduction to practice of the theory we have now imperfectly, but we hope distinctly set forth, will demand great changes, and more changes, perhaps, than anyone can foresee; and changes, too, which can be introduced at once, in no country, without violence, and probably not without bloodshed and great suffering. He who pleads for justice will not be anxious to promote violence, bloodshed, or suffering. There may be times when the kingdom of heaven must be taken by violence, and when a people should rise up and demand its rights at whatever sacrifice it may be. But there is and there can be, in this country, no occasion for any but orderly and peaceful measures for the acquisition of all we have supposed. We must not dream of introducing it all at once. We must proceed leisurely. Let the men of thought speculate freely and speak boldly what comes to them as truth; but let the men of action, men who have more enthusiasm than reflection, greater hearts than minds, and stronger hands than heads guard against impatience. Practical men, men of action, are, after all, the men who play the most mischief with improvements. Our principle is, no revolution, no destruction, but progress. Progress is always slow, and slow let it be; the slower it is the more speed it makes. So long as we find the thinkers busy canvassing all great matters, discussing all topics of reform, and publishing freely to the world the result of their investigations, we have no fears for the individual, none for society. Truth is omnipotent. Let it be uttered; let it spread from mind to mind, from heart to heart, and in due season be assured that it will make to itself hands, erect itself a temple, and institute its worship. Set just ideas afloat in the community and feel no uneasiness about institutions. Bad institutions, before you are aware of it, will crumble away, and new ones and good ones supply their places.

We hold ourselves among the foremost of those who demand reform and who would live and die for progress; but we wish no haste, no violence in pulling down old institutions or in building up new ones. We would innovate boldly in our speculations; but in action we would cling to old usages and keep by old lines of policy till we were fairly forced by the onward pressure of opinion to abandon them. We would think with the radical, but often act with the conservative. When the time comes to abandon an old practice, when new circumstances have arisen to demand a new line of policy, then, we say, let no attachments to the past make us blind to our duty or impotent to perform it. All we say is, let nothing be done in a hurry and let no rage for experiments be encouraged.

We are far from being satisfied with things as they are. We have had, perhaps, our turn with many others, of mourning over the wide discrepancy there is between the American theory and the American practice, and days and nights have given to the question, how shall the evil be remedied? The only answer, we can give, is one, perhaps, that will show little more than how ineffectually we have inquired. All we can answer is simply, let each man keep at work freely and earnestly in his own way; let all labor together, to raise the standard of thought, to give a higher, freer, and fresher tone to American literature; more purity and rationality to our theology; more depth and soundness to our philosophical speculations; to embody less of expediency and more of Christ in our systems of morality; and withal, let there be fervent prayer for more faith in God, in truth, in justice, in humanity, and then, let things take pretty much their own course. The whole that can be done may be summed up in the words, let reformers do all in their power to EDUCATE THE PEOPLE, AND THROUGH THE PEOPLE THE GENERATION TO COME.

15.

PHILOSOPHY AND COMMON SENSE[1]

Boston Quarterly Review 1 (January, 1838): 83-106

We have read with some interest an article in the Christian Examiner for November last, on Locke and the Transcendentalists. The article is written with spirit, in a sincere and earnest tone, and, for style and language, it deserves more than ordinary commendation. It is obviously the production of a mind somewhat given to philosophizing, although we should think of a mind which has not yet grappled, very closely, with the real problems of metaphysics. Its author appears to us a young writer, whose philosophical views are a little vague and fluctuating; but at the same time a writer who, if he duly apply himself, may yet do himself great credit, and exert a salutary influence on the literature and philosophy of his country.

So far as we can judge from the article before us, we differ widely from the present philosophical tendency of its author; but we nevertheless welcome him into the philosophical field and are glad to find him disposed to be one of its cultivators. We may from time to time take an account of his labors, but we will assure him, that we shall not quarrel with him, because he may chance to labor in a direction different from the one we have marked out for ourselves. They who cultivate philosophy must labor in peace. They must not call one another hard names and seek to render one another odious to the public. Into all philosophical subjects we must carry calmness of mind, a catholic spirit, and a respect for every man's honest opinions. We must carry with us a disposition to seek for truth under the forms of gross error even, and that love for man and all that is human, which will prevent us from harboring, for one moment, a single intolerant feeling, and which will prevent a single harsh word from ever escaping us. We may subject, we ought to subject, all opinions to the most rigid investigation, not for the sake of triumphing over adversaries, not for the sake of proving others in the wrong; but for the purpose of discovering the truth, and quickening our love and reverence for mankind.

[1][Ed. Review of "Locke and the Transcendentalists," by Francis Bowen (1811-90) *Christian Examiner* 23 (November 1837), 170-94.]

No greater evil can befall us than that of entering into a career of angry disputes and of passing from the calm and rational inquiry after truth to the violent and passionate crimination of individuals. In philosophizing, we ought to make an abstraction of individuals and their motives. Men honestly differ in their views. The views of all are more or less partial, and therefore defective, and therefore erroneous; and no one, therefore, has the right to condemn another. The philosopher, instead of complaining of men, charging them with folly, or with evil intentions, and seeking to render their views odious or suspicious, sets himself down to collect quietly the partial views of each, and to mold them into one systematic and harmonious whole. We insist on this point. A philosophical epoch for our country begins and we would not have it disgraced by wrath and bitterness, by personal contentions, railings at individuals or systems. We would have every man, who enters the field of philosophy, enter it with a heart at peace with mankind, and solicitous only for the truth. Let everyone guard against the trammels of a school and the pride of system. Let him beware how he adopts a darling theory, which he shall be ambitious to make prevail. Let him beware how he looks on his fellow laborers as the disciples of another school, and therefore enemies to be fought and vanquished. Let him wed himself to the truth, and give it an uncompromising support; but let him, at the same time, expect truth in all theories, and be willing to receive it, let it come to him from what quarter it may.

We young Americans, who have the future glory of our country and of humanity at heart, who would see our country taking the lead in modern civilization, and becoming as eminent for her literature, art, science, and philosophy, as she now is for her industrial activity and enterprise, must ever bear in mind the greatness and the sanctity of our mission. We must set an example worthy of being followed by the world. We must feel the dignity and immense reach of the work to which we are called. Into all our discussions we must carry a free, lofty, and earnest spirit; we must purge our hearts of all low ambition, of all selfish aims, of all wish for personal triumph. We must fix our eyes on the true, and aspire to the holy. We must be invincible in our dialectics, but still more so in our love of truth, and in our sympathy with humanity in all its forms. A great and a glorious work is given us; may we be equal to it, and worthy of achieving it!

We say we have read this article in the Examiner, with some interest, and so we have; but not altogether on account of its intrinsic merit. It interests us mainly as one of the signs of the times, as an indication of a change which has been silently taking place among us, on philosophical matters, and as a proof that our countrymen are beginning to lose some portion of their hereditary contempt for abstract thought, and that they are preparing themselves to raise hereafter the study of metaphysical science to the rank it deserves. It proves to us that the day for philosophical discussion is ready to dawn on our land and that thought with us is about to assume new and nobler forms. Intellectual pursuits are beginning to have charms for us and a future, worthy our free institutions, is beginning to be elaborated. We need not say that this gives us joy. It is what we have for years been yearning and laboring for; but which we have not generally dared hope that we should live long enough to see realized. Discussion of the great problems of metaphysics must come, and we are glad of it; for discussion in this country, of whatever subject it be, cannot fail to be followed by important and useful practical results.

The specific design of the author in this article we profess not to have discovered, and we think he himself would be somewhat puzzled to inform us. Apparently, however, the article was intended to vindicate the character of Locke as a metaphysician and to put the community on its guard against certain individuals whom its author denominates Transcendentalists. Who these Transcendentalists are, what is their number, and what are their principal tenets, the writer does not inform us. Nor does he tell us precisely the dangers we have to apprehend from their labors; but so far as we can collect his meaning, it would seem that these dangers consist in the fact that the Transcendentalists encourage the study of German literature and philosophy, and are introducing the habit of writing bad English. He may be right in this. It is a matter we do not feel ourselves competent to decide. So far, however, as our knowledge extends, there is no overweening fondness for German literature and philosophy. We know not of a single man in this country, who avows himself a disciple of what is properly called the Transcendental Philosophy. The genius of our countrymen is for Eclecticism. As to the bad English, we presume those, whom this writer calls Transcendentalists, may sometimes be guilty of it, and we shall be happy to learn that they alone are guilty of it.

This writer may be correct in his estimate of the merits of Locke. If we understand him, he does not mean to defend Locke's philosophy—although we should think him partial to it—but merely his candid spirit, and the manner in which he wrote on metaphysics. He thinks Locke wrote on metaphysical subjects in a free and easy manner, altogether more in the manner of a man of the world than of a cloistered monk. We agree with him in this; but we think several of

Locke's predecessors and contemporaries are entitled to this praise as well as he. Hobbes,[2] who preceded Locke by some years, is much his superior, so far as style and language go, and so is Cudworth.[3] Locke is transparent; there is seldom any difficulty in coming at his meaning; but he is diffuse, verbose, tedious, and altogether wanting in elegance, precision, and vigor. Hobbes, while he is equally as transparent as Locke, infinitely surpasses him in strength, precision, and compactness. He tells you more in a few short sentences than Locke in the whole of a long chapter. If the proper style and language, the proper manner of writing on metaphysical subjects, be the matter in question, we think Locke should not be named in the same year with Hobbes, a man to whom justice has never yet been done; whose name is a term of reproach; but who, as a philosopher, has exerted a thousand times more influence over the English mind, than Locke, and whom Locke himself reproduces much oftener than he acknowledges.

The writer in the Examiner, we think, also ascribes improperly to Locke the merit of delivering us from the technical phraseology and barren logic of the Scholastics. Between Locke and the Scholastics there intervened a considerable space of time, Descartes, Bacon, Gassendi,[4] and Hobbes, and the most glorious period of English history and literature. The Scholastic philosophy was shaken and nearly destroyed by the revival of letters and the study of antiquity, which so strongly marked the fifteenth and sixteenth centuries. The little dominion, it retained at the commencement of the seventeenth century was completely overthrown by those two fathers of modern philosophy, Descartes and Bacon. The Scholastics were defunct in all the world—unless Oxford offers an exception—long before Locke began his philosophical career.

But these are small matters. The article we are examining appears to us to assume that the metaphysician should always restrict himself to what may be called common sense modes of thought and expression, and that the highest philosophy may be so announced as

[2][Ed. Thomas Hobbes (1588-1679), author of the famous *Leviathan* (1651), supported political absolutism and promoted a doctrine of psychological determinism.]

[3][Ed. Ralph Cudworth (1617-88) was a Cambridge Platonist philosopher who opposed both religious dogmatism and the atheism of Thomas Hobbes' materialism, arguing that the only real source of knowledge was the Christian religion.]

[4][Ed. Pierre Gassendi (1592-1655) was a French Catholic priest, anti-Aristotelian and anti-Cartesian philosopher and scientist who argued that we cannot have knowledge of the inner essence of things, but we can develop a reliable understanding or science of the world of appearances.]

to be comprehended at once by anyone of ordinary capacity whether accustomed to philosophize or not. The article, it is true, does not expressly state the doctrine here implied; but it appears to us to proceed on the supposition of its truth, and we are unable to legitimate its reasonings without assuming it. Through the whole article there seems to us to be a striking want of clear discernment of the difference between philosophy and common sense. The writer evidently wishes to reconcile common sense and philosophy, which is laudable; but he sees no way by which this can be done, save by reducing philosophy to common sense. He asks, "what is common sense, but the highest philosophy, applied to the usual purposes of practical life? And what is philosophy, but common sense, employed in abstract investigations?" Do not these questions confound philosophy with common sense? Or rather, instead of reconciling philosophy with common sense, do they not sink philosophy in common sense? To us they betray no slight confusion in the mind of him who puts them in earnest, and they are a very good proof that he does not discern clearly, if any difference at all, the difference there is between knowledge and philosophy, two things as far asunder as intuition and reflection.

But this writer is not the only one who does not discern distinctly the difference between common sense and philosophy, in whose mind the limits and precise characteristics of each are not determined. We trust, therefore, that we shall not be doing a needless work if we undertake in what follows to aid our readers to draw the line between common sense and philosophy, and to determine what is the precise object of philosophy. Moreover, something of this is necessary to serve as a sort of introduction to a series of articles on metaphysics, which we propose to lay before our readers in our future numbers.[5]

The term *common sense* may be applied to what Hobbes calls the *cognitive faculty*, or faculty of knowing, which is common to all human beings. It is by this faculty, and only by this faculty, that we know either in the ordinary affairs of life or in abstract science. The faculty, by means of which we are capable of acquiring knowledge, is the same in all cases. Knowledge then admits of no other divisions than those of the subjects with which we may seek to become ac-

[5][Ed. Brownson's plan for a series of articles on metaphysics never really materialized, but he did write two articles on "The Eclectic Philosophy" and "Eclecticism—Ontology" that he may have considered a fulfillment of this promise. See *Boston Quarterly Review* 2 (January, 1839): 27-53; 2 (April, 1839): 169-87.]

quainted. This is what the writer of the article we are reviewing probably meant to assert. But knowledge is not philosophy; and though it is indispensable to philosophy, it can and does, in most men, exist without philosophy.

But the term common sense is also used to designate the common or universal beliefs of mankind, the simple spontaneous beliefs of humanity. These beliefs may be true, they may be acted on; but with the multitude they are taken on trust, adopted without being legitimated. Philosophy is not a contradiction of these beliefs, a substitution of something else for them, but an explanation and verification of them. This is the precise object of philosophy.

Philosophy and common sense are not opposed to one another. There is no discrepancy between them. Common sense furnishes the philosopher all his knowledge, all the data from which he reasons. His sole mission is to clear up and legitimate the universal beliefs of mankind, or the facts of common sense. The common sense man is not in the wrong; he does not err; he has the truth, but he does not know that he has it. He believes the truth, but he does not comprehend what he believes, nor wherefore he believes. He cannot tell how he came to believe what he does believe; he knows not what right he has to believe it; and when asked, why he believes it, he can only answer, he believes it because he does believe it. The philosopher believes precisely the same things, as the common sense man, but he knows what he believes, and he can tell wherefore he believes. The common sense man believes, but does not comprehend; the philosopher comprehends, and therefore believes.

We may easily bring up to our minds the common sense man by recalling our childhood and youth. In early life, faith is strong and implicit. We believe. We are conscious of no difficulties. We are conscious of no thoughts and feelings too big for words, and which cannot be easily communicated to all who will give us their attention. We see no mysteries in nature, in man, or in God. All things appear to us open and plain. Things are to us what they seem. The primrose is a primrose, and nothing more. The sun and stars are beautiful, and the rainbow is pleasant to look upon; but they contain no dark, perplexing mystery we are dying to wring out. Day and night, summer and winter, spring and fall, sickness and health, life and death, are alternations to be welcomed, or not welcomed, but they are not mysteries. They are not a book we would learn to read; hieroglyphs we would be able to decipher. We see all. The outward, the sensible, sufficeth us. Common sense satisfies curiosity, and prevents inquiry from becoming doubt. This, which is a description of the childhood and youth of all, is also a description of the greater part of men through their whole lives. All who come under this description are common sense men.

But childhood and youth, with their ready answers to all inquiries, their open brow and laughing cheek and trusting heart, for whom life is all one holiday, and all things are but their morris-men,[6] do not abide with us all forever. Some of us grow old and lose the light which plays around our heads in our younger days. One day, one hour perhaps, never to be forgotten, a sudden darkness spreads over the universe, and we no longer see where we are, or what we are. The bright sun is extinguished; the stars no longer glimmer in the firmament, and the beacon fires, which the philanthropic few had kindled here and there to cheer, to warn, or to guide the solitary traveler, are gone out. Friends drop away; we stand among the dead, by the graves of those we loved, surrounded by the ghosts of affections unrequited, hopes blasted, joys cut short, plans defeated; and there are mysteries. The universe becomes to us a scroll, a book, like that which John saw in the right hand of Him who sat on the throne, sealed with seven seals.[7] Every object we make out in the darkness is a hieroglyph, big with a meaning of fearful import, which we can divine not; we are to ourselves a riddle we can read not; and in tumult of soul, perplexity of mind, and sorrow of heart, we find ourselves standing face to face with the dread Unknown.

A change has come over us. Childhood and youth are gone forever. We have broken with the whole past. We stand alone; yet not alone, for the awful mystery of the universe is round, about, and within us. For a time our courage forsakes us; we can stand up no longer; we sink down, weak, helpless, forlorn. But this weakness passes away. After a while, in a sort of desperation, we draw ourselves up into ourselves, and bid the monster in whose presence we are, a "grim, fire-eyed defiance."[8] Little by little we become inured to the obscurity and able to discern the outline of things in the dark. By straining, by recollecting, by comparing, by reflecting, we become able to spell out, here and there, one of these fearful hieroglyphs, till we

[6][Ed. Reference may be the morris dance, an old English rustic dance in which the performers took the part of Robin Hood and other characters in English folklore. Morris-men, then, may refer to the playful and carefree life style that some lead.]

[7][Ed. Reference here is to Rev. 5:1.]

[8][Ed. The quote is from Thomas Carlyle's *Sartor Resartus*, chapter 7, "The Everlasting No." See Thomas Carlyle, *Sartor Resartus, Lectures on Heroes, Chartism, Past and Present* (London: Chapman and Hall, 1888), 103.]

obtain the word of the universe—God. Then the darkness rolls back; things become plain again; conviction supplies the place of lost faith; and foresight makes amends for the inspiration of hope which returns no more forever. A change has indeed come over us. We are no longer in the trustingness of common sense. We have become philosophers. We have looked beneath the surface, beyond the shadows of sense; in the visible we have found the invisible; in the mutable, that which changes not; in the dying, the immortal; in the evanescent, the abiding and the eternal. We have seen the world of childhood and youth vanish in the darkness of doubt; but we have found a new world, the world of truth, a new universe which is really a universe. We see and comprehend the hidden sense of that of which we saw at first only the form, the shadow. We now know what we believe, and wherefore we believe it, and are able to legitimate our belief. He who has been through this scene of darkness, doubt, perplexity, grief, and has attained to a well grounded conviction of the great truths comprised in the universal beliefs of mankind, is a philosopher.

Now, between this man whom we have pointed out as the philosopher, and the one we called the mere common sense man, is there no difference? And can they converse together with perfect ease? Can they utter themselves by means of the same symbols? Or, which is more to our purpose, will the same symbols have the same significance to them both?

Suppose a man over whose mind and heart has passed the change of which we have spoken, a man truly born again, who has been able to see that there are mysteries, and who sees a little way into them, and who looks on man, nature, God, with other eyes and other feelings too than those of childhood and youth; has he nothing within him, no thoughts, no spiritual facts, of which the mere common sense man knows nothing, has dreamt nothing; and which, therefore, he has not named; and which, therefore, are untranslated into his vocabulary? Can this man utter himself in the language of the market, in terms, the full import of which can be easily seized by them in whom no such change has been wrought? Would you talk with a blind man of colors? Couch his eyes. Will the miser comprehend you when you speak to him of the pleasures of benevolence? Can you, by any possible form of words, make the meaning of the word love obvious to him, whose heart has never thawed in presence of sweet and gentle affection? Whoever has had some little acquaintance with the world, knows to his sorrow, that he often fails to make himself understood, even when he adopts the commonest and simplest forms of speech. The words a man utters are not measured, in the minds of those to whom he speaks, by his experience, but by theirs. Words are meaningless, save to those who have, in their own experience, a significance to give them. Be they as full of meaning as they may, in the mouth of him who utters them, they fall as empty sounds on the ears of those who listen, unless they who listen have the same inward experience as he who speaks. How different is the import of the same words to different minds. How different is the import of that word death, when, with our childish simplicity and curiosity, we look from our mother's arms into the coffin to see the baby corpse, from what it is in after life, when, one by one, all our early associates and friends and companions have dropped away, and we stand alone by the new-made grave of the last, the best loved one! And how different, too, is the meaning of that same word death, to him who looks upon the grave as the end of life, and sees buried, in its darkness and silence, all that which is to him but the dearer and lovelier and more beloved part of himself, from what it is to him who regards the grave merely as the door of entrance, through which we pass from this world of trial, sin, and suffering, to our everlasting home, where is repose and joy and blessedness forever and ever! No matter what are the words one uses, nor what is the meaning he seems to himself to be conveying. If that particular fact he would communicate be not a fact of the experience of him to whom he would communicate it, let him be assured that to him it is incommunicable. No matter with what wisdom we speak, we can impart no more than they, to whom we speak, are prepared to interpret by what they have thought, felt, joyed, or sorrowed in themselves.

The darkness, we sometimes complain of in men's speech and in books, is not infrequently the darkness of our own minds. To say of a book, that it is unintelligible, is seldom anything more than to say, that we are aware of nothing in our experience, by which it can be interpreted. A wise man, especially a modest man, is slow to infer, from the fact that he does not comprehend a book that it contains nothing to be comprehended. We often fancy, too, that we understand an author, when we have not the remotest suspicion of his meaning. His words are so common, his manner is so familiar, he talks so much like one of our old friends, that we never think of asking ourselves whether we understand him or not. One day we shall read him, and be startled at the new and unthought-of meaning we discover in his words, and we shall be filled with wonder that we did not see it before. We rarely understand one another. Only they who have a common experience are mutually intelligible. This is the reason why we are so estranged one from another. Two men meet for the first time, they converse together, understand each other, and they are friends forever. Let men but understand one another, and all strife, hatreds, contentions, wars, are at an end; and of this they seem to have a secret consciousness, for this is what they imply, whether they know it or not, when they say of two or more persons, "there is a good understanding between them."

They, who, like Nicodemus, sneer at the new birth, have made as little proficiency in philosophy as in theology.[9] No man, who has not been born again, been born spiritually as well as naturally, can see the kingdom of God, in a philosophical, any more than in a religious sense.[10] There are some things which the natural man may understand, and there are some things which he cannot, for they are spiritually discerned. Spiritual things, be they expressed in what language they may, can be discerned only by spiritual men. Spiritual things are foolishness to the natural man, and the common sense man laughs outright at the profound words of the philosopher. When the natural man becomes a spiritual man, he finds that what he had called foolishness, are the deep and unsearchable things of God, and the common sense man, when he becomes a philosopher, stands in awe of that at which he had laughed. Let no man laugh at what he understands not, for the day may come when he shall weep at his folly; when he shall bitterly condemn himself, for his previous want of spiritual discernment.

We know no help for this difficulty, on the part of the unregenerate, to understand the regenerate. No matter what terms are used; the most common household words will be as dark, as unmeaning, as are said to be the most abstruse, the most far-fetched terms ever adopted by the most hopeless Germanizing Transcendentalist. Admitting then that Locke did write on metaphysical subjects in a sort of common sense phraseology, we cannot esteem it a very great merit. We have sometimes thought that by studying to adapt his style and language to the apprehension of the unlearned and the superficial, he retarded instead of accelerating the progress of metaphysical science. It is true that the manner in which he treated metaphysics made his "Essay" somewhat popular, and secured it a much larger number of readers, than it probably would have had if he had written more in the manner of the scholar; but we very much doubt whether he by

[9][Ed. The reference is to Nicodemus in John 3:3.]

[10][Ed. The reference here is to Paul's assertion that only the spiritual person can discern spiritual things. See 1 Cor. 2:14.]

this means added at all to the number of metaphysicians. He became popular because nobody found anything in his "Essay," which made anybody a whit the wiser. People read him and called themselves philosophers without having one grain more of philosophic thought than they had before they read him. By creating the impression that men can become philosophers without any severe mental discipline, he checked instead of encouraging that patient and laborious thought, without which no man becomes a philosopher; just as he, who is always telling what an easy thing it is to be a Christian hinders those efforts which alone can make us Christians. We are far from thinking that Locke himself was superficial, but he helped to make others superficial, or rather he hindered others from becoming profound. The most striking characteristic of his followers has ever been their superficialness. Few of them have ever dreamed of penetrating beneath the surface of things. English literature, during the period of his reign, contrasts singularly enough with that of the epoch which preceded him. Saving the productions of those writers who were not of his school, of those whose hearts were touched with the coals from off religion's altar, or whose souls were kindled up by the great democratic movements of the time, English Literature of the eighteenth century is, to the earnest spirits of our times, after the age of childhood, or early youth, absolutely unreadable. It is as light, as shallow, as unproductive, as the soil on one of our immense pine barrens. We look into it in vain for a new or profound thought, for a thrilling remark, for something which goes down into the deep places of the heart, and moves the soul at its bottom. We grow weary of it and pass it over in order to come at the richer and profounder and more living literature of the seventeenth century—the literature of those "giants of old," as they have been called. How far the light and shallow, cold and lifeless literature of England, during the eighteenth century, is to be attributed to the influence of Locke's philosophy, we shall not undertake to determine; but of this we are certain, that a different literature is never to be looked for, where that philosophy is the dominant one.

We trust that the design of these remarks will not be misinterpreted. We have no wish to dress up philosophy in the garb of the old Schoolmen. We are advocates for no technical phraseology, for no unintelligible jargon. We set our faces, as much as anyone, against all affected or far-fetched modes of speech. We ask for naturalness and simplicity. We ask every man to make it a matter of conscience, to speak and write as intelligibly to even the undisciplined mind, as the nature of his subject will admit. But we insist upon it, that the interests of science, literature, philosophy, are never to be sacrificed for the sake of adapting ourselves to the apprehension of men of no spiritual experience. We need not "bring philosophy down from its high places, [...] in order to add to its usefulness."[11] This is a sort of leveling which is uncalled for. Bring the masses up, if you will, enable them to comprehend the highest philosophy, if you can; but never talk of bringing philosophy down to vulgar capacities. We have heard too much, in our day, about the necessity of "adapting ourselves to the capacity of the common people," and about the danger of "shooting over the heads of the people." We have no patience with this left-handed democracy. We have no patience with men who talk of letting themselves down. There has been quite too much letting down. We would not bring the great gods down to earth, even if we could; but we would raise men to heaven, and enable them to hold fellowship with the Divinity. Philosophy is not, and never was, too high; but the people are, and ever have been, too low. Let him, who would "enhance the dignity of philosophy by adding to its usefulness,"[12] set himself seriously and earnestly at work, to elevate the people. Let him, if his heart throb with genuine love of man and his soul burn to augment the sum of human well-being, let him study to elevate the masses, to quicken their dormant energies, to create within them a craving for the loftiest range of thought, and to make them feel that they may aspire to it. But we pray him to withhold his condescension. Let him forget that the masses are below him; let him speak from his own full heart and strong convictions, to the universal heart and mind of humanity, in his own natural tones, with all the power and depth and sublimity of thought and feeling he can command. Let him speak to all men as his equals, and speak out his ripest thoughts, his profoundest reflections, and have no fear that he will speak in vain.

Assuredly we would not seek obscure modes of expression; we would ever be as transparent as possible; but we cannot consent to sacrifice depth for the sake of clearness, to dilute our thoughts for fear that they may be too strong for the intellects of our readers. We will take no pains to supersede the necessity of severe thinking on the part of those for whom we write. If we aid them, it is not by thinking for them but by compelling them to think for themselves. There is no such thing as one man's thinking for another. The real difficulty in the way of acquiring a knowledge of a given science, does not

[11] [Ed. See Bowden, "Locke," 173.]

[12] [Ed. See ibid.]

consist, and never did consist, in the language adopted by its cultivators. There are difficulties which lie deeper than words, and which no form of words can remove. Set all the world a-talking metaphysics, and nothing is gained, unless the real metaphysical problems be clearly seen, and the bearings of the proffered solutions fully comprehended; and these problems—state them in what words you will—are not perceived, and these solutions—express them in the simplest terms you can—are not and cannot be appreciated, without severe mental discipline, without long, patient, and profound thought. And thought is one's own act. It cannot be imparted from one mind to another. It is impossible to form a tunnel out of common sense phraseology, by means of which, thought may be poured from one mind into another, as we pour wine into a demijohn. Knowledge, in its higher and nobler sense, is ever the mind's own creation. It is wrought out in the mind by the mind itself. Man was to gain his bread by the sweat of his face, by hard work; and it is only by hard work, by incessant toil and mental labor, that the mind can attain to true philosophical knowledge. This may be discouraging to the indolent, and frightful to all who are wanting in robust mental health; but so be it then. There is no help for it. There is no labor-saving machinery that can be introduced into the mind's workshop, no locomotive to run by steam on the mind's railroad to philosophy. The old way is still the only way. The various inventions, christened "Thinking made easy," so numerous of late, stand us in no stead. The only machinery that will work at all, is that of patient and scrupulous observation, and calm and profound reflection. He who will not observe, he who will not reflect, can, by no process yet discovered, ever become a philosopher.

We have dwelt long on this point, not so much for the sake of replying to the writer in the Examiner, as because we deem it of some importance in itself; because we are fully convinced that a preparation is no less needed, in order to be a good hearer or a good reader, than in order to be a good speaker or a good writer; and because we have thought it neither mistimed nor misplaced, to admonish those—and many there are—who sneer at what they do not understand, and "speak evil of dignities" [Jude 1:8], that

> There are more things in heaven and earth—
> Than are dreamt of in "their" philosophy.[13]

[13][Ed. A paraphrase of William Shakespeare (1564-1616), *Hamlet*, Act I, Scene V, Lines 168-69: "There are more things in heaven and earth, Horatio, Than are dreamt of in our philosophy."]

Still we wish it to be understood, that we do not look for this preparation exclusively in saloons nor in universities. These places are not the ones in which we are most likely to find those whose hearts and minds are best prepared to hear and comprehend the philosopher. They only have the preparation needed, whose hearts have sorrowed before the mystery of the universe, and whose minds are scarred by their conflicts with doubt. And these are not seldomest found in that mighty multitude on whom we often look down from our high places, in pity or in scorn. We shall, if we seek, often find those who have the inward experience required, among those who have been to no school but nature's, and had no instructors but the internal whisperings of God's Spirit. Whoever has doubted, whoever has really sorrowed that there was no man found to open the book of God's providence, and read him the destiny of man and society, is prepared to hear and to comprehend the philosopher.

Nor let it be supposed that we would debar the people at large from the truths the philosopher professes to have demonstrated. These truths are not the peculiar possession of the philosopher. They are the truths of the universal reason, and are the property alike of all men. They are taught to all men by the spontaneous reason, which is the same in kind in every man. These truths are not the philosophy. Philosophy is the explanation and verification of them. The masses, who see nothing mysterious in these truths, and who have never thought of questioning them, do not wish to have them explained or verified. The explanation and verification, which is philosophy, are unintelligible to them. But the truths themselves, are not unintelligible to them. Whoever proclaims to the masses these truths, which the philosopher has demonstrated, cleared up, and legitimated, is sure to be heard and believed and followed.

The fact is, the great mass of mankind are not, as to their beliefs, in so sad a condition, as schoolmen sometimes imagine. The educated, the scientific are prone to look upon the masses as possessing no ideas, as having no knowledge but that which they obtain from human teachers. This is peculiarly the case with Locke and his followers. According to them, the child receives no patrimony from his father; he is born into the world naked and destitute in soul as well as in body, and with no innate power to weave himself a garment. His mind is a *tabula rasa* on which others indeed may write what they will, but upon which he himself can write nothing, save the summing up of what others have written thereon. Evil as well as good, falsehood as well as truth, may be written thereon. It depends wholly on the external circumstances, the quality of the masters secured, whether the mind's blank sheets shall be written over with truth or falsehood. The masses, after the flesh, it must be admitted, are surrounded with unwholesome influences, and provided with most wretched teachers. They must then be filled with evil thoughts and false notions. Their beliefs, their hopes and fears, likes and dislikes, are deserving no respect. Hence, on the one hand, the contempt of the masses manifested by so large a portion of the educated, even in democratic America, and, on the other hand, the pity and commiseration, the great condescension, and vast amount of baby-talk, which equally characterize another, but more kind-hearted, portion of the more favored classes. Of this last division, we presume, is the writer on whom we are remarking. He is not a man to look with contempt on human beings; he feels that we ought to labor to benefit the masses; but we presume he has no suspicion that the masses have any correct beliefs, but such as they receive from the favored and superior few. Hence his strong desire that all men, who write, should write in a simple style, and so let themselves down, that they will not be above the capacities of the many. He would not, we presume, think of learning from them, or of verifying their beliefs; but merely of teaching them what they ought to believe. We bring not this as a charge against him. It speaks well for his goodness of heart and proves him to be as good a democrat as a follower of Locke consistently can be.

But in point of fact, the masses are not so poor and destitute as all this supposes. They are not so dependent on us, the enlightened few, as we sometimes think them. We need not feel that, if we should die, all wisdom would die with us, and that there would be henceforth no means by which the millions would be able to come at truth and virtue. Reason is the true light, and it enlighteneth every man who cometh into the world. It is, as we have said, the same in all men, and therefore it is that no man is left in darkness. The reason has two modes of activity, one the spontaneous, the other the reflective. In the great majority of men, the reflective reason, which gives philosophy, is never awakened, and consequently but a small minority of mankind ever become philosophers. But the spontaneous reason develops itself in all men, in the highest and the lowest, in the uneducated as well as in the educated. This reason, the spontaneous reason, furnishes the universal beliefs of mankind, which are termed common sense. It furnishes all the ideas we ever have; teaches us all the truths we ever know. As this reason is the same in all men, it gives to all men the same ideas, furnishes them with the same truths, the same beliefs. These masses then, on which we look down with contempt or with pity for their weakness and ignorance, have all the truths we who look down upon them have; they have the same ideas, and the same beliefs. They are not so destitute then as the Lockeites thought them; they are not so erroneous then as the self-complacent aristocrat judged them, nor so dependent on their betters, as *great* men have generally counted them. Their views, beliefs, hopes, fears, likes, dislikes, are worthy to be examined, are to be respected. The masses are not to be pitied then, but respected, and herein is laid the foundation of true philanthropy.

But we are controverted. We are met by men who have no confidence in the masses, no respect for their beliefs, and who regard them as blind, infatuated, bent on evil, and only evil, and that continually.[14] Here comes then the doubt; common sense is suspected and put on trial. We may ourselves doubt. That is, we may, in looking in upon ourselves, doubt the legitimacy of those beliefs we have had in common with the rest of mankind, or, looking abroad upon the immense masses of human beings, following blindly their instincts, we may seriously doubt whether they are going in the right direction. There is a problem now in our minds. The reflective reason awakes and we reflect on this problem and seek its solution. This is to philosophize; and here is seen the utility of philosophy. We did not seek philosophy for the sake of instructing those masses; we do not need it, that we may communicate it to them; we merely desire to know whether their beliefs be well founded, whether relying, as they do, on common sense, following, as they do, the teachings of the spontaneous reason, they are safe, or not. Shall we pity or reverence them? War against them or become their allies? This is the problem. Philosophy is merely the solution we arrive at by reflection.

Well, what is this solution? Is common sense a liar? Are the teachings of the spontaneous reason false? Is humanity doomed to everlasting and universal error? So says the sceptic, so say Locke and his followers, or so they must say, if faithful to the principles they avow. But so say not we. Different from this is the solution we have obtained. We cannot now undertake to prove that our solution is the true one; but the reflective reason has with us legitimated the teachings of the spontaneous reason, legitimated common sense, assured us that it is the voice of the spontaneous reason, and that the spontaneous reason is the voice of God. True and holy for us then are the instincts of the masses; true and holy for us then are the universal beliefs of mankind. We no longer pity the many, we no longer apologize for their conduct, no longer labor to change their faith. We stand

[14][Ed. Reference here is to Gen. 6:5.]

in awe of them, and apply ourselves to the work of enabling them to march to the glorious destiny God hath appointed them, and to which his own hand is leading them.

Philosophy, as it is a solution of the problem which doubt has placed in the mind, can be understood only by those in whose minds the problem has been placed. By this fact the philosopher is, and must be, separated from the great mass of his brethren; but since the truths he has demonstrated, and which he believes, are precisely the truths of the spontaneous reason, precisely the universal beliefs of mankind, he is also connected with his race, and, by all the truth he believes, intimately bound to the humblest, as well as to the proudest, member of the human family. No stranger then is he to humanity. Not with contempt does he look on the masses, not with scorn does he treat their instincts. Nothing that is human is foreign to him. He reverences in each human being the human nature he reverences in himself, and in each human being he finds all the elements of that truth and virtue, his own reason and conscience bid him believe and obey.

Philosophy is not needed by the masses: but they who separate themselves from the masses, and who believe that the masses are entirely dependent on them for truth and virtue, need it, in order to bring them back, and bind them again to universal humanity. And they need it now, and in this country, perhaps as much as ever. The world is filled with commotions. The masses are heaving and rolling, like a mighty river, swollen with recent rains, and snows dissolving on the mountains, onward to a distant and unknown ocean. There are those among us, who stand awe-struck, who stand amazed. What means this heaving and onward rolling? Whither tend these mighty masses of human beings? Will they sweep away every fixture, every house and barn, every mark of civilization? Where will they end? In what will they end? Shall we rush before them and attempt to stay their progress? Or shall we fall into their ranks and on with them to their goal? "Fall into their ranks; be not afraid; be not startled; a Divine Instinct guides and moves onward that heaving and rolling mass; and lawless and destructive as it may seem to you, ye onlookers, it is normal and holy, pursuing a straight and harmless direction on to the union of Man with God." So answers philosophy and this is its glory. The friends of humanity need philosophy, as the means of legitimating the cause of the people, of proving that it is the right and the duty of every man to bind himself to that cause, and to maintain it in good report and in evil report, in life and in death. They need it that they may prove to these conservatives, who are frightened almost out of their wits at the movements of the masses, and who are denouncing them in no measured terms, that these movements are from God and that they who war against them are warring against truth, duty, God, and humanity. They need it that they may no longer be obliged to make apologies for their devotion to the masses, their democratic sympathies and tendencies. They who are persecuted for righteousness' sake, who are loaded with reproach for their fidelity to truth and duty, who are all but cast out of the pale of humanity, because they see, love, and pursue humanity's true interests—they need it that they may comprehend the cause of the opposition they meet, forgive their enemies, silence the gainsayer, and give to him that asks it a reason for the hope that is in them. The friends of progress, here and everywhere, need it that, having vindicated, legitimated progress, as philosophers, they may go into the saloons, the universities, the halls of legislation, the pulpit, and abroad among the people, and preach it, with the dignity and the authority of the prophet.

It will be seen from this that our philosophy, notwithstanding certain aristocratic airs, is by no means wanting in its democratic tendencies. Its aim is not utility, but the establishment of truth, and that not for the many, but for the few; nevertheless the truth established, always benefits the world, and the truth established in this case, is the truth which everybody is interested in. We by no means reject common sense; we love, we obey it, because we have legitimated its right to be loved and obeyed. All true philosophy accepts, and explains, and legitimates, the instinctive beliefs of mankind. Philosophy, therefore, though it is not common sense, is in perfect harmony with it.

Will the respect the writer in the Examiner has for common sense carry him as far as this? Does he credit common sense? Does he believe the instinctive beliefs of mankind are true, worthy to be trusted? If so, we pray him to legitimate those beliefs on the ground of Locke's philosophy. If he does not believe them true, if he denies them, we ask him what right he has to require philosophical writers to respect common sense? Moreover, if common sense, the universal beliefs of mankind, the instinctive beliefs of humanity, the teachings of the spontaneous reason, be discredited, as they must be by a disciple of Locke, we ask, how it is possible to establish the certainty of anything whatever? We ask those who rail against humanity, and look upon the instinctive beliefs of the masses with contempt, how they will save us from universal scepticism?

16.

THE CHARACTER OF JESUS AND THE CHRISTIAN MOVEMENT[1]

Boston Quarterly Review 1 (April, 1838): 129-52

From the fact that in a previous Essay[2] I undertook to set forth that the Christ was in the world before Abraham, and had been the only savior of men from the beginning, I would by no means leave it to be inferred that I see nothing peculiar in the character of Jesus, or original in the movement he commenced—in the moral, religious, and social order to which he has given his name. The character of Jesus was, in truth, strikingly original and peculiar; and the movement he commenced and to which his death gave such a mighty impulse—like his character, from which it proceeded—was alone of its kind, original and peculiar, with no prototype in the previous history of the world.

But in what consisted the originality and peculiarity of his character? And wherein does the Christian movement differ from other important movements of humanity? These are the questions which I propose to answer.

I. In what consisted the originality and peculiarity of the character ascribed by the New Testament writers to Jesus? I answer,

1. Not in his nature. If we may regard at all the reasoning of my previous Essay on this subject, or place any reliance on what seem to be the plain declarations of the writers of the New Testament, Jesus was in no respect distinguished by his nature from mankind in general. He did not belong to a separate order of being but to common humanity. The Christ was not manifested in a superior nature, in a super-angelic, nor in an angelic, nature, but in a human being, in a man, made like unto other men, subject to all the infirmities of other men, sin alone excepted. It behooved him to be made like unto his brethren, otherwise he could not have properly sympathized with

[1][Ed. The running title varies for this essay: "Originality of Jesus" (129-39) and "The Christian Movement" (140-52).]

[2][Ed. See "Christ before Abraham," *Boston Quarterly Review* 1 (January, 1838): 8-21, and Chapter 13 in this volume.]

them, and been an example unto them of what they might and should be, in order to be followers of God as dear children.

2. The originality and peculiarity of Jesus do not consist in the fact that he taught any new and peculiar truths, that he disclosed to the world any intellectual truth before unknown, nor in the fact that he pointed out any new method, or created any new means, by which men may be justified in the sight of God. This I have proved, by showing, as I think I have done, that the Christ, the only savior of men, the only redeemer of lost sinners, was before Abraham, was, in fact, the lamb slain from the foundation of the world, and that by virtue of which the wise and the good of all ages and nations had been justified. The way of salvation, the means of redemption and sanctification, were, after the coming of Jesus, precisely what they had been before his coming. Men were before Jesus just and holy in the sight of God only on the condition that they possessed the Christ, and they can be just and holy under the Christian dispensation only on the same condition. The conditions of salvation never change. Men must *be* holy, before they can be accounted holy, by Him who is not deceived by appearances; and holiness is possessed only by dwelling in love, and by love dwelling in us—dwelling in God, and God dwelling in us.

3. Nor was Jesus original and peculiar because the Christ was in him and manifested through him. The Christ, I have proved, at least think I have proved, is nothing but pure, disinterested love. Now Jesus was not the first that loved, nor was he alone in the fact of manifesting pure, disinterested love. Thousands before him had loved, and with as much purity and intensity as he did. His love was strong, was intense, and able to endure neglect, ridicule, persecution, and death; but in this he was by no means singular. Others had been able to endure all he endured, and to submit to as great, if not even greater, sacrifices than he did. His personal sacrifices were great; but, according to the record, they were by no means remarkable, nor are they difficult to be matched in any age or nation of the world. His death on the cross strikes me in no wise as remarkable; and it loses much of its merit too, if we suppose that he foresaw that it was to be only a temporary suspension of existence and that he should be alive again and well after the third day. Who of us would not joyfully consent to be crucified, if we could foresee that our crucifixion would result in the regeneration of the world, and that in three days we should be alive and well, walking about, meeting our friends, eating and drinking, and knowing that we were henceforth to die no more, but to rise at once into inconceivable glory and blessedness?

4. Nor was Jesus separated from all who went before him by the fact that he died a martyr to principle, or to convictions of duty. Socrates long before him had set an illustrious example of a noble martyrdom to principle, and Abraham had been ready to offer up his son Isaac at the command, or supposed command, of duty, which, I must believe, cost him altogether more than it would have cost him to lay down his own life. And shall we suppose that truth, principle, duty, love, had no martyrs in the countless generations which had passed on and off the earth before the coming of Jesus? Shall we so wrong our common nature, do such injustice to the patriarchs, sages, and prophets, and saints, who the writer to the Hebrews says, "had trial of cruel mockings and scourgings, of bonds and imprisonment, who wandered about in sheep-skins and goat-skins, in deserts, in mountains, in dens and caves of the earth, destitute, afflicted, tormented, stoned, sawn asunder, or slain with the sword?" [Heb. 11:36-37]. Never since the human race began its endless career of progress, has truth, science, love, faith, principle, duty, wanted martyrs, and martyrs too whose corporal and mental agonies suffer not in comparison with those of Jesus. It was noble in Jesus to die rather than be false to his mission; but this fact does not separate him from his race. Humanity is rich in martyrs, and the fact that Jesus was one, does but admit him into a numerous and a glorious company. Every page of human history is written in the precious and life-giving blood of martyrs; and the blood of martyrs is too honorable to humanity to be called the distinguishing glory of one alone. A goodly company, an august assembly was that, composed of the martyrs of all ages, which the apocalyptic John saw in the visions of his spirit, almost in the very days of Jesus, gathering round the throne of the Ancient of Days, and striking their harps to the triumphal song of Moses and the Lamb. Let no man wish to snatch the crown from one of their heads, or the palm from one of their hands, for the sake of elevating any one of their number above his equals.

But if Jesus was distinguished neither by his nature, nor the truths he taught or revealed, nor the means of man's justification which he pointed out or created, nor the strength and intensity of his love, nor by his personal sacrifices and his martyr death on the cross, in what then did the originality, the peculiarity of his character consist? It consisted in the fact that in him the Christ attained to universality, and that his love was no longer the love of family, caste, tribe, clan, or country, but a love of humanity; it was no longer mere piety, nor patriotism, nor friendship, but it was PHILANTHROPY.

I will try to explain and verify this statement. Love had existed, and been as pure, as intense, as all-unconquerable, in thousands who had preceded Jesus, as it was in him; but in none of them had it taken the form of philanthropy, or love of mankind. Take the case of Abraham, the father of the Jewish people. The Christ was in Abraham; the principle, or sentiment, which I have called love, was strong and abiding in him; but it was partial, it wanted freedom and universality; and it manifested itself in no remarkable degree, save in its religious aspect. The effort to give up his son Isaac, must, I have said, have cost him more than it would to have sacrificed himself, and could have been made only through the force of the strongest religious principle. But you see nothing of the human side of Abraham's love. The Christ in him was not the God-Man, the union of the love of God and the love of man. Faithful to God, he was often wanting in his duty to man. In his human relations, he was false, tyrannical, and in no way distinguished from ordinary chieftains of a nomad tribe. He lived by pasturage, and perhaps by carrying on a predatory warfare, as do the Bedouin Arabs today. So far as history gives us any account of him, it does not appear that he ever dreamed of loving or serving mankind. He was, so far as he is known to us, the true type of the Jewish people. That people was of an earnest race, full of noble qualities, capable of the firmest principles, the most exalted sentiments, and the loftiest deeds; but it was an Oriental race. Its brow was expanded but not elevated. It equals, if it do not surpass, all others on the religious side of our nature; but it comprehends nothing, feels nothing of the sentiment of humanity. The fullness of its heart overflows towards God, but never towards man. From the depths of its being, rise perennial springs of piety, but not of philanthropy. In the same breath it pours forth the most kindling strains of devotion and utters the most horrid imprecations upon its enemies.

Moses and David, the two most eminent names, after Abraham, of the race, partake of the same noble qualities, and are marked by the same defects. Moses was a great man. Antiquity boasts few greater names than his. The Christ was in him; but unable to attain to a symmetrical development. His love was strong, intense, all-enduring, but it was love only in its religious and patriotic, or more properly, clannish phases. Piety was his breath. He saw God at all times, and in all things; and he bowed down with profound awe before the Divine Presence. He recognized God as the only rightful sovereign of the universe, and he would have no king in Israel, but Jehovah. His love for his tribe, or, if you please, for his people, was strong, generous, and strikingly verified. Though brought up as the adopted son of

Pharaoh's daughter, and by his education, talents, genius, and position, capable of becoming virtually the first man in the kingdom, he chose to adhere to his people, a proscribed race in Egypt, to suffer reproach and affliction with them, and, if need were, to die for them. This was to him far more desirable than all the wealth, honors, pleasures, and power that Egypt had to give. But his love did not extend beyond his people. They were the whole earth to him. They were the only mankind he knew. He was willing to rob the Egyptians to enrich them, and he could command them to extirpate with fire and sword the Canaanites, even to helpless women and innocent babes. So strong is his hatred even of other nations, that he surrounds his people with laws and institutions designed to keep them forever a separate, distinct, and peculiar people. I will not say that all this, considering the age in which Moses lived, and the designs of Providence, was wrong. Nothing can come but in its time; and the time for the universal brotherhood of humanity was not yet. Moses doubtless was as perfect as his age and people admitted or demanded. All I would say is, that he was not a *whole* man, that he manifested the Christ only in its religious and patriot phases. This was much but was not all. It was enough for his time but not for all time.

The same in some respects at least may be said of David. David was a second Moses, really inferior by many degrees to the first, in himself, but in some measure compensating that disadvantage by living some centuries later. He was a poet and a warrior, a prophet and a man of blood. He was remarkable for his piety, and the strength and freshness of his devotional feelings. Even to this day, religious people can find no better medium for expressing their devotional sentiments, than his really inspired Psalms. I can conceive no language so adequate to the utterance of our religious feelings, as those astonishing Hebrew odes of his. I read them always with fresh wonder and awe. But no sooner does David sink, as it were, the priest and the prophet in himself, and withdraw his eyes from the dazzling glories of Jehovah's chariot, than he breaks forth in the most intolerant rage against all who are not of his Israel. Some of his Psalms are nothing but imprecations upon his enemies. Spite, contempt, disdain, wrath, hatred, revenge, ring forth in a sort of hellish harmony, and would seem to partake enough of the infernal to make hell's monarch himself applaud. He loved his tribe, and through the aid or intrigues of the priesthood he made it the ruling tribe. He loved his family and left it the throne, of which it retained possession for many generations. But no recognition of human brotherhood ever escaped him; no gleam of philanthropy ever broke in upon the obscure night, as to the relations of man to man as man, in which he lived and in which he died. All the nations of the earth, save the Jews, were his and Jehovah's enemies, and could be favored only by bowing their necks to his yoke. So was it with all his successors, whether among the bards and minstrels, or prophets and kings, unless an exception be made in favor of Solomon, who seems, in the latter part of his life, to have relaxed somewhat from the rigid national bigotry of his countrymen and to have felt that other nations besides his own were worthy of regard and even of imitation. Perhaps a slight exception ought also to be made in the case of Isaiah, for though he was a Jew, a stern, unrelenting Jew, and doubtless held all other nations in suitable abhorrence, he does seem to have had some dream or dim presentiment that the time would come at least when the Gentiles would enjoy a share of Jehovah's regard, though probably, in his mind, only by being converted to Judaism.

If from the Jews, we pass to the Greeks and Romans, albeit we find a difference, we shall still find the Christ only partially formed. The religious aspect of the Christ is less striking; the love of country suffers no diminution, and that of science, and in the case of the Greeks, that of the beautiful, are super added. But we do not find the sentiment of humanity. No precept betrays it, no life reveals it. There is certainly a greater approximation towards universal brotherhood, than with the Jews. You meet a more human and cosmopolitan spirit. Still the Greek looks with a sort of contempt upon all races but his own. The Roman deems liberty, freedom, the especial property, or deserving to be the especial property, of the Roman citizen alone. In either country, there is no want of men who can die for family and friends, and especially for country; but there are none to die for humanity. Instances of the most striking devotion to one's country meet us at every step. Rome up to the epoch of the Empire was always full of men ready to immolate themselves for the safety or glory of the city; but I have found no instance, recorded in her history, of a man who immolated himself for mankind. She furnished heroes and patriots, but not philanthropists.

Socrates, as Plato has given him to us, is in my judgment the greatest of the predecessors of Jesus, and the only one of them that may with any propriety be brought into comparison with him. History presents me in none of her favorites, before Jesus, a single individual who comes up so near to my conception of a complete man as Socrates; and yet he has nothing of the completeness we perceive in Jesus. He has a strong devotional spirit. The religious phase of the Christ was, perhaps, as striking in him as in Jesus. He had equal sincerity, modesty, firmness, and moral courage, though less warmth and earnestness. But he was an Athenian; the greatest of the Athenians, the noblest race of antiquity, but he was not great enough for humanity. Great as he was, it is questionable whether his love stretched beyond his native Athens, at most beyond the Hellenic race. His life and his death was a noble homage to virtue and truth and philosophy, but not a homage to philanthropy. He did not submit to death because he loved the human race but because he loved wisdom; not because he was a philanthropist but because he was a philosopher.

Now all these whom I have mentioned and to whom my remarks naturally refer though I have not given their names did much and did nobly. They prepared the way for Jesus; but he is distinguished from them all by a broad line. His originality and his peculiarity consist in the fact that he was not the man of a clique or coterie, of a tribe, or a people, that he was not a patriot nor a philosopher, but a philanthropist. In him, if we may credit history, the Christ for the first time leaped the narrow enclosures of the temple, the priesthood, the school, the sect, the family, the clan, the country, and bounded forth, with a free step and a joyous heart, over the immense plains of humanity. Then, for the first time, there was a MAN on the earth; one who might, in the significant idiom of the Hebrews, call himself the Son of Man; and who was a type of the universal man, the man of all ages, and countries, the man formed not by conventions, but by the free, full, and harmonious development of human nature itself.

I cannot say how much the prejudices of a theory, or of education, may have blinded my eyes and biased my judgment, but I think every intelligent reader of the Gospels, must admit that Jesus was singularly free from everything merely local and temporary. He has no feature of the conventional or artificial man. Though born and brought up a Jew, there is nothing Jewish in the genius and complexion of his mind. There is nothing in his character by which you can determine the age, or people, to which he belonged, nor the circumstances amid which he had grown up. Indeed it is difficult for us to conceive of his character as ever having been formed. We are almost compelled to look upon it as a spontaneous production, as coming into the world all ready formed, perfected and finished by the Creator's hand at one stroke. It is this completeness and this fidelity to universal human nature that enable him to commend himself to all men of all times, nations, sects, and creeds. Eighteen hundred years have rolled away since he was on the earth. Mighty revolutions have changed more than once the face of the moral and intellectual world;

his countrymen have been scattered to the four winds of heaven; the empires which in his day were in the pride of their strength and the zenith of their glory have passed beneath the sway of the conqueror, fallen to pieces and moldered to dust; new tribes and new peoples have issued forth from the depths of the forest, passed on and off the stage, and been succeeded by others still; new sciences, new arts, new laws, new thoughts, new feelings, new languages, new forms of government, new religions, and new modes of life, have sprung up; and yet his character is as young, as fresh, as modern, if I may so speak, as though he had been the playmate of our childhood, and the companion of our youthful studies—is as faithful a type of human nature as it is developed today in this Western world and in this free republic, as it was of human nature as it was developed in the multitudes that thronged to hear him as he went preaching through the cities of Judea and Galilee. Through the lapse of ages, and all the changes that time works in the things of this world, it has not been outgrown, has acquired nothing of the antique, the superannuated, the obsolete. Here is a proof of the universality of his nature. He was no Sadducee, no Pharisee, no Jew, no gentile; HE WAS A MAN, true to universal human nature. The elements of his mind and heart were the elements of all minds and hearts. Herein was his peculiarity. He was peculiar in that he was not peculiar, in his entire freedom from all idiosyncrasy, in being marked by nothing which does not belong to the universal mind and heart of humanity.

With this character we may readily predict that his love will not be confined to his family and friends, to the individuals of a particular caste, class, sect, party, or country; but that it will be free, impartial, and universal. His sympathy will be awakened by man and by man only. All the factitious distinctions of society will disappear before him; kings, priests, nobles, patricians, plebeians, thrones, scepters, diadems, and miters, all will vanish away, and there will stand before him only men, human beings in their moral strength or moral weakness, in their beauty, or their deformity. Man and men, not tribes and nations, man and men, not classes, orders, or estates, he will see, love, and die to redeem. This is his glory. This gives him the title, more honorable than any nobility ever bore, of the SON OF MAN. This makes him the savior of mankind. This endears him to simple humanity throughout all time and space, establishes his empire over the universal mind and heart, builds the temples which bear his name, and tunes the millions of voices which on each successive Sabbath day, throughout all the earth, shout forth his praise in glad and loud hosannas.

In this, I see the originality and the peculiarity of Jesus. He was the first of our race in whom the sentiment of the universal brotherhood of the human race was developed; the first who had died a martyr to his love of mankind. His life was the earliest revelation of philanthropy, and he was the first who, sinking all considerations of father, mother, sister, brother, friend, country, creed, school, sect, party, tribe, people, order, class, estate, could let the fountains of his love overflow for simple humanity, who could die for man as man. He was the first whose love begat humanity; and through him the human race is installed; and the good man directed henceforth to find his household and friends and countrymen in humanity; and a neighbor in whomsoever needs his kind offices. With him philanthropy, love, to man as man, was born; and well did heaven's hosts shout at his birth, "Peace on earth and good will to man," as well as "Glory to God in the highest" [Luke 2:14].

II. Having ascertained wherein consisted the originality, the peculiarity of the character of Jesus, there can be no difficulty in seizing the peculiar traits of the Christian movement. The Christian movement sprung from the life of Jesus; and as that life was the life of philanthropy, the Christian movement must needs be a movement in the direction of love to mankind. It was not a movement in behalf of piety, of patriotism, nor of art and science, but of humanity. Its end was to reconcile men to one another and to God, to bring together in Christ, all the members of the human family, however widely estranged, and to integrate them all in the unity of the spirit of love. In this consists what it may claim of the original and peculiar.

The Jewish movement, commenced by Abraham, continued by Isaac and Jacob, of which Moses was the lawgiver, Joshua the hero, David the poet, and Solomon the philosopher, was essentially a religious movement, using the word religion, as I now do, in its most restricted sense. Its main-spring was piety, the worship of God, not the weal of man; and its mission was to bring out the religious element of human nature and to institute the worship of a spiritual Divinity. This was the end of that movement and to this end was limited the mission of the Jewish people. To this mission, God, in his providence, had called the Jewish people; and this is wherefore they were denominated the chosen people of God. They were God's chosen people in an especial sense because it was their especial work to bring out the idea of God, of piety. This work, as far as, when taken exclusively, it can be accomplished, they did accomplish. When the time had come for religion to be transferred from the Jews to humanity, to be brought out of the temple at Jerusalem and placed in the temple of the universal human heart, the Jewish nation died, as die all nations, and all individuals too, when their work is done, their mission fulfilled.

Had Jesus been sent merely to effect a religious movement, he would have been only the continuator of Abraham and Moses. In this case he would have had nothing original and peculiar in his character, nor in his mission. Christians would have been called merely to engage in the work which had been assigned to the Jews, which work was finished when the veil of the Temple was rent in twain, and the Holy of Holies laid open to the gaze of the profane. The Christian movement would have had no aim peculiar to itself; it could only have tended to achieve a work already achieved.

So far as it concerns the religious element of human nature, taken as an exclusive element, I must needs believe the Jews had done all for its development that can be done. In respect to piety, Christians can make no advance on the Jews; nor do they essentially differ from the Jews. They and the Jews worship one and the same spiritual Divinity. The most religious of today find the Hebrew odes, as I have said, the best interpreters of their religious feelings. Whoever would sing the praises of God, extol his providences, or speak forth his glory and majesty, might and dominion, strikes the harp of David and pours out his soul in a Hebrew song. On the religious side of our nature, Jews and Christians are the same. In a strictly religious sense, then, Christianity adds nothing to Judaism. The Christian movement is not original and peculiar under its religious aspect.

But however perfect Judaism may have been, as a development of the religious element of our nature, as it concerns a sense of man's duty to God, it is extremely deficient in relation to other essential elements of humanity, and especially in relation to a sense of man's duty to man. The Jew was defective on what may be called the human side of his character. He had no love for man, as man, for the simple fact of his being a man. He held all nations but his own in abhorrence, and if he loved a single human being, it was because that human being superadded to his claims as a man, those of countryman or kindred, of a benefactor, or a dependent, a friend, a companion, or an acquaintance. He never conceived of the love of simple, naked humanity. This was his great defect. This defect Christianity supplies. To the Jew's piety it adds philanthropy, the love of man, as man, for his human nature, without reference to anything else. It does not take from the Jew, it simply adds to what he had. Jesus did not come to destroy Judaism, but to fulfil, perfect, complete it, to supply its deficiencies. The tendency of the movement he commenced was not to make us love God less, but man more. This was its grand characteristic. By its philanthropic tendency it was distinguished by a broad line from Judaism, and became and should be considered something more than a continuation of Judaism.

The Christian movement may also be as clearly distinguished from the Greek movement. Greece was the land of art and science, the home of the beautiful and the true. The Jews had no art, no science, and, properly speaking, no philosophy. But Greece had them all, and in a high degree of perfection. God called the Greeks to the work of developing art, science, philosophy, in like manner as he had called the Jews to that of developing religion. If Christianity were a movement in the direction of the arts and sciences, if its object were to realize the true and the beautiful, it would be merely a continuation of the Greek movement, it would be identified with that movement, and would therefore have nothing original and peculiar to itself.

In point of fact, that element of human nature which creates art, whether under the form of literature, poetry, eloquence, or under the form of music, painting, sculpture, and architecture, has received no extraordinary developments from the Christian movement. We study most of the fine arts at Athens today, as we did before the coming of Jesus. The Greek historians, poets, tragedians, orators, sculptors, architects, are still our masters in their respective spheres, as the Jewish prophets are in what relates to the worship of God. Christianity has done something. It has embodied in its painting and in its Gothic architecture, the beauty of sentiment, a species of beauty unknown to the ancient world, and which could be developed only by a religion of love. The Greeks embodied in their works of art only the beauty of form and of idea. In science we have advanced on Greece, but always in the direction of Greece. We have continued and improved Greece. In philosophy we have agitated no questions which were not agitated at Athens, and we probably must continue to agitate the same problems for ages to come, without obtaining solutions which may be regarded as definitive. However much we may have surpassed the Greeks, either in art or science, in the cultivation of the true and the beautiful, we can claim little originality. We cannot say that the world is at all indebted to Christianity, or to the Christian movement, for art, science, and philosophy, though it may be indebted to it in some degree for the progress they have made.

The Christian Movement is distinguished also from the Roman movement. The Roman world is nothing but the complement of the

Grecian world. It stands out for its contributions to patriotism and jurisprudence. Its mission was to found the state, and to teach the world to live under law. Law is truly a Roman element. Christianity has extended it, and contributed much to the improvement of legislation, both in its spirit and in its forms, but it is not the originator of law.

But there is one aspect under which the Christian world, by the side of Greece and Rome, must strike us as original and peculiar. Neither Greece nor Rome, in any of their movements, in any of their creations, ever realized the love of man as man. They give us no example of philanthropy. The word is indeed Greek, but the thing is purely of Christian origin and growth. Penetrate the Grecian and Roman city, you shall find there no institution that recognizes, no law that reveals, a love for man as man. The duty of the citizen is in no case the duty of the philanthropist. You find men with philanthropic souls, with humane feelings, men who are chaste, continent, generous, brave, heroic, but the end prescribed them, by the order of civilization to which they belong, is never the welfare of humanity, but always the glory of the city. To improve, enrich, and embellish the city, to extend its conquests and dominion, to preserve or confirm its empire, is the great end prescribed to the individual. For this he toils, studies, sings, creates, faces danger, meets the enemy and death in battle. He does not live for himself alone. Far from it. Selfishness is not the *primum mobile.*[3] Sacrifice is enjoined. The individual must be ready to give up ease, wealth, reputation, life, and that too without a murmur—but for what? For the city, the state, not for humanity.

Greek and Roman civilization advanced far beyond selfishness and beyond the mere love of family and friends; but it attained only to love of country. It could obtain the sacrifice of all the tender affections of the heart, all the endearments of home, all the pleasures of life, and life itself, at the call of duty, but merely at the call of duty to the city or state, not at the call of duty to man. The citizen rushed forth to battle and left his bones at Thermopylae, at Marathon, Platea, Sardis, Arbela, Memphis, Carthage, in Spain, Gallia, Germany, or the Isles of the Britons, but not at the voice of humanity; it was always at the voice of Sparta, Athens, or Rome.

I say not that humanity has gained nothing by Greek and Roman wars. The interests of the human race were in them all and were debated at Thermopyla, at Marathon, at Platea, at Salamis, on the

[3][Ed. Latin for"the source of motion, or the mainspring."]

Granicus and the Nile, at Arbela and Philippi, in Pontus, Parthia, Spain, Gallia, and the British Isles; but the motive which moved the Grecian phalanx, or the Roman legion, was not a sense of duty to man as man, but to the Grecian or the Roman state. Man as man, claimed as yet no regard and never did in the Grecian and Roman civilization. To promote the interests and glory of the city was the highest moral end ever imposed by that civilization. He who was conscious of fidelity to the state was acquitted of all sin in the eyes of his conscience, and felt that he had done all that Gods or men could demand of him.

This civilization, therefore, did not repel slavery. It had no conception of human brotherhood, of man's equality to man. It recognized distinctions of class, and had its nobles, patricians, plebeians, its populace, its *prolétaires*, its helots and its slaves. Sparta kept a whole nation in servitude, and if they became too numerous, hunted them down as we do wild beasts. Athens had slaves in abundance, and Rome to several times the amount of her free population. This fact of itself proves that there was no recognition of the rights of man, no love of simple humanity. For he who sees in others the same humanity he loves and reverences in himself, who loves his fellow men simply as men, because they are men, will not, cannot degrade them to a lower round of the social hierarchy than he is willing to occupy himself, will certainly never consent to reduce them to slavery.

Hence, again, this civilization did not repudiate war. In fact, it was almost purely a military civilization. Its main business and its chief glory, were war and conquest. But had it been penetrated with a love of humanity, had it seen a brother in the foreigner, a fellow man to be loved, it could not but have condemned war in principle, even if it had tolerated it in practice. But no. The same word served it to designate an enemy and a foreigner. All out of the pale of the city were out of the pale of its love.

You see, then, wherein consisted the defectiveness of the Greek and Roman civilization. It probably was far behind the Jewish in its religious phase, but it far surpassed it in art, literature, science, philosophy; yet like the Jewish, it was wanting in the love of man as man. This love of man as man, wanting in both the Jewish and the Greek and Roman civilizations, in the Oriental world and in the Occidental world, is precisely that which Jesus came to supply, and which constitutes the originality and peculiarity of the Christian movement.

The Christian movement does not tend to develop piety, as did the Jewish; it does not tend, so exclusively, to perfect the state, to bring out art, science, philosophy, jurisprudence, the sense of law and love of country, as did the Greek and Roman; but it tends to the development of genuine philanthropy. In this tendency it proves itself original and peculiar. It does not destroy piety, art, science, philosophy, nor even patriotism; but it aims to shed over them a purer light, to diffuse through them a freer and a richer sentiment, and to make them all harmonize with, and contribute to, the freest and fullest development of human nature, man's highest possible perfection.

The love of man as man is Christianity's point of departure and its point of arrival too. From this it starts and to this it comes round. By making this its starting-point, it teaches us that our duty to God, to our country, to relatives, family, and friends, is discharged in the true love of humanity, that all our duties, of whatever nature, are integrated in the love of man, in the service of mankind.

Under Judaism everything was subordinated to religion, or the worship of God. The city or the state existed only for the purpose of maintaining the priesthood and the temple-service. All human interests were sacrificed. Art could not flourish, literature could have no existence, science and philosophy no toleration. Religion must reign without a rival, and by so doing it became exclusive, despotic, tyrannical. It lost its primal character, lost sight of its legitimate end, and from a reverence for the true and spiritual, a love of the beautiful and good, it degenerated into a long, fatiguing ritual, a mass of unmeaning rites and ceremonies, as unacceptable to God as burdensome and debasing to man. Religion, when separated from our other duties, when erected into a separate, a distinct duty of itself, or even when regarded as capable of being so erected, becomes a deep and withering curse upon humanity, and inevitably awakens abhorrence, and the most unrelenting hostility in the bosom of every genuine Son of Man. Religion should be to us as the light, a medium through which we see all that we do see, but which itself remains forever unseen.

Man ought to learn, and if he studies the Christian movement he will learn that it is folly to think of doing anything for God. God stands in no need of help from man. He dwelleth not in temples made with hands, nor is he served with men's hands as though he needed anything. He is the universal Being, self-subsisting, and self-sufficing. He is above and beyond, albeit near and within us. He asks no vain oblations, no offerings of sweet incense and myrrh, gold and precious stones. His worship is no separate act, standing out by itself, distinct from all human interests and in opposition to them. This is the great lesson Christianity teaches the Jew.

The Greek and Roman citizen is taught by this same Christian movement that the city is not ultimate, that instead of living and dying for his country, he should live and die for man. The city or state to which one belongs can have no legitimate interest not identical with the interests of universal humanity. What is the true interest of one city is the interest of all cities; of one nation, of all nations; and of one man, of all men. The true way then of doing what the Jew sought to do, that is, to serve God, and of doing what the Greek and Roman sought to do, that is, to serve the city or state, is to do that which best serves man as man. He who loves man as man that is, as he loves himself, will always seek to do him all the good in his power, and by so doing will fulfil his whole duty both to God and the state. In love, then, all interests and duties unite; in love our duties to God and to man unite; in love, then, God and man meet, lose their antithesis, and become one.[4] Love is the Christ, as I have before proved, and of course then love is the mediator between God and man the universal atoner or reconciler. Hence the idea of the God-Man, the union of the divine and human natures in the same person, an idea held by the church from its birth up to the present, though in all likelihood without being comprehended in its full significance. In the love of man as man, all antitheses in matters of interest and duties will be found to meet and become identical.

The Christian movement, from what I have said, it will be seen, is not a destructive movement. It destroys no element of human nature. It accepts the piety of the Jew and the patriotism of the Greek and Roman, and absorbs them in a higher and broader sentiment than either. It takes nothing from the world, which is enduring, but it adds that which gives life and energy and a right direction to the whole.

Having ascertained the true character of the Christian movement, and wherein it is original and peculiar, I proceed to remark on its progress, and to determine who are affected by it, and what we must be and do in order to be Christians.

The progress of the Christian movement is the great matter of human history. The history of it has not yet been written; its grandeur and immense bearings on the destiny of man in this life have as

[4]See *New Views of Christianity, Society, and the Church*. Boston: James Munroe & Company. 1836. This little book, which some call a dark book, is written expressly to unfold the idea touched upon in this sentence. [Ed. That is, the idea of the atonement.]

yet been hardly conceived. The histories of the church, and especially of Christianity, at least those accessible to the English reader, are small things, and give one about as just a conception of Christianity as a single brick would of the city of Babylon.[5] We find in them little except a mass of miserable cant and nauseous details of controversies about words and unmeaning dogmas, ever renewed and never ending; contests between rival sects; contests between the civil society and the ecclesiastical society; persecutions, crusades, holy wars on a large or a small scale; facts at one time horrible, revolting to all human feelings, at other times trivial, foolish, disgusting. And this miserable detail is called the history of Christianity. The true history of Christianity is the history of the progress of philanthropy for the last two thousand years; its struggles with the old world, with old habits, old manners, old institutions, old doctrines; its struggles with the barbarian hordes issuing out of the bosom of the North, and overrunning the civilization of the South; its efforts to humanize religion, government, law, art, science, literature, the whole order of civilization, and its failures and successes. This history, so far as my knowledge extends, remains to be written, and till it is written, there will be no history of the Christian movement.

I have neither the space nor the ability, to sketch even the faintest outline of the mighty progress of this movement. I stand in awe before it and bow down in gratitude to God for it. It has been sweeping on for two thousand years, and I can hardly credit the changes it has already wrought. It has swept away Judaism and Greek and Roman civilization, as exclusive states of society; it has tamed and humanized the ruthless Barbarian, softened national hostilities, subdued national prejudices, demolished the military nobility, put an end to the hereditary nobility in the spiritual society, and struck it with death in the temporal society. It is substituting the order of merit for the order of birth, and supplanting the artificial aristocracy

[5][Ed. It is not clear which histories of Christianity Brownson is referring to here. Much of the American knowledge of Church history was derivative from translations of foreign works. Some of the more widely read Protestant histories of Christianity at the time were: Johann Lorenz Mosheim's (1694?-1755) *An Ecclesiastical History: Ancient and Modern*, 6 vols. (Philadelphia: Stephen C. Ustick, 1797), Joseph Priestly's (1733-1804), *An History of the Corruptions of Christianity*, 2 vols. (Boston: William Spotswood, 1797), and especially François Pierre Guillaume Guizot's (1787-1874), *General History of Civilization in Europe, from the Fall of the Roman Empire to the French Revolution* (Oxford: D. A. Talboys, 1837; New York: D. Appleton and Co., 1838), a translation of his *Histoire de la civilization en Europe depuis la chute de l'empire romain jusqu'a la révolution Françoise* (Paris, 1828), which Brownson cited periodically.]

by that of nature, by the aristocracy of talent and virtue. It has destroyed all distinctions of caste, and of master and slave, in principle at least, and will soon do it in practice. It proclaims the kindling doctrines of liberty and equality; it is preparing a system of universal education; it is carrying on an exterminating warfare against privilege, in whatever name or shape it may appear; it is raising up the poor and neglected, the low and oppressed; it is everywhere infusing into the human heart a deep reverence for human nature, a regard for everything human, and it issues its decree, let not man, ever again, be counted vile or vulgar in the eyes of man.

They who manifest a true love for man as man, who labor to meliorate the condition of man, who seek to obtain a greater amount of good for man, even for him who is at the foot of the social ladder, as well as for him who is at its summit, are affected by the Christian movement. They who sympathize with man, and labor for his elevation, whether it be by reforming theology or philosophy, church or state, schools or jurisprudence, by improving art or science, by infusing morality into the transactions of the business world, unmasking the pretensions of a self-styled aristocracy, or imparting dignity to the mechanic arts, and to honest though ill requited labor, whether called heretics, perfectionists, loco focos, transcendentalists, colonizationists, abolitionists, temperance reformers, or moral reformers, are affected by the Christian movement, and do show forth more or less of the Christ dwelling within them.

In order to be Christians, we must take a deep interest in whatever concerns man as man, and each in his own sphere, according to his light and strength, must do his best to elevate the human soul and enlarge its sum of good. What can be done and what ought to be done each must determine for himself. It may be the mission of one, the mother, to attend solely to household affairs, to develop in the soul of her son the principles of the gospel, to quicken his mind, and form his heart to virtue, to fit him for the love and achievement of grand and lofty deeds. It may be the duty of another, merely to prepare her own mind and heart for the duties which may await her as a wife and a mother. This one may be called merely to provide for the little ones committed to his care; that one will confine himself to the proper education of the young immortals confided to his wisdom and guardianship; this one may call out in a loud and thrilling voice to the masses, and seek to awaken the many to self-respect, to their rights, and to efforts for their melioration; that one may be commanded to thunder rebuke in the ears of a corrupt and indolent priesthood, to demand a reformed theology, a higher philosophy, a broader and more thorough education, a more equal, and therefore a more just, state of society; and another may have it in charge, to bring out the beautiful, to improve the fine arts, and adorn the world. There is a diversity of gifts and of occupations but the same spirit. Let each be true to the mission God has given; and dare neither live nor die without contributing something to make the world the wiser, the better, or the happier. We should all so live and so act that, when the moment comes in which we must leave these scenes which now know us and which shall know us no more, we can say in truth, man is the better for our having lived. Then shall we follow or be carried along by the Christian movement, and be able to die with the comfortable assurance that we are true Christians, and that we do but leave the society of our fellow men on earth to mingle with the spirits of the just made perfect in heaven.

17.

TENDENCY OF MODERN CIVILIZATION

Boston Quarterly Review 1 (April, 1838): 200-38

Very few of our readers, we presume, have ever heard of this new Association,[1] and most of them, on reading its name, will probably be somewhat puzzled to make out who may be its members, or what can be its object. Are its members abolitionists, infidels, fanatics? Or are they philosophers? What propose they to do? Why do they associate in defense of the rights of man, especially in this free country, where the rights of man are acknowledged and secured? Perhaps the following, which they have put forth as their confession of faith, may throw some light on these questions.

"*Principles.* lst. The *rights of man* are not grants or privileges; they are derived from no compacts; but are founded on the simple fact that man is man. They cannot be alienated by the individual, given nor taken away by civil authority.

"2d. Every man, by virtue of the fact that he is a man, has the right to develop freely, and to perfect all his faculties, his whole nature, as a moral, intellectual, and physical being.

"3d. Every man has a right to freedom of industry, freedom of thought, and freedom of conscience.

"4th. The rights of society can never be in opposition to the rights of the individual. If they could be, right would be able to change its nature, and become wrong, and there would be the foundation of a perpetual war between the individual and society, in which both parties would be, at the same time and in relation to the same proposition, in the right and in the wrong.

"5th. That social state, therefore, which does not respect all and every one of the rights of its members, is by virtue of that fact wrong, and needs to be revolutionized, reformed, or ameliorated.

"6th. Government is the creature of society, and is restricted in its functions to the mission of maintaining, from all encroachments, the rights of the individual and of society.

[1][Ed. Brownson is referring here to the newly established Boston Association of the Friends of the Rights of Man. I was unable to identify this association or to locate the text from which he is quoting.]

"Objects. Our objects are to ascertain in detail and to determine with precision what are the rights of man and of society; to ascertain and fix the boundaries of the legitimate province of government; to keep government within its province; and lastly, to labor for such reforms in governments, in the individual, and in society, as will secure to every member of the community the opportunity and the means to be and to do, what he is fitted to be and to do, by the nature and faculties with which he is endowed.

"*Means.* Our means are simple, but mighty, and such as can work no injustice to governments or to individuals. The causes of all existing abuses are ignorance and selfishness; abuses, therefore, can be removed only by knowledge and love; these are our means. We wish to direct our own attention, and that of the whole community, more directly than it has heretofore been, to the whole subject of the rights of man, and the means of promoting the progress of man, and of society.

"We therefore propose to inquire into the whole subject, and to inform ourselves as to what the rights of man and society really are; also to ascertain how far those rights are acknowledged, secured, or enjoyed in our present social state, and how far custom, prejudice, false notions, governments, or legislation, disregard, abridge, or attempt to disannul them.

"If we can do something by private discussions, by public debates, by lectures, and the publication of well written essays, and select libraries, to diffuse just knowledge among the people on these great subjects, and to kindle up in our own hearts and in the hearts of others a love of virtue, and the genuine sentiments of humanity, we shall at least do something to preserve our rights as far as already obtained, and to obtain them where they are yet denied.

"Let the people once perceive and understand their rights—perceive and understand what is wrong in our present systems of legislation, and defective in our social arrangements, and let them be inspired by a true sense of the worth of man as man, and they will easily and peaceably effect all the governmental and social reforms needed to place every man in the free and full enjoyment of all his faculties."

This to our way of thinking is not a bad confession of faith; and it indicates very good intentions on the part of those who make it. It proves that the members of this new association are not wholly ignorant of the subject with which they concern themselves; that they have lofty aims; that they take broad and comprehensive views; and that they contemplate a most thorough, radical reform, one which will root out nearly all existing evils, and base governments and society itself on the laws of universal, eternal, and unalterable justice. For such a reform, every heart must cry out, and every hand exert itself. The members of this association may never live to realize it; they will in all likelihood die without having been able to witness any perceptible change in the world for the better; but we cannot but deem them deserving high praise for contemplating such a reform, and for undertaking to effect it. Men who have bright and glorious dreams are never to be spoken lightly of. They have rich stuff in their souls, and may always be relied on as true friends to the cause of humanity.

We may also add that this association is composed mainly, if not exclusively, of mechanics and other workingmen; and it is this fact, more than any other, that has induced us to place its name at the head of this article. This is the age of associations. Men now-a-days associate for every purpose, great or small, good, bad, or indifferent. The simple fact of the organization of a new association deserves of itself no attention. But we confess we cannot view an association like this with indifference. We feel something of patriotic pride swelling our hearts when we find even our workingmen associating for the study and defense of the rights of man, and putting forth such declarations as the one we have laid before our readers. It is a proof that our free institutions work well, and that their quickening and elevating influences reach even to the lowest ranks of society. Nowhere but in this democratic country of ours could we think of finding an association like the one we are considering. The workingmen must have advanced far, and attained to a good share of well-being, before they could think of their rights, before they could have the leisure, the intelligence, and the means of investigating such great subjects as those set forth in this confession of faith. The fact then of the organization of this association is a proof of the comparatively good condition of the workingmen in this country, that their condition has been improved, and that though it may not yet be as good as it should be, or as it one day will be, yet that it has become tolerable. This fact should endear our free institutions to the friends of mankind, and forbid us ever to despair of popular liberty.

We have been struck, coming as it does from the workingmen, with the catholic spirit that pervades this confession of faith. It breathes peace and good will; it censures nobody, makes war upon no class of society, and manifests hostility to no existing institution. It makes war, if war it makes, upon ignorance and selfishness only; and the weapons of its warfare are those of knowledge and love; powerful weapons indeed, but harmless save against evil and evil-doers. These workingmen seem to forget themselves, to sink themselves in common humanity, and to dream of no good for themselves, which is not at the same time a good for universal man. Changes they no doubt contemplate, reforms they may demand, thorough, radical reformers they may wish to be, but not with a view to their own interests alone—not with a view to the interests of a class, sect, or party; but with a view to the interests of mankind. We commend this fact to those of our friends who are apprehending a "war of the poor against the rich," who have feared that the movements of the workingmen would render property insecure, throw the whole community into a universal hubbub, and send us all back to the savage state to go naked, to feed on nuts and the scanty and precarious supplies of fishing and hunting. The workingmen will respect the rights of property, for they have a natural love of justice, and because they have no design in what they are attempting, but that of making justice universally triumphant.

More might be said against the visionary or impracticable character of what these workingmen propose than against its dangerous tendency. It might be said, with some plausibility perhaps that hopes of a reform so vast, so thorough, so radical, of results so desirable and so felicitous as they contemplate, are perfectly idle, and that no sane man, at all acquainted with the world, can indulge them for a moment; that the world is as good, society, here especially, as perfect, as we have any right to expect; and that instead of wasting ourselves in fruitless efforts to make the world better, we ought to do our best to keep it from growing worse. This all may be so. We have a great respect for the practical men, the men of routine, who say so; that is, when they keep in their own sphere; but when they undertake to prophesy, we have no disposition to lend them our ears. We cannot but distrust their capacity to look through the whole future, and tell us exactly what can and what cannot be done. They would themselves do well to bear in mind that he, who undertakes to tell what cannot be done, may be as much out in his reckoning, as he who undertakes to tell what can be done. For ourselves, we rarely tell a man that he is a visionary, that his schemes are impracticable. We do not know everything. We have not been able, as yet, to find out the exact boundary between the possible and the impossible, the practicable and the impracticable, between the man who is verily a visionary, and the one who entertains projects which are rational and may one day be realized. We do not know what may or may not yet be done. For aught we know, man may yet rise above the loftiest and loveliest ideal, which the most rapt dreamer in his most ecstatic moments has ever bodied forth to his dreaming fancy. "The prophet that hath a dream let him tell a dream" [Jer. 23:28], for who knows but the dream may turn out to have been from God, and to contain a truth in the diffusion of which all coming ages are interested?

More than all this we would not discourage these dreamers as the world calls them. The man whose mind never strays beyond the actual, never soars into the ideal, and loses itself in that which is not and perhaps will not be realized, is never able to perform any great and glorious deed. The mind moves before the hand; and he who contemplates nothing great or good in his soul, will accomplish nothing great or good in his deeds. It is by communing with the sweet, and holy, and sublime visions which ever and anon flit across the soul, by seizing, seeking to embody, and prevent them from escaping us, that we ever become able to do anything for which the world should bless our memories. He who has a glorious ideal will achieve glorious deeds. He who hopes much will accomplish much. Never should we damp the ardor of hope, or seek to chain to the earth the soul that would rise to heaven. Never should we seek to subdue man's faith in himself or in his race. Faith is the true miracle-worker. To him that believeth, all things are possible. We know not how much injury we have done by clipping the wings of the young eagles, that were ambitious of taking their lofty flight through the heavens; how much we have dwarfed the intellect and kept back the progress of our race by our sneers at enthusiasm, and our cold-water counsels of experience poured on the ardent hopes, and burning zeal of the young prophets of humanity. Men of the world, who never had any dreams, and old men, who no longer remember the dreams of their youth, should never be suffered to open their lips, or in any way to hint a counsel. They are the Deevs of Ahriman's kingdom, the kingdom of darkness, and should ever be avoided by the children of Ormuzd, the children of the light.[2]

But we are not sure that these workingmen deserve to be accounted visionaries. We confess that we see nothing in the result they would bring about, in the end they are in pursuit of, that even *practical* men, men of routine, men wise for yesterday and not for tomorrow, men with pleasant country seats, who think only of enjoying snug quarters for the rest of life's campaign, need regard as visionary or chimerical. They, who oppose the result, who think they can arrest the workingmen's movements, and prevent this result; they are

[2][Ed. A reference to the Persian Zoroastrian doctrine of dualism, indicating the struggle between the Evil Spirit and the Good Spirit.]

the visionaries, the real dreamers. This result, this end the workingmen are pursuing, of which they have a lively sentiment, if not a clear perception, is that towards which the whole force of modern civilization is bearing us. These workingmen's movements, which have alarmed some, and which shortsighted politicians have thought to arrest by a sneer or a nick-name, by crying out "workie," "loco-foco," "agrarian," and other like terms of presumed reproach, are but so many proofs that the great law of modern civilization is still in force, and that its influence is at work in the heart of the millions. The workingmen in these alarming or visionary movements are only, consciously or unconsciously, exerting themselves to fulfil the mission of that order of civilization to which Christianity has given birth. The whole tendency of this civilization is in the direction these workingmen are looking, to the realization of such "reforms as will place every man in the free and full enjoyment of all his faculties."

They who have no faith in the progress of man and society are always very fond of appealing to history, as though history was in their favor; and they are always ready with a pile of individual facts, with which to drive back the reformer or beat out his brains; but happily for humanity, the reformer can read history today as well as they, and it shall go hard but his reading shall turn out to be as correct as theirs. According to his reading, history shows us everywhere progress and is ever with her ten thousand angel voices calling us to a loftier and lovelier future. They who find history against the reformer may perhaps be convicted of having never read history. Descriptions of some famous battles they may have read, some court anecdotes they may have picked up, and the dates of certain events they may have ascertained, but the concealed causes in operation, the invisible forces, the spiritual facts, the laws of the great events which have occurred, and to which the facts usually narrated in history owe their birth, and which are the only things in history it concerns us to know; these it is altogether likely they have not discovered, have not stumbled upon in any of their historic researches. To know history is to know these; and these, with modesty be it said, bear witness to the kindling truth that the human race is progressive, and that society is ever struggling to realize a more and more perfect ideal.

How many different orders of civilization have, each in its turn, ruled the world, we know not. Some think they catch here and there a glimpse of an earlier civilization, which they call the Cyclopean, the "golden age" of the poets; but the earliest civilization, of which we can affirm anything with certainty, is the sacerdotal civilization, as we find it in ancient India, Egypt, and Syria; in its greatest perfection, perhaps, in Judea.[3] The idea of God is the dominant idea of this order of civilization. God reigns, in principle, supreme, though, in fact, his symbol, or representative, the priesthood, possesses all the power. The state and the individual, as we have shown in another place,[4] succumb to the priesthood. Everything, all ideas and all actions, are held to be subordinate and subservient to the worship of God.

To the sacerdotal civilization succeeds the Greek and Roman, or political civilization. The dominant idea of this order of civilization is the state. The state is everything. The priesthood is a function of the state, and religion is regulated by a decree of the senate, or an edict of the emperor. The individual man is not yet born. There is no people. There is the Roman city, but no Roman people, as we understand the term people now.

The mission of this order of civilization was the realization of the majesty of the state. This mission it accomplished. We stand in awe, even today, of the majesty of the Roman state. Wherever Rome set her foot she left the imprint of her majesty. The modern traveler, over what was once her dominion, is struck with a sense of her greatness in every fragment of her antiquity he meets. The language she has left us, reveals in every phrase, in its very construction, in its single words even, her majesty. We can hardly, by imagination the most creative, conceive of the greatness and power of that City of the Tiber, which could make her presence felt, her faintest whisper heard, and obeyed as law, at the same moment, throughout the extremities of Europe, Asia, and Africa. But the majesty, before which we stand awestruck, is always the majesty of the state, never of the people as individuals. The individual is merely a member of the corporation, and aside from his corporate capacity has no recognized existence, no rights, no worth. If he is cared for, it is solely because he is an appendage to the state, a part of the body politic.

This fact becomes apparent, if we merely glance at the conquest of the Roman empire by the barbarians. In the long agony of that struggle, the barbarian encounters no forces but those of the Roman legions. In scarcely an instance does he find a people to resist him. The moment the Roman state is overthrown, nothing is to be found standing. From the general silence of history, we might almost infer that just in proportion as the Roman legions were withdrawn from

[3][Ed. Brownson probably derived his view of the primacy of the "sacerdotal civilization" from Benjamin Constant.]

[4][Ed. On this see "The Character of Jesus and the Christian Movement," *Boston Quarterly Review* (April, 1838): 147; see also Chapter 16 in this volume.]

the provinces, especially from the provinces of Gaul, they became deserts, and that of all the numerous populations which covered them none were left. In most instances of a conquered country, the conquerors do not gain at once a peaceful and undisputed possession. The conquered revolt, rebel, rise against their conquerors, and attempt to throw off their yoke. But nothing of this meets us in the history of the conquest of the Roman empire by the barbarians. When once the regular forces of the empire have been overcome, the conquest is complete. We take our stand in the heart of the Western Empire at the close of the fifth century; the Franks are seated in Gaul, the Visigoths in Spain, the Vandals in Africa, and the Ostrogoths in Italy, and of that vast empire we see nothing, unless it be a few of its municipal institutions in the city of Rome itself, and some of the larger towns. Wherever the eye extends, nothing is to be seen but barbarians, the church, and slaves. The reason of this must needs be in the fact that under the Roman civilization all authority, all energy was absorbed in the state, and none was left to the people. That civilization created a majestic city but not a majestic people. The populations which lived under it had no inherent vigor, no self-reliance, no resources in themselves. Consequently, when the protection of the city was withdrawn, they had no power to beat back the invader; and when fallen under the barbarian rule, no energy to revolt and to struggle to regain their independence.

Rome called herself a Republic, and boasted of her liberty; but the people had less freedom under her dominion than they now have under the most despotic of Christian princes. Beneath the overshadowing majesty of the government, the dazzling prosperity of the state, there was the most abject servitude, the most inconceivable wretchedness. The masses were degraded below the condition of our southern slaves. Human rights, human well-being, a regard for man simply as man, efforts to raise every man to the true dignity of manhood, were unknown, undreamed of. Now was this to be the definitive state of human society? Could this civilization be the term of human progress? It could not. Something better for man was needed, and must come. The good of humanity required a new and a different order of civilization; one which should substitute the majesty of man for the majesty of the state. This new order of civilization is the natural fruit of the Christian idea of the worth of man as man. Christianity gives to man precisely the place given by the political civilization to the state. But by its great doctrine of the universal brotherhood of humanity, the enfranchisement it demands for one man, it demands for every man.

Modern civilization is the offspring of Christianity. It is the attempt to realize the great idea of the equal worth of every individual man as man. Its mission is the perfect realization of this idea in the new society to which it gives birth. Now the perfect realization of this idea is precisely what these workingmen, of whom we have spoken, are striving after. Will this idea be realized? That is, will modern civilization fulfil its mission? Will it fail, die before its time comes? Did Judaism fail before it had fulfilled its mission? Did Greece and Rome expire before their work was done? Has a nation ever been known to die before realizing the idea on which it was founded? Are there any indications of disease, weakness, decline, decrepitude, in modern civilization? Has it ceased to extend itself, to make conquests? Is there a new order of civilization springing up and threatening to invade its territory? Is it not still vigorous, young, and full of the future? What reason have we, then, to think that it will fail to do its work?

When modern civilization began its career, the individual, we have said, was nothing, the state was everything. The first thing to be done was to break down the state and raise up the individual. But this could be done only by destroying the old order of civilization and of course not without overthrowing the Roman empire which it had created and which was its last word. This could be done only by raising up a new and vigorous society in its bosom, which should contain the germs of the new civilization, and by the influx of a new people, in whom the individual should still live in all his integrity. The first was found in the church which undermined the Roman state from within, and the second was supplied by the barbarians who invaded and conquered it from without.

In the savage state, individuality predominates. There is in that state no society. The elements of society are there, but they are isolated, and for the most part inoperative. Each man is his own center and forms a whole by himself. The city is not yet organized and counts for nothing. The tribe counts for something but it can never absorb the individual. The attachment to the tribe or to its chieftain is personal, not political. The barbarians who supplanted the Roman empire cannot be said to have been pure savages, nevertheless they had not advanced so far as to lose sight of the individual. Personal freedom was still the dominant sentiment. Individual barbarians indeed grouped at unequal distances around a chief; but he was their leader, not their master; and their attachment to him was by no means a political attachment. He was not in their eyes the representative of the majesty of the state, but a man like the rest of them, only perhaps a little taller, or the descendant of a more respected branch of the common family. The barbarians' idea of freedom was always that of personal freedom, freedom of the individual, not the freedom of the state, or body politic. In seating themselves in the Roman territory, they necessarily introduced into that territory this element of individual freedom. This is one of the benefits which has resulted from the overthrow of the Roman empire, and may induce us to regard the destruction of the Roman civilization as a blessing, not as a curse, to humanity. As we come to know more of the designs of Providence, and to see more clearly their wisdom, we shall be less and less disposed to complain of what has been.

If we take our stand again in the Western Empire immediately after the Conquest, immediately after the irruptions of the barbarians have ceased, we shall discover, already at work, all the elements of modern civilization. These elements are, first, the church, depositary of the earlier or sacerdotal civilization, invigorated by the infusion of the Christian idea of the majesty of man; second, royalty, or recollections of imperial Rome, mingled with the barbarian notions of chieftainship; third, republicanism, or recollections of republican Rome which survived in the city of Rome, in some of the Italian cities, and a few towns in southern Gaul; and fourth, feudalism, in germ, which embodied the new element, that of personal freedom.[5]

Each of these elements is good and essential to a perfect state of society. The fundamental idea of the church is that of the supremacy of moral power. Its aim is to substitute, in the government of the world, moral power for brute force. The order of civilization it represents, the sacerdotal, is that which breaks down the savage state, and rescues man from the dominion of brute force. It must necessarily precede the political civilization. Theocracy is older than monarchy, aristocracy, or democracy, as the priesthood is older than the state. The church becomes mischievous only when it becomes exclusive, and governs in the interests of the priesthood, and not according to the law of God; when it resorts to material force to make what it calls moral right prevail. It then becomes a theocracy, and practices a tyranny over man, of all tyrannies the worst; for it strikes not only the body, but the soul also, perverts conscience, and makes man a slave within as well as without.

[5]See Guizot's *Histoire generale de la Civilisation Moderne en Europe*. Paris, 1828. [Ed. See François Pierre Guillaume Guizot (1787-1874), *Histoire générale de la civilisation en Europe, depuis la chute de l'Empire romain jusqu'a la révolution Français* (Paris: Pichon and Didier, 1828).]

Royalty, as it exists in modern Europe, is a branch of republicanism. All governments, whatever their form, which represent the majesty of the state and are held to be instituted for the public, are republican. Asiatic monarchies are instituted not for the public, but for the monarch; they therefore are not republics. But the governments of France and England, for instance, are held to be instituted not for the benefit of the monarch, but to take charge of the public affairs for the public good. The real idea which lies at the bottom of republicanism, whether bearing a royal or popular form, is that of the state. The idea of the state is that of the social nature of man. Its mission is to realize the social instincts of mankind, to give order, regularity, harmony, stability, to all social actions and social intercourse. When it becomes exclusive, separated, on the one hand, from morality, and, on the other, from personal freedom, it degenerates into despotism either of the one, the few, or the many, and becomes unjust, cruel, and oppressive.

The fundamental element of feudalism is, as we have said, the element of individuality or personal freedom. It is the recognition of the fact that there are rights of man as well as rights of the priesthood and of the state. But when this element is predominant, not limited by the moral and the social elements of our nature, it breaks all social bonds, destroys everything like social order, and precipitates us into the savage state. When it is not generalized, or when it is coupled with the notion that might creates right, and that he only deserves to be a freeman who is able to assert and maintain his freedom, it establishes an order of things like that which prevailed in Europe from the sixth century to nearly the close of the fourteenth. It gives us then only here and there a man (a baron, for baron means man, a man, or the man, probably from the Latin, *vir*), while the many are his vassals, serfs, bond men, or slaves. An exemplification of this may be seen on any southern slave plantation, and a reminiscence of it in a cotton factory in our own New England.

The exclusive predominance of any one of these elements would have defeated the design of modern civilization. Has any one of these been able to obtain exclusive dominion over modern society?

Each of these elements of modern civilization has made its effort to reign without a rival. The church made the attempt, and appeared to succeed, but it did not. The progress of civilization is not backward. The past never returns. The success of the church would have been the reproduction of the sacerdotal civilization of Egypt, India, Judea, which had yielded to the political civilization of Greece and Rome. It therefore failed. It reached its culminating point under

Hildebrand, Gregory VII, and from that time, notwithstanding appearances and pretensions, it steadily declined till Luther appeared to prepare the way for its reconstruction under a more liberal form. Royalty attempted to gain exclusive dominion and under the Frank emperor, Charlemagne, seemed to have reproduced imperial Rome; but feudalism was too strong for it, and Charlemagne was hardly laid in his tomb, before his empire was dissolved. Republicanism, especially in the Italian cities and the large towns in the south of France, made an effort, threatened for a time to reproduce republican Rome on a small scale, and to cover Europe with a multitude of city-republics; but it could not succeed against royalty, feudalism, and the church. Feudalism made its effort also, and nearly plunged the European world into primeval barbarism. It resisted all the tendencies to centralization which manifested themselves under Charlemagne and Gregory VII. It held the burghers in subjection, and yet it enfranchised the slave. Under Louis XI, it was shorn of its power, and it lost itself in the public under Louis XIV. Not one of these elements has been able to succeed in obtaining exclusive dominion, and yet all the ideas they represent have ever been gaining power.

The conquest of England by the Normans hastened in that country the march of civilization, and tended to establish and develop those free institutions, which have for so long a time been the boast of Englishmen. The first effect of the conquest was a large accession of power to the central government, that is, to the monarch. This was necessary in order to keep the Saxons, or native English, in subjection, and to secure to the Norman adventurers the quiet possession of their estates. But this accession of power to the central government led to tyranny on the part of the monarch and for a time threatened the triumph of absolutism. Feudalism took the alarm and calling to its aid a portion of the burghers, principally of the Saxon race, wrested Magna Carta from king John at Runnymede, a sort of compromise between feudalism and royalty. For a time the preponderance might have been on the side of feudalism; but the barons found themselves arrested in their progress by the burghers. They had used the burghers against king John, against royalty, and these uniting with royalty under Henry VII, restrained and all but annihilated them, weakened as they had become by the Wars of the Roses.[6]

[6][Ed. The Wars of the Roses (1455-85) was a series of English civil wars that preceded the rise of the Tudors (Henry VII to Elizabeth I) to power in England.]

Royalty threatened again to become absolute under Henry VIII and Elizabeth, but it was resisted under James I and decapitated under his successor.[7] The Republic appeared with the Long Parliament; but inasmuch as sufficient account was not made of personal freedom, it gave way to the Restoration, which in its turn yielded to the Revolution of 1688, a compromise between all the elements of modern civilization, the church, royalty, feudalism, and republicanism.

Thus we see that not one of these elements has succeeded, though all have made the attempt. Each in turn has been defeated. Yet in being defeated it has not been destroyed. Defeat has brought along with it a modification, but an increase rather than a diminution of real power. Royalty, meaning by it either the central government or the representative of the majesty of the state, has been always on the advance. Order has been ever on the increase, and social relations have ever been becoming more determinate and fixed, social action and intercourse freer and more regular. The church, though shorn of some of its material splendors, has lost nothing of its spiritual power. Moral power has been continually gaining on brute force. France was more truly religious in the eighteenth century than it was in the eleventh. Feudalism had lost much of its exclusive dominion, but personal freedom and security, the ideas it represented, were much greater under Louis XIV, or James II, than under Saint Louis, or Henry III.[8] Republicanism had not succeeded in establishing the communal regime; yet in the sixteenth century, we find a PUBLIC, and the burghers sitting in Parliament as one of the three estates of the realm, and exerting an influence on public affairs, almost infinitely greater than they did in the most palmy days of the communes.

Though all the elements of modern civilization existed and were at work as soon as the barbarian conquest had been effected, yet they existed separately and were at work each on its own account. Before modern civilization could achieve its destiny, all these elements were to be brought together and molded into an harmonious whole. They must needs go through a process of fusion. The governing forces, the church, royalty, and republicanism needed to be fused into one uniform power; and the feudal or conquering population, and the con-

[7][Ed. Henry VIII (1491-1547), King of England; Elizabeth I (1533-1603), Queen of England; James I (1566-1625), King of England. Charles I (1600-49), King of England (1625-49), was executed by decapitation during the English Civil War.]

[8][Ed. References here are to Louis XIV (1638-1715), king of France, James II (1633-1701), king of England, Saint Louis IX (1214-70), king of France, and Henry III (1207-72), king of England.]

quered or indigenous population, into a uniform population, in which every member should be free and equal to every other member. This was the work to be done. How far has it been accomplished?

One great imperfection in modern society has been the separation of church and state.[9] The separation of church and state is the separation of morality and politics. The church, faithfully or unfaithfully, represents the ideas which belong to the moral order; the state represents those which belong to the social order. The church separated from the state gives us a moral, spiritual code indeed, but one which embraces no social idea, which in no wise regulates the intercourse of man with man, as a social being, or directs him to labor for the melioration or progress of society. The state separated from the church establishes a social order indeed, but a social order that embraces no moral idea, and which is supported by no appeals to conscience, or to a sense of justice inherent in man. It is founded on physical might, and is sustained by the sword, the *posse comitatus*,[10] the dungeon, the scaffold, and the gibbet. The two, not united, but, blended into one, forming a unity rather than a union, give us a government resting for its support on moral power, and a social order founded on justice. The unity of church and state is the great desideratum. Now to this unity, we think, both church and state have been tending. This is what the Puritans had a presentiment of, precisely what Vane, the Fifth Monarchy men, and the Quakers sought to realize in the English Revolution of 1648.[11]

[9][Ed. Brownson always supported the institutional and legal separation of church and state. What he protests against here and throughout his life is what he would later call "political atheism," that is, the separation of religious and moral principles from politics and from the operations of government. On the other hand, he opposed throughout his life any establishment of a "Christian Party in Politics" (on this, see the introduction to EW, 1: 21-22), any references to the United States as a "Christian nation" or "Christian commonwealth," and any attempts to use legal or political means to advance specifically religious causes.]

[10][Ed. *Posse comitatus* is Latin for "power of a count" and refers to the power a sheriff or other law keeper has to call together a group of citizens to assist him in enforcing the law, quelling a riot, or discharging an official duty.]

[11][Ed. Reference is probably to Sir Henry Vane, the younger (1613-62), a strong supporter of Oliver Cromwell in the Revolution of 1648. On Vane, see DNB (1921-22) 20:116-29. The Fifth Monarchy Men were a mid-seventeenth-century fanatical sect of revolutionaries who sought to bring about the "Fifth Monarchy" promised in the Book of Daniel 2:4. The Fifth Monarchy would, they thought, succeed the four empires of Assyria, Persia, Greece, and Rome, and during it Christ would reign for a thousand years (Rev. 20:4). For a time these revolutionaries supported Oliver Cromwell's (1599-1658) Commonwealth, believing it was a preparation for the "Fifth Monarchy," but they later turned against him and after some unsuccessful uprisings in 1657 and 1661 the leaders were executed and

There should be in no country two societies, one spiritual and the other political. During the past, this division has been doubtless the less of two evils; but it always marks an imperfect social state. Civil government should be instituted for the purpose of maintaining social order, and that social order too, which is founded on absolute justice; the means it makes use of to establish and maintain social order, should always be strictly moral, spiritual, holy. Its symbol should not be the sword, but the crosier. If this were the case, civil government would be as holy as the church has ever claimed to be. The church, as a governing or controlling body, would then be superseded, or rather, the state having become the church as well as the state, no separate church would be needed or admissible. Religion we should still have, preachers we should have, meeting houses we should have, but no ecclesiastical corporation. The duty of the preacher would cease to be that of gathering people into an outward, visible church, and become that of infusing into all hearts a love of goodness, and that of directing all minds to the decrees of strict justice, as the laws to be obeyed in all social and individual action. Clergymen might make public prayers, administer the sacraments, and wear a surplice or a black gown; but they would not constitute a separate class of men, organized into a distinct body, whose members must be accounted, *par excellence* men of God. They would be teachers of righteousness, men laboring to promote knowledge, justice, piety. Now this is precisely the condition to which, with us, both church and state are tending. The separation of church and state hardly exists in this country, especially in this Commonwealth, which stands as it should and as it becomes it, in the front rank of the advanced guard of the great army of progress. All the ecclesiastical establishments of this country are breaking up. The Episcopalians gain few converts to the doctrine of the divine right of bishops; the Methodist church has reached its culminating point,[12] and its mem-

the sect gradually ceased to exist. Reference to the Quakers during the Revolution of 1648 is difficult to understand. George Fox (1624-91), their founder, had just began preaching in public in 1647 and therefore by 1648 there were only a very few Quakers in existence.]

[12][Ed. By the mid 1830s the Methodist Church was indeed the fastest growing Protestant church in the country but, contrary to Brownson's predictions, its growth would continue throughout the nineteenth century. By 1844, it had become the "most numerous religious body in America, with 1,068,525 members, 3,988 itinerant preachers, 7,730 local preachers, and an incalculable number of regular hearers." On this, see Sydney E. Ahlstrom, *A Religious History of the American People* (New Haven: Yale University Press, 1972), 437.]

bers, democrats as most of them are, will soon see that their church establishment is an engine which may be directed with but too much success against freedom. As soon as they discover this, they will abandon it, which they may do without abandoning their doctrines or their piety. The Presbyterian church is torn by intestine divisions, and is penetrated in all directions by Congregational notions, and it must ultimately adopt the congregational form of church government, the only form of church government that can long coexist in harmony with democracy in the state. To the same result England and France are tending. To no other end can tend the writings of the Abbé de la Mennais and his party.[13]

Not only do we perceive an approximation to the unity of church and state but a sort of blending of royalty and republicanism. The notion that kings own their subjects, are their absolute lords and proprietors, is growing obsolete. Kings are beginning to be regarded as public officers, and royalty is considered, as we have said, the representative of the majesty of the state. The king is not considered now as governing for his own good, but for the public good. He is not above, but under law. The Republic, which may be said to represent the majesty of the people, is also under law. The people may do what they will, but not unless they will that which is lawful, right. All governments are now, at least in the principal states of Christendom, held to be public, to be instituted for the public, and to have it for their mission to make justice prevail. The question between monarchy and its rivals is merely a question of expediency, a question as to what form of government is most likely to secure the prevalence of justice. There is then a sort of fusion of the church, the empire, and the commune, taking place, and they must soon lose their opposition, and become one under the dominion of law—justice.

On the other hand, a similar fusion has been taking place in relation to the different populations of Christendom. At the beginning of the sixth century, all that part of Europe, which had been under the Roman dominion, was covered over by two distinct populations, one noble, and the other ignoble. The barbarians, with a very few exceptions, constituted alone the noble population. The native population, saving that portion of it which belonged to the ecclesiastical society, was ignoble, deemed an inferior and degraded race. It

[13][Ed. During the mid 1830s Brownson generally associated Félicité Robert de Lamennais and the French liberal Catholics with the worldwide movement to unite Christianity and democracy.]

was the conquered population, and to that fact, to a great extent, must be attributed the ideas which the conquerors entertained respecting its inferiority. It was everywhere oppressed. It had no rights, no protection. All employments deemed noble or honorable, except those of the church, were reserved to its masters, the barbarian nobility. It could not meet the barbarian on equal terms. It could approach him only at a humble distance. It was in relation to the conquerors what the ancient Gibeonites were to the ancient Israelites, "hewers of wood and drawers of water" [Josh. 9:21]. The distance between these two classes, two populations, was not to be passed at once. Not in one day was the slave to become the equal of his master, the serf, to stand up by the side of his lord, and all traces of conquest to be wiped out. Yet the distance between the two populations has been lessened. The two races have been brought together and so intermixed that their separation is henceforth impossible. Not all the noble families in France or in England can trace their descent to the conquerors. The descendants of the conquered have frequently risen to the highest ranks, and those of the conquerors have fallen in many instances to the lowest. The English of today are neither Normans nor Saxons, but a people formed from the union of both. Robert of Glocester says,

> The folk of Normandie
> Among us woneth yet, and shalleth evermore.
> Of Normans beth these high men thath beth in this land,
> And the low men of Saxons.[14]

But this cannot be said now. Some of the "high men" in the land are of Saxon origin and some of the "low men" are of Norman blood. In France, the Franks are not now the exclusively noble. The Franks and the Gallo-Romans have commingled. There is now a French nation, as there is a French language. In this country, the fusion of the two populations is complete. We have no noble, no ignoble race. Saving the Negroes and Indians, not included in the civilized population, we know only one race; and we have adopted in state and in society, as well as in the church, the doctrine that "God hath made of one blood all the nations of men" [Acts 17:26]. Here few traces of the

[14][Ed. Robert of Gloucester (fl. 1260-1300) was an historian, known only from his English metrical chronicle of the history of England to 1270, one of the oldest chronicles of English history. For the quotation, see *The Metrical Chronicle of Robert of Gloucester*, ed. William Aldis Wright (London: Eyre and Spottiswoode, 1887), lines 54-55, 61. It is not clear what source Brownson may have used for this quotation. It is not exactly the same as the one in Wright's edition.]

conquest are discernible. We recognize no distinction of ranks, no inferiority or superiority of classes. No honest employment unfits any one for any social circle, any office of honor, trust, or emolument. There is not here and there a baron with his army of retainers, bondmen and slaves. All are barons, that is, men. No man is more than man, and no one is less than man. At least this is our theory, though it must be admitted that our practice does not as yet fully conform to it. All Europe is tending to this same result. The distinctions of rank are wearing away; the prejudices of blood are losing their force; the burghers are up with the lords, and, in point of intelligence, influence, and social importance, even beyond them. The people have become the nation; royalty and nobility are their servants, and maintain themselves standing, only on the plea of the public good. The London Quarterly itself is forced to admit that De Tocqueville is right in saying that all Western Europe has been for several hundred years hastening to democratic equality.[15] The progress is assuredly in that direction and no earthly power seems able to arrest it, or even for a moment to divert it from its course.

How has this change been effected? What are the causes which have produced it? Are these causes still in operation? And may we hope that they will be as efficient in accomplishing what remains to be done as they have been in accomplishing what has already been accomplished?

One of the most efficient causes of this change is Christianity. By Christianity, in this connection, we do not mean exclusively the church, but the new life revealed, the philanthropic movement commenced, by Jesus for humanity, and of which we have spoken in a foregoing article.[16] Christianity surrounds every man with a bulwark of sanctity. It declares the unity of the human race, that God has made of one blood all the nations of men, and that all men are equal before him. This declaration cannot remain unfruitful. When it is once received, when the idea of man's worth as man, together with that of man's brotherhood to man, is once entertained, has once become a sincere, an earnest, a religious conviction, it becomes all-powerful for human enfranchisement. To the influence of this

[15][Ed. The London *Quarterly Review*, published from 1809 to 1962, appealed to conservative political opinion in England. Alexis Charles-Henri-Maurice Clérel de Tocqueville (1805-59) was a French political scientist, historian and politican who was best known for his *Democracy in America* (1835-40), emphasizing that a democratically organized society could retain liberty and authority in balance.]

[16][Ed. Reference is to Brownson's "The Character of Jesus and the Christian Movement," *Boston Quarterly Review* 1 (April, 1838): 129-52.]

idea must be attributed the manumission of the slaves of modern Europe, which, in nearly all cases, has been the voluntary act of their masters, done from religious motives.

The church, properly so called, has done something. It opened its bosom alike to the children of both races. In the house of God, in its services for the sick and dying, and in its solemn funeral rites, the high men and the low men were reduced to a momentary level. They were alike amenable to its discipline; they alike partook of its sacraments, and alike might aspire, so far forth as their blood was concerned, to fill the highest offices in its gift. The perpetual presence of a society that recognized no distinctions of blood, which, so far as itself was concerned, declared all men as men, equal, could not fail to weaken the prejudice of race, and to attack all social inequalities. The bondman was not wholly vile in his own estimation, for he might hope that his son would find his way to the papal chair, and make the proud monarchs of the conquering race doff their diadems before him, and the most powerful of his oppressors court his favor and sue for his benediction. The passage from equality in the spiritual order to equality in the social order was neither long nor difficult, and more than once was it made by the simple-hearted and simple-minded peasants, under the guidance of the lower orders of the priesthood. An instance of this is in the Insurrection of the Peasants, in the time of Richard II of England, led on by Wat Tyler (Walter the Tiler), John Ball, a priest, Jack Straw, Hob Carter, and Tom Miller, all men of low origin.[17]

This Insurrection of the Peasants is generally regarded as a war of the poor against the rich, and much is made of it against every man who comes forward in defense of what are termed the lower classes. If one speaks in favor of equality and bears his testimony against the inequality which obtains, but which ought not to obtain, between members of the same community, forthwith he is a Wat Tyler, or, in allusion to another leader of the peasants at a later day, a Jack Cade.[18] Yet we own we have a sort of fellow feeling with this same Walter the Tiler, who led on his sixty thousand peasants towards London, singing,

[17][Ed. Richard II (1376-1400) was king of England (1377-99) during the Peasants' Revolt of 1381. Wat Tyler (d. 1381) led the revolt, during which he also freed from prison the rebel priest John Ball, who had supported the peasants.]

[18][Ed. Jack Cade was an English rebel who died in 1450. Irish by birth he became a leader of the Commons of Kent when they rose in rebellion against the extortions practiced by the King's officers. On Cade, see DNB (1921-22) 3:623-26.]

When Adam delved, and Eva span,
Where was then the gentleman?[19]

And we are inclined to think that no man somewhat in love with humanity should feel it a reproach to be called a Wat Tyler, or even a Jack Cade. Many a name is now banded about as a term of reproach, which will be seen one day to stand high on the calendar of saints.

These peasants attempted nothing for which they should be censured. Their condition at the time of their insurrection was anything but enviable. They were serfs in person and in goods, and obliged to pay enormous rents for the small piece of land on which they raised the means of supporting themselves and families, and which they could not abandon without the consent of their lord; whose husbandry, gardening, and labor of all kinds he chose to demand, they were obliged to perform gratuitously. The lord could sell them, their houses, their utensils of labor, and their children, born and even unborn. Their condition was worse than that of our Negro slaves; for our slaves are fed and clothed and taken care of in sickness and in old age; but these were obliged to take the same care of themselves that they would have been obliged to do had they been freemen, and at the same time to labor as much for their masters as our slaves do for theirs. Resentment of the evils inflicted on them by the oppression of the noble families, joined to a total forgetfulness of the fact that these noble families were of Norman origin, since they no longer called themselves Normans, but Gentlemen, very naturally conducted them from the injustice they endured to the injustice of servitude itself, independently of its historical origin. In the southern provinces, where the population was numerous, especially in Kent, whose inhabitants preserved a vague tradition of a treaty concluded between them and William the Conqueror,[20] for the maintenance of their ancient franchises, there were strong symptoms of popular agitation near the beginning of the reign of Richard II. Expenses of the court and the gentlemen were great in consequence of the war which was then carried on against France, whither each nobleman went at his own charges, and where he sought to distinguish himself by the magnificence of his arms and equipage. The proprietors of the seigneurs and manors, loaded their farmers and villeins[21] with excessive taxes and

[19][Ed. The quotation is anonymous, but supposedly it was used by John Ball for his Blackheath speech to the peasant rebels in the uprising led by Wat Tyler against excessive taxation.]

[20][Ed. William I (1028-87), the Conqueror, was king of England (1066-87).]

[21][Ed. Brownson has "villains," but he means villeins, a class of serfs in the feudal system. I have change the spelling wherever it occurs.]

exactions, alleging, as a pretext for each new demand, the necessity they were under of going to fight the French in France, to prevent them from making a descent on England. But the peasants said to themselves and to one another, "they tax us to aid the knights and country squires to defend their possessions; we are their bond-men; we are their flocks which they fleece; and yet, taking all in all, if England were lost, they would lose altogether more than we."

To such words as these, on their return from the fields, by the way, or in the clubs where they met in the evening, after the labors of the day were ended, succeeded words of far graver import. Some of the orators at these clubs were *priests*, who drew from the *Bible* their arguments against the social order of their epoch. "Good folks," said they, "things cannot and will not go right in England until there be no more villeins, nor gentlemen; until all are equal, and the lords be no more masters than we. Why should they be? Why do they hold us in bondage? Have we not all, they and we, sprung from the same parents, Adam and Eve? They are clothed in velvet, and crimson, and fur; they have flesh-meat, and spices, and good wines, and we have only miserable orts to eat and water to drink. They have ease in their beautiful manors, and we have pain and labor, wet and cold in the fields." At such discourses as these, the multitude cried out in tumult, "There must be no more villeins; we will be treated as beasts no longer; and if we work for the gentlemen, they SHALL PAY US WAGES!"[22]

Surely this demand of the villeins was by no means an extravagant one. It was simply that they should be no longer held in bondage, that they should henceforth be treated as men, not as beasts, and that they should receive wages. They made no war on the rich as such; it entered not into their minds that these estates, held by the descendants of the conquerors, had been unjustly wrested from their fathers; they had no thought of stripping the gentlemen of their property; they merely wished to be accounted freemen, and to be paid for their labor. Was this unjust, unreasonable? Certainly not. The lower classes have never been known to make an unjust demand. They always claim altogether less than their rights, and, we may add, the terror they inspire by their demands is always in consequence of their justice, and not their injustice. The lords and gentlemen have always seemed to hear, in the faint voice of the feeble peasant, the awful voice of God summoning them to judgment. The simple demand of

[22][Ed. See Augustin Thierry's (1795-1856) *Histoire de la conquête de l'Angleterre par les Normands*, 4 vols. (Paris: Didot, 1825), 4: 309-17.]

these peasants not to be treated as beasts, and to be paid for their labor, struck all the upper classes of England with consternation. However, the peasants gained nothing. The day of their deliverance had not yet dawned. They were cajoled by a few lying words of the king, their leaders were killed, themselves dispersed, and fifteen hundred of their number put to death by the common hangman. Their movements have no great historical importance, except as showing that they drew their arguments for equality from the Bible; that they legitimated them on the ground of the unity of the human race, that high men and low men have the same parents, even Adam and Eve, and therefore are brethren and equals.

Christianity also did much to effect the change of which we have spoken, by its spirit of tenderness and compassion, by the generous and humane sentiments with which it sought to inspire men one towards another, and by encouraging the practice of the kindly charities of social and private life. It did much by exalting the sentiments; and it elevated the poor by giving them the assurance that though forsaken by men they were yet remembered by God, and though destitute, wronged, down-trodden here, they should be kings and priests hereafter. It did something too by inspiring the ministers of the church with courage to rebuke the king and the feudal lord, and to remind them, that the truest nobility they could aspire to was the practice of the Christian virtues.

Philosophy, or the spirit of inquiry, the desire for general intelligence, which had been kept alive by the church, and which took a new start after the feudal régime had become somewhat fixed, also contributed its share towards effecting the social change we have noted. The desire to philosophize, or to know the reason and nature of things, manifested itself in a striking degree in the twelfth century, and has been manifesting itself more and more strikingly ever since. The first subject to which it applied itself was theology. There was at first no disposition to disprove nor even to question the truth of theology, but a craving to establish its truth on rational conviction, and not on positive authority. Abelard attempted to do this, and gave birth to the Scholastic philosophy, a philosophy more ridiculed than understood, and whose influence on the progress of society has been altogether underrated.[23]

To the Scholastic philosophy succeeded the revival of letters, and the study of Grecian antiquity. The study of ancient literature and

[23][Ed. Peter Abelard (1079-1142) was a philosopher and theologian known particularly for his development of the dialectical method in theology.]

philosophy enlarged the modern circle of ideas, and introduced a more liberal and just mode of thinking into the affairs of the world. From the study of antiquity and the human mind, men passed to the study of nature, and opened a new career to science. Scientific discoveries followed in rapid succession, and gave a new face to war, commerce, and manufactures, which in their turn reacted upon the social state, and lessened its evils. No small portion of the evils of the lower classes was owing to their ignorance. As soon as they began to think, to find out that they had thinking faculties, and to use them, their condition was ameliorated. The low-born man by means of intelligence became the equal of the high-born; he became a minister of state, an influential prelate, one of the real nobility of his country. By means of knowledge the two classes were occasionally brought into contact and the plebeian found himself the master of the patrician.

The habit of looking into the reason and nature of things soon disclosed the unreasonableness of the pretensions of the church, the illegitimacy of the authority of the Pope, and brought about the Reformation. It carried more intelligence and order into the administration of government, into legislative enactments, and the interpretation of laws, which produced in return something like social order, and gave something like security to persons and property, facilitated industry, and by that elevated the industrious class.

But the cause, to which, more than to any other, we are indebted for this change, is to be found in the rise, progress, and dominion of the moneyed power, represented and sustained by what we term the business part of the community. Much is said against this power at present, and perhaps justly. It has attained its zenith. Businessmen have had their golden age. They have become the sovereigns of the world. Kings, nobilities, hierarchies, legislators, are their servants. The world, it may be, is growing weary of their dominion, and perhaps restless under the weight of their tyranny. A strong party is organizing itself against them; and in this country we are in the midst of a revolution which must overthrow the money-king, and inaugurate humanity. Nevertheless the money-king was once a slave, as vile a slave, as maltreated a slave, as any on whom kings and nobility trampled, and his accession to power marks the enfranchisement of industry. Whether desirous or not of prolonging his reign, we must all admit that his reign *has been* for the best interests of the human race.

Owing to conquest as the proximate, if not as the ultimate cause, the immense majority of mankind at an early day were reduced to a servile condition. Hence the reason why the workingmen, the manual laborers, the creators, in one view of the case, of all the wealth, comforts, and luxuries of a nation, are themselves, always and everywhere, poor, ignorant, degraded, accounted the lower class, an inferior order of being. This is owing to conquest, not, as the advocates of aristocracy ignorantly allege, to the natural inequality with which God creates men. The laboring class has been always the lower class, poor, and ignorant, and menial, because the tribe or nation to which it originally belonged was conquered by another tribe or nation, stripped of its possessions which went to increase the stock of the conquerors, reduced to slavery, and compelled to perform all the labor of the community, and by its labor to augment that stock still more.

Rome was conquered by the barbarians; the wealth of the Roman world, at least the greater part of it, passed into their hands; consequently the indigenous population was left destitute. Destitute of property, they were entirely at the mercy of their barbarian lords. Poor, dependent, enslaved, they of course must be regarded as inferior, and as unworthy as incapable of associating with the conquerors on equal terms. Poor, dependent, enslaved, regarded as inferior, as low, vile, they must needs be deprived of all means of improvement, excluded from what was held to be good society, and debarred from all opportunities of cultivating elegant manners and refined tastes. It needs no argument, therefore, to prove that they must cease to be dependent, that they must acquire some portion of this world's goods and a certain degree of leisure, intelligence, and refinement before they could claim to be of an equal race with those who constituted the upper classes. The laboring or conquered population could rise to a level with the conquerors, and thus regain their lost independence, only by the acquisition of wealth. They must become capitalists, proprietors. The man, who has nothing in this wide world that he can call his own, can hardly exhibit the bearing or the virtues of a man. A man must feel that he has something before he can feel that he is something.

This is not all. The laboring class, so long as they are doomed to perpetual toil, must needs be ignorant and brutish. They cannot take their place with the upper classes of society, until they have become intellectually, and in point of intelligence, their equals. But their equals they cannot become in the lowest depths of poverty. Great wealth is no doubt unfavorable to mental growth; but a certain degree of wealth is needed in order that the mind may have leisure to concern itself with something besides mere animal wants. The laborer must be able to live like a man, before he can think like a man, have a man's intelligence. The distinction between the upper classes and the lower, the conquerors and the conquered, could then be obliterated only by means of a physical amelioration of the lower or laboring class. The interests of this class, then, at first were necessarily identified with the moneyed interest. The first service to be rendered it was to open to it the road to wealth.

Now the road to wealth this depressed, enslaved population was obliged to open to itself, by its own efforts. Nothing was to be hoped from the upper classes. Whatever was obtained from them was to be obtained by main force. The conquerors will hold with all their power the conquests they have made. The conquered must rely on themselves alone. The odds are altogether against them. They are poor and naked, and the earth and nearly all the means of gain are in the hands of their masters. They are placed under almost every conceivable disadvantage. Nevertheless they must work out their own salvation; and by their own energy and perseverance rise from bondmen to freemen, and from slaves to be the sovereigns of the world. Their work is a great one, and ages must elapse before we can perceive that they have made any progress. Yet progress they do make; and after centuries of secret, silent working, ever interrupted, but ever beginning anew, perpetually thwarted, but never despairing, we see that they have made a mighty advance.

The plebeian population, on the establishment of the barbarians, though all equally vile, were not all in precisely the same condition. The agricultural portion was the most unfavorably situated. The land, whether cultivated or not, was all appropriated in the hands of a few, and for the most part locked up in entail. The agricultural laborers could therefore have no hope of becoming proprietors. All they could hope for was to be tenants on such terms as their masters should be pleased to grant. The inhabitants of the towns or cities were somewhat better situated. They were held to be as vile, as menial, and as far removed from freemen as were the villeins or agricultural bondmen; but they were mainly tradesmen and artisans, who could manufacture articles for sale, and carry on a species of traffic with the upper classes themselves. The barbarian population, calling itself noble, disdained to be traders or handicraftsmen. Consequently trade and manufactures fell to the indigenous population, and of course to the inhabitants of the towns. Trade and manufacture, though insecure, subjected to innumerable risks, and loaded with vexatious and all but ruinous exactions, nevertheless enriched the traders and the artisans, who became in due time merchants and manufacturers.

The mercantile and manufacturing population, as the most favorably situated for the acquisition of wealth, therefore take the lead in the enfranchisement of industry, and are the first of the conquered population to become free and independent.

Trade and manufactures require outlays, and when they are carried on to a great extent, they demand large capitalists. This gives rise to a division in the conquered population itself, a division between capitalists and simple operatives—a division which may one day lead to a war between capital and labor, but which at this epoch could work no ill. The amount of capital in the hands of the industrious class, including the mercantile and manufacturing portion, in comparison with that possessed by the feudal population, was exceedingly small, and it was necessary to concentrate it in as few hands as possible, in order to increase its productiveness and augment its power. It was so small that if equally distributed among the whole population, it would have been lost, at least have had no power to redeem the class. Every trader or manufacturer, who had capital which he invested in commercial or manufacturing enterprises, became a public benefactor because he was increasing the amount of wealth belonging to the industrious class and throwing into its hands the power with which it was one day to conquer equality with the feudal lord.

Trade and manufactures, though they did not distribute wealth equally among all the members of the industrious class, nevertheless augmented the gross amount of its wealth, enriched it as a class. But for them the capital of the world would have remained in the hands of the feudal society, in the hands of the nobility and of the church. In their hands it must have remained virtually unproductive. No addition to its amount would or could have been made. But just in proportion as capital came into the hands of the trader and the manufacturer, it became productive, and the wealth of the world was augmented. Individuals amassed large estates; but not by impoverishing others, as was the case when a nobleman became rich, or richer. The wealth they amassed they had called into existence; not, it is true, with their own hands, but by the profitable employment of the hands of others. In creating this additional amount of wealth, they did a real good, without doing any injury. The operatives they employed, indeed, did not become rich themselves, but they did not become the poorer. Their condition, on the contrary, was much improved. The laborer at wages, though his wages were below what they ought to have been, was in a condition altogether superior to that of a bondman, which he was before he became a workman at wages.

Trade gives a spring to manufactures. It finds out markets and thus creates a demand for them. By creating a demand for them, it aids their growth, calls a greater number of workmen into the factories. This in its turn increases the demand for agricultural products, and with this increased demand for the products of agriculture, agricultural labor rises in importance, and as a necessary consequence the agricultural laborer finds his condition improving. The smaller nobility, proprietors of a portion of the soil, turn their attention to the better cultivation of their lands, and take pains to increase their productiveness because they find a market for their produce or because they wish to obtain a larger supply of the articles furnished them by the merchant and the manufacturer. An additional amount of capital, a portion of that invested in land, is thus added to that employed in the interests of industry.

As the merchant and manufacturer, the tradesman and artisan, increase in wealth, they form a sort of middle class, or a class of commoners. Gradually they give to their children a decent education, and prepare them to compete, successfully in many respects, with the children of the nobility. Intelligence, polished manners, and refined taste are, after a while, associated with the names of some wealthy commoners. Some casual intercourse is commenced between them and the nobility. A marriage between one of their daughters and one of the sons of the nobility, desirous of replenishing his estate, now and then occurs—and the process of amalgamation begins, never to cease till it becomes complete.

It is only by slow degrees that the money power is instituted, and businessmen obtain an influence in the affairs of the world. Businessmen require a fixed order, security for persons and property. They can do little for themselves or for the cause of industry when they can count with no tolerable certainty on a return for their outlays. Now through long ages of modern Europe, order, security for property or persons, there was little. The banker was not always a nobleman. The capitalist was not always a lord. From the fifth century to the tenth, moneyed men in no sense of the word constituted an aristocracy. No class of the community were more harassed or more exposed than they. Kings, lords, and bishops, harassed, vexed, taxed, despoiled them at their will. Nevertheless they contrived to prosper. Their wealth, power, importance, were ever on the increase. This is seen in the communal movement, in the eleventh, twelfth, and thirteenth centuries, of which we have already spoken. The burghers were then able, in a multitude of cases, to force the kings, lords, and even bishops, to grant them charters of incorporation, securing to them important privileges, and allowing them, within the walls of their town, to live under laws of their own making, and magistrates of their own choosing. Some, we are aware, pretend that these charters were granted to the towns, through the generosity or policy of the kings; on the one hand to aid the people, and on the other to secure their assistance in controlling the feudal lord, of whose power the kings were jealous. But they who attribute the least of the good, which they find the people enjoying, to the generosity or policy of kings, are the worthiest interpreters of history. Kings play a much less conspicuous part in the real history of the world than they do in the narratives of historians. The communal charters, in nearly all cases where they secured any important franchises, were obtained because the commune was powerful enough to conquer them, or rich enough to buy them. That the kings of France and of England as well as some of the great feudal lords and perhaps now and then a bishop did grant charters of incorporations to some old towns, and to some new ones, is very certain; but they did it as a means to obtain money. Whether, therefore, the burghers conquered or purchased their charters of incorporation, the fact of the charters being granted proves their growing importance, their increasing wealth, and their efforts to obtain a fixed order, favorable to trade and manufactures.

The communal movement failed before the end of the fourteenth century, and in the fifteenth century, the towns and boroughs, as a sort of petty republics, have no longer any significance. But the wealth and influence of the burghers or commoners have increased. They constitute now one of the three estates of the States-General. They were first compelled to send their deputies to the Parliament to vote the supplies demanded by the king, that the town or borough might be held to pay it, because voted by its deputy. But this, which was at first a compulsory duty, becomes with the improved condition of the commoners, a valued right, not to be surrendered, and the origin of representative government. The commons remembering that they originally voted supplies, and forgetting that they did it because compelled, and in the interest of the king, not of themselves, come to claim the exclusive right to vote them, and therefore become masters of the government, and from an estate, become the nation.

These, of course, are only loose hints on the influence of the moneyed power in elevating the plebeian class, in creating the commons, and in amalgamating the two populations which occupied the European territory at the commencement of modern history. We should be glad to be more explicit and minute; but we have been enough so for our present purpose. The moneyed power has been one of the great agents by which modern civilization has advanced, and the businessmen have contributed their full share to the progress of popular liberty. By means of trade and manufactures, the majority of the available wealth of Christendom has been thrown into the hands of the commons, and this has given the commons a preponderance in the government of the world. It must be added, too, that trade and manufactures have not robbed the feudal lord of the wealth they have placed in the hands of the commons. They have created it, and by so much augmented the wealth of Christendom, of the world. Having now, at least in England, France, and America, a majority of the wealth on their side, the commons are the real rulers. They have as a class risen from their degradation, broken the yoke of the conqueror, and recovered their independence.

The progress of society has brought up the industrious class as far as it was identified with the moneyed power. But the work of modern civilization is not completed. The feudal lord restrained the absolutism of the monarch; the moneyed power has restrained, supplanted, taken the place of the feudal lord, and made the government of the world pass from the hands of the soldier to those of the banker, and substituted the pen for the sword. But it places that government still in the hands of a class, not in the hands of humanity. It has brought up a much larger class than the old feudal nobility, and a class, too, which has come out from the bosom of the people and can claim no preeminence over them in point of blood or race; but still it leaves the immense majority below the proper estate of man. The distinction between the capitalist and the laborer now manifests itself and becomes an evil. Till the moneyed power had triumphed over the old nobility and lodged the government in the hands of the businessmen, the interests of capital and labor were one and the same. It was necessary to secure the victory to the moneyed power, in order to redeem the people, that population to whom the businessmen belong. That victory is gained; the class is redeemed, as a class; and the work now is to redeem the class *as individuals*, that henceforth the government of the world shall be in the hands of no class, but in those of humanity.

This new work was seriously begun with the American Revolution. The world had, here and there, attempted it before, but without success. It was attempted in England, in the seventeenth century, but the agricultural population were too weak to perform their share of it. The soil, or the greater part of it, was in the hands of the nobility, and its cultivators were too poor and too dependent. The work failed, or rather was suspended, adjourned. This country had been discovered. The land here was unappropriated. Its cultivators became its owners. The agricultural population here became, therefore, independent proprietors, without ceasing to be laborers. Their influence, and a powerful influence too, was therefore capable of being thrown into the scale, not, as in England, against the laborers in towns, cities, and factories, but against the power of any dominant class.

Our Revolution was effected not in favor of men in classes; not in favor of orders or estates; but in favor of man, men as integers. It marks a new epoch in human progress. The influence of capital, or the moneyed power, as the ruling power, had then ceased to be legitimate. Man, not money, was then to be sovereign; and the whole people, not the businessmen merely, were to hold the reins of government. But this was not fully understood at the time. Alexander Hamilton[24] and his party thought matters stood as they ever had done, and that the moneyed power was still the legitimate sovereign. They were doubtless sincere. They had not that order of mind which is first to discern when old watchwords change their meaning. The country, in consequence of the war of the Revolution, was embarrassed with a national debt and the aid of the businessmen was needed to pay it off. A national bank was therefore established, and the money-king suffered to wear the crown yet longer. In 1800, an effort was made to dethrone the money-king, and enthrone the people, and attended with partial, which would have been complete, success, had it not been for the war of 1812. That war plunged us again into debt, and made it necessary, in 1816, to recall the money power. The debt is now paid off; the nation owes not a cent; and the great contest has recommenced between capital and labor, or more properly, between man and money—between the moneyed power supported by the businessmen, and the entire people sustained by a majority of the agricultural and mechanical population.

It is not likely that this contest will be immediately ended, yet we cannot doubt the final result. Modern civilization has brought up the nobility against the king, and maintained them; it has brought up the businessmen against the nobility, enfranchised capital and capitalists, and sustained them; it now brings up the laborer, that portion of the plebeian class whose enfranchisement was adjourned, so as not to prejudice the interests of capital; and shall it fail now? It shall not. Humanity, from the depths of her universal being, utters

[24][Ed. Alexander Hamilton (1755/57-1804), the major author of the *Federalist Papers* and the first secretary of the Treasury of the United States (1789-95), was an advocate of a national bank that would cement the relationship between businessmen and a strong national or central government.]

the word, it shall not fail. The struggle may be long, arduous, and perhaps bloody; the oppressed may have to groan yet longer; the friends of humanity may experience more than one defeat; but they will never give over the struggle or despair of ultimate success. They have been too long victorious, and too often have they gained the victory, in darker days than these and with feebler forces than they now have at their command, to despair, or "bate a jot of heart or hope."[25]

All classes, each in turn, have possessed the government; and the time has come for all predominance of class to end; for man, the people to rule. To this end all modern civilization has been tending, and for this it gives valiant battle today. Its forces appear to us as numerous, as well disciplined, as skillfully drawn up in battle array, as ever; and unless God has changed his purposes, and inverted the order of his Providence, it shall come off conqueror; and man be redeemed; and the work for his friends henceforth cease to be the melioration of society, and become that of perfecting the individuals of each successive generation, as they appear in time and pass off into eternity. This done, and the wish of the workingmen is fulfilled; the visions of the prophets are realized; and the prayers of the philanthropist are heard in heaven, and answered on the earth.

[25][Ed. Quotation from John Milton (1608-74), Sonnet 22 ("To Cyriak Skinner, upon His Blindness"), line 7-8. See *The Works of John Milton*, vol. 1, part 1 (New York: Columbia, 1931), 68. Milton congratulates himself in this sonnet, written after he went blind, for wearing out his eyes "In libertyes defence, my noble task" (line 11). Personal costs, Brownson is saying above, cannot be counted in the struggle for freedom.]

18.

SLAVERY–ABOLITIONISM[1]

Boston Quarterly Review 1 (April, 1838): 238-60

We have not introduced this little volume of Dr. Channing's for the purpose of reviewing it. It has been too widely circulated and too generally read to permit such a purpose to be either necessary or proper. The public have long since made up their minds respecting its merits and are quietly giving it the high rank it deserves. In our opinion, though not wholly unexceptionable, it is the best book that the present discussion of slavery among us has called forth and the only one we have met that we can read with anything like general satisfaction. With its general estimate of slavery, its lofty moral tone, and its profound reverence for the rights of man, we sympathize with our whole soul; but some of its special views, and the traces of a doctrine tending somewhat to centralization, which we here and there discover, and of which we believe the author to be unconscious, we cannot entirely approve.

We place this work at the head of this article merely for the purpose of testifying in general terms our high appreciation of its merits, and because it gives us an occasion of expressing our own views at some length on the subject of slavery. The subject of slavery is fairly before the public and it must be met. However much we may regret its agitation at this time, when all thoughts should be turned to the settling of the financial affairs of the nation, we must suffer it to be discussed and take part in its discussion. We would merely add, let it be discussed calmly, without passion, and in a truly Christian spirit.

We say without any hesitation that we are wholly and totally opposed to slavery and that we do not consider it any question at all with the American people, whether it be a good or an evil. We believe that question is decided by the Declaration of Independence and forever put at rest. To attempt to prove that slavery is wrong, that it is not to be perpetuated, and that it ought to be abolished, as soon as it can be, is to insult every true American's mind and heart, and

[1][Ed. Review of William E. Channing's [1780-1842] *Slavery*, 4th edition, revised (Boston: James Munroe & Co., 1836).]

that too, whether he live north or south of Mason's and Dixon's line. We have much mistaken the character of our southern brethren, if there be one among them that will for one moment contend that slavery is the proper estate of a man.

That man has no absolute right to hold his brother man in slavery is but a necessary inference from the fact that slavery is wrong. It can never be right, no man can ever have the right, to do wrong. Every slaveholder, then, ought to do all he can do to rescue his fellow beings, whether black or white, from the servitude in which he finds them, or to which he may have reduced them. If slavery be wrong, his duty is plain. He must, if in his power, remove it. Here is no room for dispute, no need of argument.

Again, we hold that slavery must and will be abolished. The whole force of modern civilization is against it, and before the onward march of that civilization it must be swept away. To this result we do not believe that our southern brethren are opposed. Some of them may believe that slavery is fixed upon them forever, may believe that its abolition is impossible, and therefore may undertake to invent good reasons for its continuance; but secretly none of them love it and the immense majority of them would rejoice to be rid of it.

But while we contend that slavery is wrong, that it is wrong to hold slaves, and that the slaveholder ought to labor with all his power for its abolition, we do not agree with our friends the Abolitionists in denouncing slaveholders, and in declaring that no slaveholder can be a Christian.[2] Reformers should war against systems not against men. Paul was always careful to have it understood, that he did not "wrestle against flesh and blood, but against principalities, against powers, against the rulers of the darkness of this world, against spiritual wickedness in high places" [Eph. 6:12]. For ourselves, we have learned that men may profit by institutions opposed to the best good of humanity without necessarily being bad men. Many practices, which, in one view of the case, strike us as altogether wrong, in another point of view, appear to us as excusable, if not even as justifiable. The older we grow, the more we see—we speak personally—the less and

[2][Ed. William Lloyd Garrison had frequently asserted that slaveholders could not be considered Christians and should be removed from their churches. In a speech of 15 October 1830, for example, he asserted that the emancipation of the slave "could not be withheld by his master an hour without sin" and that there was no such thing as a "Christian slaveholder." For this quotation, see Henry Mayer, *All on Fire: William Lloyd Garrison and the Abolition of Slavery* (New York: St. Martins Press, 1998), 103.]

less are we disposed to be censorious. The world is *not* all wrong, everything is not out of place, and every man is not a devil. Thank God! We every day acquire fresh faith in human virtue; and while we bate nothing in our zeal or efforts for progress, we become able to look with more and more complacency on the world, and to feel that, of all God's prophets, we are not the only one that is left alive. There are more than we who have not bowed the knee to Baal.

If slaveholding were purely an individual act, we confess, we should doubt the possibility of the slaveholder's being a good man save at the expense of his intelligence. But slaveholding, in our southern states, for instance, is not an individual but a social act. Slavery is not an individual but a social institution, and society, not the individual conscience alone, is responsible for it. The question is not, Is slaveholding wrong? But, can a man who adheres to, and attempts to profit by a wrong social institution be a good Christian man? Must he necessarily be a sinner? This is the question and we wish our moralists and divines would answer it. It is an important case of conscience, and reaches, perhaps, further than we are ordinarily aware of. Society always has been and everywhere is imperfect. All its institutions are more or less imperfect, more or less in opposition to absolute justice. We may all of us be getting our living today by means of institutions, as unjust in themselves as abolitionists have shown slavery to be. If no man who adheres to, or profits by, a wrong social institution, can be a good man, that is, a Christian, what shall we do with the upholders of monarchy, hereditary nobility, corrupting hierarchies, with Mahometans, Brahmins, all who live in an imperfect social state and profit by unjust social institutions? Nay, what shall we do with ourselves; for who of us has anything which we can say positively has come into our possession without the aid of any wrong social institution? We should, it seems to us, view with suspicion all rules of judgment, which in their operation must overstock hell and leave heaven an unpeopled desert.

For ourselves, we ask no questions of the slaveholder that we do not of any other man. Is the slaveholder faithful to all his engagements, in the discharge of all the private virtues? Does he cultivate piety towards God and love to man? Does he make slavery as light a burden as he can; that is, does he treat his slaves with kindness and respect? Does he inquire into the character of his social institutions and do what he can to perfect them? If so, we must call him a good Christian. We know the abolitionists may say that it is his duty to free his slaves at once; and so should we, if it depended on his individual will whether he should free them or not. But this matter of freeing the slaves is a matter for the community rather than the individual slaveholder. As a member of the community, the individual should do all he can do to hasten the period when the community shall unfetter the slave and let him go free. Before that period he cannot free his slaves even if he would.

But we are told by the South, that this is their affair and not ours, and that we have no right to meddle with it. Is the South right? This brings us to the question, what rights have we at the North in regard to southern slavery? This after all is the real question before the American people, and unhappily this question has become so entangled with other questions, that it is difficult to give it a separate and distinct answer. Our own opinion on the matter we have hinted in a foregoing article,[3] but we deem it necessary, in justice to ourselves and to the cause of liberty, to go more fully into it and to state more at large the grounds of our opinion. We do this the more readily because nobody can for one moment suspect us of any desire to palliate slavery or to prolong it. All who know us, know well that we are heartily opposed to every form of slavery, and that our whole life is devoted to the cause of universal liberty to universal man—a cause for which we have made some sacrifices and for which we are ready, if need be, to make more and greater sacrifices.

In all that concerns their internal regulations, institutions, and police, we regard the several states which compose the Union, as distinct, independent communities.[4] We are to be regarded as one people, as one nation, only in the several respects specified in the Constitution of the United States. In all other respects we are not one nation, but twenty-six independent nations, and stand in relation to one another, precisely as the United States as one nation stands in relation to France, England, or Mexico. We of Massachusetts have no more concern with the internal policy and social institutions of South Carolina, for instance, than we have with the internal police of Russia, Austria, or Turkey. Slavery, then, in the states is not a national institution; that is, not an institution over which the people of the United States, in the sense in which they are one people, have any control. The right of the people of the non-slaveholding states, in

[3][Ed. Brownson may be referring to "The Character of Jesus and the Christian Movement," *Boston Quarterly Review* 1 (April, 1838): 129-52, especially 145-46; see also Chapter 16 in this volume.]

[4][Ed. In what follows Brownson articulates his basic agreement with John C. Calhoun's state rights theory of government, emphasizing the sovereignty of the states.]

relation to slavery in the southern states, is precisely what it is in relation to it in Constantinople, or in any foreign slaveholding state.

In one respect slavery may in this country be regarded as a national and not as a state institution. The Constitution of the United States allows slavery to form one of the bases of national representation. All the states have a legal right to concern themselves with this question. We of the North, if we choose, may undoubtedly use all just means to amend the Constitution so that slavery shall not be represented in Congress. Whether it is desirable so to amend the Constitution, is a question of policy, which we do not now undertake to decide. Slavery in the District of Columbia and in the territories belonging to the United States is a different matter from slavery in the states, and, for aught we can see, may constitutionally be acted upon by the Congress of the United States. Whether Congress should act upon it in the District and the territories is a question on which good men will differ. For our own part, we wish slavery, when abolished, to be abolished by a concert of all the slaveholding states, together with the Congress of the United States. We can see little utility in abolishing it at present in the District of Columbia and the territories. To petition Congress to do it is only to petition Congress to do indirectly what all parties agree it may not do directly, that is, abolish slavery in the states.

Here is the ground of the objection, which the South makes to the reception of anti-slavery petitions by Congress. These petitions literally touch the question of slavery only in the sections of the slaveholding country, over which Congress has exclusive jurisdiction, but really, and in the minds of those who get them up, they are petitions for the abolition of slavery in the states themselves. Does any body believe, that, if Congress should grant the prayer of the petitioners, slavery would stand a year in this country? Do not all the abolitionists believe that the abolition of slavery in the District of Columbia and the territories, by Congress, would necessarily involve its abolition in all the slaveholding states? Is not this also the belief of the South? What, then, is the true character of the petitions with which Congress is flooded in regard to slavery? Are they not in fact, though not in name, petitions for Congress to interfere with the internal police of the southern states? So the South regards them, and on this ground it opposes their reception. Is the South right in this? Have we a right to petition Congress to abolish slavery in South Carolina? Have we a right to petition Congress to violate the Constitution of the United States? A right to petition it to do indirectly, what it may not do directly, openly, avowedly? Yet we have unquestionably the right to petition Congress to abolish slavery in the District of Columbia and the territories, and the South have been unwise and impolitic, to say the least, in denying it. By denying it, they have mixed up with the question of abolition that of the right of petition, which has in reality no connection with it. The abolitionists have by this means been able to make themselves regarded as the defenders of the right of petition, a right dear to all New England men, from the memory of the struggle of their fathers of England in the seventeenth century with Charles Stuart.[5] And yet, virtually, the South are, in this very controversy, truer defenders of constitutional rights than the abolitionists. The abolitionists are technically, literally right, and the South technically, literally wrong; and hence their efforts work altogether against them and recruit the ranks of abolitionists by thousands. Abolitionists never rejoiced more sincerely than they did at the passage of Mr. Patton's Resolution.[6] Congress, we believe, ought to receive the petitions as the less of two evils and to treat them with all proper respect.

But to return to the question of the right of the people of the free states to interfere with slavery. What is this right? How far does it extend? The right of the people of the non-slaveholding states in relation to southern slavery is precisely their right in relation to any of the social institutions of France or England. They have the same right to labor for the abolition of monarchy or the House of Lords in England that they have for the abolition of slavery in any of the southern states. What is this right? How far does it extend? In our opinion simply to the free and full discussion of the question. As men, as citizens, in this respect, of independent communities, and therefore divested of none of our natural rights by any other community, we have the right to discuss freely, and give our views unreservedly, on all questions which concern humanity. We have, for instance, a perfect right to question the legitimacy of monarchy, to show, if we can, that it is a bad institution, that it is founded in usurpation, that it does great wrong to man, and that it ought to be abolished forthwith. We may also throw all the light in our power on the means of abolishing it, and offer what we believe to be sound and cogent rea-

[5][Ed. Reference is to Charles I (1600-49), king of England (1625-49) during the English Civil War. Prior to the war he had refused to call Parliament and to listen to the Puritan Commons who set out their complaints against the government in the Petition of Right in 1628.]

[6][Ed. Probably a reference to John Mercer Patton (1797-1858), a Virginia politician and lawyer who was a United States Representative (1830-38). He was adamant in his defense of slavery.]

sons for abolishing it. So of slavery. We may examine it, publish all the facts we can collect respecting it, speak, print, publish, in the limits of our respective states, fully and freely, our honest convictions of its nature, tendency, justice, injustice, the necessity, the duty, the means of its preservation or removal. This we believe is the extent of our right of interference. A step further than this contravenes international law and encroaches upon the rights of the slaveholding states.

The right here stated and to this extent we claim for ourselves. We claim it on the ground that we are men and have therefore a right to interest ourselves in whatever concerns men as men. We claim it on the ground that we are citizens of a state which allows, which guarantees free discussion, freedom of speech and the press, and which no other state has any right to interfere with or seek to control. This right the South must not presume to deny us. While we respect her rights, she must respect ours. If we may not interfere with her legislation, she must not interfere with ours. Moreover, neither the North nor the South has any right to abridge or restrain freedom of discussion because freedom of discussion is one of the rights of man and therefore older than governments and raised above their legitimate reach. The South has erred in denying us this right. In doing this she has struck a blow at our independence, made the abolitionists, with no great consistency however, appear to be the champions of free discussion and induced not a few to join them under this character, that never would have joined them as simple abolitionists.

Still, we are inclined to believe, that the South has never intended to deny us the right to discuss in our own way the abstract question of slavery. All she has really intended to do is to assert her right to manage her internal police as she judges proper, and to deny, as a necessary inference from this, our right to interfere with it. The real question at issue between the abolitionists and the South is not whether slavery be good, bad, or indifferent, but whether one state has the right to avow the design of changing the institutions of another state, and of adopting a series of measures directed expressly to that end? This is the question. In all that concerns them as states, these United States are as independent on one another as are England and France. France has as much right to interfere in the internal police of England, as Massachusetts has in the internal police of South Carolina. Slavery is unquestionably a matter which falls within the powers of the states, as independent, sovereign states. In relation to this question, then, all the states stand to one another precisely as foreign nations. The question then comes up in this shape: have we the right to avow the design and to adopt measures to control the internal legislation of a foreign nation? The question needs no answer. Everybody knows that we have not, at least so long as we acknowledge the independence of that nation.

Nor does it alter the nature of the question, that the actual interference is by individual citizens and not by the state. What the state is prohibited from doing, it can never be lawful for the citizens to do. Interference in the affairs of foreigners is as unlawful on the part of individual citizens as of states. Who will pretend that La Fayette had any more right to interfere in the quarrel between this country and England, than France herself had? And who will pretend to justify La Fayette's interference by international law? France was at peace with England, and La Fayette, as a subject of France, was bound to keep that peace. We adduce not this case to censure La Fayette, whose chivalrous aid to the cause of American Independence we appreciate as highly as do any of our countrymen, but simply to show that the obligations of the state bind the citizen. Our Canadian neighbors are now in a quarrel.[7] Has this nation a right to interfere in that quarrel? Certainly not under its existing treaty obligations to England. It may side with the Canadians, but not without involving itself in a war with England. Its duty, if it would preserve its peace relations with England, is to remain neutral. Is not the duty of the citizens the same? Can an American citizen take up for the Canadians, without losing his character of American citizen, and forfeiting the protection of American laws?

If the individual citizens may do in relation to an independent state, what the state may not do, the consequences are not difficult to be foreseen. If the citizens of this State may associate to do what the State itself may not do, all that is requisite to enlist the whole force of the State in that which it is unlawful for the State to do, is to waive the State, and band all the citizens together into what shall be called a voluntary association. If half a dozen citizens may unite in an abolition society, pledged to emancipate the slaves, all the citizens of the state may do it. And when all the citizens of the state have thus formed themselves into an association, what is that association but the state

[7][Ed. Brownson is probably referring to French Canada's protests against what many French Canadian nationalists considered the tyrannical imperial policy of the British government. In the summer of 1837 in particular public protests, boycotts of British goods, and organizing for possible military action indicated the rebellious nature of the Canadian "quarrels." On this see Peter Burroughs, *The Canadian Crisis and British Colonial Policy, 1828-1841* (London: Edward Arnold, 1972), 74-94.]

under a different name? The interference of such an association would be as efficient, to say the least, as that of the state itself. And if the citizens of a state may thus lawfully associate for changing the institutions of foreign nations, we ask, what security can one foreign nation ever have in relation to another? It is of the greatest importance to the peace and safety of nations that citizens or subjects observe with scrupulous fidelity the engagements of their respective governments. The abolitionists themselves were of this opinion in relation to the interference of our citizens in the affairs of Texas.[8]

Nor, again, will it do to say that slavery is an institution of so peculiar a character that we may claim the right of interfering with it without claiming the right to interfere with the whole internal police of foreign nations. In the first place, it is not an institution peculiar in its kind. Something similar to it is found in every state in which the law makes any discrimination between individual citizens. The principle which legitimates southern slavery may be found incorporated, if we are not much mistaken, into the constitution and laws of every state in the Union. In every state in which restrictions are placed on eligibility, as in this state, or in which the law presumes to say who may and who may not exercise the right of suffrage, or in which there are monopolies or exclusive privileges recognized by law, there is the seminal principle of slavery. But waive this as not essential to our argument. In the next place, we say we have no right to make any inquiry concerning the institutions of foreign nations, for the purpose of ascertaining which of them we have or have not the right of undertaking to abolish. We cannot do this without denying the independence of the nation in question. Do we acknowledge South Carolina, for instance, to be a free and independent state? Do we acknowledge her sovereignty to be absolute so far as not limited by the Constitution of the United States? Then what right have we to take the revision of her doings? Can we do this without virtually denying her sovereignty? Can we deny her sovereignty without giving her just cause of offence? And when we admit her sovereignty, do we not acknowledge her right to establish such institutions as she pleases? If then she pleases to establish slavery, is it not her affair, and one of which we have debarred ourselves, by the acknowledgment of her sovereignty, from taking any cognizance?

[8][Ed. Brownson himself and the abolitionists had protested against the annexation of Texas at an 1837 meeting of the Massachusetts Anti-Slavery Society in Worcester. On this, see the Introduction to this volume and *The Liberator* 7 (October 6, 1837): 163.]

But it may be said, that slavery is unjust, that no state has the right to establish an unjust institution; therefore, South Carolina has no right to establish slavery. Grant it. What then? Who has the right to determine the question, as to the justice or injustice of the institution, South Carolina or we? If she be an independent state, she has the right to be her own judge as to the rectitude of her decisions. She is not accountable to us, and we have no right to arraign her before our tribunal. If we believe her decision unjust we may undoubtedly tell her so; but so long as we admit her independence, we must speak to her as an equal, not as a culprit. We must concede her right to judge for herself; we must disavow the right and the intention of dictating to her; and we must confine ourselves to the simple statement of our reasons, as one man may state to another man his reasons for not agreeing with him in opinion. If, however, instead of doing this, we begin by formally declaring her in the wrong, by denouncing her as awfully wicked, by stirring up wrath and indignation against her, by solemnly pledging ourselves not to cease our exertions till we have compelled her to reverse her decision, and by adopting all the measures in our power which we believe conducive to that end, do we not then fail to treat her as an independent state, refuse to acknowledge her right to judge for herself, and are we not, to all intents and purposes, waging war against her?

It will be seen from what we have said that we do not question the proceedings of the abolitionists on constitutional grounds. We do not believe that we of the North have made a compact with the South, by which we are debarred from interfering with slavery. We find in the Constitution of the United States no such compact. None such in fact was needed. Slavery exists in the states by virtue of no constitutional guarantee, but solely by virtue of state sovereignty. The question in relation to it stands precisely as it did before the formation of the national government, and we have precisely the same rights, and only the same rights, of interference with it that we should have had, had no national government ever been formed. The states are older than the Union, and they retain in their own hands all the rights of sovereignty not, in so many words, conceded to the Union. Now as the disposition of slavery is not conceded to the Union, it belongs as a matter of course to the states. By belonging to them it stands precisely as it did before the Union was consummated. As the states before the Union were so many independent nations, the question of slavery in them is to be treated solely as a question between foreign nations. Interference with it in one state by the citizens of another state is to be regulated by international and not by constitutional law. Had the Union not been effected, everybody knows that efforts by the citizens of Massachusetts to free the slaves in South Carolina, efforts begun and carried on with express reference to that end, would have been a violation of international law, especially if accompanied with perpetual denunciation of South Carolina, and by their very character threatening to disturb her internal peace and tranquillity. Now this, which would have been true without the Union, we contend, is true under it. The South, we think, must therefore place her defense on the ground of state sovereignty. It is as striking against state sovereignty, as denying the independence of the several states, as claiming for the citizens of one state jurisdiction over the legislation of another, that we view the proceedings of abolition societies with suspicion and alarm. To say the least, they assert the justice of a species of propagandism, which, if admitted, must strike at all national independency, and which will not fail to disturb the peaceful intercourse of nations, embroil them in war, and deluge the earth in blood. He who comes forth as the champion of liberty must bear in mind that he is under no less obligation to defend the rights of communities than he is the rights of individuals. He who loves America and would live and die for American liberty should look well before he adopts a course which may embroil the several states in a civil war, or in the end change the relations which now subsist between the national government and that of the several states. Liberty is as much interested in maintaining inviolate the rights of the national government, on the one hand, and especially of the several states which compose the Union, on the other hand, as she is in freeing the slave. In the measures the abolitionists adopt there is a deeper question involved than that of Negro slavery. All who are accustomed to look below the surface of things may see that it is a question of no less magnitude than that of changing the whole structure of the government of this country, and possibly that of destroying the liberty of the whole American people. When hundreds and thousands of our citizens are banded together to trample on the rights of independent communities in the holy name of freedom herself, we confess we are not a little alarmed for the rights of the individual. One barrier leaped, another may be; and when communities can no longer make their rights respected, what can the individual do?

But we shall be told that all our fears are idle, all our reasonings groundless, for abolitionists do not propose to do anything more than we have conceded them the right to do; that is, to express freely their honest convictions on the question of slavery. We deny this. The abolition societies, as everybody knows, are not formed for the discussion of slavery but for its abolition. Their members are pledged to the "immediate emancipation of the slaves without expatriation." Lawyers may have been consulted and the wording of their constitutions may be technically within the letter of the law, but we know, and everybody knows, that the real end, the avowed end, of their formation is not merely to give utterance to certain opinions on the question of slavery, but to effect its abolition. They are not formed for deliberation, for discussion, but for action, and action, too, within the limits of states of which abolitionists are not citizens.

But we shall be told again that, admitting the abolition societies are formed for the abolition and not the discussion of slavery, they do not contravene international law because they adopt for the purpose of carrying their end only legal and constitutional means, such means as the laws of nations permit them to adopt. This undoubtedly is the real ground on which the abolitionists rest their defense. We object to it because we are not yet able to perceive that the legitimacy of the means, in themselves, can legitimate an unlawful end. It is admitted that the abolitionists have no legal right to emancipate the slaves. Yet the emancipation of the slaves is what they propose to do. They propose to do what the laws of nations prohibit them from doing. Are any means directed to that end lawful to be used?

The abolitionists, it will be said, do not propose to emancipate the slaves, except as the effect of the expression of their opinions and feelings on the subject of slavery. We question this statement; but admit it for a moment. The abolitionists—unless they choose to break with the slaveholding states, to refuse to sustain the relation of friends to them, and to come into open war with them—are bound by the laws of nations to refrain from all words and deeds which will disturb their peace and tranquillity, stir up insurrection in them, sully their reputation, or excite public indignation against them. Now we may undoubtedly discuss the question of slavery, but not so as to produce any of these results. Free discussion is itself subjected to this restriction. So long as we wish to be at peace and amity with foreign nations, we are bound to treat all their institutions, as their institutions, with respect. We have no more right to denounce them, to slander them, to speak to their prejudice, or to injure them in any way, because their institutions differ from ours, or from what we believe just, than we have an individual whose creed we happen to disbelieve. We may reason against such a man's creed, but we are bound to see that our reasoning against it do not result in any injury to him. If we should represent him as one with whom his neighbors should hold no intercourse, brand him as a sinner of the deepest dye, hire editors of papers to publish him to the world as such, and hold public meetings and pass public resolves to the effect that, if he do not change his creed instantly, he shall be placed out of the pale of humanity, we should most assuredly transcend our rights in regard to him, and give him just cause of complaint against us. Now the abolitionists pursue a course like this towards the slaveholding communities, and they do this for the express purpose of freeing the slave. They may in all this be only giving utterance to their honest convictions and feelings, but have they, under plea of free discussion, a right to utter themselves in this manner? Can they do this and be in a state of peace with those communities?

The abolitionists say they use only moral and rational means, merely arguments addressed to the reason and the conscience. Is it so? To what kind of a reason or a conscience is denunciation addressed? Is it so? What mean then these fifteen hundred affiliated societies, spread over the non-slaveholding states, pledged to the immediate emancipation of the slaves? Are these societies' arguments addressed to the individual reason and conscience of the slaveholder? What is the rationale of this argument? What is its legitimacy? Many hundreds of thousands of men, women, and children, all solemnly pledged to effect the immediate emancipation of the slaves, are banded together in some fifteen hundred societies; therefore slavery is a sin; therefore no slaveholder is a Christian; and therefore every slaveholder must immediately emancipate his slaves! We confess this is a species of logic that passes our comprehension. That these societies, by banding together the majority of our population, may so concentrate public opinion, and bring it to bear with such force on the institution of slavery, that the slaveholder shall feel himself unable to withstand it, and therefore compelled to free his slaves, is what we can understand very well; but this is neither a rational nor a moral argument for the abolition of slavery. A man finds a loaded pistol presented at his breast, and to save his life gives up his purse; and the slaveholder finds the community pointing the finger of scorn at him, and to save his reputation, which he holds dearer than life, emancipates his slaves; which is the more moral and rational argument of the two? An army, organized and marching upon the South to free the slaves at the point of the bayonet, would, in principle, be an argument to the individual reason and conscience of the slaveholder, equally as forcible, appropriate, and convincing, as an associated multitude pointing the finger of scorn, or shouting denunciation, and threatening the vengeance of heaven.

Nor is it true that our abolitionists contemplate no action on the subject, but the action of truth and moral suasion. They do contemplate political action. They let pass no possible opportunity of bringing the subject of slavery before the state legislatures; and they are constantly at work to get it discussed on the floor of Congress. What, we ask, is all this agitation for? Why is abolitionism organizing a political party in the states and the nation? Why does it want abolition members in our state legislatures? Why does it interrogate candidates for office as to their views of slavery? Is there no political action intended? Give it a majority in Congress and will it not legislate on the subject? It will at once abolish slavery in the District of Columbia, and in the territories. Will it stop there? Who so simple as to believe it? It will usurp, or alter the United States Constitution so as not to need to usurp the power to abolish it in the states. What are paper constitutions in the way of a body of men, women, and children, inflamed, drunken with a great idea, and so much the more drunken because the idea with which they are filled is a holy one—what are paper constitutions in their way, when they have in their hands the actual power to advance? He knows nothing of the power of an enthusiastic multitude, who thinks such feeble barriers would arrest their progress. Their leaders might rush before them, the wise and prudent might beg them to pause; but leaders, and the wise and prudent are as chaff before the wind, and on will the multitude press, sweeping them away, or trampling them under their feet, to the realization of the idea which inspires them. Here is the danger. Let the abolitionists get the majority banded together in or under the control of their affiliated societies, pledged to the immediate emancipation of the slaves, and they will throw into Congress the power to do it; that is, power to regulate the internal institutions of the states; gone then is the independency of the states; and then goes individual freedom; and then all power is in the central government; Greece or Rome is reproduced; the absolutism of the state is established, which merely preludes the absolutism of the emperor. God grant that in the honest and earnest defense of liberty we dig not her grave!

We speak on this subject strongly but we have no fears of being misunderstood. There is not a man or woman living that can accuse us of defending slavery. This whole number of our Review is devoted to the defense of the rights of man, not to the rights of one man, of a few men, but of every man. We can legitimate our own right to freedom, only by arguments which prove also the Negro's right to be free. We have all our life long sympathized with the poor and the oppressed, and we yield to no abolitionist in the amount of the sacrifices we have made, wisely or unwisely, needlessly or not, in the cause of human freedom. It is not today, nor this year, that we have pledged ourselves, for life or for death, to the holy cause of universal liberty. But everything, we say, in its time. First, we must settle the bases of individual freedom, settle the principle that man measures man the world over, and establish our government upon it, and secure the action of the government in accordance with it and then we may proceed to make all details harmonize with it.

To explain ourselves; the work to be done in this country today is to place the government in the hands of the people, not only in principle, but in fact. Hitherto the government, in point of fact, has been in the hands of the businessmen, who have shaped legislation to their especial interests. We are struggling now to get it out of their hands, not to the disadvantage of the businessmen, but to hinder them from having an exclusive control over it. The businessmen form a part of the people, a large part, and a respectable part, and we must not wish to turn the government in any respect against them; but we must seek so to arrange matters, that they shall share only an equal protection with all the other sections of the community. The object is to effect such changes, that there shall henceforth, in all governmental relations and actions, be no classes, but simply the people. This done, we shall have established the principle of universal liberty and opened the door for every man to enter into the possession of entire freedom under the dominion of equal laws. We shall then have all the individual freedom of the savage state with all the order and social harmony of the highest degree of civilization. This is the end to be gained as we have attempted to show in the article which precedes this.[9]

Now, our danger is not from an excess of individuality, but from centralization. The danger to be apprehended is from the strength, not the weakness of the government. Nearly the whole North has a strong tendency to merge the individual in the state. The North is enterprising, fond of undertaking great things, which are to be accomplished only by concentrating the power of masses, to be wielded by a few directing minds. This tendency is good, and springs from noble qualities; nevertheless it may, in its eagerness to reach its end, so centralize power, that the individual from an integer may become a mere fraction of the body politic. It therefore needs a check, a counterbalancing power, at least until the bases of legislation and social

[9][Ed. Reference may be to "Tendency of Modern Civilization," *Boston Quarterly Review* 1 (April, 1838): 200-38.]

action become so fixed, that there shall henceforth be no danger that the state will swallow up the individual.

This check is found in the strong individuality of the South, arising from the individual importance which each man there possesses in consequence of being himself a sort of petty sovereign. The southern planter keeps alive here the very element of individual freedom, represented by the feudal baron in Europe. The South therefore becomes the defender of individual freedom, as the North is the great advocate of social freedom. One represents the individual element, as the other does the social element of human nature. Hence the North demands a strong government, and the South a strong people. The North have been Federalists, the South Democrats. Now if we weaken the southern individuality before the northern centralization be fixed by laws, which leave the individual in possession of all his natural rights, we destroy the equilibrium between the individual and the state, and endanger the freedom of both. This is one reason why we regret the present agitation of the slave question, and why we see danger, not to the Union merely, but to liberty herself in the abolition movements.

This strong individuality of the South is the effect of the institution of slavery. The South without slaves would have had the same tendency to centralization that we have at the North. The cause of it here is the fact that no individual here feels himself of much importance by the side of the state. Individually he can do but little and feels himself small. Hence his strong desire to lean on the state, his uncommon fondness for associations, corporations, partnerships, whatever concentrates power and adds to individual strength. Then again our commercial and manufacturing pursuits also tend to make us desire somewhere the social power, we can call in to supply our individual deficiency in strength, capital, or skill. The southern planter is a sort of prince. Living in the center of his plantation, of his own principality, absolute lord and proprietor of a number of human beings, he feels that he, individually, is a man; that his rights as a man are of too much consequence to be swallowed up in the rights of the state. It is true, he ought to reflect that his Negroes have the same rights by nature, as himself, and so he will one day; but first he must secure his own rights. After he has secured his own rights as a man, and finds them no longer in danger from the northern tendency to centralization, he will perceive that he has, in defending them, been defending those of his Negroes; and then he will take up in earnest the matter of freeing them. To free them before were of no use, because before he has secured his own rights, there can be no security for theirs.

Here is the aid which slavery itself, through the providence of God, is made to contribute to liberty. Good always comes out of evil; and southern statesmen are nearer the truth than we commonly think them, when they say, that "southern slavery is the support of northern liberty." We confess, that as things were, we see no way in which freedom could have been established in this country, without the strong sense of individual freedom which slavery tends to produce in the planter. When the world has become Christianized, we shall support individual freedom on the maxim, that "you are as good as I"; but in an earlier stage of social and individual progress, we must do it by means of this other maxim, "I am as good as you." Now this feeling of personal importance, of egotism, if you please, was in no way, that we can see, to be introduced but by slavery, and without this, our Republic would not have had the checks and balances needed. The time will come, when this will not be needed, and then slavery will cease. Before, it will not.

Another means of saving individual freedom is in the sovereignty of the individual states. Destroy the states as sovereignties and make them only provinces of one consolidated state, and centralization swallows up everything. The individual finds the government so far from him, and his own share in it comparatively so insignificant, that he soon comes to feel himself individually of little or no importance, and when he so feels he ceases from all manly defense of his rights, and loses himself in the mass. Now the South, in consequence of having peculiar state institutions to defend, has been the foremost in defense of state rights, the sovereignty of the states in its plenitude, so far at least as all their internal affairs are concerned. It is because they have had slaves, not to be retained without the supreme control of all state institutions, that they have been so earnest in defense of state sovereignty. There is some analogy between the relation a state holds to the Union, and that held by the individual to the state. The arguments which defend the rights of the individual defend those of the state, and those which defend the rights of the state defend those of the individual. The South may have sometimes carried her doctrine of state rights too far, but her repeated assertion of it has done not a little to save American liberty.

Now, until we have settled the controversy about state rights and individual rights, and obtained the amplest security for both, it is as unwise as it is useless to touch the question of slavery. As yet there is no security given, or capable of being given, that the slave will be a free man even if declared free by the laws. Let this security be obtained before you attempt to emancipate him. He is now, paradoxical as it may seem, aiding in laying the foundation of universal liberty to universal man, and when the superstructure is reared, and the multitude throng its courts, he shall appear in the temple a free and equal worshiper.

Hard undoubtedly is it that liberty should be purchased at the slave's expense, and we confess we have no fondness for the idea; but less injustice is done the slave than we commonly imagine. The Negro on a southern plantation is unquestionably a superior being to the Negro in his native Africa. By being enslaved, he has been elevated, not degraded. Degraded he no doubt is in comparison with his master, but his captivity shall redeem his race. The years of his bondage shall not be so long, his labors, sufferings, and sacrifices in becoming a civilized man shall be far less, than ours have been. So far as we may judge from the past, it is the settled order of God's providence, that man shall be saved only by crucified redeemers. Man is never to receive freedom and civilization as a boon; he can obtain them only by toil and struggle and blood. Why it should be so is one of the mysteries of Providence for which we might perhaps assign some good reasons, but which we do not undertake to solve. The world is full of mysteries, and this is no more dark and perplexing than a thousand others. Time will clear it up.

19.

LETTER TO WILLIAM LLOYD GARRISON[1]

Liberator 8 (May 11, 1838): 73

Dear Sir, I read in your paper of yesterday,[2] some strictures upon the second number of the Boston Quarterly Review, and upon me personally, which I cannot in justice to myself suffer to pass without some comment. Had I less confidence in the purity of your motives, less respect for your talents and reverence for the warmth of your philanthropy, I should do by your strictures as I have invariably done with all similar ones—pass them over without notice. I have had much, one time and another, written and alleged against me, but I have rarely if ever appeared in my defense. My aim is to pursue the course I believe to be right, steadily and without much regard to the applauses I may obtain, or the censures I may call forth. If I do any good, it will live and be a sufficient protection to my character, while the opinion men may form of me will at longest be soon forgotten. But my regard for you personally, and my deep reverence for the rights of man of which you stand before the public as a conspicuous champion, induced me for once, to depart from my settled rule, and to complain of the injustice I believe you have done me.

I find no fault with you, sir, for not agreeing with me in opinion, nor for endeavoring to show that my views are not always correct.

[1]Mount Bellingham, April 14, 1838. [Ed. William Lloyd Garrison (1805-1879), the American abolitionist, and editor of *The Liberator*. Brownson's letter was originally published in the *Boston Reformer and Anti-Monoplist* 16 (April 20, 1838):1-2. Garrison reprinted the letter in his *The Liberator*. On this see Garrison to Samuel J. May, April 24, 1838, in *The Letters of William Lloyd Garrison*, vol. 2 *A House Divided Against Itself, 1836-1840*, edited by Louis Ruchames (Cambridge, Mass.: Harvard University Press, 1971), 347.]

[2][Ed. WLG, "Extraordinary Somerset," *The Liberator* 8 (April 13, 1838): 59. Garrison had supported the *BQR* when it was first published, but withdrew his support after Brownson's article on "Slavery-Abolitionism" of April 1838. Garrison had assumed that Brownson supported immediate abolition, which he had not, and, therefore, charged that Brownson had reversed his view in the "Slavery-Abolitionism" article. Garrison, therefore, recalled "every word of praise we have bestowed upon it [*BQR*] and now declare that it is as oppressive and servile in its spirit, and as unprincipled in its doctrines, as the veriest slave-driver at the south could desire."]

My publications are public property. Every man has a right to criticize them as much as he pleases, and with what scrutiny may seem to him proper. I shall neither complain nor be offended. I was gratified when you commended the first number of my Review.[3] You spoke kindly of it, and I thanked you then, and I thank you now, notwithstanding you have recalled what you then said. Had my present number met your approbation, I should also have been gratified. But I find no fault with you because it has not. I do not complain of you, since you do not approve it, for expressing your strong disapprobation of it. Still, sir, I think your allusions to me are unkind and needlessly caustic. But of this I do not complain. You are not the first man who has spoken unkindly of me. I complain that *you have denounced me to your readers without stating clearly my offences, or attempting to show that my statements at which you appear to be displeased are not true*. I complain that you call me hard names, make false charges against me, instead of refuting my arguments. Were you not a man of more than ordinary pretensions to purity of character and Christian perfection, I should not notice even this. But you, sir, are a reformer. You denounce the Christian churches as being below the Christian standard, and call out in a voice that rings through the land for a purer and more elevated morality than the world as ever yet seen, save in the person of Jesus of Nazareth. You are a professed peace man. You denounce war, all resort to force, to everything like coercion, and contend that we should all practice on the law of disinterested love as manifested in our Savior. I cannot but respect the man who is and does this, and I almost necessarily attach no little importance to his statements. But in proportion as I respect him, do I feel hurt, when he turns the force of his character against me, and denounces me as servile, as looking with complacency on the slave trade, as departing from my principles, and making myself a moral harlequin, and I put it to yourself, sir, whether, were you in my case you would deem such denunciation consistent with that elevated morality for which you contend?

You charge me with having "thrown a somerset," as you express yourself, with having once acted in concert with the abolitionists, spoken in their defense, eulogized their labors, and cheered them on to the conflict with slavery, but now in the twinkling of an eye facing right about, using a southern dialect, opposing abolition societies, and looking with complacency even upon the piratical slave trade.

[3][Ed. Garrison himself acknowledged that he had praised Brownson's review when it was first issued. See, "Extraordinary Somerset."]

You speak of me as having once advocated doctrines respecting the rights of man, which were sound and trustworthy, but as now putting forth doctrines so "detestable and fatuous," so inconsistent with those I recently cherished, that I can no longer be looked upon as worthy of any confidence. Now, I regard this as a serious charge. Had you called me a loco-foco, a horrid radical, an agrarian, or by any of the sobriquets which are terms of reproach in the estimation of those who are opposed to reformers, I could have borne it without uneasiness. But, sir, by many years of hard labor I have gained the name of a horrid radical, brash and headstrong innovator. This name is my all on earth. I have worn it so long that it is dear to me, and I am unwilling to have it torn from me.

Now, sir, you must be aware that it is hardly true to say that I have for some time acted in concert with abolitionists. I have from my earliest recollection been opposed to slavery, but I have never been in the technical sense of the term an abolitionist. Once I appeared, and once only, as a member of one of your society meetings.[4] I attended a meeting of the Anti-Slavery Society at Worcester last fall[5] and took an active part in its proceedings. I went there, sir, almost solely out of respect to yourself. On the evening before that meeting, two abolitionists called at my house, and told me an effort was to be made at Worcester to put down Mr. Garrison, and they wished I would go and do what I could to sustain him. I knew something of the nature of the contest; I had strong sympathy with you and no confidence in the clerical gentlemen who were opposed to you; and after much solicitation, and after being assured that the fact that I was not a member of the Anti-Slavery Society would be no bar in my way, I consented. The course I took when there you yourself well know. This is the only act of my life that could identify me with the abolitionists, and this I had not done, had I not wished to do what I could to save you from an unjust, and, in my opinion, a cruel persecution. Twice I have lectured on the subject of slavery, taking care, however, on both occasions, to state that I was not lecturing as a member of any society, but as an individual speaking for himself, and himself only. When your abolition friends have been impeded in their efforts to *discuss* the subject of slavery, I have spoken in their

[4][Ed. See *Liberator* 8 (January 5, 1838): 1-2, where Brownson gave a speech commemorating the death of Elijah P. Lovejoy at a December 22, 1837 meeting of the Massachusetts Anti-Slavery Society (MAS).]

[5][Ed. On the MAS September meeting in Worcester and Brownson's participation in it, see *The Liberator* 7 (October 6, 1837): 163. See also "Remarks of Dea[con] John Gulliver," *The Liberator* 7 (October 20, 1837): 170-71.]

favor, and vindicated as I could for them, as for all, the right of free discussion. When Lovejoy[6] was inhumanly murdered at Alton, for doing what he considered his duty, I spoke as I felt in regard to the tragical event, both in my own pulpit, and by request before the Anti-Slavery Society.[7] But, in neither instance, did I profess myself an abolitionist, or speak as an abolitionist, but as a man, as a friend to humanity and the advocate of the right of free discussion. When listening to the eloquent and thrilling appeals of your orators against slavery, I confess, sir, I have wished to join with you; I have for the moment been for "marching against Philip," and probably have said so; but all my friends know that my views of abolition were and ever have been essentially different from those of the abolitionists. How can it be said that I have acted in concert with them?

What is the "somerset" I have thrown? The opinions I have always expressed are that slavery is wholly and totally wrong; that no man has a right to hold his fellow man in slavery, that it is every man's duty to do whatever as a good Christian and a good citizen he may do to abolish it; that it is folly to pretend that slavery can be perpetuated, for it is doomed, and must be swept away before the onward march of civilization. These are the sentiments I have uniformly held; and these are the only sentiments I have ever advanced, that you can suppose me to have abandoned. You *will find all these, sir, clearly stated in the article you so strongly denounce*. I still hold them, and trust I ever shall. I am not conscious of having undergone any change on these points, since you have known my name, or I yours.

With regard to abolition societies, I have always been opposed to them, a fact which may be inferred from my having had no more connection with them. I am and always have been opposed to the associations which are so characteristic a feature of our times. Good I see in them; good I trust will grow out of them; good is the end they propose; and indications are they [are] of a good spirit abroad; but I

[6][Ed. Elijah P. Lovejoy (1802-1837) was the abolitionist editor whose murder by a pro-slavery mob in Alton, Illinois, became an abolitionist cause. Contemporary accounts include Edward Beecher, *Narrative of Riots at Alton: In Connection with the Death of Rev. Elijah P. Lovejoy* (Alton, Illinois: G. Holton, 1838) and Joseph Cammett Lovejoy and Owen Lovejoy, *Memoir of the Rev. Elijah P. Lovejoy* (New York, 1838). See also John Gill, *Tide Without Turning: Elijah P. Lovejoy and Freedom of the Press* (Boston: Starr King Press, 1958), Merton L. Dillon, *Elijah P. Lovejoy: Abolitionist, Editor* (Urbana, Illinois: University of Illinois Press, 1961), and *American National Biography*, 14: 4-5.]

[7][Brownson's speech is published in the *Liberator* 8 (January 5, 1838): 1-2.]

have always stood aloof from them. With a temperance society I have sometimes been connected; a part I have sometimes taken in Lyceums, but I believe I have never been a member of any other of the numerous voluntary associations of the day. I have stood aloof from these associations partly because I have had other things to attend to, partly because I have seen at the head of them, men with whose religious or political views I have been unable to sympathize, but mainly because I have regarded them as unfriendly to freedom, as striking at individual liberty, and merging the individual in the mass. I will, sir, be in bondage to no man. I love liberty too well to become a slave to a huge association, even though that association have for its object universal emancipation. Though I have never approved abolition societies, I have always contended that their members have a right to discuss the subject of slavery. Moreover, I have always had the deepest sympathy with the subject they have in view, and the greatest reverence for their zeal and disinterestedness. This I have always expressed, but more than this I am not aware of having ever uttered. No thing of this am I conscious of having contradicted. Where then is the "somerset" I have thrown?

I must needs think, sir, that you have not carefully read my article on slavery and abolitionism.[8] The account you give of it can hardly fail to make those of your readers who have not perused it, suppose that it is an article in defense of slavery. Now I am not willing to believe that you would knowingly misrepresent me. It makes up, I presume, no part of your religion to misrepresent any man. Yet that article is by no means in defense of slavery. If you have read it, you must know that it is not. It lays down principles as well as makes express statements which are directly opposed to slavery, and also to the doctrine of the South upon the subject. Its propositions are that slavery is wrong, that it can never be right to hold slaves, and that every slaveholder is bound to labor to remove it as soon as it can be. Is this in favor of slavery? It also asserts our right to discuss the subject of slavery, fully, freely and unreservedly, and bases our right to do this on the ground that we are men and have therefore the right to interest ourselves in whatever concerns humanity, and on the ground that the right of free discussion is one of the rights of man, which no government can legitimately restrain. Is this to defend slavery, or to speak a southern dialect? Moreover, I say in my article on

[8][Ed. A review of William Ellery Channing's *Slavery*, 4th ed.. rev. (Boston, 1836), Brownson's "Slavery-Abolitionism," *Boston Quarterly Review* 1 (April, 1838): 238-60.]

Grund's Americans, in the same number of the Review,[9] that the discussion of slavery cannot be, and *ought* not to be prevented, and that "so far as the abolitionists, are merely addressing arguments to the reason and consciences of the community against slavery, I am with them."[10] Does this look like abandoning the free principles I have generally been supposed to cherish?

The position I have assumed in my article, to which you as an abolitionist may object, are by no means positions in favor of slavery, or against the discussion of its character, and the use of all the moral and rational arguments in our power against it. This would seem to be all that a moral and a rational man need ask. In that article, I assume four positions to which I suppose you must, with your views, object. 1. A man may hold slaves and yet be a Christian. I regard slavery as a social institution, a wrong one indeed, but one which the individual cannot in his individual capacity correct. But before I allow him to be a Christian I contend that he must do *all he can* to correct it. 2. Societies, not for the *discussion* but for the *abolition* of slavery, since they are societies formed to control the institutions of foreign states, contravene international law. Consequently, if we mean to respect the rights of the slaveholding states, as states, we of the North cannot bond ourselves into abolition societies. You may say that humanity is older than state rights, that justice is paramount to law, and these both demand that we associate to free the slave. My article does not deny this. There may be cases when a man *may* set laws at defiance, and throw himself upon abstract justice. I would only add that a man should not do this hastily without deliberating long, and assuring himself in the most positive manner that justice requires him to do it. 3. The slave on a southern plantation is a superior being to the Negro in his native Africa. It is easy to sneer at this position, but that does not prove it false. I will only say such has been my deliberate conviction ever since I have thought on the subject, yet this opinion does neither make me "look with complacency on the piratical slave trade" nor lessen my abhorrence of slavery. 4. It is impossible to free the slaves before we have laws and institutions capable of guaranteeing the rights of man. No man's rights as a man are yet secure in this country; and till we have laws that will secure to the Negro the certainty of being a freeman, it is of little use to declare

[9][Ed. A review of Francis J. Grund (1805-63), *The Americans in their Moral, Social, and Political Relations*, 2 vols. in one (Boston: Marsh, Capen and Lyon, 1837) in "Grund's *Americans*," *Boston Quarterly Review* 1 (April, 1838): 161-92.]

[10][Ed. "Grund's *Americans*," 191.]

him free. You, I suppose would consider the slave freed, should he be declared free, and converted into a laborer at wages, with legally all the rights of citizenship. I consider that as things are he would be a slave in reality then as well as now, and his condition would be but slightly improved. I ask something more for the slave than the abolitionists propose to give him. These are I suppose the objectionable points in my article. I wish, sir, it had pleased you to have taken them up and shown wherein they are unsound, instead of speaking so harshly of me as you did. You know my article was calm and candid; I called the abolitionists no hard names; I did not sneer at them, nor ridicule them; I merely stated fairly and in as unobjectionable a form as I could, my honest objections to abolition societies. Was I to be denounced for this, and represented in a light which you know must be abhorrent to my feelings, and that too by a champion of free discussion and of the rights of man? Why was I not to be met in a spirit as candid, as little abusive, as the one I myself displayed?

If, sir, you had reflected a moment, you must have perceived that to speak of me as you did, was not the way to convince me that my objections to abolition societies are unfounded. If you wished to convince me of my errors, you took altogether a wrong course. If you intended your remark as a rebuke, you overlooked the fact that I am also a man as well as you, with notions of right and wrong for myself, and that I am more likely to receive them as an abuse than as a brotherly reproof. If you intended to render me odious to all whom you are capable of influencing, I would ask, if it comport with your idea of Christianity to blacken the reputation of those whose crime consists in their not agreeing with you in opinion? Is it a part of the policy of abolitionists to overawe, browbeat, denounce every man who does not agree in all respects with them? Is this to respect free discussion, to defend the rights of man? Is it less important to respect the rights of a white man than it is of a black man!

Again, sir, you knew that my Review would be opened to an article from yourself or any of your friends who should feel disposed to take the opposite side of the question. If my views are as "detestable and as fatuous" as you consider them, it were a very easy matter to disprove them, and by fair and manly argument to arrest their evil tendency. I wish, therefore, that you had forborne somewhat your severity, especially since you are a friend to free discussion, and know that so far as depends on me, free discussion may be had.

I have expressed myself thus freely to you, because I have felt hurt in being denounced as an enemy to freedom, as taking unworthy views of the rights of man, and as abandoning the free principles

I have professed to cherish. If any man can read the second number of the Boston Quarterly Review, and call its editor a man of servile spirit, or fail to see in him a fearless friend of human freedom, a bold, uncompromising defender of universal liberty to universal man, he can do more than I can conceive it possible for a man to do. If you can show me a man that takes broader or more comprehensive views of freedom than are taken in my essay on Democracy[11] and in that on the Tendency of Modern Civilization,[12] I will bow down to him with a reverence but little short of idolatry, and I will consent then to be called the advocate of principles servile and cringing enough to justify your epithets of "detestable and fatuous." I am willing, sir, any day to compare in this respect my writings with your own, and abide the issue.

You must bear with me, sir, yet longer. I respect you as the eloquent and indefatigable friend of the slave. You regard the slave. Slavery of the Negro is the chief evil you see, though I am ready to admit, not the only one. For this I give you no slight praise. But I, sir, see other evils, and if not greater ones, at least evils which must be removed before we can remove that one. I will not yield to any man, not even to yourself, in my sympathy with the Negro slave. I will go as far as you or any other man in my efforts to give him his freedom. But I cannot reach him. He is buried beneath the rubbish of the old social fabric. Do not call me his enemy because instead of crying out, "the slave is dying where he is, release him, release him," I set myself at work to clear away that rubbish with what strength and diligence I can command. I regard the progress and triumph of true democracy in the non-slaveholding states, as the certain abolition of slavery at the South. Just so much as you and I do to bring out the rights of man as man, and to cause them to be respected here at the North, just so much do we do for the abolition of slavery at the South, even though we never mention the abolition of slavery by name or have it in our minds.

You early engaged in the work of freeing the slave. You have struggled hard, you have suffered much; you have had infinitely harder things said about you, than you have said about me. You have done much. You have gained a name that is linked with your country's history. If much is said against you, many voices cheer you onward. Voices from across the Atlantic come to you as angels-music, and sustain you in your severest struggles. Abolition has made you one of

[11][Ed. See Chapter 14 in this volume.]
[12][Ed. See Chapter 17 in this volume.]

the great men of the nation. If, therefore, you have suffered for it, you have gained something by it. When you commenced you were alone, but you are alone no longer. You have already a mighty army, and are irresistible. How can you remember your sacrifices now, or sympathize thoroughly with reformers who are less noted?

I, too, early commenced the work of freeing the slave, but not of the Negro slave alone. My voice was raised against slavery, I will venture to say, before yours was, and that, too, against every species of slavery. I have warred against the slavery of the poor and of the rich, of the one to want, and the other to luxury, against the slavery of the mind, and of the heart. I have been less fortunate than you. My work has been vaster and yet less showy. I have labored steadily, and with untiring perseverance, in poverty, in neglect, alone, unaided, uncheered. Rarely has there a voice bid me be of good courage; rarely has the hand of fellowship been extended to me. Opposition I have encountered, but open opposition that I could meet and crush, not often. My fate has been to persevere in my efforts in the cause of freedom amid neglect, that most trying of all oppositions the reformer can encounter. I have persevered, sir, amid trials more difficult to bear than yours have been for as many years as you have advocated the rights of the Negro. I have done it, too, without any of the encouragement you have had, either from fast friends or avowed enemies. Is it not ungenerous, then, on your part to attempt to take from me the only thing which has sustained me, the conviction that I am a friend to free principles. Why hold I the position I do in this city?[13] Is it not because I have spoken out for the oppressed and the downtrodden? I have suffered for free principles, long and intensely, and therefore I love them. I love them today as well as ever I did, and I cannot consent to be branded as their enemy because I do not believe that abolitionists have a monopoly of them, or take the only or the best methods of raising them to universal empire.

The charge you bring against me affects me singularly. I have ever been reproached for entertaining views directly the opposite of those you represent me as holding. I have, however, often been accused of sudden and unaccountable changes of opinion. The fact is, the world, so far as it has concerned itself with the matter, has done

[13][Ed. The reference here is not entirely clear. It may refer to his position as Unitarian minister of the Society for Union and Progress, but more than likely it refers to his editorship of the *Boston Quarterly Review* or his post as Steward of the United States Marine Hospital in Chelsea, a position he obtained in January of 1837.]

me justice in neither respect. An advocate for universal freedom, I have always been; that rash, violent, heedless radical, I have been called, I have never been. My position has not always been the same; but my opinions, except as to growth, I can say have undergone comparatively very few changes. The reason for the changes which one makes in his position are rarely comprehended by the world. These changes may be great while the modifications of opinion which justify them are almost too slight to be indicated by words. We should therefore view them with great charitableness, and not be in haste to accuse a man of throwing a somerset because we see not clearly the reasons which govern his conduct. Now you convey the idea to your readers that I have contradicted in the second number of my Review, principles I laid down in my first number. You doubtless really believe that there is a discrepancy between the doctrines of the one and those of the other. Now I see no such discrepancy, admit no such contradiction. There is nothing in my Review of Whittier[14] that is contradicted in my article on slavery. I defy you, with all your sagacity, to point out a single principle in one number that is not consistent with everything of mine in the other. There is not a sentence nor a word in my first number so far as concerns the doctrine it teaches that I would recall or that I could not write with my present convictions.

Principles, sir, are eternal and universal. In stating them, the philosopher has and should have no reference to time or place; but the practical man who comes forward to embody those principles, or to translate them into actions, is bound by every law of morality to regard both. This sentence, sir, may serve as a key to any discrepancy you may seem to find in my writings, and to the misapprehension people have labored under in regard to me. In stating principles I aim to state them in their universality and eternity. But when I come to the question of practice, then I regard the time and the place. Nothing can come before its time. The human race is in progress. It goes onward, but it is step by step. One step only can be taken at a time. Which is the step to be taken *now*? This is the practical question. With regard to this question my mind sometimes may vacillate. From the best observations I can make, I conclude it is *this*; I accordingly call attention to it; subsequently, as the result of further inquiry, and of having a broader field of observation before me, I may

[14][Ed. "Whittier's Poems," a review of John Greenleaf Whittier's *Poems Written during the Progress of the Abolition Question in the United States, between the years* 1830 *and* 1838 (Boston: I. Knapp, 1837), in *Boston Quarterly Review* 1 (January, 1838): 21-33.]

conclude *this other* step is the one, and govern myself accordingly. Here is the principal amount of the changes which can be alleged against me. They all come to this, that I thought yesterday that one piece of work should be done before another, and today perhaps, I think differently, *as to that question*, but precisely the same as to the value of the work itself, and the importance and necessity of doing it.

One word more and I end this protracted letter. I made my first appearance before the world as an advocate for reform, a radical reform in church and state and in the individual. I have ever continued the same. I have never faltered, I have never wavered in my efforts for reform. The progress of man and society, the creation or establishment of the kingdom of God on earth, has ever been present to my thoughts, the object of my aspirations, and the end of all my exertions. Yet, sir, I will own to you, that as I increase in years and experience, as I go deeper into the philosophy of man and of history, I become less and less disposed to countenance revolutionary movements, and less and less sanguine in my hopes of much good from sudden and violent changes. My faith in the final result, in the indestructible nature of the law of progress, is every day more and more confirmed; but I expect less and less from immediate results. I look to time and the slow but sure action of innumerable causes which I see at work, but over which we have, at best, only a partial control. I keep at work, aim to fulfill the command, "What thy hand findeth to do, do it with all thy might" [Eccles. 9:10] and rest confident that in due time the fruits of my labors, so far as they have been in the Lord, will appear. This may seem to you to be cold, chilling, "detestable and fatuous"; but, sir, it is the conclusion to which years of hard thinking and still harder buffetings with the world have finally brought me, and I believe no one will accuse me of any want of warmth and earnestness—at least of temperament.

Allow me, sir, in conclusion to subscribe myself, notwithstanding our differences of opinion as to the best means of promoting universal emancipation, your friend and brother.

20.

RELIGION AND POLITICS[1]

Boston Quarterly Review 1 (July, 1838): 310-33

This is a work written with some ability, possibly with a sincere intention, and probably for a good end. Most religious people, not accustomed to much reflection on the subject it treats, will think it an admirable book and be inclined to receive it as a sort of second gospel. In our judgment it is the production of a man who has very little knowledge of religion in general and none of Christianity in particular. The author designs to point out the relation which should subsist between Christianity and civil government, and to place certain matters, which have not hitherto been very well understood, in a new and clearer light; but so far as we can come at the results of his *Inquiry*, he merely makes "confusion worse confounded."[2]

Who the author of this book is we know not; but, be he who he may, we should like to know his name, that we might give him an immortality, which he has not secured to himself by this production. He belongs to the "Blue Ruin" party, both in politics and religion. He is a genuine croaker, though somewhat cunning, and withal, capable of croaking in a tolerable voice, and is less disagreeable than most of his family connections. Our country, to believe him, is assuredly ruined; the altars of religion are all desecrated; pestilential heresies are rife in the land; Socinians and Jews, and even unbelievers, vote, and are sometimes voted for; and the awful visitations of God's wrath cannot be delayed much longer. One may almost fancy him a second Jonah, lately disgorged from some whale's belly, come to denounce divine judgments upon another Nineveh. The good people of America, it is devoutly hoped, may take warning and repent, ere the "forty days" be run out.

[1][Ed. Review of Henry Whiting Warner's [1787-1875], *An Inquiry into the Moral and Religious Character of the American Government* (New York: Wiley & Putnam., 1838). Arthur Schlesinger, Jr., *Age of Jackson*, 352, n4, attributed this pamphlet not to Warner but to Theodore Frelinghuysen (1787-1862), at one time a United States Senator of New Jersey (1829-35). On Frelinghuysen, see *American National Biography* 8: 456-57.]

[2][Ed. John Milton, *Paradise Lost*, Book 2, Line 996.]

The sum of all his complaints is, he tells us, "that one way or another, that religion, which has given us a name among the states of Christendom, and which many of us deem essential to our future well-being, as a people, is everywhere *politically set at nought*; regarded as an outlaw to the institutions of the country; a feather in the scale of its interests; as useless, if not discreditable in public life; and in reference to the elective sovereignty itself not to be thought of!" Surely this is a grievous complaint. But on what facts does the author rest for its justification? And what kind of political recognition of religion does he demand?

The facts, which justify the complaint, and prove all here set forth, are: 1st. President Jefferson refused to appoint a fast when some of his political opponents wanted one, for the purpose of fasting over some of his political sins, and alleged in his own defense, that he could not find any power delegated to him by the Constitution of the United States, authorizing him to interfere with religious doctrines, institutions, discipline, or exercise. 2dly. The refusal on the part of General Jackson to appoint a fast, to keep off the cholera, when certain religious people requested him to do it. 3dly. The assertion of a United States Senator,[3] that a reference to the Bible, in the Senate, as authority, was not fortunate, that book not being the statute book of that body. 4thly. The refusal on the part of Congress to stop the mail from running on Sunday. 5thly. The fact that the New York Legislature, during its last session, refused to appoint a chaplain. 6thly. The fact, that the legislature of pious Connecticut debated the question, whether they would not do the same. 7thly. Electors do not inquire whether candidates for office are orthodox or not, and orthodox electors do sometimes vote for anti-orthodox, or heterodox candidates.

These are the facts which justify his complaint and authorize him to call our government an irreligious one. What would he have as a remedy for the evil? What kind of connection between religion and politics does he demand? A union of church and state? No; that is not to be thought of. Have the state become the servant of the church? Most likely; but he does not say so. Have the state decree a body of Divinity, which all must embrace, a ritual all must observe? No. What then? Enact that the Bible is the holy word of God; that no man who does not profess to believe it shall be eligible to any

[3][Ed. The Senator may have been Colonel Richard M. Johnson (1780-1850) from Kentucky who had opposed the Sunday mails in the 1820s. On Johnson, see EW 1:268 n. 2.]

office; that to deny the existence of God, the truth of the doctrine of the Trinity, or the inspiration of the Old and New Testaments, is blasphemy, to be punished as a criminal offence; to prohibit by strong penal enactments all profane swearing, and all Sabbath-breaking, and to appoint fasts whenever the clergy or the church say the occasion demands them.

The author of the book contends that ours is a Christian commonwealth, and therefore infers that all which comes or may come under the denomination of Christian ethics should be legally enforced. He divides Christianity into two parts, *Ecclesiastical Christianity* and the *Ethics* of Christianity. The first belongs exclusively to the church, which is a body distinct from all civil polity, and raised infinitely above the reach of the civil legislature; it asks and will submit to no civil protection or control. The ethics of Christianity are binding on legislatures, and are proper objects of legislation; it is the duty of civil governments to respect them and to cause them to be respected.

That the government of this country is a Christian government is inferred from the fact that in no case is it positively declared not to be. The Constitution of the United States repudiates some of the abuses of Christianity, but says nothing against Christianity itself. The first settlers of this country were Christians and in nearly all cases designed to found a Christian commonwealth, and did found one. Nearly all the state constitutions originally recognized Christianity, and the greater part of them do it even now. Christianity is part and parcel of the common law of England [doubted],[4] which was brought here by our fathers, and which is still in force. The majority are Christians; and as the majority have an absolute right to rule, it follows that they have a right to form a Christian commonwealth and to insist upon Christianity as the religion of the government. Moreover, in practice, the government in all its branches—saving the cases of Presidents Jefferson and Jackson, the majority of the committee on Sabbath mails, the New York legislature in dispensing with a chaplain—has always recognized Christianity and respected it as the religion of the country.

Ours being a Christian commonwealth, it follows that our government must regard Christian ethics as its own, and that it can have no right to introduce pagan, Jewish, or Mahometan ethics; and it also follows that none but Christians can really be citizens or members of the commonwealth. Governments are instituted to protect

[4][Ed. Brackets in original.]

rights, not to create them; and its mission is to protect the rights of all its citizens. For this end the American government was instituted. It was instituted by Christians to nurse and maintain their rights as Christians. Christians did not institute it for unbelievers, Socinians, and Jews, but for themselves. Its functionaries are then under no obligation to consult the prejudices, beliefs, or pretended consciences of these. These have no rights in a Christian commonwealth; and if they choose to live in one must take up with such franchises as Christians choose to grant them.

This, then, is the amount of freedom secured to us, or designed to be secured to us, by our boasted free institutions. It is freedom to Christians but to none others. The people here comprise not the whole population, but the Christian majority. Christians are the favored class. The rest are out of the pale of citizenship, are denied to have any rights, and are reduced to virtual slavery, liable at any moment to be prosecuted and punished as criminals. This is the doctrine of a professed Christian, and of a pretended friend of liberty! After avowing this doctrine, he has the effrontery to say Christianity is favorable to liberty! So is Christianity favorable to liberty, but not such Christianity, not such liberty as this.

The pretense set up by some religious people that our government is a Christian government, that our commonwealths are Christian commonwealths, deserves more than a passing notice. Mischief lurks beneath it. If it be sustained, we undergo a revolution and must bid farewell to liberty. The several states or commonwealths, which form the confederacy of the United States, are not Christian commonwealths, in the sense in which our author and those who think with him, contend they are. The design of our fathers when first landing in this country was not to found a Christian commonwealth. The idea that brought them here was liberty, still more than it was religion. Their dominant idea was freedom. They wanted and they aimed to establish a free commonwealth. They may not have fully possessed their idea, they may not have generalized it to the extent it will bear, but nevertheless they have it from the first moment fermenting in them.

The age in which the colonies were planted was an age in which all great ideas appeared in a theological envelope. Our fathers wanted liberty. This was their first want. But they had no conception of a liberty worth having, not founded on justice. In this they were right. Liberty is derived from justice. But justice, in their minds, was Christianity, and Christianity was their theology and church polity. Hence the reason why Christianity held the place it did in the commonwealths they founded. Their mistake was a natural one, an inevitable one in their age. It consisted merely in taking their notions of Christian ethics as their measure of natural right, instead of taking, as we do, man's innate sense of natural right, as the proper measure of Christian ethics. If they disfranchised all but Christians, it was not because they sought to found a commonwealth for Christians alone, but because they regarded all who were not Christians, either as having not as yet risen to man's estate, or as having forfeited their rights as men, and fallen into the class of the guilty. They did not know, did not admit, that men were men, and possessed of all the rights of men, though opposed to the Christian faith, and they made that crime, which is not crime; but they did not do this to secure a monopoly to those who professed to be Christians, but to secure a liberty supported on justice, an order of government founded on their highest idea of right, and maintaining it in the state.

That the real idea of our fathers was liberty, that liberty was the dominant idea of the institutions they founded, is evident from the history of these institutions. The institutions of a nation rarely if ever receive a new idea. The history of the nation is but the history of the practical development of the ideas with which it starts. A theocracy can never grow naturally into a government in which the interests of man are paramount to all others; a monarchy never softens down into an aristocracy, especially not into a democracy. The old nation is destroyed, and a new one takes its place, whenever a change similar to any of these is observed to occur. The natural growth of a nation is the natural unfolding of the ideas with which it begins its career. If theocracy had been the dominant idea of our fathers, if their leading design had been to found Christian commonwealths, then the natural growth of our institutions would have manifested this idea, this design, more and more clearly. But instead of this, the idea of liberty, of the rights of man, is the idea which has been gradually unfolding itself from our institutions. Every advance, every change has tended to bring out this idea. The tendency from the first has been to prune away whatever conceals the majesty of man or overshadows his rights. Church membership was at first made a prerequisite to citizenship, because at first it was thought none others were really men. But this is no longer the case because we have ascertained that individuals, who are not church members, may be men. Property qualifications for the exercise of the right of suffrage have, in most cases, been abandoned; for it has been ascertained that a man has rights, though he have not property; religious tests have been dispensed with, not because the people have become less religious, but because it has been found that religious tests are inconsistent with the rights of man. In every case of amendment to our state constitutions, the idea of the rights of man has been brought out more clearly, and liberty extended or surrounded with new guarantees. This fact is decisive. It proves that freedom, not religion, is the dominant idea of our institutions. Our commonwealths are free commonwealths, rather than Christian commonwealths. Their genius is liberty, not Christianity, *anthropocratic*, if we may use the term, not theocratic.

Now, should we find in our institutions certain provisions favorable to a theocracy—which we take it is what is meant by a Christian commonwealth, in the sense the term is used by this author and his friends—we must regard them as exceptions, anomalies, which are not yet brought under the general rule, not as indications of their real character and design. All these provisions must be interpreted in favor of liberty, as much in accordance with the genius of our institutions as they will bear. The fact that the author finds some such provisions in the constitutions and laws of the several states is not, and should not be regarded by him as a proof, that our commonwealths are Christian commonwealths, in his sense of the term; but merely as a proof, that many of our ideas are yet in their theological envelope, and that we have not brought all our constitutional and statutory provisions into perfect keeping with our great, our dominant, idea of liberty.

Assuming then, as we do, that the great idea, the genius, of our government, is that of a government instituted for nourishing and maintaining the rights of man, we deny that a Christian as such has any preeminence over any other man. We speak now of Christianity as a positive system of religion, a positive institution. In this sense Christianity is younger than man. Man existed in all his integrity and with all his rights as a man before it was instituted. His rights as a man are older than his claims as a Christian. They are not derived from Christianity, they are not dependent on Christianity; then their enjoyment and exercise cannot be made to rest under a government which professes to recognize and is bound to maintain them on the fact of embracing Christianity. Give Christianity, or take it away, man and his rights remain the same. Governments, then, that are instituted for the purpose ours are, have precisely the same rights to recognize and maintain in the case of him who is not a Christian, as in the case of him who is. If there are any provisions in the constitutions and laws of our several states in opposition to this, they are inconsistencies, incongruities, made null and void, in justice, by the genius of our institutions.

It behooves professed Christians to beware how they controvert this position. On what ground will they do it? On what ground will a man pretend that he has a right to be a Christian, if he denies to his brother the right not to be one? The right of any one to be a Christian can be legitimated only by the admission of that more general right of every man to choose his own religion. And, as religion is in all cases a matter of opinion, of belief, the right of a man to choose his own form of religion can be legitimated only by admitting a right still more general, that of the entire liberty of every man to form and express his own opinions. This last right is virtually recognized and secured in those constitutional provisions which guarantee us the freedom of speech and the press. The greater always includes the less. It would be absurd to admit that we have the liberty to propagate by speech or by the press our opinions, whatever they may be, and yet to deny us the right to form our opinions by the free action of our own understandings.

The Christian claims protection under our government, not by virtue of the fact that he is a Christian, but by virtue of the fact that he is a man, and because it is one of the rights of man to be protected in the peaceable enjoyment of his religious belief. If he withhold this right from another, if he prohibit another from the free enjoyment of his religious belief then he denies that this right to the enjoyment of one's own religious belief is one of the rights of man. In doing this, he denies his own right as a man to be a Christian, and bases his right to protection in his religious faith on mere accident, on the accident that he lives under a government favorable to his views, or that he has the good fortune to be of the majority. But, if he claim his protection on the ground that he is a man, and ought not to be molested in his belief, then his plea is equally good for every other man, whatever may be that other man's belief.

Lay down the rule that government has a right to protect one belief in preference to another, or to make any exceptions to a man in any case on account of his belief, and where shall we stop? If the state may declare it necessary to believe in a God in order to be a citizen with all the rights and immunities of a citizen, then it may declare what God must be believed in, whether it must be the Hindoo God, the Greek and Roman God, the Jewish God, the Mahometan God, the Catholic God, the Calvinistic God, the materialist's God, or the spiritualist's God. If it may do this, it may do more. It may declare the Bible to be the word of God; and if this, still more; it may determine the interpretation that may be put upon the Bible; it may decide whether the Trinitarian or the Unitarian commentators shall be the orthodox commentators whom it is lawful to read. In fine, once begin, there is no stopping place, this side of absolute religious despotism. Is our author in favor of this? O no. The doctrines of religion belong to the church, and the state may not meddle with them. What then? He merely asks that Christians be protected in their religion. What, protected in the enjoyment of their religion, as all men are protected in their opinions? If this be all, he asks nothing unreasonable; but he asks what he already has. This, however, is not all. He asks as a Christian to be protected in his religion, not only so far as concerns his own freedom of professing it, but also in preventing anybody from opposing it. He thinks it a grievous wrong that in this country, where the majority are Christians, he must submit to hear the truth and sacredness of that religion he embraces and reveres, questioned and even ridiculed. He wishes not that anybody should be required by law to believe it, but merely that nobody shall be permitted by law to oppose it, and that whoever does oppose it shall not only be without note, but also without civil rights in the commonwealth.

Very well. On what grounds does he make this modest demand? Is what he asks one of the rights of man? Does he claim it on the ground that he is a man, and therefore has a right to profess his faith without being opposed or questioned? If so, his plea is equally available in the case of any one who adopts a different faith. If the atheist may not question his faith in God, then may he not question the atheist's faith in No-God. If the disbeliever in the inspiration of the Old and New Testaments may not speak against his belief in that inspiration, what right has he to speak against disbelief in it? If he have a right to demand that the legislature decree it blasphemy to deny the doctrine of the Trinity, the Unitarian has an equal right to demand that it decree it blasphemy to assert it. Will our author do as he would be done by, treat the beliefs and disbeliefs of others as he would have his own treated? Not at all. He wants a preference shown to himself and all of his way of thinking. Very well, we say again. But we beseech him to tell us on what ground he legitimates his right to the preference he demands. Not on the simple ground that he is a man, for all men are equal as men, and he must give what he asks to receive, and this excludes all idea of preference. On what ground then? That his faith is true, and therefore must not be opposed? But they, who oppose him, say his faith is false, and therefore ought in justice to truth and humanity to be opposed. Why shall the government credit him rather than them?

But our author claims this preference to his faith because it is the faith of the majority. The majority are Christians; and as the majority have a right to rule, they have a right to enact that their religion shall be respected as the religion of the country, which may not be lawfully denied. But will he admit the soundness of this argument? We ask why the majority have any more right to decree that their religion is the religion of the land than the minority have to decree the same thing of theirs? We should like to know why a man has any more right to have his religion respected because he is in the majority than he would have if he were in the minority? Are the rights of man matters dependent on the will of the majority? Does one's rights as a man vary as he chances to be in the majority or in the minority? What may be one's rights today, then, may not be one's rights tomorrow, for majorities may change.

Our author, we presume, is a Christian as he understands Christianity. There are countries in which Christianity is in a feeble minority. Suppose our author should have his lot cast in one of those countries, would he think that it would be wrong for him to profess his religion there, or that it would be right, if born there, that he should not be permitted the freedom of the commonwealth, because the majority embraced a religion different from his own? Jesus and the apostles were once a small minority, a little band with the whole world against them. Were they justified in opposing the religious notions of the majority? And were those Roman laws wise and just, which required the early Christians to respect the pagan Gods? Luther and Calvin were in a small minority; they denounced the religion of the majority. Were they right, or were they wrong? The author has arraigned the report of the majority of the committee of Congress on Sunday Mails.[5] As that report was the report of the majority, would our author, had he been on that committee, have deemed himself justified in making a minority report against it? Had he been in Congress at the time, would he have spoken against it, in the minority, as he would have been? Nay, was he not there? And did he not make a speech there against the opinions of the majority of the House? This book reminds us very much of a certain speech made on the occasion by a distinguished Senator from New Jersey,[6] who, for aught

[5][Ed. On the Sunday mails controversy, see Introduction of EW, 1: 268-75, 330.]

[6][Ed. Brownson is referring to Senator Theodore Frelinghuysen (1787-1862) who was in Arthur M. Schlesinger, Jr.'s view "the special champion of religion in politics." He was considered by many, not just Brownson, to be the author of *An Inquiry*. See *Age of Jackson*, 351-52.]

we know may be its author. But what right would he have had to say anything against the opinions of the majority? If the majority have a right to prohibit all speech against their opinions, the rule is absolute; and it applies to the majority of a committee, or of Congress, as well as to any other majority. Will the author follow his doctrine to this, its logical result? If not, where will he stop? Why stop there, rather than somewhere else?

We have spoken of the rights of man. Now the rights of man go with man wherever he goes. He does not acquire them by being in the majority, nor does he forfeit them by falling into the minority. The Christian has a right to be protected in his honest belief, and in the peaceable exercise of his religion, because this is one of the rights of man. Faith and worship are individual matters; and so long as they are not made pretexts for injuring the rights of others, the individual has a perfect right to enjoy them. It is the grossest tyranny, either by legislative enactments or by public opinion, to make him suffer for them. If the Christian has the right, as a man, to defend his honest belief, the deist, the Jew, the atheist must have the same right. A law making it criminal to disavow faith in God, in the Scriptures, or in the Trinity, is as much an infringement upon the rights of man, as a law making it criminal to profess to believe either one or the other. If one man has as much right to avow atheism as another has theism, one must have as much right to speak against theism as the other has against atheism. If the majority today have a right to decree that Christianity is the religion of the country, and to make it criminal to speak against it, it may decree, if it choose, the reverse tomorrow. If the majority have the absolute right to rule, it has the same right to make a law against asserting the existence of a God, that it has against denying his existence. All which our infidels want then to justify them in making strong penal enactments against Christianity, is merely to become the majority. Has our author thought of this?

Christianity itself is decidedly against this author. It recognizes the great brotherhood of men, and teaches that all are equal. It teaches this when it commands us to do unto others as we would have others do unto us. This command can be legitimated only on the ground that man is everywhere equal to man. Man being everywhere equal to man, it follows that whatever it is proper for one man to do by another, it is proper that other should do by him. Men are men, whatever their beliefs. The respect one claims for his belief, he must show to the belief of others. This is the Christian law. Our author as a Christian is bound to obey it. As he would have infidels treat his belief, so let him treat theirs then. If he does this, how can he demand the preference to be shown to his faith by the government, which he has pointed out, and on which he so earnestly insists?

The writer falls into the common mistake in relation to liberty of conscience. He thinks he has a right to enjoy liberty of conscience, and that his conscience, as a Christian, should be respected. Is he not correct, justifiable in this? But he forgets that other men have consciences as well as he, and that government is as much bound to respect their consciences as his. He forgets that to construe one's own liberty of conscience, so as to interfere with another's liberty of conscience, is to misconstrue it.

We hold to liberty of conscience. Conscience we regard as the supreme law for the individual in all cases whatsoever. It is more ultimate than the *lex scripta*, than the *lex non scripta*, of paramount authority to all creeds, confessions, rituals, dictates of fashion, public opinion, or decrees of the majority. It is to the individual, the voice of God, which he may not disregard without sin, and which he is bound to follow, though it lead to reproach, poverty, the dungeon, the scaffold, or the cross. But by the very fact, that we recognize the supremacy of the individual conscience, we necessarily restrict the sphere of its supremacy to the individual himself. Conscience cannot be divided against itself. Consequently the persuasion one may have, which would lead him to force or restrain the exercise of conscience in another, can never be conscience. The liberty of conscience in each individual must then be always so construed as to leave an equal liberty in every other individual. They pervert conscience, who make it the plea for exercising a control over others, which they will not suffer others to exercise over them. One's conscience leads him to observe the Sabbath. It is well. Let him obey his conscience. But let him at the same time remember that he must not impose his conscience on another. That other has a conscience of his own, which is his supreme law.

Our author we suppose would, in part, admit this. But he does it on the ground that unbelievers have no conscience. We shall not dispute this ground. We should prefer to question whether he who assumes it has a conscience or not. The man who really supposes that unbelievers are destitute of moral feelings and moral judgments, or who supposes them in general less conscientious than Christians, has no right to set himself up as one capable of instructing the commonwealth. If he assert it without seriously believing it, what is his own conscience worth? Unbelievers are to be compassionated because they want that serenity of soul, that inward repose which faith alone can give; but we are never to suppose them necessarily more deficient in the moral qualities of human nature than the rest of mankind. Indeed, in the majority of instances, we presume, the unbeliever is so called, because he has more faith than his neighbors. We shall make little progress in the work of converting unbelievers to Christianity, till we learn that they are men, to be respected and loved as brothers. The arguments which will convince their understandings, or win their hearts, are not those which exclude them from the freedom of the commonwealth, and deny them to be human beings. Christianity is most grievously wronged when we make it the pretext for imposing on others burdens, which we would not submit to have others impose on us. Jesus wept with unbelievers and died on the cross that they might have faith in man and in God. It was in enduring, not in inflicting, legal penalties that the early Christians arrested the attention of the world and prepared the way for its conversion.

"Our fathers," says this author, "had no conception of some of the modern notions of what are called state-rights; and I believe they would have stood amazed at the kind of suggestion now current in the country, that a government, such as they have left us, so respectful of the rights of man, ought yet to be administered with as little avowed deference as possible for those of the Supreme Being." What is meant by the rights of the Supreme Being? Are governments instituted for God, or for man? Is it their especial province to guard the rights of God? Does God stand in need of human governments, and look to them for protection? God is his own guardian, his own avenger. He asks no aid of man, no human arm to be raised in his defense. But suppose it not so, we would ask, how can we better respect his rights than by protecting those of his children? If we have studied Christianity to any purpose, it teaches us that we serve and honor God by loving and serving his children, our brethren.

Our author contends that we ought to respect Christianity legally, politically, because Christianity is favorable to liberty. If he means by this that our laws should be enacted and administered in accordance with the great principles of justice, meekness, and love, which constitute the essence of Christianity, assuredly we have no controversy with him. We contend earnestly, in season and out of season, for the same. But if he means that Christianity is to be recognized legally, politically, in its character of a positive religion, we do not agree with him. Religion is an individual concernment. It is what there is most intimate and holy in man. Governments have no right to interfere with it. They must put off their shoes when they approach it, and stand in awe before it, as Moses did before the burning bush. Its place is in the interior sanctuary of the individual heart, where it should be screened from all human observation, save as it manifests itself through a sweet and gentle, a just and beneficent life.

Christianity, no doubt, forms the moral sense of this community, and therefore should always be consulted by government and its functionaries; but it is Christianity only as the religious name for what we usually term natural morality, or in its broadest sense, natural right. In this sense, nearly all men embrace it, and all desire to have it respected. But to conclude from this to legal and political sanctions, either to the dogmas or discipline of Christianity, as a positive system of religion and ethics, though our author does it, is bad logic. He concludes from this, if we understand him, though he says not so in just so many words, that the denial of the existence of God, of the inspiration of the Bible, profane swearing, and Sabbath-breaking, should be deemed offences against the peace of the community. Here is his error. He will find few atheists or deists, who will question the gospel morality, or who will differ with him in any rational interpretation of natural justice. The moral worth of men, so far as regards their actions towards one another, is not to be judged of by their faith, or their want of faith, in moral or religious codes. Unbelievers, saving the positive duties of the church, are, in general, as good Christians as Christians themselves. They have as warm a love for man, take as much interest in the progress of man and society, are as honest, as upright, as conscientious, as believers. They are no more immoral, unless conventionalism be called morality, than any other class of the community. The charge of licentiousness brought against them, if understood to mean licentiousness in regard to natural morality, or even the moral precepts of the gospel, cannot be sustained.

The error of our author and those who agree with him is in confounding *natural* and *positive* morality. Natural morality is that which is founded in human nature, and is the same wherever man is; positive morality rests merely on arbitrary authority, and varies with time and place. The former is immutable, save that it is more fully comprehended in proportion as civilization advances; the latter varies with the opinions, fashions, and usages of different ages and countries. The one comes from within, the other from without. The first is developed, the last is imposed. Now the first is the only morality that may be legitimately recognized by government. All legislation in this country has reference to it, and professes to aim at its realization. So far as this morality is concerned, and this is Christian morality—

the gospel being, as Bishop Butler[7] well remarks, only a republication of the law of nature—all men of whatever sect, party, or religion, agree that it may and should be legally and politically recognized. The dispute is in reference to the positive morality. Positive morality, as our author understands it, acknowledges no man to be moral, who does not admit the existence of God, the inspiration of the Old and New Testaments, and the doctrine of the Trinity; who does not keep the Sabbath holy, refrain from profane swearing, and maintain some form or other of public worship. The several moral qualifications here implied he requires in every candidate for office, and all these are to be enjoined and enforced by law, not under plea of maintaining religion, but that of maintaining morality. He wishes every man, who does any one of the things here prohibited, or neglects any one here enjoined, to be declared by law an offender against the peace of the commonwealth, and punishable as such. And he alleges that he and his friends cannot enjoy their rights of conscience, unless it be so. Now, if he will reflect a moment, that all these injunctions are injunctions of positive, not of natural morality, resting upon an arbitrary authority for their obligation, he must see that they cannot be legally recognized and enforced, without denying all freedom of opinion. Whether they have anything to do with real worth of character or not, is a matter of opinion. They are not felt to be universally obligatory. This man may contend for them, that one may oppose them. I may believe that I ought to be just and merciful, to do no harm, and to do all the good I can, and I may labor to be true to my faith; yet I may regard all this positive morality as of no binding force, and think that I am at liberty to observe it or not, according to my own convictions. Bring in the government now with its positive law, and it reduces me to slavery. If it may command me to observe the first day of the week as holy time, it may enjoin any religious observance it pleases. If it may forbid me to labor on that day, if it may command me to attend church on that day, it may tell me on what days of the week I shall plough my ground, what days hoe my corn; indeed prescribe to me every act of my life, I am permitted to do, and the time and manner of doing it. The same may be said of all the other particulars specified.

The only safe rule is for government to confine itself to natural morality, and leave positive morality to everyone's own conscience.

[7][Ed. Joseph Butler (1692-1752) ranks among the great exponents of natural theology. He attempted to meet the criticisms of deists and other Enlightenment critics of Christianity, publishing his famous *Analogy of Religion* (1736) in response to those charges.]

They who believe in the Trinity ought to be protected in the enjoyment and expression of their belief; they who do not believe it, should have full liberty to oppose it. So of all other matters of belief. They who regard the first day of the week as holy should have the right to keep it holy; but not, as they claim to have, the right to force those to keep it holy who do not regard it as holy. They who reverence the Bible should have full liberty to reverence it, but no authority from government to exact reverence from those who do not believe it worthy of reverence. It may hurt the feelings of Christians to hear it spoken against, and so may it hurt the feelings of unbelievers to hear their favorite books spoken against; and if it be blasphemy to hurt the feelings of the one, there is no reason in the world why it should not be blasphemy to hurt the feelings of the other. If the Christian demands a law prohibiting unbelievers from reviling his sacred books, he must submit to a law prohibiting him from reviling the sacred books of unbelievers. He has not always done this. He has said as hard and as malignant things against the Age of Reason, as believers in the Age of Reason have ever said against believers in the Bible.

We are aware that this rule, so far as government is concerned, places men of all opinions on a par, and gives the Christian no legal or political advantage over the infidel. Shall the Christian object to this? Shall the Christian ask for a legal and political advantage over his unbelieving brother? Has he not God and truth on his side, and is not this advantage enough? Has he not also the majority, fashion, public opinion on his side; all the schools and colleges and most of the means of influence in his hands; and does he ask for more? Shall the Christian intimate that he is unwilling to meet the infidel on equal terms? Let him blush then to call himself a Christian. *He* is the infidel who wants faith in reason, and fears to trust it.

It is often alleged that atheism is incompatible with the stability of government, and the peace and welfare of the community, and may therefore be punished as an offence. We have not the space to enter far into the matter involved in this statement. We hold that no government can have any right to maintain itself by the sacrifice of private right. The powers of government are not made up from the individual rights surrendered to it. The notion that individuals give up a portion of their natural rights to society, in order to secure protection for the remainder, is a false notion.[8] Government is not a contract, a bargain. It rests on Divine right. The *Jus Divinum* must be reasserted if there be any government to be maintained. The mag-

[8][Ed. Brownson argues here against John Locke's contract theory of government.]

istrate is ordained of God. Define the legitimate powers of government and those powers are sacred and are derived from God. But as they are derived from God, they can never be in opposition to individual rights, which are also derived from God. If then we have established the fact, that a man has a natural right to profess atheism, the consequences of professing it, to the government, be they what they may, can never invalidate one's right to profess it. The good of the community may be consulted and ought to be; but only in harmony with the good of each part. The greatest good of the greatest number is not the end to be sought, but the greatest good of the whole. The few may never be sacrificed to secure the safety and well-being of the many. No individual, however lowly, may be overlooked. No individual can ever be without significance; and whenever the rights of one individual are disregarded, be the end what it may, the rights of every individual and of the whole community are invaded.

But let this pass. Atheism, we deny to be dangerous to communities, and we might quote as high authority for our assertion as that of Lord Bacon,[9] but that we are not much given to quotations. An atheistical community cannot be found. The history of our race contains the record of no such community. Mankind almost universally regard the atheist with horror. This horror, which we naturally feel at the denial of God, and the declaration of our own orphanage, is a sufficient protection against the spread of atheism. If it were a seducing doctrine, one, to the profession of which there were many and strong temptations, then it might, perhaps, be necessary to consider whether we have the right to suppress it. It has hitherto been rarely if ever professed for its own sake, but because it has been a refuge from oppression. Men oppressed, despoiled of their possessions and their rights, overwhelmed with the weight of tyrannical kings, nobilities, and hierarchies, professing to reign in the name of God, and by divine ordination, have sought relief in atheism, and denied God, that they might shake off a tyranny which had become too grievous to be borne. Give the atheist perfect liberty to profess his atheism, take away from him the conviction that in professing it he is warring against an arrogant authority, and he will himself be disgusted with it, and no longer have any wish to profess it. When men are permitted to see in God a father, they have no disposition to deny him; and

[9][Ed. Francis Bacon (1561-1626), empirical scientist and philosopher, wrote an essay "Of Atheism" that he included in his *The Essays or Counsels Civil and Moral* (1625). On this see *Francis Bacon, 1561-1626*, edited by Brian Vickers (Oxford: Oxford University Press, 1996), 371-73.]

when they see belief in him drawing mankind together as brothers, they will love that belief and do their best to acquire it.[10]

Similar remarks may be made in regard to Sabbath keeping and attendance on public worship. The first question is always, whether the government have a right to enforce them? The Sabbath, it is said, should be kept holy, but they only will keep it holy who believe it to be holy time, law or no law; and they who believe it to be holy time will keep it holy, although not legally enjoined. They who believe in the propriety of public worship, and who would profit by attendance on it, will attend it, if they can. They who do not believe in its propriety, and have no relish for it, would not worship, though compelled to attend the places of worship. Religious worship, to be acceptable, must be free and sincere. If it be not offered freely, from the spontaneous promptings of the heart, it can have no worth. All laws, having for their object the enforcement of religion, or a respect for its ordinances, are therefore useless in the case of those who are religious, and can only produce hypocrisy in the case of those who are not. And hypocrisy in our estimation is a much more heinous sin in the sight of God than Sabbath-breaking or neglect of public worship.

We have spoken, as we have, from no indifference to religion or to its ordinances, but from the overflowings of our zeal for Christian freedom. We would by no means encourage atheism, Sabbath-breaking, non-attendance on public worship, or the habit of elevating to office men deficient in high moral and religious worth. But we are convinced that the best way to secure belief in the existence of God,

[10]It may also be remarked, that society depends not on religion for its subsistence, but on the social instincts of human nature. Man lives in society, not because he has a religion, but because he is man, and is created with a social nature. The instinct of society is a primitive, not a secondary instinct. It is not a result of a belief in God, nor of any other belief. Men have not reasoned themselves into society; they have not said to themselves, Let us create society. They have always lived in society. Society is as old as man himself. God, in giving us social instincts, social affections, and cravings, which society alone can satisfy, has amply provided for its subsistence. If men would believe more in God, and understand a little more of human nature, and rely less on their positive creeds, they would have fewer fears of the disastrous effects of the propagation of error. He who really believes in God believes that the power which controls all worlds and events is mightier than any false opinion. They who think a little heterodoxy can bring the world to an end, or essentially alter its course, who fear that it can dissolve society, and prevent men from uniting with one another, be they called what they may, or profess they what faith they will, are the genuine infidels, the real atheists, against whom the friends of religion should be most on their guard, and against whom, if against any, laws of blasphemy should be enacted and enforced.

reverence for religion, its ordinances, and the practice of the Christian virtues, is for Christians to be just, to respect all the rights of man, and to attempt to secure no legal or political advantages to themselves. We would leave religion perfectly free, and rely solely on arguments addressed to the reason and the conscience for its maintenance and prosperity.

The disposition on the part of churchmen to arrogate to themselves rights they will not concede to others, the practice believers indulge of denouncing unbelievers, treating them with bitterness, scorn, and contempt, of ridiculing their notions and their writings, publishing from the pulpit and the press gross exaggerations of their doctrines, and utter falsehoods about their personal characters, the low and vulgar rank to which they seek to sink them in the social scale, and their unwillingness to respect them for what is just and true in their doctrines and characters, may be set down among the chief causes of existing indifference to religion, and the spreading infidelity, which every true Christian deplores; and till the church become Christianized, and professed Christians imbibe the spirit and follow the example of their Master, it will be of little avail to demand laws against unbelievers and Sabbath-breakers, to speak against infidels, or to labor for their conversion.

21.

SUB-TREASURY BILL[1]

Boston Quarterly Review 1 (July, 1838): 333-60

We regard the Sub-Treasury Bill as one of the most important measures which our government has proposed since its organization. It constitutes now, and will probably for some time to come, the great question in federal politics. Its adoption or rejection will have an immense bearing on our whole future history. We believe, therefore, it may be well to devote a few pages to the consideration of the principal arguments for it and chief objections against it.

The principle of the Sub-Treasury Bill is simply that of providing for collecting, safe-keeping, and disbursing the public revenues without recourse to banks. We shall not trouble ourselves or our readers with the details of the Bill. They are, we presume, in the main satisfactory; for we have heard little or nothing said against them. The principle of the Bill is all that we feel much interest in; it is all the friends of the Bill are very tenacious of, and all its enemies very strenuously oppose. To the principle of the Bill, as we have stated it, shall we, therefore, confine the greater portion of the remarks we have to offer.

It may be assumed in the outset that the government has the right to collect, keep, and disburse its revenues by means of its own officers without any recourse to bank agency. It may also be assumed that the banks have no natural claim on the government to be employed as its fiscal agents, and that they will have no injustice to

[1] [Ed. Brownson's review of Daniel Webster's (1782-1852) *Mr. Webster's speech on the currency . . . Delivered in the Senate of the United States. September 28, 1837* (Washington: Printed by Gales and Seaton, 1837]; John C. Calhoun's (1782-1850) *Speech of Mr. Calhoun . . . on the Sub-Treasury Bill: Delivered in the Senate of the United States, February 15, 1838* (Washington: Hamilton and Denham, 1838); Daniel Webster's *Mr. Webster's second speech on the Sub-Treasury Bill. Delivered in the Senate of the United States, March 12, 1838* (Washington, 1838); John C. Calhoun's *Speech of Mr. Calhoun . . . in reply to Mr. Clay, on the Sub-Treasury Bill. Delivered in the Senate of the United States, March 10, 1838* (Washington: Washington Chronicle Office, 1838); John C. Calhoun's *Speech of Mr. Calhoun . . . in reply to Mr. Webster's rejoinder. Delivered in the Senate of the United States, March 22, 1838* (Washington, 1838).]

complain of if they are not so employed. Moreover, it may be assumed again that the government can if it choose manage its fiscal concerns without any connection with banks or banking institutions. Banks are a contrivance of yesterday; but governments are older than history, older even than tradition; and there can be no doubt that they had fiscal concerns, which they managed, and in some instances very well too, a considerable time before banks were dreamed of. What has been done may be done. The question, then, on the side we are now viewing it, is one of expediency. Is it expedient for the government to dispense with banks and all bank agency in the management of its fiscal concerns?

Our government, in its measures and practical character, should conform as strictly as possible to the ideal or theory of our institutions. Nobody, we trust, is prepared for a revolution; nobody, we also trust, is bold enough to avow a wish to depart very widely from the fundamental principles of our institutions; and everybody will admit that the statesman should study to preserve those institutions in their simplicity and integrity, and should seek, in every law or measure he proposes, merely to bring out their practical worth and secure the ends for which they were established. Their spirit should dictate every legislative enactment, every judicial decision, and every executive measure. Any law not in harmony with their genius, any measure which would be likely to disturb the nicely adjusted balance of their respective powers, or that would give them, in their practical operation, a character essentially different from the one they were originally intended to have, should be discountenanced and never for a single moment entertained.

We would not be understood to be absolutely opposed to all innovations or changes, whatever their character. It is true, we can never consent to disturb the settled order of a state, without strong and urgent reasons; but we can conceive of cases in which we should deem it our duty to demand a revolution. When a government has outlived its idea, and the institutions of a country no longer bear any relation to the prevailing habits, thoughts, and sentiments of the people, and have become a mere dead carcass, an encumbrance, an offence, we can call loudly for a revolution, and behold with comparative coolness its terrible doings. But such a case does not as yet present itself here. Our institutions are all young, full of life and the future. Here, we cannot be revolutionists. Here, we can tolerate no innovations, no changes, which touch fundamental laws. None are admissible but such as are needed to preserve our institutions in their original character, to bring out their concealed beauty, to clear the field for their free operation, and to give more directness and force to their legitimate activity. Every measure must be in harmony with them, grow as it were out of them, and be but a development of their fundamental laws.

The government of the United States is a congress rather than a government. It is not instituted for the ordinary purposes of government, but for a few, and comparatively a very few, special purposes. The ordinary rules for interpreting the powers of government can be applied to it only to a limited extent, and even then with great caution. The principal governments of the country, according to the theory of American institutions, are the state governments. These were intended to be the governments for the people in all their civil, municipal, domestic, and individual interests and relations. The federal government was designed merely to take charge of the external relations of the confederated States with foreign nations, and, to a certain extent, with one another. It was never intended to be a government affecting the private interests of the people as individual citizens. It in fact repudiates every measure which would make it a great central government, giving law to the states, or which tends to give it a direct or indirect control over the private fortunes and affairs of the people; and it can own only such measures as tend to keep it within its province, to preserve its original idea, and enable it to discharge its legitimate functions.

Undoubtedly the federal government may take such measures, though they affect the private fortunes and relations of individual citizens, as are *necessary* to the exercise of its delegated powers. But they must be necessary, not merely convenient. The rule always to be observed is, the federal government must touch the individual citizen as seldom and as lightly as possible, consistently with the faithful discharge of its constitutional duties. Should two measures be proposed for accomplishing a constitutional end, one of which has very little bearing on individual citizens, leaving them almost entire freedom, the other connecting the government intimately with all the business of the country and bringing it into a close relation with every individual citizen, the first ought to be adopted instead of the last, although the last might be the more feasible of the two and likely to be attended with more beneficial results. What may not be consulted openly and done directly, must never be consulted covertly and done indirectly. We must avoid, as far as practicable, all incidental action of the government—and that too, when it promises to be useful as well as when it threatens to be injurious.

These principles we believe are sound. We do not mean to say that some persons may not be found who will controvert them; for there are persons to be found who do not very well comprehend the relations, which were originally established between the federal government and the state governments, and who have a strong desire to make the federal government the supreme government of the country. But they are the only principles we can adopt, if we mean to avoid the charge of being revolutionists, and to preserve our institutions in their real character; if we mean to preserve to the states, as we ought, the main business of government, and to restrict the federal government in its action to the special purposes for which it was originally instituted.

Yet these principles have been departed from. The federal government, in point of fact, has become the supreme government of the land. It is no longer a congress for regulating our relations with foreigners, for adjusting the intercourse of the states with one another, and providing for the general defense; but it has become a grand central government, affecting, by its measures, individual interests and relations more powerfully than the action of the state governments themselves. The people, at least a large and influential portion of them, have come to regard it as the supreme government. They think of it as such; speak of it as such; commend it as such; condemn it as such. All eyes turn towards it. Do capitalists want to change their mode of investment, Congress must provide for the change; do their profits turn out to be less than their wishes, Congress must raise the tariff of duties to make them greater. Is there distress in the money market, commercial embarrassment, the federal government has caused it; are our factories closed, ships hauled up to rot, industry paralyzed, and the laborer seeking in vain for employment, the federal government is in fault, and Congress must afford relief.

Federal politics, too, absorb state politics. State legislators vote on a bill for the organization of a primary school, or for constructing or repairing a bridge, according to their opinions on a bill before Congress, or the fitness or unfitness of this or that man to fill the presidential chair. A federal warrant must be obtained before one feels himself authorized to support a measure of state policy; and the merits or demerits of any given measure will be determined by the fact that it is or is not opposed by the federal administration. Federal politics therefore decide everything and reduce state politics to insignificance.

Is this the order of things demanded by the genius of our institutions? Does this comport with the divine idea with which our fathers were inspired? Was the federal government framed to be the supreme government, and intended to invade by its acts even our domestic fire-sides? Does the theory of our institutions make the state governments mere prefectures, dependent on and accountable to the federal government? Most assuredly not. Widely then have we departed from that theory, and fearfully rapid has been our progress towards centralization, which is only another name for despotism. Without delay, then, should we hasten to retrace our steps, and return to the special purposes for which the government was instituted and beyond which it should never have strayed.

The people are honest and they mean to preserve their democratic institutions. They never would have suffered this departure from first principles had they clearly perceived the precise nature of the federal government. Our system of government, though exceedingly simple, has nevertheless the appearance of being exceedingly complex. Foreigners rarely if ever comprehend its real character. They regard the federal government as the supreme government, the state governments as inferior and subordinate. Their view of it presupposes the federal government to have possessed in the outset all the powers of government and to retain in its possession now all not conceded to the states. Many of our own citizens seem to fall into the same error. They appear to regard the Constitution of the United States as a limitation, rather than as an enumeration, of the powers of the federal government. They seem to forget that the sovereignty exercised by the federal government is after all vested in the states, and is exercised by the federal government only because the states have by mutual compact agreed that portion of their sovereignty shall be so exercised. They have therefore felt that the federal government, instead of being at liberty to do only what it has the express leave to do, is at liberty to do whatever it is not forbidden to do; that where it has not the power to act directly, it may act indirectly; and while in the pursuit of a constitutional end, it may accomplish, incidentally, any object it can, providing that object promises to be of general utility. They have therefore been able to see, without alarm, the government touching more interests and exerting almost infinitely greater control incidentally, than it can directly, in the plain, straight-forward exercise of its constitutional powers. They have also, in consequence of adopting this principle of interpretation, been able to solicit without compunction a continual extension of this incidental action, and to allege pretexts for so extending it as to bring it home to every man's "bosom and business." Had they clearly perceived the true character of the federal government, they had not seen this without lively alarm nor done it without poignant remorse.

In consequence of adopting the rule that the government may do incidentally what it may not do directly, and what is not necessary to the discharge of its constitutional functions, three systems of policy have grown up, which not only create obstacles to a return of the government to its legitimate province, but also perpetual inducements for it to depart further and still further from it. These are the system of internal improvements, the American system, as it is called, and the connection of the government with banking. There is no constitutional grant of power to the federal government in favor of any one of these. Congress has the right to establish post offices and post roads and to provide for the general welfare; therefore it has been contended that it may intersect the whole country with great roads and undertake any work of internal improvement that promises to be generally useful. It has no right to lay a protective tariff, but inasmuch as it has the right to lay imposts for the purposes of revenue, it may lay them to double the amount needed for revenue, and so lay them as to tax one portion of the community to enhance the profits of another, and in point of fact so as to affect all the business relations of the whole country. Under the grant of power to regulate commerce, to coin money and fix the value thereof, it is contended that it has the right to be connected with the banks and the whole business of banking. By means of its connection with the banks and banking business, it is brought into the closest connection with every man, woman, and child in these twenty-six confederated states. We say nothing against banks or the banking system. We are not now inquiring whether the system be a good or a bad one. What we are contending for stands above and independent on any views anybody may entertain of banks or banking. The banks are intimately connected with all the business concerns of the community; they affect the private fortune of every individual; they determine, to a great extent at least, the price of every article bought or sold, produced or consumed. The government, by being connected with them, becomes connected with the business concerns of every individual citizen, and controls those concerns, just in proportion as it is connected with the banks or exerts a controlling influence over their operations.

By means of the internal improvement system, of the American system, and its connection with banks, the federal government has become the supreme government of the land. We say *has* become, perhaps it were as well to say, *had* become. The tendency to centralization was unchecked till the accession of General Jackson to the presidency. During his administration it began to be arrested. Some may indeed question this fact and we will not insist on it so far as concerns the executive department of the federal government. Circumstances, not sought by General Jackson, and which we see not well how he could have controlled, threw into the hands of the executive an uncommon share of power, and gave to administrative measures an influence and an importance, which we hope never to see possessed by the measures of any subsequent administration. Nevertheless, the tendency—excepting always a certain proclamation—so far as the doctrines promulgated and measures recommended were concerned—was arrested. The internal improvement system was vetoed, the American system was modified, compromised, and sent on its way to the place whence it came. And now, if we mean to finish the work, and arrest completely and perhaps forever, this dangerous tendency, we must disconnect the government from all banks and bank agency and adopt the principle of the Sub-Treasury Bill.

Now, as we have taken it for granted that nobody amongst us is for changing the fundamental laws of our institutions or for disturbing the relations which our fathers saw fit to establish between the federal government and the state governments, we see not well how any man can avoid coming to the above conclusion. There are only two courses for us to take. One course is to make the federal government, by its connection with the banking business, and through that with private credit, which is, in this country, the basis of most business transactions, the supreme government, the government controlling all the state governments, and the one which most vitally affects the people. We can take this course if we will. Revive the Deposit system, or charter a national bank, and we shall have taken it. But then our institutions are radically changed; the wisdom of our fathers set at naught; and we ourselves afloat on the tide of a new experiment. We trust that we are, as a people, yet too near the cradle of our institutions, and that we yet feel too much of the joy that thrilled our hearts, when we were told the young child, Liberty, was born, to be prepared for this. We trust also that we have too much stability of character, firmness of purpose, and self respect, to disappoint at once the hopes of the friends of freedom throughout the world who have been looking to us for encouragement, and for a triumphant answer to those who allege that society cannot subsist without kings, hierarchies, and nobilities.

The other course is to adopt the principle of the Sub-Treasury Bill, and divorce the government from its destructive alliance with the business of banking. It is to follow out the policy already commenced; and as we have abandoned the internal improvement system, and the protective system, so now to abandon the banking system. We mean not by this that the government is to wage a war against the banks but that it shall let them alone. If the states have not yielded up to the general government their right to institute banks, the banks are matters wholly within the jurisdiction of the states, and we should be the first to repel any attacks the federal government might be disposed to make on them; and this too whether we approved the banking system or not. The states are competent to manage their own affairs. We ask nothing of the federal government in relation to banks, but to provide for the management of its fiscal concerns without making any use directly or indirectly of their agency.

The adoption of this principle will be for the federal government to withdraw itself within its legitimate province, from which we can see nothing very soon at least likely to tempt it forth again. This will leave a broader field and weightier matters to the state governments, which will raise their importance in the estimation of the people, make them objects of more serious attention, enlist more talent in their administration, and make them altogether more practically useful. We have no wish to underrate the federal government. If the tendency of the times were to lessen its importance, we would set forth its claims in as strong terms as we do now those of the states.[2] Because we value the rights of the states, it must not be inferred that we do not value the Union. The Union is by no means likely in our days to be underestimated. The centripetal force is altogether too strong for that. Should we, however, see the centrifugal force predominating, and be led to apprehend any danger from a tendency to individuality, to disunion, dissolution, we trust we should be found among the fast friends of the Union. But we are not one of those who neglect the danger which now is, to utter warnings against a danger, which may possibly never come. Sufficient for the day is the evil thereof. The federal government is indispensable, and in its sphere, it

[2][Ed. Brownson would indeed reverse his support and emphasize the role of the federal government during and after the Civil War when he believed the greatest threat to society came from the revolutionary tendencies of the era in the United States as in Europe, and from an over-emphasis upon the rights of states independent of the Union. See, e.g., "The Great Rebellion," *Brownson's Quarterly Review* 23 (July, 1861): 378-402, and especially *The American Republic: Its Constitution, Tendencies, and Destiny* (New York: P. O'Shea, 1865).]

should be preserved at all hazards. But it is after all less essential than our state governments. Our external relations, our affairs as communities, which it belongs to the federal government to watch over and regulate, are of far less consequence than our relations as individual citizens. The former are few, and comparatively remote, while the latter are many and intimate. The first affect us only occasionally, the last continually, every moment. The federal government is also so far removed from the individual citizen, and permits so few to take part in its deliberations or administration that it can never legislate for private interests, wisely, usefully, and safely, even if it have the constitutional right to do it. The states are therefore the more important institutions of the two. They should therefore claim our first attention. If the principle of the Bill under consideration be adopted, they will receive our first attention. Political men will not be thinking perpetually then of what may be thought at Washington. They will have leisure to bestow their best thoughts on state legislation, on the means of removing abuses which weigh heavily on the individual citizen, of improving our systems of jurisprudence, increasing the facilities for popular education, encouraging literature and the arts, and elevating the individual man. The balance between the state and the individual, between the federal government and the state governments, may be readjusted, and we be at liberty to develop the resources of our noble country, to avail ourselves of our commanding position, and to prove ourselves a people worthy to be studied and imitated.

The principle of this Bill ought also to be adopted because it simplifies the fiscal concerns of the nation, and keeps them clear of the complicated financial systems of the old world. The real governments of the old world are at this moment on Change or the Bourse,[3] and the regulation of funds is the principal business of government. Government, instituted for the social weal of the people, becomes thus the mere instrument of private interest, of stock- jobbers, speculators in the funds. We do not want this state of things here. We want a government, simple, open, and direct in its action, performing in the simplest and plainest manner possible the functions assigned to it.

We have also commenced in this country a new system of government, not in form only, but in spirit. We reject the maxim that it is necessary to deceive the people for the people's good, and adopt

[3][Ed. "Change or the Bourse" refers to a building in which the merchants of a town assemble for the transaction of business.]

the maxim, that honesty is the best policy. To carry out this maxim, it is necessary that the government should always tell the truth, both in its words and its deeds. It has a right to impose taxes, but only for defraying the expenses incurred in the legitimate exercise of its constitutional powers. It may lay imposts and collect revenues, for this purpose, and for this purpose only. It has then no right to use its revenues or to suffer them to be used for any other purpose. Now, when it deposits its revenues in the banks, whether in a national bank or in a state bank, in general deposit, as it is contended it should, it uses its revenues, or suffers them to be used, for other purposes than those of defraying its expenses. They are not deposited there for safe keeping, as the people are taught to believe, but to be made the basis of loans to the business part of the community. They serve the purpose of sustaining the credit of the banks and, through the banks, of the merchants and manufacturers. This is to collect the revenues for one purpose and to appropriate them to another. This is to deceive the people and to depart from the fundamental maxim of our state policy. If it be necessary to tax the community some thirty millions of dollars annually to sustain the credit of businessmen, and to enable them to carry on their extensive operations, let them be so taxed; but let it be openly and avowedly. The people will know then what they are taxed for. But so long as the revenues are avowedly collected for the purpose of defraying the expenses of the government, they should be sacred to that end. If in this way a portion of the funds of the nation be useless, it may operate as an inducement to make the taxes as light as possible, which in its turn will relieve the people, and keep the government poor; and by keeping it poor, keep it honest, free from corruption.

The greatest objection, or one of the greatest objections to the deposit system, in either a national bank or in state banks, is that it gives to the banks the use of the government funds. Being given to the banks, the use of these funds is virtually given to the business community. The business community, so long as it has the use of them, will not be anxious to reduce the revenues. It will prefer high taxes and favor the accumulation of a surplus because by having the use of the funds to sustain its credit, it gets back more than it is obliged to pay in taxes. This part of the subject, Mr. Calhoun, in his speech of February 15th, has set in a clear light, and his remarks deserve to be read and pondered well by every freeman. The policy of our government should be to make the taxes as light as possible, consequently to look with distrust on all measures the direct tendency of which must be to increase them.

It may also be maintained with some plausibility at least that it is for the true interest of the banks themselves to have no connection with the fiscal concerns of the government. Nobody, we presume, is hardy enough to contend that the banks should control the government. It has never, we believe, been the intention of the people to place the real government of the country in the hands of bank corporations. They have, we believe, always intended that the government should maintain its supremacy, and follow its own interest and that of the country, regardless of the special interests of the presidents and directors of banks. In case the government maintains its supremacy, the amount of its funds, the time, place, and extent of its appropriations, must always be matters beyond the control of the banks, and also matters which they may not always foresee or be prepared to meet. Government will have it in its power to disturb, whenever it chooses, their nicest business calculations, and thwart them in their most cherished plans. It may call upon them for its funds when they are all loaned out, and when they cannot be called in without great detriment to the business operations of the community, often not without producing a panic, financial embarrassment, commercial distress. If there be but one bank, or if there be one mammoth bank, it may, perhaps, profit by panics, financial embarrassments, commercial distress, but the banks generally cannot. Their interest is one and the same with that of the business community; it is best promoted by sustaining credit, by keeping the waters smooth and even, the times good and easy. They ought, then, to be free from all connection with a partner over whose operations they have no control, and who may choose to withdraw his investments at the very moment when they are most in need of them. It is altogether better for them to trust to their own means and keep to their proper vocation, than it is to mix up their interests with those of the government. The history of the late deposit banks may be thought to afford some evidence of the truth of this.

We did intend to adduce several other considerations in favor of the Sub-Treasury Bill, but our limits forbid. We have barely room left to offer a few brief remarks on the principal objections we have heard urged against it.

The Bill is said by some to be objectionable because in its original form it contemplates the disuse of bank notes in payment of the public dues. But this is essential to the principle of the Bill. It is impossible to separate the government from the business of banking, so long as it receives or pays out bank notes. There is no difference in principle between receiving a bank note and making a bank deposit.

A bank note is merely a certificate of deposit in the bank in favor of its holder, to its nominal amount. If the bank be solvent it will be paid on demand, and so will be the deposit made in any other form.

Then again, why should the government receive the notes of banks rather than of individuals? Bank notes are not money, currency. Their value consists in the confidence entertained by the community that their promises to pay money will be redeemed on demand. Notes of individuals may be as likely to be redeemed as these bank notes, may be worth as much, and be in as good credit; why not take them? Why demand payment of the revenues at all? Why not take the notes or bonds of the government debtors, as sufficient? The principle would be the same with that of taking bank notes. What would the people think of a provision for receiving the notes of certain individual merchants or manufacturers in payment of the public dues?

Bank notes, we have said, are not currency. Currency is that which passes current in the legal discharge of debts. In no case, except that of the government, are bank notes ever made a legal tender. No creditor but the government is under any obligation to receive them. Why shall the government be compelled to receive them? Why may not the government, as a creditor, be placed on an equal footing with any other creditor?

Bank notes are no doubt convenient and highly useful in commercial transactions. A change in the source and method of their emission, together with additional securities for their redemption, is unquestionably demanded, and must ere long be effected; but no one at all acquainted with the business operations of the commercial world will think of dispensing wholly with their use. But when they have no legal value in the discharge of debts, when they are left for their circulation, so far as the law is concerned, to the free-will and confidence of the community, they have even then a natural tendency to become superabundant and to stimulate individual credit beyond what is consistent with its soundness. Should the government receive them in payment of the public dues, it would strengthen this tendency, and greatly aggravate its evil consequences. Bank notes will become sufficiently abundant and be in as good credit as they deserve, although the government should have nothing to do with them, neither receiving them nor paying them out.

We are also disposed to concur with Mr. Calhoun in the position he has assumed that the federal government cannot place its funds in the banks in general deposit without violating an express clause of the Constitution. He contends that when the revenues are collected and deposited in the banks, they are, if ever, in the Treasury. The Constitution says expressly that "No money shall be drawn from the Treasury but in consequence of appropriations made by law."[4] The public funds deposited in the banks are drawn from them for other purposes than those of meeting appropriations made by law; they are made by the banks the basis of discounts, and are frequently all loaned out to their customers. Can this be done without violating the Constitution?

If the principle involved in this statement be admitted, it follows as a necessary consequence, that the government cannot receive bank notes in payment of the public dues. In denying the right to make the deposit, we necessarily deny the right to receive the notes. To receive the notes of the banks, since these notes are only certificates of deposits, is only an indirect way of making bank deposits. The right to receive them can then rest only on the right to make the deposits.

Mr. Webster promised to reply to this constitutional objection, but, unhappily, he failed to redeem his promise. He merely proved that the government had been in the habit of receiving bank notes in payment of the public dues—a fact well known and admitted by Mr. Calhoun. The fact that the government has been in the habit of receiving bank notes does not prove that it has a constitutional right to receive them. In establishing the fact, therefore, Mr. Webster did not establish the right—the only point he was called upon to establish. As he did not do this, since it was what was essential to be done, we presume he could not. If Mr. Webster could not, who can? We conclude, therefore, that Mr. Calhoun is correct that the government has no constitutional right to place its funds in the banks in general deposit, nor to receive bank notes in payment of the public dues; and consequently the objection to the Bill we are considering is not an objection to the Bill itself, but to the Constitution.

Mr. Webster's main objection to the Bill is that it does not provide for a uniform currency, safe and of equal value throughout the Union. This objection is about as reasonable as would be the objection to a bill fixing the weight and fineness of the dollar, that it does not fix the length of the yardstick. The Bill professes simply to provide for collecting, safe-keeping, and disbursing the public revenues, without any recourse to banks or to bank agency. To object to it that it does not effect another object, and one which it does not contemplate, is hardly fair. Is it Mr. Webster's creed that all governmental

[4][Ed. *Constitution of the United* States, article 1, sec. 9.7.]

measures should be avowedly adopted for one object, but really and intentionally for another and a different object? If so, he must pardon us; we cannot with our present notions of honesty and plain-dealing consent to embrace it.

Mr. Webster insists upon the obligation of the federal government to provide for a uniform currency, safe and of equal value throughout the Union. He reiterates this, and dwells upon it with as much earnestness, as if he verily thought he was bringing out a novel and unadmitted theory. But really, in the constitutional sense of the term currency, nobody disputes him. It was unquestionably the intention of the framers of the Constitution, that the federal government should provide for a currency which should be uniform and of equal value throughout all the states. The Union of the states was desired and effected, principally to facilitate their commercial intercourse with one another and with foreign nations. Commerce craved and effected the Union, made us one people. Without the Union, the states would have been to each other foreign nations, and the commercial transactions between the citizens of one state and those of another would have been subjected to the laws, which govern the trade of our citizens with the subjects of England, France, or any other foreign nation. This was a thing to be avoided. It was desirable to bind the states together in a closer intimacy than that of foreign states, and to make the business intercourse between the citizens of one state and the citizens of another state, as facile and as safe, as the business intercourse between citizens of the same state.

But this was to be effected only by giving to the federal government the power to provide for a uniform currency, to "coin money and regulate the value thereof."[5] Had this power over the currency been retained by the states individually, there might have been as many currencies as states. What was coin in one state would have been bullion in relation to another. Coins of the same denomination might have varied in value as you passed from state to state, and there would have been no currency in the Union with which debts could be discharged alike in all the states. To avoid this last result, the states were prohibited from issuing bills of credit, and from making anything but gold and silver a legal tender. This prohibition was not laid on the states for the purpose of protecting the citizens of the same state against one another, but the citizens of one state against those of another state. The object in view was still a uniform currency. It was

[5][Ed. *Constitution of the United* States, article 1, sec. 8.5.]

to secure to every creditor payment in a currency which would be of equal value in whatever part of the Union he might wish to use it.

Now thus far we contend as earnestly as Mr. Webster that it is the duty of the federal government to furnish a uniform currency. We contend that this is one of the chief duties of the government, not merely that it may equalize taxes and provide a uniform currency in which to collect its revenues, as we have heard it suggested by some, but also to provide for the wants of commerce, to facilitate the business intercourse between the citizens of one state and those of another. But we do not find that this implies an obligation on the part of the federal government to provide a currency of bank paper, which shall be safe and of uniform value throughout the states. We cannot find that the Constitution and laws know any other currency than that of gold and silver; and when we consider the object which led to the prohibition of the states from issuing bills of credit, and from making anything but gold and silver a legal tender, we may safely conclude that it was the intention of the framers of the Constitution that gold and silver alone should constitute the legal currency. Bank notes may circulate because they are convenient and because it may be believed that they will be redeemed in specie on demand, as may bills of exchange and the promissory notes of individuals; but however much they may circulate they do not constitute a legal currency. It is always optional with the creditor, whether he will receive them or not. So far as the law is concerned he may always insist on payment in gold and silver. If he consents to take bank notes and discharge his debtor, the law regards it, and treats it as a private contract, bargain, or agreement.

Mr. Webster himself, when it suits his purpose, contends that gold and silver constitute the only currency known to the Constitution and laws. The following extract from a speech of his in Congress in 1816, which we find in Mr. Calhoun's speech of March 22, is very clear and satisfactory on this point.

"Mr. Webster first addressed the House. He regretted the manner in which this debate had been commenced, on a detached feature of the bill, and not a question affecting the principle; and expressed his fears that a week or two would be lost in the discussion of this question, to no purpose, inasmuch as it might ultimately end in the rejection of the bill. *He proceeded to reply to the arguments of the advocates of the bill.* It was a mistaken idea, he said, which he had heard uttered on this subject, *that we were about to reform the National currency. No nation had a better currency,* he said, than the United States; there was no nation which had guarded its currency with more care; for the framers of the Constitution, and those who enacted the early statutes on this subject, were *hard money men*; they had felt, and therefore duly *appreciated the evils of a paper medium*; they, therefore, sedulously guarded *the currency of the United States from debasement. The legal currency of the United States was gold and silver coin*; this was a subject in regard to which Congress had run into no folly.

"'What, then,' he asked, 'was the present evil? *Having a perfectly sound national currency, and the Government having no power in fact to make anything else current but gold and silver, there had grown up in different States* a currency of paper issued by banks, setting out with the promise to pay gold and silver, which they had been wholly unable to redeem: the consequence was, that there was a mass of paper afloat, of perhaps fifty millions, which sustained no immediate relation *to the legal currency of the country*—a paper which will not enable any man to pay money he owes to his neighbor, or *his debts to the Government.* The banks had issued more money than they could redeem, and the evil was severely felt,' &c. Mr. Webster declined occupying the time of the House, to prove that there was a depreciation of the paper in circulation: *the legal standard of value was gold and silver*; the relation of paper to it proved its state, and the rate of its depreciation. *Gold and silver currency, he said, was the law of the land at home, and the law of the world abroad; there could, in the present state of the world, be no other currency.*"[6]

Nevertheless Mr. Webster means a bank currency, when he contends the federal government is bound to provide a safe and uniform currency of equal value throughout the states. He infers the government is bound to provide this currency not only from its general power over the currency, but also from its special power to regulate commerce. Its general power over the currency extends merely to coining money and regulating its value. The power to regulate commerce, even he in his sober moments can hardly contend, reaches his case. On this point Mr. Calhoun's reply to him is sufficient.

"The last argument of the Senator, on the question at issue, was drawn from the provision of the Constitution, which gives to Congress the right to regulate commerce, and which he says involves the right and obligation to furnish a sound circulating medium. The train of his reasoning, as far as I could comprehend it, was, that, without a currency, commerce could not exist, at least to any considerable extent, and, of course, there would be nothing to regulate:

[6] [Ed. *Speech of Mr. Calhoun . . . in reply to Mr. Webster's rejoinder. Delivered in the Senate of the United States, March 22, 1838.* (Washington, 1838), 13, 14.]

and, therefore, unless Congress furnished a currency, its power of regulating commerce would become a mere nullity; and from which he inferred the right and obligation to furnish not only a currency, but a bank currency! Whatever may be said of the soundness of the reasoning, all must admit that his mode of construing the Constitution is very bold and novel. To what would it lead? The same clause, in that instrument, which gives Congress the right to coin money and regulate the value thereof, gives it also the kindred right to fix the standard of weights and measures. They are just as essential to the existence of commerce as the currency itself. The yard and the bushel are not less important in the exchange of commodities, than the dollar and the eagle; and the very train of reasoning which would make it the right and duty of the Government to furnish the one, would make it equally so to furnish the other. Again: commerce cannot exist without ships and other means of transportation. Is the government also bound to furnish them? Nor without articles or commodities to be exchanged, cotton, rice, tobacco, and the various products of agriculture and manufactures. Is it also bound to furnish them? Nor these in turn, without labor; and must that too be furnished? If not, I ask the Senator to make the distinction. Where will he draw the line, and on what principles? Does he not see that, according to this mode of construction, the higher powers granted in the Constitution would carry all the inferior, and that this would become a Government of unlimited powers? Take, for instance, the war power, and apply the same mode of construction to it, and what power would there be that Congress could not exercise, nay, be bound to exercise? Intelligence, morals, wealth, numbers, currency, all are important elements of power, and may become so to the defense of the union and safety of the country; and according to the Senator's reasoning, the Government would have the right and would be in duty bound to take charge of the schools, the pulpits, the industry, the population, as well as the currency of the country; and these would comprehend the entire circle of legislation, and leave the State Governments as useless appendages of the system."[7]

Mr. Webster contends, that since a paper currency has sprung up in the states under the auspices of state legislation, which answers in many respects all the purposes of the legal currency, it ought, in order to be uniform, current alike in all parts of the Union, to come under the control of the federal government. Now, if he be right in

[7] **[Ed. Ibid., 14, 15.]**

this, he must admit that the federal government has the supreme control over all the banks of the country, the full right to determine the mode and extent of their issues, and the securities they must give the public for the redemption of their notes. A power less unlimited than this will not meet the exigencies of the case. But the federal government can have this power over only the banks of its own creation. Nobody can be mad enough to contend that it may have this power over state institutions. State institutions for furnishing a paper currency must then be abandoned, and federal banks alone be tolerated.[6] If the power supposed be vested in the federal government, the constitutional right of the states to incorporate banks must be given up. Our state banks are all unconstitutional, and the recent act of the legislature of the State of New York, authorizing private banking is unconstitutional also. Will Mr. Webster go this length? Is he aware that the ground he assumes is incompatible with the constitutionality of the state banks? We believe he is, and notwithstanding his professions of regard for them, that he is very nearly prepared to abolish them. No man has said harder things against them, and we believe his soberest convictions are that the federal government only has a right to incorporate a bank. It becomes the friends of state banks to look well to Mr. Webster's arguments for a sound, uniform, national bank paper currency. Just as much power as he claims for the federal government over the paper currency of the country, just so much does he deny to the states; and as he claims the supreme control for the federal government, he of course leaves nothing to the state governments.

The Bill under consideration is also accounted objectionable, by some, because it will lock up the money of the country in the govern-

[6]It will not alter the state of the case at all, to say that Congress need not exert this control directly; that it may do it indirectly through the agency of a great national bank. Granting, what however we much doubt, that a national bank would exert the control over state banks here supposed, Congress has no more right to establish a bank for exerting that control, than it has to exert it immediately, by direct federal legislation. Nothing is clearer than that a government may not do mediately what it may not do immediately. If it have no right to control state banks by direct legislation, it of course has no right to establish a bank to do it. Consequently if the federal government is bound to regulate the circulation and value of bank paper, it must have the supreme control over the sources of its emission. It can have this control over no institutions but those of its own creation. Either then the federal government must, after having done its duty in relation to a gold and silver currency, leave bank issues entirely to the people and the states, or else all state banks, or institutions created by the states to furnish a paper currency, must be given up. We yield Mr. Webster either horn of the dilemma.

ment vaults and keep it from general use. But this can be the case only to a limited extent. It is not the policy of modern governments to hoard money. The true theory of our government is to collect no more money than is wanted for its necessary expenditures. Consequently what is collected must always be immediately disbursed in payment of government creditors and go again into general circulation. Very little will be kept constantly on hand. Mr. Wright[8] thinks about five millions, Mr. Calhoun, in our judgment more correctly, thinks three millions will be nearer the truth. The Bill will tend if adopted to keep down the taxes or revenues. The business portion of the community, who are now for high taxes, because they have the loan of the government funds, will, when they find they can make no use of them, and derive no advantage from them, exert their whole influence to keep them down to the wants of government, and also to keep the wants of government as few as is compatible with its free and healthy action. In this way altogether more will be gained to the country than will be lost by suffering a few millions of dollars to lie idle in the government vaults.

It is said that the Bill increases the patronage of the government. It adds nine additional clerks to the present list of government agents, and creates four new offices of receivers general. This is not much, not sufficient to alarm a man possessed of any tolerable nerves. As for the power of the government over the public funds, it remains precisely the same under the new arrangement as under the old. The change in this respect is merely taking away the control of the banks over the public money without increasing that of the government. The objection would be nearer the truth if it read, the Bill diminishes the influence of the banks over the fiscal concerns of the government. Put it in the worst light possible, all that can be said is, the safe-keeping of the government funds is placed in the hands of government officers, instead of the hands of irresponsible bank presidents and directors. Is this a weighty objection?

The money will not, it is said, be safe. All safety is comparative. They who have money must run the risk of losing it. Government vaults may be made as safe as bank vaults, and perhaps there may be government officers, who are as honest, as trustworthy, as the officers and agents of banks, whether state or national. The chances against loss are much greater under the Bill, than under the deposit system,

[8][Ed. Silas Wright (1795-1847), United States Senator of New York, was a Jacksonian Democrat who favored President Martin Van Buren, his fellow New Yorker, and the Sub-Treasury Bill.]

in either of its forms. Under the Bill honesty and ordinary prudence alone will suffice to keep them safe, for they are locked up. Under the deposit system they are loaned out, and it depends on the sagacity and accurate calculations as well as the honesty of the bank agents, and on the honesty and ability of the bank debtors, whether they shall be kept safe or not.

These are the principal objections which we have heard urged against the Bill. It is in reality unobjectionable, and the opposition to it does not arise from any conviction that the measure itself will not work well, but from the fact, that it does not give to the business community the use of the government funds during the period which elapses between their collection and disbursement. From the organization of the federal government up to the present moment, the business community, by means of the funding system and bank agency, have had, in a greater or less degree, the use of the public funds, and made them to a great extent the basis of their credit and business operations. They have had the use of these funds so long that they seem to have forgotten that they were originally collected not for them but for the government. They seem to think that long possession has given them a right to them. And now that the government proposes to reclaim them, and to make them sacred to the uses for which they were collected, they feel themselves sorely grieved, and talk of the government, as though it were doing them a wrong. We hope, however, they will moderate their wrath, and reflect with a little soberness. If they do, we think they must be satisfied that the government is not wronging them.

For ourselves, we can see no reason why the business portion of the community should have, directly or indirectly, the use of the government funds. We will charge upon no class of our fellow citizens the doctrine that the government ought to protect, or specially favor one portion of the community, as the means of benefitting other portions of the community. We do not believe that the businessmen will maintain in general thesis that government ought to favor them, facilitate their operations, in order to enable them to advance the interests of the farmer and the artisan. There is, we devoutly hope, nobody among us to contend that the government should hire one class to take care of another. For, here, everybody knows, government can give to one class only what it takes from another. We go against all special protection, against all special favors. We wish well to commerce, well to manufactures, well to agriculture, well to the mechanic arts. These are all sister interests; and when government does not choose to single out one as the special object of its caresses, they all live harmoniously together, and add to each other's comfort.

If, however, any interest in this country needs to be protected more than another, it is the interest of what may be termed productive labor. Commerce and manufactures do not need with us any especial care of the government. Of all interests among us they are those which can best take care of themselves. Money always secures the influence needed for its own protection. It is those who come not into the moneyed class, honest, but humble laborers, who are usually deficient in the power to protect themselves. But for these we ask no special protection, no special governmental action. Leave industry free, unshackled, and they will work out their own salvation.

If this Bill become a law, it will, in our judgment, mark a new era in the history of our government. It will greatly diminish the business of the government, lessen the demand for legislation, and leave more to individual freedom, skill, and enterprise. Some inconveniences at first must doubtless be anticipated. It will take some little time for things to settle down, business to find a smooth and safe channel. No important change, however beneficial or desirable, can be effected without more or less of inconvenience and suffering. We gained not our national independence, without inconvenience, without long and painful sacrifices. Yet it is thought now to be worth all it cost us.

If this Bill become a law, we shall have gained, in addition to our political independence, social independence, which is still more valuable. The moneyed interest will be prevented from converting our government from a democracy into a timocracy, and the people, the whole people, will be in fact, not in name only, the state, under justice, the real sovereign. Our Republic will continue its peaceful march of freedom and realize the idea of its venerated founders. There is a glorious future before us. If we only possess the wisdom to decide rightly the great questions, as they from time to time come up, we shall assuredly realize it. We love to contemplate the destiny which may, and which we trust will be ours; and we could expatiate with no little enthusiasm on it; but we forbear. Whatever may be the fate of the Bill, we despair not of the Republic. The people here are strong; and though they may err for a moment, or for a moment be deceived, they will come round right in the end, and prove that "*vox populi*" is, after all, the surest rendering of "*vox Dei.*"

22.

THE AMERICAN DEMOCRAT[1]

Boston Quarterly Review 1 (July, 1838): 360-77

The creator of *Natty Leatherstocking* and the author of the *Bravo* can hardly write a book that shall be read without interest, or fail to deserve the respectful consideration of his countrymen.[2] He possesses talents of a high order, is not wholly without genius, and has, in the course of his reading and travels, amassed much useful information. He has contributed something to American literature and gained a name that will not be forgotten for some time to come.

It would be interesting to ourselves, and perhaps to our readers, were we prepared to do it, to enter into the consideration of Mr. Cooper's merits as a writer, into a critical examination of his works, and some speculations as to their probable influence upon the thought and literature of this country. The thing is to be done and will be done; but is not for us, at present at least, to do it. His earlier novels amused us; his later productions have done something to quicken our thinking powers, and to instruct us.

We have a high regard for Mr. Cooper, for his love of independence, and his willingness to hazard his literary reputation in the cause of the people. We respect him for the fact that he had the moral courage to approve and defend some of the measures of General Jackson's administration, and those measures, too, the most assailed by that portion of the community on which literary men are thought to be the more immediately dependent and with which they are the more intimately connected. We respect him for his rebellion against cant, for his earnest defense of individual freedom, and his manly assertion of every individual's right to form and express his own opinions without being called to an account, abused, insulted, injured in

[1][Ed. Review of James Fenimore Cooper, *The American Democrat, or Hints on the Social and Civic Relations of the United States of America* (Cooperstown: H. & E. Phinney, 1838).]

[2][Ed. Brownson refers to James Fenimore Cooper's (1789-1851) *Natty Leatherstocking*—a series of Leatherstocking novels, which included *The Pioneers* (1823), *The Last of the Mohicans* (1826), and *The Prairie* (1827)—and to *The Bravo: A Tale* (Philadelphia: Carey & Lea, 1831).]

his person, feelings, or reputation, for so doing. We respect him because he loves his country and would make her true to the democratic creed she avows, as independent on foreign nations in her thoughts, as she is in her politics. In these particulars at least, he deserves the gratitude of his countrymen, and we trust he will receive it. He is willing to be known as a democrat, and the literary man, not ashamed to be called a democrat, in this democratic country, deserves to be held in more than ordinary consideration.

The work before us is written with ability, in a clear, strong, and manly style, and handles a subject with great freedom and with much justice, on which American citizens, shame to say, need to be instructed. Mr. Cooper thinks he sees two tendencies among us, which are alike dangerous to the stability and beneficial working of our free institutions. The upper classes, the affluent, the fashionable, he thinks are somewhat anti-American in their thoughts, principles, and affections. They do not accept heartily our free institutions, and set themselves seriously at work to develop the practical good they contain. They imbibe too readily the notions as the fashions of foreign countries, especially of England, and sigh to reproduce an order of things, which can never exist and which ought never to exist on this continent. They magnify the evils of the American system of government and society, and laud beyond measure the excellences of the monarchical or aristocratical institutions of the old world. "Fifteen years since," he says, "all complaints against our institutions were virtually silenced, whereas now it is rare to hear them praised, except by the mass, or by those who wish to profit by the favors of the mass."

The lower classes, or the mass, he thinks, are governed by an opposite tendency, which is pushing them to a dangerous extreme. Notions that are impracticable, and which, if persevered in, cannot fail to produce disorganization, if not revolution, are getting to be widely prevalent; and there is a multitude who are looking ahead in the idle hope of substituting a fancied perfection for the ills of life. This disorganizing tendency in the mass, he thinks, if not arrested, will check civilization, destroy the arts and refinements of civilized life, and reduce us all to a dead level of barbarism. This book, it may therefore be readily conjectured, is a double battery, charged alike against those who believe too much in the past, and those who believe too much in the future. The author aims to demolish those who have too much democracy and those who have too little. To be democratic over much is ungentlemanly and may lead to a kind of leveling not agreeable to those who are ambitious of being distinguished, and to be democratic not enough is unwise, not to say absolutely foolish.

This is, no doubt, to a certain extent, true, and the author's efforts to recall his countrymen from extremes, and to induce them to maintain the golden mean, are, no doubt, praiseworthy; but that they will be successful is not altogether so certain. Men in masses, as well as in their individual capacity, are logicians, and have an irresistible tendency to push their first principles to their last consequences. They can never be arrested by being pointed to the dangerous extremes into which they are running. Wise, practical observations are useless. The masses go where their principles logically developed require them to go. To arrest them we must change their principles, alter or enlarge their premises. But this is what Mr. Cooper has not done, and what he has not attempted to do. He does not seek for the causes of these opposite tendencies to dangerous extremes, to point out the defects in our first principles, and by changing our logical direction, to change also our practical direction. He does not appear to believe that the practice of a nation is merely its experimenting in verification of its theory, or the mere practical application of its theory. Change the theory, the philosophy of a nation, its ideas, and you change its history. But Mr. Cooper has no faith in theories, no love for the abstract. He affects the character of a wise man, who has seen the world; of a shrewd observer, who is above the speculations of the student, and not at all dependent on closet thinkers. He has seen, and he knows. He is a common sense man, and says, away with your visionary theories, and let us have a little common sense. All this is very well. Common sense is unquestionably a very excellent thing, and Mr. Cooper, no doubt, has it; but if it be *common* sense, we see not why we may not claim it as well as he. We think he ought to pronounce the word with fewer airs, for, if what he calls common sense, really be common sense, it must be common to all men, and he can in no wise claim a monopoly of it.

Again; Mr. Cooper, though he abjures all theories, and has many a biting sarcasm at theorizers in general, is himself a theorizer, and that too of no commendable sort. Does he not theorize when he lays it down as a general proposition that common sense is worthy of credit? Does he not theorize when he declares this notion is practicable and that is not? When he tells us this amount of equality may be attained, and this other amount cannot be? He affects to have analyzed the powers of the human mind, and to have ascertained how much it is wise to aim at, and what it is merely visionary to attempt. And what are his views on these matters, but the theories he has adopted respecting the desirable and the undesirable, the wise and the foolish, the attainable and the unattainable? Has he not speculated in coming to his conclusions? Or has he jumped to his conclusions? And is it his theory that all men ought to jump to their conclusions? If so, we say he is a theorizer, whom a wise man may well hesitate to follow. Mr. Cooper does not, we must needs think, prove himself so wise in declaiming against theorizing, which is in fact declaiming against reasoning, reflection, as he fancies; and his common sense, we imagine, may, in many instances, be found to be very uncommon sense, a very peculiar sense, even an idiosyncrasy.

This is not all. The man who is accustomed to analyze the works he reads, and reduce them to their lowest denominations, will, without much difficulty, perceive that Mr. Cooper's common sense rests, in most cases, for its support on the philosophy of Hobbes. We presume he has never read Hobbes, perhaps he has never heard of him, certainly, we presume, is unconscious of ever coinciding with his philosophic theory. But Hobbes's philosophy is, in political matters, the common sense of most Englishmen and Americans; and all Englishmen and Americans, who eschew philosophy and professedly follow common sense, are sure to be Hobbists. Mr. Cooper, we are sorry to say, forms no exception to this remark. For proof of what we allege we refer to his definition of liberty, and to the fact, that he seems to have no faith in abstract justice. Liberty with him is the right to do what one pleases. Perfect liberty, or a state of society, if society it may be called, in which there is no restraint placed on men's natural right, is a state of war, oppression, injustice. Government is instituted for the purpose of maintaining peace and order, by restraining natural liberty. This is Hobbism, and it is the doctrine of the book before us; only Mr. Cooper thinks we may leave men a larger portion of their natural liberty than Hobbes believed could be done with safety.

Now we contend that the design of government is to maintain to every man all his natural liberty. Liberty, according to our definition of it, is freedom to do whatever one has a natural right to do; and one has a natural right to do whatever is not forbidden by natural or absolute justice. Mr. Cooper admits the right of governments to restrain the natural liberty of the citizen, to a certain extent, but we admit no such right. The government that restrains or abridges in any sense, in any degree, the natural liberty, that is the natural rights, of any, the meanest or the guiltiest citizen, is tyrannical and unjust. In checking the tendency to extremes then, which Mr. Cooper deplores and against which he arms himself with so praiseworthy a zeal, we should endeavor to point out the precise limits prescribed by justice. We should deny the justice of all restraints upon natural rights.

We should then check at once the tendency to arbitrary government. Mr. Cooper, however, permits restraint to a certain extent. Why not to a greater extent? Say his fashionable, affluent, and polite acquaintances. Why to so great an extent? Why not give more liberty yet? Say the visionary mass, in pursuit of an ideal perfection never to be realized. What can he answer? Nothing that will satisfy either, because the question is in both cases, not a question of principle, but merely a question of more or less. This book, therefore, we think, will hardly succeed in arresting the tendency to extremes, because it leaves both parties their starting-points, and with their faces in the same direction, and merely beseeches them not to go quite so far as they have hitherto been disposed to go.

But notwithstanding our want of faith in the great influence of this book in accomplishing the object for which it has been sent forth, and notwithstanding our objections to its want of faith in reasoning, and to the Hobbian philosophy which lies at the bottom of the author's common sense, we still welcome the book as a very timely and a very valuable publication. It is full of wise and just observations; it is in most cases characterized by good sense, and its views, on all the great political topics it treats, are in the main just and democratic. It corrects many false notions, separates numerous matters which had become confounded, and gives much useful information, for the want of which our citizens have suffered, and our free institutions been endangered. We have more faith in the masses and more sympathy with them than Mr. Cooper appears to have; and we have altogether a stronger love for progress. He seems to be a little sour, half mad at mankind, and to do little for their cause, because he loves it. He too often confounds the actual with the possible, and mistakes what is for what ought to be. But his book breathes in the main a free and independent spirit, and may be said to be written in the interests of the people. It preaches democracy, not exactly according to our reading, nevertheless it preaches it; and if, as we have heard it contended, as much through spite as through love, we complain not. We are thankful that democracy is preached, though it be through spite, through ill-will to the aristocracy.

The following chapter on an Aristocrat and a Democrat, gives a very good idea of the whole work, at least of the spirit in which it is written.

AN ARISTOCRAT AND A DEMOCRAT

"We live in an age, when the words aristocrat and democrat are much used, without regard to the real significations. An aristocrat is one of a few, who possess the political power of a country; a democrat, one of the many. The words are also properly applied to those who entertain notions favorable to aristocratical, or democratical forms of government. Such persons are not, necessarily, either aristocrats, or democrats in fact, but merely so in opinion. Thus a member of a democratical government may have an aristocratical bias, and *vice versa.*

"To call a man who has the habits and opinions of a gentleman, an aristocrat, from that fact alone, is an abuse of terms, and betrays ignorance of the true principles of government, as well as of the world. It must be an equivocal freedom, under which every one is not the master of his own innocent acts and associations, and he is a sneaking democrat, indeed, who will submit to be dictated to, in those habits over which neither law nor morality assumes a right of control.

"Some men fancy that a democrat can only be one who seeks the level, social, mental, and moral, of the majority, a rule that would at once exclude all men of refinement, education, and taste from the class. These persons are enemies of democracy, as they at once render it impracticable. They are usually great sticklers for their own associations and habits, too, though unable to comprehend any of a nature that are superior. They are, in truth, aristocrats in principle, though assuming a contrary pretension; the ground work of all their feelings and arguments being self. Such is not the intention of liberty, whose aim is to leave every man to be the master of his own acts; denying hereditary honors, it is true, as unjust and unnecessary, but not denying the inevitable consequences of civilization.

"The law of God is the only rule of conduct, in this, as in other matters. Each man should do as he would be done by. Were the question put to the greatest advocate of indiscriminate association, whether he would submit to have his company and habits dictated to him, he would be one of the first to resist the tyranny; for they, who are the most rigid in maintaining their own claims, in such matters, are usually the loudest in decrying those whom they fancy to be better off than themselves. Indeed, it may be taken as a rule in social intercourse, that he who is the most apt to question the pretensions of others, is the most conscious of the doubtful position he himself occupies; thus establishing the very claims he affects to deny, by letting his jealousy of it be seen. Manners, education, and refinement, are positive things, and they bring with them innocent tastes, which are productive of high enjoyments; and it is as unjust to deny their possessors their indulgence, as it would be to insist on the less fortunate's passing the time they would rather devote to athletic amusements, in listening to operas for which they have no relish, sung in a language they do not understand.

"All that democracy means is as equal a participation in rights as is practicable; and to pretend that social equality is a condition of popular institutions, is to assume that the latter are destructive of civilization; for, as nothing is more self-evident than the impossibility of raising all men to the highest standard of tastes and refinement, the alternative would be to reduce the entire community to the lowest. The whole embarrassment on this point exists in the difficulty of making men comprehend qualities they do not themselves possess. We can all perceive the difference between ourselves and our inferiors; but when it comes to a question of the difference between us and our superiors, we fail to appreciate merits of which we have no proper conceptions. In face of this obvious difficulty, there is the safe and just governing rule, already mentioned, or that of permitting every one to be the undisturbed judge of his own habits and associations, so long as they are innocent, and do not impair the rights of others to be equally judges for themselves. It follows, that social intercourse must regulate itself, independently of institutions, with the exception that the latter, while they withhold no natural, bestow no factitious advantages beyond those which are inseparable from the rights of property, and general civilization.

"In a democracy, men are just as free to aim at the highest attainable places in society, as to obtain the largest fortunes; and it would be clearly unworthy of all noble sentiment to say, that the groveling competition for money shall alone be free, while that, which enlists all the liberal acquirements and elevated sentiments of the race, is denied the democrat. Such an avowal would be at once, a declaration of the inferiority of the system, since nothing but ignorance and vulgarity could be its fruits.

"The democratic gentleman must differ in many essential particulars from the aristocratical gentleman, though in their ordinary habits and tastes they are virtually identical. Their principles vary; and, to a slight degree, their deportment accordingly. The democrat, recognizing the right of all to participate in power, will be more liberal in his general sentiments, a quality of superiority in itself; but, in conceding this much to his fellow man, he will proudly maintain his own independence of vulgar domination, as indispensable to his personal habits. The same principles and manliness that would induce him to depose a royal despot, would induce him to resist a vulgar tyrant.

"There is no more capital, though more common error, than to suppose him an aristocrat who maintains his independence of habits; for democracy asserts the control of the majority, only, in matters of law, and not in matters of custom. The very object of the institution is the utmost practicable personal liberty, and to affirm the contrary would be sacrificing the end to the means.

"An aristocrat, therefore, is merely one who fortifies his exclusive privileges by positive institutions, and a democrat, one who is willing to admit of a free competition, in all things. To say, however, that the last supposes this competition will lead to nothing, is an assumption that means are employed without any reference to an end. He is the purest democrat who best maintains his rights, and no rights can be dearer to a man of cultivation, than exemptions from unseasonable invasions on his time, by the coarse-minded and ignorant."[3]

Great men are rarely above taking notice of small things. Mr. Cooper forms no exception to this remark, and small things at his touch become matters of considerable magnitude.

"Some changes of the language are to be regretted, as they lead to false inferences, and society is always a loser by mistaking names for things. Life is a fact, and it is seldom any good arises from a misapprehension of the real circumstances under which we exist. The word 'gentleman' has a positive and limited signification. It means one elevated above the mass of society by his birth, manners, attainments, character, and social condition. As no civilized society can exist without these social differences, nothing is gained by denying the use of the term. If blackguards were to be *called* 'gentlemen,' and 'gentlemen,' 'blackguards,' the difference between them would be as obvious as it is today.

"The word 'gentleman,' is derived from the French gentilhomme, which originally signified one of noble birth. This was at a time when the characteristics of the condition were never found beyond a caste. As society advanced, ordinary men attained the qualifications of nobility, without that of birth, and the meaning of the word was extended. It is now possible to be a gentleman without birth, though, even in America, where such distinctions are purely conditional, they who have birth, except in extraordinary instances, are classed with

[3] [Ed. *The American Democrat,* 94-98.]

gentlemen. To call a laborer, one who has neither education, manners, accomplishments, tastes, associations, nor any one of the ordinary requisites, a gentleman, is just as absurd as to call one who is thus qualified, a fellow. The word must have some especial signification, or it would be synonymous with man. One may have gentleman-like feelings, principles, and appearance, without possessing the liberal attainments that distinguish the gentleman. Least of all does money make a gentleman, though, as it becomes a means of obtaining the other requisites, it is usual to give it a place in the claims of the class. Men may be, and often are, very rich, without having the smallest title to be deemed gentlemen. A man may be a distinguished gentleman, and not possess as much money as his own footman.

"This word, however, is sometimes used instead of the old terms, 'sirs,' 'my masters,' &c., &c., as in addressing bodies of men. Thus we say 'gentlemen,' in addressing a public meeting, in complaisance, and as, by possibility, some gentlemen may be present. This is a license that may be tolerated, though he who should insist that all present were, as individuals, gentlemen, would hardly escape ridicule.

"What has just been said of the word gentleman is equally true with that of lady. The standard of these two classes rises as society becomes more civilized and refined; the man who might pass for a gentleman in one nation, or community, not being able to maintain the same position in another.

"The inefficiency of the effort to subvert things by names, is shown in the fact that, in all civilized communities, there is a class of men, who silently and quietly recognize each other, as gentlemen; who associate together freely and without reserve, and who admit each other's claims without scruple or distrust. This class may be limited by prejudice and arbitrary enactments, as in Europe, or it may have no other rules than those of taste, sentiment, and the silent laws of usage, as in America.

"The same observations may be made of relation to the words master and servant. He who employs laborers, with the right to command, is a master, and he who lets himself to work, with an obligation to obey, a servant. Thus there are house, or domestic servants, farm servants, shop servants, and various other servants; the term master being in all these cases the correlative.

"In consequence of the domestic servants of America having once been negro-slaves, a prejudice has arisen among the laboring classes of the whites, who not only dislike the term servant, but have also rejected that of master. So far has this prejudice gone, that in lieu of the latter, they have resorted to the use of the word boss, which has precisely the same meaning in Dutch![4]How far a subterfuge of this nature is worthy of a manly and common sense people will admit of question.

"A similar objection may be made to the use of the word 'help,' which is not only an innovation on a just and established term, but which does not properly convey the meaning intended. They who aid their masters in the toil may be deemed 'helps,' but they who perform all the labor do not assist, or help to do the thing, but they do it themselves. A man does not usually hire his cook to *help* him cook his dinner, but to cook it herself. Nothing is therefore gained, while something is lost in simplicity and clearness by the substitution of new and imperfect terms, for the long established words of the language. In all cases in which the people of America have retained the *things* of their ancestors, they should not be ashamed to keep the names."[5]

It is devoutly to be hoped that all this and much more like it in the volume before us will be duly regarded by our democratic friends. It is very important that our democrats should be taught good manners, and probably no man amongst us is better qualified to be their teacher than Mr. Cooper. He has resided long abroad, traveled much, seen much, observed much, and is himself, we presume, *au fait* in all that appertains to good manners. We hope he will meet with success, proportioned to the zeal and diligence with which he takes himself to his task. An unmannerly democracy must always be distasteful and even revolting to a *gentleman.* In sober earnest, he who improves the manners of a nation, does much for its morals. Let there be care, however, that the improvement attempted be something more than the transplanting of the conventionalisms of one country to another. "The wise are polite the world over; fools are polite only at home," says, very truly, the Citizen of the World.[6] True politeness is made up of good sense and good nature, and no man, who has good sense and good nature, can ever be wanting in the manners of the gentleman, in the only worthy sense of the term, though he may be wanting in the conventionalisms of different countries, or of a particular clique or coterie. Really good manners always have their foundation in hu-

[4] [Ed. The Dutch *baas*, from which the English boss comes, means master.]

[5] [Ed. Ibid., 120-22.]

[6] [Ed. Oliver Goldsmith, *The Citizen of the World*, in *Collected Works of Oliver Goldsmith*, vol. 2 *The Citizen of the World*, edited by Arthur Friedman (Oxford: Clarendon Press, 1966), 166, lines 26-27.]

man nature, and must always take their hue from the age and circumstances of the individual, and the institutions of the country. The manners most appropriate to an aristocracy, or to a monarchy, can never be the most appropriate to a democracy. But we beg pardon of Mr. Cooper for trespassing on his peculiar province.

Mr. Cooper thinks the application of the terms *gentleman* and *lady,* to footmen and cooks, is very unbecoming, and ought not to be tolerated. We are sorry not to sympathize with him in this, as fully as he may desire. We applaud his motives, but we confess that we look with pleasure on the fact, that footmen and cooks are rising to the dignity of gentlemen and ladies; and it is also an article in our creed that all who are born at all are well-born. Every human being, in our belief, is of noble, ay, of royal birth, and may stand up and claim to be a king, and demand regal honors. This is the foundation stone of our democracy, and he, who has yet to learn that no human being is or can be ignoble, is in our judgment a sorry democrat.

We confess that as concerns this leveling tendency, we are unable to sympathize with the fears Mr. Cooper seems to indulge. We see no disposition among our countrymen to bring all down to a dead level of ignorance and barbarism. They, against whom the charge of desiring to do this is sometimes brought, are in no sense obnoxious to it. The workingmen, agrarians, loco-focos, Jacobins, or by whatever name they may be designated by themselves or by their enemies, have made certain movements which have created some alarm, and made some say that they are for arresting civilization, and for plunging us into primitive ignorance and barbarism; but these same dreaded levelers have been the first in this country to advocate equal, universal education. They demand reforms, radical reforms, it is true; but they expect them almost solely from an improved system of education. They propose to raise the standard of education, to breathe into education a free and living spirit, and to extend it equally to all, to every child born in the land, whether rich or poor, male or female. Is this to show a love for ignorance and barbarism? Is this a kind of leveling that should alarm a wise man, a Christian, and a democrat?

Distinctions there are in society and distinctions there always will be; but distinction implies diversity not necessarily inequality. The footman is diverse from the cook, but not necessarily inferior or superior to the cook. There is a difference between Mr. Cooper's gentleman and his footman, yet the two may be equal in moral worth, in knowledge, in wealth, and social position. Nevertheless admitting inequalities, they may be real, not factitious. Now all the war which has been carried on against the inequalities which do obtain in society has had for its object, not the suppression of those inequalities which are founded in nature, or which rest on merit, but those which have no real foundation but an ignorant and barbarous public opinion, or an ignorant and barbarous state of society. Factitious inequalities, not natural, not moral inequalities, are the ones that the radicals are striving to destroy. Beyond these they have no thought of going. There is in every man, in Jacobins as well as in conservatives, a natural instinct which leads him to bow down to superior worth. The great man can never be lost in the crowd. He who is really and intrinsically superior to the common mass will always be permitted to tower above them. Carlyle is right in his remarks on hero-worship.[7] It is the natural and earliest religion of mankind, and it remains and will remain, though all other religions be outgrown, their altars broken down, and their temples moldered to dust. No man, who is conscious that the royal blood flows in his veins, that the royal heart beats under his ribs, need fear that the honors of royalty will not be decreed him. Let a man be a king, and as a king shall he be owned, reverenced, and obeyed. Human nature is rich in loyalty and will pour out her blood like water in honor of even a semblance of a king. Let the wise man be ashamed then to tremble at a supposed tendency to wipe out all distinctions, and to confound the great with the little.

One tendency we do discover and that is to strip off disguises and compel people to pass for what they are. There is a growing disgust at all make-believe, at all shamming, and a demand for reality. Therefore is there danger that some men may not always succeed in bearing the characters they once contrived to obtain. The men rather short by nature, but who have hitherto been accounted tall, because they were standing on stilts, may hereafter be taken at their true altitude, and laughed at into the bargain for the pains they have taken to add a cubit to their stature. Mr. Cooper has nothing to apprehend from such a leveling tendency as this, nor has any other man who is conscious of true worth, and who is willing to be estimated at his real value. Others may fear—let them.

[7][Ed. Thomas Carlyle (1795-1881), Scottish essayist and biographer, had a great influence upon American Transcendentalists. Carlyle saw hero-worship as the "tap root of all religion." On this, see B. H. Lehman, *Carlyle's Theory of the Hero: Its Sources, Development, History, and Influence on Carlyle's Work* (Durham, N.C.: Duke University Press, 1928), 67. Carlyle's idea of hero-worship has its foundations in "The State of German Literature" *Edinburgh Review* October 1827, and in his essay on Goethe in the *Foreign Review* of July, 1828, but Brownson more than likely found the idea in *Sartor Resartus* (1836), book 3, chapter 7, a book which he had definitely read.]

Mr. Cooper's remarks "On the Public" are to the point, and deserve to be read and pondered well. We should be glad to extract them, but have not the room.

We must bring our remarks to a close, and we do it by throwing out a few suggestions for the consideration of American Democrats. The democracy of the last century was materialism applied to politics; it sought equality by lopping off the heads of kings and priests, and its natural tendency was to universal anarchy. We do not complain of it on this account. Kings and priests, when they have lost the true kingly and priestly nature, have no more right to wear their heads than they have to wear crowns and miters. But democracy has changed its character. The democrat of today is not destructive, but constructive; he does not lop off the heads of kings and priests, but he seeks to arrive at equality by making every man a king and a priest. He is a leveler, but he levels upward not downward. He is not affected by the fact that some are higher than others, but by the fact that some are lower than others. He grieves over the fact that human nature is wronged, that its inborn nobility is not brought out, that the mass of men are not true men, but something less than men; and he sets himself seriously at work to remove all obstacles to the full development of the true man, and to call forth the might which has for so many ages slumbered in the peasant's arm. He holds up the standard of the true man, and labors to bring all men up to it. He therefore is eminently religious, eminently Christian, eminently philosophic. He avails himself of all the means and influences, of all the arts, sciences, literature, everything, by which the universal soul of humanity may be quickened, thought awakened, moral power increased, and the majesty of man made to appear. Be assured then that the democrat of today is no barbarian. He is a man, a free man, a Christian man, who believes in the powers and capacities of all men to be men, in the full significance of the term, and who labors to make them so or to induce them to make themselves so.

Again, in a more restricted sphere, the American democrat is one who is jealous of power, and always interprets all doubtful questions so as to increase the power of the people, rather than of the government. In this, his first duty is to watch that the federal government do not swallow up the state governments. Power has a perpetual tendency to extend itself. The functionaries of government, whether executive, legislative, or judicial, almost inevitably so exercise their functions as to enlarge the sphere of government. There is a tendency in the federal government, from its central character, to engross as much of the public business of the country as possible.

The first danger to our liberty is to be apprehended from this quarter. Cooks may be called ladies, and footmen gentlemen, and still our liberty be tolerably secure; but when the federal government has succeeded in getting under its control, directly or indirectly, nearly all the internal affairs of the states, and is able to make its acts, like the frogs of Egypt, reach to our domestic hearths, and to come up into our sleeping chambers and kneading troughs, we may be assured that the first barriers to a consolidated despotism have been leaped. This was well nigh done. The friends of freedom have made an effort to arrest the dangerous tendency; but whether with success or not time must determine. The universal tendency throughout Christendom to centralization, a tendency accelerated a hundred fold by the "thousand and one" voluntary associations of the day, is somewhat alarming, and should teach our democrats, that this is no time to sleep at their posts, or to expect a victory without a long and obstinate struggle. They must be awake, always prepared for the battle, well armed, and stout of heart.

Lastly, the American Democrat must be on his guard against the tendency of the state governments to enlarge the dominion of the state at the expense of that of the individual. There are two antagonist tendencies at work; one to individual freedom, a tendency we traced in our April number, in our remarks on modern civilization;[8] the other, a tendency to centralization, to the merging of the individual in the state, in the mass. This last is the only dangerous tendency in this country. The philosopher cannot fail to perceive that we have much more to apprehend from our reverence for law than from our disregard of it. Mobs, bad as they are, are not half so threatening to liberty, to the true working of our institutions, as the prosecution of a man for advocating an unpopular doctrine,[9] or as is the prevalence of that modern doctrine of "vested rights," a doctrine, which, if admitted and practiced upon, may in time cover all the property of the state with charters, and lock it up forever in close corporations. We are called upon as democrats by every consideration that can touch our sensibility, arouse our patriotism, or our love of humanity, to contend manfully for individual rights, and re-

[8][Ed. See Chapter 17 in this volume.]

[9][Ed. Reference is to the four blasphemy trials against Abner Kneeland. Early in 1834 he was indicted for publishing in his *Boston Investigator* of 20 December 1833 a "scandalous, impious, obscene, blasphemous and profane libel of and concerning God." It took four trials before a jury finally convicted him of blasphemy and the judge sentenced him to sixty days in jail. On this, see *The Age of Jackson*, 356-59.]

sist at the threshold every encroachment of power. We must frown upon every legislative enactment, upon every judicial decision, that restricts the sphere of individual freedom, and especially upon all those huge associations which cover the land, though called moral, religious, benevolent, which tend to swallow up the individual, and are a device of the devil, by which the same control under a free government may be exerted over individual opinion and action, that is exerted over them by despotisms and hierarchies. We must throw around each individual a bulwark of sanctity, and not permit society to break through it, though it were to do the individual an unspeakable good. God leaves man his freedom, and does not control it, though man in abusing it brings damnation to his soul. Let the divine government be a model of ours. We may not control a man's natural liberty even for the man's good. So long as the individual trespasses upon none of the rights of others, or throws no obstacle in the way of their free and full exercise, government, law, public opinion even, must leave him free to take his own course. In order to secure this end we must breathe a freer spirit into our schools, place men at the head of our colleges and higher seminaries of learning who sympathize with our democratic institutions, demand, will, create, and sustain a truly democratic literature.

23.

ULTRAISM[1]

Boston Quarterly Review 1 (July, 1838): 377-84

The author of this volume is a worthy and we would fain believe a useful man. He is sincere, earnest, and ambitious to do what in him lies for the advancement of his race. He is quite a reformer and appears to doubt not that he shall soon be able to recover for mankind the long lost Eden.

According to him, so far as we have been able to collect his theory, the seat of life, thought, and virtue is in the stomach, and the Devil, or soul-destroyer, always makes his appearance in the form of roast beef, pig, mutton, fish, rich sauces, or some savory dish or other, and is to be vanquished only by inducing mankind to feed on apples, mush, cold boiled potatoes, with now and then a dessert of parched corn. Apples are the author's favorite dish for reforming the world, and curing all the ills that flesh and spirit are heirs to. His love for apples seems to be very great, even surpassing the love of women; and we cannot help fancying that should he be admitted into paradise and find no apples there, it would be no paradise to him. May apples go with him wherever he goes. We too are fond of apples. But as for mush, to be eaten without milk, butter, sugar, or molasses, Yankee dish under the name of hasty-pudding, and immortalized by the immortal Barlow's song,[2] though it be, we will none of it. Cold boiled potatoes unsalted, and no water even to wash them down—may the author of the delectable book before us enjoy the sole monopoly of digesting them!

We have no doubt that many of the ills of life come from indigestion. We certainly would not be ungrateful to the man who labors to give us a good digestion. We moreover do by no means object to a simple diet. A simple diet, and by simple diet we mean one into

[1][Ed. Review of William Andrus Alcott (1798-1859) *The Mother in her Family; or Sayings and Doings at Rose Hill Cottage,* by the author of "The Young Wife" (Boston: Weeks, Jordan & Co., 1838).]

[2][Ed. The reference to Barlow's song may be a reference to Joel Barlow's (1754-1812), American businessman, diplomat and poet, *The Prospect of Peace* (1778), a verse oration delivered at a Yale commencement.]

which little animal food enters, is the most favorable to health and to enjoyment. But because a man wishes to recommend a simple diet, he need not run mad. The earth is filled with a profusion of good things, suitable for food, and we see no reason why we should reject all of them, save apples, mush, and cold potatoes. The way to preserve health and enjoy life is not to starve oneself to death, or to compel oneself to feed on the coarsest and least nutritious provender. Why, therefore, may not the advocates of a simple diet speak with moderation, and content themselves with urging such changes only as the good sense of the community will approve?

The author of this book doubtless means well and so may all those who are laboring with him; but we confess that we are sorry to find them calling themselves reformers. They almost make a sensible man ashamed to enroll himself among the friends of reform, as the shape and tricks of monkeys do sometimes make us ashamed of our humanity. It is well to be reformers; it is our duty to labor for the progress of our race; but we should do it with a becoming modesty, feeling that it is but dimly we can see the new good to be obtained, and but little that we can do to obtain it. It is an unpleasant sight to a wise man, that of one of our modern reformers astride the millionth part of an idea, cantering away as a Tenth Avatar, and fancying that he bears with him the universal palingenesia of man and nature.

In fact, are not our modern reformers carrying the joke a little too far? They are becoming, it strikes us, a real annoyance. The land is overspread with them, and matters have come to such a pass, that a peaceable man can hardly venture to eat or drink, to go to bed or to get up, to correct his children or kiss his wife, without obtaining the permission and the direction of some moral or other reform society. The individual is bound hand and foot, and delivered up to the sage doctors and sager doctresses, who have volunteered their services in the management of his affairs. He has nothing he can call his own, not even his will. There is left him no spot, no sanctum, into which some association committee cannot penetrate, and dictate to him what he may do or what he ought to suffer. What is most intimate and sacred in his private relations, is laid before the public, and he is told that he ought to be thankful that there is no dearth of disinterested lecturers, ready in public discourses to explain to his wife all the mysteries of the conception and birth of a human being.

Now this in our judgment is to be philanthropic overmuch. It is making philanthropy altogether too great an annoyance. No real good can come to the community from sacrificing the individual. There are things which an individual ought to be allowed to call his own, and over which he shall have the supreme control. Around each individual there should be traced a circle, within which no stranger should presume or be suffered to enter. It is no service to virtue to keep us all forever in leading-strings. If we are to be men and to show forth the virtues of men, we must be permitted to think and act for ourselves. That philanthropy which proposes to do everything for us, and which will permit us to do nothing of our own accord, may indeed keep us out of harm's way, but it is a left-handed philanthropy, and will be found always to diminish our virtues in the same proportion that it does our vices.

It must joy the heart of every benevolent man to see efforts made for the advancement of humanity. There is room enough for reform. But we do wish our modern reformers would enlarge their conceptions and seek to add knowledge to their zeal. It is well to be zealously affected in a good cause; but zeal in a good cause, if not guided by just knowledge, may work as much evil as good. The world is not to be regenerated by the exertions of reformers who have but one idea, and who fancy that one idea embraces the universe. Life is a complex affair. The good and the evil it is subject to are so intermixed, and run one so into the other, that it is often no easy matter to say which is which. There is no one sovereign remedy for all the ills of life, no one rule which is applicable at all times to all cases for the production of good. Good and evil both have their source in human nature. The one cannot be greatly increased, or the other essentially diminished, but in proportion as human nature itself is more fully developed; but in proportion to its general culture and growth. The tree of evil is not destroyed by pruning away a branch here, and a branch there. So long as its root remains in the earth, so long will it live, and flourish. All classes of reformers see and deplore its growth. One class thinks all evils come from the breach of the seventh commandment, another class ascribes them all to the eating of flesh or fish, to the drinking of rum, wine, or cider; this class fancies the world would move on as it should, if women were but allowed equal civil and political rights with men; that class is sure all things will be restored to primitive innocence, love, and harmony the moment Negroes are declared to be no longer slaves; and this other class, when nations shall no longer appeal to arms to decide their disputes. Each of these classes of reformers mounts its hobby and rides away, condemning all as children of the past, as wedded to old abuses, as the enemies of truth and virtue, who will not do the same. But not one or another of these classes shall succeed. All these classes of evils are mutually connected, and no one of them can be cured separately. The cause of them all lies deep in human nature, as now developed, and they must be regarded as inseparable from the present stage of human progress. The doctors, who are vaunting their skill to cure them, are merely prescribing for the symptoms, not the disease. War is a melancholy thing. Philanthropy cannot but weep over its doings. But as long as the passions of the human heart remain as they are, and the interests of the world continue in their present complicated state, it is perfectly idle to talk of the cessation of war. Everything manly in our nature rises indignant at the bare name of slavery; but should the Negroes be declared free, and all other things remain as they were, slavery would not be abolished. One of its forms might be slightly changed, but its substance would continue the same. Give woman equal civil and political rights with man, and if her present tastes and culture remain, her influence will be just what it now is. Intemperance is not a mother-evil. It is the symptom, not the disease. Temperance lectures will not cure it. It will remain in spite of Temperance Societies, in spite of law, in spite of religion, till the causes producing it are removed, and men are able to find an innocent source of the excitement they crave. Chastity may be commended, but it will not be universal, till the whole community is so trained that it can find more pleasure in sentiment than in sense. The object of each class of reformers is, we are willing to admit, good, and praiseworthy; but it can in no case be insulated and gained as a separate object.

The work of reforming the world is a noble one. The progress of man and society goes on. But it goes on slowly, much more so than comports with the desires of our one-idea reformers. These reformers, with one idea, are no doubt worth something. Each class of them may contribute something to aid on the work. But no one of them can do much or run far ahead of the general average of the race. The evils of life rise as lofty mountains in our path. We cannot go over them nor turn our course around them. They rise alike before all of our race and form the same barrier to the onward march of all. We must remove them. If we take ourselves to the work with faith and energy, we can remove them. But we can do it only a little by little. Our generation works its brief day at the task, and worn out gives way to another; another comes and removes its portion, and gives way to yet another. Thus do generations labor, and yet centuries elapse before we can perceive that they have made any impression on the mountain. Ever and anon a company may undermine a portion of rock and earth, which come down with thundering noise and raise much dust, and some of the spectators may fancy the work is done.

But when the noise has subsided, and the wind has brushed away the dust and smoke, it is seen that many of their number have been crushed under the falling masses, and that fragments have rolled back and blocked up the path which had already been cleared. There may be something sad and depressing in this view. Life is full of deep pathos to the wise man. Sorrow springs from experience. He, who knew most of man and his trials, was said to be a "man of sorrows and acquainted with grief" [Isa. 53:3]. Man's path from the cradle to his union with God is not of smooth and easy ascent, strewed with flowers, and shaded by groves from which the sweet songsters are ever warbling their wild notes. It is steep and rugged and we ascend not without labor and difficulty. Yet is there no cause for complaint. Man has some strength; let him use it, and not murmur because he has also some weakness. Something he can do; let him do it, and complain not that there is something he cannot do. Each generation has its allotted work; let it take itself cheerfully to its performance. The race is immortal; and as one generation does its work and passes off to receive its reward, a new generation comes on to take up the work where its predecessor left it. The work shall then go on and the race be ever achieving its destiny. What is it then, though this generation cannot do so much as to leave nothing to its successor?

We have no fellowship with the philosophy that teaches us to regard with indifference the efforts of a single individual, however puny, to advance the cause of humanity. True philosophy teaches us to find a sufficient reason for whatever occurs and to see good in everything. We ought therefore never to condemn outright any class of reformers or plan of reform we may meet; but we cannot refrain from regarding most of the reformers who fill our age and country as extremely short-sighted, and their plans as most woefully defective. We would not make war upon them, nor in our sober moments treat them otherwise than with great tenderness; but we cannot bring ourselves to act with them. Whoever would pass for a man of correct feelings, and of some degree of philosophic wisdom, must see and deplore the ills that afflict himself and brethren; he must labor with all his might to cure them; but he will proceed always calmly, with chastened hopes, and with the conviction that the only way to cure many evils is to bear them. The lesson, to bear, though difficult to learn, and one that many of us never do learn, is one of the lessons most essential to man in his earthly pilgrimage. Even these evils, of which we complain, may be made the ministers of our virtues and the means of our spiritual growth.

INDEX OF BIBLICAL REFERENCES

INDEX OF NAMES AND SUBJECTS

D

E

F

G

H

J

K

M

N

O

P